THE SYNTAX OF RELATIVE CLAUSES

Relative clauses play a hugely important role in analysing the structure of sentences. This book provides the first evidence that a unified analysis of the different types of relative clauses is possible – a step forward in our understanding. Using careful analyses of a wide range of languages, Cinque argues that the relative clause types can all be derived from a single, double-headed, structure. He also presents evidence that restrictive, maximalizing, ('integrated') non-restrictive, kind-defining, infinitival, and participial RCs merge at different heights of the nominal extended projection. This book provides an elegant generalization about the structure of all relatives. Theoretically profound and empirically rich, it promises to radically alter the way we think about this subject for years to come.

GUGLIELMO CINQUE is Professor of Linguistics at Ca' Foscari University, Venice.

CAMBRIDGE STUDIES IN LINGUISTICS

General editors: P. AUSTIN, J. BRESNAN, B. COMRIE,
S. CRAIN, W. DRESSLER, C. J. EWEN, R. LASS,
D. LIGHTFOOT, K. RICE, I. ROBERTS, S. ROMAINE,
N. V. SMITH

In this series

THE SYNTAX OF RELATIVE CLAUSES

A UNIFIED ANALYSIS

GUGLIELMO CINQUE

Ca' Foscari University, Venice

CAMBRIDGE
UNIVERSITY PRESS

CAMBRIDGE
UNIVERSITY PRESS

University Printing House, Cambridge CB2 8BS, United Kingdom

One Liberty Plaza, 20th Floor, New York, NY 10006, USA

477 Williamstown Road, Port Melbourne, VIC 3207, Australia

314–321, 3rd Floor, Plot 3, Splendor Forum, Jasola District Centre,
New Delhi – 110025, India

79 Anson Road, #06–04/06, Singapore 079906

Cambridge University Press is part of the University of Cambridge.

It furthers the University's mission by disseminating knowledge in the pursuit of
education, learning, and research at the highest international levels of excellence.

www.cambridge.org
Information on this title: www.cambridge.org/9781108479707
DOI: 10.1017/9781108856195

First published 2020

A catalogue record for this publication is available from the British Library.

ISBN 978-1-108-47970-7 Hardback
ISBN 978-1-108-79058-1 Paperback

Contents

Acknowledgements

This book has had a long gestation. Earlier versions of (parts of) it were presented in lectures at the University of Venice (spring 2002), and University of California, Los Angeles (winter 2003), at the Workshop on Antisymmetry and Remnant Movement at New York University (31 October–1 November 2003); in classes at the Linguistic Society of America summer school at the Massachusetts Institute of Technology (July 2005), the Ecole d'Automne de Linguistique (EALing) in Paris (September 2009), the Workshop on Syntax-Semantics Interface, Taipei (17–18 June 2011), and New York University in the spring of 2014; at the London Advanced Core Training in Linguistics summer school (23–27 June 2014), the University of Siena (31 March 2015), and the University of Tel Aviv in June 2016; and in the Linguistics Department of the Higher School of Economics in Moscow in the spring of 2017. I wish to thank here the many people who commented on various aspects of the analyses on these occasions, and in particular Klaus Abels, Adriana Belletti, Valentina Bianchi, Peter Cole, Christopher Collins, Michael Daniel, Francesca Del Gobbo, Yoshio Endo, Alex Grosu, Hubert Haider, Gaby Hermon, Roland Hinterhölzl, Julia Horvath, Jim Huang, Richard Kayne, Hilda Koopman, Yury Lander, Peter H. Matthews, Friederike Moltmann, Marie-Claude Paris, David Pesetsky, Cecilia Poletto, Andrew Radford, Luigi Rizzi, Ian Roberts, Ken Safir, Ur Shlonsky, Tal Siloni, Andrew Simpson, Dominique Sportiche, Tim Stowell, Peter Svenonius, Anna Szabolcsi, Adam Szczegielniak, Henk van Riemsdijk, and Gert Webelhuth.

Special thanks are due to Paola Benincà, Wayles Browne, Iliyana Krapova, Yen-Hui Audrey Li, Akira Watanabe, and Niina Zhang for their observations on specific points of my analysis. I am particularly indebted to Željko Bošković, Alex Grosu, Jaklin Kornfilt, Andrew Radford, Alain Rouveret, and Adam Szczegielniak, who went over the entire manuscript providing many valuable comments of both substance and form.

My grateful thanks also go to Cambridge University Press's publishing team, especially Andrew Winnard, for encouraging me to produce this volume, Gordon Lee for his exceptionally careful copy-editing of the manuscript and Grace Morris for her constant guidance.

Specific thanks will also appear in the chapters that follow.

Introduction

In this work I would like to propose that the different types of relative clauses (RCs) attested cross-linguistically – externally Headed post-nominal, externally Headed pre-nominal, internally Headed, double-Headed, Headless (or 'free'), correlative, and adjoined (Dryer 2005) – can all be derived from a single, double-Headed, universal structure via different, independently motivated, syntactic operations – movement, deletion (non-pronunciation), and replacement by a proform – with 'raising' or 'matching'.[1]

With 'raising' I refer to derivations where the overt Head is the internal Head, which raises to the Spec,CP of the RC (Kayne 1994: ch. 8), causing the deletion of the external Head. With 'matching' I refer instead to derivations in which the overt Head is the external Head. The term 'matching' will actually cover a number of distinct cases here. In one (see Lees 1960, 1961; Chomsky 1965; Sauerland 1998, 2003; Hulsey & Sauerland 2006, among others) the internal Head is a full match of the external Head, and is deleted completely, under identity (non-distinctness) with the external Head, as in constructions displaying invariant relativizers (Italian *che*, English *that*, etc.), or partially deleted, stranding a determiner/modifier, as is arguably the case in the Italian art. + *qual-* non-restrictives and English *which* non-restrictives, discussed in §3.1[2] (as well as in the kind-defining RCs discussed in §3.2). In other cases the internal Head is represented by a proform (see Montague 1970; Partee 1976; Chomsky 1973, 1977; Jackendoff 1977; Heim & Kratzer 1998, among others). This proform can be an overt *wh*-pronoun moved to the Spec,CP of the RC, as is arguably the case in

---

[1] The analysis shares the idea that both 'raising' and 'matching' are needed with Carlson (1977), Åfarli (1994), Sauerland (1998, 1999, 2003), Aoun & Li (2003) and other works cited in fn. 1 of the Appendix, though it differs from them in assuming a single, double-Headed, structure for both, compatible with Antisymmetry.

[2] In non-integrated non-restrictive RCs the overt internal Head may also be only loosely related semantically to the external one (see §3.1).

Italian RCs with *cui* (§2.1.2.1), in English restrictive RCs with *who/which/where*/etc. (see §2.1.2.2), and in similar constructions in other languages, or an overt 3rd person pronoun in situ, or ex situ, as in languages like Hebrew making use of resumptive pronouns (see §4.3), or a PRO as in (some) participial relative clauses (see §3.4), or an overt (or silent) 1st and 2nd person pronoun in argument position, as in certain non-restrictive RCs modifying 1st and 2nd person pronouns (see §3.1.8). These different options seem to depend on the semantic type of the relative clause involved (whether it is 'amount/maximalizing', 'restrictive', 'non-restrictive', or 'kind-defining'), in turn related to the different height of the respective merger within the nominal extended projection (see §3.5)[3], as well as on the match or mismatch between the external and the internal Heads. For example, in restrictive RCs, only when the internal Head exactly matches the external one (which is smaller than DP as it is the portion of the nominal extended projection c-commanded by the RC, merged below strong determiners and above weak ones, called here dP) will deletion be licit (in the possible presence of an invariant relativizer). Whenever the internal Head is instead bigger than the external one, because it is a full (oblique) DP/KP or a DP/KP inside a PP, no deletion will be possible, for lack of identity, and a relative *wh*-phrase or a resumptive pronoun or epithet (preceded by a preposition) will be employed.

Some movement operations (like the relative clause internal Ā-movement that builds an operator-variable structure in some languages) are specific to the relative clause construction, others (like the movement of the external Head that yields the post-nominal position of the RC) appear instead to be tied to the word order type of the language (head-initial, head-medial, or non-rigid head-final).

In Chapter 1, after briefly introducing the cross-linguistic syntactic and semantic typologies of relative clauses, I present what I take to be the unique, double-Headed, structure underlying all attested types of relative clauses in both the 'raising' and the 'matching' derivations.

Under the assumption which I tried to motivate in Cinque (2003, 2009a), briefly summarized here in §1.4, that RCs are merged in a specifier modifying (immediately c-commanding) the external Head (pre-nominally, if order is part

---

[3] Non-restrictives (attached above DPs) have an external Head (which includes strong determiners) bigger than that of restrictives (which only includes weak determiners), while participial RCs have an even smaller external Head.

of narrow syntax)[4], the different 'matching' derivations to be discussed will prove to be compatible with Antisymmetry.

Chapter 2 is the core of the volume as it attempts to illustrate in more detail how the cross-linguistic attested types of restrictive and maximalizing RCs can be derived from the single double-Headed structure made available by Universal Grammar (UG), under 'raising' and 'matching'.

Chapter 3 will then consider the derivation, from the same double-Headed structure, of other types of RCs (finite non-restrictive, kind-defining, infinitival, participial), as well as their (external) Merge positions, which are distinct from each other and from that of the restrictive and maximalizing RCs.

Chapter 4 recapitulates the different 'strategies' with which the internal Head can be represented (as a gap, in the possible presence of an invariant relativizer, as a relative pronoun, as a full or partial repetition of the external Head, or as a resumptive pronoun or epithet) and considers how these different forms interact with the 'raising' and 'matching' derivations.

Chapter 5 addresses a number of residual cases (including 'hydras', RCs with split antecedents, and 'double dependence' RCs) and some of the questions they raise, some of which will remain open.

The Appendix reviews several phenomena which appear to suggest that a 'raising' derivation is not sufficient to derive all types of RCs.

---

[4] The question whether linear order is determined in narrow syntax, or only at the PF interface, is still a moot question (see Chomsky, Gallego & Ott 2017/2019 and Kayne 2018, among others). The present proposal is compatible with either possibility provided that the (meaningless) movements 'required to yield the proper hierarchies' (Chomsky 2004: 110 and n. 27) that determine the different linear orders of languages under Kayne's (1994) Linear Correspondence Axiom (LCA) are part of narrow syntax. For possible evidence that some meaningless movements should be permitted in narrow syntax, see Cinque (2018).

1 *Preliminaries*

1.1 The Syntactic Typology of Relative Clauses

As noted in the Introduction, in the languages of the world RCs appear to take one of the following forms (see Dryer 2005): externally Headed post-nominal (1a); externally Headed pre-nominal (1b); internally Headed (1c); double-Headed (1d), Headless (or 'free') (1e); correlative (1f), and adjoined (1g).[1]

(1) a. The [**book** [$_{RC}$ that/which we read]] *English* (externally Headed post-nominal)
b. [[$_{RC}$ nuna ranti-shqa-n] **bestya**] ... *Quechua* (Cole 1987: 279) (externally Headed pre-nominal)
man buy-PERF-3 horse.NOM ...
the horse the man bought ...
c. [[$_{RC}$ nuna **bestya-ta** ranti-shqa-n]] (alli bestya-m) *Quechua* (Cole 1987: 279) (internally Headed)
man horse.ACC buy-PERF-3 good horse ...
the horse the man bought (was a good horse)
d. [[**doü** adiyano-no] **doü**] deyalukhe *Kombai* (De Vries 1993: 78)
(double-Headed)
sago give.3PL.NONFUT-CONN sago finished.ADJ
'The sago that they gave is finished.'
e. [$_{RC}$ **what** you did] (is nice) *English* (Headless, or free)
f. [$_{RC}$ **jo laRkii** khaRii hai] **vo** *Hindi* (Dayal 1996: 196) (correlative)
(**laRkii**) lambii hai
which girl standing is that girl tall is
'The girl who is standing is tall.'
g. ŋatjulu-lu φ-na **yankiri** pantu-nu [$_{RC}$ kutja-lpa ŋapa ŋa-nu] *Walrpiri* (Hale 1976: 78) (adjoined)
I-erg AUX emu spear-PAST COMP-AUX water drink-PAST
'I speared the emu which was/while it was drinking water.'

---

[1] Strictly speaking the correlative is not a separate type, as it involves one or the other of the first five types as one of its components (see Cinque 2009b and §2.6, below), nor is the 'adjoined' relative (Hale 1976). Keenan (1985: 165), Dayal (1996: 152), Bhatt (2003: 491) and Nordlinger (2006: §1) analyse the latter as a correlative RC. However, to judge from Hale (1976), in addition to the correlative type, some adjoined relatives (like that in (1g)) are plausibly to be analysed as extraposed RCs (see §2.7). For a more detailed discussion of the syntactic typology of RCs see De Vries (2002: ch. 2) and Chapter 2 of the present volume.

1.2   The Semantic Typology of Relative Clauses

The classical semantic typology of RCs distinguished two types: *restrictive* RCs, which are standardly assumed to denote sets that combine with the sets denoted by the Head through set intersection (for finer distinctions within the class of restrictive RCs, see Cabredo Hofherr 2014), and *non-restrictive* RCs (which simply add information concerning a Head whose reference is already established). To this first distinction, Carlson (1977) added a third type, *amount* RCs, which have since been generalized by Grosu and Landman (1998) to the wider class of what they call 'maximalizing' RCs.[2] What Grosu and Landman (1998) suggest (but also see Carlson 1977 and Heim 1987) is that the operation of maximalization takes place in RCs when the Head noun is semantically interpreted CP internally, as opposed to when it is semantically interpreted CP externally, as is the case in ordinary restrictives (and non-restrictives). This semantic distinction will be argued to correlate with the syntactic distinction of 'raising' and 'matching' derivations. Benincà (2003, 2012a, 2012c) has argued for the existence of a fourth class of RCs, *'kind-defining'*, which are also generally lumped together with restrictives but in fact share a number of properties with non-restrictives (though differing from them). Prince (1990, 1997) has also recognized a separate type of 'kind' RCs. For further discussion see Benincà & Cinque (2014) and §3.2 below. Here I will especially consider the syntactic aspects of these four different semantic types, and try to integrate them in a unified picture with the syntactic typology mentioned above and the 'raising' and 'matching' derivations proposed in the literature for the analysis of RCs. Non-restrictive RCs will be argued, following Cinque (2008a), actually to belong to two different types (see §3.1), neither of which is derived by 'raising' of the internal Head.

---

[2] See Grosu & Landman (2017), McNally (2008), and Loccioni (2017, 2018: §5.4) for finer distinctions within maximalizing RCs. As Salzmann (2017) notes, in an amount relative like *Jill spilled the milk that there was in the can* '[t]here is [...] no restrictive interpretation where only the milk that is in the can is spilled while some other milk (e.g., that in the fridge) is not' (p. 7). Also see Mendia (2017) for the idea that amount relatives are a form of non-intersective relative clause (different from ordinary restrictives). Here I will not be concerned with such Spanish constructions as *Juan no es lo ágil que era en el pasado* 'Juan is not as agile as he was in the past.' (Rivero 1981: 189), *Juan vio lo mal que respondió María* 'Juan saw how badly Mary responded' (Ojeda 1982: 412), sometimes referred to as '"comparative" or degree relatives'. They appear to involve the raising of different categories ($[_{AP/AdvP/PP}$ DEGREE adj/adv/P] to the Spec of a comparative or interrogative or exclamative clause, alternating with the raising of a *wh*-determiner + adj/adv/etc. (*Juan no es tan ágil como lo era en el pasado/Juan vio cuan mal respondió María*), and it is not clear if they involve a double-Headed structure.

1.3   A Unified Double-Headed Analysis

Despite the apparent differences existing among the various syntactic and semantic types of RCs, these will be argued to instantiate one and the same double-Headed structure (whether they involve a 'raising' or a 'matching' derivation).[3]

If English-type, post-nominal, relatives were to be taken to (most closely) reflect the structure of (external) Merge, with pre-nominal ones (and others) derived from them, the [$_{DP}$ D CP], plus Head raising, analysis of Kayne (1994: ch. 8 – see (2)) would, as Kayne notes, be virtually forced by Antisymmetry.[4]

(2)   [$_{DP}$ the [$_{CP}$ book [$_{C'}$ that [$_{IP}$ we read t]]]]

Here I explore an alternative analysis, also compatible with Antisymmetry, suggested in Cinque (2003) and which takes (if linear order is part of narrow syntax) pre-nominal relatives to be the ones, if any, that more directly reflect the structure of Merge of RCs, with post-nominal and other types of relatives derived from them.[5]

This change of perspective finds some basis, I submit, in the more general observation that constituents found to the right of a lexical head (N, V, A, etc.) are arguably never *merged* there, but come to be there as a consequence of the

---

[3] The present analysis is in accord with Grosu (2002: 145), where the existence is assumed 'of distinguished syntactically represented elements in both the matrix and the relative clause'.

[4] The other possible antisymmetrical option for post-nominal RCs, with CP as the complement of N, appears not to yield the right semantics (see Kayne 1994: 87), nor can it accommodate the fact that the relative clause Head is phrasal (Kayne 1994: 154 fn. 13). For modifications which essentially remain within the [D CP] analysis plus Head raising (for restrictive relative clauses), see Bianchi (1999, 2000a, 2000b), De Vries (2002), Sportiche (2015, 2017a), among others.

[5] A pre-nominal analysis of RCs (where pre-nominal ones may involve extra movement steps from the 'base' pre-nominal merger) is reminiscent, modulo phrasal- rather than head-movement, of Fukui and Takano's (2000) idea that RCs are left-adjoined and that postnominal ones require additional movement across the RC. Kim (1997: §3) and Borsley (2001) also mentioned the pre-nominal merger of RCs as a possibility. Aoun and Li (2003) argue for a left adjunction of the RC to the Head NP, for Chinese. Isac (2001, 2003), and Ouhalla (2004) for Semitic, propose generating RCs in a left branch specifier, of a Conj(unct)P and NP, respectively.

Should linear order prove to be a PF phenomenon (see fn. 4 of the Introduction, and Cinque 2017b, 2018 for discussion), different types of movement will have to apply in narrow syntax to an unordered structure to build the appropriate hierarchical configurations that yield the different orders in PF under the LCA. The trees in this and later chapters should in fact be seen as neutral between a conception of linearization as a narrow syntax or a PF phenomenon, although their two-dimensional representation will necessarily manifest a linear order.

lexical head, or one of its projections, moving leftwards, past them (in head-initial languages). The main evidence for this sweeping conclusion comes from a pervasive left-right asymmetry found across languages, which I briefly illustrate in the next section (for more detailed discussion see Cinque 2009a).

1.4 The Pre-nominal Origin of Relative Clauses If Linear Order Is Part of Narrow Syntax

Quite generally, across languages one finds that to the left of a head (N, V, A, etc.) the order of complements, adjuncts, and modifiers, is unique, while to the right of the head more possibilities exist; either the same order as that found to the left of the head, or, more frequently, its mirror image. Greenberg's (1963) Universal 20 exemplifies this state of affairs with N and some of its modifiers:

(3)   'When any or all of the items (demonstrative, numeral, and descriptive adjective) precede the noun, they are always found in that order. If they follow, the order is either the same or its exact opposite.'

In other words, we find the pattern in (4):[6]

Order of Demonstratives, numerals, and adjectives (Greenberg 1963; Cinque 1996, 2005)

(4)   a.   Dem > Num > A > **N**   (English, Malayalam, . . .)
        b.   *A > Num > Dem > **N**   0
        c.   **N**> Dem > Num >A   (Abu', Kikuyu, . . .)
        d.   **N** > A > Num > Dem   (Gungbe, Thai, . . .)

Exactly the same pattern is found with the relative order of A(djective)P(hrase)s ((5)), A(dverb)P(hrase)s ((6)), circumstantial PPs ((7)), and Mood, Tense, and Aspect morphemes ((8)):

Order of (attributive) adjectives: (Hetzron 1978; Sproat & Shih 1990; Cinque 1994, 2010a; Plank 2003: 11–12)[7]

---

[6] This is in fact a simplification, which however does not affect the thrust of the argument. While the pre-nominal order is Dem > Num > Adj without exceptions (or virtually so; see Cinque in preparation, where out of more than 1800 languages only one language, Dhivehi, appears not to conform, in ways, however, that are not entirely clear), more possibilities than the two Dem > Num > Adj and Adj > Num > Dem are actually attested post-nominally (see Cinque 2005 and in preparation for a review and for an illustration of how they can be derived by different leftward movements).

[7] These orders are rigid in some languages but just the unmarked ones in others. In the latter case, the rigidity of the class of direct modification adjectives (those not derived from RCs) is obscured by the existence of a second class of adjectives (those derived from RCs). See Cinque (2010a: §3.3.2).

(5) a. $A_{size} > A_{colour} > A_{provenance}$ $> N$ (English, Bulgarian …)
   b. $*A_{provenance} > A_{colour} > A_{size}$ $> N$ 0
   c. $N > A_{size} > A_{colour} > A_{provenance}$ (Welsh, Irish …)[8]
   d. $N > A_{provenance} > A_{colour} > A_{size}$ (Indonesian, Yoruba, …)[9]

Order of adverbs: (Rackowski 1998, Rackowski & Travis 2000, Pearson 2000, Cinque 1999: 42–3)

(6) a. $Adv_{\text{'no longer'}} > Adv_{\text{'always'}} > Adv_{\text{'completely'}}$ $> V$ (English, Chinese, …)
   b. $*Adv_{\text{'completely'}} > Adv_{\text{'always'}} > Adv_{\text{'no longer'}}$ $> V$ 0
   c. $V > Adv_{\text{'no longer'}} > Adv_{\text{'always'}} > Adv_{\text{'completely'}}$ (Italian, (main clause) German, …)
   d. $V > Adv_{\text{'completely'}} > Adv_{\text{'always'}} > Adv_{\text{'no longer'}}$ (Malagasy, Niuean, …)

Order of circumstantial PPs (Boisson 1981, Cinque 2002, Hinterhölzl 2002,[10] Schweikert 2005a, 2005b)

(7) a. Temp > Loc > Manner **V**   (German/Korean/Turkish – Haider 2000, Kornfilt pers. comm.)[11]
   b. *Manner > Loc > Temp > **V**   0
   c. **V** > Temp > Loc > Manner   (Otomi, V2 clause German)
   d. **V** > Manner > Loc > Temp   (English/Italian/Norwegian – Nilsen 2000: 60 ff)
   e. Dutch: Temp > Loc > Manner **V** & **V** > Manner > Loc > Temp (Barbiers 1995)

Order of Mood, Tense, and Aspect morphemes (Cinque 2013a)[12]

(8) a. Mood Tense Aspect **V**   (Nama, Yoruba, …)
   b. *Aspect Tense Mood **V**   0
   c. **V** Mood Tense Aspect   (Comox, …)
   d. **V** Aspect Tense Mood   (Korean, Malayalam, …)

---

[8] While the relative order of post-nominal adjectives of size, colour, and provenance in Welsh is the same as the order of the same adjectives in pre-nominal position in English (see Rouveret 1994: 213), other adjectives (among which quality, age, the functional adjective *other*, and demonstrative adjectives) show a (post-nominal) order which is the mirror image of the English order (see Willis 2006, and references cited there):

N A_{size} A_{colour} $A_{provenance}$ A_{age} $A_{quality}$ 'other' Dem.

If movement of phrases containing the NP rather than N movement is responsible for DP internal orders (Cinque 2005), this mixture of direct and mirror-image orders of nominal modifiers can be reconciled (*pace* Willis 2006) with Antisymmetry and a unique, universal, structure of (external) Merge.

[9] Concerning Yoruba, see Ajíbóyè (2001) and Cinque (2010a: §3.5.1.2 n. 15).

[10] '[…] Time, Place and Manner adverbs occur preverbally in the order T > P > M in OV languages, but in exact mirror image in VO languages' (Hinterhölzl 2002: 276).

[11] Temp > Loc (> Ben) > Manner > V is also the order given by Kroeker (2001: 3) for SOV Nambikuara.

[12] Mood refers, here and in Cinque (2014), only to morphemes encoding Declarative, Interrogative, or Imperative force. See Cinque (2014: §2) for some apparent counterexamples to the absence of the order in (8b).

The same pattern is also found within one and the same language (see (9) concerning the orders of auxiliaries and restructuring verbs in Hungarian, and (10) and (11) concerning the order of clitics in Modern Greek and Occitan varieties, respectively), or within one and the same language family (see the order of lexical verbs, modals, and auxiliaries in Germanic – Barbiers 2005, Abels 2016). To the left of the lexical V only one order is possible, while to the right of the lexical V two orders are possible – either the same order as the preverbal one or its mirror image.

Order of auxiliary and 'restructuring' verbs (Koopman & Szabolcsi 2000: 80–1)

(9) a   Aux 'begin' 'want'   **V**   (Hungarian, …)
     b   *'want' 'begin' Aux   **V**   0
     c   **V** Aux 'begin' 'want'   (Hungarian, …)
     d   **V** 'want' 'begin' Aux   (Hungarian, …)

Order of dative and accusative clitics in Modern Greek (Terzi 1999: 86)

(10) a   **Mou to** edoses
          me$_\text{Dat}$ it$_\text{Acc}$ gave.2sg
          'You gave it to me.'
      b. ***To mou** edoses
          it$_\text{Acc}$ me$_\text{Dat}$ gave.2sg
          'You gave it to me.'
      c. Dos' **mou to**
          give me$_\text{Dat}$ it$_\text{Acc}$
          'Give it to me!'
      d. Dos' **to mou**
          give it$_\text{Acc}$ me$_\text{Dat}$
          'Give it to me!'

Order of dative and accusative clitics in Occitan varieties (Ordóñez 2002: 217)

(11) a. **Lo me** dussèt pas veire
          it$_\text{Acc}$ me$_\text{Dat}$ let not see
          'You did not let me see it.'
      b. ***Me lo** dussèt pas veire
          me$_\text{Dat}$ it$_\text{Acc}$ let not see
          'You did not let me see it.'
      c. Daussa-**lo me**
          let it$_\text{Acc}$ me$_\text{Dat}$
          let me it
      d. Daussa-**m lo**
          let me$_\text{Dat}$ it$_\text{Acc}$
          let me it

In Cinque (1996) I suggested that the left-right asymmetry displayed in (4) could find a revealing account in Kayne's antisymmetric framework, which bans the symmetrical Merge of modifiers both to the left and to the right of a head. In particular, I suggested that if we were to take the order of (external) Merge to be that in (4a) (see (12)), and if we were to take the NP to optionally raise successive-cyclically, either by itself (see (13)) or by pied-piping each time the projection to whose Spec it raises (see (14)), the unique order to the left of the head, and the two orders to the right of the head, would follow (also see Cinque 2005):[13]

(12)   Dem Num A N

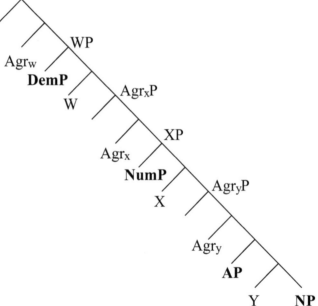

---

[13] See now Cinque (2017b) for the possibility that even (4a) involves movement with pied-piping of the *picture-of-whom* type, which does not alter the order of modifiers, rather than with pied-piping of the *whose-picture* type, which reverses their order.

(13)   N Dem Num A

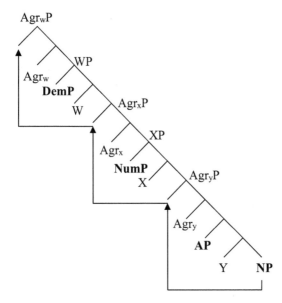

(14)   N A Num Dem

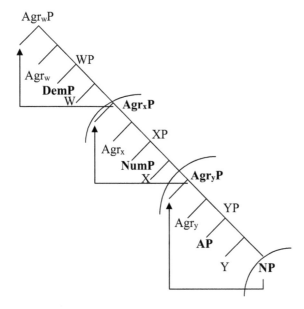

This amounts to saying that the orders of modifiers found to the right of the N are a function of the NP raising (sometimes within a larger phrase) past them, merged in hierarchically higher specifiers (preceding the head if linear order is part of narrow syntax). Similar considerations hold for the other instances of the same pattern noted above. It is in fact difficult to see how this pattern could be derived otherwise from a *single* universal structure. Under the widespread idea that complements and adjuncts to the right of a head are in their Merge position there, one would have to base generate the two orders to the right of the head, as well as the one to the left of the head, independently of the others even if we feel that they are the *same* order (literally the same in the case of the (a) and (c) cases, and in the (d) case the mirror-image order, which is, at a more abstract level, the same order). If one assumes that all complements, adjuncts, and modifiers of the extended projection of N, as well as those of the extended projections of V, A, P, etc., are (externally) merged higher up, pre-nominally, pre-verbally, etc. (if linear order is part of narrow syntax), the observed left-right asymmetry necessarily follows, as noted, from independent properties of movement (phrasal movement with, or without, pied-piping).

All this has the direct consequence that the only possible (external) Merge position of a relative clause is the pre-nominal one (if linear order is part of narrow syntax), and that its post-nominal position is derived by leftward movement of the relative clause 'Head' past it (a consequence, in fact, of the general derivation of head-initial languages from the universal structure of external Merge). See Cinque (2017b) for more detailed discussion.

In what follows I argue that the external Head corresponds to the extended projection of the NP which is immediately below the projection that hosts the relative clause (the complement of X, in (15)):

(15)   [. . .[$_{XP}$ **RC** [$_{XP}$ X [. . . [$_{NP}$ **N**]]]]]

As to the precise location of RCs with respect to other (pre-nominal) modifiers some typological evidence, to be reviewed in §3.5, seems to indicate that the restrictive and maximalizing types are introduced between the determiner or demonstrative and the (cardinal) numerals (see (16) below)[14], the participial type lower down, between the (cardinal) numerals and the adjectives, and the finite non-restrictive type higher up, above determiners and demonstratives. See §3.5 for evidence to this effect and for the (external) Merge position of kind-defining and infinitival RCs.

---

[14] For the time being I take finite maximalizing RCs to have the same (external) Merge position of finite restrictive RCs, but see §3.5 for possible evidence that they occupy two distinct, possibly contiguous, positions. As shown below in head-initial/medial languages they end up in post-nominal position, and in head-final languages they can also come to occupy a pre-demonstrative position (also see below the discussion concerning Chinese in §3.6).

(16)   [DemP D° [RC X° [Num$_{card}$P Y° [AP Z° [NP]]]]]

As already mentioned, not much would change if linear order were a property of the PF interface rather than of narrow syntax. The external Merge of the RC CP in a Spec asymmetrically c-commanding the external Head (i.e., the portion of the extended nominal projection below it) would ensure, if nothing happens, that the RC is linearized under the LCA to the left of the external Head. If on the other hand the external Head were to raise to a Spec asymmetrically c-commanding the RC CP, the latter would be linearized to the right of the external Head (thus appearing in post-nominal position).

The external Merge position of restrictive and maximalizing RCs between Det/ Dem and (cardinal) numerals ((16)) also has the semantically desirable property of having the restrictive or maximalizing RC and its external Head both under the scope of D°.[15] If the external Head of the RC is whatever is c-commanded by the RC (namely, [Num$_{card}$P Y° [AP Z° [NP]]] in (16)) (cardinal) numerals are part of the Head. That cardinal numerals are part of the Head is indicated by the family of Head Internal RCs that show an indefinite restriction on the internal Head, which can apparently contain them (see Cinque 2008b, and §2.3).[16]

---

[15] The role of D° is to express the uniqueness (or maximality) of the intersection between the set of entities contributed by the external Head and the set of entities contributed by the RC (Grosu & Landman 1998: §1). This analysis bears some resemblance to an early analysis of RCs (the so-called Art-S (Det-CP) analysis of Smith 1964; also see Chomsky 1965: 128 ff and Larson & LaTerza 2017), in which the RC is merged with the determiner to form a constituent, from which it is later extraposed. This analysis was meant to capture the apparent fact that with certain nouns (proper names, *way*, *kind*, etc.) a determiner cannot occur unless there is a full or reduced relative clause (**la Venezia* 'the Venice' vs *la Venezia che amo di più ...* 'the Venice (that) I love more ...', **he did it a/the way* vs *He did it the way (that) you had prescribed*). Notice however that a determiner appears to be licensed also in the presence of modifiers that do not have a relative clause source (*l'altra/la futura/la povera Venezia* 'the other/the future/poor Venice', *He did it that way*), which might suggest that the presence of a determiner is dependent on modification in general rather than on modification by a RC. The obligatory restrictive RC after the German complex definite determiner *der-/die-/dasjenige* (Blümel 2011, Blümel & Liu 2019) is no clear evidence for a D CP structure with 'raising', as the determiner plus the Head can be stranded by extraposition of the RC (*Jens hat **diejenige Musikerin** nach dem Konzert ausgelacht, die das einfache Stück nicht spielen konnte* 'Jens laughed at the/that musician after the concert who couldn't play the easy piece.'). The present analysis of restrictive or max-imalizing RCs is closer to the Nom-S analysis of Stockwell, Schachter & Partee (1973: ch. 7) and Partee (1976), which has a natural semantic compositional analysis. For complications introduced by coordinated DP Heads ('hydras'), see §5.1. The present analysis also differs from the Art-S one in not having the RC ever form a constituent with the determiner and in not extraposing the RC, which will be seen to acquire its postnominal position (when it does) via raising of either the internal or the external Head.

[16] It is also apparently supported by those cases where a cardinal numeral within the Head can be understood in the scope of a quantifier in the RC (as in *I met the two students that each professor invited* – see Bianchi 1999: 45–6), though perhaps not all such cases constitute an

1.5   Pre-nominal Merge, Antisymmetry, and a Unified Double-Headed Structure for 'Raising' and 'Matching'

As noted, under a pre-nominal Merge of RCs, both 'raising' and 'matching' are compatible with Antisymmetry. This may prove a welcome result if both types of derivation must be available, as some evidence brought up in the recent literature seems to suggest. See the Appendix for a list of works advocating this position and for a survey of the evidence that a 'non-raising' derivation must be available in addition to the 'raising' one. My attempt in the next chapters will be to show the feasibility of deriving from *a single, double-headed, structure* the attested types of RCs, in both the 'raising' and the (different types of) 'matching' derivations. As apparent from (17) below, which is to be thought of as built bottom up (with Merge and Move interspersed), this unified structure has both an external and an internal Head. This generalizes to all relatives (even those involving 'raising') the double-Headed structure assumed in the early literature for 'matching'.

Given that the external Head (the chunk of the extended projection of the NP modified, c-commanded, by the RC) is 'indefinite' (only contains weak determiners in Milsark's 1974 terms), the internal Head, when the two Heads are exact matches of each other, is also 'indefinite'. The exact match case is at the base of the (hidden) indefiniteness of the internal Head of restrictive RCs with invariant relativizers (*che, that, co*, etc.),[17] and of the indefiniteness restriction of Internally Headed RCs of Lakhota-type languages, to which I return in §2.3.[18]

---

argument for the syntactic 'raising' (and reconstruction) of the internal Head. See Chapter 2: fn. 11 and related text for discussion. Bhatt (2002) takes also ordinal numerals to be reconstructable inside the RC (thus suggesting their being part of the internal Head). Ordinals in fact appear to be merged in two distinct positions, one to the left and one to the right of cardinal numerals; two positions that can both be filled. See the following Italian, French, and Russian examples *i miei* **ultimi** *due* **primi** *giorni di scuola, mes deux* **derniers premiers** *jours de l'école* 'my last two first days of school', **poslednie** *pjat'* **pervyx** *učitelej* 'the last five first teachers' – Kagan & Pereltsvaig, 2012: 171) (see Cinque 2015b: fn. 4).

[17] See Browning (1987: 129 ff), Cinque (2008b) and references cited there. For simplicity, I am taking *che, que, that, co*, etc. to be complementizers inserted under a C head, but see Kayne (2014a [2010]), Sportiche (2011) and Koopman & Sportiche (2014) for arguments that they may be (weak) invariant relative phrases, which would require merging them in the specifier of an additional (silent) C head. This is especially true if Kayne (2015a) is right in his suggestion that all overt elements are merged in specifier position, heads being necessarily silent. For evidence that RCs actually involve multiple CP projections and a rich left periphery see §2.1.3/ §2.1.4.

[18] For simplicity the representation in (17), as well as all subsequent ones in this and later chapters, will abstract away from the pre-verbal merger of objects and the head-final merger of V, I, C. In such a merger the position of the V(P) *wrote* of (17) would be the result of its crossing over the

(17)

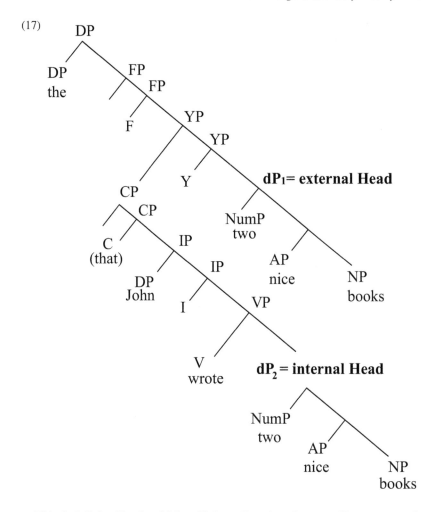

This indefinite Head, which will be referred to here as dP, may contain multal/paucal quantifiers, cardinal (and possibly ordinal) numerals, adjective phrases, and, as already mentioned, an overt or silent indefinite determiner, apparently sandwiched between cardinal numerals and adjectives (see the Ladin dialects of Val Badia and Val Gardena, where, as noted in Haiman & Benincà 1992: 152, the feminine cardinal numeral *øna/una* 'one' co-occurs with, and precedes, the feminine indefinite determiner *na*, itself apparently a reduced form of the cardinal numeral, which in turn precedes a pre-nominal

---

dP$_2$ object merged in a specifier position (to a position lower than I, though higher than the lowest adverbs: *well, early,* etc.). See Cinque (2017b).

adjective, if present: *øna na (bela)* 'skwadra 'one a (nice) team'; *una na (bela) rama* 'one a (nice) branch' – see Rasom 2008: 296, 310).[19]

This indefinite dP, although smaller than a full DP (which contains also strong determiners), can still function as the antecedent of a 'definite' pronoun (see (18a)), or of PRO (see (18b)), and can license parasitic (DP) gaps (see (18c)) (see Borsley 1997: 632):

(18)   a.   The [boy]$_i$ that t$_i$ said he$_i$ would come …
       b.   The [boy]$_i$ that t$_i$ refused PRO$_i$ to work for you …
       c.   The [boy]$_i$ that John invited t$_i$ without really knowing e$_i$ well …

This appears to be corroborated by the possibility of resuming even a *non-specific* indefinite nominal phrase with an apparently 'definite' pronoun in Italian. See (19), and also Aoun & Li (2003: §6.1.2) for evidence that the Head of Chinese RCs is smaller than DP:

(19)   a.   **Una ragazza**$_i$ prima o poi **la**$_i$ troverà   (Cinque 2008b: 20)
            a girl sooner or later her he.will.find
            'Sooner or later he will find some girl or other.'
       b.   **Una sorella**, ce l'ha anche Gianni   (Kayne 2016b: fn. 27)
            a sister, there her has also Gianni = 'Gianni has a sister, too.'

Exemplifying with English externally Headed post-nominal restrictive or maximalizing RCs, 'raising' and 'matching' can be seen as two different derivational options open to this double-Headed structure. I briefly consider here just the case in which the two Heads are exact matches of each other, i.e. dPs, leaving to the next chapter the case where the internal Head is not an exact match of the external one. As noted, in the 'raising' derivation, it is the Head internal to the relative clause that ends up being the **overt** Head by raising to Spec,CP and licensing the deletion of the external Head (see (20))[20]. The invariant relativizer *that* may or may not be spelled out. In this derivation

---

[19] This comes close to Kayne's (1994: 124) suggestion that the English indefinite determiner *a* does not occupy D but is lower and moves together with the internal Head to Spec,CP, and to Bianchi's (2000a: §1) proposal that what is raised is a DP with an empty D. On the relation between numeral 'one' and the indefinite article, see Kayne (2015b).

[20] Under Kayne's (1994: 16) definition of c-command, dP$_2$ in the Spec,CP of (20) c-commands dP$_1$ as it is not contained in CP, nor in YP. In some variants of the 'raising' analysis (Schachter 1973, Vergnaud 1974, 1985, Cecchetto & Donati 2011, 2015) the internal Head is taken eventually to raise outside the CP (what Sportiche 2017a: §2.2 calls 'High Promotion'). This however may have undesirable consequences, as it leads to the expectation that the RC of amount/maximalizing relatives can extrapose stranding the Head, contrary to fact (see the discussion in §2.5.6 and in A4 of the Appendix). Also see the evidence from Bulgarian (exx. (62) of Chapter 2 and related text) and from Croatian clitic second syntax (mentioned in fn. 160 of Chapter 2) that in 'raising' derivations the internal Head remains inside the RC CP.

reconstruction and island effects are detectable as the ***overt*** Head is in a chain with the RC internal position. As to the Case borne by the Head in 'raising' derivations, which is the one assigned externally, see below.

(20)

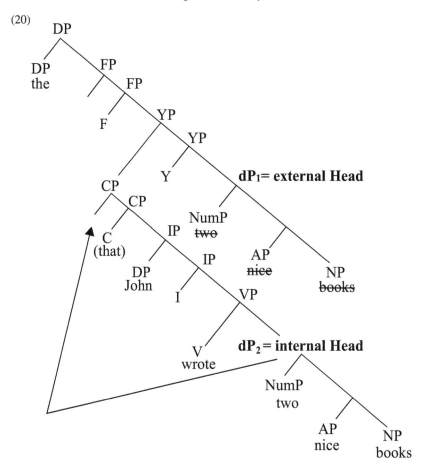

If on the other hand it is the external Head that raises to Spec,FP (as a consequence of the movement options characteristic of head-initial/medial languages – see fn. 1 of the next chapter and Cinque 2017b), licensing the deletion of the internal one, we have one (type of) 'matching' derivation. In this derivation reconstruction effects are not detectable as the ***overt*** Head, the external one, is not in a chain with the relative clause internal position (see (21)).[21]

---

[21] Island effects may still be detectable if the Head internal to the relative clause also raises before being deleted, but here variation exists. See the resumptive strategy discussed in §4.3. The two

(21)

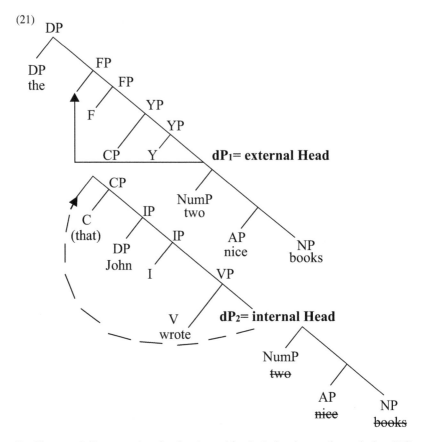

In Chapter 2 I argue that in the 'matching' derivations of restrictive RCs, where the overt Head is the external one, the internal Head need not be an

derivations in (20) and (21) bear some resemblance to the 'promotion' and the 'matching' derivations of Aoun & Li (2003: ch. 4) for head-initial English and Lebanese Arabic, modulo our pre-nominal Merge of the RC and their direct Merge of the external Head in a position higher than CP. Aoun and Li in fact abandon the idea of deriving all RCs from a single universal structure ('We have entertained and rejected the possibility of a universal structure for relative constructions' (p. 210) because the [D CP] structure proposed for post-nominal RCs cannot extend to Chinese pre-nominal RCs, for which they propose that the RC left adjoins to NP. The pre-nominal merger of RCs assumed here does however permit the unification of both post-nominal and pre-nominal RCs in Chinese-type languages, as shown in the next chapter (also see the discussion of Chinese RCs in §3.6). The potential Relativized Minimality violation, in (21), induced by dP$_1$ crossing over dP$_2$, which c-commands it under Kayne's 1994 definition of c-command (see Szczegielniak 2016) can perhaps be avoided if in the 'matching' derivation the internal Head does not need to raise to the highest CP projection of the RC multiple CP structure discussed below in §2.1.3/§2.1.4.

exact match of the external one; for example, when the relativized internal Head is bigger than an indefinite dP, i.e. a DP/KP or an DP/KP inside a larger phrase (PP, DP, etc.) no deletion of the internal Head is possible. In these cases of categorial distinctness the internal Head is represented by a *wh*-pronoun or a resumptive one.[22]

---

[22] The structures in (20) and (21) reflect the version of the structure I had proposed in Cinque (2003), later modified by taking the RC to be just an IP, with the CPs hosting the internal and the external Heads part of the extended projection of the NP (see Cinque 2008b). I return here to the original proposal because this better fits the derivation of head-initial structures suggested in Cinque (2013a, 2017b) and some considerations put forth in Poletto & Sanfelici (2014, 2018).

2 Deriving the Cross-Linguistically Attested Types of Restrictive and Maximalizing Relative Clauses from a Double-Headed Structure

In this chapter I consider only finite restrictive and maximalizing RCs (see Chapter 3 for the derivation of finite non-restrictive and other kinds of RCs). The goal here is to show how the seven attested syntactic types of restrictive and maximalizing RCs can be derived through independently motivated operations (movement, deletion, and replacement by a proform) from the unique, double-Headed, structure presented in §1.5.

Let me begin with the externally headed post-nominal type already introduced, and refine certain aspects of it. I take from now on a simplified version of the external and internal Heads, ignoring weak determiners and adjective phrases, which may be part of the external and internal Heads.

2.1 Externally Headed Post-nominal Relative Clauses

As noted, the 'raising' and 'matching' derivations can be seen as two different derivational options open to the double-Headed structure in (1), which will be enriched as we proceed. For the time being I just indicate the structure and labels that are relevant, in X-bar format; the trees can also be taken to indicate just the hierarchical structure prior to linearization, if this takes place on the PF side under the LCA.

(1)

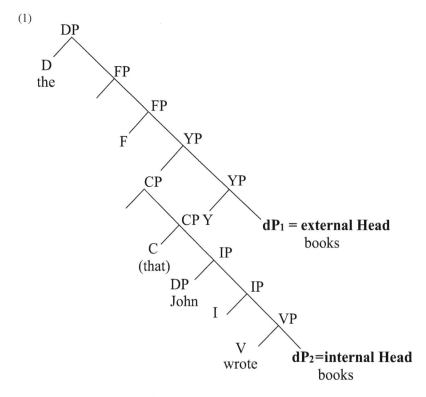

In the 'raising' option, it is the Head internal to the relative clause that, raising to the Spec of the RC CP, licenses the deletion (non-pronunciation) of the external Head and ends up being the **overt** Head. In the 'matching' option, it is instead the external Head (which in head-initial languages raises to a projection higher than the RC CP, the Spec,FP in (1))[1] that licenses the deletion of the internal Head, thus ending up as the **overt** Head.[2] But see §2.1.2 for other types of 'matching'.

---

[1] As evident from the properties and derivation of head-initial and head-final languages suggested in Cinque (2017b) the movement of the external Head to Spec,FP, above the RC CP, is a consequence of the regular derivation of DP-structure in head-initial languages, where the NP, or a projection of the NP, raises above its modifiers in a roll-up fashion; above all of the modifiers in rigid head-initial languages ($[[[[[N]_i A t_i]_j Num t_j]_k RC t_k]_m Dem t_m]$), or of only some of them in non-rigid head-initial (or head-medial) languages like English (Dem [Num A N]$_i$ RC t$_i$).

[2] In both cases, depending on the language and other factors, the presence of an invariant relativizer (*that, che,* etc.) may be necessary. For the time being I represent the invariant relativizer in the head of the same CP projection that hosts in its specifier the raised internal

2.1.1   The 'Raising' Derivation

This derivation appears to be forced in those cases where the overt Head has to be interpreted inside the RC (Carlson 1977; Grosu & Landman 1998, 2017; Sauerland 2003: 244); and hence must be in a chain with the copy left under movement inside the RC, as in amount RCs, 'Headless' (or Free) RCs, RCs relativizing a predicate, (some) RCs with Inverse Case Attraction, etc.[3]

Consider a sentence like (2) under the maximalizing 'amount' interpretation of *libri* 'books' ('the (ENTIRE) NUMBER OF books'), and its derivation, sketched in (3):[4]

(2)   Se avesse continuato a fare il preside non avrebbe potuto scrivere i libri che ha scritto.[5]
       Had he continued to be a dean, he could not have written the books that he wrote.

Head, although it is plausible that it is merged, as a head (or possibly as a phrase), in a distinct, lower, CP projection, as in (i):

(i) $[_{DP}$ D $[_{FP}$ F $[_{CP1}$ dP_i $[_{CP2}$ *that* $[_{IP}$ t_i]]] dP]

[3] Bhatt and Pancheva (2012) argue that the Head must be interpreted inside the RC also in certain cases involving superlatives (e.g., *the boy who Mary likes the most* …). Also see Loccioni (2018: §5.4).

[4] The maximalizing interpretation of the amount reading vs the not necessarily maximalizing interpretation of the substance reading is clear in a pair of sentences like the following:

(i)   a.   It will take us the rest of our lives to drink the champagne that they spilled last night. (Heim 1987: 38)
       b.   Did you drink the champagne that was served last night at the party?

In the case of (i)b the more natural interpretation is that we drank *some* of the champagne that was served at the party (or that we drank, not necessarily at the party, the kind/brand of champagne served there – Alex Grosu, pers. comm.), while in the case of (i)a the natural interpretation is: *the total amount* of the champagne that was served at the party.

[5] The sentence is in fact ambiguous in three ways. In addition to 'the (entire) number of books', one can also interpret it as 'the kind of books' (that he wrote) or 'the specific individual books' (that he wrote). This may suggest that *books* is actually merged as the specifier of a functional noun like NUMBER, KIND or THING, respectively. That NPs may always be headed by a functional noun was suggested in Kayne (2007b: Appendix) as a consequence of his Principle of Decomposition. It remains to be seen whether the 'kind' reading also forces a 'raising' derivation like the 'amount' reading (see Sauerland 1999), possibly unlike the 'thing' reading, which may not necessarily force it. For discussion of amount RCs see Grosu & Landman (1998, 2017), Fintel (1999), Herdan (2008a, 2008b), McNally (2008), Meier (2015) and Mendia (2017), and for additional references Radford (2019: 14 fn. 6).

(3)

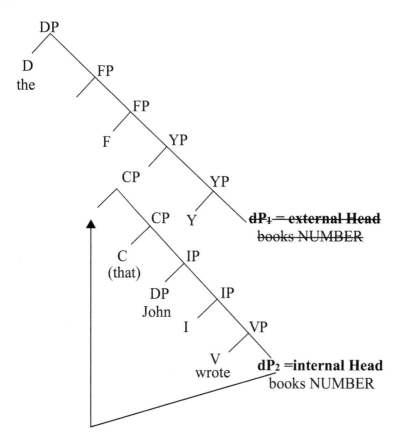

In this case both 'reconstruction' ((4a)) and island sensitivity, of the strong ((4b)), and weak type ((4c)) are expected, as the **overt** Head is in a movement chain relation with the relative clause internal position and is non-referential.[6]

---

[6] I take the Spec,CP to which the internal Head raises to be an intrinsic operator position, which endows the raised dP_2 with operator status, capable of licensing the copy/trace of the internal Head as a variable, much like the Spec of FocusP in Italian (*QUEL FILM, ho visto __ (non questo)!* 'That film (focus) I saw (not this one)!') vs the Spec of TopP of Italian Clitic Left Dislocation (pragmatically, a kind of Topicalization), which doesn't (thus requiring a clitic to locally bind the IP-internal empty category – see Cinque 1990: ch. 2): *Quel film, *(l') ho già visto.* Lit.: That film, (it) I have already seen = 'That film, I already saw.' I take the internal Head not to raise out of the RC into Spec, FP, for the reason mentioned in fn. 20 of Chapter 1. I also assume that *that*, and the analogous invariant relativizers *che* in Italian, *que* in French, *deto* in

(4)   a.   ... the degree x such that he wrote x many books (see Carlson 1977; Grosu & Landman 1998)

         b.   *Se avesse continuato a fare il preside non avrebbe potuto scrivere i libri che è stato premiato per aver scritto.

                Had he continued to be a dean, he could not have written the books that he got a prize for having written.

         c.   Se avesse continuato a fare il preside non avrebbe potuto scrivere i libri che mi sono sempre chiesto quando avesse scritto (impossible under the 'amount' interpretation, though not under the individual reading)

                Had he continued to be a dean, he could not have written the books that I always wondered when he had written.

The 'raising' analysis of relative clauses has been extensively discussed in the past (either as the only derivation available for RCs or as one of the possible derivations). See, among many others, Schachter (1973), Vergnaud (1974, 1985), Carlson (1977), Åfarli (1994), Kayne (1994), Sauerland (1998, 1999, 2003), Bianchi (1999, 2000a, 2004), Zwart (2000), Bhatt (2002, 2015), De Vries (2002), Szczegielniak (2005, 2012), Radford (2016).[7] Because of that, here I will limit myself to summarizing the main properties of the 'raising' derivation, manifested in maximalizing RCs such as amount/degree RCs, 'Headless' (Free) RCs, correlatives, (some) RCs with idiom chunk Heads, etc.

Bulgarian (Krapova 2010), *še* in Hebrew (Cole 1976), *co* in Czech and Polish, and *što* in Russian (Szczegielniak 2004, Šimík 2008b), etc., are directly merged in CP (possibly in one CP below the CP targeted by *wh*-phrases) as these relativizers seem also to be found in structures where there is no evidence of movement given the construction's insensitivity to islands. See §4.3. Cross-linguistically, invariant relativizers of (postnominal) RCs fall into a number of different classes. They can be drawn from the demonstrative paradigm (as the distant demonstrative adjective *that* of English, or the 'near speaker' demonstratives of the Bantu languages Basaá – Jenks, Makasso & Hyman 2017: 19 – and Nugunu – Ambadiang 2017: 69); or, as the Romance *che/que*/etc. invariant relativizers, from an interrogative one. That Italian *che* is an invariant relativizer rather than a relative determiner – *pace* Manzini & Savoia (2003: §2.1; 2011: ch. 1), Kayne (2014a: §8) – appears to be shown by the fact that it can never be followed by a lexical noun, even in non-restrictives, which allow the *il quale* paradigm to be followed by a lexical noun: *I nostri soci, che (*soci) non sono mai in regola con i pagamenti,* ... vs *I nostri soci, i quali (soci) non sono mai in regola con i pagamenti,* ... 'Our members, which members never effect all payments, ...'. Invariant relativizers can also be related to the verb 'say' (as in many Niger-Congo and creole languages – Frajzyngier 1984). The relative clause markers that close off pre-nominal RCs are also often related to the verb 'say' (see Bayer 1999 on Indo-Aryan and Dravidian final 'complementizers'). For other sources, see Heine & Kuteva (2004: 114).

[7] Michael Brame is credited as the first to have proposed the raising derivation in an unpublished manuscript (Brame 1967 – see Chomsky 1973: fn. 70). An abridged version was published in Brame 1976: §6.1.

Some, though not all, of the cases of anaphor binding, pronominal binding, scope reconstruction, and idiom chunk reconstruction may involve 'raising' (see below and §A4.4 of the Appendix). One first property of the 'raising' derivation, stemming from the fact that the Head is in a chain with the RC-internal gap, is (obligatory) **'reconstruction'** of the Head inside the RC (see Bianchi 1999: 46; Aoun & Li 2003: §5.1 and *passim*).[8] See for example (5a), where the anaphor within the Head can only be bound by the lowest subject (see Bianchi 2004: 82), or (5b) and (5c), where the obligatory reconstruction of the R-expression (or the pronominal) within the Head leads to a violation of Principle C (or B):[9]

(5)   a.   L'immagine di se stesso$_k$/*?se stessa$_j$ che Maria$_j$ dice che lui$_k$ si è fatto è tutta sbagliata
              The image of himself/herself that Maria says that he has created is completely wrong.
       b.   *The responsible guardian of Bill$_i$'s sister that he$_i$ claims to be ...
              (Krifka 2011: §3.3)
       c.   *The picture of John$_i$/him$_i$ that he$_i$ took yesterday ...[10]

---

[8] According to Carlson (1977: §2.1) and Aoun & Li (2003: §4.2.3) reconstruction is only possible if the determiner is of the strong type ('the', 'every', 'all', etc.), which induces maximalization (weak determiners blocking or rendering reconstruction very marginal). For Sportiche (2017b) reconstruction, possibly apart from certain special cases like pseudo-clefts (Sharvit 1999a), is a property of movement only, though it may be optional in certain cases.

[9] Bianchi (2004: 82) also gives (i) as ungrammatical, due to a Principle C violation forced by total reconstruction:

   (i)   Se tu immaginassi i pettegolezzi su Gianni$_k$ che lui$_k$/pro$_k$ può aver sentito alla festa, capiresti perché sono preoccupata.
          If you could imagine the gossip concerning Gianni that he may have heard at the party, you would understand my being worried.

For me (i) is, however, acceptable in the variant with *lui* (though not in the one with pro). Also see Bianchi (1999: ch. 4, §2.1) and Bianchi (2004: 85), where she gives a simple question mark to comparable sentences with *lui* instead of pro, and Bianchi (2004: n. 21). Also see Adger et al. (2017) for experimental evidence that reconstruction for Principle C in RCs is weak, if at all present, as opposed to that found with A-bar movement of adjectival predicates.

For the potential problem stemming for the 'matching' derivation under a copy theory of movement from cases like *The pictures of John$_i$ that I think even he$_i$ would consider ~~pictures of John$_i$~~ inappropriate* ... see fn. 51 below.

[10] The violation in (5c) could also be due to the presence of a PRO subject of the dP [*picture of John/him* ...] controlled by *he* (see Chomsky 1986: 167, but also Reinhart and Reuland 1993: §5.2, and Salzmann 2019: fn. 3 and §3.4). Also see the wellformedness of *The picture of Bill$_i$ that he$_i$ thinks I took,* which adds a level of embedding to (5c) thus allowing Vehicle Change to rescue the structure (Salzmann 2019: 207) and *The picture of John$_i$ that he$_i$ took of himself$_i$ is on the mantle,* noted in Duncan (2004: 64), which presumably has an internal Head consisting of just *a picture* rather than *a picture of John,* as well as *This picture of himself, which,*

I adopt here a syntactic approach to reconstruction for the standard cases (see Fox 2000), as it extends also to the reconstruction of Principles A, B, and C of the Binding Theory, which do not (necessarily) have the interpretive consequences of scope reconstruction or the reconstruction of pronominals bound by quantifiers inside the RC, which have motivated semantic reconstruction.[11] Whenever a Condition A, B, or C effect is found (as in (5) above, but see §A.4.4.2 of the Appendix), syntactic reconstruction seems to be involved. As noted, I take reconstruction of the **overt** Head into the RC to be found only when the 'raising' derivation is forced. In the 'matching' derivations the **overt** Head is the external one, which does not reconstruct into the RC (reconstruction of the internal Head will however take place *within the RC* if the internal Head moves to Spec,CP). In sum, reconstruction obtains only within a movement chain (under a copy theory of movement, syntactic reconstruction can be achieved in a number of ways. For concreteness I adopt here Fox's 2000, 2002 proposals).

A second property (deriving from the raising of the internal Head) is **sensitivity to strong islands** (Complex NPs, Adjunct clauses, etc.), and, even more telling, **sensitivity to weak islands** (embedded *wh*-interrogatives, negative ('inner') islands, factive islands, etc.), which unites the variable left by maximalizing RC constructions to that left by adjuncts.[12]

---

incidentally, John took just yesterday, which Safir (1999: 613 fn. 23) takes not to involve 'raising' as it is a non-restrictive RC.

[11] RCs like (i)a–c, where the RC internal quantifier appears to bind a pronoun that it does not c-command, may possibly involve some version of semantic 'reconstruction' (on which see Cresti 1995, Rullmann 1995, Sharvit 1999b, Sternefeld 2001, Ruys 2011, Barker 2012, 2019, Jacobson 2002, 2019, among others). Barker (2012) goes even so far as to claim that 'a quantifier need not c-command a pronoun in order to bind it'. (p. 625)

(i)   a.   The woman that every man$_i$ loves is **his**$_i$ mother. (Sharvit 1999: 448)
       b.   The assignment [that every student$_i$ gave her$_j$] [that every phonology professor$_j$ most praised him$_i$ for] was the last one **he**$_i$ handed to **her**$_j$. (Jacobson 2002: 152)
       c.   What [everyone$_i$ hates most] is to have **his**$_i$ mother insulted. (Barker 2012: 625)

For critical discussion and possible arguments in favour of either syntactic or semantic reconstruction see Cecchetto (2006) and Heycock (2019), as well as the other contributions in Krifka & Schanner 2019.

[12] Sensitivity to strong islands does not distinguish maximalizing RCs from ordinary restrictive, kind-defining and non-restrictive RCs in those languages where they also involve movement of the internal Head. Sensitivity to weak islands does however distinguish maximalizing RCs from the other relative clause types, as the latter are not sensitive to weak islands. The reason is arguably that the latter have access to a 'matching' derivation, where the copy/trace is specific/referential (kind-defining and non-restrictives RCs will in fact be argued in Chapter 3 to have access only to a 'matching' derivation, *pace* Bianchi 2004, whose analysis for non-restrictives

So, for example, factive predicates block the low reading of ordinal adjectives (see Whitman 2013: 365):

(6)   the first book that John informed Mary that Tolstoy wrote ...
- a.   *High reading*: the ιx first [book, x] [John told Mary that Tolstoy wrote x] (the first book in reference to which John told Mary that Tolstoy wrote it)
- b.   *Low reading* (disallowed): the ιx [John told Mary that [first [Tolstoy had written [book, x]]]]

Similarly negative islands and *wh*-islands block the reconstruction of quantifiers inside the RC:

(7)   a.   Ho conosciuto i due pazienti che ogni medico non ha voluto visitare. (2 > every; *every > 2)
       I got to know the two patients that every doctor did not want to visit.
    b.   Ho conosciuto i due pazienti che mi chiedo se ogni medico sia riuscito a visitare. (2 > every; *every > 2)
       I got to know the two patients that I wonder if every doctor was able to visit.

The factor that unites the variable left by maximalizing RCs and the variable left by adjuncts may be due to the **non-specific/non-referential** nature of the copy/trace left by both (for discussion on the case of maximalizing RCs see Bianchi 2004: §3.3 and on that of adjuncts Rizzi 1990: Appendix 1, Cinque 1990: 29).

Their non-specific/non-referential nature may also be at the base of two more properties of maximalizing RCs pointed out in Bianchi (2004: §4.4 and §7.3): the fact that they are **refractory to resumptive pronouns** and the fact that they occur in Postal's (1998: ch. 2) **anti-pronominal contexts**, i.e. those that preclude the occurrence of definite pronouns, like existential *there* constructions (**There are them on the table*), change-of-colour contexts (*... but I refused to paint mine it*), name positions (*... but I didn't name mine it*), predicate nominals (**Frank became it*), adverbial DPs (**I talk that way, but Harry rarely talks it*), idiomatic V + DP structures (**Herbert claimed to have made headway on the project but he never made it*), etc.

Another possible property of amount/maximalizing RCs is their **incompatibility with relative pronouns** (of the *which/who* type), although there are apparent differences of judgement among speakers. Carlson (1977: §2.2)

I will not follow as it involves LF movement, whose existence should perhaps be dispensed with – see Kayne 1998).

explicitly says that 'A[mount]R's, unlike R[estrictive]R's, are introduced by *that* (or 0), and never by WH-forms' (p. 541), giving examples like those in (8):[13]

(8)   a.   *Every man who there was disagreed. (p. 526)

        b.   *{Those, The, Any} bugs which there were on the windshield were harmless. (p. 526)

        c.   *That's all which there is. (p. 526)

        d.   Marv put {everything, those things, the things}({that,*which}) he could in his pocket. (p. 528)

        e.   {The, Those, Any} hours {that,*which} the movie lasts beyond my bedtime make very little difference. (p. 530)

        f.   {The, Those, What, Every} (few) mile(s) {that,*which} the road went on for _ past Dry Gulch were tough ones indeed. (p. 530)

        g.   {The, Those, What, Every} (few) pounds {that,*which} Max weighs make little difference. (p. 531)

        h.   {The, Those, What, Every} feet/foot {that,*which} the javelin fell short were/was predicted by Mrs. Tivini. (p. 531)

---

[13] Also see Butler (2002), and Aoun & Li (2003: 113–4), who report Barry Schein's judgement that no reconstruction of *two* under the scope of *every doctor* is possible in (i)b:

(i)   a.   I phoned the two patients (that) every doctor will examine tomorrow. (2 > every or every > 2)

        b.   I phoned the two patients who every doctor will examine tomorrow. (2 > every but *every > 2)

Andrews (1975: 168) and Kwon, Polinsky & Kluender (2006: fn. 4) also report that some speakers find the contrasts in (ii), with relativization of idiom chunks, and Jespersen (1949: 92) points out that *wh*-pronouns are never found in exclamatory RCs like those in (iii) (which seem to receive an amount interpretation):

(ii)   a.   the headway that/*which they made on the project was impressive

        b.   the crow that/*which he ate was substantial

(iii)   a.   The money that/*which I've spent xeroxing!

        b.   The time that/*which I've wasted transmuting lead!

Bare *which* cannot be used to relativize time and manner nominal adjuncts either: *the day that/ *which we met, the way that/*which you walk* (Hendery 2012: 141 fn. 42).

    Yadroff and Billings (1998) note a similar distinction in Russian: a Head with approximative inversion (which has an amount interpretation) 'is bad if modified by relative clauses with *kotor-* 'which', but far better if the relative is with *čto* 'that'.' (p. 332). Also see Gagnon & Mitrović (2012: §3) for differences in Serbian between RCs introduced by *koj*-relative pronouns and those introduced by the invariant relativizer *što*, with only the latter open to a 'raising' derivation. Grosu & Landman (2017: §2.2), where further cases and a general discussion of this diagnostic are provided, suggests that *who/which* indicate that the abstraction is over individuals while *that*/0 are not so restricted, being compatible with abstraction over individuals, amounts, kinds, properties, etc. For a different appraisal of the distinction between *that* and *which*, see Kayne (2007a, 2014a: §16).

i.   {The, What, Those, Every} dollar(s) {that,*which} Max owes Bill will be repaid by the end of the month. (p. 531)

l.   Ted saw {everything, all} of Alice {that,*which} he wanted to see. (p. 531)

m.   ˈHuns will exhibit {any, what, the, that} courage {that,*which} they find necessary to conquer the palace. (p. 533)

n.   Mary will do {any, what, the, that} travelling {that,*which} she wants to do tomorrow. (p. 533)

o.   They are all the daughters {that,*which} he has. (p. 534 fn. 12)

p.   Coach Hayes put the best players {that,*which} he could into the game. (p. 541)

Huddleston (1984) and Šimík (2008a, 2008b) report similar judgements concerning cases of relativization of a predicate NP (9a–b) (also see Smits 1989: 288), and cases where the relative clause forms a comparison class to a superlative contained in the Head (9c–d).[14]

(9)   a.   *[He was no longer the kind and gentle person] who/which he had been when we first met him. (Huddleston 1984: 394)
      b.   Peter is not the idiot that/*which we took him for.   (Šimík 2008a: 277)
      c.   Anna Karenina is the best book that/*which I've read. (Šimík 2008a: 277)
      d.   *The best movie which I have ever seen …   (Šimík 2008a: 194)

Šimík (2008a) also claims (§2.2) that pair-list readings (involving reconstruction of the Head under the scope of a universal quantifier) are available with *that*-relatives but not with *wh*-relatives. See (10a–b):[15]

(10)   a.   The man that every woman invited, namely Paul in case of Mary, Steve in case of Ann, …
       b.   The man who every woman invited, namely *Paul in case of Mary, Steve in case of Ann, …

---

[14] Emonds (1976: 190) notes the similar illformedness of *wh*-phrases with Heads modified by *same* (also see Carlson 1977: §5 on other 'specifiers of uniqueness'):

(i)   a.   He bought the same type of cereal as/that/*which I bought yesterday.
      b.   He likes the same people as/that/*who you like.

Huddleston (1984: 394) notes that prepositionless datives are also unacceptable with *who(m)* (see (ii)a), but other (British) speakers who accept *They had sent him it/the book* find (ii)b bad with either *who(m)* or *that*:

(ii)   a.   *[John wasn't the one] whom they had sent it.
       b.   *[John wasn't the one] whom/that they had sent the book.

[15] As opposed to functional readings: *The man who every woman invited, namely her husband* …
On functional readings in RCs see Cresti (1995) and Sharvit (1997, 1999b).

As noted, other speakers find no particular difference between bona fide 'raising' RCs introduced by *that* or 0 and those introduced by a *wh*-phrase. For these speakers I would like to follow Andrew Simpson's suggestion (reported in Aoun & Li 2003: 244 n. 15), that they reanalyse such pronouns as stylistic variants of *that*/0.[16] Aoun and Li report in the same note that reconstruction (a hallmark of 'raising') is no longer possible even for the more liberal speakers if the *wh*-form is more complex, and clearly phrasal, like [*whose* NP]. See their examples (i) and (ii), given here as (11a–b):

(11)   a.   *I saw the girl of his$_i$ dreams whose pictures (John said) every boy$_i$ was showing off.
        b.   I saw the two students whose friends (John thought) every teacher visited. (no narrow scope for *two students*)

Lee (2001: 324–5) also notes that RCs introduced by *that* but not those introduced by *wh*-pronouns allow the Head to take narrow scope with respect to a RC internal quantifier (also see the discussion in Bianchi 2004: 87):

(12)   a.   We are looking for someone that knows every application. (some > every and every > some)
        b.   We are looking for someone who knows every application. (some > every and *every > some)

A comparable situation is found in Italian. RCs introduced by the invariant relativizer *che*, but not those introduced by (P) *cui* or art. + *qual-* allow reconstruction of a quantifier:

(13)   a.   I due bambini che saranno affidati ad ogni coppia provengono tutti dall'Africa. (every > 2; #2 > every)
        b.   I due bambini a cui ogni coppia vorrebbe dare il proprio nome sono qui. (*?every > 2)
              'The two children to whom each couple would like to give their name are here.'
        c.   I due bambini i quali saranno affidati ad ogni coppia provengono tutti dall'Africa. (*every > 2)
              'The two children who will be assigned to each couple all come from Africa.'

For further discussion see Aoun & Li (2003: §4.2.2) and §2.1.2.1 below.

Amount/maximalizing RCs also appear **refractory to stacking** (Carlson 1977: §4.3; Grosu & Landman 2017: §2.2), and **to extraposition** (Hulsey &

---

[16] Also see Pesetsky and Torrego's (2006: §5) analysis of *who* and *which* in English finite restrictives as agreeing variants of the complementizer *that*.

Sauerland 2006), although once again many cases of extraposition of RCs apparently involving 'raising' are judged as possible or not completely ill-formed by a number of speakers. See the discussion in A4 of the Appendix, where stacking, extraposition, and weak island sensitivity will be taken to discriminate between 'raising' and 'matching', based on the fact that bona fide maximalizing RCs ('Headless', or Free, RCs, amount and existential-*there* relatives, and relatives relativizing predicate DPs) do seem to be incompatible with them. We speculate that those cases putatively involving 'raising' that allow for stacking, extraposition, or extraction from weak islands also have access to a 'matching' derivation. See §A4.4 (this is also how I would reinterpret Bianchi's 2004 idea that restrictives can involve either a non-specific/non-referential chain or a specific/referential one). Summarizing, I take the properties listed in (14) to be characteristic of 'raising':

(14)   a.   (obligatory) reconstruction (the Head has to be interpreted inside the RC)
        b.   sensitivity to strong islands
        c.   refractoriness to resumptive pronouns
        d.   possible occurrence in anti-pronominal contexts
        e.   incompatibility with *wh*-pronouns (unless these are assimilated to an invariant relativizer)
        f.   no extraposition
        g.   no stacking (with proper intersective import)[17]
        h.   sensitivity to weak islands

Returning to the tree in (3), one question that arises is whether dP_2, once moved to Spec,CP, c-commands dP_1. Under Kayne's (1994) definition it does.[18] Since CP is not included in YP (only in one of its segments) and dP_2 is not included in CP (only in one of its segments), dP_2 does c-command dP_1. A further question is whether c-command is necessary for the internal Head to license the deletion of the external one. To judge from 'VP deletion', which can apply both forwards and backwards when the two VPs do not c-command each other, c-command by some antecedent would seem not to be required for deletion in general. In fact, in §2.3.1 I consider a case of backwards and forwards 'dP deletion' in one class of

---

[17] Grosu & Landman (2017: §2.3.4) notes that the (in)felicity of stacking with amount RCs depends on the interpretation of the stacked construction (basically, intersective singletons give rise to infelicity, but certain amount constructions not relying on singletons are possible). I am indebted to Alex Grosu for clarifying this point.

[18] 'X c-commands Y iff *X and Y are categories* and X excludes Y and every category that dominates X dominates Y' (1994: 16), where 'X excludes Y if no segment of X dominates Y' (p. 133 n. 1).

Head-external pre-nominal RCs and Head-internal ones, where neither of the two Heads c-commands the other. There may still be a difference between VP-deletion and the dP-deletion taking place in RCs. VP deletion is generally not obligatory, for example not in English (*He didn't leave because I left.*), though we lack a representative cross-linguistic survey. The dP-deletion obtaining in RCs instead appears to be obligatory in many languages (though not in those that allow double-Headed RCs – see §2.4.[19]

Another question that arises is why under the 'raising' derivation in a double-Headed structure a *wh*-internal Head raised to Spec,CP does not license the non-pronunciation of the external Head, as shown in (15):

(15)   *[the [which$_i$ (book) he bought t$_i$] (~~that~~) ~~book$_i$~~] was expensive.

To account for the impossibility of (15) one may adopt Safir's (1986: §2 and §4) or Browning's (1987: 52–63) suggestions that *wh*-relative pronouns have to enter a special relation with the Head of the RC ('R-Binding', or Agreement, under c-command by the Head).[20] In (15) there is no Head that can R-Bind, or enter into an agreement relation with, the relative *wh*-phrase (unless *book* is raised above it so as to c-command it, in which case it is no longer deletable – fn. 19). In fact I will suggest below that something like R-Binding/Agreement may be at the base of the typological observation that pre-nominal RCs (at least those that are exclusively pre-nominal) systematically lack relative pronouns of the 'which' type (although rare cases exist of pre-nominal RCs with initial invariant relativizers).[21]

[19] Possibly the deletion of the c-commanding dP by the c-commanded one has to be barred, by extending to non-chains Kayne's (1994: 96) condition (50), so that 'XP$_k$ can license the deletion of XP$_i$ (under non-distinctness) only if XP$_i$ does not c-command XP$_k$'. For the 'matching' case of English RCs, Sauerland (1999) proposes a special rule of Relative Deletion, which is similar in its obligatory character to the deletion occurring in comparative constructions. See also Bhatt (2002: 77–9). But see the next section for the different options open to the 'matching' derivation under the interpretation adopted here.

[20] Also see Chomsky (1977: 81) and Fukui & Takano (2000: 231). But see Kayne (1994: 90) for a different suggestion. The R-Binding relation may be strictly local, as in English or Italian, where no constituent can intervene between the Head and the relative *wh*-phrase, or less local, as in those languages where it may admit the intervention of Topic and Focus phrases (see §2.1.4 below). In rarer cases the relative pronoun may be related long-distance to the Head, in that it can remain in situ or undergo only partial movement, as in Punjabi (see again §2.1.4). On other, more limited, in situ usages of relative *wh*-phrases in Chinese, Polish, and English, see the last part of §2.1.4.

[21] Thinking of Italian and French *il quale/lequel* 'article + which' and the possibility of *the which* in older stages of English (up to the nineteenth century; see Emily Dickinson's '*Work while the day lasts for the night is coming in the which no man can work.*' The Letters of Emily Dickinson – 11–20 www.emilydickinson.it/l0011-0020.html – and the examples of *the which* in Allen 1977: 229, Nevalainen & Raumolin-Brunberg 2002: 114–5, and Lassiter 2011: fn. 5)

In the next section I will argue that in restrictive RCs *which* is not a deter-
miner/modifier modifying a lexical noun but (in contrast to the interrogative,
non-restrictive, kind-defining and 'Headless' relative clause *which*) a pronoun
obligatorily co-occurring with the silent functional noun THING; whence its
incompatibility with +human antecedents. See fn. 55 below.

Under the copy theory of movement (Chomsky 1993) a potential problem for
a double-Headed analysis of RCs involving a 'raising' derivation would seem to
be posed by RCs relativizing an idiom chunk (*the **headway** that John made was
satisfactory; I would like to know the **strings** that he pulled to get her a job;* etc.).
If the overt idiom chunk Head has to be reconstructed inside the RC to combine
with the other part of the idiom, the external Head, which exactly matches the
internal one, apparently has no idiom part with which to combine:

(16)

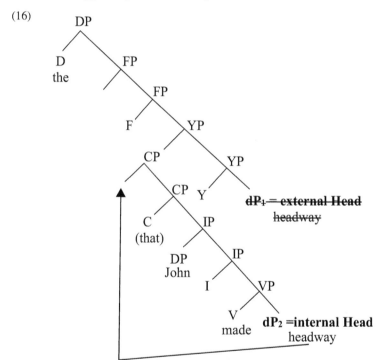

For such cases I would like to propose that a partial match between the two
Heads is (as in other cases to be seen below) sufficient, and perhaps independently justifiable. Recall the ambiguity of a sentence like (2) above, repeated

---

Modern English *which* might also be preceded by a silent determiner, recalling Bianchi (2000a:
§1).

here as (17), and the suggestion made in fn. 5 that such an ambiguity could be accounted for if *libri* 'books' was actually the specifier of a silent functional noun/classifier (either NUMBER, or KIND, or THING).

(17)   Se avesse continuato a fare il preside non avrebbe potuto scrivere i libri che ha scritto.
'Had he continued to be a dean, he could not have written the books that he wrote.'

This opens up the possibility that a sentence like *The headway that John made was satisfactory* may receive the following representation, with partial match (see Watanabe 2016 concerning Japanese amount RCs, whose analysis would be compatible with an external Head – Akira Watanabe, personal communication):[22]

(18)

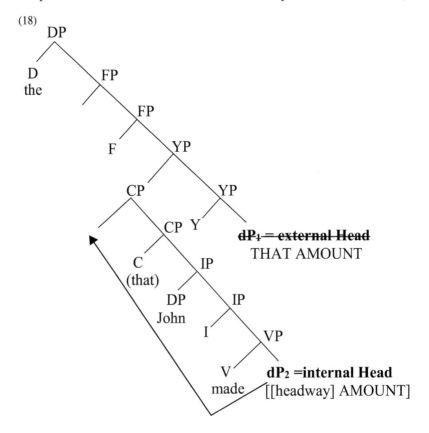

[22] See perhaps *L'enorme numero che scrive di articoli ...* 'the enormous number that he writes of articles ...'; *Mi ci vorrebbe un anno intero per bere la quantità che lui ha bevuto di champagne*

Possible support for this suggestion comes from French Sign Language (LSF). Geraci and Hauser (2017) point out that an amount reading is available only if there is an overt classifier of size and shape following the noun (see (19a)). Otherwise only a restrictive reading is available (see (19b)):

(19)   a.   IX-1 CANNOT EAT RICE **SIZE&SHAPE-CL** Rel FALL SPREAD.
       'I cannot eat the amount of rice that fell and spread on the floor.'
       b.   IX-1 CANNOT EAT RICE Rel FALL SPREAD
       'I cannot eat the rice that fell and spread on the floor.'
       '*I cannot eat the amount of rice that fell and spread on the floor.'

A partial match ((*strings*) NUMBER/KIND) may also be involved in those cases where the idiom chunk combines with the matrix verb (see (20)):[23]

(20)   Parky pulled the strings [that got me the job].   (McCawley 1981: 137)

Similar partial matches are plausibly involved also in the 'matching' derivation, where the overt Head is the external Head. Partial match of this type between the internal and external Head is in fact directly observable in languages with overtly double-Headed RCs. See the case of the Trans-New Guinea Papuan language Kombai – De Vries 1993: 77 ff) in (21), where 'man' is presumably 'man PERSON' and 'pig' 'pig THING' (also see (86) in §2.3.4 from Chamorro, and §2.4 for examples from a variety of languages):

---

ieri sera. 'I would need an entire year to drink the quantity that he drank of champagne last night.' Other idiom cases (*I was offended by the lip service that was paid to civil liberties; the careful track that she is keeping of his expenses pleases me,* etc.) may instead involve a partial match with one of the other functional nouns/classifiers (KIND or THING). The availability of partial match may also dispense with the need to assume full 'matching' with deletion of the idiom chunk in the external Head, as in Citko (2001). Alternatively, thinking of the virtually compositional nature of relativizable idioms and the relatively independent reference under specifiable conditions of the relativized idiom chunk (see section A.4.4.1 of the Appendix and the references given there), the external Head could be a full match: [[headway] AMOUNT]. I thank Alex Grosu for discussion of this point.

[23] No problem instead arises either (*pace* Douglas 2016: 22–3) in those cases, like (i), where the idiom chunk has to combine with both the matrix and the embedded verb:

(i)   a.   He managed to get out of Berlin by pulling strings that no other reporter seemed able to pull (McCawley 1991: 51)
      b.   John never *pulled* the *strings*ᵢ [that his mother told him should be *pulled* tᵢ] (Salzmann 2006c: 43; example is attributed to Henk van Riemsdijk)
      c.   They *made the headway* that they had hoped to *make* (Bhatt 2015: 732)

So for example in (i)c the overt Head *headway* AMOUNT can be the external Head of the RC matched by a deleted internal Head *headway* AMOUNT raised to Spec,CP of the RC whose copy is interpreted in the object position of *make.*

(21)   a.   [[**kho** khumolei-n-o]   **mogo**] ...
              [[**man** die.3SG.NF-TR-CONN] **person**] ...
              'The man who died ...'
        b.   [[**ai** fali-khano]   **ro**]   nagu-n-ay-a.
              [[**pig** carry-go.3PL.NF]**thing**]   our-TR-pig-PRED
              'The pig they took away is ours.'

Another potential problem, noted in Borsley (1997: §3), is represented by those 'raising' cases where the Case of the Head appears to be determined by the matrix context rather than the RC context. Apart from limited cases where the Head retains the Case assigned inside the RC (so-called Inverse Case Attraction cases – see A4.1.5 of the Appendix), some Case overwriting may have to be admitted. See for discussion Bianchi (2000a: 129–30), De Vries (2002: ch. 4: §3.4), among others.

2.1.2   The 'Matching' Derivation

This derivation will be taken to be available in those cases where the overt Head does not need to be interpreted inside the RC (as is arguably the case of the individual reading of *the books that John wrote* ... – see (22)):

(22)

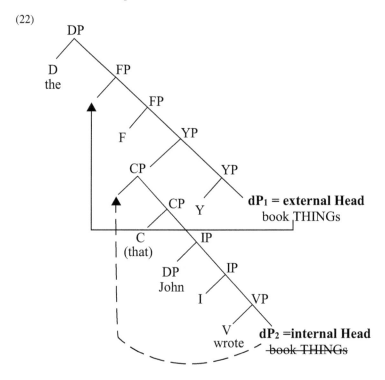

or where the 'raising' derivation is not accessible for one reason or other (to be reviewed below). When the external and the internal Heads are categorially non-distinct (dPs), as in (22), the raising of the external Head to Spec,FP causes the deletion of the internal one, which in English-type languages has raised to the Spec of the RC CP (inducing island sensitivity). On the other hand, when the external and internal Heads are categorially distinct (the external one being a dP and the internal one a DP/KP, or a DP/KP inside a PP) the external Head cannot cause the deletion of the internal Head under non-distinctness. In such cases, the internal Head will be realized by a *wh*-pronoun or *wh*-phrase, or by a resumptive pronoun or epithet, depending on the language, or on the particular relative construction (whether finite restrictive, finite non-restrictive, kind-defining, infinitival, etc.), or on particular factors within one and the same construction (as in certain cases of the Hebrew restrictive RC, discussed in §4.3). In all such cases no reconstruction of the overt Head inside the RC is available. The different 'matching' possibilities found in finite restrictive RCs will be illustrated in the next sections, and those found with finite non-restrictives, kind-defining, infinitival and participial RCs in the next chapter, although some of them may be briefly mentioned here for comparison. Before discussing the English case, I present in §2.1.2.1 the restrictive relative clause constructions of Italian.

2.1.2.1   The Restrictive Relative Clause Constructions of Italian

In this section the two Italian restrictive relative clause constructions (the one involving the invariant relativizer *che* and the invariant relative pronoun *cui*, and the more formal one involving the art. + *qual*- paradigm) will be briefly presented. While the 'raising' derivation proves possible in RCs with *che*, it appears to be impossible in RCs with (P) *cui* and with art. + *qual*-phrases.[24]

2.1.2.1.1   The che-cui *Relative Clause Construction of Italian*   The main properties of the Italian *che-cui* RC construction can be summarized as follows (see Cinque 1978, 1982 for a more detailed presentation of the facts):[25]

---

[24] This recalls Szczegielniak's (2004: ch. 2) observation that Polish and Russian RCs with the invariant relativizers *co/čto*, and no resumptive pronouns, may (apparently, must in Polish – though perhaps not in Russian – Giltner 2017: 16) involve a 'raising' derivation, while those employing the *który/kotoryj* paradigms only involve a 'matching' one. The former, but not the latter, can have degree/amount readings, can have idiom chunks as Heads, and can reconstruct into the RC for scope, and binding.

[25] These properties hold of both the restrictive and the non-restrictive construction with *che-cui*, though only the former will be illustrated here. *Che/cui* non-restrictives will be discussed in §3.1.

I.   subjects and direct objects (as well as temporal nominals and nominal predicates) are relativized with the invariant subordinator of embedded finite clauses, *che*:[26]

(23)   a. La proposta che è stata fatta è assurda.   (Cinque 1978: 35)
            The proposal that has been made is absurd.
        b. Il vestito che hai comprato non ti sta bene.   (Cinque 1978: 35)
            The suit that you have bought does not fit you.
        c. Il giorno che arrivi telefonami.   (Cinque 1978: 109 fn. 31)[27]
            The day that you arrive, call me.
        d. Non era l'attore di avanguardia che pretendeva   (Cinque 1978: 39)
            di essere.
            He wasn't the avant-garde actor that he
            pretended to be.

II.   complements/circumstantials introduced by a functional preposition (*di* 'of', *a* 'to', *da* 'from', *in* 'in', *su* 'on', *con* 'with', *senza* 'without', *verso* 'towards', *tra* 'between') are relativized not with *che* but with *cui* preceded by the preposition:[28]

(24)   a. Il ragazzo di cui/a cui/con cui/senza cui/su cui ho parlato ...
            The boy of whom/to whom/with whom/without/about whom I spoke ...

---

[26] The generalization thus appears to be based on a categorial (nominal, dP/DP, vs everything else) rather than on a functional, distinction (the higher vs the lower functions of an accessibility hierarchy, as in Keenan & Comrie 1977, 1979; see the discussion and references in Cinque 2013b: ch. 10). This is similar to the situation of French and Hebrew as presented in Kayne (1976) and Cole (1976), respectively. The invariant relativizer *che* appears to differ from interrogative *che* in at least two ways. In contrast to the latter, it is never used as a determiner (see fn. 39 of this chapter) and it allows the elision of the final vowel (see (?)*quello ch'era successo* ... 'that that had happened ...' vs **Non so ch'era successo.* 'I don't know what had happened.' – Paola Benincà, pers. comm.). For a different analysis of Italian relative *che* (and French relative *que*) see Kayne (2014a: §8). For other differences between relative and interrogative *che* in Italian see Cinque (1988: last part of p. 465).

[27] See *Arrivò lo stesso giorno* 'He/she/it arrived the same day.'

[28] P + *cui* can in fact be followed by *che* in certain northeastern Italian dialects. See (i), from Vedovato & Penello (2007: 101), comparable, as they note, to the *which that* sequences found in Middle English (for which see §2.1.3 below):

(i)   El frutat a cui che tu volevis dà al libri al è partì. (Friulian dialect of Nimis (Udine))
        the boy to whom that you wanted to give the book has left

Cui could also be followed by *che* in old Italian (with a 'Headless' relative clause interpretation equivalent to *chi*). See:

(ii)   non si potè avere concordia da cui che si rimanesse. (Vocabolario Universale Italiano, Naples 1830, p. 518)
        'One could not have harmony from he who was staying.'

b. Le persone verso/in cui nutre una stima profonda sono poche.
   The people towards/in whom he has a deep esteem are few.

III. any pied-piping larger than a PP headed by a functional preposition is
      disallowed (see Cinque 1982: §1.1):

complex (axial) PPs[29]

(25) a. *Il giorno dopo di cui/prima di cui/durante cui si è assentato ...
          The day after which, before which, during which he left ...
      b. *Il paese fuori da cui/lontano da cui vive ...
          the village out of which/far from which he lives ...

Complex DPs

(26) *I ragazzi [le famiglie di cui] siano già state convocate ...[30]
      the boys the families of whom have (subjunctive) already been summoned ...

VPs

(27) *L'uomo [fuggita da cui] non era ...
      the man fled from whom she hadn't ...

APs

(28) *Gli animali [affezionata a cui] non la ritenevamo ... (Cinque 1978: 115
      fn. 59)[31]
      the animals fond of whom we did not consider her ...

AdvPs

(29) a. *Questo è l'uomo [diversamente da cui] avete agito. (Cinque 1982: 256)
          This is the man unlike whom you have acted.

---

[29] The only apparent exception is provided by those complex (axial) prepositions which take a PP
complement headed by the functional preposition *a* 'to'. See (i), to which I return in fn. 38 below:

(i)   Il ragazzo accanto a cui/davanti a cui/vicino a cui, etc. era seduta ...
      the boy besides whom/in front of whom/near whom, etc. she was sitting ...

[30] For the acceptable alternative *I ragazzi le cui famiglie siano già state convocate ...* 'The boys
whose families have (subjunctive) already been summoned ...', which belongs to the same
grammar as art. + *qual-*, see Cinque (1978: §3.11; 1982: §1.6; 1988: §1.1.6.1.3).

[31] Note that extracting [(*a*) *cui*] out of the AP gives a wellformed sentence:

(i)   Gli animali (a) cui$_i$ non la ritenevamo [affezionata t$_i$] ...
      the animals (of) whom we did not considered her fond ...

On bare dative *cui* I assume that it enters a PP headed by a silent (functional) preposition *a*. Note
that the functional preposition *a* cannot be left silent in complex axial PPs of (i): *accanto/
davanti/vicino cui.

b.   *Il libro [dopo aver parlato di cui] fui insultato ... (Cinque 1978: 69)
the book after having spoken about which I was insulted ...

CPs

(30)

*L'unica persona [di aver parlato a cui] non possiamo rammaricarci è Gianni.
the only person to have talked to whom we cannot regret is Gianni

In Cinque (1978, 1982) these properties did not receive a satisfactory account. Let me explore here a different, possibly more promising, one.

Consider property I. The relatives introduced by the invariant relativizer *che*, which relativizes subjects and objects (as well as, as noted, temporal nominals and nominal predicates), are in principle derivationally ambiguous between a 'raising' and a 'matching' derivation. In the first case, the overt Head is the internal one raised to the highest CP projection of the RC, causing the deletion of the c-commanded external Head:[32]

(31) $[_{DP}$ Il $[_{FP}$ F $[_{CP1}$ vino AMOUNT$_i$ $[_{CP2}$ che $[_{IP}$ t$_i$ è stato versato]]] ~~vino AMOUNT~~]]
the wine that was spilled

In the second case the overt Head is the external Head, raised (as characteristic of head-initial languages) to the Spec of a functional projection, FP, dominating the external Head and the relative clause CPs, causing the deletion of the internal Head, which in Italian must have been raised to (the higher) CP of the RC given the island sensitivity of the construction:[33]

(32) $[_{DP}$ Il $[_{FP}$ vino THING$_i$ $[_{CP1}$ ~~vino THING$_k$~~ $[_{CP2}$ che $[_{IP}$ t$_k$ è stato versato]]] t$_i$]]
(i = k)

In the first case, as noted, given Kayne's (1994: 16) definition of c-command, the internal Head c-commands the external one, from Spec,CP1. In the second, it is the external Head, moved to Spec,FP, that c-commands the internal one (in

---

[32] One must assume that nothing prevents the presence of overt material in both CP$_1$ and CP$_2$ if the occupant of CP$_1$ is not a *wh*-phrase (as opposed to the impossibility of **il quale che* 'which that' case – for which see below). The entire issue of the availability or non-availability of doubly filled COMPs, clearly a low level parameter distinguishing languages and language varieties, is complex. See Kayne (1994: 91), Koopman (2000), and especially Radford (2018: 144–60) and the detailed discussion of the various factors involved in the parameterization of the spellout of complementizers in English in ch. 3 of that book.

[33] As already noted, I take the Spec of the highest RC CP to have inherent operator status (like that of FocusP), allowing the phrase moved into it to license the copy/trace inside the RC IP as a variable.

Spec,CP1). In both cases it is the c-commanding Head that causes in Italian the *obligatory* deletion of the c-commanded one, under non-distinctness (see fn. 19).

Concerning property II, whereby complements and adjuncts introduced by a functional preposition are relativized with *cui* preceded by the preposition, a question that arises is: why isn't the pronoun *cui* also deleted in Spec,CP1 as a consequence of its being c-commanded by the external Head in Spec,FP? If *cui* stands for an entire DP/KP it counts as distinct from the external Head, a dP. Furthermore, its deletion would lead to the stranding of the functional preposition, which in Italian is not permitted.[34] Deletion of P + *cui* is not permitted either. As Bayer & Bader (2007: §2.3) observes, functional Ps contribute features to DP which belong to DP, as shown by the fact, among others, that functional Ps + (simple) *wh*-pronoun behave the same as (simple) *wh*-pronouns (vs heavier pied-pipings) in successive cyclic multiple copying. See (33) (and Boef 2012: §2.6.3 and §2.7.2 for similar facts in Dutch), but also Rett 2006: 359 on the different behaviour of functional Ps like *mit* and axial Ps like *unter* in successive cyclic multiple copying:

(33)   a.   **Wem** glaubst du, **wem** Anita meint, **wem** wir vertrauen können
                whom believe you whom Anita thinks whom we trust can
                'Who do you believe Anita thinks we can trust?'

            b.   [**Mit wem**] glaubst du, [**mit wem**] Anita meint, [**mit wem**] wir uns treffen sollten?
                with who believe you with who Anita thinks with who we REFL meet should
                'Who do you believe Anita thinks we should meet with?'

            c.   *[**Wie schön**] glaubst du, [**wie schön**] wir singen müssten . . .?
                how beautifully believe you how beautifully we sing should . . .?
                'How beautifully do you believe we would have to sing . . .?'

If so the deletion of P + *cui* would not be deletion under identity (non-distinctness). The antecedent, as noted, is a dP category (the portion of the nominal extended projection including weak determiners below the Merge position of the RC), while the deletee would at the very least be an (oblique)

---

[34] While preposition stranding in Spec,CP is possible in Afrikaans (du Plessis 1977: 724), and was apparently possible in Middle English (see fn. 78 of the next chapter), it is no longer possible, for reasons that need to be elucidated, in Modern English, an otherwise preposition stranding language (see Postal 1972b, and Collins & Radford 2015: §6 for a possible account in terms of their Preposition Dangling Constraint/PDC). Also see Bošković (2018) for a possible relation of stranding in COMP and (non-)successive-cyclic movement.

DP/KP category, if not a PP category[35], thus leading to a violation of Chomsky's (1980: 21 ff) principle of recoverability. This conclusion seems to run counter to the claim I made at the very outset that the external and the internal Heads are a match of each other, smaller than DP; i.e. dP, as a consequence of the fact that the RC is merged above the external Head containing only weak determiners, and the fact that the internal Head should ordinarily match the external one.

I take this at face value, continuing to assume that in (gapped) *che* RCs the external and the internal Heads are (indefinite) dPs, smaller than DP (as is the internal Head of Lakhota-type internally Headed RCs to be discussed below), while assuming that when the internal Head is neither a subject nor an object nor a temporal or predicate bare nominal, but an oblique object or adjunct preceded by a functional preposition (P + *cui*), it is necessarily larger (DP/KP/PP) than the external dP Head (DPs with (inherent) Case may have a silent prepositional layer – see Emonds 1985: 224). This categorial distinctness is what prevents the deletion of the internal Head under the 'matching' derivation. This implies that subjects, direct objects (and temporal/predicate bare nominals in Italian) can be dPs and are not necessarily DPs/KPs. This may be due to the fact that their (structural) Case is retrievable, as Bayer, Bader & Meng (2001), Bayer & Salzmann (2013), and Czypionka, Dörre & Bayer (2018) also propose on independent grounds for Swiss German RCs with the invariant relativizer *wo*, where subjects and objects are gaps while indirect objects and other oblique arguments require a resumptive pronoun (as their Case must be overtly marked in a KP).[36]

---

[35] See Caha (2009: §1.5) for the idea that functional prepositions may represent Case in languages with poor Case morphology, where Case is plausibly the highest functional layer of the extended projection of NP ($[_{CaseP} .. [_{QP} .. [_{DP} .. [_{NP}]]]]$) interfacing the clause, as it indicates the role (subject, object, etc.) that the nominal has in the clause.

[36] '[...] German oblique Cases require morphological licensing. Case morphology may, of course, also appear on the structural Cases nominative and accusative, but it is not required there. Nominal categories which are necessarily without morphological Case such as CPs and indefinites like *nichts* ('nothing') were shown to function as nominatives and accusatives but not as datives [...]. We have made the proposal that oblique Case is phrase structurally manifested in terms of a functional projection of K(ase)P which comprises not only inflectional but also adpositional Case' (Bayer, Bader & Meng 2001: §2.12). What can fail to be a DP/KP is subject to variation. Salzmann & Seiler 2010 report a few Swiss German varieties where indirect objects may also be gaps, in addition to subjects and direct objects. On Swiss German relatives see Van Riemsdijk (1989, 2003, 2008), Georgi & Salzmann (2014, 2017) and references cited there. Case morphological (non-)distinctness is involved in determining whether an object can be a gap or a relative pronoun in Bavarian German (Bayer 1984), and a gap or a resumptive pronoun in Bosnian/Croatian/Serbian (Bošković 2009, Gračanin-Yüksek 2010, 2013) and other slavic languages with Case (Hladnik 2015: §3.4), also determining whether the RC involves reconstruction effects ('raising') or not ('matching').

For cases where even the external head is larger than an indefinite dP as in non-restrictives, or in those restrictive constructions where the Head is represented by the coordination of two or more full DPs (known as 'hydras'),[37] categorial non-distinctness will allow deletion of the internal Head. For the case of non-restrictives I refer to §3.1.

The perfect match of the external and the internal Heads with subject and object relativization and the non-perfect match of the two Heads with the relativization of oblique DPs/KPs/PPs appears to be at the base of properties I and II. What about property III?

If, as noted above with reference to Caha (2009), functional prepositions may represent Case in languages with poor Case morphology (also see Grimshaw's 2005: ch. 1 idea of P being part of the nominal projection), pied-piping of a functional P (but not that of axial Ps, nor a fortiori that of complex DPs, VPs, APs, AdvPs, CPs) may be simple sharing of the *wh*-feature within the nominal extended projection that allows the agreement relation with the external Head. An alternative, after Kayne (2004b: Appendix), would be to take the pied-piping of functional prepositions (as opposed to that of every other category) not to be a case of pied-piping at all. According to his suggestion, functional prepositions can be taken to merge above the agreement/Case projection targeted by oblique DPs. If such an agreement/Case projection were to be optionally merged in the CP domain, the oblique DP would raise without pied-piping anything. See Kayne (2004b) for further discussion.[38]

---

37 (i)   a.   [[il ragazzo] e [la ragazza]] che si sono incontrati a Vienna ... (see Jackendoff
               1977: 190)
               the boy and the girl that met in Vienna ...
        b.   [[l'austriaco] e [la canadese]] che si sono sposati ... (see Bobaljik 2017: 13)
               the Austrian and the Canadian who married each other

Possibly in such cases the coordination of the two singular DPs intersects with the RC under the scope of a higher, silent, plural D° (see §5.1 for more discussion):

   (ii)   [$_{DP}$ D$_{pl}$° [[$_{DPsing}$ il ragazzo] e [$_{DPsing}$ la ragazza]] [che si sono incontrati a Vienna]] ...

38   As to the exception represented by the complex (axial) prepositions which take a PP complement headed by the functional preposition *a* 'to' (see fn. 29 above), it is to be observed that they are the only ones that allow their complement to be extracted. See for example (i)a vs (i)b–c (see Rizzi 1988: §3.3 and Cinque 1988: §1.1.12):

   (i)   a.   Il ragazzo a cui$_i$ si era messa accanto/davanti/vicino, etc. t$_i$ ...
               Lit.: the boy to whom she put herself beside/in front/near, etc.
        b.   *il ragazzo di cui$_i$ ho parlato dopo/prima t$_i$ ...
               the boy of whom I talked after/before ...
        c.   *un paese da cui$_i$ vivo fuori/lontano t$_i$
               Lit.: a village of which I am living outside/from which I am living far away

Concerning the type of derivation involved in this restrictive construction, 'raising' appears to be available with *che*, but not with (P) *cui*. See the following contrasts, with phenomena that may require a 'raising' derivation (reconstruction of quantifiers; pronominal binding under reconstruction, and idiom chunk reconstruction):[39]

(34)   a.   I due medici **che** ognuno di loro vedrà domani sono già arrivati.[40] (2 > every and every > 2)
'The two doctors that every one of them will see tomorrow have already arrived.'

           b.   I due medici **da cui** ognuno di loro è stato visitato sono già arrivati (2 > every and *every > 2)
'The two doctors by whom every one of them has been visited have already arrived.'

(35)   a.   Il successo dei suoi$_i$ figli **che** [ogni genitore]$_i$ si augurava ...
the success of his children that every parent wished ...

           b.   *Il successo dei suoi$_i$ figli **su cui** [ogni genitore]$_i$ conta ...[41]
the success of his children on which every parent counts ...

This makes it tempting to think that the functional PPs headed by *a*, but not the other functional PPs that do not extract, can raise to a functional projection above the axial PP (as they presumably do before extracting: [[a cui]$_k$ [accanto t$_k$]] – see Van Riemsdijk 1978: ch. 6 and Kayne 1994: §3.5), after which [accanto t$_k$] raises above [a cui], which possibly does not count as an intervener because only one link of the chain intervenes: [[accanto t$_k$]$_i$ [[a cui]$_k$ [accanto t$_k$]$_i$]).

[39] Also note that unlike art + *qual-* in infinitival RCs, to be seen in §3.3 (as well as in non-restrictive and kind-defining ones, to be seen in §3.1 and §3.2), *cui* cannot be followed by a nominal constituent, suggesting that it is a pronoun rather than a relative determiner/modifier. See:

(i)   a.   Sta cercando un laboratorio in cui (*laboratorio) poter condurre le sue ricerche.
He is looking for a lab in which (lab) to be able to conduct his research.

       b.   Sta cercando un laboratorio nel quale (laboratorio) poter condurre le sue ricerche.
He is looking for a lab in which (lab) to be able to conduct his research.

Similarly, *che* (as opposed to art. + *qual-*) in restrictive, non-restrictive, and kind-defining RCs, cannot be followed by a nominal constituent, suggesting that it too is not a relative determiner/modifier (see for example the contrast in (9) of Chapter 3).

[40] See Bianchi (1999: 46).

[41] Less clear is the case of functional RCs (Sharvit 1999b), which have the special property of apparently allowing a RC internal quantifier to scope outside the RC (thus permitting an analysis that does not need syntactic reconstruction to account for the binding of a pronoun within the Head). See (i) and fn. 11 above:

(i)   L'unico dei suoi$_i$ amori di cui nessuno$_i$ parla volentieri è il suo$_i$ primo amore.
'The only one of his loves about which nobody talks willingly is his first love.'

(36)   a.   La pazienza **che** ha avuto non è stata sufficiente.[42]
             The patience that he had was not sufficient.
        b.   *La pazienza **di cui** si era armato non è stata sufficiente.[43]
             The patience with which he had armed himself has not been sufficient.

2.1.2.1.2 The art. + qual- *marked Restrictive Relative Constructions of Italian* In Cinque (1978: §3.8; 1982: §1.5) it is observed that Italian has a more formal restrictive construction employing the same art. + *qual-* paradigm that is used in the non-integrated non-restrictive construction (for which see here §3.1), and apparently also in kind-defining relatives (see §3.2), and in (marked) infinitival relatives (see §3.3). The basic properties of this construction are: 1) the retention of subject and (more marginally) object relative pronouns (see (37) from Cinque 1988: 452),[44] and 2) the possibility of heavy pied-piping (see (38a–b), from Cinque 1978: 84, and (38c)):[45]

---

[42] The idiom is *aver pazienza* 'to have patience'. The lack of an article before the object, otherwise obligatory before singular common nouns in Italian, shows that it is an idiom, despite its relative transparency.

[43] The idiom is *armarsi di pazienza* 'to arm oneself with patience'. Also see the minimal pair *aver simpatia per qualcuno* and *aver qualcuno in simpatia*, both meaning 'to like someone':

    (i)   a.   La simpatia **che** ha per Gianni ...
               Lit.: the sympathy that he has for Gianni ...
          b.   *La simpatia **in cui** ha Gianni ...
               Lit.: the sympathy in which he has Gianni ...

As far as I can tell, no relativization of prepositional complements of idioms is possible. Bianchi (1993) distinguishes three categories of idioms according to which movement types they allow. Interestingly, those that she lists as permitting restrictive relativization all relativize objects (see her §5.1; and also Bianchi 1999: 43 ff).

[44] The obligatory retention of art. + *-qual* with subjects and (more marginally) objects is obscured by the existence of the parallel unmarked *che/cui* construction, where deletion of subjects and objects is obligatory. The obligatory retention of the internal Head in one construction and the obligatory deletion in the other gives the illusion of optional deletion. On a possible reason for the marginality of object relativization with the art. + *qual-* ((37b)), see Cinque (1978: §3.7). In this more marked restrictive construction, deletion of part of the Head stranding art. + *qual-* appears to be virtually obligatory (compare (38a) with *?I lavoratori i figli dei quali lavoratori abbiano superato le prove d'esame sono pregati di presentarsi al più presto.*) in contrast to the non-restrictive and kind-defining constructions employing the same art. + *qual-* paradigm (for which see §3.1 and §3.2), in which deletion of the part of the Head following art + *qual-* appears to be optional. In Cinque (1978: 84 ff; 1982: §1.5) I suggested that the internal Head can be retained in this very formal art + *qual-* restrictive construction. Yet such cases are more accurately analysable as kind-defining RCs (previously lumped together with restrictives). See §3.2.

[45] French appears to have a similar (archaic or poetic) marked restrictive RC construction employing the *lequel* paradigm. See the examples in (i)a–d (where relativization of object DPs is judged more marginal, as the corresponding Italian cases):

(37)   a.   Gli iscritti i quali non abbiano ancora versato la quota annuale sono
             esclusi dall'assemblea dei soci.
             'The registered members who have (subjunctive) not yet paid the annual
             fees are excluded from the members' assembly.'
       b.   ?Gli studenti i quali non abbiate ancora potuto esaminare dovranno
             presentarsi agli scritti.
             'The students who you have (subjunctive) not been able to examine yet
             will have to sit the written exams.'

(38)   a.   I lavoratori i figli dei quali abbiano superato le prove d'esame sono
             pregati di presentarsi al più presto.
             'The workers the children of whom have (subjunctive) passed the exams
             are requested to come as soon as possible.'
       b.   Questo è un lampadario osservando il quale si possa avere l'intuizione
             della legge del pendolo.
             'This is a chandelier observing which one can have (subjunctive) the
             intuition of the law of the pendulum.'

(i)   a.   Il n'y a pas un air de music-hall lequel ne soit un souvenir poignant et
             délicieux. (Aragon, *Anicet ou le panorama*, L.P., p. 165, cited from Grevisse
             1993: 1056)
             'There is no music-hall atmosphere that is not a touching and delicious souvenir.'
       b.   Il y a des replis de nous-mêmes lesquels nous n'époussetons pas, de peur d'y faire
             tomber les étoiles qui s'y accrochent. (Aragon, *Anicet ou le panorama*, L.P.,
             p. 228, cited from Grevisse 1993: 1056)
             'There are folds of ourselves which we do not dust lest we make the stars fall
             which cling to them.'
       c.   Vous voyez ici les romans les auteurs desquels sont des espèces de poètes.
             (Grevisse 1969: 489)
             'You see here the novels the authors of which are kinds of poets.'
       d.   ???l'homme la femme duquel tu aimes est très jaloux. (Pollock 1992: 442)
             'The man whose wife you love is very jealous.'

The same marginality is found with *qui* in heavy pied-piping of objects vs PPs. See the contrast
between (ii)a and b:

(ii)   a.   L'homme avec la femme de qui tu t'es disputé s'appelle Georges.
                                                                    (Kayne 1976: 261)
             'The man with the wife of whom you argued is named Georges.'
       b.   L'homme la femme de qui tu as insulteé . . .
             'The man the wife of whom you have insulted . . .'

Kayne (1976: 261; 1994: 89) assigns to (ii)b an asterisk, while Pollock gives to a comparable
example (see (i)d above) three question marks; a judgement of intermediate grammaticality
apparently shared by Michal Starke (see Pesetsky 1998: 343 fn. 7). Also see Sportiche (2011:
§2.1).

    c.   Gli studenti gli esiti degli esami dei quali non siano risultati sufficienti potranno ripetere la prova a settembre.[46]
'The students the results of whose exams were (subjunctive) not sufficient will be able to take the exam again in September.'

As apparent from (37) and (38) this marked restrictive construction typically involves in Italian the subjunctive mood. The heavy pied-piping property that it shares with the art. + *qual-* ('non-integrated') non-restrictive construction in particular appears to indicate that the relation between the art. + *qual- wh*-phrase and the Head is fundamentally different from the sentence grammar relation between the invariant *cui* relative pronoun and the Head seen above; as with the discourse grammar character of the non-integrated non-restrictive construction to be seen in §3.1 this special restrictive based on it has obligatory retention of art. + *qual-* with subjects and objects.[47]

This more marked restrictive construction involving art. + *qual-* and subjunctive mood appears to allow for the 'matching' derivation, but not for the 'raising' one. See (39)–(40):

---

[46] Similar examples are found in the French marked restrictive construction:

    (i)   L'homme à l'ami du frère de qui vous vous êtes adressé est un ministre influent.
                                              (Tellier & Valois 2006: 22)
        'The man to the friend of the brother of whom you addressed yourself is an influential minister.'

Example (38c) shows that heavy pied-piping in Italian does not show the intervention effect discussed in Sportiche (2017a: §7.3).

[47] Retention of subject and object art. + *qual-* with the indicative mood is instead highly marked, if at all possible, though P + art. + *qual-* is possible (at a high stylistic level). See (i)a–c:

    (i)   a.   *?Gli studenti i quali non hanno superato l'esame possono ripeterlo a settembre.
                  'The students who (lit. the which) have (indicative) not passed the exam can take it again in September.'
        b.   *Gli studenti i quali non ho ancora potuto esaminare dovranno presentarsi agli scritti.
                  'The students whom (lit. the which) I have (indicative) not been able to examine will have to sit the written exam.'
        c.   Gli studenti ai quali avete dato la sufficienza vi saranno riconoscenti.
                  'The students to whom (lit. to the which) you have (indicative) given a pass will be grateful to you.'

It is tempting to analyse these facts as involving the **integrated** non-restrictive structure, where the RC modifies an entire DP. If so subject and object art. + *qual-* would be obligatorily deleted under non-distinctness with the Head while PPs would still be categorially distinct from the Head; hence non deletable.

(39) a. I due esercizi i quali siano già stati assegnati ad ogni studente saranno considerati sufficienti.[48] (2 > every and *every > 2)
The two exercises which have (subjunctive) been assigned to every student will be considered sufficient.

b. *La recensione del suo$_i$ libro la quale sia stata inviata ad ogni scrittore$_i$ ...[49]
The review of his book which was (subjunctive) sent to every writer ...

c. *Tutta la pazienza la quale abbia non sarà sufficiente.
'All the patience which he may have (subjunctive) will not be sufficient.'

(40) a. Questi sono i soli due pazienti con i quali ogni medico abbia avuto a che fare. (2 > every and *every > 2) 'These are the only two patients with whom each doctor had (subjunctive) to deal.'

b. *La recensione del suo$_i$ libro per la quale ogni scrittore$_i$ possa diventare famoso ...
'The review of his book because of which every writer may (subjunctive) become famous ...'

c. *Tutta la pazienza della quale si possa armare non sarà sufficiente.
'All the patience with which he may arm (subjunctive) himself will not be sufficient.'

2.1.2.2   The Restrictive Relative Clause Constructions of English

It is tempting to take the English restrictive construction employing the invariant relativizer *that* to parallel the Italian construction employing the invariant relativizer *che*, with obligatory 'deletion' of the external Head under 'raising' ((41a)) and of the internal one under 'matching' ((41b)), and to take the construction employing *wh*-phrases (*which, who*, etc.) to parallel the art. + *qual-* more marked restrictive construction of Italian, with pied-piping, even of the heavy type ((42)), and with obligatory retention of the subject and object *wh*-phrase due to the categorial distinctness of the two Heads (the external one being a dP and the internal one a DP) ((43)):[50]

---

[48] Cf. *Due esercizi sono già stati assegnati ad ogni studente* 'Two exercises have already been assigned to every student' (2 > every and every > 2).

[49] Cf. *Una recensione del suo$_i$ libro è stata inviata ad ogni scrittore$_i$* 'A review of his book was sent to every writer'.

[50] If this is correct, the apparently optional deletion of the *wh*-pronouns (*the man (who(m)) I saw; the man that I saw*) would be an illusion due to the existence of the parallel unmarked restrictive construction employing the invariant relativizer *that* (or 0) with obligatory deletion of subjects and objects. As to the relativization of the object of prepositions (possible in English owing to the preposition stranding option available to the language: *the article (that) I referred to ...; the man that we bought a car from ...*), I tentatively assume that the preposition may take an indefinite

(41)   a.   [The [$_{CP}$ [pictures of himself$_i$]$_k$ that John$_i$ took [~~pictures of himself$_i$~~]$_k$ last
            year] ~~pictures of himself$_i$~~]] were hanging on the wall.
       b.   [The [$_{FP}$ pictures of John$_i$'s children] [$_{CP}$ [~~pictures of John$_i$'s children~~]$_k$
            that even he$_i$ considered [~~pictures of John$_i$'s children~~]$_k$] to be ugly were
            hanging on the wall.[51]

(42)   a.   the man [to whom] we have spoken . . .
       b.   the man [whose son] we met yesterday . . .
       c.   The boy [[[[whose] brother's] friend's] father] was recently arrested . . .
       d.   the book [the first chapter of which] is being widely discussed . . .
            (Kayne 2017b: 368)
       e.   reports [the height of the lettering on the covers of which] the
            government prescribes . . . (Ross 1967: 198)

(43)   a.   The book which is here/which I bought . . .
       b.   The boy who came yesterday/who I saw yesterday . . .

In other words I take restrictive *which*, in fact (THE) *which* (see fn. 21 above),
not to be a determiner/modifier modifying a lexical noun but, in contrast to the
interrogative, non-restrictive and kind-defining relative *which* (see (i) and
(ii) of fn. 55 below), a pronoun obligatorily occurring in the Spec of the
non-human silent functional noun/classifier THING; whence its general

---

dP, in addition to a definite DP, as complement. The pied-piping possibilities available in the
more marked restrictive art. + *qual-* and *who/which* constructions are apparently less natural
than those available in the art. + *qual-* and *who/which* 'non-integrated' non-restrictive and kind-
defining constructions of Italian and English, discussed in §3.1 and §3.2. Here I assumed *that* to
be an invariant relativizer/weak relative pronoun rather than a determiner. One possible piece of
evidence is that, unlike *which*, *that* can never be followed by a nominal constituent in non-
restrictive and kind-defining RCs (much like Italian *cui* and *che* – fn. 39). See (i)a vs (i)b and
§4.2 for further differences between relative pronouns and invariant relativizers:

(i)   a.   He rode twenty miles to see her picture in the house of a stranger, **which stranger**
            politely insisted on his acceptance of it. (Jespersen 1949: §6.5, p. 126)
       b.   *He rode twenty miles to see her picture in the house of a stranger, **that stranger**
            politely insisted on his acceptance of it.

For a different analysis see Kayne (2014a).

[51] The potential violation of Principle C induced by the lower internal copy could be assumed,
following Safir (1999) and Sauerland (1999: §3.2), to be avoided by applying Vehicle Change,
to yield: [*The* [$_{FP}$ *pictures of John's children*] [$_{CP}$ [~~*pictures of his$_i$ children*~~]$_k$ *that even he$_i$
considered* [~~*pictures of his$_i$ children*~~]$_k$] *to be ugly were hanging on the wall.*
For discussion and further evidence for Vehicle Change see Salzmann (2019). Alternatively
the internal copy could be just a partial match of the external one (i.e., *pictures*) (see Sauerland
2003: 211; Radford 2019: 51 fn. 48), perhaps like such non-restrictive cases as *These pictures of
John$_i$'s children, which pictures he himself$_i$ considered to be ugly, . . .*

incompatibility with human nouns: *the boy which came yesterday* . . . – Aoun & Li 2003: 121; also see Lassiter 2011: §4.5).[52]

Similarly, I take *who* to obligatorily occur in the Spec of the human silent functional noun(s)/classifier(s) PERSON/PEOPLE (see Jackendoff 1977: 174; Lassiter 2011: 82, and Radford 2019: §1.5).

This idea can in fact be extended to other *wh*-relative phrases: *when* will be *when* TIME, *where where* PLACE, etc. (see Kayne 2004a; 2005a). This means that *the restaurant where we met* . . . and *the day when you were born* . . . would be something like [*the* [*restaurant* PLACE [*where* PLACE$_i$ *we met* AT t$_i$]]] . . ., [*the* [*day* TIME [*when* TIME$_i$ *you were born* AT t$_i$]]] . . .,[53] after movement of the external Head (restaurant PLACE, day TIME), with partial match.[54] This would allow one not to have to postulate phrases like *where restaurant* or *when day*, with *where* and *when* determiners/modifiers of a lexical noun (see Aoun & Li 2003: 120). Also see the discussion of these phrases in 'Headless' ('Free') RCs below (§2.5).

In addition to the impossibility of *the boy which came yesterday* . . ., possible evidence for taking *which* to be a pronominal DP (rather than a determiner), which obligatorily occurs in the Spec of a silent noun THING

---

[52] But see Radford (2019: ch. 1 fn. 27) for some examples of *which* used with a human antecedent, possible in certain varieties of English. The contrast between (i)a and (i)b, noted in Browne (1986: 115, ex 20), might be related to *which* being in the Spec of THING and moving with it to Spec,CP1 (*That* THING [$_{CP1}$ *which* THING$_i$.. t$_i$]) vs the case of the invariant relativizer *that*, which we take to be directly merged in CP2, not in the Spec of THING despite it being sometimes sensitive to the +/- human status of the head of the relative (Kayne 2014a: §6).

(i)   a.   That which he has written is an inspiration to us all.
        b.   *That that he has written is an inspiration to us all.

The corresponding Italian cases appear to have a reverse grammatical status: *Quello che/*il quale non sia stato ancora detto dovrà essere detto al più presto.* 'That that/which has (subjunctive) not yet been said will have to be said as soon as possible.'. This holds of neuter *quello* (identical to *ciò*: *ciò il quale/al quale penso* . . .), not of masculine animate or inanimate *quello* as the following grammatical sentences show (for the lack of extraposition with neuter *quello che* see §2.5.3):

(ii)   a.   Quello che non sia stato ancora inviato dovrà esserlo al più presto.
              'That (animate or inanimate) which has (subjunctive) not yet been sent will have to be sent as soon as possible.'
        b.   Quelli che non siano stati ancora inviati dovranno esserlo al più presto.
              'Those (animate or inanimate) which have (subjunctive) not yet been sent will have to be sent as soon as possible.'

[53] Concerning the silent preposition AT see Caponigro & Pearl (2008, 2009) and fn. 137 below.

[54] For reference to a language that pronounces the functional noun associated with *where*, see fn. 137 below.

(see (45)), may come from the impossibility, even in more formal restrictive vs more formal non-restrictive and kind-defining RCs, for *which* to be followed by a copy of the Head:

(44)   a. *This is the only film which film they liked.[55]

   b. *No pictures which pictures John sold . . .   (Sportiche 2017a: §1.2.2)

(45)

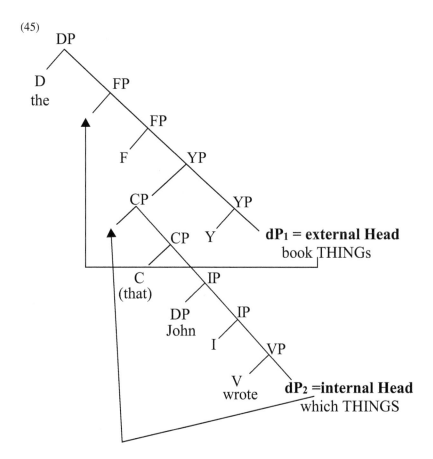

---

[55] When they modify an overt noun, the relative *which* of non-restrictive, ((i)a), (also see (i)a of fn. 50 above), kind-defining, ((i)b), and 'Headless' RCs, ((i)c), must then be closer to interrogative *which* ((i)d), as they are compatible with a +human NP:

(i)   a.   . . . a young woman with a wedding-ring and a baby, which baby she carried about with her when serving at the table (Jespersen 1949: §6.5, p. 126)

As noted, I take 'matching' not to imply in all cases what Sportiche (2017a) calls 'strong matching', namely a full copy of the Head, which, as he notes, would rather arbitrarily always require obligatory ellipsis of the matching copies in restrictives.[56]

2.1.3   Co-occurrence of Relative Pronouns and Invariant Relativizers

Though nothing principled should rule out their co-occurrence (*pace* Cecchetto & Donati 2015: 61), *that* may not co-occur with relative *wh*-phrases in Modern English (but see Zwicky 2002: §5.3 for some examples in

---

    b.   'There was one Brussels bureaucrat without the help of which (individual/?? bureaucrat) they would have been unable to draft the revisions to the backstop clause.' (Andrew Radford, pers. comm.)

    c.   'I'll give it to whichever man happens to be passing by.'

    d.   'Which boy did you see?'

The contrast between (ii)a and b, noted in Kayne (2014a: 195) may then stem from the fact that (ii)a is restrictive while (ii)b is non-restrictive:

(ii)   a.   *the person to which I was alluding ...

        b.   ?There were lots of linguists there, only some of which were known to us.

In Modern English *which/who* and *that* are in complementary distribution, as opposed to Middle English (see §2.1.3 below).

[56] According to Bhatt (2015: §5.2.4) and Sportiche (2017a: §1.2.2), the crossover effect present in cases like **Pictures of anyone$_i$ [which he$_i$ displays t prominently]* ... (where the quantifier *anyone*, as opposed to a referential expression like *John*, cannot be vehicle-changed to *him* – Safir's 1999: §6) appears to argue for a full representation of the internal Head even in 'matching' derivations, i.e. for 'strong matching'. Also see the discussion in Salzmann (2019: §3.3). Note however that the crossover effect is not present in other, comparable, cases, like (i)a below, which seem quite acceptable and in stark contrast with (i)b, which represents the putative structure resulting from reconstruction:

(i)   a.   [Le foto compromettenti di [ogni aiutante del presidente]$_i$] che [il poveretto lì ritratto]$_i$ non si aspettava di veder pubblicate sono apparse su tutti i giornali nazionali.

            Compromising pictures of [every aide of the president]$_i$ that [the poor guy in them]$_i$ did not expect would be published have appeared in all the national newspapers.

    b.   *[Il poveretto lì ritratto]$_i$ non si aspettava di veder pubblicate [le foto compromettenti di [ogni aiutante del presidente]$_i$].

            '[The poor guy in them]$_i$ did not expect that compromising pictures of [every aide of the president]$_i$ would be published.'

Ken Safir, who I thank for discussing this point with me, finds the English translation of (i)a moderately good also in English.

colloquial varieties). In any event it could in Middle English, in both restrictive and non-restrictive RCs. See (46) and Keyser (1975), Allen (1977), Maling (1978), Radford (2009: 486) and Gisborne & Truswell (2017) for discussion:[57]

(46)   a.   ... the partie of the orisonte **in which that** the sonne ariseth (A Treatise on the Astrolabe. 31, from Grimshaw 1975: 218)

        b.   And telle you, as pleynly as I kan, the grete effect **for which that** I bygan (Allen 1977: 256)

        c.   Only the sighte of hire, **whom that** I serve, ... (Chaucer, Knight's Tale 1231: line 373; from Keyser 1975: 9)

        d.   What wol my dere herte seyn to me, **which that** I drede never-mo to see? (Chaucer's *Troilus and Criseyde* 4. 858–9)[58]

Like Middle English are Macedonian ((47a)), Montreal French ((47b)) Bavarian ((47c), and even certain varieties of modern English ((47d)):[59]

(47)   a.   Čovekot [**čija što** žena ja sretnavme] ...   (Tomić 2006: 259)
               man.the.M.SG whose.F.SG what (=that) wife 3SG.F.ACC.CL
               meet.1PL.PERF.PAST
               the man whose wife we met ...

        b.   L'homme [**avec qui que** j'ai travaillé] ... (Lefebvre & Fournier 1978: 284)
               the man with whom that I have worked ...
               the man with whom I worked ...

[57] As Grimshaw (1975: n. 5) observes, while the co-occurrence of a *wh*-pronoun and *that* is possible in Middle English the co-occurrence of two *wh*-pronouns (*which which*) is never found. On doubly-filled COMPs and their possible relation to cleft structures see Kayne (2014a: §18), though to judge from Paduan the relation does not seem entirely natural. See the contrast between interrogatives and relatives: *Dove ze che te si sta*? Lit.: 'Where is it that you have been?' vs *el posto dove (*ze) che te si sta* ... 'the place where (it is) that you have been ...', the latter of which cannot have an overt copula and more crucially lacks the informational status of a cleft. I thank Paola Benincà for discussion and for the examples reported.

[58] A modern rendition is: 'What can my dear heart [my sweetheart] say to me, whom I fear never to see again?' In Middle English relative *which* could apparently still be accompanied by a silent +human NP even in restrictive RCs, like (more marginally) in Modern English non-restrictives (see fn. 55 above).

[59] See also the Friulian dialect mentioned in fn. 28 above, the Frisian dialects discussed in Hoekstra (2002: 64 and fn. 1) and colloquial Dutch (Boef 2013: 136). In Tyrolean RCs with extraction from the complement of a bridge verb the relative pronoun plus the invariant relativizer can be doubled in intermediate position. See (i), from Alber (2008: 146):

(i)   I kenn es Haus **des wos** du gplasch **des wos** die Maria gekaaft hot.
       'I know the house which you think Maria bought.'

    c.   der Mō [**dem wo** mir g'hoifa hom] ...   (Bayer 1984: 215)
          the man whom where (= that) we have helped
          the man who we have helped ...
    d.   I'm aware of the speed [**with which that** they work]. (Radford 2019: 37)

If *that* and similar invariant relativizers in other languages are phrasal weak relative pronouns (see Kayne 2008b, 2014a; Sportiche 2008, 2011), the relative clause CP structure must be taken to contain at least two CP projections, one, lower, hosting the invariant relativizer and the second, higher, hosting the internal Head when this moves. This is also the case under Koopman's (2000) ban on filling the specifier and head of the same projection (if such invariant relativizers are heads). Certain German dialects discussed in Grewendorf & Poletto (2015) (see (48)), and the African languages Buli and Ngemba mentioned below (see (50)), appear to suggest the presence of a third CP (also see the three CP layers of Danish – Vikner 1991 – and possibly Dutch – Zwart 2000, Boef 2013: §4.3, as well as the decomposition of d-complementizers in Germanic and their relation with embedded V2 – Leu 2015):[60]

(48)   Der Mo **der wo dass** des gsogt hot ...   (Grewendorf & Poletto 2015: 397)
            the man who where that this said has
            the man who said this ...

If we adopt a strong version of Chomsky's (2001: 2) Uniformity Principle (also see Sigurðsson 2003, Kayne 2005a and Miyagawa 2010: §1.4.1), even evidence of a rich left periphery in a single language suggests the presence of a rich left periphery in the RC of every language, with languages differing in the targets of movement and in how many and which projections they come to express overtly.

---

[60] For interesting suggestions concerning the different role of the higher and the lower relativizers in German dialects like those in (47c) and (48), which may carry over to those of other languages, see Catasso & Hinterhölzl (2016), as well as Weiß (2013) and Trutkowski & Weiß (2016a), where it is suggested that RCs in German are always introduced by a 'complementizer' *wo/was* (overtly in dialects and covertly in standard German). On dialectal German *wo*, see Van Riemsdijk (1989, 2003, 2008), and for a possible correlation with its capacity of incorporating with prepositions (*wovon*, etc.) Kayne (2014a: fn. 75).

For example, there are also languages that show two invariant relativizers (typically deictic elements) sandwiching the RC, one at the beginning and one at the end (in some cases the two morphemes are identical, in others they are different). Kuteva and Comrie (2006: 222) refer to this case as 'bracket relativization'. See for example the cases of Jabêm (Oceanic) in (49a) (and see Bradshaw 2009 for other Oceanic languages), Kukú (Nilo-Saharan) in (49b), and Banjoun (Ghomala) (Bantoid) in (49c):

(49)   a.   ŋa? [naŋ   ka-keŋ   ɛŋ ge-ya   pola? naŋ]   ge-mu ge-meŋ   (Ross 2002: 281)
            man   DEM1sg-give 3sg 3sg-go:3 Polac   DEM 3sg-go.back 3sg-go:1
            'Has the man I sent to Polac come back or not?'
       b.   e ŋutu? [lɔ   a kita   lɔ]   a   ŋesu   (Bretonnel Cohen 2000: 46)
            person COMP   NEG work   COMP NEG   eat
            'A person who doesn't work cannot eat.'
       c.   mo   [yə   e   jó   sáŋ   á'á]   (Watters 2003: 255)
            man   Rel   3ps see.Past bird   Rel
            ... the man who saw the bird

This suggests that the relative IP possibly raises to the left of the lowest of the relative CPs.

The Grassfield Bantoid language Ngemba (Kuteva & Comrie 2006: 223), and the Gur language Buli (Hiraiwa 2003: 46), in addition to the two invariant relativizers sandwiching the RC, show the presence of the third CP seen in the dialectal German example (48), which hosts the internal Head in the form of a relative pronoun. See (50a–b) and the tentative richer structure in (51), with English glosses, later to be amended to make room for Focus and Topic projections:[61]

(50)   a.   nyung [wá [bah   a-keshung-ne   mung wa   la]]   a-kung atsang (Ngemba)
            man   REL COMP he-TNS.beat-ne child DET   subord.particle he-enter prison
            'The man who beat the child went to prison.'
       b.   kpàrʷà-[wā:y [ālī   tà   nā:b   lá]] ... (Buli)
            farmer-REL   COMP have cow(indef.)   Subord.Particle
            'The farmer who has the cow ...'

(51)

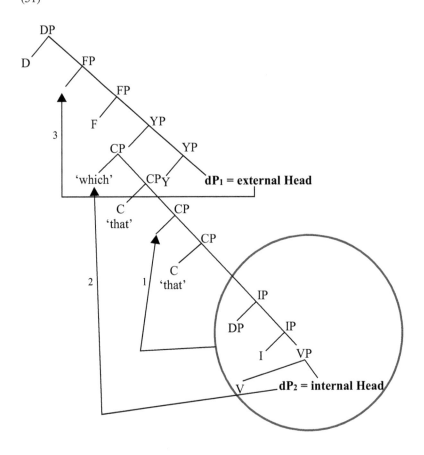

It thus becomes possible to think that the 'which that IP' languages have the lowest CP silent while the 'which IP' languages have the two lower CPs silent and the 'that IP' languages have the highest CP and the lowest CP silent, and that the 'IP that' languages (with post-nominal RCs)[62] have only the lower CP pronounced.

---

[62] See the case of Dhaasanac (Cushitic) in (i)

(i)   [ɲigéɲ [ká   comii   ka]]   ʰé ku   ʔargiyyi (Tosco 2001: 283)
       young here   come:PERF **Rel**   3A 2O   see:PERF
       'The young man who came saw you.'

and the comparable cases of Teribe (Chibchan) and Slave (Na-Dene) reported in Cinque (2013b: 136).

In addition to the 'which that IP' languages there appear to be 'that which IP' languages. See the case of Polish in (52a), that of Moroccan Arabic in (52b), that of the Bantu language Nzadi (52c), and that of one of the relativization possibilities of West Rumelian Turkish in (52d):[63]

(52)   a. Marysia zna   chłopków **co których** Ania lubi.   (Szczegielniak 2004: 15)
           Mary   knows   boys   **that who** Ann likes
           'Mary knows some boys who Ann likes.'
       b. 1-bnt   **lli**   **m'a-men** xrejti . . .   (Ouhalla 2006: 650–1)
           the-girl   **RelMarker** **with-whom** you.went.out . . .
           the girl with whom you went out . . .
       c. bàán   **na**   **ŋgo**   kɔ′t   kó   ńdzɔ
                                  (Crane, Hyman & Tukumu 2011: 194)
           children   **that**   **WH.PAST** enter LOC house
           the children who entered into the house
       d. Madem-ljer ičun **ći**   **angi-ljer** daa čok   iš-e   dir-en . . .
                                    (Dombrowski 2012: 83)
           mineral-PL for   **COMP** **which-PL** more much work-DAT enter-PART
           about the mines that are most often worked . . .

Whether this should be taken to show the existence of a further CP layer above that hosting 'which'-type pronouns or simply that languages can vary as to the location of the 'which' and 'that' CPs remains to be seen.

2.1.4   *Non-contiguity of Relative Pronouns and Invariant Relativizers with the Relative Clause Head*

Languages also appear to differ as to where Topic and Focus phrases are located with respect to the invariant relativizers and/or the relative pronoun. While in Italian Topic and Focus phrases necessarily follow the relative pronouns (*cui,* art. + *qual-*) (see (53)–(54)) and the invariant relativizer *che* (see (55)) (Cinque 1979, Rizzi 1997, Benincà & Poletto 2004), and in

---

[63] Murelli (2011: 101) gives similar examples from Old Russian and Russian dialects. Varieties of colloquial Dutch also display a similar pattern. See (i), from Boef (2012: fn. 11), with *of,* an invariant subordinator, and *wat* a relative pronoun:

(i)   Het boek **of wat** ik gelezen heb is mooi geschreven.
      the book **if what** I read have is beautifully written
      'The book that I read is beautifully written.'

Nez Perce appears to be both a 'which that' and a 'that which' type of language, which Deal (2016) analyses in terms of a different spell-out of chain links. Also see Radford (2019: 37 fn. 34) for certain examples in colloquial English, which however might be production errors.

Venetian, where the single relative pronoun *dove* 'where' and *che* co-occur, both of them (see (56))[64], in some languages Topic and Focus phrases may come to occupy a position between the RC Head and the relative *wh*-pronoun or relativizer. This is for example the case of Latin, Hungarian and the Trans-New Guinea language Bine in (57a–c) (also see the case of the Bantu languages Chishona and Luganda mentioned in fn. 10 of Chapter 4):

(53) a. Questa è la babysitter a cui **mio figlio** non lo affiderei per nessuna cosa al mondo.
      this is the babysitter to whom of my child (topic) I would grant custody for nothing in the world

   b. *Questa è la babysitter, **mio figlio**, a cui non lo affiderei per nessuna cosa al mondo.
      'This is the babysitter of my child (topic) to whom I would grant custody for nothing in the world.'

(54) a. L'uomo al quale **quésto** dovevi dare (non altro) era Gianni.
      The man to whom this (focus) you should have given (not other things) was Gianni.

   b. *L'uomo **quésto** al quale dovevi dare (non altro) era Gianni.
      The man this (focus) to whom you should have given (not other things) was Gianni.

---

[64] This is also true in English where topics, and negative foci triggering subject auxiliary inversion, follow the relative pronoun, and *that*. See (i) and Radford (2019: §1.3) for illustration of the ordering of left-peripheral constituents in English RCs:

(i)   a. the man to whom liberty we could never grant (Baltin 1982: 17)

   b. a candidate who/that under no circumstances would I vote for … (see Culicover 2011: n. 2)

   c. He said that his password, on no account, normally, would he divulge (it) to anyone. (Andrew Radford, pers. comm.)

   d. A university is the kind of place where, that kind of behaviour, under no circumstances will the authorities tolerate. (Radford 2019: 20)

In (ii) it is the relative *wh*-phrase in negative topic position that triggers subject auxiliary inversion:

(ii) these candidates, none of whom would I vote for, … (Culicover 2011: n. 2)

Culicover (2013: fn. 26) suggests that the negative phrase raises first to a Polarity Phrase (PolP) of the Split CP, triggering subject auxiliary inversion and then moves to Spec,CP. If PolP is a criterial position in Rizzi's (2006) sense, a derivation similar to that concerning interrogative clefts in Rizzi's (2010) analysis could be proposed, non-restrictives being less selective than restrictives concerning the type of phrase that moves to CP$_{Rel}$.

(55) a. So di un lattaio che **il vino** lo vende a 100 lire   (Cinque 1979: 107)
          I.know of a milkman that the wine it he.sells at 100 liras
          'I know a milkman who sells wine at 100 liras.'
      b. *So di un lattaio **il vino** che lo vende ancora a 100 lire (Cinque 1979: 107)
          I.know of a milkman the wine that it he.sells at 100 liras

(56) a. Conosso un posto dove   che **il vino**   i   o vende ancora a   buon marca'
          I.know   a   place where that the wine they it sell   still   cheap
      b. *Conosso un posto dove **il**   **vino**   che i   o vende ancora a buon
                                                                                  marca'
          I.know   a   place where the wine   that they it sell   still   cheap
      c. *Conosso un posto **il**   **vino** dove   che i   o vende ancora a buon
                                                                                  marca'
          I.know   a   place the   wine where   that they it sell   still   cheap
          'I know of a place where they still sell wine cheap.'

(57) a. **meus vicinus** [meo viro] **qui** liberum praehibet locum, . . .
                                                (Latin – Bianchi 1999: 97)
          my neighbour$_{Nom}$ my husband$_{Dat}$ who$_{Nom}$ free$_{Acc}$ offers place$_{Acc}$
          my neighbour, who offers a free place to my husband, . . .
      b. **a könyv**, Janos **amit** említtet, . . .
                                (Hungarian – Haberland & van der Auwera 1990: 136)
          the book John which mentioned, . . .
          the book which John mentioned . . .
      c. **kaakesea-cäco biname**   taun cabu   **lui** yaa-craj-u-ge, . . .
                                                (Bine – Fleischmann 1981: 2)
          work-without person   town in   rel 3ob-live-hab-3sg.s
          people without work who live in towns, . . .

In Canariense Spanish and Georgian a topic can also occur between the relative *wh*-pronoun and the invariant relativizer. For Canariense Spanish Brucart (1992: 134) reports the possibility of a sentence like (58), where *el*, which is plausibly followed by a silent 'which'-type relative pronoun, precedes a topic which in turn precedes the invariant relativizer *que*:[65]

(58)   el amigo **con el** más confianza **que** tengo . . .
         the friend in the (whom) most confidence that I have . . .

---

[65] This casts doubt, as Brucart notes, on the possibility that *el* and *que* make up a constituent.

The same appears to be the case in Georgian even though the relative *wh*-pronoun and the invariant relativizer cannot co-occur. As noted in Callegari (2014), the two types of Georgian relativizers, *rom* and *romeli*, behave differently. *Rom* is an invariant subordinating conjunction. It can function as a relativizer but it can also introduce declarative complement sentences (where it has to be initial – Foley 2013: §5.2). In RCs it must be separated from the Head by at least one constituent (or perhaps a single remnant not containing the verb – see Foley 2013; *pace* Kojima 2005: §4, 2014, and references cited there).[66] *Romeli* only introduces relative clauses, inflects for gender, number and Case and is followed by the relative/ focus marker *c*. It cannot be separated from the Head by anything. See (59) and (60), from Callegari (2014: §4) (for other cases like (59a) see Harris 1994: 132):

(59) a. Biči   Vanos   rom c'igns   miscems.
          boy-Nom Vano-Dat that book-Dat he-will-give-it
          the boy that will give a book to Vano
      b. *Biči   rom   Vanos   c'igns   miscems.
          boy-Nom that   Vano-Datbook-Dat he-will-give-it

(60) a. K'aci   romelsac   nobelis   p'remias   aucileblad   miscemen.
          man-Nom who-Dat   Nobel-Genprize-Dat undoubtedly they-will give-it
          a man to whom the Nobel Prize they will give it undoubtedly
      b. *?K'aci   nobelis   p'remias   romelsac   aucileblad   miscemen.
          man-Nom Nobel-Gen prize-Dat who-Dat   undoubtedly they-will-give-it

These data show that relative *wh*-pronouns or the invariant relativizer occupy in some languages CP projections lower than the FocusP and TopicP of the RC split CP (in contrast to languages like Italian, where they necessarily occupy CP projections higher than TopicP and FocusP – see Rizzi 1997 and Benincà & Poletto 2004).

---

[66] The same is true of the relativizer of Luganda and, optionally, of that of Lunyole, two Bantu languages. See Walusimbi (1996: §1.5) and fn. 12 of Chapter 4 below for an example from Luganda.

(61a) represents the case of Italian- and Veneto-type languages, (61b) that of Latin (and Hungarian) type languages, and (61c) the case of Canariense Spanish (and Georgian) type languages.

(61a)

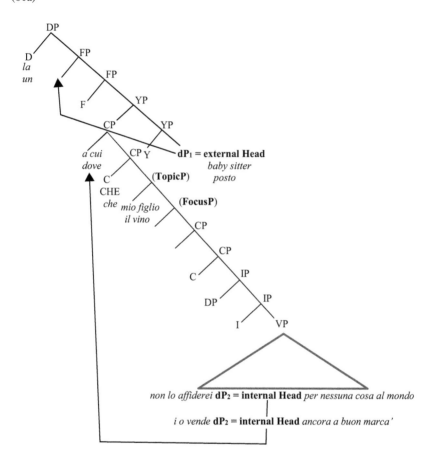

(61b)

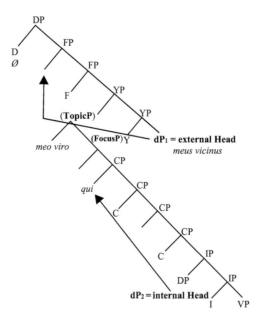

(61c)

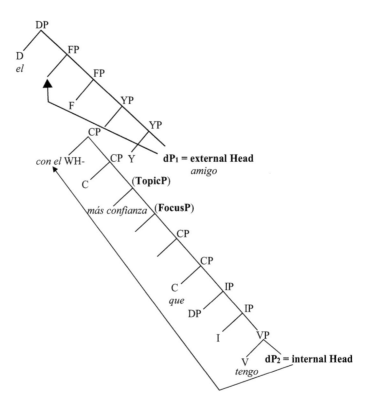

Krapova (2010: §4.2) observes an interesting contrast in Bulgarian between cases where there is no apparent necessity for a 'raising' derivation, like (62a), and cases plausibly involving 'raising', as with the relativization of certain idiom chunks, like (62b). In the former a topic or focus phrase can come to occupy a position between the RC Head and a relative pronoun or the invariant relativizer *deto*. In the latter, the *overt* Head cannot be separated from the invariant relativizer *deto* by a topic or focus phrase, which, rather, can marginally precede it. See (62c) (her (33c)):

(62)   a.   Tova e **ženata** [$_{Top/FocP}$ naj-složnite pesni] **kojato/deto**   (Rudin 1986:
            peeše ...   128)
            this is woman.the most complex.the songs who/that sang.3sg
            'This is the woman who sang the most complex songs.'

       b.   *[**Natiskăt** [$_{Top/FocP}$ zaradi zdravnata reforma]$_i$ **deto** Evropa okazva na
            Bălgarija t$_i$] e neprestanen
            pressure.the because-of health-care.the reform that Europe exert.3sg on
            Bulgaria is constant

       c.   ?[$_{Top/FocP}$ Zaradi zdravnata reforma]$_i$ **natiskăt deto** Europa okazva na
            Bălgarija t$_i$] e neprestanen
            because-of health-care.the reform pressure.the that Europe exert.3sg on
            Bulgaria is constant
            'The pressure that Europe puts on Bulgaria for the health care reform is
            constant.'

The contrast between (62a) and (62b) becomes understandable if in Bulgarian the internal Head targets a Spec,CP lower than TopP/FocP, when these are present[67] (much like the Latin case in (57a) above), and cannot raise out of the

---

[67] Rudin (1986: 127) in fact notes the ungrammaticality of (i), where the relative pronoun (the internal Head) precedes the Topic/FocusP.

(i)   *Ženata **kojato** [$_{Top/FocP}$ naj-složnite pesni] peeše ...
         woman.the who most complex.the songs sang.3sg
         the woman who sang the most complex songs ...

I take the contrast between (62a) and (62b) to support the 'raising' analysis of the internal Head in (62c) and that of the external Head in (62a). This appears confirmed by the possibility of reconstructing the quantifier 'two (books)' in (ii)a (every > 2; as well as 2 > every) vs the impossibility of reconstructing it in (ii)b, whose interpretation is that the two books are the same type of books for every student (Iliyana Krapova, pers. comm.). The target of the internal Head able to reconstruct inside the RC thus appears to be necessarily lower than Topic/FocusP:

(ii)   a.   Dvete knigi deto vseki učenik e kupil ot knižarnitsata ...
              two-the books that every student has bought from bookstore-the ...
              the two books that every student bought from the bookstore ...

RC split CP to Spec,FP (the target of the external Head), perhaps due to a locality violation (see Kayne's 2010b: §1).[68]

Certain languages appear to allow an even more radical non-contiguity of relative pronouns with the Head. In the post-nominal relatives of the Indo-Aryan language Punjabi,[69] when the relativization is from a deeply embedded clause, the relative pronoun can remain in situ in its (external) Merge position ((63a)) (in defiance of Safir's 1986: 678 'Locality Condition on R-Binding'), or move to any of the intermediate CPs ((63b)), or move all the way up to the CP of the highest clause ((63c)):[70]

(63)   a.   o kuRii [mona soch-di hagi [rani **jeenu** pasand kardi hai]] (Yang 2006: 146)
            Dem girl Mona think-HAB is Rani REL-ACC like do is
            the girl who Mona thinks Rani likes ...
    b.   o kuRii [mona soch-di hagi [**jeenu** rani pasand kardi hai]] (Yang 2006: 147)
            Dem girl Mona think-HAB is REL-ACC Rani like do is
            the girl who Mona thinks Rani likes ...
    c.   o kuRii [**jeenu** mona soch-di hagi [rani pasand kardi hai]] (Yang 2006: 147)
            Dem girl REL-ACC Mona think-HAB is Rani like do is
            the girl who Mona thinks Rani likes ...

---

    b.   Dvete knigi, ot knižarnitsata, deto vseki učenik e kupil ...
        two-the books, from bookstore-the, that every student has bought
        the two books that every student bought from the bookstore ...

[68] Thinking of Kayne (2017b: (1): 'Wh-movement in relatives cannot (normally) land below ForceP (or TopP) because of locality requirements holding between the 'head' of the relative and the *wh*-phrase.'), the landing of Bulgarian *wh*-relative pronouns below TopP may suggest that the relation can exceptionally be less strictly local. Also see the cases below concerning in situ *wh*-relative pronouns. The additional raising of the internal Head from Spec, CP to Spec,FP (in 'raising' derivations) would also incorrectly make the 'raising' and 'matching' derivations non-distinct in their behaviour with respect to extraposition (see A4.1 of the Appendix).

[69] Punjabi also has an extraposed variant of the embedded post-nominal RC, and a correlative construction (Yang 2006: §6.2.1).

[70] It can also appear simultaneously in the (external) Merge position and in the highest CP ((i)a) or in the CP of an intermediate clause and the highest CP ((i)b), other possibilities being excluded (see Yang 2006: §6.3.3):

(i)   a.   o kuRii [**jeenu** mona soch-di hagi [rani **jeenu** pasand kardi hai]] (Yang 2006: 150)
            Dem girl REL-ACC Mona think-HAB is Rani REL-ACC like do is
            the girl who Mona thinks Rani likes ...
    b.   o kuRii [**jeenu** mona soch-di hagi [**jeenu** rani pasand kardi hai]] (Yang 2006: 150)
            Dem girl REL-ACC Mona think-HAB is REL-ACC Rani like do is
            the girl who Mona thinks Rani likes ...

Li (2002: fn. 14), Huang, Li & Li (2009: §6.2.4) and Lin & Tsai (2015: 114) report similar cases from Chinese, where the *wh*-forms *weishenme* 'why' and *zenyang* 'how' show a relative pronoun in situ predicated of the Heads 'reason' and 'way', respectively (in possibly light headed Free RCs). See (64):[71]

(64)   a.   [[ta **weishenme** bu lai] de **yuanyin**].   (Li 2002: fn. 14)
           he   why   not come DE reason
           the reason why he didn't come . . .
     b.   ?[[ta (**ruhe$_i$/zenme$_i$**) xiu che] de **fangfa$_i$**] meiren zhidao.
                            (Huang, Li & Li 2009: 222)
           he how fix car de method nobody know
           'Nobody knows the way (how) he fixed the car.'
     c.   [[xiaozhang **zenyang** chufa zuobi] de   (Lin & Tsai 2015: 114)
           fangshi] . . .
           chancellor how punish cheating DE way . . .
           the way how the chancellor will punish cheating . . .

2.2   Externally Headed Pre-nominal Relative Clauses

As with externally headed post-nominal ones, externally headed pre-nominal RCs appear in some languages to involve both 'raising' and 'matching' derivations (e.g., Chinese), while in others possibly just the 'matching' one (e.g. Pharasiot Greek). Before considering some of the relevant evidence, I briefly address two properties that are characteristically attributed to pre-nominal RCs: **the absence of (initial or final) relative pronouns** (Schwartz 1971: 144; Downing 1978: 392 ff; Keenan 1985: 149; Kayne 1994: 93; Dik 1997: vol. 2, 46; Song 2001: 220, 232; De Vries 2001: 235, 240, 2005: 147; Kroeger 2005: 238; Creissels 2006: vol. 2, 239, 242; Andrews 2007: 208, 218, 222; Wu 2011: §3.3) **(and of initial invariant relativizers** – Andrews 1975: 44), and **their non-finite status** (Keenan 1985: 160; Dik 1997, vol. 2: 55; Andrews 2007: 208; De Vries 2001: 235; among others). While the general-

---

[71] For further properties of this construction (island sensitivity, etc.), see Huang, Li & Li (2009: §6.2.4). Similar, though more marginal, cases of relative *wh*-in situ are reported for Polish in Szczegielniak (2005: 180) (see (i)), and for a second relative *wh*-phrase in English, (ii), from Kayne (1994: 155 fn. 16), and (iii), from Kayne (2017b: §3):
    (i)   ?Kobietę [$_{RC}$ mężczyzna rozpoznał **którą** wczoraj]] Janek zna od lat
           woman(acc) man(nom) recognized which yesterday Janek knows for years
           a woman who a man recognized yesterday Janek knows for years
    (ii)   ?the man whose wife's love for **whom** knows no bounds . . .
    (iii) ?that car over there belongs to my old friend John Smith, whose long-standing attachment to **which** is well known to all his friends

ization that pre-nominal RCs lack initial (or final) relative pronouns appears virtually exceptionless,[72] which calls for an explanation, the absence of initial invariant relativizers (or weak invariant relative pronouns), and the necessarily non-finite status of pre-nominal RCs, appear not to be clearly supported.

See for example the cases in (65), where the obligatorily pre-nominal RC is introduced by an initial invariant relativizer:[73]

(65)   a.   [[**kiát** [íra]] perí] ...
                        (Silli Greek – Song 2001: 256 and reference cited there)[74]
               COMP saw-I boy ...
               the boy that I saw ...

---

[72] Enrico (2003: 365) reports some cases of initial relative pronouns in the pre-nominal RCs of Haida (Na-Dené; or a language isolate according to some authors), which appear to involve an (interrogative) pronoun also used in 'Headless' RCs. See e.g. (i):

(i)   [tll guud 'll tlaalra qaajuu-gaang-aa-s] k'iw-aay ...
        [where on 3p husband hunt-FREQ-EVID-PR] trail-DF
        the trail on which her husband sends to hunt

[73] In other cases, the pre-nominal RC with the initial invariant relativizer can also be found in post-nominal position. This last case may be interpreted as involving an additional fronting of the RC from the (itself derived) post-nominal position. See, for example, the case of Galla/Oromo (Cushitic) in (i), from Mallinson & Blake (1981: 289), and that of Xong (Miao-Yao) in (ii), from Sposato (2012: 51–2). Also see the comparable cases of Yurok (Berman 1972: 257), of Latin (Bianchi 1999: §6.4 and 2000b: §4.4), of the SVO Bantu language Kikuria (Gould 1988: 57), of the Austronesian language Hainan Cham (Thurgood, Thurgood & Li 2014: §8.3.4), and of the SVO Sinitic-Malayic language Jambi Teochew (Peng 2011), where RCs can either precede or follow the Head.

(i)   a. [**kan** [kalēsa gale]] namtiĉĉa an arge.
               Rel yesterday arrived(finite) man-def I saw
            b. nam-tiĉĉa [**kan** kalēsa gale] (sana) an arge
               man-def Rel yesterday arrived (Dem) I saw
               'I saw the man that arrived yesterday.'
(ii)   a. [**max** nonx hlit] miex ...
               [REL eat cooked.rice] person ...
               the person who's eating rice ...
            b. miex [**max** mex bib] wel yanb.
               person [REL exist hair] 1SG like
               'I like people who have hair.' (i.e. who are not bald)

[74] The same is true of other Asia Minor Greek dialects with obligatory pre-nominal RCs, Cappadocian (see (i)), and Pontic Greek (Bağrıaçık & Danckaert 2016: §5):

(i)   [**tú**-érxunde i=misafúr-i]   pésu   džó=pérun=ta
                                                     (Cappadocian Greek – Janse 1999: 459)
        REL-come   the=stranger-PL.NOM inside   not=take=them
        the strangers who come, they do not take them in

b. [[**tu** [čú-ši γéna]] o nomát] . . .

(Pharasiot Greek – Bağrıaçık 2014: 3)[75]

COMP not-has.3s beard the man . . .

the man who does not have a beard . . .

Analogously, while the non-finite status of pre-nominal RCs is clearly found in a number of languages and language families (Dravidian, Turkic, Tungusic, Mongolic, many Uralic and Tibeto-Burman languages, and Quechuan languages),[76] where the RC 'exhibits a reduction in tense-aspect marking and in verb agreement morphology' (Keenan 1985: 160), often being participial (like the pre-nominal reduced RCs of German and Finnish), or nominalized, this is not true for many other languages and language families. See the Silli Greek example in (65a), the Papuan languages Awtuw (Feldman 1986: §10.2.7), Kamano (Payne & Drew 1970: §4.3), Menggwa Dla (de Sousa 2006: 420), Mian (Fedden 2007: 453), Oksapmin (Loughnane 2009: §7.5.4), Tauya (Mac-Donald 1990: 289 ff), Usan and Gahuku (Reesink 1987: 217–8), as well as the Qiangic (Sino-Tibetan) language Japhug (Jacques 2016: §5), the Omotic language Maale (Amha 2001: §8.1.1), the Ethio-Semitic languages Amharic (Fulass 1972: 497; Wu 2011: 602), Chaha (Abebe 1990), Silt'i (Rawda Siraj 2003: 4.1.1.1), and Tigre (Palmer 1961, Wu 2011: 602), the Munda language Kharia (Peterson 2006: §7.7.2 Ia; 2011: §7.6.2), the non-Pama-Nyungan language Bunuba (Rumsey 2000: 120), the Iranian language Sarikoli (Kim 2014: ch. 3; 2017: §10.2.1), the isolate language Kusunda (Watters 2006: §9.1), the South Caucasian language Laz (Lacroix 2009: 749), the Yeniseic language Ket (Nefedov 2012: 197–8), among others, all of which display finite pre-nominal RCs. As noted by Wu (2011) 'prenominal relatives are not non-finite intrinsically, but owing to the fact that prenominal-relative-clause languages use non-finite subordination in general [. . .] it is meaningful to insist on prenominal relative clauses being non-finite only if the language in question uses non-finite forms merely for prenominal relatives, but not for the other subordinates. Nonetheless, I have not found such a language.' (p. 601).

---

[75] The RCs of Pharasiot Greek 'are exclusively pre-nominal at least in the texts written prior to the population exchange and for decades after that (1886–1960s)' (Bağrıaçık & Danckaert 2016: §1.2.1).

[76] But see the recently emerged finite pre-nominal RC of Imbabura Quechua, preferred by some speakers over the non-finite alternative (Hastings 2004: ch. 4 fn. 2).

2.2.1   The 'Raising' Derivation

Here, the internal Head, dP_2, is attracted to the RC Spec,CP, from where it licenses the deletion of the external Head, dP_1. After that the RC remnant raises outside of the CP (see (66)). Reconstruction effects are expected as the **overt** Head is the 'internal' one. And so is sensitivity to islands, due to the movement of the 'internal' Head.

(66)

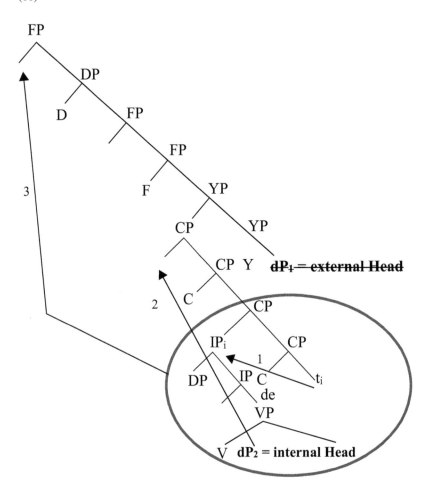

Chinese is one language with pre-nominal RCs which shows the presence of 'raising' derivations: RCs display island sensitivity (see (67), from Aoun & Li 2003: 178), allow for the relativization of idiom chunks (see (68), from Aoun & Li 2003: 138), and show anaphor and pronominal binding reconstruction (see (69a–b), from Aoun & Li 2003: 132–3), though apparently not reconstruction of numerals under the scope of a RC internal quantifier (see (70), from Aoun & Li 2003: 133). Aoun & Li (2003) suggest that the latter property is related to the possibility in Chinese to reconstruct NPs but not DPs. I take this to be a consequence of the Merge position of Chinese pre-nominal RCs which is below not only strong determiners (as we should expect for restrictives) but also below cardinal numerals (and classifiers), much like the participial RCs of German and English (see §3.5.7): Dem Num CLF RC N, which is one of the canonical orders of RCs, the alternative one (RC Dem Num CLF N) being arguably derived by movement.[77] This implies the external Head (and the internal one, which reconstructs in 'raising' derivations, is only constituted by [AP N]). In other words, Aoun and Li's observation concerning the non-reconstructions of numerals in Chinese may be a consequence of the position which RCs enter in the language.

(67) *[wo xihuan [[t$_i$ chuan de] yifu] de] na-ge ren$_i$ ...
      I   like   wear DE clothes   DE that-cl person
      the person$_i$ that I like the clothes he$_i$ wears ...

(68) [[ta chi e$_i$ de] cu$_i$] bi shei dou da.
      he eat vinegar compare who all big
      Lit.: 'The vinegar he eats is greater than anyone else's.'
      'His jealousy is greater than anyone else's.'

(69) a. [[wo jiao zhangsan quan mei-ge-ren$_i$ kai t lai de] ziji$_i$ de chezi ...
          I ask Zhangsan persuade every-CL-person drive come DE self DE car
          'The self's car that I asked Zhangsan to persuade everyone to drive over ...'

      b. ni hui kandao [[wo xiwang mei-ge xuesheng$_i$ dou neng dai t lai de] wo gei ta$_i$ de shu].
          you will see I hope every-CL student all can bring come DE I give his book
          'You will see the book that I gave to him$_i$ that I hope every student$_i$ will bring.'

(70) wo hui zhengli [[mei-ge-ren dou hui kan t DE] san-ben shu].
      I will arrange every-CL-person all will read de three-CL book (same 3 books)
      'I will put the three books that everyone will read in order.'

---

[77] Hsu (2017) takes the pre-Dem RC to be in focus. See §3.6 and references cited there for further evidence of the derived nature of the pre-demonstrative position of Chinese RCs.

The interpretation of Chinese RCs in post-numeral and in pre-demonstrative positions has long been a controversial issue. Chao (1968: 286) (also see Huang 1982: 68 ff) proposed that the pre-demonstrative position is interpreted restrictively (though the same interpretation is available in post-numeral position if the RC is stressed) while the unstressed post-numeral position is characteristically 'descriptive' or non-restrictive. This runs counter to the semantics (whereby restrictives must be interpreted under a definite determiner or demonstrative, while non-restrictives must be interpreted above definite determiners and demonstratives as they modify an autonomously referential DP). Perhaps a way to avoid this paradox would be to take Chinese RCs to be a type of non-finite (participial) RCs (see §3.6, for possible evidence to this effect).

The situation of Japanese is only partially similar, as restrictive RCs appear between demonstratives and cardinal numerals and (as expected) show reconstruction of cardinals for scope interpretation as well. See the detailed discussion in Whitman (2013). They can also appear in pre-demonstrative position, like non-restrictive RCs but when they do they follow non-restrictive RCs (Kameshima 1989: 233 ff, *pace* Ishizuka 2008b). Malayalam (Mohanan 1984: §2), as well as Modern Tamil (Annamalai & Steever 1998: 123, and Vasu 1994: 50), and Turkish (Kornfilt 1985: §6), all of whose pre-nominal relative clauses are unbounded and sensitive to islands (see for example (71) from Malayalam), may be other languages allowing for a raising derivation (although sensitivity to islands can also be displayed, as seen, by raising of the internal Head, subsequently 'deleted' by the external one in a 'matching' derivation – for which see the next section):

(71)   a. [[[[kuṭṭi __ ṇuḷḷi] eṇṇa] amma paranna] aana] uraṇṇi.
                 child-N pinched that mother-N said-P elephant-N slept
                 'The elephant that mother said the child pinched slept.'
        Complex NP island
             b. *[[[[kuṭṭi __ ṇuḷḷi eṇṇa] kaaryam] amma paranna] aana] uraṇṇi.
                 child-N pinched that fact-N mother-N said-P elephant-N slept
                 the elephant such that mother stated the fact that the child pinched the
                 elephant slept
        Adjunct island
             c. *[[[kuṭṭi __ _nuḷḷiyappooḷ] amma ciricca] aana] uraṇṇi.
                 child-N pinched-then mother-N smiled-P elephant-N slept
                 the elephant such that mother smiled when the child pinched the
                 elephant slept

Indirect evidence for the fronting of the RC across its Head may possibly come from the apparent non-local agreement with the RC subject found on the Head of Sakha relative clauses discussed in Kornfilt (2005a), which she takes as stranded by the RC when this is fronted above the DP (or rather DemP): [RC Subj$_i$ VP] (Dem) Head-agr$_i$.[78]

2.2.2 The 'Matching' Derivation

In this derivation dP$_1$ directly licenses the deletion of dP$_2$ (in situ) backwards (see (72)). In this case, no reconstruction effects are expected, as the *overt* Head is the 'external' one, nor is sensitivity to islands as no movement of the internal Head has occurred.

As mentioned above, while Pharasiot Greek used to have exclusively pre-nominal RCs (Bağrıaçık & Danckaert 2016: §1.2.1), in more recent times it developed post-nominal relative clauses as well, but the two differ with respect to reconstruction and weak island sensitivity. Only post-nominal RCs allow amount readings, show (obligatory) reconstruction of idiom chunks and quantifiers and are sensitive to weak islands (Bağrıaçık & Danckaert 2016: §2). On the basis of this, Bağrıaçık and Danckaert conclude that pre-nominal RCs are derived by 'matching' only while post-nominal ones can also be derived by 'raising'.

Lander and Khozukhar (2015: 5) report that RCs in Tanti Dargwa (East Caucasian) do not show sensitivity to islands, as do Comrie & Polinsky (1999) for another East Caucasian language, Tsez, though more recently Polinsky (2015, Part III, ch. 10) notes that relativization into a relative clause in Tsez is not possible, and that the apparently possible relativization into adjunct clauses may involve silent resumption.

It is not clear whether languages exist that only employ this in situ 'matching' derivation. Kwon, Polinsky and Kluender (2006: fn. 4) claim that Korean might be one such language, as it does not permit relativization of idiom chunks,[79] and only has a high reading of 'first' and 'last', but more work needs to be done as Korean RCs seem to display island sensitivity (Han & Kim 2004), despite occasional claims to the contrary.[80]

---

[78] Similar considerations (modulo the post-nominal character of the RC) may apply to Wolof, which also displays (optional) stranding of adverbs belonging to the RC after the determiner:

[N [$_{RC}$ t$_i$]]$_k$ D AdvP$_i$ t$_k$. See Torrence (2005 and 2013: ch. 4).

[79] For the observation that idiom chunks cannot be relativized in Korean also see Jo (2002: 122).

[80] Sensitivity to islands is per se compatible with a 'matching' derivation, provided that the internal Head raises to a position that does not c-command the external Head (see fn. 19 above). As here too the overt Head would be the external Head, no reconstruction would be found, even in the presence of sensitivity to islands.

(72)

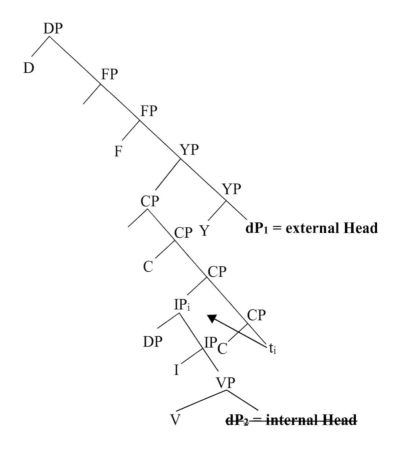

The matching analysis just reviewed in terms of backwards deletion of the internal Head by the external one seems to find the exact converse (forwards deletion) in one family of Internally Headed RCs, which are examined in §2.3 below.

2.2.3   On the Absence of Relative Pronouns in Pre-nominal Relative Clauses

Concerning the systematic absence of relative pronouns in pre-nominal RCs (whether initial, '[[which you bought] book] . . .', or final, '[[you bought which] book] . . .'), in §2.1.1 I mentioned the possibility that this may depend on their having to be R-bound by the Head, which requires that the Head c-command the pronoun in Spec,CP.[81] But this obtains neither in the 'raising' nor in the 'matching' derivation of pre-nominal RCs. If indeed R-Binding (or lack thereof) is at the base of the presence (or absence) of such pronouns, then pre-nominal and post-nominal RCs must differ in terms of structure. Pre-nominal ones must not be c-commanded by the Head, which thus cannot bind a relative pronoun in Spec,CP, while post-nominal ones must be. This is also at the base of their different linear order with respect to the Head, as determined by the LCA. This in turn requires (in head-initial languages) some meaningless movement – see Cinque (2018b). If they had the same hierarchical structure, externalization at PF would not be able to capture the generalization that such pronouns are not found in pre-nominal RCs.

2.3   Internally Headed Relative Clauses

Internally Headed RCs are not a unitary RC type (see Grosu 2001, 2002; Hiraiwa 2017: 7). Like externally Headed ones, they turn out to belong to distinct types (at least, the restrictive and maximalizing ones),[82] involving distinct derivations. In the following I discuss how their properties could be derived within the double-Headed syntactic structure developed above (which recalls Cole's 1987 analysis), attempting to integrate it with Grosu's (2002, 2012) semantic typology.[83] Given the fragmentary information we have of the syntax and semantics of the IHRCs of some of the languages to be discussed, the conclusions reached here must be considered quite tentative.

2.3.1   The Lakhota Exclusively 'Matching'/Restrictive Type

One type, discussed in detail in Williamson (1987), is that of the Siouan language Lakhota. This type is characterized by the following cluster of

---

[81] For a different account, see Kayne (1994: ch. 8: §8.3).

[82] As well as the non-restrictive ones in (some of) the IHRCs that do not display an indefiniteness restriction. See §3.1.6.3.

[83] Grosu's (2012) typology of IHRCs (also see Grosu 2002: §1) distinguishes between Plain-Restrictive, Maximalizing, and Mismatch-restrictives, with the following respective properties:

> *Plain-Restrictive* (Lakhota, Mojave): Range of Ds outside the IHRC, an indefinite internal Head, stacking with intersective import, island-insensitivity.
> *Maximalizing* (Japanese, Quechua): No Ds outside the IHRC, strong Ds allowed with the internal Head, no stacking, island-sensitivity.
> *Mismatch-Restrictive* (Navajo): No Ds outside the IHRC, strong Ds allowed with the internal Head, with external scope, stacking with intersective import, island-sensitivity.

> Also see the cases of Dogrib (Athapaskan) and Washo (Hokan/isolate), whose RC internal Heads can apparently be preceded by strong determiners and allow stacking of IHRCs (see Saxon 2000 and Hanink 2016, respectively, although the authors do not discuss the issue of island sensitivity).

properties (also see Culy 1990: 153; Basilico 1996: §7, Grosu 2002: §2; 2012: §3.1; Cinque 2008b: 14 ff):

(73) a. *presence of an indefiniteness restriction* (see Williamson 1987: §7.1.3–4 and §7.3.2; Grosu 2012: §3.1): the RC internal Head can only be preceded by adjectives, and weak determiners, the same as those possible in the English *there*-existential construction (indefinite articles, cardinal numerals, multal/paucal quantifiers). Strong determiners (like demonstratives, definite articles, universal quantifiers, etc.) are outside of the RC.[84]

     b. *possibility of stacking* (Williamson 1987: 173)[85]

     c. *absence of island sensitivity* (Williamson 1987: §7.2)[86]

     d. *impossibility of non-restrictives* (Williamson 1987: 175)[87]

The possibility of stacking, which Grosu and Landman (1998) show to be incompatible with maximalizing RCs, and especially the absence of island sensitivity, suggests that this type of IHRC cannot involve the 'raising' derivation, but just a 'matching' one, where the internal Head does not move.[88] This

---

[84] In addition to Lakhota the indefiniteness restriction appears to be found in other Siouan languages (Hidatsa – Boyle 2007: §6.2.4.2; 2016: §4.1 and §2.3.5 below – and Crow – Andrews 1975: 167; Graczyk 1991: 500 ff), in Yuman languages (Mojave – Munro 1974: §3.1; Basilico 1996: 507; and Grosu 2012: 12–3 – and Diegueño – Gorbet 1973: 68; 1976, 1977), in the Dogon language family (McPherson 2014: ch. 4; Heath 2015), in the Papuan language Marori, which also allows stacking (Arka 2016). It is also found in Gur languages. See fn. 111 below. To judge from Colburn (1984: §5.1) the Trans-New Guinea Madang language Erima also has an indefiniteness restriction in its IHRCs, with bare NPs or Num + NP internal Heads and RC external demonstratives. To judge from Shougrakpam (2014) the indefiniteness restriction is also found in Manipuri, which according to Subbãrão (2012: §8.5) belongs (together with Mizo and Hmar) to the Tibeto-Burman family whose IHRCs have no overt Case markers on the internal Head.

[85] One of the examples of stacked RCs given in Williamson (1987: 174) is:

    (i)   [[[wowapi wą] Deloria owa cha] blawa cha] . . .
             book a Deloria write ind.art. I.read ind.art . . .
             a book that Deloria wrote that I have read . . .

[86] See for example (i), where the Head is within a complex NP, and the discussion in Williamson (1987: §7.2) and Grosu (2002: §2; 2012: 11):

    (i)   Wichota wowapi wą Ø-yawa pi cha ob woʔẽglaka pi ki he L.A. Times Ø-e
             many-people paper a read PL ind.art. with we.speak PL the that L.A. Times be
             the newspaper that we talk to many people who read (it) is the L.A. Times

[87] Williamson says that proper names and definite pronouns 'are excluded from the position of internal head'. Grosu (2002: n. 1) reports that in Lakhota 'appositive constructions [. . .] appear to be externally headed'.

[88] '[T]he IHs of Lakhota do not undergo Head-Raising' (Grosu 2009b: abstract). Semantically they have restrictive import, deriving from the operation of λ abstraction, as in the corresponding English externally Headed restrictives (see Grosu 2002: §2; 2012: §3.1 for further relevant discussion). This could perhaps be captured by externally merging a null operator into Spec,CP, which binds the internal Head as a variable much like in McCloskey's (2002) analysis for Irish and Irish-like RCs with resumptive pronouns (see Vincent 2017: fn. 10).

is in fact the exact converse of the backwards deletion derivation seen above for the 'matching' derivation of pre-nominal RCs. Instead of dP_1 deleting backwards dP_2 here it is dP_2 that deletes dP_1 forwards, as shown in (74):[89]

(74)

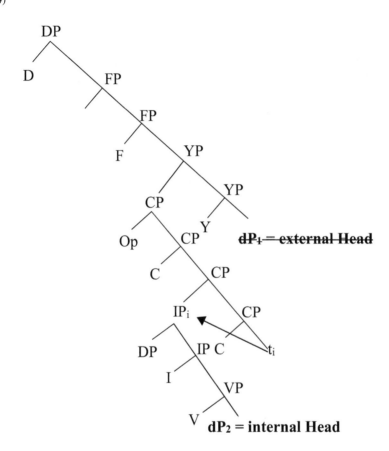

[89] The double-Headed structure in (74) is reminiscent of those posited by Platero (1974) and Cole (1987), if we abstract away from minor differences. Platero (1974) also assumed backwards and forwards deletion of the Heads under identity to derive the pre-nominal and the Head internal variants of Navajo RCs, but later (Hale & Platero 1974) pointed out that in Navajo movement rather than deletion must be involved, given the island sensitivity of its RCs. See also Grosu (2002, 2012). Kayne's (1994: 95 ff) analysis of IHRCs is similar in spirit, modulo the remnant movement of IP after raising of the internal Head, and pronunciation of the tail of the chain. Also see Bianchi (1999: §6.1).

In the 'matching' derivation of Lakhota type IHRCs ((74)), as well as in the 'matching' derivation of externally headed pre-nominal RCs seen earlier ((72)), neither Head c-commands the other from its in situ position.[90] Like VP deletion, which can take place either backwards or forwards in the same language, one should expect deletion here to apply freely either backwards or forwards, with the consequence that the language may give the impression of having two separate strategies of relative clause formation (external pre-nominal and internal). See Cole's (1987) observation that often Externally Headed pre-nominal RCs alternate with Internally Headed RCs within the same language. Perhaps in languages that have Head-Internal but no pre-nominal RCs (like the Siouan languages and Dogon – Boyle 2007: 327), or those that have pre-nominal but no Head-Internal RCs (like Chinese), the direction of dP-deletion is fixed (either forwards or backwards).[91] The situation (and Cole's generalization) is rendered more complex by the existence of those IHRCs which (also) involve 'raising' (to be considered in the next sections), and by the fact that in some languages one of the two strategies is more limited than the other in what it can relativize (for example, in Tibetan and Behlare, IHRCs can only relativize absolutive DPs, other DPs being

---

[90] This is reminiscent of Kayne's (1994: ch. 8) analysis, modulo 'matching' instead of 'raising'.

[91] While rare, dP deletion in RCs may fail to apply in certain languages (see §2.4 below on double-Headed RCs, which alternate with externally Headed pre-nominal or post-nominal RCs). The case of Wenzhounese (Sinitic, Wu) is particularly interesting in that it has double-Headed RCs as in (i)a, Head-external pre-nominal RCs as in (i)b, Head-internal RCs as in (i)c (with a final complementizer), as well as 'Headless' (Free) RCs as in (i)d (see Hu, Cecchetto & Guasti 2018: §2), which I would tentatively interpret as deriving from the double-Headed source ((i)a) with either (movement and) deletion of the internal Head ((i)b), or deletion of the external Head (with possible movement of the internal one) ((i)c) or deletion of both Heads (with possible movement of the internal one) ((i)d):

(i)   a.   ŋɑ^{52} bo^{21} fio^{31} mɜ^{42} ŋ^{33} kə$ʔ^0$ mɜ^{42} ŋ^{33}(double-Headed RC)
            grandma draw child REL child
            the child that the grandma draws

       b.   ŋɑ^{52} bo^{21} fio^{31} __ kə$ʔ^0$ mɜ^{42} ŋ^{33} (externally Headed pre-nominal RC)
            grandma draw REL child
            the child that the grandma draws

       c.   ŋɑ^{52} bo^{21} fio^{31} mɜ^{42} ŋ^{33} kə$ʔ^0$ __   (internally Headed RC)
            grandma draw child REL
            'the grandma that draws the child' or 'the child that the grandma draws'

       d.   ŋɑ^{52} bo^{21} fio^{31} __ kə$ʔ^0$ __   ('Headless' RC)
            grandma draw REL
            (the one) that the grandma draws

relativizable only through the pre-nominal strategy – Mazaudon 1978: §7 and Bickel 1995: §4). Also see the discussion in Grosu (2012: §1).

Within the double-Headed structure assumed here, the external Head can license the deletion of the internal one provided that the internal Head does not come to c-command the external Head by raising to Spec,CP (with the internal Head remaining in situ). By the same token the internal Head can license the 'deletion' of the external one provided that the 'deleted' external Head does not come to c-command it by raising to Spec,FP.

In those languages where, in spite of what was once believed (see Downing 1978: 399), Internally Headed RCs do alternate with Externally Headed *post-nominal* RCs[92] one must assume that the external Head can either raise to Spec,FP (giving rise to the Externally Headed post-nominal version) or stay in situ where it is 'deleted' by the internal Head.[93]

Mojave (Yuman) appears to have the same properties (see Basilico 1996: 505 ff, 522 after Munro 1974).

2.3.2 Deriving the Indefiniteness Restriction and the Impossibility of Non-restrictives in Lakhota Type IHRCs

The indefiniteness restriction on the internal Head found in Lakhota-type IHRCs, where nothing moves, is a direct consequence of the double-Headed structure assumed here. The necessary indefinite character of the internal Head follows from the fact that in order to delete the external Head the internal Head has to exactly match the external one, which is the portion of the extended nominal projection c-commanded by the RC. As this Head contains only weak determiners (paucal and multal quantifiers, cardinals, and a low indefinite

---

[92] As for example in the Gur languages Dàgáárè (Bodomo & Hiraiwa 2010), Dagbani (Wilson 1963, Lehmann 1984: 117), Mooré (Peterson 1974: 73–4) and Buli (Hiraiwa 2005, 2008); in the Amerindian languages Crow (Siouan – Lehmann 1984: 268), Slave (Athabaskan – Rice 1989: ch. 47), ThchoYatiì (Dogrib) (Athabaskan – Hucklebridge 2016; also see Saxon 2000), Western Shoshoni (Uto-Aztecan) (Crum & Dayley 1993: 190), Passamaquoddy (Algonquian) (Bruening 2001: §3.3 and §4.4.4), Haida (isolate) (Enrico 2003: ch. 10), Kiowa (Kiowa-Tanoan) (Adger, Harbour & Watkins 2009: §1.2.2), Upper Necaxa Totonac (Totonacan) (Beck 2016), Ika (Chibchan) (Rijkhoff 2002: 195); in the Austronesian languages Chamorro (see §2.3.4 below), Tukang Besi (Donohue 1999: ch. 15) and Seediq and Tagalog (Aldridge 2004, 2017); in the Papuan language Skou (Donohue 2004: §8.3); in the Yun variety of the Tai language Shan (Moroney 2018); in American Sign Language (Fontana 1990; Culy 1990: 225 ff; Wilbur 2017: §1.1), and possibly in Italian Sign Language (see Bertone 2006; Brunelli 2006, 2011; Cecchetto, Geraci & Zucchi 2006; Branchini & Donati 2009, Branchini 2014).

[93] For this case not to overgenerate, it must be that a deleted external Head cannot raise to Spec,FP and conversely that a non-deleted external Head *must* raise to Spec,FP.

article), strong ones being above the RC, the internal Head can also only contain weak determiners.[94]

The impossibility of non-restrictive IHRCs in Lakhota type languages (see fn. 87) follows from the indefinite restriction. If the internal Head must be indefinite (for the reason just mentioned) it cannot contain definite DPs, nor pronouns, nor proper names, which are definite.

2.3.3   The Exclusively 'Raising'/Maximalizing Type of Japanese and Some Quechuan Languages

As Japanese IHRCs have been the object of many in-depth investigations, to which I have nothing to add, I summarize here the main properties that have been isolated, specifically in the work of Grosu and his colleagues (see Grosu 2001, 2002, 2009a, 2012, Grosu & Landman 2012, Grosu, Hoshi & Sohn 2013, Grosu & Hoshi 2016, 2018, and references cited there). They appear to be virtually the opposite of those of Lakhota, except perhaps for the impossibility of non-restrictives, for which see Grosu & Hoshi (2016: §5), *pace* Kitagawa (2005, 2019) and others mentioned below. See (75) (to which Kuroda's 1976 Relevancy Condition could be added):

(75)   a.   *Absence of the indefiniteness restriction*
        b.   *impossibility of stacking*
        c.   *sensitivity to islands*
        d.   *impossibility of non-restrictives* (?)

The absence of the indefiniteness restriction, the apparent impossibility of stacking,[95] and the sensitivity to islands (but see Kitagawa's 2019: §5 for critical discussion) suggest that they have maximalizing import with movement taking place within the RC. See (76), where one can take the internal

---

[94] As observed in Graczyk (1991: 502) the indefiniteness restriction is 'a matter of purely formal syntax: head nouns of [Crow] relative clauses are marked with the indefinite determiner even if they are already given in the discourse and identifiable by the hearer'.

[95] *Pace* Hiraiwa et al. (2017), where an example of Japanese stacked IHRCs is reported to be possible (see (i)), and where the claim is made that 'stacking may not offer a reliable test for semantic classification' (p. 25).

(i)   Ken-wa [Naomi-ga [teeburu-no ue-ni ringo-ga at-ta no]-o kitte-kure-ta no]]-o tabe-ta
       Ken-Top Naomi-Nom table-Gen on-Dat apple-Nom be-Past C-Acc cut-Ben-Past C-Acc eat-Past
       'Ken ate the apple that was on the table that Naomi cut for him.'

Head to have to raise to Spec,CP deleting the external one, with some constituent moved across it:[96]

(76)

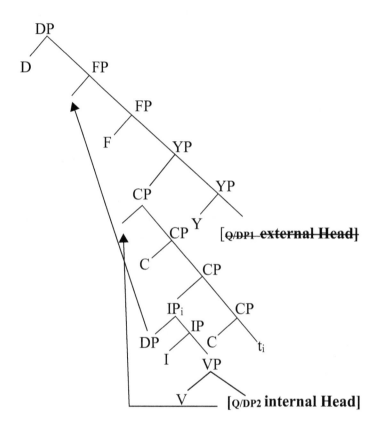

Possible alternatives would be the raising on an empty determiner/operator to Spec,CP, triggering abstraction in the semantics, or raising of the internal Head with pronunciation of the tail of the chain (see Bonneau 1992: 298, Watanabe 2004 and Grosu 2012: 21).

---

[96] If the strong determiners are RC-internal and are interpreted inside the RC (see Grosu 2002: §4, 2012: §3.2), this maximalizing relative construction could have, if the two Heads have to be non-distinct, the RC merged above the strong determiners (perhaps still under a higher D as with hydras: *all the boys and all the girls of the classroom who were in love with each other* – see §5.1).

Kitagawa (2005, 2019), Fuji (2010), and Shimoyama (1999) report examples like those in (77), where the Head of the IHRC appears to be proper name (also see Culy 1990: 255):

(77)   a.   Naomi-ga [Ken-ga naku no]-o nagusameta.   (Kitagawa 2005: 1245)
              Naomi-Nom Ken-Nom weep no-Acc comforted
              'Naomi comforted Ken, who was crying.'
        b.   [Ken-ga ie-kara deteki-ta] no-o tukamae-ta.   (Fuji 2010: 49)
              [Ken-Nom house-from come.out-Past] Nmn-Acc catch-Past
              'I caught Ken, who came out of the house.'
        c.   Taro-wa [[daidokoro-no mado-kara Lucky-ga haitte kita]-no]-o
              tukamaeta   (Shimoyama 1999: 173)
              Taro-Top [[kitchen-Gen window-from Lucky-Nom came_in -NM-Acc
              caught
              'Taro caught a white cat/Lucky/Isadora's cat as she came in from the
              kitchen window.'

This might be taken to indicate that non-restrictives are possible after all, but (77b–c) could well be pseudo-relatives of the Romance type (see *Hanno colto Mario che rubava negli spogliatoi* 'They.caught G. stealing in the dressing room' – Cinque 1995: §2.9).[97] Also see Shimoyama's (1999: 173) observation that an example like his (77c) could be 'analogous to the so-called *tokoro* circumstantial adverbial construction', and Grosu (2001: §5.2), where an ungrammatical example is given of a non-restrictive IHRC:

(78)   ?*[[Daidokoro-no mado-kara Lucky-ga haittekita]-no]-ga sakana-o totte
        nigeta
        kitchen-Gen window-from Lucky-Nom came-in-the-Nom fish-Acc stole
        ran-away
        Lucky came in from the kitchen window, it stole a fish and ran away

---

[97] Non-restrictive IHRCs also seem possible in Korean, the internally Headed construction of which displays the same characteristics of the Japanese one (see Grosu 2009a, Grosu & Landman 1998, Grosu, Hoshi & Sohn 2013, Hiraiwa 2017: n. 26). See (i), but once again they could correspond to the Romance pseudo-relative construction, given the character of the matrix verb (see *Ho incontrato Gianni che stava uscendo dalla stanza.* 'I met Gianni who (lit. that) was coming out of the room.'):

(i)   [Kim-ssi-ka pang-eyse naonun kes]-lul manasse   (Jung 1995: 241)
       K.-Mr.-Nom room-from coming.out kes-Acc met
       'I met Mr Kim, who was coming out of the room.'

Kim (2007: §4.1) argues that Korean IHRCs have a structure which is smaller (lacking a TP) than the corresponding Externally Headed RCs.

On the range of IHRCs in Japanese and their complexities see Grosu & Landman (2012) and Grosu & Hoshi (2016), Kitagawa (2019) and references cited there. Kitagawa's (2005, 2019) proposal that Japanese IHRCs have an external Head pro may be taken to support the double-Headed analysis pursued here.

The derivation of the Japanese externally-Headed option, which is sensitive to islands and has restrictive import (Grosu 2012: §3.2), could instead involve CP-internal movement of a determiner/operator, followed by backwards deletion of the stranded internal Head:[98]

(79)

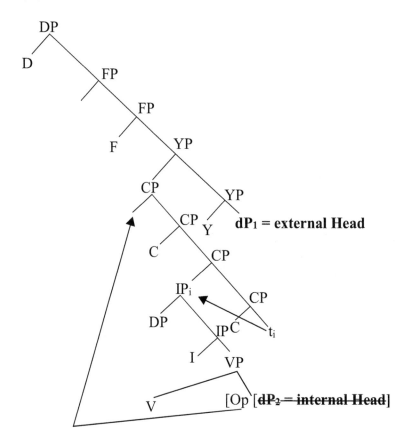

This deletion is apparently optional given the possibility of double-Headed RCs like (80a–c) reported in Kuno (1973: 237), Inada (2009: 94–5) and Erlewine & Gould (2016: 2), respectively:

(80)   a. [[watakusi ga **sono hito**   no namae o   wasurete-simatta] **okyaku-san**] …
            [I NOM   **that person**'s name   ACC   have forgotten] **guest**]
            a guest whose name I have forgotten …

        b. [[[Taro-ga   **aru gaku**-o   kaseideru]   **sono gaku**]-no   hanbun-o] …
            [[[Taro-NOM **a certain amount**-ACC   earns]   **that amount**]-GEN half-ACC]
            half of the amount (of money) that Taro earns …

        c. Junya-wa   [[Ayaka-ga   **ringo-o**   mui-ta]   **sono ringo-o**]   tabe-ta.
            J.-TOP   A.-NOM   apple-ACC peel-PAST that apple-ACC   eat-PAST
            'J. ate the apples that A. peeled.'

Concerning Quechua, Ancash Quechua (Srivastav 1991a: 103; Dayal 1996: 216) and Imbabura Quechua (Hastings 2004: §2.6 and ch. 3) also display maximalizing IHRCs. For example, unlike the corresponding externally Headed RCs, an Ancash Quechua IHRC like (81) 'entails that the total number of horses bought by the man is two [… so that …] the sentence could not be continued with '… *and two were bad*" (Dayal 1996: 216):

(81)   nuna ishkay bestya-ta   ranti-shqa-n alli   bestya-m   ka-rqo-n
        man   two   horse-ACC buy-PERF-3 good horse-VALID. be-PAST-3
        'The two horses that the man bought were good horses.'

Cole (1987: §5) also shows that, unlike Lakhota's IHRCs, those of Quechua display sensitivity to islands (and to ECP) (pp. 249–50) and Cole & Hermon (1994) mention that, again unlike Lakhota, Quechua IHRCs 'present […] no evidence that the internal head must be indefinite' (fn. 12).[99]

The next types of IHRCs appear to involve a different mix of the above properties. Within the limits of the available evidence, I will attempt to illustrate how the properties displayed by Chamorro, Hidatsa, Navajo, the Gur languages, and the Tai language Shan could be derived under the

---

[99] According to Hastings (2004), Cuzco Quechua appears to have both maximalizing and restrictive RCs, and Imbabura Quechua RCs involving 'raising' of the internal Head and RCs where the Head is external to the RC (§2.6 and ch. 3).

double-Headed analysis assumed here, and reconciled with Grosu's semantic typology of IHRCs.

2.3.4   *The Chamorro Type*
To judge from Vincent (2017), the IHRCs of the Malayo-Polynesian language Chamorro appear to display the following cluster of properties:

(82)   a.   *presence of the indefiniteness restriction.* Strong determiners (the definite and an indefinite article, universal quantifiers) are CP-external. In fact, CP-internally, not even weak determiners are possible, an apparent extreme version of the indefiniteness restriction. Vincent (2017: §4) makes the interesting observation that weak determiners in Chamorro focus and *wh*-interrogative constructions can split from their complement, stranding it. Capitalizing on this possibility he suggests that IHRCs involve the split of an empty weak determiner/operator, which is in complementary distribution with other weak determiners (thus accounting for the extreme version of the indefiniteness restriction) and which raises to Spec,CP, causing the construction's island sensitivity. This appears to be confirmed by the obligatory presence of a linker (*na*) preceding the internal Head (a linker which is otherwise found to obligatorily intervene between determiners and the nominal Head). See (83) below.

        b.   *stacking* (apparently impossible, although it seems that the impossibility may be due to independent factors – Vincent 2017: §3.1.1.4)

        c.   *sensitivity to islands* (present) (Vincent 2017: 23)

        d.   *impossibility of non-restrictives.*[100]

(83)   Sen-malångu   på′gu i   [k<um>ekeha   **na** **haga-n Dora**   nigap].
        SG.R.AGR.very-ill now the <SG.R.AGR>complain.PROG LK daughter-LK Dora yesterday
        'The daughter of Dora's who was complaining yesterday is now very sick.'

I thus take the derivation of Chamorro's IHRCs to be as shown in (84), with the silent operator raising to Spec,CP and with the internal Head deleting forward the external one:

---

[100] In Vincent (2017) there is no discussion of non-restrictive RCs, but a plausible conjecture, given the extreme version of the indefiniteness restriction holding of Chamorro IHRCs is that the internal Head cannot be an independently referential DP (like a proper name or a pronoun).

(84)

IHRCs occur alongside 'two more frequently used externally headed RC types: head-initial [(85a)] and head-final [(85b)] (Vincent 2017: 1):[101]

(85)　　a.　K<um>áti　　　i　　patgun　　[ni　　　ha　　　　lalátdi　si　　Maria].
　　　　　　<SG.R.AGR>cry the　child　　　　COMP　3SG.R.AGR scold　UNM　Maria
　　　　　　'The child that Maria scolded cried.'
　　　　b.　K<um>áti　　　i　　[ha　　　　lalátdi　si　　　　Maria] na　　pátgun.
　　　　　　<SG.R.AGR>cry the　3SG.R.AGR scold　UNM　　　　Maria LK　child
　　　　　　'The child that Maria scolded cried.'

---

[101] Head-initial (post-nominal) RCs are introduced by the complementizer *ni*, while the linker *na* separates Head-final (pre-nominal) ones from the Head. I tentatively take the former to involve movement of the external Head to Spec,FP in a structure like (84), deleting the internal Head, and the latter to involve backwards deletion of the internal Head by the external one.

According to Vincent (2017: 62) 'Chamorro provides evidence of a different sort that both the external and the internal position are available'. Both can host overt material simultaneously, resulting in a double-Headed relative clause. See (86):

(86)   Asta på′gu ti hu   fa′nana′an   i   **ga′-hu** [ni hu adopta na **katu** gi ma′pus na
                                                          simåna]
       up.to now   NEG 1SG.R.AGR   name.PROG   the **animal**-1SG.POSS COMP1SG.R.AGR adopt LK
                                                          cat LOC last LK week
       'I still haven't named my pet cat that I adopted last week.'

As with some of the double-Headed RCs discussed below in §2.4, Chamorro's external head is a generic functional noun 'classifying' the internal Head lexical noun. In (86), one of Vincent's (2017: 63) examples of double-Headed RCs, a selective deletion is plausibly involved whereby the two Heads are merged as identical copies (with the lexical NP a specifier of the functional N), and with deletion of the lexical N in the external Head and deletion of the functional N in the internal Head:

(87)   asta på′gu ti hu fa′nana′an i   [k̶a̶t̶u̶ [ga′-hu]][ni hu adopta na[katu [g̶a̶′̶h̶u̶]] gi ma′pus na
                                                          simåna]
                        [c̶a̶t̶ [animal]]   [cat [a̶n̶i̶m̶a̶l̶]]

Concerning Chamorro's IHRCs Vincent (2017) claims that they constitute an additional subtype of restrictive IHRCs, as the collection of properties exhibited by them matches none of the subtypes of Grosu's typology ('The possibility of determiners outside the IHRC and impossibility of determiners local to the IH rules out both the Maximalizing and the Mismatch-Restrictive analyses. But the island-sensitivity rules out the analysis proposed for Plain-Restrictive IHRCs', p. 23). However, see below for the possibility that Navajo, which in Grosu's typology represents the Mismatch/restrictive type, may after all have the indefiniteness restriction like Hidatsa below.[102]

---

[102] Moroney (2018) argues that IHRCs of the SVO Yŭn variety of the Tai language Shan, which also has externally Headed post-nominal ones (see (i)a–b below), are 'island sensitive and non-maximal, which complicates the typology of IHRCs'. (p. 198). In the present context (i)a possibly has the derivation sketched in (84) for Chamorro, while (i)b involves raising of the external Head to Spec,FP, followed by deletion of the internal Head:

(i)   a.   ʔăn   háw   hăn lik   nâj mán   lĕŋ (IHRC)   (Moroney 2018: 197)
           COMP1.SG   see   book   this3.SG.   red
           'The/A book that I see is red.'
      b.   **lik**   ʔăn   háw hăn   nâj mán   lĕŋ (post-nominal)   (Moroney 2018: 197)
           book   COMP   1SGsee   this3.SG   red
           'A book that I see is red.'

2.3.5   The Hidatsa Type

As shown in Boyle (2007, 2016) the IHRCs of the Siouan language Hidatsa display the following properties, minimally different from those characterizing the Lakhota IHRCs (the difference lying in their sensitivity to islands):[103]

(88)   a.   *presence of an indefiniteness restriction* (see Boyle 2007: §6.2.4.2; 2016: §4.1): the RC internal Head can only be preceded by weak determiners (indefinite articles, cardinal numerals, multal/paucal quantifiers) and adjectives. Strong determiners (like demonstratives, definite articles, universal quantifiers, etc.) are outside of the RC CP.[104]

    b.   *possibility of stacking*[105]

A comparable case may be provided by Upper Necaxa Totonac, a predicate initial language with Internally Headed and post-nominal RCs. See (ii), from Beck (2016: 2–3):

(ii)   a.   [tiː taliːtatsɛ́ʔa **ʔawačą́n** i̱stsi̱ːką́n]
            [tiː taliː–ta–tsé̱ʔ–a ʔawa̱čá̱–n i̱š–tsi̱ː–ka̱n]
            HREL 3PL.SUB–INST–DCS–hide–IMPF boy–PL 3POSS–mother–PL.PO
            those boys that hide behind their mother('s skirts)

        b.   **ʔawačą́n** [tiː taliːtatsɛ́ʔa i̱stsi̱ːką́n]
            ʔawa̱čá̱–n [tiː taliː–ta–tse̱ʔ–a i̱š–tsi̱ː–ka̱n Ø_SUB]
            boy–PL HREL 3PL.SUB–INST–DCS–hide–IMPF 3POSS–mother–PL.PO __
            those boys that hide behind their mother('s skirts)

[103] Arka (2016) reports the same properties (indefiniteness restriction, restrictive import, and stacking) for the Papuan language Marori. Should Marori display island sensitivity, it would be like Hidatsa; otherwise it would pattern with Lakhota. Bošković (2012: §1.9) claims that Head-internal relatives display island sensitivity in languages without articles, but not in languages with articles; yet, to judge from Hidatsa, Chamorro (Vincent 2017: §3.1.1.5 and §5.1.2), and the Gur languages analysed in Hiraiwa (2005, 2008, 2009) and Hiraiwa et al. (2017), all of which have determiners and whose Internally Headed RCs show island sensitivity, this does not always seem to be the case. On the inaccuracy of this correlation, which Hiraiwa et al. (2017) attribute to Bonneau (1992), see their n. 22.

[104] See (i):

(i)   wacéeš   wašúkawa   akutíheeš   (šipíšac)   (Boyle 2016: 260)
        [wacée-š   wašúka-wa   aku-tí-hee]-š   (šipíša-c)
        [man-DET_def dog-DET_ind REL.S-die-3.CAUS.D.SG]-DET.D (black-DECL)
        'The dog that the man killed is black.'

[105] Although Boyle (2007) does not explicitly discuss RC stacking, he gives on p. 337 one example that appears to be a case of stacking:

(i)   Alex waaʔáakaši aku-ákakaši-š Lyle aku-íka-š ihtía-c
        Alex book REL-S.-write-DET.D Lyle REL-S.-read-DET.D. big-DECL
        [the book_i [that Alex wrote e_i [that Lyle read e_i]]] is big

   c.   *sensitivity to islands* (Boyle 2007: §6.2.5),[106]
   d.   *impossibility of non-restrictives* (Boyle 2007: §6.2.4.2)[107]

The possibility of stacking in Hidatsa clearly shows that, even in the presence of movement within the RC (given its sensitivity to islands), the restrictive construction must be available (see Grosu 2002, 2012). I take this to involve the same derivation as Chamorro's IHRCs 'matching'; namely, raising of a silent determiner/operator of the internal Head to Spec,CP, followed by forwards deletion of the external Head by the internal one:

(89)

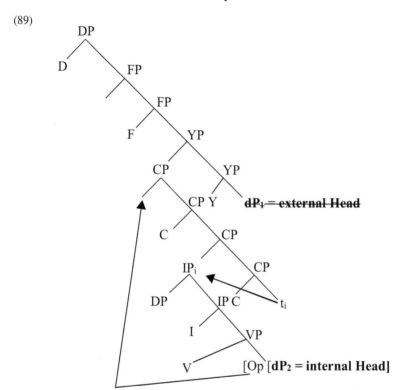

---

[106] Boyle (2007: 336) explicitly notes that examples with 'nouns inside of a RC may not be the Head of another RC', so that examples like (i), which are good in Lakhota, are impossible in Hidatsa (he also reports that Hidatsa IHRCs are sensitive to the Coordinate Structure Constraint and the ECP, in that the internal Head cannot be found in the subject position of a clause embedded within the IHRC):

  (i)   *wašúka   wacée-wa wirúkʰa aku-kúu-š   aku-náhci-š   wahúu-c
        dog   man-DET.Igun   REL-.S-get-DET.DREL-S-bite-DET.D bark-DECL
        'The dog who bit the man that picked up the gun is barking.'

[107] This follows from the indefiniteness restriction.

2.3.6   The Navajo Type

(90)   a.   *apparent absence of the indefiniteness restriction* (Grosu 2002: §3; Fuji 2010: §3.2.2)

　　　　b.   *possibility of stacking* (Barss et al. 1989: 323; 1992: 29; Grosu 2002: §3)

　　　　c.   *sensitivity to islands* (Platero 1974: §2.2; Grosu 2012: 25)

　　　　d.   *impossibility of non-restrictives* (Fuji 2010: §3.2.1)[108]

Fuji (2010: §3.2.2) argues that Navajo, despite the apparent CP-internal presence of strong determiners, which are in fact interpreted CP-externally (Grosu 2002: §3), displays in fact the indefiniteness restriction, like Lakhota.[109] For example, in sentences in which there are both a strong and a weak NP only the weak NP can be interpreted as the internal head. See for example his example (91):[110]

(91)   [t'áá'aɫtso at'ééd yí'dísooɫ-ę́'é] deezgo'
　　　　[everyone girl whistle-Nmn] fall
　　　　'*Everyone who was whistling at the girl fell.'
　　　　'The girl that everyone was whistling at fell.'

He also argues that given that both the indefiniteness restriction and the proper name condition (see fn. 108) hold in Navajo, replacing the weak NP with a proper name renders the sentence in (91) ungrammatical (see (92)):

(92)   *[t'áá'aɫtso Mary yí'dísooɫ-ę́'é] deezgo'
　　　　*[everyone Mary whistle-Nmn] fall
　　　　*everyone who was whistling at the Mary fell
　　　　*Mary who everyone was whistling at fell

---

[108] Fuji (2010: §3.2.1) claims that Navajo IHRCs cannot have a proper name as internal Head, just like Lakhota. See his example (i):

(i)   *[John aɫhosh-ígíí] aɫhą́'ą́'
　　　　*[John imp.3.sleep-Nmn] imp:3:snore
　　　　'*John, who is sleeping, is snoring.'

[109] Bogal-Allbritten, Moulton & Shimoyama (2016) and Bogal-Allbritten & Moulton (2017) claim that some quantifiers in Navajo are interpreted CP-internally, with maximalizing import, as in Japanese. But see Grosu (2002, 2012) and Fuji (2010) for the fundamental semantic difference between the Japanese and the Navajo IHRCs.

[110] This remains to be seen as Grosu (2001: §3), after Faltz (1995: 305), gives an example of IHRC in Navajo which appears to have a universally quantified internal Head. See (i):

(i)   Łééchąą'í   t'áá'aɫtsoashki   deishxashígíí   nidahaɫ'in
　　　　dog   all   boy   bite-REL   bark
　　　　'All the dogs who bit the boy are barking.'

If Navajo were to turn out to show the presence of an indefiniteness restriction, it would be like Hidatsa, and susceptible to the same analysis sketched in §2.3.5.

2.3.7   The Gur Type

The IHRCs of the Gur languages Buli, Dagbani, Gurenɛ, and Kabiyé appear to show the following properties, also displayed by Hidatsa, and possibly Navajo (and Chamorro):

(93)   a.   *presence of an indefiniteness restriction.*[111]
        b.   *possibility of stacking* (Hiraiwa 2003: §3.9)
        c.   *sensitivity to islands* (Hiraiwa 2005: §5.3.2 on Buli; Hiraiwa et al. 2017)
        d.   *impossibility of non-restrictives* (Hiraiwa 2003: 75 on Buli)[112]

In addition to in situ IHRCs, Buli, Dagbani, Gurenɛ, and Kabiyé have what Hiraiwa et al. (2017: §2.2) call 'left-headed IHRCs', which appear to involve raising of the internal Head within the relative CP, to the left of C (also see Munro 1974 and Basilico 1996 for the existence of short leftward movements of the internal Head in the Mesa Grande dialect of Diegueño and Mojave).[113] The internal Head of Mooré, is reported to license parasitic gaps (Tellier 1989: 302), suggesting that the raising is to an A-bar position, but see fn. 15 of Hiraiwa et al. (2017).

This suggests that the internal Head does move, though not as high as to cross over the strong determiners (which is precisely what the 'left-headed' variant of the same construction apparently does. See (94)):[114]

---

[111] See what Hiraiwa et al. (2017) have to say concerning the determiners that follow the internal Head, which they refer to as 'relativizers': 'The relativizers in Gur languages share a function of indefiniteness marking. Indeed, just as Williamson (1987) observes for Lakhota, they are morphologically identical with specific-indefinite determiners in Dagbani and Gurenɛ [...]. The relativizer in Buli is not a specific indefinite determiner per se, but still it yields Indefiniteness.' (p. 8). 'The relativizer in Kabiyé does not function as a specific-indefinite determiner by itself, either. But at least it has an indefinite meaning.' (p. 9). The same indefiniteness restriction is found in Mooré, another Gur language, where the internal Head is followed by 'the specific-indefinite determiner *ninga*', never by a definite determiner (Peterson 1974: 74). Strong determiners (like demonstratives and definite articles) are outside of the RC CP, to its right.

[112] Hiraiwa et al. (2017) do not mention the impossibility of non-restrictive IHRCs in Dagbani, Gurenɛ, and Kabiyé, but their impossibility is expected if the indefiniteness restriction holds of the internal Head of the IHRCs of these languages too.

[113] In Dàgáárè IHRCs this leftward movement appears to be obligatory (Bodomo & Hiraiwa 2004, 2010).

[114] From the discussion in Hucklebridge (2016) ThchoYatiì (Dogrib) may instantiate yet another type, as its IHRCs are island insensitive, allow stacking but show no indefiniteness restriction. Pending further information little can be concluded about this type.

(94)   [[ná:-m′ʊ   [àtì   núrú-wá   swà]]   lá]   (Hiraiwa 2005: 198)
        cow-the   COMP   man-the   own   Dem
        the cow that the man owns

2.4   Double-Headed Relative Clauses

The clearest support for a generalized double-Headed analysis of RCs comes, it seems, from the existence of overtly double-Headed RCs in a number of languages.[115]

Dryer (2005) reports the existence of one such case in the Papuan Trans-New Guinea OV language Kombai, which he refers to as *double-headed*. As he phrases it, 'relative clauses in Kombai combine the features of externally-headed and internally-headed relative clauses in a single structure: they have both an external head noun and a noun corresponding to the head noun inside the relative clause. While the two nouns are sometimes the same, as in (6a) [=(95a)], the external noun is usually more general than the one inside the relative clause, as in (6b) [=(95b)], where the external noun is simply *ro* 'thing'.' (p. 366). Dryer cites (95a) and (95b), from De Vries (1993: 78 and 77) [to (95b), I added the missing main predicate]. (95c–e) are additional examples given in De Vries (1993: 77 ff):[116]

(95)   a.   [[**doü**   adiyano-no]   **doü**]   deyalukhe.
              [[sago   give.3PL.NONFUT-CONN]   sago]   finished.ADJ
              'The sago that they gave is finished.'

        b.   [[**gana**   gu   fali-kha]   ro]   na-gana-y-a.
              [[**bush.knife**   2SG   carry-   thing]   my bush.knife-
                                                    go.2SG.NONFUT]   TR-PRED
              'The bush knife that you took away is my bush knife.'

        c.   [[yare   gamo   kherejabogi-n-o]   **rumu**]   na-momof-a.
              [[old.man   join.SS   work   DUR.do.3SG.   person]   my-uncle-
                                                    NF-TR-CONN]   PRED
              'The old man who is joining the work is my uncle.'

        d.   [[kho   khumolei-n-o]   mogo] ...
              [[man   die.3SG.NF-TR-CONN]   person]
              the man who died ...

        e.   [[ai   fali-khano]   ro]   nagu-n-ay-a.
              [[pig   carry-   thing]   our-TR-pig-PRED
                        go.3PL.NF]
              'The pig they took away is ours.'

---

[115] This section draws from Cinque (2011b), to which I refer for a comparison between bona fide double-Headed RCs, like those of Kombai, and apparent double-Headed RCs, which should rather be analysed as correlatives.

[116] Also see the case of Chamorro, which in addition to post-nominal and pre-nominal externally Headed RCs, and IHRCs, has post-nominal double-Headed ones, like (86) above, where the external Head is more general than the internal one.

In addition to the case of Kombai, where double-Headed RCs constitute the prevalent RC strategy, double-Headed RCs are also found in several other languages and language families, even if they do not constitute the prevalent RC strategy, but only an alternative strategy, available in selected contexts.

I will for convenience group the languages displaying overtly double-Headed RCs in the following three classes.

The first is represented by a number of OV languages, belonging to the Papuan, the Niger-Congo, the Tibeto-Burman, the Northwest Caucasian, and the Altaic families, whose basic RC type is of the *Internally Headed* one or the *pre-nominal* Externally Headed one, or both.

The second is represented by VO languages with *pre-nominal* Externally Headed RCs.

And the third is represented by VO and OV languages with Externally Headed *post-nominal* RCs (with or without *wh*-pronouns), belonging to the Papuan, the Austronesian, the Chadic, the Pama-Nyungan, and the Indo-European, families.

I will just mention a selection of cases from each class, referring to Cinque (2011b) for a fuller treatment of these types, and for cases of double-Headed RCs in child languages.

2.4.1   Double-Headed Relative Clauses in OV Languages with Internally Headed or Externally Headed Pre-nominal Relative Clauses

In addition to Kombai, another (non-Austronesian) Papuan OV language which appears to document doubled-Headed RCs is Yagaria:[117]

(96)   a.   [[hemeti dete'   **ge**   hu-d-u-ma']   **ge**] ...   (Renck 1975: 173)
             [[today morning **word** say-PAST-1.SG-PIV] **word**]
             the word I spoke this morning ...

        b.   ... [[hemeti   **yo'**   gi-ta   su ho-d-u-pa'] yo]-se' ...   (Renck 1975: 174)
             [[today   **house** build-1.PL   finish-PAST-1.PL-PIV] **house**]-BEN
             ... for the house which we finished building today ...

---

[117] In addition to double-Headed RCs (which constitute a significant number of Renck's 1975 examples of RCs), Yagaria appears also to have Internally Headed, Externally Headed pre-nominal, and 'Headless', RCs (see Renck 1975: §3.2.2.15). Another OV Papuan language with double-Headed RCs appears to be Isarawa (Oguri 1976: 91) '... no referent (even the referent which is coreferential with the noun head) has to be deleted'. An OV Oceanic language in contact with Papuan languages which appears to have double-Headed RCs is Motu. See (i) and other examples in Taylor (1970: ch. 3):

    (i)   [(pata) henunaio-helai-mu]   pata-na   na   tama-gu ese   e-kara-ia.   (Taylor 1970: 67)
          (table) under (SP) sit (ASP) table (REL)(OM) father-my(TSM) (SP) make (OS)
          'My father made the table that you are sitting under.'

A second OV language family with Internally Headed RCs as its basic type, which documents at least some double-Headed RCs, is the Dogon family (Niger-Congo). Double-Headed RCs are attested in Jamsay (Heath 2008: §14.1.1) and in Najamba Dogon (Bondu-So) (Heath 2017: §14.2.9).

For example, in Jamsay, whose basic RC is Internally Headed, 'it is also possible to expand this core relative clause structure [. . .] by adding a copy of the head N (not the full head NP), as a special kind of **external head**'. See (97), from Heath (2008: 481–2):[118]

(97)　a.　[[dà: ŋà-nɔˇ:　**ùrò**　mà　bèrè kùn-ó-Ø]　　　mà　**úró**]　kɔ̀:-rɔ́.
　　　　　[[water.jug　[**house**　Poss　in be.in-Neg-Ppl.Nonh]　Poss　**house**]　be.Nonh-Neg
　　　　　'There is no house that a water jug is not in.'
　　　b.　[[**ìjè**　　è　　íjé　bèrɛ:-Ø]　　　　mà　**ìjɛ**] . . .
　　　　　[[**position.L**　2PlS.L　stand can.Impf-Ppl.Nonh]　Poss　**position**]
　　　　　'(In) the position (or: situation) where you-Pl are . . .'

A third OV language family which documents at least some double-Headed RCs in at least some of its languages is the Tibeto-Burman family. They are reported to exist (alongside Externally Headed pre-nominal, Internally Headed, and 'Headless' RCs) in Ronghong Qiang (see, for example, (98)), in Sherpa (Givón 1975: 100), and in Tibetan (Keenan 1985: 152).[119]

(98)　　a.　[[**khuə**　mi-ta　　ʁdʑe　le-m]$_{RC}$　**khuə-le:**]$_{NP}$　hə-la.
　　　　　　　　　　　　　　　　　　　　　　　　　　　　　　(Huang 2008: 741)
　　　　　[[**dog**　person-DAT　bite　exist-NOM]　**dog-DEF:CL**　DIR-come
　　　　　　　　　　　　　　　　　　　　　　　　　　　　　　]
　　　　　'The dog who would bite people is coming out.'
　　　b.　[[**zəp**　iɐtɐimaqa　ʐawa　tshu-tshu]$_{RC}$(-tɐ)　　　**zəp**　tha-kua]$_{NP}$ . . .
　　　　　　　　　　　　　　　　　　　　　　　　　　　　　　(Huang 2008: 761)
　　　　　[[**place**　usually　rock　drop-REDUP(-GEN)]　**place**　that-CL]
　　　　　the place where rockslides often occur . . .

---

[118] In addition to IHRCs and double-Headed RCs, Jamsay also has pre-nominal and 'Headless' RCs (Heath 2008: 482, 490).

[119] In the Tibeto-Burman language Sema it is used as a last resort strategy, to relativize on ablative PPs which otherwise cannot be relativized with an Internally Headed RC. See (i):

　　(i)　　nɔ – nɔ　　a-zɨkiki　lɔnɔ　　　azɨ　sɨ̈e – ke- u　　zɨkiki- ye　miṭhe mɔ
　　　　　　　　　　　　　　　　　　　　　　　(Subbārāo & Kevichüsa 2005: 261)
　　　　　you [+TR] gm poss well from water bring noz def well(?) [-TR] clean neg
　　　　　'The well from which you brought the water is dirty.'
　　　　*'The water which you brought from the well is dirty.'

Japanese (Altaic), which has both externally Headed pre-nominal and Internally Headed RCs also seems to allow for certain types of double-Headed RCs. See the examples in (80) above.

2.4.2 Double-Headed Relative Clauses in VO Languages with Externally Headed Pre-nominal Relative Clauses

Double-Headed RCs have also been reported for certain Sinitic VO languages with predominant pre-nominal RCs. One such language is Wenzhounese (Wu). See (i)a of fn. 91 above from Hu, Cecchetto & Guasti (2018: §2), also reported in Arcodia (2017: 46), repeated here as (99):[120]

(99)   ŋa33-bo21   fio342   **na42-ŋ́44**   ke?0   **na42-ŋ́44** ...
        grandma   draw   **child**   rel   **child**
        the child who the grandma draws ...

2.4.3 Double-Headed Relative Clauses in VO and OV Languages with Externally Headed Post-nominal Relative Clauses

Four (non-Austronesian) Papuan languages with externally Headed postnominal RCs which appear to have some cases of double-Headed RCs are Abun (SVO – Berry & Berry 1999: 162), Bine (SOV – Fleischmann 1981: 5), and Moskona (SVO – Gravelle-Karn 2010: §10.1.7). See for example the case of Abun in (100) and Cinque (2011b) for examples from the other languages.

(100)   Abun (Berry & Berry 1999: 162)[121]
        An ndo-bot [**su-git** dik yo [to men ye bok ne git **su-git** ne]].
        3sg ask-about [**food** one det.I [Rel 1pl people several anaph eat **food** det]]
        'He asked about some (kind of) food which all of us would eat.'

Double-Headed RCs are apparently possible also in the Chadic language Mina (see (101)), and in the Pama-Nyungan language Yidiɲ (see (102)):

---

[120] Hu, Gavarró & Guasti (2016: 9) also report this possibility for (Wenzhounese) colloquial Mandarin:

(i)   māma   qīn xiǎopéngyou   de xiǎopéngyou ...
        grandma   kiss child   rel child
        the child that the grandmother kisses ...

[121] Berry & Berry (1999: 162) reports that the double-Headed strategy is not common, and is limited to non-restrictive RCs.

(101)   [**skɔ̀n** [nàm dzán **skɔ̀n** syì]] há diyà gáy kà. (Mina – Frajzyngier & Johnston 2005: 433)[122]
[**thing** [1DU find **thing** COM]] 2sg put spoil POS
the thing (= what) we found, you are ruining it

(102)   ŋaɳɖi binaŋaɭɲu [**duŋur**   [**duŋur**   wuna-ɲunda]] (Dixon 1977: 328)[123]
we.SA hear.PAST [**noise.ABS** [**noise.ABS** lie-COMP]]
'We heard a noise, which was lying [over the whole country].'

Double-Headed RCs appear to be possible, under certain conditions, also in a number of Indo-European VO and OV languages with Externally Headed *post-nominal* RCs that have *wh*-pronouns moved to the front of the relative clause.

In Cinque (1978: 88–9), Italian examples like (103) were noted where the external Head is matched by an identical phrase preceded by the relative modifier (art +) *qual-* within the RC:[124]

(103)   Non hanno ancora trovato una **sostanza** [dalla quale **sostanza** ricavare un rimedio contro l'epilessia].
they have not found a substance from which substance to obtain a remedy against epilepsy

Keenan (1985: 153) reports a comparable example from Latin (modulo the extraposition of the relative clause, stranding the external Head):[125]

(104)   **Loci** natura erat haec **quem locum** nostri delegerant
Of the ground nature was this which ground our (men) chose
'The nature of the ground which our men chose was this.'

---

[122] Frajzyngier & Johnston (2005) explicitly say that '[t]he relativized object may be coded twice, once at the beginning of the clause as the head of the relative clause, and the second time after the verb, in the position of object' (pp. 432–3). Mina has both pre- and post-nominal RCs.

[123] Dixon says that example (102) 'features two occurrences of the common noun' (p. 328), adding that there are also instances 'in which at least part of the common NP occurs twice' (p. 327), appearing once as 'a generic noun' and once as 'a specific noun' (in Dixon 2009: 335–6 the 'generic noun' is called 'classifier').

[124] As Diego Pescarini (pers. comm.) observed, this possibility may be restricted to Benincà's (2012a) *relative definitorie* ('kind-defining' RCs, for which see §3.2; a class of relatives which though usually lumped together with restrictive relatives displays a number of properties that set them apart from ordinary restrictive relatives, which in fact do not seem to allow for the pronunciation of the two Heads. See (i) (and the example in fn. 44 above):

(i)   *Questo è l'unico libro dal quale libro sono rimasti affascinati.
this is the only book by which book they were fascinated

[125] Cases like (i), also cited by Keenan, and similar cases in other European languages (see (ii) from English and other cases cited in Cinque 2008a and Cardoso & De Vries 2010, which involve a *wh*-phrase resuming the external Head *ad sensum*) appear to be non-integrated non-

The same appears to be true in emphatic contexts in (some) Indo-Aryan languages, where a left dislocated Externally Headed post-nominal RC entering the correlative construction can be double-Headed, with the internal Head moved to the front of the relative clause. See the examples in (105), and §2.6 for their sources.[126]

(105)   a.   [vo laRkii, [jo laRkii khaRii hai]],   vo laRkii lambii hai.   **(Hindi)**
            [that girl   [which girl standing be-PRES]], that girl tall be-PRES
            the girl who is standing, that girl is tall

       b.   [ba   moRii   [jo moRii ThaRii hɛ]],   ba moRii lambii hɛ. **(Bundeli)**
            [that   girl   [which girl standing is]],   that girl tall   is
            'The girl who is standing is tall.'

       c.   [(o) panc-sab [jaah[i] panc-sab-kE[n] ham niik jakaan[n] janait chalianh[i]]ₛ]ₙₚ o panc-sab
            ... **(Maithili)**
            (the) Panch which Panch-PL-OBJ I good way know.PART BE.PAST.AGR, the (same)
            Panch ...
            the Panch whom I knew very well, the same Panch ...

2.4.4   Summary

The existence of structures in which the external Head is 'doubled' by an internal Head thus seem to provide direct evidence that at least some RCs in some languages are double Headed, and that, by the Uniformity Principle, we should generalize this structure to all languages and to all RCs (whether they involve a 'matching' or a 'raising' derivation).

While the copy theory of movement (Chomsky 1993) might offer a technical means to capture this fact even in an exclusively 'raising' analysis (by the simultaneous spell out of the copies in the external Merge and in the final

---

restrictive RCs (see §3.1) (what Touratier 1980 and Bianchi 1999: ch. V: §4.4 call 'relatifs de liaison'):

     (i)   roman o ratu, koje delo prevodim   (Serbo-Croatian – Keenan 1985: 153)
             novel about war, which work I am translating
             a novel about war, which work I am translating, ...

     (ii)   This book, which masterpiece I have read twice, ...   (Kayne 1994: 165 fn. 73)

[126] Also see the examples of double-Headed (especially kind-defining) RCs given in Radford (2019: §2.6) from colloquial English:

     (i)   a.   That was **a game** [that we should have put **the game** out of reach].
            b.   I'm just worried that Liverpool are buying **players** [that **the players** don't relate to the crowd].

For examples of double-Headed RCs in child languages see Cinque (2011b: §3), where it is noted, after Utzeri (2007), that children do not employ options which are not found in some adult grammar, which may be different from the one to which they are exposed.

derived position), it seems that this possibility should not be allowed too freely as no comparable spelling out is found in other clear movement cases (e.g. *wh*-movement in interrogatives and Free relatives and focus movement – see below). This weakens the possibility, it seems, of adopting such a solution just for relatives. While I do not have relevant data for most of the languages discussed above concerning the possible existence of copies in their other movement constructions, some suggestive evidence from Italian can be offered that makes a copy spell-out approach dubious. So, for example, whereas it is possible in literary styles of Italian to repeat the Head inside some RCs (see (103) above), no comparable repetition in literary or other styles is permitted in *wh*-interrogatives, Free relatives, and focus constructions.[127] See the sharp ungrammaticality of (106a–c):

(106) a. ****Che sostanza** (dicono che) hanno ricavato **che sostanza**?
           which substance (they say that) they.have obtained which substance?
           'Which substance (do they say that) they have obtained?'
       b. ****Qualunque sostanza** (si dice che) possano ricavare **qualunque sostanza** sarà pericolosa.
           whatever substance (they say that) they.have obtained will be dangerous.
       c. ****Questa sostánza** (non quélla) (dicono che) hanno ricavato **questa sostanza.**
           this substance (not that one) (they say that) they.have obtained this substance.

A particularly noticeable feature of the double-Headed RCs of some of the languages reviewed above, and in Cinque (2011b), is the fact that the two Heads are often very general terms (functional nouns) referring to 'thing', 'person', 'place', 'time', etc., or the fact that the external Head represents a more general class of which the internal Head is a specific member or vice versa (e.g. 'cat', 'animal', 'novel', 'work', etc.). As already noted, a possible conclusion suggested by this phenomenology is that a DP is always associated with a functional N classifying it ($[_{FP}$ $[_{DP}$ guest] person], $[_{FP}$ $[_{DP}$ table] thing], etc., much as we see with proper nouns and common nouns ($[_{FP}$ $[_{DP}$ New

---

[127] Even though in some constructions in some languages there can be copies of the fronted phrases in intermediate positions. Labelle (1996: fn. 11) makes a similar point concerning child French.

York] city], [FP [DP Mississippi] river], etc.).[128] The variation we observed would then be due to the conditions on the pronunciation of the different pieces of the internal and external Heads. Usually functional nouns are the first pieces which fail to be pronounced: *New York* instead of *New York city*; *The Mississippi* instead of *The Mississippi river* (presumably with a silent CITY and RIVER, respectively).

In most languages functional nouns are unpronounced in both the external and the internal Head positions (as is generally the case also for the associated non-functional noun in the internal Head position, or in the external one in 'raising relatives', and head-internal relatives). But, as observed above, certain languages may retain the functional noun in the position of the external Head, while not pronouncing the associated non-functional noun.

The necessary presence of functional nouns like 'thing', 'person', 'place', 'time', generally unpronounced, generalizes to other functional nouns like 'amount/number/degree' and 'kind', which seem semantically implicated in certain RCs, as in, for example, the three-way ambiguity of (2) of this chapter.

2.5 'Headless' or Free Relative Clauses and Light-Headed Ones[*]

A particular challenge for the generalized double-Headed analysis of RCs proposed here comes from 'Headless' (or Free) RCs, especially under the analysis which takes the *wh*-pronoun to be in the Spec,CP of the RC, the so-called 'COMP analysis' convincingly argued for in Hirschbühler (1978), Groos & Van Riemsdijk (1981), Hirschbühler & Rivero (1983), Harbert (1983a), Borsley (1984), Suñer (1984), Grosu (1986/87, 1994, 2003a, 2003b), Knowles (1990), Kayne (1994), Pittner (1995), Grosu & Landman (1998), Benincà (2007, 2012b), Gračanin-Yüksek (2008), and Assmann (2013), among others.[129]

---

[128] This is the conclusion also reached by Inada (2009: fn. 15) ('... the amount expression *100man yen* 'a million yen' [...] contains the semi-lexical expression *gaku* ['amount'] ([*gaku* [*100man yen*]] as a so-called 'big DP'. In this case, only the amount expression *gaku* is relativized and it also yields the A[mount]R[elative] reading, with the copy of *gaku* unpronounced in the base position').

The order proper noun > common noun is typical of head-final languages, and the order common noun > proper noun of head-initial languages (though there are inconsistencies). See Cinque (2011a) and references cited there.

[*] This section has many points in common with the analysis presented in Cinque (2020).

[129] The alternative 'Head analysis' which takes the *wh*-phrase to be outside of the RC CP, in the external Head position (see Bresnan & Grimshaw 1978; Larson 1987, 1998; Haïk 1985: §4.4; Roberts 1997; Bury 2003; Citko 2002, 2009; Donati & Cecchetto 2011; Cecchetto & Donati 2015: §3.2), cannot account for the extraposition facts of German (and

In following this analysis, I take the CP containing the *wh*-pronoun to be embedded in a larger DP structure, where it is merged in a specifier that modifies the portion of the nominal extended projection which constitutes the external Head 'matching' the internal one, as in every other RC type. If so, the question arises as to the nature of the external Head in 'Headless' RCs.[130]

2.5.1   *Languages Lacking 'Headless' Relative Clauses*

A first step towards answering the question of the nature of the external Head of 'Headless' RCs is the observation that in many languages the 'construction' is not Headless at all. In structures corresponding to the 'Headless' RCs of

---

Dutch) 'Headless' RCs pointed out in Groos & Van Riemsdijk (1981), nor for the reconstruction of anaphors in Polish and Croatian 'Headless' RCs discussed in Borsley (1984) and Gračanin-Yüksek (2008), nor for the Case mismatches in certain languages (Pittner 1991, 1995, Grosu 1994). See below §2.5.6 and §2.5.11. It also cannot easily account for such cases as (i) in English, where *whoever* appears to act as the subject of the matrix even though it is embedded in the larger NP *whoever's woods* (see fn. 152 below for some discussion of such cases):

(i)   [Whoever's woods are these] is a good judge of real estate. (Andrews 2007: 214)

For additional arguments against the 'Head analysis' see Borsley (1984), Grosu (1994: Study I, ch. 4) and Jacobson (1995), among others. The obligatory presence of an overt antecedent in German when the extraposed 'Headless' RC is part of a PP (*Der Reporter hat sich auf *(das) gestürzt [was man ihm zeigte]* 'The reporter jumped on what one showed to him' – Haider 1988: 120) may suggest that a silent DP is not sufficient to avoid a violation of the ban on preposition stranding (see the grammaticality of *Der Reporter hat sich darauf gestürzt [was man ihm zeigte]*).

[130] In the case of '-ever' 'Headless' RCs, which occur either as arguments (as in *I'll do [whatever you do]*) or as clausal adjuncts (as in *I won't change my mind, [whatever you do]*) only in the former case does the question arise. As shown in Izvorski (2000), where they are dubbed 'Free adjunct Free RCs', the latter are just CPs with no external Head. Setting these CP adjuncts aside for the moment, the bare CP analysis for all 'Headless' (Free) RCs suggested in Åfarli (1994), Rooryck (1994), Vogel (2001) and others does not seem tenable. Their DP nature is clearly indicated by a number of properties, which make them differ from both Free adjunct Free RCs, and indirect questions, and point to a [DP [CP ...]] structure: for example, strong island sensitivity (Alexiadou & Varlokosta 1996: §6) and same distribution as DPs (Grosu 1994: 3–4), e.g., under Subject Auxiliary Inversion. See (i):

(i)   Is [that idea/what she suggests/*that she proposes to go alone] unreasonable? (Huddleston & Pullum 2002: 1069)

For further properties distinguishing standard 'Headless' RCs from Free adjunct Free RCs see §2.5.10 below and for differences between them and indirect questions Rizzi (1982: 75–6 and n. 32), Daskalaki (2005), Benincà (2010, 2012b) and Bertollo & Cavallo (2012: §4).

English or Italian, several languages display an overt Head taking the form of one of the functional/light nouns/classifiers 'thing', 'person', 'place', 'time', etc. This is the case of the Gbe languages (see (107a) from Gungbe (Enoch Aboh, pers. comm.), (107b) from Gengbe (Huttar, Aboh & Ameka 2013: 118), and, for Fongbe, see Lefebvre & Brousseau 2002: 164). This is also the case of many other language families with Externally Headed post-nominal RCs (see Cinque 2020: §2).

(107)   a.   Nú   ɖĕ   à   ná   mì   wɛ   nǎ   yí
             thing   REL   2SG   give   1SG   FOC   1SG.FUT   take
             'I will take whatever you give me.'

        b.   Ame-ke gbe dzi be ye la ple gbɔ, yi-na asi ya me
             person-rel ever desire that 3sg FUT buy goat go-CNT market that in
             'Whoever wants to buy goats comes to this market.'

'Headless' RCs with functional/light Heads are also attested with Externally Headed pre-nominal RCs (see, for example, (108a), from Afar – Cushitic), with IHRCs (see (108b), from Lakhota – Siouan), with double-Headed RCs (see (108c) from the Tibeto-Burman language Ronghong Qiang), and with correlative RCs (see (108d) from the Mande language Mwan):

(108)   a.   a'nu   ge'd-a-**kke**   'isin   t-amaa'too-n-u   'ma-dud-d-a-n
                                                                         (Afar – Bliese 1981: 29)[131]
             I   go-impf-**place**   you   you-come-pl-juss neg-able-you-impf-pl
             'Where I am going you are not able to come.'

        b.   [[Mary   [**taku**]   kağe]   ki] ophewathĕ
                                                                         (Lakhota – Williamson 1987: 188 n. 4)[132]
             Mary   **something**   make   the I.buy
             'I bought what Mary made.'

        c.   [[**mi**   qɑ   nə-xeᴵ-m]RC   **mi**]NP-le: kə-ji
                                                                         (Ronghong Qiang – Huang 2008: 762)
             [[**person** 1SG   DIR-scold-NOM]   **person**]-   go-CSM
                                                           DEF:CL
             'He who scolded me has gone.'

        d.   Mɛ̃ɛ̃   lá   klélé   klálàá   g`ɛ,   à   zā á blĩ̀ŋ!
                                                                         (Mwan – Perekhvalskaya 2007: 47)
             person Rel   trash   throw.Prf   ici,   3Sg.Acc own 3Sg.Acc.Anaph take.off
             'Whoever threw the trash here he himself should take it off!'

---

[131] Functional nouns include 'place', 'time', 'reason', 'something', 'amount', 'manner' (Bliese 1981: ch. 2).

[132] Lakhota may in fact also drop the indefinite pronoun. Compare (108b) with (i):

(i)   [[Mary   [*e*] kağe]   ki] ophewathĕ   (Lakhota – Williamson 1989: 189 n. 4)
       Mary   make   the I.buy
       'I bought what Mary made.'

For other such cases, see Culy (1990: 249–50).

I take such functional nouns to also be present, if unpronounced, in the 'Headless' RCs of English (and English-type languages), as shown in (109).[133] In English each *wh*-pronoun is associated with a specific silent functional noun: *what* with THING (or AMOUNT or KIND), *who* with PERSON/PEOPLE, *where* with PLACE (Kayne 2004a), etc.:[134]

(109)   a.   (We gave him) [DP THE [CP what THING$_i$ [C [we bought t$_i$]]] (THAT) THING][135]

   b.   (He weighs) [DP THE [CP what AMOUNT$_i$ [C [you weigh t$_i$]]] (THAT) AMOUNT]

   c.   (I hate) [DP THE [CP who(ever) PERSON$_i$ [C [t$_i$ does that to me]]] (THAT) PERSON][136]

   d.   (This is) [DP THE [CP where PLACE$_i$ [C [they slept P t$_i$]]] THERE PLACE][137]

---

[133] The argument is admittedly more suggestive than conclusive, as Andrew Radford (pers. comm.) points out, in that one could argue that languages lacking 'Headless' relatives will resort to Headed RCs (as semantically rather than syntactically equivalent). Although a single-Headed analysis with 'Raising' in a [DP D° [CP]] structure is also conceivable for the examples in (108), I will sketch here what a double-Headed analysis with 'raising' would look like for them.

[134] As mentioned at the end of the preceding section possibly all DPs are *always* merged as modifiers of one such (silent) functional/light/classifier noun, whether the DP contains a proper name or a common noun: [John [PERSON]], [dog [ANIMAL]], [table [THING]], etc. – see Kayne (2007: Appendix) (capitals signal non-pronunciation). This is rendered plausible by the existence of languages where some such functional/light nouns/classifiers can actually be pronounced (see, e.g., (i), from the Australian language Yidiɲ):

   (i)   bama:l   yabuɽuŋgu miɲa   gangu:l   wawa:l   (Dixon 1977: 480)
         person-erg   girl-erg   animal-abs wallaby-abs see.past
         Lit.: 'the person girl saw the animal wallaby' ('the girl saw the wallaby')

[135] The Oceanic language Motu seems to confirm the abstract representation in (109a) in that it may overtly spell out the external Head THING. See (i), from Taylor (1970: 59):

   (i)   [oi   dahaka o-kara] gau-na   na-ita-ia
         you   what   (SP)do thing (REL) (1SSP) see (OS)
         'I saw what you did.'

[136] Bare *who* RCs are generally quite marginal, if possible at all (though some such examples are reported in McCawley 1991: 50). Richard Kayne, pers. comm., tells me that for him the otherwise impossible *I'll invite who you want me to invite improves if *exactly* is added (?*I'll invite exactly who you want me to invite). The normal way is to use 'light Headed' RCs (see §2.5.14 below): *he/(any)one who . . .* For recent discussion see Patterson & Caponigro (2016).

[137] See the Western Malayo-Polynesian language Bih for the pronunciation of the 'generic/functional' noun PLACE:

   (i)   ti   anôk   ŏng dôk?   (Nguyen 2013: §6.2.1.5)
         where place you stay
         'Where are you?'

In Malay 'place' and 'time' are used in headed RCs as relative 'pronouns' with 'where' and 'when' plausibly deleted (see Yanti et al. 2012: 5; and the example *kantor **tempat** mereka dibayar*. Lit.: office **place** 3PL DI:pay 'the office where they were paid', from Hendery 2012: 59).

e. (He was born) [$_{DP}$ THE [$_{CP}$ when TIME$_i$ [C [I was born P t$_i$]]] THEN TIME]

f. (This is) [$_{DP}$THE [$_{CP}$ how MANNER$_i$ [C [we'd like to behave P t$_i$]] (THAT) MANNER]

The structures in (109) represent the double-Headed structure of 'Headless' RCs in English. Within the (pre-nominal) RC the internal Head moves to Spec, CP, licensing the deletion of the external Head in what amounts to a 'raising' derivation, the external Head remaining in situ.[138] The overt part (*what*, etc.) of the Head (*what* THING, etc.) is a *wh*-proform (also used in interrogatives and other constructions – see Caponigro (2003: ch. 3) for the specific semantic contribution compatible with all of its uses) which does not need a c-commanding antecedent in contrast with relative *wh*-proforms.[139]

For arguments that *where, when, how* are necessarily merged with a silent preposition stranded by *wh*-movement, see Caponigro & Pearl (2008, 2009). They assume that preposition stranding may be possible with silent prepositions even in languages like Italian that do not allow it with overt (non-axial) prepositions. This appears confirmed by sluicing cases such as *Stava parlando con qualcuno. Non so chi/con chi.* 'He was talking with someone. I don't know who/with whom.' Also see Abels (2003: 238) and Almeida & Yoshida (2007).

[138] For the maximalizing nature of 'Headless' RCs, see Carlson (1977), Grosu (1994: §3.2), Grosu & Landman (1998), Caponigro (2003). The non-existence of non-restrictive uses of 'Headless' RCs (Emonds 1979: 232, Kayne 1994: 114) is taken here to be related to their maximalizing, hence 'raising', nature and to the exclusively 'matching' nature of non-restrictive RCs (see §3.1).

[139] A possible argument for the presence of a light noun Head in 'Headless' RCs comes from a cross-linguistic generalization mentioned in Šimík (2017a: §1.1). Whenever Light Headed RCs (see §2.5.14 below) have relative *wh*-pronouns distinct from interrogative *wh*-pronouns (as in Modern Greek and Bulgarian), 'Headless' RCs employ the same *wh*-pronouns used in Light Headed ones. 'Crucially, there seems to be no language with a difference between interrogative and [Light Headed Relative] *wh*-words that would choose to use interrogative *wh*-words in ['Headless' RCs]' (Šimík 2017a: fn. 1). Hanink (2018) also argues that 'Headless' RCs 'are not Headless at all; instead they have a super light (i.e. unpronounced) head [...]. The proposal therefore draws an analogy between 'Headless' and light-Headed relatives (Citko 2004) in German, proposing that the former are derived from the latter.' (p. 248). Also see Kornfilt (2005b) for an analysis of Turkish Free relatives as light-Headed RCs, and Catasso (2013) for the claim that the external Head of 'Headless' RCs is a light demonstrative, which can be spelled out in languages like German ([*das* [*was Maria kocht*] ... Lit.: 'that what M. cooks ...', and §2.5.14 for a discussion of light-Headed RCs. Another possible argument may be based on Benincà's (2012b) observation that the *wh*-pronouns of 'Headless' RCs in Italian, although morphologically identical to interrogative *wh*-pronouns, target in the Split CP not the position targeted by interrogative *wh*-pronouns, but that targeted by relative *wh*-pronouns in Headed RCs.

In certain languages, the silent determiner of (109) is pronounced, as in Yucatec Maya (see (110a), from Gutiérrez-Bravo 2013: 29) or in the Iroquoian language Tuscarora (110b), from Mithun (2012: 279):[140]

(110)　a.　[le　　[ba'ax　　　k-in　　　　tsikbal-t-ik-Ø te'ex]-a'
　　　　　　　det　　what　　　　HAB-ERG-1SG　chat-TRNS-IND-ABS.3SG 2PL-CL
　　　　　　　this (thing) which I'm telling you about
　　　　b.　Nyękwa'tikęhriyúhθe　　**ha'**　　　**tawę:te**　　kakurihwíhs'ę.
　　　　　　　it is pleasing to us　　　**the**　　　**what**　　they have promised
　　　　　　　'We are pleased with what they promised.'

2.5.2　*Pronunciation/Non-pronunciation of the External and Internal Heads*

While in English (and English-like languages) the external but not the internal Head can be silent (see Kayne 1984: 65; except perhaps in hidden temporal relative clauses like *Liz left before* THE TIME [WHEN TIME$_i$ *you said* $<t_i>$ *she had* LEFT $<t_i>$ – Geis (1970), Larson (1987), Haegeman (2012: §5.2.2.3), in other languages the external and the internal Heads can both be silent while the determiner is pronounced as in the Lakhota example (i) of fn. 132 above. In others it is the external functional noun Head that is pronounced while the internal Head is not. See the example (111) from the Dogon language Jamsay:

---

[140] Also see Chomsky (2013: 46) on the presence in Spanish and French 'Headless' RCs of a determiner, possibly reduced in English. As a matter of fact the determiner happens to be pronounced in certain varieties of English. See (i), from Nakamura (2009):

(i)　a.　That is **the what** you do against the Rams these days. (*The Los Angeles Times*, Nov 14, 1994)
　　　b.　[we talked] on consumption, and **the why** [= the reason why] it was so connected with what is beautiful and interesting in nature. (Jespersen 1949: 529)
　　　c.　A pocket money allowance of pounds 14.10 is set for all **the who** receive state help towards their nursing home fees. (*The Observer*, Apr 27, 1997)
　　　d.　Some observers feel that Mr Ayling devoted far too much of his time to this protracted wrangle and failed to notice **the where** things were going wrong at the airline's core. (*The Guardian*, Mar 11, 2000)
　　　e.　In this country, cheating has mainly involved tampering with the time clocks that register **the when** the birds are released and **the when** they return. (*The Guardian*, Mar 29, 1997)
　　　f.　'LIKE walking into a Christmas card' is **the how** tour operator Sherpa describes winter walking holidays in the picturesque resort of Meiringen, Switzerland. (*The Times*, Oct 6, 2001)

(111)   c`ɛ: ù   kúnó-sà-Ø   cêw   (Heath 2008: §14.1.11)
        thing.L   you   put-Reslt-Ppl.Nonh   all
        whatever you have put (in it)

In still other languages the determiner and the two Heads can all be silent. See (112a–c) from Sinhala (Indo-Aryan), Nivkh (isolate) and Turkish (Turkic), respectively:

(112)   a. [redi hodənə]   Nuwanwə   taraha   æwisuwə   (Walker 2005: 170)
           clothes wash-PRES-REL Nuwan-ACC anger induce-PST
           'The one washing the clothes made Nuwan angry.'
        b. [Ṭ'o+řa-d-ɣu]   p'u-d-ɣu   (Nedjalkov & Otaina 2013: 285)
           fish+fry-NML-PL   go.out-IND-PL
           'Those who have fried the fish went out.'
        c. Mary   [John-un   pişir-diǧ-in]-i   yedi   (Demirok 2017a: §3)
           Mary   John-gen. cook-nomin-3sgPoss]-acc.   ate
           'Mary ate what John cooked.'

Also see De Vries (2002: ch. 2, §6.3). Thus the pronunciation or non-pronunciation of the external and/or the internal Head seems parameterized across languages, or depends on other aspects of their grammars; something that remains to be investigated.

2.5.3   A Note on the Italian Equivalent of 'What' in 'Headless' Relative Clauses

Standard Italian displays a gap in the *wh*-paradigm used in 'Headless' RCs. While it employs interrogative *chi* 'who', *dove* 'where', *quando* 'when', *come* 'how', *quanto/quanti* 'how much/many', it cannot employ (*che*) *cosa* lit. '(what) thing' (see *(**Che**) **cosa** mi ha detto non è vero*. 'What he told me is not true.') (see Cinque 1988: 497; Benincà & Cinque 2010: §4.5; Bertollo & Cavallo 2012: §3; Cecchetto & Donati 2015: 48–9).[141]

   What is used in its place is the complex form *quello che* (or *ciò che*, in more formal registers) '(demonstrative) that + (invariant relativizer) that' (*Quello che mi ha detto non è vero*). A possible question that arises is whether *quello* is the external Head, outside of the RC CP, or the internal one raised to the Spec of (the highest) CP, much like the *wh*-forms used in 'Headless' RCs, for which there is evidence that they remain inside the RC CP. In fact some evidence exists that *quello* is not an external Head, but is raised to the Spec of (the highest) CP just like the other *wh*-forms (modulo its obligatory co-occurrence with the invariant relativizer *che*):

---

[141] In some regional varieties of Italian *cosa*, or *che*, can apparently also be used in 'Headless' RCs (see Caponigro 2003: 26 and Manzini 2010: 171).

(113)   [$_{DP}$ [$_{CP}$ quello THING$_i$ [che [mi ha detto t$_i$]]] THING] non è vero

A first piece of evidence is that *quello che* can replace interrogative (*che*) *cosa* 'what' in embedded interrogatives, suggesting that, just like (*che*) *cosa*, *quello che* is in the Spec of the CP selected by the interrogative predicate. See (114), from Munaro (2000: 99; 2001: §3), and see Touratier (1980: 135) for comparable interrogative uses of *ce que/qui* in French:

(114)   a.   Non so [$_{CP}$ quello   [*(che)[ha comprato]]]
              not know.I that   that   has.he bought
              'I don't know what he has bought.'
         b.   Ho chiesto loro [$_{CP}$ quello [*(che) [hanno visto]]]
              have.I asked them   that   that have.they seen
              'I have asked them what they have seen.'

The CP status of interrogative clauses introduced by *quello/ciò che* is confirmed by the possibility of extracting out of them just as it is possible to extract out of a *wh*-island. See example (39) of Chapter 5. A second piece of evidence has to do with the impossibility of extraposing the constituent introduced by *che*. Unlike Headed RCs that allow the extraposition of that constituent (see (115a)), and like the impossibility of 'stranding' the *wh*-phrase of a 'Headless' RC extraposing the rest (see §2.5.6 below for discussion, based on an original observation by Groos and Van Riemsdijk), *quello* cannot be 'stranded' while the constituent introduced by *che* is extraposed (see (115b):

(115)   a.   E' successa una cosa ieri in dipartimento [che mi ha lasciato senza parole]
              is happened a thing yesterday in the department that left me without words
              'Something happened yesterday in the department that left me without words.'
         b.   *E' successo quello/ciò ieri in dipartimento [che tutti temevamo][142]
              is happened that yesterday in the department that we all feared

---

[142] See in particular the minimal pair constituted by (115b), where *quello/ciò che* is interpreted as 'what' and (i) where *quello* is interpreted as a deictic determiner with a silent noun (e.g. *libro* 'book'):

(i)   Gli ho dato quello ieri in dipartimento [che mi avevi consigliato tu]
       to.him I.have given that yesterday in the department that me you.had recommended
       'I gave him that one yesterday in the department that you had recommended to me'

Also see the contrast in French between **J'ai dit ce hier à Jean qu'il voulait entendre. Lit.: 'I said that yesterday to Jean that he wanted to hear' and ??J'ai donné le tableau hier à Jean qu'il voulait acheter l'année dernière. Lit.: 'I gave the painting yesterday to Jean that he wanted to buy last year.' (Michal Starke's judgements, pers. comm.). Also see the contrast between *ce*

2.5.4 Definite and Universal/Free Choice 'Headless' Relative Clauses

I take the structures in (109) to underlie both *definite* 'Headless' RCs (*Il mese prossimo sposerò proprio chi(*-unque) mi hai presentato l'anno scorso* 'Next month I will marry precisely who(*-ever) you introduced to me last year', '... the very person who ...'; *Sarà ammesso alla festa solo chi(*-unque) porterà una bottiglia di vino* 'Only he who brings a bottle of wine will be admitted to the party'; *Yesterday I left when(*ever) Daniel arrived* '... at the very time that ...')[143] and *universal/free choice* 'Headless' RCs (*I see him when(ever) I can* '... every time I can') (Dayal 1997, von Fintel 2000, Caponigro 2003, Van Riemsdijk 2006: §5.2).

For a discussion of the interpretational possibilities of bare and '-ever' 'Headless' RCs, see Larson (1987), Grosu (1994, 1996), Jacobson (1995), Dayal (1997), Izvorski (2000), von Fintel (2000), Caponigro (2003), Tredinnick (2005) Šimík (2018), and references cited there.

2.5.5 Modal Existential Headless wh-Relatives

As to Modal Existential Headless *wh* relatives (Grosu 1994, 2004), like (116), also called 'non-indicative *wh*-clauses of existential predicates' or 'Irrealis Free Relatives' (Izvorski 1998, 2000, Pancheva Izvorski 2000: ch. 2; Grosu & Landman 1998: §3), or 'existential free relatives' (Caponigro 2003), or

---

and ordinary Heads concerning the intervention of parenthetical material between them and *que* in Quebec French, noted in Kemp (1981: 253):

(i)   a.   J'ai pas trouvé les coupes, tu sais, que tu voulais.
            I haven't found the cuts, you know, that you wanted.
        b.   *J'ai pas trouvé ce, tu sais, que tu voulais.
            I haven't found what, you know, that you wanted.

[143] That the definite reading is made impossible by the presence of '-ever' is pointed out in Dayal (1997), who gives contrasts like the following (also see Jacobson 1995, Caponigro 2003: 112 and Tredinnick 2005: 2):

(i)   What(*ever) Mary bought was Barriers. (Dayal 1997: 103)

(ii)   What(*ever) Mary is cooking, namely ratatouille, uses onions. (Dayal 1997: 109)

For the possibility that the apparent universal/free choice reading of *wh*- and *wh*-'ever' reduces to a maximal (plural) definite reading, see Jacobson (1995: §5). A 'definite' *what* as the associate of a *there* existential construction in English is generally impossible: *There is what you ordered on the desk* (Wilder 1999: 686). When possible (*There is what you need: wine in the cellar and food in the fridge*) it may be compatible with Kayne's (2016a) analysis if the definite determiner is actually embedded within the associate, as in some of the cases that he discusses (*There is* [THE what KIND] THING(S) *you need*).

'kind-defining headless relatives' (Benincà & Cinque 2014: §2.2), or 'indefinite free relatives' (Kotek & Erlewine 2016: §3.2), they differ from standard 'Headless' RCs in several respects.

(116)   a.   Maria are [cu cine să voteze].   (Grosu 1994: 138; also see Grosu 2004)
                Maria has with whom SUBJ vote
                'Maria has (someone) for whom to vote.'
         b.   Ima   koj   kâde da   me zavede.   (Izvorski 2000: 41)
                have.3sg who   where Part$_{subj}$ me take.3sg
                'I have someone to take me somewhere.'
         c.   Non ha con chi parlare.   (Caponigro 2003: ch. 3)
                not he.has with whom talk.INF
                'He doesn't have anyone to talk to.'
         d.   Non c' è a chi chiedere informazioni.   (Benincà & Cinque 2014: §2.2)
                not there= is to who ask.INF informations
                'There's nobody who you can ask for
                information.'

They are typically introduced by verbs with existential import ('be', 'have', 'look for', 'find', etc.), they are not maximalizing, they do not require category and Case matching, they disallow *wh*-'ever' phrases, they allow multiple *wh*-fronting in languages which allow it in questions,[144] and they are not strong islands. See Izvorski (1998, 2000: ch. 2) and Grosu (1994: Study I, ch. 5; and 2004), where they are in fact analysed as bare CPs (even if there is perhaps a silent object, THING, PERSON, etc., of 'have', 'there is') with which the CP does not form a complex DP, recalling the RCs discussed in §5.5 below, which are also insensitive to islands. Also see Šimík (2008c, 2011), and Šimík (2017b) for a comprehensive bibliography.[145]

---

[144] For apparent multiple *wh*-pronouns in Bulgarian 'Headless' RCs, which have no special '-ever' *wh*-forms, see §2.5.12 below and references cited there.

[145] The conclusion that they are distinct from standard 'Headless' RCs may find some support from Italian, where, as noted above in §2.5.3, *(che) cosa* 'what' has no 'Headless'-RC usages. For in these irrealis/existential/indefinite genuinely Headless RCs, *(che) cosa* sounds possible (just as in *wh*-interrogatives):

   (i)   a.   Adesso avrei/ho trovato finalmente cosa fare
                Lit.: now I would.have at last/I found what to do
          b.   Per noi, adesso, ci sarebbe cosa dire
                Lit.: for us now there would.be what to say

Another indication that they may be just CPs can be based on the fact that embedded interrogative CPs but no standard 'Headless' RCs (which are DPs) permit Gapping (see Rizzi 1982: 75 fn. 32). Interestingly, these irrealis/existential/indefinite truly Headless RCs allow Gapping, just like embedded interrogative CPs. Compare (i)a–b with a bona fide 'Headless' RC ((i)c) and an ordinary embedded interrogative CP ((i)d):

Šimík (2008c), after Čeplová (2007), claims that the *wh*-phrase in Czech is not in the highest CP projection but is in the periphery of the VP (much like the VP topic and focus projections proposed by Jayaseelan 2001 and Belletti 2004), entering a monoclausal configuration as shown by the possibility for clitics to climb above the *wh*-phrase:

(117)   a.   Včera jsem **ho$_i$** nevěděl [kde potkat t$_i$]   Šimík (2008c: 124)
                  yesterday AUX.1sg **him** not.had where meet$_{INF}$
                  'Yesterday there was no place where I could meet him.'
      b.   Nemám **ti$_i$** [co dát t$_i$]   (Rezac 2005: 134 n. 9)
                  NEG.have.1sg **you$_{DAT}$** what$_{ACC}$ give$_{INF}$
                  'I don't have anything to give you.'

The same is apparently true of Bosnian/Croatian/Serbian. See (118), from Pancheva Izvorski (2000: 40):

(118)   Nemam   **ga$_i$**   [kome   t$_i$ dati]
       not-have-1sg   it.Acc   whom.Datgive.inf
       'I have no one to give it to.'

In other languages (e.g., Italian) the *wh*-phrase appears instead to sit in the highest CP in what may be a biclausal configuration, as clitic climbing is barred (see (119a–b), unlike in monoclausal restructuring embedded interrogatives (see (119c)):

(119)   a.   *?Non li ho a chi dare.
             not them I.have to whom to give
             (cf. *Non ho a chi darli.* I don't have to whom to give them)
      b.   *Non ce n'è con chi condividere.
             not there of.it is with whom to talk
             (cf. *Non c'è con chi condividerne.* there isn't with whom to share them)
      c.   Non li saprei a chi dare.
             Not them I.would.know to whom to give
             'I don't know who I could give them to.'

(i)   a.   Avrebbero chi invitare oggi e chi __ domani
             Lit.: they would.have who to invite today and who tomorrow
      b.   C'è chi preferisce la pasta e chi __ il riso.
             Lit.: there is who prefers pasta and who rice
      c.   *Ho punito chi ha telefonato a Maria e chi __ a Giuliana
                                       (Rizzi 1982: 75 fn. 32)
             I punished who called Maria and who __ Giuliana
      d.   Non ho ancora capito chi ha telefonato a Maria e chi __ a Giuliana
                                            (Rizzi 1982: 75 fn. 32)
             I haven't understood who called Maria and who __ Giuliana

As for the 'identifier' of the particular functional noun postulated in (116), I follow Grosu (1986/87: 47) in taking the *wh*-phrase of the 'Headless' RC to be 'the only reasonable candidate for the role of formal identifier [of the external Head]'.[146]

2.5.6   The Nature and Position of the wh- in 'Headless' Relative Clauses

The present analysis, which takes the *wh*- to be a phrase in the Spec of the RC CP, is not compatible with Donati's (2006), Donati & Cecchetto's (2011), Cecchetto & Donati's (2010: §4.2; 2015: ch. 3) proposal (see fn. 3 of their 2011 article for precedents of this idea) that 'Headless' RCs only involve a bare (X-bar) head which raises and projects, as a determiner, to DP:[147]

(120)

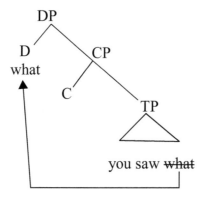

For one thing, as already mentioned, some languages provide direct evidence that the *wh*-phrase in 'Headless' RCs is within the RC CP, not outside. In particular, a structure like (120) would lead one to expect that the corresponding German *wh*-free relative pronouns could not extrapose together with the

---

[146] Also see Van Riemsdijk (2006: 363) and Assmann (2013).

[147] In their system if C rather than the raised *wh*- projects the result is a standard interrogative CP rather than a 'Headless' RC. This leaves to be seen how best to capture Beninca's (2007, 2012b) finding mentioned in fn. 139 that despite the morphological similarity of the *wh*-forms in the two constructions, the target of the *wh*- in (Italian) 'Headless' RCs is higher (above Topics) than that of the *wh*- in interrogatives (below Topics).

rest of the 'Headless' RC, contrary to fact, as will be seen below.[148] Secondly there are two constructions which appear to front to Spec,CP complex *wh*-phrases; the 'paucal' relatives in sentences like (121), and the *wh*-'ever' relatives in sentences like (122) (also see Caponigro 2019 for similar observations and arguments):[149]

(121) a. **What beer** we found was flat. (Andrews 1975: 75)
       b. Fred hid **what (few) weapons** were on the table. (Andrews 1975: 76)
       c. We gave him **what little money** we had. (Kayne 1994: 154 n. 13)
       b. [I]t begins to fit with **what little** we know about evolutionary history. (Chomsky 2015: 74)[150]

(122) a. I'll read **whatever book(s)** he tells me to read. (Jacobson 1995: 451)
       b. I shall visit **whatever town** you will visit. (Donati & Cecchetto 2011: 552)

Donati and Cecchetto (2011) may be right in suggesting that in some languages some '*wh*-ever' phrases can also be Heads of Headed RCs. See the Italian – *unque* case in (123a), from Battye (1989: 230), where such sentences are dubbed

---

[148] Cable (2005) acknowledges that this is a serious challenge for the Move-and-Project analysis though he also advances some speculations on how it could be resolved. A worse challenge for the Move-and-Project analysis comes from missing-P 'Headless' RCs for which there is evidence, from German locality condition on P + *w*- contraction and colloquial German overt copies of P + *w*- in intermediate Spec,CPs, that the constituent structure in such cases as (i) is the one indicated there: (see in particular Grosu 1996: §5 and 2003b: Appendix, modulo THING instead of *pro*) and Hanink (2018: §5):
    (i) I believe [IN (THAT) THING [CP in what THING] you believe]]

[149] The discussion in Andrews (1975: §1.1.2.2) provides evidence that what he calls 'paucal' (Free) relatives cannot be taken to be *wh*-'ever' relatives with a silent '-ever'. Apart from their special meaning of insufficiency, 'paucal' (Free) relatives, as opposed to *wh*-'ever' phrases, can only be used with mass or plural nouns (**Fred hid what weapon was on the table* vs *Fred hid whatever weapon was on the table*). Also, they are compatible with paucal modifiers like *few* and *little*, but not with multal or numeral quantifiers (**I saw what many/three people arrived early*), while exactly the opposite holds for *wh*-'ever' phrases (**I greeted whatever few people came to the door* vs *I hid the coats of whatever three people he brought*). Should they co-occur with a different ('paucal') silent element (possibly LITTLE/FEW), this would likely be within CP, like '-ever', given the extraposition facts to be mentioned below concerning the German *w*- *auch immer* phrases (the analogues of English *wh-ever* phrases), which necessarily extrapose with the rest of the 'Headless' RC. Also see examples like *You can take which (one) you like!* (Smits 1989: 297), *I shall take what measures I think proper* (Kuroda 1968: 249 fn. 8), which however may involve a silent *–ever*.

[150] Which we take to be: … *with* [THE [*what little* AMOUNT THAT *we know* …] (THAT) AMOUNT]. In the next page, the following variant is used: … *with the little that we know* (i.e., *with* [*the* [WHAT *little* AMOUNT *that we know*] (THAT) AMOUNT]. For the degraded status of overt *that* if *what* is also overt see fn. 154 below.

'pseudo-free relatives', and the English *-ever* case in (123b), from Bresnan & Grimshaw (1978: 346), and (123c), from Chierchia & Caponigro (2013: 7):[151]

(123)   a.   **Chiunque a cui** tu avessi parlato ti avrebbe dato la stessa risposta.
              'Whoever to whom you had spoken would have given you the same reply.'
        b.   **Whatever food that** there may be in the pantry is probably infested with moths.
        c.   John would read **whichever book that** he happened to put his hands on.

There are however indications that the same does not hold for other languages and possibly for other *wh-* forms in English (for at least some speakers). Citko (2008c: 930 ff) points out three phenomena with respect to which RCs with *wh-*'ever' phrases pattern with standard 'Headless' RCs with bare *wh-*words rather than with Headed RCs. They are: incompatibility of most forms with overt 'complementizers' in English (see (124)),[152] strict Case matching in Polish (see (125)),[153] and RC extraposition in German (see (126)).

---

[151] The contrast between (123a), grammatical (for me) with a slight pause between *chiunque* and *a cui*, and its English translation, ungrammatical, is to be related to the possibility of using *chiunque*, but not *whoever*, as an indefinite pronoun (= *anyone*). See *Parlerebbe con chiunque* 'He would speak with anyone (lit. whoever)' – Cecchetto & Donati 2011: Appendix) vs *He would speak with who(m)ever*. For the special status of *–unque* 'Headless' RCs in Italian and their Romanian analogues, see Caponigro & Fălăuş (2018a). (123b–c) should perhaps be kept distinct from the apparently similar cases found in 'doubly-filled COMP' languages like Middle English (Benincà 2007: §5.2), Quebec French (Bonneau 1990: 149), and Paduan (Benincà 2012b: 36–7), where both the *wh-*phrase and the 'complementizer' are within the (split) CP, although it shouldn't if the same speakers who accept it also accept *that* with an interrogative *wh-*phrase, as Andrew Radford does (see fn. 154 below).

[152] On the general inability of bare 'wh-ever' phrases to be ordinary arguments in Head position in English, see Jacobson (1995: 460 ff), Grosu (2003b: §2.1) and Groat (2012). For examples like *[[Whoever's father's family] has a lot of money] will get rich* (or Smits's 1989: 216 *Whose condition worries us most is Alan*) it is the *wh-* possessor at the edge that can enter into an Agree relation with the external silent Head, which I take to be PERSON, matched by $who_{person}ever·s/who_{person}se$. Also see Citko (2009: 61–2). As Andrews points out, such sentences are less problematic if the phrase is preposed within the RC than it would be if it were in the external Head position. Saddy, Sloan & Krivochen (2019: §3.1) appear to say on the basis of the contrasts in (i) and (ii) that only the possessor can enter an Agree relation with the external silent Head, never the possessee:

  (i)   whosever book this is better come up and claim it/*is a first edition

  (ii)   whosever room this is should be ashamed/*has dirt in the corners

But see *?I'll buy whoever's books he's selling* (McCawley 1998: 457), and sentences like *[Whosever dog bit me] should have been on a leash*, which is putatively ambiguous between a 'dog reading' and a 'man reading' (Knowles 1990).

[153] Wh–*kolwiek* (*wh-*'ever') RCs require Case matching, like simple 'Headless' RCs, and unlike Headed RCs.

(124) a. We'll hire whichever man (*that) you recommended to us (Citko 2009: 931)[154]

     b. I'll read whatever book (??that/which) you'll read (Jacobson 1995: 461)

     c. I'll buy whatever (*that) he's selling (see McCawley 1998: 455)

     d. I'll talk to [whatever students (*who) are problematic] (Caponigro 2019: §3.2)

(125) a. Zatrudnimy [któregokolwiek studenta nam polecisz t_{ACC}]$_{ACC}$ (Citko 2008c: 931)
       Hire.1PL whichever.ACC student.ACC us recommend.2SG
       'We'll hire whichever student you recommend to us.'

     b. *Zatrudnimy [któremukolwiek studentowi ufamy t_{DAT}]$_{ACC}$ (Citko 2008c: 931)
       hire.1PL whichever.DAT student.DAT trust.1PL
       'We'll hire whichever student we trust.'

     c. *Zatrudnimy [któregokolwiek studenta [ufamy t_{DAT}]]$_{ACC}$[155]   (Citko 2008c: 931)
       hire.1PL whichever.ACC student.ACC trust.1PL
       'We'll hire whichever student we trust.'

(126) a. Der Hans hat zurückgegeben   **[welches Geld auch immer** er gestohlen hat]
       the Hans has returned   which money even ever he stolen has
       'Hans has returned whatever money he has stolen.'

     b. *Der Hans hat **welches Geld auch immer** zurückgegeben [er gestohlen hat][156]
       the Hans has which money even ever returned he stolen has

---

[154] The same is true of 'paucal' 'Headless' RCs. See (i), from Andrews (1975: 78),

    (i)   I drank what beer (*that) was on the table/we found.

though he finds the ungrammaticality of (i) less severe than that with ordinary Free relatives with *that* (*I ate what that he brought*). Andrew Radford, pers. comm., who generally accepts both *wh*-'ever' and paucal *wh*- followed by a nominal to co-occur with *that* (see exercise 7.4 of Radford 2016), still finds a difference between *What little beer that was left, he drank* (perfect) and the much worse *What (little) that was left, he drank*. The fact that he has a similar contrast in *wh*-interrogatives (*I wonder what *(kind of celebration) that he has in mind*) may suggest that even in the Free RC construction the *wh*-'ever' or paucal phrase and *that* are for him both in CP. For further complexities concerning the occurrence of *that* with *wh*-ever phrases, see Saddy, Sloan & Krivochen (2019).

[155] Compare it with:

    (i)   *Zatrudnimy*   [*tego człowieka*$_{ACC}$ [*któremu ufamy* t_{DAT}]$_{ACC}$ (Citko 2008c: 931)
         hire.1PL   this.ACC man.ACC whom.DAT trust.1PL
         'We'll hire the man that we trust.'

[156] Also see the following, provided by Henk van Riemsdijk, pers. comm.:

    (i)   a.   [[Wessen Buch auch immer] von Reich Ranicki gelobt wurde] hat sich immer sehr gut verkauft
             whose book even ever by Reich Ranicki praised was has REFL always very well sold
             'Whoever's book was praised by Reich Ranicki always sold very well.'

         b.   **[Wessen Buch auch immer] hat sich immer sehr gut verkauft, von Reich Ranicki gelobt wurde

Borsley (1984: 11–12) discusses another case from Polish which suggests that *wh*-'ever' phrases, like bare *wh*-pronouns, and unlike the Head of Headed RCs, are located in Spec,CP.

The possessive anaphor *swój* must occur in the same local domain (IP/CP) as its antecedent. When inside the *wh*-phrase of an embedded interrogative it can only be bound (under reconstruction) by an antecedent inside the embedded interrogative (see (127a)), and cannot be bound by an antecedent in the matrix clause (see (127b)). When inside the Head of a Headed RC containing a *wh*-pronoun *swój* must instead be bound from an antecedent located in the matrix clause (see (128a)), not by one located in the relative clause (see (128b)):[157]

(127)   a.   Jan   zapytał   [[którą   ze   swoich$_i$ piosenek]$_k$ pro$_i$ lubisz t$_k$]
             John   asked   which   from self.poss   songs   you.like
             'John asked which of your songs you liked.'
        b.   *Jan$_i$ zapytał   [[którą   ze   swoich$_i$ piosenek]$_k$ lubisz t$_k$]
             John   asked   which   from self.poss   songs   you.like
             'John asked which of his songs you liked.'

(128)   a.   Jan$_i$ zaśpiewa [[każda ze   swoich$_i$ piosenek] jaką$_k$ wybierzesz t$_k$]
             John   will.sing each   from self.poss songs   which you.will.choose
             'John will sing each from his songs that you choose.'
        b.   *Jan zaśpiewa [[każda ze swoich$_i$ piosenek]$_k$, jaką ty$_i$ wybierzesz t$_k$]
             John   will.sing each   from self.poss songs   which you will.choose
             'John will sing each from your songs that you choose.'

Crucially, when *swój* is contained inside the 'wh-ever' phrase of a 'Headless' RC, it can**not** be bound by an antecedent in the matrix clause (see (129a)); it can only be bound by one within the RC (under reconstruction) (see (129b)), as when it is contained within a *wh*-phrase in the Spec,CP of an embedded interrogative clause (see (127) above).

(129)   a.   *Jan$_i$ zaśpiewa [[którąkolwiek ze   swoich$_i$ piosenek]$_k$ pro$_j$ wybierzesz t$_k$]
             John will.sing whichever   from self.poss songs   (you) will.choose
             'John will sing whichever of his songs you choose.'
        b.   Jan$_i$ zaśpiewa [[którąkolwiek ze   swoich$_j$ piosenek]$_k$ pro$_j$ wybierzesz t$_k$]
             John will.sing whichever   from self.poss songs   (you) will.choose
             'John will sing whichever of your songs you choose.'

---

[157] This appears to show that the RC Head cannot reconstruct inside the RC, pointing to the presence of a 'matching', rather than a 'raising', derivation in (128).

This clearly suggests that 'wh-ever' phrases (in Polish) are in the Spec of the 'Headless' RC, not in an external Head position.[158]

The same pattern is displayed by the Croatian possessive anaphor *svoj* (Gračanin-Yüksek 2008: §2.2–3). When *svoj* is within the *wh*-phrase of an embedded *wh*-question it can only be bound by an antecedent within the embedded *wh*-question (under *total* reconstruction), not by one in the matrix clause:

(130) Ivan$_k$ ne zna   koje   je   svoje$_{j/*i/*k}$ slike Vid$_i$ mislio da je Dan$_j$ poslao na natječaj
      Ivan not know which Aux self's pictures Vid thought that Aux Dan sent   on contest
      Ivan$_k$ doesn't know which pictures of himself$_{j/*i/*k}$ Vid$_i$ thought Dan$_j$ sent to the contest

The opposite holds in Headed RCs. *Svoj* can only be bound by an antecedent in the matrix clause, not by one within the RC. See (131):[159]

(131)   Vid$_i$ će negraditi ono svoje$_{i/*j}$ dijete koje Dan$_j$ preporuči
        Vid will reward that self's child which Dan recommends
        Vid$_i$ will reward the one of his$_{i/*j}$ children who Dan$_j$ recommends

Wh-'ever' phrases of 'Headless' RCs behave like *wh*-phrases in *wh*-questions. The possessive anaphor *svoj* contained within them can only be bound (under total reconstruction) by an antecedent within the RC, not by one in the matrix clause (thus pointing to their location in the Spec,CP of the 'Headless' RC):[160]

---

[158] For Citko (2009: §3.3) 'however many' *wh*-phrases in Polish Free relatives also allow for non-reconstructed interpretations. Adam Szczegielniak informs me that for certain speakers *swój* can also function as a pronominal, so that for them no comparable clear contrasts should be expected to exist. He himself finds the contrast between a 'Headless' RC ((i)a) and a Headed one ((i)b) striking:

(i)   a. Jan$_n$ zaśpiewa [[którąkolwiek ze   swoich$_{i/*n}$ piosenek]$_k$ pro$_i$ wybierzesz t$_k$]
          John will.sing whichever   from   self.poss   songs   (you) will.choose
          'John will sing whichever of your songs you choose.'
      b. Jan$_n$ zaśpiewa [którąkolwiek ze swoich$_{*i/n}$ piosenek]$_k$ [[którą pro$_i$ wybierzesz t$_k$]
          John will.sing whichever   from your   songs   which (you) will.choose
          'John will sing whichever of your songs which you choose.'

[159] Gračanin-Yüksek notes that '[R]econstruction of the head NP into the relative clause is impossible. The head NP and the matrix subject seem to belong to the same clause' (2008: 281), which points to a 'matching' rather than a 'raising' derivation. The only exception is 'H[eaded] R[elative]s denoting degrees' (2008: fn. 8), which since Carlson 1977 are taken to involve 'raising'.

[160] The clitic second syntax of Croatian also shows conclusively that they cannot have raised out of Spec,CP (Gračanin-Yüksek 2008: §3), so that 'move-and-project analyses [...] cannot be the right account of Croatian FRs' (Gračanin-Yüksek 2008: fn. 22).

(132)   Vid$_i$ će negraditi koje god svoje$_{j/*i}$ dijete Dan$_j$ preporuči
        Vid will reward which ever self's child Dan recommends
        Vid$_i$ will reward whichever of his$_{j/*i}$ children Dan$_j$ recommends

Other languages show that even *definite* 'Headless' RCs (those that plausibly do not involve a silent '-ever', as seen above) can be introduced by a complex *wh*-expression *who/what/which* + NP.

One such case is provided by Chuj (a Mayan language from Guatemala) (see (133), from Kotek & Erlewine (2015a: §5.2.3), who explicitly say that they 'may include overt nominal domains' (p. 34):[161]

---

[161] Another case appears to be Melchor Ocampo Mixtec (Caponigro, Torrence & Cisneros 2013: §4.3 and §5.6).

Cecchetto & Donati (2015: 51) point out that there appear to be no 'Headless' RCs with in situ *wh*-pronouns (see also Kayne 1994: 158 n. 30) and that this follows from the need for the Free relative CP to project into a DP via raising of the *wh*-pronoun/determiner (a case in point could in fact be French: *[Tu as rencontré qui] est malade* 'He whom you have met is sick' (see [*Qui tu as rencontré est malade*]) vs interrogative *Tu as rencontré qui?* 'Who have you met?'). In the present context this might instead be related to the non existence in French (and languages like French, as opposed to languages like Punjabi – see §2.1.4 above) of in situ *wh*-pronouns in Headed RCs (whatever the principle is that forces their movement in French-like languages). As a matter of fact the ban on in situ *wh*-pronouns in 'Headless' RCs does not seem to be completely general. Though rare (see Demirok 2017b, and his proposal of two types of *wh*-in situ, only one of which is compatible with *wh*-in situ in 'Headless' RCs), 'Headless' RCs with in situ *wh*-pronouns appear to be documented in at least some languages. See (i)a from Punjabi (Indo-Aryan), which also has, as noted, in situ *wh*-pronouns in Headed RCs, (i)b from Crow (Siouan), which also has Internally-Headed RCs, (i)c from Tsez (Northeast Caucasian), and (i)d from Dogrib (Athapaskan):

(i)   a.   mãi   náïï   vekhiaa   [ó   ne   jo   vekhiaa]   (Bhatia 1993: 59)
           I   neg.   see.pst.ms   he   erg.mk   rel   see.pst.ms
           'I did not see what he saw.'
      b.   Bill-sh   ak   dapp-é-:sh   sahí:-k   (Andrews 1975: 129)
           Bill-NM   who   kill-DEF   Cree-DECL
           'The one who killed Bill was a Cree.'
      c.   huł   babi-y-ä   **šebi**   žek'-ä-*(zo-)r   magalu   teƛ!
                                                                        (Polinsky 2015: 296)
           yesterday   father-OS-ERG   who/what.ABS   hit-PST.WIT.INTERR-ATTR.OS-LAT
                                                       bread.ABS.III give.IMPER
           'Give the bread to whomever Father beat yesterday.'
      d.   done   sìi   **ʔayìi**   t'à   ʔedegeadàa   sìi ...   (Saxon 2000: 102)
           person   Foc   what   by   3pS.Pf.survive.C   Foc ...
           what people survived with ...

On languages like Turkish with in situ *wh*-pronouns in correlatives (also present in Burushaski (isolate) – Yoshioka 2012: 199; Wappo (Yukian) – Thompson, Park & Li 2006: 123; and Koṇḍa (South-Central Dravidian) – Lakshmi Bai 1985: 185), see Kornfilt (1997, 2005b, 2014, 2015), Iatridou (2013) and Demirok (2017a, 2017b).

(133)   a.   Ix-Ø-w-ilelta [FR **mach** (**winh** **unin**) ix-Ø-ulek'-i].
PRFV-B3-A1S-meet who (CL.MASC boy) PRFV-B3-come-ITV
'I met (the boy) who came.'

        b.   Ko-gana [FR **tas** (**libro-al**) ix-Ø-s-man waj Xun].
A1P-like what (book-NML) PRFV-B3-A3-buy CL.NAME Juan
'We like the book that Juan bought.'

Thus, a raising and projection of the *wh*-form in 'Headless' RCs does not seem viable.

2.5.7   *The Lack of 'Headless' Participial Relative Clauses*

'Headless' participial RCs appear not to be possible. See (134), explicitly noted in Jacobson (1995: 460) (and confirmed by other speakers):

(134)   a.   *What(ever) lurking outside my windows scares me.[162]
        b.   *What(ever) displayed in this window will be sold by midnight.
        c.   *Whatever house cheaper than mine will sell quicker.

The pattern follows if no Case is assigned to Spec,IP as a consequence of the lack of finite Tense within the participial RC (see Kayne 1994: §8.4), and if there is no other way of assigning Case to the *wh*-phrase from the outside.[163]
    The same seems true of Italian:

(135)   *Chi invitato alla festa dovrà portare una bottiglia
        who invited to the party will have to bring a bottle.

---

[162] The ungrammaticality of (134a) should be contrasted with the grammaticality of *Anything lurking outside my windows scares me* (Andrew Radford, pers. comm.). He however accepts paucal 'Headless' participial RCs like *What little time remaining should be used to our advantage, What little money remaining was donated to charity.*

[163] On the IP nature of reduced RCs see Cinque (2010a: §4.2 and §5.1), where evidence from Fanselow (1986) is cited for the presence of a PRO subject with both present and past participles (*pace* Siloni 1995). Also see here §3.4. The fact that 'Headless' participial RCs appear not to be possible even where no Case licensing is plausibly at issue (see (i)), may suggest that they contain no CP capable of hosting a *wh*-phrase:

(i)   a.   *L'articolo sarà recensito dove pubblicato.
        'The article will be reviewed where published.'
        b.   *Quando addormentata, Gianna si mise a russare.
        'When fallen asleep, Gianna started snoring.'

(vs *Appena addormentata*, ... 'Once fallen asleep, ...', where *appena* is an AdvP plausibly in IP).
    Also see Siloni (1995) for the different structure to be attributed to present and past participle reduced RCs in French and Italian, IP and ParticipialP, respectively. If she is right that these categories are contained within an extra DP layer, no 'government' issues should arise for the presence of a PRO.

Apparent exceptions, like (136), can be accounted for if, as suggested in Donati & Cecchetto (2011: Appendix), *qualunque cosa* and *chiunque* can be external Heads, which receive Case in the matrix clause. See (137), where they stand by themselves (similar considerations hold for *quanto* 'how much/ what' – see Chapter 3: fn. 118):

(136)   a.   (?)Qualunque cosa persa da uno di voi non verrà ricomprata
             whatever thing lost by one of you will not be bought again
        b.   (?)Chiunque sorpreso a rubare verrà multato
             whoever caught stealing will be fined

(137)   a.   Farei qualunque cosa per aiutarti
             I would do whatever thing to help you
             'I would do anything to help you.'
        b.   Parlerebbe con chiunque
             (s)he would talk with whoever
             '(S)he would talk with anyone.'

For the same reasons I take *newspapers* in (138a–b) to be an external Head, assigned Case in the matrix clause. If it could receive, in Spec,CP (or Spec,IP), the Case assigned by the matrix Tense to the matrix DP containing the CP (IP), we would expect the 'Headless' RCs in (134) and (135) above also to be possible, contrary to fact.[164] For further discussion, see §3.4.2.4.

(138)   a.   The [newspapers [recently arrived]] were eagerly read by everyone.
        b.   The [[recently arrived] newspapers] were eagerly read by everyone.

2.5.8   The Lack of 'Headless' Infinitival Relative Clauses

Although 'Headless' (Free) RCs have been claimed to be infinitival as well (in contrast to *wh-*'ever' Free RCs) (Donati & Cecchetto 2011: Appendix), the examples putatively showing this possibility have been shown in Pancheva Izvorski (2000: ch. 2) and Caponigro (2019: §3.2) to belong to a distinct construction, called 'Irrealis Free Relatives' (Pancheva Izvorski 2000), 'modal existential *wh*-construction' (Grosu 2004, Šimík 2011), or 'existential free relative' (Caponigro 2003, 2004). Recall §2.5.5 above, where the following properties distinguishing them from ordinary 'Headless' (Free) RCs were mentioned: they are typically introduced by verbs with existential import

---

[164] By the same token, contrary to Cinque (2010a: 56), the Head *headway* of a reduced RC like *The headway made so far is not negligible* must be an external Head (the coindexed PRO within the reduced RC perhaps satisfying the idiom requirements). On idiom chunks with present participle reduced RCs see fn. 117 of Chapter 3, and related text. On the non-decisive diagnostic nature of idiom chunks for 'raising', see the Appendix, A4.4.1 and references cited there.

('be', 'have', 'look for', 'find', etc.), they are not maximalizing, and they do not require category and Case matching, they disallow *wh-*'ever' phrases, they allow multiple *wh-*fronting in languages which allow it in questions, they are not strong islands. They also allow for *wh-*phrases that cannot be used in ordinary 'Headless' (Free) RCs, like (*che*) *cosa* 'what' (see §2.5.3 above), *di che* 'of what' in Italian (Caponigro 2019: §3.2).[165]

The evidence reviewed in §2.5.7 and §2.5.8 thus points to the conclusion that 'Headless' (Free) RCs have to be full finite RCs.

2.5.9   *The Position of the External Head in 'Headless' Relative Clauses*

If 'Headless' RCs indeed have an external Head, as argued here, the question arises as to its position with respect to the RC. The expectation is that in languages with post-nominal restrictive or maximalizing RCs, the external Head should precede the 'Headless' RC, and in head-final languages with pre-nominal RCs it should follow the 'Headless' RC, while in languages with Internally Headed RCs it should be internal to the RC. The latter case is clearly shown by Lakhota 'Headless' RCs as they alternate with a functional/light internal Head ('something'). See (108b) and (i) of fn. 132 above.

In languages lacking 'Headless' RCs (see §2.5.1 above) the external Head will be pronounced and will appear overtly where the Heads of corresponding Headed RCs appear.

2.5.10   *Wh-'ever' in Argument and in Adjunct Clausal Position*

As mentioned in fn. 130, there are reasons to distinguish argument 'Headless' RCs from Free adjunct Free RCs (Izvorski 2000, Pancheva Izvorski 2000: ch. 4; Grosu 2003b: fn. 1; Van Riemsdijk 2006: §5.1, Rawlins 2008), which are close in meaning to *no matter* clausal adjuncts (even if the two may share a common semantics at a more abstract level – see Hirsch 2016, Kayne 2017b: fn. 2, and Šimík 2018).

As noted in Van Riemsdijk (2006: §5.1) argument 'Headless' RCs (as opposed to Free adjunct Free RCs) do not yield natural paraphrases with *no matter* concessive clauses (see *This dog attacks whoever/?*no matter who crosses its path.*).[166] Free adjunct Free RCs also differ from standard argument

---

[165] On the absence of infinitival 'Headless' (Free) RCs also see Pancheva Izvorski (2000: ch. 2).

[166] He also notes that there is no standard argument 'Headless' RC that corresponds to *no matter whether* Free Adjunct Free RCs (such as *No matter whether Carl talks or not, he will be convicted*). Andrew Radford, pers. comm., however, finds *This dog attacks no matter who crosses its path* acceptable.

'Headless' RCs in requiring '-ever'(*Co*(kolwiek) się stanie, jedziemy jutro do Paryża/What*(ever) happens, we are going to Paris tomorrow* – Citko 2010: 238).[167]

Listed here are a few additional phenomena which show that *wh*'-ever' phrases in argument and adjunct positions behave differently.

a) Although *–unque wh*-phrases in Italian 'Headless' RCs may (also) be external heads followed by a relative pronoun, as seen above, they cannot be followed by a relative pronoun in Free adjunct Free RCs. This is expected if these are bare CPs, with no external Head:

(139)   *Qualunque cosa di cui lui si vanti, noi non ci lasceremo impressionare.
whatever thing of which he may boast, we won't let ourselves be impressed
(vs *Di qualunque cosa lui si vanti, noi non ci lasceremo impressionare* 'Of whatever thing he may boast, we won't let ourselves be impressed.')

b) To judge from German, Free adjunct Free RCs also appear to occupy a position different from the position occupied by arguments, where standard 'Headless' RCs are internally merged. While the latter, as DPs, target ordinary DP positions, argument or topic and focus positions in the left periphery, counting as occupiers of the first position and yielding V2 (see (140)), Free adjunct Free RCs occupy an adverbial position higher than topics and foci, forcing the finite verb to be in third position (see (141)), like other 'conditionals of irrelevance' ((142)):[168]

(140) | Wen | auch | immer | du | einlädst, | wird | Maria | gut erhalten |
         |-----|------|-------|----|-----------|------|-------|--------------|
         | Who | also | ever | you | invite, | will | Maria | welcome |

'Maria will welcome whomever you invite.'

(141)   a. Wen auch immer du einlädst, Maria wird nicht kommen (d'Avis 2004: 141)
         Who also ever   you invite, Maria will not come
         'Whomever you may invite, Maria will not come.'
         b. *Wen auch immer du einlädst, wird Maria nicht kommen   (d'Avis 2004: 148)

(142)   Ob es regnet oder nicht, wir gehen spazieren   (d'Avis 2004: 141)
         'Whether it rains or not, we go for a walk.'

---

[167] Among the 'Headless' *wh*-phrases of Italian *quanto* 'how much/what' cannot take the '-ever' suffix *–unque* (see Donati & Cecchetto 2011: 552) and, as opposed to those that do, it cannot be used in Free adjunct Free RCs (**Quanto possa aver fatto, noi ce ne andremo* 'How much/ what he may have done, we will leave').

[168] I thank Roland Hinterhölzl for discussing this point with me.

c) In Appalachian English (AppE) the '-ever' of Standard American English (SAE) precedes, rather than follows, the *wh*-phrase (Johnson 2015). See (143):[169]

(143)   a. You should return everwhat you have finished reading to the   (AppE) library.
        b. You should return whatever you have finished reading to the   (SAE) library.

This ordering is however banned in AppE Free adjunct Free RCs. See (144):

(144)   *You will win the competition, everwho judges the final round.

d) Free adjunct Free RCs allow multiple *wh*-phrases whereas 'Headless' RCs in argument position do not. See the contrast between (145a) and (145b) (Pancheva Izvorski 2000: §4.2.1.4; Grosu 2003b: fn. 1; Hirsch 2016: §4):[170]

(145)   a. (?)Whoever said what to whom, we've got to put this behind us (Hirsch 2016: §4)
        b. *John talked to whoever said what to whom (Hirsch 2016: §4)

e) While 'Headless' RCs in DP positions can be followed by restrictive RCs, which need to modify an (overt or silent) nominal Head, Free adjunct Free RCs, which are CPs, cannot. See the contrast between (146a) and 146b:

(146)   a. I'll move to wherever you want to live that isn't too far from Boston (McCawley 1998: 460)
        b. *Wherever you want to live that isn't too far from Boston, I won't move.

2.5.11   *(Morphological) Case (Mis)Match in 'Headless' Relative Clauses*

The (morphological) Case matching requirement holding of 'Headless' RCs has been the object of intensive research, which has come to distinguish essentially three types of languages: (1) fully matching languages (like

---

[169] We may take Standard English *wh-ever* phrases to be complex phrases derived by raising of the *wh-* part, from a structure essentially like the Appalachian English *ever-wh*, across *-ever* (which is possibly itself complex: AT ever(y) TIME *wh-*. See Kayne 2005a: 14).

[170] Although modality/aspect may make a difference. See *He's the kind of guy who would admire whoever said whatever to whomever*, which Andrew Radford (pers. comm.) finds acceptable. Zwicky (2002: 239) notes that the *wh*-phrase of 'concessive Free relatives' can be followed by *the hell* much like interrogative *wh*-phrases.

English, Italian, Polish, etc. – Grosu 1994, Citko 2000) where the category/ Case of the *wh*-phrase in Spec,CP and the category/Case of the external Head have to match exactly,[171] (2) non-matching languages where conflicts between the internal and external category/Case are resolved in favour of the internal category/Case (certain varieties of German – Pittner 1991, 1995, sometimes referred to as German B – Vogel 2001), and (3) non-matching languages where Case conflicts are resolved in favour of the external Case (like Classical Greek, Gothic, etc. – Harbert 1983a, 1983b, 1989). See the discussion and references in the above works as well as the general discussions in Grosu (1994), Van Riemsdijk (2006), and Daskalaki (2011).

I have nothing to add to these discussions. I will only comment briefly on a generalization holding of type (2) (where the Case conflict is resolved in favour of the internal Case).[172]

Type (2) non-matching appears to obey the following generalization: when different from the Case assigned externally, the *wh*-phrase can bear the Case assigned within the relative clause (as expected if it is in Spec,CP) *provided that such Case is lower in the Case hierarchy* (NOM > ACC > GEN > DAT > OBL) *than the Case assigned externally* (see Pittner 1995: 211).[173] (147) and (148) provide some illustrative examples from German B:

---

[171] Andrew Radford (2016: 468), however, reports non-matching cases like (i) even in English:

(i)   [*Whomever* you elect] will serve a four-year term.

Also see (ii)a from Poutsma (1916: 987) and (ii)b from Salzmann (2017: 117):

(ii)   a.   Whom the Gods love die young.
        b.   It is a picture of voters venting their frustration on *whomever* happens to be in power.

[172] For type (3), and its complexities, see Harbert (1989, 1992) and especially Grosu (1994, Study I, ch. 4) in terms of Case Attraction, which in some languages also holds true of the corresponding Headed RCs, whereby the internal Head comes to bear the Case of the external Head instead of that assigned within the RC, a possible extended effect of the agreement relation between the two Heads. On this type of Case attraction, see, in addition to the works just mentioned, Touratier (1980: 213–38), Bianchi (1999: 94 ff) and references cited there.

[173] The generalization appears to hold independently of the differences which may exist among the selective non-matching languages with respect to which structural positions admit non-matching: left dislocated positions (in German but not French – Harbert 1983a: §4) or subject positions, if distinct from clitic left dislocated positions in null subject languages. This recalls the possibility of Inverse Case Attraction in Headed RCs in left dislocated and subject positions in certain languages (Farsi varieties and Albanian dialects), analysed as 'raising' relatives in Cinque (2007: 99 ff) and references cited there. See here A4 of the Appendix. On Case conflict in matching languages like German A and its resolution in the presence of syncretism see van Riemsdijk (2006) and Hanink (2018) for different analyses.

(147) a. Sie lädt ein$_{\rightarrow Acc}$[$_{FR}$ wem$_{Dat}$ sie zu Dank verpflichtet ist] (Pittner 1995: 208)
           (ACC [$_{FR}$DAT]])
           she invites to.whom she to thanks obliged is
           'She invites who she is obliged to.'
      b. Jeder muss tun$_{\rightarrow Acc}$, wofür er bestimmt ist(Pittner 1995: 208)   (ACC [$_{FR}$BENEF])
           everybody must do what-for(PP) he destined is
           'Everybody must do what he is destined for.'
      c. [$_{FR}$Wen$_{Acc}$ Maria$_{Nom}$ mag$_{\rightarrow Acc}$]$_{Nom}$ wird eingeladen (Vogel 2001: 903)
           (NOM [$_{FR}$ACC])
           who.acc Maria likes is invited
           'Who Maria likes gets invited.'

(148) a. *Er zerstört$_{\rightarrow Acc}$ [$_{FR}$ wer$_{Nom}$ihm begegnet] (Vogel 2001: 904)   (ACC [$_{FR}$NOM])
           he destroys   who   him   meets
           'He destroys he who meets him.'
      b. *Ich vertraue$_{\rightarrow Dat}$ [$_{FR}$ wen$_{Acc}$ich   einlade] (Vogel 2003: 283)   (DAT [$_{FR}$ACC])
           I   trust   who   I   invite
           'I trust whom I invite.'

In a double-Headed configuration like, say, V_{matrix} [$_{DP}$ D [$_{CP}$ [$_{XP}$ *what* THING]$_i$ $V_{embedded}$ t_i] (THAT) THING]], the matrix V assigns Case to DP (which percolates to the external Head (THAT) THING). The internal Head, [*what* THING] instead receives Case from the embedded V.

The double-Headed configuration may derive the full matching case and the non-matching case where the Case conflict is resolved in favour of the internal Case without having to resort to non-local relations spanning over two maximal projections, DP and CP.

The parametric variation between fully matching languages like English (but see fn. 171), Polish, or Italian and non-matching languages like German B appears to be expressible in terms of Caha's (2009: §1.6) Universal (Case) Containment (149), which is motivated by Case syncretism and other generalizations:

(149)   Universal (Case) Containment
      a.   In the Case sequence, the marking of Cases on the right can morphologically contain Cases on the left, but not the other way round.
      b.   The Case sequence: NOM – ACC – GEN – DAT – INS – COM

Each Case in the sequence contains the Cases to its left though not those to its right, NOM being the poorest, for example: [$_{AccP}$ ACC [$_{NomP}$ NOM]].

In fully matching languages the raised internal Head licenses the deletion of the external Head, which it c-commands (under Kayne's 1994 definition), only if the category and (morphological) Case of the two Heads are identical. In German B type languages, the licensing is less strict. For the deletion of the external Head it is enough (for identification) that the internal Head, which c-commands it, has a Case which contains the Case of the external Head.[174]

2.5.12   Absence of Multiple 'Headless' Relative Clauses and
Their Apparent Presence in Bulgarian and Romanian

Even though 'Headless' RCs share a number of properties with *wh*-questions, no languages, even those that have multiple *wh*-questions, dispose of multiple *wh*-'Headless' RCs in argument position. As Citko and Gračanin-Yüksek (2016: §3) suggest, this derives from a fundamental difference between 'Headless' RCs and *wh*-questions. The former modify a silent Head, while the latter do not.[175] Even if Bulgarian has been claimed to display multiple 'Headless' RCs (see (150) and Rudin 1986, 2007, 2008)[176] there is reason to be sceptical.

(150) a.   Vzemajte   [koj kakvoto može]. (Rudin 2007: 290)
        take-imp.   who what can
        'Everyone take whatever you can.'
     b.   Sâbrahme [na kogo(to) kakvoto bjaha izpratili]. (Dimova & Tellier 2015: 1)
        gathered-1pl. to whom what aux. sent-3pl.
        'We gathered what they sent to everyone.'

Only one of the two *wh*-phrases is construed with both the matrix and the embedded predicate. In Bulgarian, the one that fulfils the categorial, Case-matching and selectional requirements of the main and the embedded predicate is systematically the second *wh*-phrase (Rudin 1986: 169; Dimova 2014) while the first is interpreted as a universally quantified expression in Topic position

---

[174] (147a–c) are thus fine as DAT/BENEF contains ACC (and NOM) and ACC contains NOM. If the opposite is the case, as in (148a–b), an ungrammatical result obtains, presumably for lack of Case recoverability. See Assmann (2013) for a similar treatment in terms of Case features containment, though she takes Nominative to be 'richer' than Accusative, which is richer than lower Cases. Within analyses that do not assume an external Head (as in $[_{DP} D [_{CP}]]$) it is not clear why in the selective non-matching cases it is enough for the Case of the *wh*-phrase (say, DAT) to contain the Case of D (say, NOM), but not vice versa (why could the Case of D not contain the Case of the *wh*-, with D DAT and the *wh*- NOM if no recoverability issue is involved?).

[175] Under a bare CP analysis of 'Headless' RCs (see fn. 130 above) or a $[_{DP} D° [_{CP}]]$ one without an external Head, it is not entirely clear what would prevent the movement of more than one *wh*-pronoun to CP (particularly in languages which have multiple *wh*-fronting in interrogatives).

[176] Rudin shows that these structures are different from multiple correlatives – on which see §2.6 below. For example, they can occur in argument position and are incompatible with correlative demonstratives.

(Dimova & Tellier 2015: 2; 2018: §3). For comparable conclusions, see Citko & Gračanin-Yüksek (2016: fn. 13).[177]

2.5.13 'Headless' Relative Clauses and Stacking

Although 'Headless' RCs cannot stack (see Grosu & Landman 1998: 155, and Appendix A4.2, for examples), a restrictive can be stacked on a 'Headless' RC (see (151)):

(151)   a.   I will read whatever you recommend that Bill wrote.
                                                              (Weisler 1980: 626)
          b.   What John has that I want is a video recorder.   (McCawley 1991: 50)

2.5.14 Light Headed Relative Clauses

Related to 'Headless' RCs are the so-called Light Headed RCs (Citko 2000, 2004; Kholodilova 2017).[178] Unlike fully Headed RCs, rather than a lexical Head they display a demonstrative/pronominal Head, and, more crucially for present concerns, they employ the same *wh*-forms used in 'Headless' RCs rather than those used in Headed ones (or in interrogatives when these are different from those used in 'Headless' RCs – see Šimík's 2017 generalization mentioned in fn. 139 above).[179] See (152) from Polish (Citko 2004: 98) and (153) from Italian:

(152)   a.   Jan czyta **to, co** Maria czyta.
              Jan reads this what Maria reads
              'John reads what Mary reads.'

---

[177] The apparent Romanian analogues of (150) (see (i) below), may have a different semantic analysis. See Caponigro & Fălăuş (2018b). At any rate it seems that these constructions are not genuine multiple 'Headless' RCs.

  (i)   a.   Am mâncat [ce când mi-ai adus].   (Caponigro & Fălăuş 2018b: 567)
              have.1SG eaten what when CL.1SG-have.2SG brought
              Roughly: 'I ate the thing/things you brought me to eat at the moment(s) appropriate for it/them.'
          b.   Ţi-am arătat [ce cum a fost instalat].   (Caponigro & Fălăuş 2018b: 568)
              CL2SG-have.1SG shown what how has been installed
              Roughly: 'I showed you the thing(s) that were installed in the way(s) it/they were installed.'

[178] In Smits (1989: §1.4) they are termed 'semi-free relatives', in Pancheva Izvorski (2000: 4.2.1.5) 'Determiner-Headed Free Relatives' and in De Vries (2002: ch. 2: §6.3; 2006) 'false free relatives'. Another term is 'pronominally Headed relatives' (Lipták 2015: 189).

[179] Light Headed RCs nonetheless differ from 'Headless' RCs in not requiring category/Case matching and in being incompatible with 'ever' (e.g. *Jan śpiewa to, cokolwiek Maria śpiewa.* Lit.: 'Jan sings that whatever Maria sings' – Citko 2004: 105).

> b. Jan czyta **tam, gdzie** Maria czyta.
>   Jan reads there where Maria reads
>   'John reads where Mary reads.'
> c. Jan czyta **wtedy, kiedy** Maria czyta.
>   Jan reads then when Maria reads
>   'John reads when Mary reads.'
> d. Jan czyta **tak, jak** Maria czyta.
>   Jan reads thus how Maria reads
>   'John reads the (same) way Mary reads.'

(153)   a. L'ho riposto **lì dove** l'avevi messo tu ieri.[180]
            it I.put.back there where it had.you put yesterday
            'I put it back where you had put it yesterday.'
        b. Si è comportata **così come** avevi previsto tu.
            she.behaved thus how you had foreseen
            'She behaved (exactly) how you had foreseen.'

I thus take such cases to pronounce part of the external Head of the corresponding 'Headless' RC:

(154)   a. Jan czyta to_{THING}, co_{THING} Maria czyta   (cf. (152a))
        b. L'ho riposto $lì_{PLACE}$ $dove_{PLACE}$ l'avevi messo tu ieri (cf. (153a))

For more discussion, see Grosu (1994: §8.3), Citko (2000, 2004), De Vries (2002), Catasso (2013), Kholodilova (2017), and Hanink (2018). On the 'missing-P' phenomenon (*I'll move to whatever town you move* – Bresnan & Grimshaw 1978: 358), where both the matrix and the embedded verb select for a PP but only one is apparently present, see for recent discussion Grosu (1996: §5; 2003b: Appendix) and Hanink (2018).[181]

---

[180] There may exist gaps in the paradigm. For example, in Italian, in addition to the systematic gap represented by the absence of (*che*) *cosa* 'what' in 'Headless' RCs (see §2.5.3 above), *allora quando* 'then when' is ackward. Also see (*Tanto) *quanto dici è falso* '(That (much)) what/ how much you say is false.'

[181] The Venetian case in (i), discussed in Bianchi (1999: 48–9), where there is also a missing preposition, is possibly similar (see (ii) – see also fn. 148 above)), and is also reminiscent of the Inverse Case Attraction type involving movement discussed in the Appendix (A4.1.5).

(i)   a. Nea situassion che semo (no se pol far gnente).
          in.the situation that we.are (not one can do nothing)
          'In the situation in which we are (we can do nothing).'
      b. *Ea situation che semo (ze bruta).
          the situation that we are (is bad).

(ii) [IN (THAT) THING [$_{CP}$ [$_{PP}$ in [$_{DP}$ the situation THING]]$_i$ that [we are t_i]]

2.5.15 Summary

So far evidence has been reviewed that renders it at least plausible to conceive of a double-Headed analysis even for 'Headless' RCs, where the external Head of the bare *wh*-forms (*what, who,* etc.) – or, for that matter, that of complex *wh*- 'ever' forms – is one of the functional/light nouns/classifiers THING, AMOUNT, PERSON, PLACE, TIME, etc., also silently present with the *wh*-forms themselves raised to the Spec,CP of the RC (*what* THING, *whatever book* THING). If so, 'Headless' RCs appear not to be an independent RC type, but an (incompletely pronounced) variant of one or the other RCs types: externally Headed post-nominal (see (155a)), externally Headed pre-nominal (see (155b)), internally Headed (see (155c)), or double Headed (see (155d)) (see De Vries 2002: ch. 2: §6.3):

(155) a. ʔExactly (he) **who** you wanted me to invite, ...
     b. [[tamen yào mai] de] **[e]**] (Waltraud Paul, pers. comm.)
         they want buy SUB
         what they want to buy ...
     c. [[Mary **[e]** kağe] ki] ophewathě (Lakhota – Williamson 1987: 189 n. 4)
         Mary make the I.buy
         'I bought what Mary made.'
     d. [skə̀n [nàm dzán **skə̀n** syì]] há diyà gáy kà (Mina – Frajzyngier & Johnston 2005: 433)
         [thing [1DU find thing COM]] 2sg put spoil POS
         'What we found, you are ruining (it).'

In this respect it is no wonder that no language has 'Headless' RCs as the only RC type.

2.6 Correlative Relative Clauses[*]

2.6.1 Simple Correlatives as 'Left Dislocated' DPs Resumed by an Anaphoric DP in the Matrix Clause[†]

Following a certain tradition, by 'simple correlatives' I mean those correlatives that contain a single *wh*-phrase, like those in (156) (see §2.6.3 below for the non-relative status of multiple correlatives):

---

[*] This section is an updated version of the analysis of correlatives presented in Cinque (2009b).

[†] See Rebuschi (1999: 68) for the similar idea that the correlative clause may just be 'la partie visible d'une véritable relative libre topicalisée'. ['the visible part of a genuine topicalized free relative'], and especially Gupta (1986: ch. 5), who concludes: 'Thus, internal [correlative] and postnominal relative constructions display characteristics of 'left dislocated' NPs. These same traits are not evident in extranominal [extraposed] relative sentences' (p. 91). Also see Lipták (2004), Dasgupta (2006), Butt, Holloway King & Roth (2007: §4.3), and Rebuschi (2009: §3.3). As we see below, the term 'left dislocated DP' corresponds in different languages to different

(156)   a.   jo   laRkii khaRii   hai,   vo (laRkii/badmanash) lambii hai

(see Srivastav 1991b: 135)

which girl   standing be-PRES,   she/that (girl/rascal)   tall   be-PRES

which girl is standing, she/that girl/that rascal is tall

b.   jo c^hatr   vəhã k^həra   hε   vo   lərka   mera   dost   hε

(McCawley 2004: 300)

which   student   there   standing   is   that   boy   my   friend   is

which student is standing there, that boy is my friend

An influential analysis of this construction takes the left peripheral relative to be a bare CP, adjoined to the matrix IP, which contains a correlate DP bound by that CP as a variable. See Srivastav (1991a, 1991b), and Dayal (1996).[182]

---

types of 'left dislocation' constructions, where the element resuming the relative in the matrix IP may be represented either by a full DP (see for example (i) below, from Marathi – Renuka Ozarkar, pers. comm. – which incidentally redresses McCawley's 2004: 300 generalization), or by a demonstrative (optionally followed by a head noun which can also be different from the correlative head noun if it is a more general term), as shown in (156), or by an anaphoric pronoun, which can also be silent, depending on the Case it bears, and the particular language involved, or a *wh*-phrase as in Isbukun Bunun (see fn. 202 below).

(i) [jyaa aattaa-c   aalyaa aahet] **Tyaa laal Dres**   **ghaat-le-lyaadon**   **Chotyaa mulii** ...

which now-emph come-PAST.FEM be-PRES.PL those red dress wear-PAST.PART-FEM two small

girls ...

those two small girls wearing a red dress who have just arrived ...

In languages that have both demonstratives and special anaphoric correlative pronouns, the two may have different semantic consequences. See Bagchi's (1994) discussion on Bangla.

Sometimes the phrase in the matrix IP which resumes the left peripheral relative is considered as the (external) Head of the relative clause. But this is misleading if the correlative pronoun (phrase) is nothing other than a phrase resuming a 'left dislocated' DP. For multiple correlatives, see §2.6.3 below.

[182] Also see Andrews (1975) and Hale (1976). Among the works that essentially adopt this analysis are Bagchi (1994), Bianchi (1999: ch. 3, §4.1), De Vries (2002: ch. 5, section 6), Cecchetto, Geraci & Zucchi (2006), Leung (2007c), Wu (2016), and various contributions in Lipták (2009b). Grosu & Landman (1998: 167) however points out that the correlative element can be a universally quantified expression ('all DP'), and thus cannot qualify as a variable bound by the CP conceived of as a generalized quantifier. Unlike Srivastav (1991a, 1991b) and Dayal (1996), Bhatt (2003, 2005) argues that the CP is not base-generated as an adjunct to the matrix IP, but is moved there from a position inside the matrix IP adjoined to the correlative DP (Mahajan 2000: fn. 10 also proposes a movement derivation of the left peripheral relative). In this way, the fact that the relation between the CP and the correlative pronoun or demonstrative in the matrix IP is sensitive to islands (in Hindi) can be made to follow. A similar analysis is actually adumbrated in De Vries (2002: 149 fn. 49), and Dayal herself (1996: ch. 6: §2.4) admits that the CP can in certain cases be adjoined to the DP containing the correlative pronoun/demonstrative/epithet, and also mentions elsewhere (p. 183) that the relation between the two, when they are separated, is subject to island constraints.

The merger together of the correlative relative and the correlative pronoun/demonstrative followed by their split, is however not a property of correlatives in all languages that have them. See for example the case of Bulgarian below (ex. (163) and related text).

This analysis is the only conceivable one if both simple correlatives and multiple correlatives (those containing more than one *wh*-phrase, like (157)) are taken to represent one and the same construction.

(157) jis laRkii-ne$_i$ jis laRke$_j$-ke saath khelaa, us-ne$_i$ us-ko$_j$ haraayaa   (Dayal 1996: 197)
       which girl-ERG which boy-GEN with play.PAST, she-ERG he-ACC defeated
       which girl played with which boy, she defeated him

Clearly a DP analysis for the latter cases is out of the question since the correlative CP cannot have two external Heads (see Downing 1973: 13; Dasgupta 1980: 291; Srivastav 1988: 148; De Vries 2002: 147; Bhatt 2005: 9; Anderson 2005: 5 fn. 3).[183] Correlatives would thus seem to pose a problem for any unified analysis of relative clauses that takes them to be embedded in a DP within a double-Headed structure. There is however evidence (discussed in Bhatt 2003, 2005) that multiple and simple correlatives do not constitute a homogeneous construction and thus should not be forced under one and the same analysis that (in Montague's terms) 'generalizes to the worst case' (that of multiple correlatives).

Some of this evidence will be recalled in §2.6.3 below, where multiple correlatives will actually be argued to be Free adjunct Free RCs (in Izvorski's 2000 sense), along the lines of Dayal's original analysis.[184]

Note that simple correlatives like those in (156) containing a left-dislocated 'Headless' RC may alternate with a left-dislocated Externally Headed post-nominal relative. Compare (156a) with (158):

(158) vo laRkii jo   khaRii hai,   vo   lambii hai (see Dayal 1996: 152)
       that girl which standing be-PRES, she/that tall   be-PRES
       that girl who is standing, she is tall

---

[183] In addition to (simple and multiple) correlatives, Hindi has externally headed embedded ((i)a), and extraposed ((i)b), post-nominal relatives, which share properties setting them apart from (simple and multiple) correlatives (see, among others, Srivastav 1991a, Mahajan 2000, McCawley 2004, Leung 2007a, 2007b, Butt, Holloway King & Roth 2007: §3). Here I will not be concerned with these other types of Hindi RCs.

   (i)   a   vo laRkii **jo khaRii hai** lambii hai (Srivastav 1991a: 642)
             that girl which standing is tall is
         b   vo laRkii lambii hai **jo khaRii hai** (Srivastav 1991a: 642)
             that girl tall is which standing is
             'The girl who is standing is tall.'

[184] Butt, Holloway King & Roth (2007: §5) also give a non-relative clause analysis for multiple correlatives (adjunction to IP) distinct from the one they give for simple correlatives (generation in a specifier of the correlative DP).

Taking (156) and (158) together into consideration, and the double-Headed analysis of 'Headless' RCs given in §2.5, it becomes possible to interpret (156) as having a silent external Head, as shown in (159):[185]

(159)   [$_{DP}$VO LARKII [$_{CP}$ jo laRkii khaRii hai]] vo laRkii lambii hai
         THAT GIRL which girl standing be-PRES, that girl tall be-PRES
         the girl who is standing, that girl is tall

Veneeta Dayal (pers. comm.) tells me that she in fact marginally accepts (160), which shows the underlying structure (159) of (156) and (158) on its sleeve, so to speak:[186]

(160)   vo laRkii jo laRkii khaRii hai, vo laRkii lambii hai
         that girl which girl standing be-PR, that girl tall be-PRES
         the girl who is standing, that girl is tall

The same full structure is apparently acceptable (under the appropriate conditions of emphasis) in two other Indo-Aryan languages: Bundeli ((161a) – Ruchi Jain, pers. comm.) and Maithili ((161b), from Singh (1980), according

---

[185] Gupta (1986: 36 fn. 2) explicitly proposes that a Hindi correlative like (i) derives from an externally headed RC like (ii), via deletion of the external Head (also see Mahajan 2000: 215):

    (i)   jo   laRka: la:l kami:j pahne   hai vo   mera: bha:i: hai
         which boy   red shirt   wearing is   that/he I.gen brother is
         'The boy who is wearing a red shirt is my brother.'
    (ii) [[vo laRka:] [jo   laRka: la:l kami:j pahne   hai]] vo   mera: bha:i: hai
         That boy   which boy   red shirt   wearing is   that/he I.gen brother is
Junghare (1973) also proposes to derive the Marathi correlative forms in (iii) from a structure essentially like (iv), which however is not acceptable for her. Also see Wali (1982):

(iii)	a	to	**manus**	[jo	Ø	ith∂	kam	k∂rto]	to	**manus**	ajari ahe
	b	to	Ø	[jo	Ø	ith∂	kam	k∂rto]	to	Ø	ajari ahe
	c	to	Ø	[jo	Ø	ith∂	kam	k∂rto]	to	**manus**	ajari ahe
	d	Ø	Ø	[jo	**manus**	ith∂	kam	k∂rto]	to	Ø	ajari ahe
	e	Ø	Ø	[jo	Ø	ith∂	kam	k∂rto]	to	**manus**	ajari ahe
	f	Ø	Ø	[Ø	Ø	ith∂	kam	k∂rto]	to	**manus**	ajari ahe

        (that)(man)(which)(man) here work does   that (man) sick is
        'The man who works here is sick.'

    (iv) **to manus** [jo **manus** ith∂ kam k∂rto] **to manus** ajari ahe (*)

[186] Alice Davison tells me that (160) was accepted by many speakers she consulted. Wali (2006: 289) claims that in Marathi too, the left dislocated DP may sometimes surface unreduced. See (i) (Renuka Ozarkar tells me that this is indeed possible if one wants to emphasize 'that particular girl', stressing *ti* at the beginning of the main clause. Otherwise, it is slightly odd ('?')):

    (i)   **Ti**   **mulgi** [**ji**   **mulgi** ghari geli] **ti**   ithe   rähte
         That   girl   which girl   home went that here lives
         'The girl who went home lives here.'

to whom it is 'cumbersome, though acceptable' (p. 34)). It is apparently also possible in the Trans-New Guinea language Bine ((161c)) – from Fleischmann 1981: 5):[187]

(161) a. [**ba moRii** [**jo   moRii**   ThaRii hɛ]],   **ba moRii**   lambii hɛ
            that girl   which girl   standing is,   that girl   tall   is
            'The girl who is standing is tall.'

       b. [(**o**) **panc-sab** [jaah[i] **panc-sab-kE**[n] ham niik jakaan[n] janait chalianh[i]
            ]s]NP **o panc-sab** ...
            (the) Panch which Panch-PL-OBJ I good way know.PART
            BE.PAST.AGR, the (same) Panch ...
            'The Panch whom I knew very well, the same Panch ...'

       c. puga **pui cewe** tabe lui **cewe cabu** a-tyaramt-ø-i-ge **pui cewe cabu** iyeta
            miiji gwidape aletnena ...
            there that village 3sg rel village at intr-arrive-P2-i-3sg.s that village at all
            good things buying ...
            'That village at which he arrived, at that village there were all the good
            things to buy, ...'

The 'left dislocated' DP, containing the RC, is matched by a resumptive DP (often pronominal or demonstrative) in the matrix clause. Depending on the language, the 'left dislocated' DP containing the correlative clause may apparently be either an English-type Left dislocation/Hanging Topic (Kashmiri), or a German-type Contrastive Left Dislocation (German, Bulgarian), or a Romance-type Clitic Left Dislocation (as in the 'correlatives' of Italian).

As opposed to the other Indo-Aryan languages, Kashmiri is an (SOV) V2 language. Its finite verb, in main (and complement) clauses, necessarily occupies the second position, following either the subject or a scene-setting adverb, or a focused phrase or a *wh*-phrase (Hook & Koul 1996, and especially R. M. Bhatt 1999: ch. 4).[188] However, if a left dislocated/hanging topic is present, resumed by a demonstrative or pronominal inside the clause, the finite verb is systematically found in *third* position, with a subject or a focused/*wh*-phrase occupying the second position. In other words, the left dislocated/hanging topic phrase does not count as a filler for the 'first position'.[189]

---

[187] The same full structure is instead not readily acceptable in Nepali (Samar Sinha, pers. comm.).

[188] As Richard Kayne reminds me, Kashmiri, as opposed to Germanic V2 languages, allows multiple *wh*-fronting, with the consequence that the verb in such cases may end up not being in strict second position. See Koul (2003: §6.2.1.4), and also R. M. Bhatt (1999: §4.1.2.2).

[189] See for example (i) a–b, from R. M. Bhatt (1999: 103):

(i) a. Tem   dop   ki,   coon   kalam,   shiilaayi   tshooND   su
         he   said   that, your   pen,   Sheila   found   that
         'He said that as for your pen, it is Sheila who found it.'

Now, as Hook and Koul (1996: 98) show, a correlative clause too 'does not count in the V-2 calculation, with the result that the finite verbal element comes in *third* position'. See (162a), which contrasts minimally with (162b), characterized by a topicalized Headed postnominal relative (not resumed by a correlative element):

(162) a. [yus   naphar raath   aay]   bi chus yatshaan temyis   samikh-un
          [which person yesterday came]   I am   wanting him.DAT meet-INF
          'I want to meet the man who came here yesterday.'
       b. [temyis naphras yus   raath   aav]   chus bi yatshaan samikh-un
          [the   person who yesterday came]   am   I wanting meet-INF
          'I want to meet the man who came here yesterday.'

Thus Kashmiri provides direct evidence that one type of correlative clause can occupy the position of left dislocated/hanging topics, preceding the CP space which contains a fronted phrase (in first position) and the finite verb (in second position).[190]

Hindi, possibly in addition to an English/Kashmiri-type left dislocation construction (Dwivedi 1994a: §2.2.2), appears to have a topicalization construction involving movement, possibly similar to Romance Clitic Left Dislocation, modulo the presence of a non-clitic resumptive DP (either a full DP, or a demonstrative pronoun, or an epithet) (Mahajan 1990; Srivastav 1991a, 1991b; Dwivedi 1994a, 1994b). See, in particular Mahajan (2000: fn. 10) and Bhatt (2003) for arguments that the correlative relative acquires its left adjoined position by movement, and Bhatt (2003) for the idea that it starts out together with the correlative pronoun (as seen from the possibility of

---

       b.   Coon kalam, su   goyi me   garyi   mashith
            your pen,   that gone I   home-at forget
            'As for your pen, that (is what) I forgot at home.'

R. M. Bhatt (1999: 103–4) gives two arguments for the extra-clausal nature of left dislocated/hanging topics in Kashmiri. The first is that it is possible to insert a parenthetical phrase after them, and the second is that they are 'always in the nominative case', whereas the coreferential pronoun in the clause is in the appropriate Case, much like what happens with Italian Hanging Topics (Cinque 1990: ch. 2) and with the Latin *nominativus pendens*.

[190] If the left dislocated phrase containing the relative clause in Kashmiri is base-generated in the left peripheral position rather than moved there, no reconstruction of the left dislocated DP should be possible, nor should its relation with the correlative element be subject to island constraints. This remains to be ascertained.

   Hungarian correlatives, which, as Lipták (2004) shows, do not reconstruct inside the main clause to a position adjoined to the correlative element, nor display sensitivity to islands, also appear (*pace* her own conclusion) to be Hanging Topics. The two putative differences which according to Lipták (2004: 302) distinguish Hanging Topics from Hungarian correlatives may turn out not to be real. Both correlatives and Hanging Topics seem to be root phenomena and indeed, just as with correlatives, there is in general no more than one Hanging Topic per clause (see Postal 1971: 136 fn. 17; Cinque 1990: 58).

their making up a constituent), and optionally moves out to a left peripheral position stranding the correlative DP.

I follow this analysis here, in particular assuming the RC to be internal to a DP which together with the correlative DP forms a 'big DP' ([[Head RC] correlative]), much like the 'big DP' taken to underlie French Complex Inversion (Kayne 1972) and Romance Clitic Left Dislocation ([DP DP [D Clitic]] – Uriagereka 1995: 81).

In Bulgarian, unlike Hindi (and other Indo-Aryan languages), the left dislocated DP of the correlative construction is never found adjoined to the resumptive element (Bhatt 2003: 529). Rather, it appears to be base-generated in situ and matched by a correlative element which obligatorily moves to the front of the main clause (see Izvorski 1996: 12):

(163)   [Kolkoto pari Maria$_k$ iska], tolkova$_i$ tja$_k$ misli če šte j dam t$_i$
Hewever much money M. wants, that much she thinks that will her I.give
'She thinks that I will give her as much money as Maria wants.'

This is indicated by the fact that, unlike Hindi (Bhatt 2003: §3.3.1), the left dislocated DP in (163) does not reconstruct, as no Principle C violation is to be observed there.

The same holds of the correlative relatives of Hungarian (see fn. 190) and the Austronesian (Formosan) language Isbukun Bunun. Wu (2016: 201–2) argues that 'the correlative and its associated anaphoric element never form a constituent at any level'. In Isbukun Bunun, unlike in Hindi, it is not possible to coordinate two [correlative – correlate] sequences. See the contrast between (164a) and (164b):

(164) a. *Na ludah-un-ku   [sima ma-tushung   uvaaz   saia   tu   bunun]
                                                                                      (Isbukun Bunun)
            FUT hit-PV-1sg.OBL who AV-bully   child   3sg.NOM   LNK person
            mas [sima tanhaiu   tulkuk   saia   tu   bunun]
            and who AV.steal   chicken   3sg.NOM LNK   person
            Intended: 'I will hit the person who bullies a child and the person who steals chickens.'
       b. Rahul a:jkal [[[jo kita:b Saira-ne likh-i:]k vok] aur [[jo cartoon Shyam-ne bana:-ya:]j voj
            ]] parh raha: hai.
            Rahul nowadays REL book Saira-ERG write-PFV that and REL cartoon Shyam-ERG
            make-PFV that read PROG be
            'Nowadays, Rahul is reading the book that Saira wrote and the cartoon that Shyam made.'
            Lit.: 'Nowadays, Rahul is reading what book Saira wrote, that and what cartoon Shyam
            made, that.' (Bhatt 2003: 504)

Furthermore, again unlike Hindi, and like Bulgarian, the relation between the correlative relative and the correlate shows no island-sensitivity (see examples (17) and (18) of Wu 2016), nor Principle C violations under reconstruction. See (165):

(165)   [Sima mazima Abus$_k$]$_j$ na   kahaitas sain$_k$ saicia$_j$.   (Wu 2016: 202)
        Who   AV.like Abus   FUT AV.hate 3sg.NOM 3sg.ACC
        Lit.: '[Who likes Abus$_k$]$_j$ she$_k$ will reject him/her$_j$.
        'Abus hates the person that likes her.'

This appears parallel to the non-connectivity variant of German contrastive Left Dislocation. See (166a), where no Case connectivity is present, which is at the base of the correlative form in (167) (vs (166b), which shows Case Connectivity):

(166)   a.   Der Karl, dem will ich vertrauen
             the(Nom) Karl, him(Dat) will I trust
             'Karl, I will trust him.'
        b.   Dem Karl, dem will ich vertrauen
             The(Dat) Karl, him(Dat) will I trust
             'Karl, I will trust.'

(167)   [Wer das sagen wird], dem will ich vertrauen
        who.NOM that say will that.DAT will I trust
        'I will trust who(ever) says that.'

In Italian, the element resuming the 'correlative' relative is normally a run-of-the-mill clitic, actually the usual resumptive clitic associated with the Clitic Left Dislocated DP that contains the relative clause ((168a)), or a null pro ((168b)) (though a demonstrative, itself clitic left dislocated, can resume the correlative relative when this is a hanging topic, as in (168c)):

(168)   a.   **Qualunque promessa** lui potrà farti, non prender**la** sul serio
             whatever promise he will.be.able.to make to you, not take it seriously
             'Whatever promise he may make to you, do not take it seriously.'
        b.   **Chi fa cose del genere**, credo Ø non debba essere seguito
             who does such things, I.think not has to be followed
             'I do not think that one should follow someone who does such things.'
        c.   **Chi ti ha appena telefonato, quello lì,** proprio non **lo** sopporto
             Who to you has just phoned, that there really not him I.can.stand
             the one who just called you, that one really I cannot stand

From this perspective, the impossibility of stacking correlatives (Dayal 1996: 175–7; Grosu & Landman 1998: 165; McCawley 2004: §5; Butt, Holloway King & Roth 2007: §2) should be limited to those containing a left dislocated 'Headless' (Free) relative (as 'Headless' (Free) relatives are also known not to be able to stack – see Carlson 1977).[191] It should not extend to those

---

[191] Stacking of correlatives is claimed to be possible in some Indo-Aryan languages: Konkani (Almeida 1989: 304 – see (i)a), and Bhojpuri (Shukla 1981: ch. 19: §4, p. 206 – see (i)b):

(i) a. jo   a:j   aila, ja-ka   g^{h}or na, jace   poise sãdlyat, tya mons-ak pedru adar dita.
       who today come, who-dat house not, whose money lost,   that man-dat Peter help gives
       'Peter helps the man who has come today, who has no home and whose money is lost.'
    b. ham jaon p^{h}al pa:k-i:,   jaon   tu: bec-ba: taon   k^{h}a:-b
       I which fruit   ripe-3sg.m.fut, which you sell-2sg.m.fut that   eat-1sg.fut
       'I will eat that fruit, which will ripen, which you will sell.'

correlatives that contain a left dislocated externally headed (pre- or post-nominal) relative clause, or an internally headed one whose Head has not moved, all of which are known to be able to stack. In §2.6.2 I am actually suggesting that all major types of relative clauses can be left dislocated, and thus enter the correlative construction. To reserve the term 'correlative' just to left dislocated 'Headless' (Free) RCs seems, from this point of view, arbitrarily limiting. Equally arbitrarily limiting is any analysis that takes 'correlatives' to occur necessarily in sentence initial position, preceding the 'resumptive' phrase in the matrix clause (Lehmann 1986: §2.2). In a number of languages 'correlative' clauses can also appear after the matrix clause. See the cases of the Tibeto-Burman language Bhujel in (169a) (from Regmi 2012: 66), of Eastern Armenian in (169b) (from Hodgson 2018: 6), of the Uralic language Meadow Mari in (169c) (from Shagal forthcoming, ex. (5a)), and of the Western Mande language Mandingo in (169d) (from Dramé 1981: 125):[192]

(169) a. **dyo   mayo** gruti muna   [**gau   mayo** kak^h-haŋ   mulak-na]
        that child sick   stay-NPST   **which child** lap-LOC   sit-NPST
        'The child who is sitting in the lap is sick.'

   b. **Ayn   guynov**   kmeŕnem,   [**inč' guynov**   vor   tsnvel   em]
      DEM3 colour.INSTR FUT.die.1SG, **what colour.INSTR** COMP   be.born.PART be.1SG.PRES
      'I will die with the colour I was born with.'

   c. **Məj tud-əm** əšt-em,   [**mo-m**   ere   šon-en   košt-ən-am]
      I that-ACC do-PRS.1SG, **what-ACC** always dream-CVB   go-PRT-1SG
      'I did what I always dreamt about.'

   d. Táálíboo   ye   **keó**   je,   [**keó   miŋ**   ye   kában   dii   Baabá la]
      student-SP TA   **man-SP** see, **man-SP which** TA   bottle give   B.to
      'The student saw the man who gave the bottle to B.'

This is not surprising if 'correlatives' in sentence initial position are left dislocated DPs containing a RC, since DPs (containing a RC) can also be right dislocated.

2.6.2   Simple Correlatives as a Non-independent Relative Clause Type

It is often assumed, in both the typological and the generative literature, that correlatives are an entirely separate type of RC, but if they are DPs (containing a

---

Also see Davison (2009: §2.2.5) for the apparent possibility of stacking in Sanskrit correlatives. However, given that the impossibility of stacking seems to be a general property of RCs involving 'raising' of the internal Head ('Headless' RCs, correlatives with a left peripheral 'Headless' RC, etc. – Carlson 1977; Grosu 2002), one should determine whether such cases truly involve stacking rather than simple asyndetic coordination (see McCawley 2004: 306). Also see the discussion in Vai (2018: ch. 6).

[192] Correlative RCs may also follow the main clause in the Western Mande language Kakabe. See Vydrina (2017: 157).

relative clause) in TopP, resumed by a coindexed resumptive DP in the matrix IP, then one should expect them to be just a particular manifestation of Externally Headed post-nominal, Externally Headed pre-nominal, Internally Headed, double-Headed, and 'Headless' RCs, not an independent, sixth, type.[193]

This indeed seems to be the case as the 'left dislocated' DP can contain, depending on the language, any of the other types of relatives. We have already seen that it can contain an externally headed postnominal relative clause (see (158)), or a 'Headless' relative clause (see (156) and the Bulgarian, German, and Italian examples given above). It can also contain an Externally Headed pre-nominal RC resumed by a coindexed phrase in the matrix IP, as shown by the Sinhala (Indo-Aryan) example in (170):[194]

(170)   [ara [hitagena inna] gaenu lamaya], ee lamaya usa i
         that [standing being] woman child, that child tall is
         'That girl who is standing, that girl is tall.'

Finally, the 'left dislocated' DP can also contain a double-Headed RC, like the Hindi, Bundeli, Maithili and Bine in (160) and (161a–c) above, as well as an Internally Headed RC, as in the Wappo example (171a), in the Hopi Tewa example in (171b), in the Bribri example in (171c), or in the Mandingo example (171d):

(171) a. [?i   čhuya-ø   t'um-ta]   cephi   šoy'i-khi?   (Li & Thompson 1978: 108)[195]
          me   house-ACC   bought   it(nom.) burned down
          Lit.: I house bought, that one burned down (= 'the house I bought burned down')
      b. [he'i   sen   c'a:ndi   ě:bap'o   mánsu'+n]   'i   dokumq   (Gorbet 1977: 272)
          that   man   yesterday wine   3>3-drink DS 3sg   1>3-bought
          'I bought the wine which that man drank yesterday.'

---

[193] More precisely, not an independent fifth type, given that as shown in §2.5 'Headless' RCs are also not an independent RC type.

[194] I owe this example to Lalith Ananda (pers. comm.). The phonetic transcription follows the one utilized in Ananda (2008).

Sinhala is generally reported (Bhatt 2003: 491; Leung 2007c; Lipták 2009a: 10) as not having correlatives (as it does not have 'Headless' RCs nor embedded post-nominal RCs with relative pronouns). But, if correlatives are not limited to left dislocated 'Headless' RCs, this is strictly speaking not true.

Languages with both correlatives and pre-nominal RCs have also been claimed (Downing 1978: 400) not to exist. But, in addition to the case of Sinhala, Dravidian languages and the language isolate Burushaski have both correlatives and pre-nominal RCs, even though, unlike Sinhala, for correlatives they utilize a 'Headless' RC (containing an interrogative adjective/ pronoun) resumed by a correlative proform (see Lakshmi Bai 1985 for Dravidian, and Tiffou & Patry 1995 for Burushaski).

[195] Wappo (a Californian language whose genetic affiliation is unclear – Thompson, Park & Li 2006: xi) also has Free relatives resumed by a demonstrative correlative pronoun:

c. [Be' tö ù sú] ye' tö ù e' yö'.[196]
  [You ERG house.ABS see-PRF] I ERG house.ABS DEM build-PRF
  'I built the house that you saw.'

d. [Suŋólu ye lííbúroo miŋ suuñaa, Íssáá ye a je (Dramé 1981: 121)[197]
  thieves TA book-SP which steal, I. TA it see
  'Íssáá saw the book that the thieves stole.'

2.6.3 Multiple Correlatives as Non-relative, Free Adjunct Free CPs

In addition to the possibility for simple, but not for multiple, correlatives to alternate with Externally Headed post-nominal relatives, there is further evidence that one should distinguish between two separate constructions: one, a left-peripheral DP (containing a relative CP), adjoined in some languages to the resumptive correlative DP, which it can strand in its movement to the left-periphery of the matrix IP (as shown in (172a with English glosses)); and another, a necessarily base-generated CP, containing one or more *wh*-phrases, paired in the matrix IP with corresponding correlative anaphoric DPs, as in (172b, exemplified again with English glosses) (see Izvorski 2000):[198]

(i) [te **ita** čo?-me] **cew** ah te-k'a čo:-si?
   (Thompson, Park & Li 2006: 123)
  3SG where go-DUR:DEP there 1SG:NOM 3SG–COM go-FUT
  'I'll go wherever s/he goes.'

Thompson, Park & Li (2006) say that '[t]he demonstrative pronoun seems to be required when it is *cephi*, the nominative form, but optional when it is *ce*, the accusative form' (p. 116). Also see Keenan (1985: 165).

[196] From Coto-Solano, Molina-Muñoz & García Segura (2016: 34). Also see Villalobos (1994).

[197] Bambara (another Western Mande language) has both left peripheral Internally Headed RCs resumed by an anaphoric phrase/pronoun (i.e. correlatives), or Internally Headed RCs in argument position, as in (i), below (in both cases the internal Head is marked by a following modifier, *mi(n)*). It also has Externally Headed post-nominal (preferably extraposed) RCs (Bird 1968, Fachner 1986, Zribi-Hertz & Hanne 1995).

(i) Tyɛ ` be n ye so min ye dyo (Bird 1968: 46)
  man the PRES [I PAST house wh see] erect
  'The man is building the house that I saw.'

In the Kita Maninka dialect extraposition is apparently obligatory (Bird 1968: 40).

[198] Multiple correlatives are also marginally possible in a number of European languages. See the English case in (i)a and the Italian case in (i)b:

(i) a. You can be sure that whichever girl you envy for whatever reason, that girl is envying someone else (for some other reason).

  b. Qualunque cosa tu abbia a dire a chiunque altro di loro, sono sicuro che quella cosa non lo toccherà.
    'Whatever thing you may say to whoever else of them, I am sure that that thing will not affect him.'

(172)   a.   Ram, which CD is on sale, that CD bought

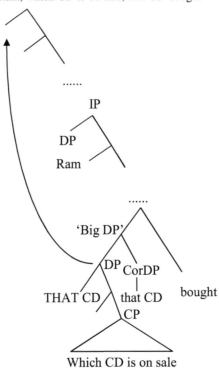

b.   which girl which CD heard, that girl that CD bought

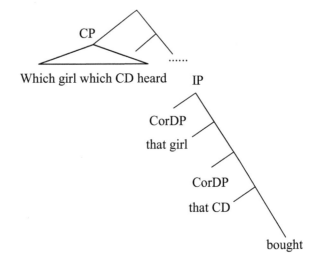

As shown most extensively in Bhatt (2003, 2005) for Hindi, this dual analysis receives support from the fact that in simple, but not in multiple, correlatives the relation between the relative clause and the correlative pronoun is sensitive to islands (also see Dayal 1996: 183; Mahajan 2000: fn. 10); and from the fact that in simple, but not in multiple, correlatives there is obligatory reconstruction of the fronted relative clause, as evidenced by pronominal binding facts and Principle C violations. For exemplification, see Bhatt (2003: §3.3.3), and Bhatt (2005).[199]

---

[199] Anderson (2005) makes the interesting observation that Nepali shows a semantic distinction between the two structures (172a) and (172b). The former is associated with a specific interpretation, the latter with an indefinite (free choice) interpretation. The evidence for this comes from the fact that when the correlative is in absolute initial position both interpretations are available while only one, the specific interpretation, is possible when the correlative is adjacent to the correlative pronoun. See (i)a and b:

(i) a. jun manche-lai bhok lag-eko cha, ma us-lai khana din-chu   (= Anderson's 2005: ex. (15))
        REL man-DAT hunger attach-PFPT 3SG.PR, 1SG.NOM 3SG.DAT food give-1SG.PR
        either: 'I will give food to the man who is hungry.' (specific man)
        or: 'I will give food to any man who is hungry.' (any hungry man)
    b. ma jun manche-lai bhok lag-eko cha, tyo manche-lai khana din-chu(= Anderson's 2005: ex. (16))
        1SG.NOM REL man-DAT hunger attach-PFPT 3SG.PR, DEM man-DAT food give-1SG.PR
        'I will give food to the man who is hungry.' (specific man)

This makes sense, according to Anderson (2005), if the initial position can either be filled by movement of the correlative relative from the internal position adjacent to the correlative DP (which gives the specific interpretation) or by base generating the simple correlative CP (like multiple correlatives) in initial position (which gives the free choice interpretation). It remains to be seen whether this holds of other Indo-Aryan languages as well. Dayal (1996: ch. 6: §2) suggests that multiple correlatives in Hindi have a functional reading, which apparently 'can also be used to refer to a unique pair of individuals in the contextual domain' (p. 204).

Additionally, it should be observed that if simple correlatives can also access the base-generated structure of multiple correlatives, they would be expected to show no necessary island sensitivity nor obligatory reconstruction. The facts here are contradictory. While Mahajan (2000: 227 fn. 10) and Bhatt (2003, 2005) claim that the correlative pronoun cannot be found within an island (see (ii)), McCawley (2004) gives one case of a correlative pronoun within a relative clause complex NP island judged possible by his informants (his orthography has been uniformized to the one used here after that of Mahajan and Bhatt). See (iii):

(ii)   *[jo si:ta:-ko acha: lagta: hɛ] mɛ [$_{DP}$ yah ba:t [$_{CP}$ki vo a:dmi: pa:gal hɛ]]
         (= (ii) of fn. 10 of Mahajan 2000)
         who Sita-DAT nice seem be-PRES I this fact that that man crazy be-PRES know be-PRES
         'I know the fact that the man who Sita likes is crazy.'
(iii)   [jo laRkii vaha khaRii hai], ram ne vo paRha, jo us ne likha
         which girl there standing is, Ram read the letter that she wrote

Further investigation is needed here, also in relation to the apparent possibility of extracting from correlatives (and *if* clauses) vs the impossibility of extracting from embedded postnominal and extraposed relatives reported in Dwivedi (1994a, 1994b). Perhaps extraction is possible from the adjunct CP correlative but not from the DP correlative.

A further difference between multiple and simple correlatives is represented by the possibility of omitting the correlative pronouns when the relative phrases have overt Case. As noted in Bhatt (1997), who attributes the observation to Veneeta Dayal, this is possible in multiple correlatives ((173)) but not in simple correlatives ((174)) (also see Bhatt 2003: §4):

(173) [jis$_i$ ne   jo$_j$ chahaa] (us$_i$ ne   vo$_j$)   kiyaa (= (24) of Bhatt 1997: 64)
REL.obl ERG REL want.Pfv DEM.obl ERG DEM do.Pfv
whoever whatever wanted, they did that

(174) [jis   laRkii=ko Srini pasand hai]   *(vo) khaRii   hai (=(9)b of Bhatt 1997: 57)
REL.obl girl=DAT S.   like   be.PRES DEM standing be.PRES
'The girl who likes Srini is standing.'

For further differences between simple and multiple correlatives, see Srivastav (1991b: §4.4).

That simple and multiple correlatives should not be treated as a homogeneous construction is also shown by the fact that not all languages having correlatives allow for multiple correlatives: for example neither Bambara, as reported in Pollard & Sag (1994: 229 fn. 10), nor Basque, as reported in Rebuschi (1999: 59), allow them.

2.6.4   *Correlatives as a Non-exclusive Relativization Strategy*

To judge from the substantive lists of languages with correlatives given in De Vries (2002: 388 and 412), Bhatt (2003: 491), and Lipták (2009a: 10–11) it seems that there may be no single language for which correlatives are the only relativization strategy available. Correlatives invariably appear to co-occur either with embedded post-nominal or extraposed relatives (most Indo-Aryan languages, Slavic languages, Warlpiri, etc.), or with pre-nominal non-finite relatives (Dravidian languages, Sinhala, etc.), or with Internally Headed RCs (Bambara, Wappo, etc.), or with double-Headed RCs (Hindi, Bundeli and Maithili). From what I have been able to gather from the literature, no language is described as having correlatives as its only type of relative clause.[200]

---

[200] Actually, Creissels (2009: 43) states that '[l]e malinké n'a pas de relatives adnominales: les seules relatives du malinké sont les relatives correlatives [...].' ['Malinke has no adnominal relatives: the only relatives of Malinke are correlative relatives'], but, as he makes clear, the correlatives of Malinké are left dislocated Internally Headed relatives, which in contrast to the closely related languages Bambara (see fn. 197 above) and Mandingo (Bokamba & Dramé 1978), appear not to be able to occur in argument position (Creissels 2009: 51). Also see the case of Kita Maninka cited in Bird (1968: 40 ff). This, if true, remains to be better understood.

This fact (assuming it to be a fact) should actually not be surprising if one thinks that simple correlatives (setting multiple correlatives aside, which are no relative clauses) are just left dislocated DPs containing a relative clause of one or another of the existing types (Externally Headed post-nominal, Externally Headed pre-nominal, Internally Headed, double-Headed, and 'Headless') resumed by an anaphoric DP in the matrix clause.[201]

2.6.5   Correlatives in Head-Final and Head-Initial Languages

Unlike what was originally thought to be the case, namely that correlatives are only found in (non-rigid) head-final languages (Downing 1973, 1978: 400; Keenan 1985: 164–5), the existence of correlative RCs has since been documented in both rigid head-final languages (e.g. Dravidian languages, Yukaghir, etc.), in non-rigid head-final languages (Indo-Aryan languages, Tibeto-Burman, languages, etc.) and rigid and non-rigid head-initial languages (e.g., Formosan and Slavic languages).

2.6.6   The DP, Rather than the Bare CP, Nature of the 'Correlative Relative'

The Hindi, Bundeli, Maithili and Bine examples in (160) and (161) and the Marathi example in (i) of fn. 186 above show that correlative relatives can be DPs (in a left dislocated position). I have in fact suggested that all correlative relatives (excluding multiple headed ones) are DPs which contain an external Head modified by a RC containing a corresponding internal Head. As noted this analysis runs counter to some classic and recent analyses of correlatives that view them as bare CPs, which are taken to act as generalized quantifiers binding the correlate as a variable (e.g. Dayal 1996). But this is an extension of the usual notion of 'generalized quantifier', which typically applies to noun phrases ('all XP', 'some XP', 'most XP', 'at least five XP' – see Barwise & Cooper 1981: §1.3). If anything one would expect the correlate to be bound as a variable by a quantified noun phrase. The DP analysis assumed here (something like: $[_{DP}$ THAT THING $[_{CP}$ which thing ...]] that THING ...) can thus be taken to be a more appropriate case of binding of the correlate by a generalized quantifier.

De Vries (2002: 40) advances the following generalizations as arguments for the non-DP status of correlatives:

(175)   a.   Correlatives do not occur in DP positions.
         b.   Correlatives never have an external determiner.
         c.   Correlatives never have an external Case ending or another nominal marking.
         d.   Correlatives never have an external (affixed) adposition.

---

[201] On non-restrictive correlatives see §3.1.6.6, *pace* De Vries (2002: 29 fn. 28).

However, they do not seem cogent.

Concerning (175a), if correlative relative clauses are typically left dislocated constructions resumed by a correlate in the matrix clause it is to be expected that they typically do not occur in argument DP positions within the matrix clause. But even this is not always the case. Bhatt (2003: §3.2.1) argues that the ultimate left-peripheral position of the correlative relative in Hindi is due to its movement from a matrix clause internal position adjoined to the correlate demonstrative with which it makes a 'big DP', offering examples like the following, where the correlative relative can in fact remain in a matrix clause DP argument position:

(176)   Rahul a:jkal [DP[DP [jo kita:b Saira-ne likh-i:] vo] aur [DP [jo cartoon Shyam-ne bana:-ya:] vo]] parh raha: hai
Rahul nowadays [[Rel book.F S.-Erg write-Pfv.F] Dem] and [[Rel cartoon S.-Erg make-Pfv] Dem]] read Prog be.PRES
'Nowadays, Rahul is reading the book that Saira wrote and the cartoon that Shyam made.'
(Lit.: 'Rahul nowadays [[which book Saira wrote] that (book) and [[which cartoon Shyam made] that (cartoon) reading is')

A similar situation is found in Punjabi (see Bhatia 1993: 58).

Nikitina (2012) argues that the Southeastern Mande construction in (177) (from Wan) 'qualifies for a special case of a correlative construction with a correlative clause embedded inside the main clause' (p. 324) (rather than on its periphery), owing to the properties that it shares with ordinary (maximalizing) correlatives, including the possibility of fronting to the left periphery of the matrix clause:

(177)   gà   màŋ yā   [kó   yī   lē   è   plá] à   lέŋ
go   rice with   [1+2DU slept   woman DEF   at] 3sg   to
'Take some rice to the woman at whose place we slept.'
(Lit.: go with rice – we slept at the woman's place – to her)

She connects this possibility to a clause internal extraposition found in Southeastern Mande languages.

As for (175b), it does not seem to be always true. See, for example, (178), from Itzaj Maya (Hofling 2000):

(178)   I   a' tu'ux xu'l-ij u-telchaak-il-ej te' t-in-yul-aj-i'ij   (Hofling 2000: 480)
and DET where end-3sg.B 3A-buttress-POS-TOP LOC COM-1sg.A-trim-CTS-LOC
'And the (place) where the buttress ended, there I trimmed it.'

Concerning (175c), see perhaps the case of the Austronesian (Formosan) language Isbukun Bunun ((179)), where the correlative is followed by a TOP nominal marking.

(179) Na [$_{PP}$ ku-[isa kasu]] (**hai**), na ku-isa amin saikin[202] (Isbukun Bunun – Wu 2016: 198)
Fut to-where 2sg.NOM (**Top**), Fut to-where also 1sg.NOM
'I will go wherever you go.' (Lit: to where you will go, to where I also will go)

Finally, (175d) appears to be contradicted by the possibility of having the correlative relative preceded by a preposition in Italian ((180)), which clearly points to the DP-status of the correlative:[203]

(180) a. [$_{PP}$ Da [$_{DP}$ [$_{CP}$ chi inviteranno]]], da lui o da lei capiremo cosa vogliono.
from whom they'll invite, from him or from her we'll understand what they want

I thus conclude that the DP status of correlative relatives is confirmed.

2.7   Adjoined Relative Clauses

The term 'adjoined relative clause' has become part of the classification of relative clauses since Hale's (1976) classical study of Warlpiri relatives.[204]

As noted in Chapter 1: fn. 1, Keenan (1985: 165), Dayal (1996: 152), Bhatt (2003: 491), and Nordlinger (2006: §1) analyse them as correlative RCs (also see Andrews 1975: §1.1.3; 2007: §1.3). While this is clearly the case for examples like (181a), where an externally headed post-nominal RC in left dislocated position is resumed by a (fronted) anaphoric DP in the main clause, and plausibly for examples like (181b), with a possibly silent anaphoric DP in the main clause, examples like (182) appear rather to be cases of RC Extraposition of an Externally Headed post-nominal RC:

(181) a. **yankiri-li kutja-lpa**   ŋapa ŋa-nu,   ŋula   ø-na pantu-nu ŋatjulu-lu (Hale 1976: 79)
emu-erg   COMP-AUX water drink-past, that.one AUX spear-past I-erg
the emu which was drinking water, that one I speared/while the emu was drinking water, then I speared it

       b. **yankiri-li kutja-lpa**   ŋapa ŋa-nu,   ŋatjulu-lu ø-na pantu-nu   (Hale 1976: 78)
emu-erg   COMP-AUX water drink-past, I-erg   AUX spear-past
'The emu which was drinking water, I speared it/While the emu was drinking water, I speared it.'

(182) ŋatjulu-lu ø-na **yankiri** pantu-nu, **kutja-lpa**   ŋapa ŋa-nu   (Hale 1976: 78)
I-erg   AUX   emu   spear-past, COMP-AUX water drink-past
'I speared the emu which was/while it was drinking water.'

---

[202] The correlate in Isbukun Bunun can also be a *wh* (Wu 2016: 198).

[203] Note that the preposition *da* in Italian cannot take a CP complement (see Cinque 1990: 35).

[204] Since then the same construction has been documented in several other Australian languages. See for example Austin (1981: 210) on Diyari; Bowern (2012: §7.2) on Bardi; Meakins & Nordlinger (2014: ch. 9) on Bilinarra; and Nordlinger (2006: §2) for references to other Australian languages.

The ambiguity between an ordinary RC and a 'while/when' adverbial clause in some of the cases, like those in (181) and (182), should not be overstated. Hale is careful in observing that when the main and subordinate clauses share an argument while making distinct temporal references only the relative clause interpretation is available. See (183) (only when the two clauses 'share an identical argument' and 'make identical time reference' does the ambiguity arise – Hale 1976: 79):

(183)   ŋatjulu-lu kapi-na **wawiri** pura-mi, **kutja-npa** pantu-nu njuntulu-lu.   (Hale 1976: 79)
         I-erg AUX kangaroo cook-nonpast, COMP-AUX spear-past you-erg
         'I will cook the kangaroo you speared.'

Also note that under exactly the same conditions, the same ambiguity or non-ambiguity is found in Italian with the general subordinator *che*, which introduces RCs and a number of other adverbial subordinate clauses. See, for example (184):

(184)   a.   Hanno filmato l'emu (ieri) che stava ancora dormendo
               They.have filmed the emu (yesterday) that it was still sleeping
               'They filmed the emu (yesterday) which was still sleeping/while it was still sleeping.'
         b.   Filmeranno l'emu (domani) che stava ancora dormendo
               They.will.film the emu (tomorrow) that was still sleeping
               'They will film the emu (tomorrow) which was still sleeping/*while it was still sleeping.'

This does not mean that the RC and the 'while' adverbial clause are syntactically the same in Italian (and analogously perhaps in Warlpiri – see Nordlinger 2006 on Wambaya). Clear evidence exists in Italian that they are structurally different, one piece of evidence being the fact that the DP preceding the clause is a non-extractable RC Head in one case (*Lo_i filmeranno (domani) t_i che stava ancora dormendo* – see *filmeranno (domani) l'emu che stava ancora dormendo*) but forms no constituent with the adverbial clause in the other, thus being extractable (*Lo_i hanno filmato (ieri) t_i [che stava ancora dormendo]*, which has only the adverbial clause reading 'They filmed it (yesterday) while it was still sleeping.'[205]

There is thus no reason to think that Warlpiri lacks a relative clause construction per se, *pace* Keenan (1985: 166), or that the 'adjoined RC' constitutes an entirely separate type of RC. It appears to be an externally headed post-nominal RC though it apparently occurs only in peripheral positions – either to the left, in a correlative configuration, or to the right, in extraposed position.

---

[205] It is thus doubtful that the relative and the adverbial readings should be unified (as in Larson 2016).

3 Deriving the Other Types of Relative Clauses from a Double-Headed Structure

3.1 Finite Non-restrictive Relative Clauses[*]

Finite non-restrictive RCs are usually conceived of as a unitary type of relative clause (semantically and syntactically opposed to both restrictive and 'amount' RCs).

In the literature, they have been analysed either as a sentence grammar phenomenon, specifically as clauses internal to the nominal projection that contains the Head, like restrictive and amount RCs (see, among others, Smith 1964, Kuroda 1968, Jackendoff 1977: ch. 7; Huot 1978; Perzanowski 1980; Cornilescu 1981; Kayne 1994: ch. 8; Bianchi 1999: ch. 5; Potts 2002; Kempson 2003; Arnold 2007), or as a discourse grammar phenomenon, i.e., as sentences generated independently of the sentence containing the Head, whose pronouns relate to the Head much like (E-type) pronouns/demonstratives relate to an antecedent across discourse[1] (see, for instance, Ross 1967, 434 ff; Aissen 1972; Taglicht 1972; Thorne 1988; Emonds 1979; Stuurman 1983; Sells 1985; Haegeman 1988; Fabb 1990; Demirdache 1991; Espinal 1991; McCawley 1998: 446 ff; Peterson 2004; Grosu 2005, Authier & Reed 2005: §3; Del Gobbo 2007; Erlewine & Kotek 2015a, 2015b).[2]

---

[*] Parts of this section draw from Cinque (2008a), an earlier version of which appeared as 2006a. I thank Paola Benincà, Valentina Bianchi, Patricia Cabredo Hofherr, Francesca Del Gobbo, Alexander Grosu, Richard Kayne, and Tong Wu for their helpful comments on those previous versions.
[1] Authier and Reed (2005) actually note that 'the subclass of QPs that can serve as heads of [non-restrictive] RCs is the same as the subclass that can serve as antecedents for E-type pronouns' (p. 639), namely *some, many, a few*, etc. but not *every, any* or *no*.
[2] This distinction roughly corresponds to what Emonds (1979: 212) calls the Subordinate Clause Hypothesis and the Main Clause Hypothesis, the one he defends. I abstract away here from the different executions that these two hypotheses have received in the literature, and from those analyses, like those of Safir (1986), Demirdache (1991: ch. 3), and Del Gobbo (2003, 2007, 2010, 2017) that combine the two. For recent overviews, see De Vries (2002: ch. 6; 2006) and Griffiths (2015: ch. 6).

In Cinque (2008a) I suggested that these two analyses should not be seen as competing analyses for a single construction, but as complementary analyses for two distinct non-restrictive constructions; what I called there the integrated and non-integrated non-restrictives. Some languages (including Italian and other Romance languages) display both. Other languages display only one. As argued in §3.1.4.2 below, languages with pre-nominal RCs have just the sentence-grammar, integrated, construction (for principled reasons); others (like English, Romanian, and Polish – Cinque 2008a, Citko 2016) have only the discourse-grammar, non-integrated construction (*pace* Potts 2005 and Arnold 2007). Still others appear to lack non-restrictives entirely, resorting to other strategies.

In what follows, I first review the evidence (in §3.1.1) for distinguishing two types of non-restrictives in Italian, by examining a number of syntactic properties which differentiate the two (the integrated one introduced by the invariant relativizer *che* and the relative pronoun *cui*, and the non-integrated one introduced by the art + *qual-* relative paradigm). To give a preview of the main properties of each type, those characterizing the non-integrated one will appear to have:

(1)   a.   illocutionary independence;
      b.   the possibility of occurring across discourse (and also across different speakers);
      c.   the possibility of split antecedents;
      d.   the possible full retention of the internal Head;
      e.   the possible non-identity of the external and the internal Heads;
      f.   the possibility of a Head other than DP;
      g.   no licensing of parasitic gaps;
      h.   no reflexive antecedents;
      i.   possible coordination of the *wh*-phrase with another DP;
      l.   heavy pied-piping (with certain restrictions).

Those characterizing the integrated type will instead appear to have the following (virtually opposite) properties, syntactically non-distinct from those of restrictive RCs (except for the different height of merger – see §3.5 below – and other, minor, differences):

(2)   a.   no illocutionary independence (only declarative force possible);
      b.   no occurrence across discourse (and different speakers);
      c.   (ordinarily) no split antecedents possible (but see §5.1);
      d.   no full retention of the internal Head;
      e   impossible non-identity of the external and internal Heads;
      f.   Head other than DP impossible;
      g.   parasitic gaps possible;

    h.   possible reflexive antecedents;
    i.   no possible coordination of the *wh*-pronoun with another DP;
    l.   pied-piping limited to functional PPs.[3]

I will then consider English, whose non-restrictives will be seen to systematically pattern with the non-integrated art. + *qual-* non-restrictives of Italian (see §3.1.2).[4]

    One general consequence of the analysis (if correct) is that the properties which have been attributed to the non-restrictive construction, because of the earlier focus on English, turn out to be representative only of the non-integrated type. Conversely, the high Merge position of non-restrictives in the extended projection of the NP containing the Head mentioned in §3.5 below is characteristic only of the integrated type (the non-integrated one being outside of the sentence containing the Head). In §3.1.3 an antisymmetric analysis of the two types of non-restrictives will be suggested, even though both will be argued to lack the 'raising' derivation. §3.1.4 will conclude with some comparative remarks.

3.1.1   Differences between the Integrated che/cui *and the*   Non-integrated art. + quale *Non-restrictives of Italian*[*]

Illocutionary Independence

Il quale non-restrictives can be of a different illocutionary type (declarative, interrogative, or imperative) from that of the matrix, while *che/cui*

---

[3] For additional syntactic differences between the two types, and for properties which instead they share, I refer to Cinque (2008a: §2 and §3). Also see Schlenker (2009) for the claim that (in French) even integrated non-restrictives can have matrix scope, as well as Schlenker (2013, 2017). Del Gobbo (2015) proposes a further distinction in the class of integrated non-restrictives between what she calls (fully) integrated non-restrictives (in languages like Chinese) and semi-integrated ones in languages like Italian, which displays the same properties as Chinese except apparently for the binding of a pronominal inside the non-restrictive. This however appears dubious as some such binding cases do seem possible in Italian (see (i)), and even in the English non-integrated construction, as noted in Lin & Tsai (2015: §2.1.1), who report Constant's (2011, §3.1.3) observation that Del Gobbo's examples are examples of what Fox (2000) refers to as 'telescoping illusory binding' (see (ii)), unavailable in both English and Chinese with downward entailing quantifiers.

    (i)   Ogni studente$_i$ si dimostrò grato al suo$_i$ professore, che lo$_i$ aveva aiutato in più di un'occasione
        'Every student showed gratitude to his professor, who had helped him in more than one occasion.'
    (ii)   Each contestant$_i$ was asked ten questions about his$_i$ wife, who had to sit behind the screen and couldn't help him$_i$.

[4] See Truswell (2012) for a possible refinement concerning the non-adjacency property.

[*] The c. examples of this section contain *che/cui* restrictives, with which, as noted, the *che/cui* non-restrictives pattern. For some of the syntactic properties of the Italian *che/cui* and art. + *qual-* pronouns, see Cinque (1978, 1982, 2008b) and, more briefly here, §2.1.2.1.1. Henceforth '*il quale*' will stand for the entire art. + *qual-* paradigm.

non-restrictives, like restrictives, can only be declarative (irrespective of the illocutionary force of the matrix clause), See the contrasts in (3) and (4):[5]

(3) a. L'unico che potrebbe è tuo padre, **il quale** potrà, credi, perdonarci per quello che abbiamo fatto?
the only one who could is your father, by whom will we ever be forgiven, you think, for what we have done?

   b. *?L'unico che potrebbe è tuo padre, **che** potrà, credi, perdonarci per quello che abbiamo fatto?
the only one who could is your father, whom (lit. that) will ever forgive us, you think, for what we have done?

   c. *Questa è la sola persona **che** potrà, credi, perdonarci per quello che abbiamo fatto? (restrictive)
this is the only person that will he ever manage to forgive us, you think, for what we have done?

(4) a. Ci sono poi i Rossi, **per i quali**, ti prego, cerca di trovare una sistemazione!
there are then the Rs, for whom please try to find an accommodation!

   b. *Ci sono poi i Rossi, **per cui**, ti prego, cerca di trovare una sistemazione!
there are then the Rs, for whom, please, try to find an accommodation!

   c. *Sono loro le sole persone **per cui** cerca di trovare una sistemazione! (restrictive)
it's them the only people for whom please try to find an accommodation!

---

[5] For similar cases in French, see Muller (2006: 328–9):

(i) a. Il n'est pas sûr qu'il vienne à l'heure, auquel cas voulez-vous l'attendre?
'It is not certain that he will come on time, in which case would you like to wait for him?'

   b. Il n'est pas sûr qu'il vienne à l'heure, auquel cas ne l'attendez pas!
'It is not certain that he will come on time, in which case don't wait for him!'

Also see (ii), from Del Gobbo (2017: 26), citing Bernard Tranel (pers. comm.):

(ii) Ton père, lequel/*qui nous pardonnera-t-il jamais?, est un grand homme
your father, the.which/that us forgive.FUT-t-he ever?, is a great man
your father, who will he ever forgive us?, is a great man

Note that the matrix need not be declarative when the non-restrictive is non-declarative. In (iii) the main clause and the non-restrictive RC are both interrogative:

(iii) (?) Sarebbe stato tuo padre, **al quale** potremo mai rivolgerci ora per aiuto?, ben disposto nei nostri confronti?
would your father, to whom will we ever be able to refer now for help?, have been well disposed towards us?

Occurrence across Discourse and Also across Different Speakers

Il quale-non-restrictives can belong to a separate sentence (and also to a separate speaker) in the discourse, unlike *che/cui*-non-restrictives (and restrictives), which cannot. See (5) and (6):[6]

(5)   a.   **A**: Ha difeso la sua tesi contro tutti. **B: La quale** sosteneva la necessità del non intervento
        He defended his thesis against everyone. Which asserted the need for non-intervention.

    b.   **A**: Ha difeso la sua tesi contro tutti. **B**: *?**Che** sosteneva la necessità del non intervento.
        He defended his thesis against almost everyone. That asserted the need for non-intervention.

    c.   **A:** *Ha difeso la sua tesi contro tutti **B: che** sosteneva la necessità del non intervento.(restrictive)
        'He defended his thesis against everyone that asserted the need for non-intervention.'

(6)   a.   **A:** Non ho mai parlato dei miei parenti$_j$ a Clara$_i$. **B: Ai quali$_j$** d'altronde non serve alcuna presentazione.
        I never talked about my relatives to C. For whom in any event no introduction is necessary.

    b.   **A:** Non ho mai parlato dei miei parenti$_i$ a Clara$_i$. **B:** *A cui$_j$ d'altronde non serve alcuna presentazione.
        I never talked about my relatives to C. For whom in any event no introduction is necessary.

    c.   **A:** *Non ho mai parlato dei miei parenti$_j$ a Clara$_i$ **B: a cui$_j$** non serve alcuna presentazione. (restrictive)
        'I never talked about my relatives to C. to whom no introduction is necessary.'

Split Antecedents

Il quale non-restrictives, but not *che/cui* non-restrictives (and restrictives), can have split antecedents. See the contrasts in (7) (adapted from Cinque 1988: 450) and (8):[7]

---

[6] See Cinque (1978: 79–80). For similar examples of non-adjacency in French with *lequel*, see Gross (1977: 136) and Fuchs & Milner (1979: 57), among others. These cases are called in the literature 'relatifs de liaison'. See, among others, Touratier (1980: 408 ff) and Bianchi (1999: 151–2).

[7] For similar cases in French see Del Gobbo (2017: 26). Also see Cardoso & De Vries's (2010: §7.7) example (i) in Dutch:

    (i)   Ik zwaaide naar Anna$_i$ en Jan zwaaide naar Marie$_k$, die$_{i+k}$ overigens dezelfde jurk aanhadden.
        I waved at Anna and Jan waved at Marie, who by.the.way the.same dress wore:PL
        'I waved at Anna, and Jan waved at Marie, who were wearing the same dress, by the way.'

(7)   a.   Se Carlo$_i$ non amava più Anna$_j$, **i quali**$_{i,j}$ d'altra parte non si erano mai voluti veramente bene, una ragione c'era.
if C. was no longer in love with A., who at any rate never really loved each other, there was a reason

        b.   *Se Carlo$_i$ non amava più Anna$_j$, **che**$_{i,j}$ d'altra parte non si erano mai voluti veramente bene, una ragione c'era.
if C. was no longer in love with A., that at any rate never really loved each other, there was a reason

        c.   *Se il ragazzo$_i$ non amava più la ragazza$_j$ **che**$_{i+j}$ si erano voluti bene, una ragione c'era. (restrictive)
if the boy no longer loved the girl that loved each other, there was a reason

(8)   a.   Se Piero$_i$ non si trova più tanto bene con Ida$_j$, **tra i quali**$_{i+j}$ d'altronde non c'è mai stata una vera amicizia, ... (Cinque 1981/82: 263)
if P. no longer gets along very well with I., between whom in any event there never was a real friendship, ...

        b.   *Se Piero$_i$ non si trova più tanto bene con Ida$_j$, **tra cui**$_{i+j}$ d'altronde non c'è mai stata una vera amicizia, ...
if P. no longer gets along very well with I., between whom in any event there never was a real friendship, ...

        c.   *Se il ragazzo non si trova più tanto bene con la ragazza **tra cui** non c'era stata una vera amicizia ... (restrictive)
if the boy no longer gets along very well with the girl between whom in any event there never was a real friendship, ...

Full Retention of the Internal Head

In more careful styles of Italian the internal Head, in spite of its identity with the 'external' one, can be retained in *il quale* non-restrictives, but not in *che/cui* non-restrictives (nor in *che/cui* restrictives):[8]

Their analysis, however, 'predict[s] that an appositive relative clause containing a split antecedent cannot be in the middle field, since having a split antecedent depends on an extraposition configuration'. This appears to be contradicted by an (Italian) example like the following:

(ii)   Io ho salutato Anna e Jan ha salutato Maria, le quali indossavano lo stesso vestito, proprio mentre stavano uscendo.
'I waved at Anna, and Jan waved at Maria, who were wearing the same dress, just as they were going out.'

[8] French *lequel* non-restrictives display the same property. They too can retain the internal Head. See for example Sandfeld (1936: 179), Huot (1978: 119), Touratier (1980: 159), Togeby (1982: 463), and Muller (2006: 325). Relativization of objects is quite marginal in non-restrictives, whether they retain the full internal Head or just the modifier *lequel* (Kayne 1976: 270), as was observed for the more marked restrictive construction with *lequel* (see Chapter 2: fn. 45).

(9) a. Se quel farmaco, **il quale farmaco** è il frutto di molti anni di lavoro, non
         è stato messo in commercio, una ragione ci dev'essere.
         if that medicine, which medicine is the result of many years' work, was
         non-commercialized, there must be a reason

     b. *Se quel farmaco, **che farmaco** è il frutto di molti anni di lavoro, non è
         stato messo in commercio, una ragione ci dev'essere.
         if that medicine, lit. that medicine is the result of many years' work, was
         non-commercialized, there must be a reason

(10) a. Giorgio riuscì a sposare quella ragazza. **Della quale ragazza**, devo dire,
          ero invaghito anch'io. (see Cinque 1988: 449)
          G. managed to marry that girl. Which girl, I must say, I was also in love with.

      b. Giorgio riuscì a sposare quella ragazza. *Di cui ragazza, devo dire, ero
          invaghito anch'io.

      c. *Giorgio riuscì a sposare quella ragazza di cui ragazza ero invaghito
          anch'io.

Non-identity of the External and Internal Heads

Il quale non-restrictives, as opposed to *che/cui* non-restrictives (and restrictives), do not require absolute identity of the internal and external Heads. See Cinque (1988: 449) (and Sandfeld 1936: 179; Kayne 1975: ch. 1 fn. 20; Touratier 1980: 174 for corresponding facts in French):

(11) a. Ha raggiunto la fama con *Il giardino dei Finzi-Contini*, **il quale
          romanzo** ha poi anche avuto una riduzione cinematografica.
          he became famous with *Il giardino dei Finzi-Contini*, which novel was
          then also made into a film

      b. All'appuntamento erano venuti quaranta studenti. **Il qual numero** non
          impressionò nessuno.
          To the rendezvous forty students had come. Which number impressed
          nobody.

The examples in (12) represents a different type of non-identity (where the external and the internal Heads differ in number features):[9]

(12) a. Prima che fosse terminata quella lunga lite, le quali alla corte di Roma
          non pare abbiano mai fine, ... (Cinque 1978: 81)

---

[9] Number mismatch is instead impossible in restrictive RCs (*La lunga lite alle quali abbiamo assistito* ... 'the long law-suit to which(pl.) we were witnesses ...'. Cases of gender mismatch like (i) may only be apparent if the relative pronoun actually agrees with a non-pronounced noun (*città* 'city', feminine; see *la città del Cairo* 'the city of Cairo' taking *Il Cairo* as its specifier (on non-pronunciation see Kayne 2005a, 2005b):

(i) Il Cairo, la quale/*il quale è la capitale dell'Egitto, ...
     Lit.: the (masc.) Cairo, the which (fem./*masc.) is the capital of Egypt, ...

> Before that long law-suit was ended, which(pl.) at the Rome justice
> court appear never to have an end, . . .

b.   Giorgio non era certo un romanziere, la prima virtù de**i quali** è quella di
       catturare l'interesse del lettore. (Cinque 2008a: §2.3.5)
       G. was no novelist (sing.), the first virtue of whom (pl.) is that of
       catching the reader's interest (see (28) below)

Possibility of a Head Other than DP

Il quale and *che/cui* non-restrictives also differ with respect to the categorial
nature of the antecedent that they can take. While *che/cui* non-restrictives (and
restrictives) only take nominal antecedents, *il quale* non-restrictives can take a
class of antecedents larger than DP, as shown in (13) to (15):[10]

(13)   a.   Carlo lavora troppo poco. **La qual cosa**   (**CP**) (Cinque 1988: 467)[11]
                verrà certamente notata.
                C. works too little. Which thing will certainly be noticed.
        b.   Carlo lavora troppo poco. *****Che** verrà certamente notato.
                C. works too little. That will certainly be observed.
        c.   Carlo lavora troppo poco. *****Di cui** si è reso conto anche il suo principale.[12]
                C. works too little. Which even his boss realized

---

[10] *Il quale* non-restrictives modifying a CP can precede the 'antecedent'. See (i):

(i)   E poi, la qual cosa verrà certamente notata, Carlo lavora troppo poco.
        And then, which thing will certainly be noticed, C. works too little.

For Latin and French comparable cases see Touratier (1980: 129, 135, respectively).

[11] In (13), (14), and (15) one can have, in addition to *la qual cosa*. Lit.: 'the which thing', *il che*.
Lit.: 'the that', and the pseudo-free relatives *cosa che* 'thing that' and *ciò che* 'that that'. Also
see Bianchi (1999: 151). On similar cases in French, see Canac Marquis & Tremblay (1998: 9),
also reported in Del Gobbo (2017: 27).

[12] *Cui*, when preceded by *per* 'for', appears to be able to resume a CP (e.g. *Lei si e' ammalata, per
cui ha dovuto smettere di fumare* 'She got ill, so that she had to quit smoking'). As *per* is the
only preposition that seems to permit such a usage in non-restrictives (see (i)) below, I am
inclined to interpret it as a fixed expression. This is confirmed by the fact that *per cui* is not
exactly synonymous with *per la qual cosa* 'for which thing', as apparent from (i)e:

(i)   a.   Se il governo vacilla, **alla qual cosa/*a cui** ho fatto riferimento anch'io, . . .
              if the government is shaky, to which I too have referred, . . .
        b.   Da quando la società è sull'orlo del fallimento, **con la qual cosa/*con cui**
              dovremo fare i conti tutti, . . .
              since the company is going bankrupt, with which all of us will have to deal, . . .
        c.   Il prezzo del petrolio è sceso, **dalla qual cosa/*da cui** tutti hanno tratto benefici.
              the oil price lowered, from which thing/from which everybody benefitted
        d.   Gianni un giorno si riprenderà, **nella qual cosa/*in cui** tutti confidano.
              One day Gianni will recover, on which thing/on which everyone is relying.
        e.   Gianni non ha pagato le tasse, **per la qual cosa** =/= **per cui** dovrà pagare una
              multa salata, . . .
              Gianni did not pay his taxes, for which thing/so that he will have to pay an
              expensive fine, . . .

(14)   a.   Maria è suscettibile. **La qual cosa** sua sorella di certo non è.   (**AP**)
            M. is touchy. Which thing her sister certainly is not.
       b.   Maria è suscettibile. *****Che** sua sorella di certo non è.
            M. is touchy. That her sister certainly is not.
       c.   Maria è suscettibile. *****Di cui** non si era resa conto neanche sua madre.
            M. is touchy. Which not even her mother realized.

(15)   a.   Maria interveniva sempre. La qual cosa faceva anche sua madre.   (**VP**)
            M. was always speaking up. Which her mother also used to do.
       b.   Maria interveniva sempre. *****Che faceva anche sua madre.
            M. was always speaking up. That her mother also used to do.
       c.   Maria interveniva sempre. *****Da cui sua madre si asteneva.
            M. was always speaking up. From which her mother abstained.

Parasitic Gaps

Parasitic gaps, which can appear in restrictives (see (16c)), can also marginally appear (for some speakers) in *che/cui* non-restrictives, but not in *il quale* non-restrictives. See the contrast between (16a) and (16b):

(16)   a.   ?Una persona$_i$ che i Rossi, **che** conoscono e$_i$ bene, hanno sempre
            ammirato t$_i$ è Gianni.
            One person that the Rossis, who (lit. that) know well, have always
            admired is G.
       b.   *Una persona$_i$ che i Rossi, **i quali** conoscono e$_i$ bene, hanno sempre
            ammirato t$_i$ è Gianni.
            Una person who the Rossis, who know well, have always admired is G.
       c.   La sola persona$_i$ che quelli **che** conoscono e$_i$ bene non possono non
            ammirare t$_i$ è Gianni.
            The only person that those that know well cannot but admire is G.

Reflexive Antecedents

While *che/cui* non-restrictives can have reflexives as antecedents *il quale* non-restrictives cannot. See (17a–b):

(17)   a.   Facendo questo rovinerà anche se stesso$_i$, che$_i$ non avrebbe certo
            bisogno di altre disgrazie.
            by doing this he will also ruin himself, that would certainly not need
            another blow now
       b.   *?Facendo questo rovinerà anche se stesso$_i$, il quale$_i$ non avrebbe certo
            bisogno di altre disgrazie
            by doing this he will also ruin himself, who would certainly not need
            another blow now

Coordination of the *wh*-Pronoun with Another DP*

(18)   a.   Gianni e Mario, tra le rispettive consorti e i quali non c'era mai stato un
             grande affiatamento, ...

        b.   *Gianni e Mario, tra le rispettive consorti e cui non c'era mai stato un
             grande affiatamento, ...
             G. and M., between their respective wives and whom there never was a
             real understanding, ...

        c.   *Il vicino del piano di sopra e quello del piano di sotto tra le rispettive
             consorti e cui non c'era mai stato un grande affiatamento, ...
             (restrictive)
             the neighbour upstairs and the one downstairs between their respective
             wives and whom there never was a real understanding, ...

Heavy Pied-Piping
See §3.1.5 below for the additional difference in the possibility of pied-piping
between non-integrated non-restrictives and integrated non-restrictives, in the
latter of which pied-piping is limited to functional prepositions, as with
restrictive or maximalizing RCs (see §2.1.2.1).

3.1.2   English Non-restrictives

As the data in the following section show, English non-restrictives pattern with
Italian *il quale*-non-restrictives. They appear to lack the equivalent of the
Italian integrated *che/cui*-non-restrictive construction.[13]

In all of the contrasts between *che/cui*- and *il quale*-non-restrictives
discussed in §3.1.1 above, English non-restrictives side with Italian *il
quale*-non-restrictives.

Illocutionary Independence
As with *il quale*-non-restrictives (and unlike *che/cui*-non-restrictives) (see (3)–
(4) above), English non-restrictives can also be non-declarative. See (19a),

---

* Also see Cardoso (2010: §3.2.2.3) for coordination of relative *wh*-pronouns with other DPs in
older stages of Portuguese:

(i)   [As quais razões e outras muitas que o padre-mestre Francisco lhe dava] ... (Cardoso
       2010: 310)
       Lit.: the which reasons and other many that the Father.Master F. to.him.CLused to give ...

[13] See in particular the general impossibility of using *that*, especially with human antecedents
(certain cases of *that* in non-restrictives are occasionally found with inanimates. See Sonoda
2006; Kayne 2014a: §6; Radford 2019: ch. 1 fn. 1; among others) and the possibility of 'heavy'
pied-piping (of phrases other than functional PPs); a possibility, as just seen, not available to the
ordinary *che/cui* non-restrictives of Italian.

where the non-restrictive is interrogative, and (19b) and (19c), where they are imperative and optative, respectively:[14]

(19)   a.   It may clear up, in which case would you mind hanging the washing out? (= (10ii) of Huddleston & Pullum 2002: 1061)

        b.   He said he'd show a few slides towards the end of his talk, at which point please remember to dim the lights! (= (10i) of Huddleston & Pullum 2002: 1061)

        c.   My friend, who God forbid you should ever meet, . . . (John Lyons, reported in Werth 1974: fn. 4)

Related to this is the fact, noted in Emonds (1979: 239–40) (also see Loock 2010: §2.1.2), that speech act adverbs are possible in English non-restrictives, but not in restrictives. See (20a–b) (though Andrew Radford, pers. comm., finds a restrictive RC like (20c) perfect, as is for me the corresponding restrictive of Italian – see Cinque 2008a: 109):

(20)   a.   The boys, who have frankly lost their case, should give up.

        b.   *The very boys that have frankly lost their case should give up.

        c.   The very boys that frankly should never have been admitted to Eton are now creating havoc there.

Occurrence across Discourse and Also across Different Speakers

Various examples of the occurrence of non-restrictives across discourse are cited in works on English non-restrictives. See for example (21a), cited in Cinque 2008a: 112), and (21b), from Tao & McCarthy (2001: 671):

(21)   a.   She borrowed a history book. Which suggests that her teacher was having some influence on her.

        b.   (Speaker A) You said 12 till 10.

            (Speaker B) Which is fine, isn't it?

---

[14] Also see Radford (2018: 94; 2019: 15) for the independent illocutionary force of English non-restrictives. It thus appears that, contra Emonds (1979: 241), Subject-Auxiliary Inversion can apply in English non-restrictives. On the related question of why Verb Second is unavailable in Dutch and German non-restrictives, see Emonds (1979: fn. 4). Even though certain Verb Second relatives are actually possible in German (and Dutch), they appear to be semantically restrictive only. See Gärtner (2001), Catasso & Hinterhölzl (2016), and Sanfelici, Schulz & Trabandt (2017) (and Zwart 2005 for Dutch). But see §3.2 below for the possibility that they are more likely of the kind-defining type. McCawley (1998: 447) also notes that in English interrogative tags can only be hosted in non-restrictives.

Split Antecedents

As was the case with Italian *il quale-* (but not *che/cui-*) non-restrictives, English non-restrictives also allow for split antecedents (*pace* McCawley 1996: n. 4). See (22), from Arnold (2007: 274) (also see Arnold 2004: 30):

(22)   Kim likes muffins$_i$, but Sandy prefers scones$_j$, which$_{i+j}$/*that they eat with jam.

According to Demirdache (1991: 118) another such case is Perlmutter & Ross's (1970) celebrated split antecedent relative (23a), which she compares to a case of anaphora across discourse like (23b), although a restrictive reading seems to be possible too (see §5.2):[15]

(23)   a.   A man$_i$ entered the room and a woman$_j$ went out who$_{i,j}$ were quite similar.
       b.   A man$_i$ entered the room and a woman$_j$ went out. They$_{i,j}$ were quite similar.

Full Retention of the Internal Head

As with (formal) *il quale-* (but not *che/cui-*) non-restrictives (see (9)–(10) above), in (formal) English non-restrictives the internal Head can also be retained. See (24):[16]

(24)   a.   He rode twenty miles to see her picture in the house of a stranger, which stranger politely insisted on his acceptance of it. (Jespersen 1949: section 6.5, p. 126)
       b.   ... a young woman with a wedding-ring and a baby, which baby she carried about with her when serving at the table. (Jespersen 1949: section 6.5, p. 126)
       c.   The French procured allies, which allies proved of the utmost importance. (Poutsma 1916: ch. XXXIX: §4, p. 961)
       d.   An accident on the road, in which accident several people were hurt, ... (Browne 1986: 117)
            (vs *The accident on the road in which accident several people were hurt ... (restrictive))

---

[15] Also see the examples given in Huddleston & Pullum (2002: 1066 fn. 13) and De Vries (2006: fn. 38). Indeed, according to my informants, replacing *who* with *that* renders such cases much worse.

[16] Jespersen (1949, section 6.5, p. 126) says that such retention is possible 'in a peculiar kind of non-restrictive clause; very often the clause is at some distance from the antecedent, and some substantive is repeated so as to avoid any doubt as to what word is to be taken as the antecedent'.

Non-identity of the External and Internal Heads

The internal Head which is retained can even be distinct from the external one, as we saw above with *il quale*-non-restrictives of Italian. Various examples are cited in the literature. See, e.g., (25) to (28) (and Jespersen 1949: 126–8):

(25)   a.   Mark belongs to the Knights of Columbus, which organization has been condemned by the Jewish Defense League. (= (33a) of McCawley 1981: 118)

       b.   *Mark belongs to a club which organization has been condemned by the Jewish Defense League. (restrictive) (= (33a') of McCawley 1981: 118)

(26)   a   This book, which masterpiece I have read twice, ... (= (ii) of Kayne 1994: 165 fn. 73)

       b   *The book which masterpiece I have read twice ... (restrictive)

(27)   a   There were only thirteen senators present, which number was too few for a quorum. (Arnold 2007: 289)

       b   *These are the only thirteen senators present which number we had forgotten. (restrictive)

As with *il quale* non-integrated non-restrictives in Italian (see (12)) the internal Head of an English non-restrictive may display non-identity in number with the external Head, at least for some speakers. See for example (28), from Cantrall (1972: 22):

(28)   Since John is a lexicalist, all of whom are badly confused, I never listen to him.

Possibility of a Head Other than DP

As noted by many authors,[17] non-restrictives in English differ from restrictives in allowing non-nominal antecedents (as was the case with *il quale-*, but not with *che/cui-*, non-restrictives in Italian). See (29):[18]

---

[17] See, for example, Jackendoff (1977: 171), Fabb (1990: 60), Demirdache (1991: 106 ff), Borsley (1997: §5), McCawley (1998: 447), De Vries (2002: 185), Arnold (2007: 274), Lassiter (2011: §2.2), Radford (2019: §1.2). In German, non-restrictive RCs modifying CPs, VPs, etc. are introduced by interrogative *wh*-phrases (*was, wofür, weswegen, welch-* + NP). See Holler (2003, 2005) and references cited there.

[18] As with Italian non-integrated non-restrictives modifying a CP (see (i) of fn. 10), English non-restrictives can also precede the 'antecedent' (see Seki 1983 and Lee-Goldmann 2012):

   (i)   a.   Moreover, which you may hardly believe, the examiners had decided in advance to fail half of the candidates. (Seki 1983: 39)

         b.   And – which is more – you'll be a Man, my son! (Lee-Goldmann 2012: 579)

(29)   a.   Sheila was beautiful, which was too bad. (Ross 1969a: 357) (**CP**)
        b.   She was fond of her boy, which Theobald never was. (Jespersen 1949: §6.4, p. 124) (**AP**)
        c.   Joe debated in high school, which Chuck did too. (Thompson 1971: 84) (**VP**)
        d.   Sam is at home, which is where Sue is. (Radford 2019: 9). (**PP**)[19]
        e.   They dressed carefully, which is also how they talk. (**AdvP**) (Arnold & Borsley 2008: 331)

Parasitic Gaps
As noted in Safir (1986), parasitic gaps, which can appear within English restrictives (see (30a), cannot appear in English non-restrictives (see (30b), just as they cannot appear in *il quale*-non-restrictives in Italian (see (16b) above)):

(30)   a.   John is a man who everyone who knows e_i admires t_j. (Safir 1986: 673)
        b.   *John is a man who Bill, who knows e_i, admires t_j. (Safir 1986: 673)

Reflexive Antecedents
Similarly to the *il quale* paradigm in Italian (see (17b)), a reflexive in English cannot constitute the antecedent of a non-restrictive RC (Carmel Coonan, pers. comm.):

(31)   *?By doing this he will ruin himself$_i$, who$_i$ surely would not need another blow now.

Coordination of the *wh*-Pronoun with Another DP
As in the Italian non-integrated formal non-restrictives with *il quale* (see (18a) above), and in older stages of Portuguese – see (18)d above), in archaic and formal English non-restrictives it is possible to coordinate a *wh*-pronoun with another DP. See (32a–b), *pace* Ross's (1967: 206) Pied-Piping Convention, which was meant to exclude restrictive RCs like (32c):[20]

---

[19] Also see *They hid the books under the bed, which is a good place.* (Arnold & Borsley 2008: 331). Fabb (1990: 60) gives an alternative with *where* (*Peter put it under the table, where I had put it earlier.*), pointing out that non-restrictive *where*, but not restrictive *where*, can have the entire PP, like *under the table*, as an antecedent.

[20] The contrast between the non-restrictives (32a–b) and the restrictive (32c) casts doubt on the analysis of non-restrictives proposed in De Vries (2006) and Sportiche (2017a: §5), according to which non-restrictives are restrictive RCs modifying a light noun in apposition to the Head. For example, (32b) would be analysed as: ... the solicitor, [$_{apposition}$ A PERSON [$_{restrictiveRC}$ between whom and himself there had been occasional correspondence]] ..., which should then be as bad as (32c) Also see the second part of fn. 31 below.

(32) a. The faithful Sam, between whom and his master there exists a steady
          and reciprocal attachment, ... (Charles Dickens, *The Pickwick Papers*,
          cited in Touratier 1980: 407)

      b. He recalled the name of the solicitor, between whom and himself there
          had been occasional correspondence ... (Jespersen 1949: 191)

      c. *The boy Bill and who(m) I watched is vain (Ross 1967: 202)

Heavy Pied-Piping

Interestingly, English non-restrictives, which pattern with Italian non-
integrated ones, are freer than restrictive or maximalizing RCs in the pied-
piping they admit (not only [*whose* XP] and functional PPs). See Emonds
(1976: §5.7 and 1979: §2.1).[21]

Griffiths and De Vries (2013) propose an 'integration' approach to English non-
restrictives (their Appositive RCs) on the basis of the fact that they immediately
follow the Head. They argue, after De Vries (2009, 2012), that the non-restrictive
'is 'parenthetically coordinated' to the anchor [Head], mediated by a syntactic
functional head that can be dubbed Par' (p. 333). For similar ideas, see Rebuschi
(2005). This functional head has something in common with the 'Discourse
Grammar' functional head H which Cinque (2008a) proposed for the non-
integrated type of non-restrictives (also see §3.1.3.2 below). This head, as is the
general rule for sentences in a discourse, is assumed to block every 'Sentence
Grammar' relation between the two discourse fragments (internal Merge, Reconstruction, Binding, etc.), despite the asymmetric c-command relation existing
between the two under the extension of the LCA to Discourse Grammar. Given
the possible occurrence of the RC across discourse (and speakers), it seems more
appropriate to think of non-restrictives of the English type as non-integrated,
especially if compared with the integrated ones of Italian and other languages.

On pied-piping in non-integrated non-restrictives (and restrictions thereon)
see §3.1.5 below.

3.1.3   An Analysis of the Two Types of Non-restrictives

3.1.3.1   The Integrated Non-restrictive

The analysis of the integrated non-restrictive that I propose is a natural extension
of the analysis I presented for restrictives in Chapter 2. There I proposed that

---

[21] The following contrasts between English non-restrictives and restrictives, pointed out in
McCawley (1991: 51) (also see Smits 1989: 294) is another difference between the two
constructions, which possibly depends on English non-restrictives being non-integrated in the
DP (see §3.1.3.2):

(i) a. *John, who I don't trust,'s wife ...
     b. The man who I don't trust's wife ...

restrictive relatives are merged (pre-nominally, if linear order is part of narrow syntax) as CPs in the specifier of a functional projection above the specifiers which host attributive adjectives and numerals and below the projection hosting determiners and demonstratives (i.e., the position in which restrictive relatives overtly appear in many (rigid) OV languages. Following Kayne (1999, 2000, 2002), I also proposed there that their eventual postnominal position in most VO, and non-rigid OV, languages is due, in the 'raising' variant, to the movement of the internal Head to the Spec of (the highest) CP with deletion of the external Head, and in the 'matching' variant, to the movement of the external Head to the Spec of an FP dominating the RC CP licensing the deletion or the internal Head (whether moved or not), or its replacement by a proform.

Integrated non-restrictive RCs minimally differ in that the CP is merged in the specifier of a nominal projection dominating DP; i.e., outside the scope of the definite determiner or the demonstrative, as is generally assumed for non-restrictives (Lehmann 1984: 261–2; Kayne 1994: 112).[22]

(33)

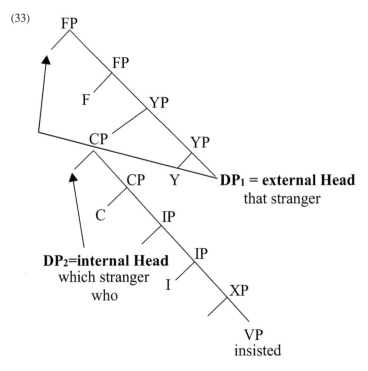

---

[22] So, for example, in languages in which restrictives remain inside the demonstrative, non-restrictives are found outside. See §3.5.2 below for illustration.

In such a structure both a 'raising' and a 'matching' derivation should in principle be possible, but in actual fact, plausibly for semantic reasons, a 'raising' one involving reconstruction of the Head inside the RC appears to be impossible (see §3.1.8 below for evidence to this effect).

3.1.3.2 The Non-integrated Non-restrictive

The analysis to be proposed for the non-integrated non-restrictive is more tentative. As mentioned at the outset, the construction appears to belong to what Williams (1977) calls Discourse Grammar, whose basic properties, distinguishing it from Sentence Grammar, are the ability to apply 'across utterance boundaries', and to be immune to island constraints (Williams 1977: 101–2).

We have already seen that *il quale*-non-restrictives in Italian and *which/ (who)*-non-restrictives in English can relate to an antecedent across discourse (and across speakers). They also appear to be able to do so across islands. So, for example, in such pied-piping cases as (34) and (35) the pronoun can relate to its antecedent across the adjunct, sentential subject, and complex NP, island boundary between them:[23]

(34)   a.   Questa macchina, [per comprare la quale] Gianni si è indebitato fino al collo, . . .
                This car, to buy which G. is up to his ears in debt, . . .
        b.   Questa macchina, [comprare la quale] voleva dire per lui rinunciare a tante altre cose, . . .
                This car, to buy which meant for him giving up many other things, . . .
        c.   Gianni, [le ragioni per non invitare il quale] erano davvero tante, . . .
                G., the reasons for not inviting whom were really many, . . .

(35)   a.   The lecture [(in order) to attend which] Sally drove 50 miles, . . .
                (Nanni & Stillings 1978: 312)

---

[23] The more formal cases of 'double dependence' like (i), where a *wh*-pronoun is fronted to the left edge of the island (possibly into the Spec of a TopicP above the subordinator, if any – see the discussion in §5.4) show the same thing.

    (i)   (?)Una tale ipoteca,[*della quale$_i$ se voi vi liberaste* t$_i$] sareste certamente più felici, non l'ho mai veduta.
              such a mortgage, of which if you could get rid you would certainly be happier, I have never seen

For such cases as (34) and (35), rather than assuming covert movement of the *wh*-phrase to the front of the island (problematic in the case of (34c)) I will (tentatively) assume that the *wh*-phrase is related to the Head via Agree, not followed by movement in narrow syntax. See §3.1.5 for further discussion.

b.   ... delicious entertainments, [to be admitted to one of which] was a privilege, ... (Jespersen 1949: 194)

c.   John, [the many reasons for not inviting whom] you are old enough to understand ... (adapted from Jespersen 1949: 194)

If we assume Kayne's (1994) Linear Correspondence Axiom (LCA) to hold of Discourse Grammar as well (the null hypothesis), linear precedence in a discourse must also reflect asymmetric c-command. One way to achieve this is to merge the linearly preceding sentence in the specifier of a (silent) head, which takes the following sentence as a complement. Concretely, the discourse fragment *John is no longer here. He left at noon.* would have the structural representation in (36):

(36)

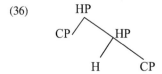

Discourse fragments do not consist of just concatenations of CPs. Other categories can apparently be concatenated; for example, DPs, APs, CPs, etc. (*A pink shirt? I will never wear any such thing in my life!; Ricco? Non è mai stato ricco* 'Rich? He never was rich!'), which would yield the structural representation in (37):[24]

(37)

I will take the configurations in (36) and (37) to underlie the non-integrated non-restrictive, (36) for the across discourse cases, and (37) for the cases in which the non-restrictive is adjacent to its antecedent.[25] In both cases, the movement internal to the non-integrated non-restrictive CP is likely to be

---

[24] The configuration in (37) possibly also underlies English-type Left Dislocation, and the Romance Hanging Topic construction, where the relation between the left dislocated phrase and the following CP appears to be one of Discourse Grammar (root character, no island sensitivity, no reconstruction, etc.; see Cinque 1990: ch. 2). As a matter of fact, the Head of non-integrated non-restrictives can have the same intonational contour as a Hanging Topic: *Quel collega? Il quale, tra l'altro, gli è sempre stato antipatico, credo proprio che di lui farebbe volentieri a meno.* 'That colleague? Who, incidentally, he never liked, I really think he would very gladly do without him.'

[25] For a similar idea concerning non-restrictive RCs see Bianchi (1995: IV.3).

different in target from that of integrated non-restrictives (and restrictives). If the target is a CP initial TOP position, as occasionally suggested (see Arsenijević & Halupka-Rešetar 2013), one could perhaps make sense of certain properties typical of the non-integrated construction, namely the fact that objects cannot easily be relativized with *il quale*-phrases in Italian (see Cinque 1978: 3.7), except in such cases as *Le stesse cose negò persino il suo avvocato* 'Lit.: The same things denied even his lawyer', belonging to the topicalization construction called 'Resumptive Preposing' in Cinque (1990: §2.5), where no clitic is required.[26]

Unlike the (Romance) Hanging Topic construction, which is only possible at the Root, presumably due to the discourse head which concatenates DP with CP, non-integrated non-restrictives can be subordinate clauses. This can be obtained from the same structure if, in the non-restrictive case, like in unbalanced coordination (Johannessen 1998), the features of the phrase in specifier position (here the categorial features of DP/XP) are able to percolate up and determine the categorial features of the dominating category (rendering HP non-distinct from DP/XP). See Rebuschi (2005: §3.2).

In the spirit of Williams (1977), we must also assume that the 'Discourse Grammar' head H, as is the general rule for sentences in a discourse, blocks

---

[26] See *Queste stesse cose, le quali negò persino il suo avvocato, . . .* 'These same things, which even his lawyer denied, . . .'. Given that non-integrated non-restrictives can also be adjacent to a Head internal to an island (*The Ferrari which Pietro, who Sofia adores, bought from me cost him a bundle* – Ross 1967: 174), an analysis in terms of extraction (from the island) followed by remnant movement does not seem a plausible alternative. The present analysis is reminiscent of the 'ColonP' analysis advanced in Koster (2000) for both restrictive and non-restrictive relatives, to the ParatacticP analysis which Gärtner (2001: §2) suggests for V2 relatives in German, and to the analyses proposed in Rebuschi (2005) and Frascarelli & Puglielli (2005) (except that we would limit it here to the non-integrated non-restrictive). De Vries (2002; 2006) and Cardoso & De Vries (2010) modify Koster's analysis to one of balanced coordination of the Head with a Headless false (or light) free relative in apposition to the Head ($[_{\&P}Ann_i$ [& $[_{DP}she_i$ [t_i who t_i is our manager]]]] – De Vries 2006: 248 – a proposal also adopted in Sportiche 2017a: §5), even though De Vries has to admit the availability of unbalanced coordination for the cases of non-nominal antecedents (De Vries 2006: fn. 25 and K of section 5.2). This modification however implies, contrary to fact, that *il quale*-pronouns in Italian should be found in false (or light) free relatives, which are taken to be a necessary component of non-restrictives. See Citko (2008a: §2.3) and **Quella/la persona la quale è di là è mia sorella.* Lit.: 'That/the person who is in the other room is my sister', **Ciò il quale mi hanno detto è falso* 'that which they told me is false' (a comparable problem is raised by French *lequel* as noted by Alexander Grosu, pers. comm.). Against a coordination analysis of non-restrictive RCs see Thorne (1988: 429–30), Schmitt (2006: §1.2.1.2.2.2), Lassiter (2011: §3.4) and Citko (2016: §3.2). The criticism levelled there against (specifying) coordination do not seem to carry over to the discourse head H of Cinque (2008a) adopted here.

every 'Sentence Grammar' relation between its specifier and complement (Movement, Agree, Binding, etc.), despite the asymmetric c-command relation existing between the two under the extension of the LCA to Discourse Grammar.[27]

3.1.3.3   Deriving the Properties of the Two Types of Non-restrictives

Let us start from the differences between the two types of constructions noted in §3.1.1, beginning with the non-integrated type.

The fact that *il quale-* (but not *che/cui-*) non-restrictives can have illocutionary independence, can be separated from the Head across discourse, can have split antecedents (whereby at least one of the antecedents is not adjacent to the relative clause), can have non-nominal antecedents, and cannot host a parasitic gap licensed by an operator in the matrix, appears to depend directly on the non-restrictive CP being, in both (36) and (37), an independent sentence at the discourse level, connected to the antecedent by the same kind of (abstract) heads which concatenate discourse fragments.

The other properties (possible retention of the 'internal' Head; possible non-identity of the internal and external Heads; possibility for *il quale*-pronouns to be coordinated with other DPs, and the possibility of heavy pied-piping) appear related to the E-type character of *il quale/which*-phrases (Evans 1980: 340).[28]

---

[27] Interesting confirmation of the fact that non-integrated non-restrictives are impermeable to outside influences is the absence of Principle C violations. See:

(i)   Lui$_i$ sostiene che Maria, la quale/*che a Giorgio$_i$ non è mai stata simpatica, sia la vera colpevole.
      He$_i$ claims that Maria, who John$_i$ by the way had never been fond of, might be the real culprit.

Andrew Radford judges coreference possible in the English translation of (i) if *he* is unstressed and the relative has a parenthetical intonation.

[28] For the proposal that *wh*-phrases in English non-restrictive RCs are interpreted as E-type pronouns see Sells 1985, Demirdache 1991, Del Gobbo 2007 and Erlewine & Kotek 2015b. It should be noted that *wh*-phrases are, with respect to Binding Theory, neither anaphors nor pronominals, but more like demonstratives (nominals) since they obey Principle C, as is apparent from multiple relativization (Kayne 1983a: §2.3, and here §5.3). The notion of reference appropriate for E-type pronouns should also be somewhat qualified given the possibility for such pronouns of having indefinite antecedents under the scope of a quantifier ((i)a), and even a negative quantifier if certain pragmatic conditions hold ((i)b) (for discussion see Authier & Reed 2005: 641 and references cited there):

(i)   a.   Every guest will bring a bottle. It/Which will almost certainly be a bottle of wine.
      b.   The professor saw no students in class Thursday. They/Who had all gone to the beach instead.

In that, they behave just like demonstrative pronouns (and adjectives) which can resume an antecedent across discourse, can be followed by an identical or non-identical copy of the antecedent, can be coordinated with other like categories, and can be freely embedded in other phrases.[29]

On the other hand, the strictly complementary behaviour of the *che/cui*-non-restrictives appears related to their being an integral part of the DP containing their antecedent. As a consequence of that they lack illocutionary independence, they must be adjacent to the Head (except for the limited cases where extraposition is allowed), and cannot have split antecedents. Being merged within the DP that contains their Head (an extended projection of NP), they can take only a nominal antecedent, and are c-commanded by whatever c-commands their Head, thus allowing a parasitic gap to be licensed by an operator binding another variable in the matrix. The remaining properties (no retention of the internal Head and pied-piping limited to functional PPs) may instead be related to *cui* being a pronoun rather than a determiner/modifier of a larger phrase and to functional prepositions being part of the nominal extended projection (see the discussion in the second part of §2.1.2.1.1).

Concerning Weak Crossover, both types of non-restrictives (as opposed to restrictives) are immune to it. This seems to be due to the fact that the Head of *il quale-* and of *che/cui*-non-restrictives has independent reference, so that the possessive may directly relate to the Head rather than to the relative clause internal trace.

3.1.4   Some Comparative Remarks

An in-depth typological study of non-restrictives is not available. The few observations that are found in the literature are sketchy and do not even always converge, as the following quotes illustrate:

> The properties of non-restrictive RCs are quite different from those of restrictive RCs across languages. Some languages apparently have no non-restrictive RCs; in others they are syntactically quite distinct; in others restrictive and non-restrictive RCs are syntactically indistinguishable.   (Downing 1978: 380)

> Formal distinction between restrictive and non-restrictive relatives is found sporadically across languages [...]   (Comrie 1981: 132)

---

[29] See Jackendoff (1977: 175): '[r]elative pronouns in non-restrictives can be anaphoric to the same constituents as ordinary demonstrative pronouns can'. Unlike demonstrative or personal pronouns *wh*-phrases in non-integrated non-restrictives nonetheless require a linguistic antecedent, possibly across discourse (and speakers). See also Lassiter (2011). On pied-piping in non-integrated non-restrictives (and restrictions thereon) see §3.1.5 below.

> [...] the syntax of non-restrictives in a language will be largely similar to that of
> restrictives, modulo some small differences, [...]   (Keenan 1985: 169).[30]

The remarks that follow thus cannot be but tentative.

As noted in the quote from Downing (1978), not all languages have non-restrictives. In fact Jeng (1977: 195), Lehmann (1984: 268), Berg (1989: 231), Carlson (1994: 487) and Aboh (2005: fn. 2) explicitly claim this to be the case of Bunun, Dagbani, Muna, Supyire and Gungbe, respectively.[31] Andrews (1975: 73) and Aygen (2003: 199) mention Navajo as another language lacking non-restrictives.

Most languages however do have non-restrictives, although the question now arises whether they have one, the other, or both, of the two non-restrictive constructions discussed above. Apparently, it so happens that in addition to languages with both types, there are languages which only have one: either the integrated or the non-integrated non-restrictive. The disagreement concerning non-restrictive relative clauses illustrated in the quotes above is possibly due to the fact that where 'restrictive and non-restrictive RCs are syntactically indistinguishable' only the integrated type is present, which we saw is virtually identical to the restrictive construction (in Italian), while in those languages in which restrictive and non-restrictive relative clauses are syntactically distinct it is tempting to think that just the non-integrated, Discourse Grammar, type of non-restrictives is present, which was seen above to pattern quite unlike restrictives (and integrated non-restrictives).

---

[30] Also see Mallinson & Blake (1981: §5.5), Andrews (1975: 27–8; 2007: 207), and De Vries (2005: ch. 6). According to Watters (2000) the difference between restrictive and non-restrictive RCs 'is generally not marked in African languages' (p. 225).

[31] Aboh (pers. comm.) points out that Gungbe (perhaps all Gbe languages – but see Dzameshie 1995: n. 5, on Ewe) resorts to overt or covert coordination instead, as does Bunun (Jeng 1977: 195). Another strategy, utilized in Yoruba (Sadat-Tehrani 2004: §5), as well as in a number of Mixtecan languages (see Bradley & Hollenbach 1992), consists of inserting a generic noun like 'person' in apposition, followed by a restrictive clause ('John, a person that no woman would like to marry, ...' – possibly a sort of false or light free relative). According to Canac Marquis & Tremblay (1998) 'all appositive relatives are in fact restrictive relatives contained in an appositive DP': *John, pro/(he) who is usually not late, ...*) (p. 129), a position also defended, as noted in fn. 20 above, by De Vries (and Cardoso & De Vries 2010). While this may be a possibility exploited by some languages it is dubious, as noted, that this strategy should be generalized to all non-restrictives in all languages that possess them. As observed in Burton-Roberts (1975), McCawley (1998) and Kayne (2008b, 2014a) true appositions appear to differ in many languages from non-restrictive RCs in a number of ways, including extraposition and modification by 'namely'. Also see Krapova & Cinque (2016: §4.3).

3.1.4.1   Languages with Both Integrated and Non-integrated Non-restrictives

Italian appears to possess both types, and so does French (see the discussion above and Cinque 1982: §2.1). Spanish, Catalan and (European) Portuguese, which can use either the complementizer or a *wh*-pronoun, also display both types plausibly (see Brucart 1999, Solà 2002, and Brito 1991, respectively).

Germanic languages (except for Nynorsk, modern spoken Faroese and Icelandic, and certain dialects of Swedish – Karlsson & Sullivan 2002: 103 – which only use the relative complementizer *som/sum/sem*), possibly have both types too (Platzack 2002). They employ either *wh*-pronouns, like English, or *d*-pronouns. Since only *d*-pronouns appear compatible with raising of the Head in restrictives (only *d*-pronouns can relativize amounts and idiom chunks – Prinzhorn & Schmitt 2005: 498 fn. 2; Salzmann 2006d: ch. 2), it is plausible that when they appear in the non-restrictive construction, they instantiate the integrated type (while *wh*-phrases presumably enter the non-integrated one).[32]

Judging from Camilleri & Sadler (2016) Maltese also disposes of both types of non-restrictives, and so does Albanian (Sotiri 2006: fn. 5), but not Arbëresh, the Albanian spoken in Southern Italy (Giuseppina Turano, pers. comm.).[33]

3.1.4.2   Languages with Only Integrated Non-restrictives

All northern Italian dialects lack *il quale*-non-restrictives (Paola Benincà, pers. comm.).[34] Hence, they plausibly have just the integrated construction.

The same appears to be true of Chinese. As shown in great detail in Del Gobbo (2001, 2003, 2004, 2005, 2007, 2010, 2015), Chinese relatives receiving a 'non-restrictive' interpretation behave with respect to many of the properties reviewed above like English and Italian restrictives (and Italian *che/cui*-non-restrictives) rather than like English non-restrictives (and *il*

---

[32] This implies that a restrictive relative like *Ich kenne nicht den Mann der da ist* 'I do not know the man who is there' the *d*-'pronoun' is actually an agreeing complementizer, much as Pesetsky and Torrego (2006: n. 22) and Boef (2013: §4.5.2.2) propose for the corresponding *d*-pronouns of Dutch.

[33] Like Italian, Albanian can utilize either an invariant finite subordinator (*që*) or a *wh*-phrase (*cil-in* 'which-the'). See Morgan (1972b: §I), Kallulli (2000: 359–60) and Sotiri (2006: §2).

[34] In fact, they utilize no *wh*-pronoun (except for *dove* 'where'), but just the invariant relativizer of finite complement clauses and either a gap or a pronominal (clitic, where possible) within the relative clause, depending on the complement position being relativized.

quale-non-restrictives of Italian). For example, they can only have nominal antecedents, cannot have split antecedents nor can they have illocutionary independence.[35] All of this suggests that the only type available in Chinese is the integrated non-restrictive (see, in fact, the conclusion in Del Gobbo 2007, 2015 and Lin & Tsai 2015); but see §3.6 below, where I tentatively suggest, given their Merge position and their syntactic and semantic properties, that they may actually be non-finite participial RCs, which are open to a restrictive or maximalizing or non-restrictive interpretation (as participial RCs are).

Judging from Kuno (1973: 235), Andrews (1975: 48–9), Emonds (1979: fn. 4), Kameshima (1989: 4.3.3) and Del Gobbo (2015), Japanese non-restrictives, which are identical syntactically to restrictives (*pace* Yuasa 2005), also appear to be of just the integrated type (for example, they cannot have illocutionary independence or have split antecedents, and can only have nominal antecedents).[36]

Similarly, Basque and Yoruba non-restrictives (De Rijk 1972: 134, and Sadat-Tehrani 2004, respectively) cannot have a whole sentence as antecedent, again suggesting that those languages may only have non-restrictives of the integrated type (De Rijk 1972 also notes that 'Japanese, Tamil, and Turkish do not allow sentential relatives, either' (p. 135), and connects this to the SOV character of all these languages). Following Kayne (1994: 174 fn. 71), I will rather take this to be related to the fact that all of these languages have pre-nominal relative clauses, which lack (for principled reasons – see Chapter 2: §2.2.3) *wh*-pronouns, which alone can enter the non-integrated type of non-restrictives, given their demonstrative-like character and related usage as E-type pronouns.[37]

---

[35] Tong Wu also pointed out to me (pers. comm.) that Chinese non-restrictives have to be strictly adjacent to the Head, and never show full retention of the internal Head.

[36] Andrews (1975: 49 and 62), Emonds (1979: fn. 4), and Fukui (1986: 235) take the fact that non-restrictives can stack in Japanese and Korean (while they cannot in English) as further indication that non-restrictives in these languages are like restrictives. More generally Andrews claims (1975: 63) that languages with exclusively pre-nominal relatives do not mark the restrictive/non-restrictive distinction; i.e. only have, in our terms, integrated non-restrictives (also see Kuno 1973: 235; Keenan 1985: 169; and Kayne 1994: 111). This does not mean that in these languages restrictives and integrated non-restrictives are alike in every respect. For example, there is evidence, reviewed in §3.5 below, that non-restrictives are merged higher than demonstratives while restrictive and maximalizing RCs are merged below demonstratives.

[37] That the presence of *wh*-pronouns with an E-type interpretation is a prerequisite for having (non-integrated) non-restrictives is implicitly or explicitly assumed also in Demirdache (1991), Del Gobbo (2003, 2007, 2010), Authier & Reed (2005), Cinque (2008a), Citko (2016), among others.

3.1.4.3   Languages with Only Non-integrated Non-restrictives

As argued above, English has just the non-integrated non-restrictive construction.

Another language that appears to be like English is (modern standard) Romanian, whose non-restrictives only employ *wh*-pronouns of the *care* paradigm (also used in interrogatives), and never show the presence of the finite indicative complementizer *că* (Dobrovie-Sorin 1994: 213; Grosu 1994: 212). See Cinque (2008a: §6.3) for evidence for this conclusion.[38] Citko (2016) claims that Polish non-restrictives are also only of the non-integrated type.

3.1.5   On Pied-Piping in Non-integrated Non-restrictives and Restrictions Thereon

The range of constituents which can be pied-piped differs from construction to construction in one and the same language and across languages (see Ross 1969b: 263–4). Here attention will be limited to pied-piping in non-integrated non-restrictives, with special reference to Italian.[39]

As opposed to integrated non-restrictives, which only allow the pied-piping of functional (and certain axial) PPs, as in ordinary restrictive or maximalizing RCs,[40] non-integrated non-restrictives like Italian *il quale*-non-restrictives (and English non-restrictives) allow the pied-piping of heavier constituents (see Ross 1967, §4.3, 1986: §4.3; Cinque 1978, 1988; Nanni & Stillings 1978; Kayne 1983a: §8.3; Ishihara 1984; Bianchi 1995: ch. VI; Kotek & Erlewine 2015a, 2015b, 2016 and the examples in (38) to (44)), provided certain conditions are not violated (for which see §3.1.5.1 below).

1   Complex DP

(38)   a.   New York, l'altezza degli edifici della quale non può che colpire, ...
New York, the height of the buildings of which cannot but strike one, ...

---

[38] Archaic literary Romanian *ce* 'what' (also used in Headless RCs) and modern colloquial Romanian *care* followed by a clitic introduce non-restrictives possibly of the integrated type (see Cinque 2008a: §6.3 and references cited there).

[39] For pied-piping in RCs and other Ā-constructions, in English and other languages, see Kayne (1983a: §8.3; 1994: 24–5; 2017b), Webelhuth (1992: ch. 4), Heck (2008, 2009), Cable (2010a, 2010b, 2012, 2013), Kotek & Erlewine (2015a, 2015b, 2015c, 2016), Horvath (2017), and references cited there.

[40] See §2.1.2.1.1 and fns 29 and 38 of Chapter 2 for possible accounts of this restriction, which carries over to the integrated non-restrictive construction.

b.   (?)Berlusconi, [$_{DP}$ l'uscita [$_{PP}$ di qualunque indiscrezione [$_{CP}$ che riguardasse il quale]]] era sempre vista con sospetto, . . .
      Berlusconi, the publication of any indiscretion concerning whom was always viewed with suspicion . . .

2 Non Functional Axial PPs

(39)   a.   Mario, [$_{PP}$ a fianco del quale] si erano schierati tutti, . . .
              'Mario, with (lit. beside) whom everybody sided, . . .'
        b.   Mario, [$_{PP}$ a destra del quale] c'era sua moglie, . . .
              'Mario, to the right of whom there was his wife, . . .'

3 VPs

(40)   a.   Gianni, [$_{VP}$ inviato al quale] l'avviso non era ancora stato, . . .
              'Gianni, sent to whom the notification had not been yet, . . .'
        b.   Gianni, [$_{VP}$ parlato col quale] ancora non ho, . . .
              'Gianni, spoken with whom, I haven't yet, . . .'

4 APs

(41)   a.   Sua moglie, [$_{AP}$ orgoglioso della quale] non è mai stato, . . .
              His wife, proud of whom he has never been, . . . (see Webelhuth 1992: 130)
        b.   Carla, [$_{AP}$ più magro della quale] non sei mai stato, . . .
              Carla, slimmer than whom you have never been, . . .

5 AdvPs

(42)   Gianni, [$_{AdvP}$ diversamente dal quale] io ero d'accordo, . . .
        Gianni, differently from (i.e. unlike) whom I agreed, . . .

6 IP

(43)   a.   Queste disposizioni, [$_{IP}$ PRO illustrando le quali] faremo capire il nostro pensiero . . .
              These provisions, illustrating which we'll disclose our thought, . . .
        b.   Le feste eleganti [$_{IP}$ PRO essere ammessi ad una delle quali era un privilegio], . . .
              The elegant parties, to be admitted to one of which was a privilege, . . .
              (see Nanni & Stillings 1978: 312)

7 CPs

(44)   I dimostranti, [$_{CP}$ quanti dei quali siano stati arrestati] è tutt'altro che chiaro, . . .
        The demonstrators how many of whom were arrested is far from clear, . . .

3.1.5.1 Restrictions on Heavy Pied-Piping

A popular analysis of pied-piping is one in which the *wh*-phrase that pied-pipes a larger phrase moves to the front of the larger phrase in LF (Safir 1986: 678–81). This is prima facie rendered plausible by the fact that this movement is apparently overt, at least marginally, in English (see Bianchi 1999: 143, where Ross's 1967: 197 sentence in (45) is cited):

(45)   ?Those reports, [which$_i$ the height [of the lettering [on t$_i$]]]$_j$ the government prescribes t$_j$, are tedious.

While some movement may be involved in certain cases (see the overt movement of a *wh*-phrase to the front of a pied-piped island in the 'double dependence' construction discussed in §5.4),[41] it does not seem to be generalizable to all cases, in particular to such cases as (45).

There is in fact reason to think that the front position of *which* in (45) is not due to movement. While the progressively larger pied-pipings that Ross (1967: 197–8) gives as wellformed all involve 'fronted' DPs (see (46), in addition to (45)), he notes that 'fronted' PPs give illformed results. See (47a–c):[42]

(46)   a.   Reports [$_{DP}$ the covers of which] the government prescribes the height of the lettering on almost always put me to sleep.
         b.   Reports [$_{DP}$ the lettering on the covers of which] the government prescribes the height of are shocking waste of public funds.
         c.   Reports [$_{DP}$ the height of the lettering on the covers of which] the government prescribes should be abolished.

(47)   a.   *Reports [$_{PP}$ of which] the government prescribes the height of the lettering on the covers are invariably boring.
         b.   *Reports [$_{PP}$ on the covers of which] the government prescribes the height of the lettering almost always put me to sleep.
         c.   *Reports [$_{PP}$ of the lettering on the covers of which] the government prescribes the height are shocking waste of public funds.

This is reminiscent of the DP/PP contrast in extraction discussed by Chomsky (1982: 72–3) in relation to an observation by Adriana Belletti (see (48)),

---

[41] Namely in cases like (i)a–b

(i)   a.   (?)Un circolo, [al quale$_i$ [essere ammessi t$_i$ a tali condizioni]] è senza dubbio un privilegio, ... (Cinque 1978: 59 ff)
               a club, to which to be admitted under such conditions is certainly a privilege ...
         b.   The most piteous tale [... [which$_i$ [in recounting t$_i$]] this grief grew puissant ...
               (Jespersen 1949: 184)

[42] '[T]here seems to be a constraint [...], which prohibits noun phrases which start with prepositions from being relativized.' (Ross 1967: 201).

(48)   a.   the man that I went to England without speaking to ___
        b.   *the man to whom I went to England without speaking ___

Chomsky took (48a), as opposed to (48b), not to involve movement, but a base-generated silent pronoun in the DP gap; a conclusion generalized to further cases in Cinque (1990: ch. 3).

Under this analysis, the illformedness of the PP cases in (47) would then be a consequence of the movement of the PP across one (or more) islands, while the (relative) wellformedness of (46) would follow from a base generation of the 'pied-piped' DP at the front of the RC resumed by a silent pronominal ([$_{DP}$ pro]) – an option not open to PPs.

Another difficulty in taking the *wh-* to raise to the front of the pied-piped constituent (whether in LF, or more plausibly in narrow syntax followed by remnant movement) is provided by the wellformedness of (49a) vs the illformedness of the corresponding case with overt movement ((49b)):

(49)   a.   (?)Berlusconi, [$_{DP}$ l'uscita [$_{PP}$ di qualunque indiscrezione [$_{CP}$ che riguardasse il quale]]] era sempre vista con sospetto, ...
              Berlusconi, the publication of any indiscretion concerning whom was always viewed with suspicion ...
        b.   **Berlusconi, [il quale$_i$ [$_{DP}$ l'uscita [$_{PP}$ di qualunque indiscrezione [$_{CP}$ che riguardasse t$_i$]]]] era sempre vista con sospetto, ...
              Berlusconi, whom the publication of any indiscretion concerning was always seen with suspicion ...

If the illformedness of (49b) is due to the extraction of the *wh-* out of (compounded) islands, as seems plausible, the wellformedness of (49a) must then be due to the fact that *il quale* does not move (whether in narrow syntax, followed by raising of the remnant, or in LF, which is presumably to be dispensed with).

There is also the converse situation, where extraction of the *wh-* out of an apparent island is possible (see §5.6 on such cases) while pied-piping with the same *wh-* is impossible. See (50a) vs (50b)

(50)   a.   Ecco Giorgio, [al quale$_i$ non conosco nessuno che sarebbe disposto ad affidare i propri risparmi t$_i$]!
              'Here is Giorgio, to whom I don't know of anyone that would be ready to give his savings.'
        b.   *Giorgio, [non conosco nessuno che sarebbe disposto ad affidare i propri risparmi al quale], sembra una brava persona
              'Giorgio, I don't know of anyone that would be ready to give his savings to whom, looks like a nice guy.'

The above cases also cast doubt on the idea that the overt Head is the internal Head that has 'raised' stranding *il quale*, for one would then expect (46) and

(49a) to be ruled out as violations of island constraints, just as (47) and (49b) are.

'Raising' of the Head in (non-integrated) non-restrictives is also rendered problematic by the possibility of (51a)–(52a) vs the impossibility of (51b)–(52b)

(51)   a.   Gianni e Mario, i quali tuoi due amici non hanno esitato ad aiutarti, . . .
              Gianni and Mario, the which your two friends have not hesitated to
              help you, . . .
              'Gianni and Mario, which two friends of yours have not hesitated to
              help you, . . .'

        b.   *I due amici$_i$, i quali tuoi t$_i$ non hanno esitato ad aiutarti, . . .
              the two friends, which your have not hesitated to help you, . . .

(52)   a.   Gianni e Mario, i quali due tuoi amici non hanno esitato ad aiutarti, . . .
              Gianni and Mario, the which two your friends have not hesitated to
              help you, . . .

        b.   *I tuoi amici$_i$, i quali due t$_i$ non hanno esitato ad aiutarti, . . .
              the your friends, which two have not hesitated to help you, . . .

Erlewine & Kotek (2014, 2015a, 2015b) also note that relative pronouns in heavy pied-piping in (non-integrated) non-restrictives are insensitive to syntactic barriers such as islands (although they are susceptible to intervention effects, on which see the quoted articles by Erlewine & Kotek, and Sauerland & Heck 2003):

(53)   a.   This portrait, [$_{RC}$ [$_{RPPP}$ the background [$_{RC}$ that was chosen for which]]
              is quite stunning], sold for a million dollars at auction. (Erlewine &
              Kotek 2015b: ex. (12)b)[43]

In fact Erlewine & Kotek (2015b) propose that in non-restrictive relatives, relative pronouns are interpreted in situ within the pied-piped constituent via a Rooth-Hamblin alternative computation.

A Tensed Clause Restriction[*]

(54)   a.   *Giorgio, [che voi abbiate scritto al quale] credo sia stato un errore, . . .
              (Cinque 1982: 273)
              Giorgio, that you have written to whom I think was a mistake, . . .

---

[43] Although they note that some speakers (but not the majority) find this sentence ungrammatical. The same speakers do not detect any intervention effects.

[*] See Ross (1967: 203–4) for a comparable observation concerning English RCs. The tensed clauses in (54) contrast in Italian with the corresponding infinitival clauses:

(i)   a.   Giorgio, [l'aver scritto al quale] credo sia stato un errore, . . .
              Giorgio, having written to whom I think was a mistake . . .

        b.   Maria, dopo aver visto la quale, Gianni ammutolì, . . .
              Maria, after seeing whom, Gianni became dumb, . . .

b. *Giorgio, [che voi abbiate scritto al quale] nessuno può credere …
Giorgio, that you have written to whom, nobody can believe, …

c. *Maria, [dopo che ebbe visto la quale], Gianni ammutolì, …
Maria, after he saw whom, Gianni became dumb, …

The much better (55), where the tensed clause is within a complex DP shows that the restriction may only hold for subject/object and adjunct tensed clauses, the reason for which remains to be elucidated:[44]

(55)   a.   ?Giorgio, [il solo fatto [che abbiate scritto al quale]] non depone a vostro favore, …
Giorgio, the very fact that you have written to whom does not argue in your favour, …

b.   ?Giorgio, [l'idea [che possiate rivolgervi al quale]] non vi deve neanche sfiorare, …
Giorgio, the idea that you could refer to whom should not even come to your mind, …

c.   ?Giorgio, [le voci [che hanno riferito al quale]] sono pura fantasia …
Giorgio, the rumours that they reported to whom are pure fantasies …

A Restriction on the Presence of a (Lexical) Subject

In both Italian and English, the presence of a subject in a pied-piped infinitival sentence gives questionable results. See (56a) and (56b):[45]

(56)   a.   Le feste eleganti [$_{CP}$ (l')esser (*?gli studenti) ammessi ad una delle quali era stato senz'altro un privilegio], …
The elegant parties, for the students to be admitted to one of which was certainly a privilege, …

b.   The elegant parties, (*for us) to be admitted to one of which was a privilege. (Nanni & Stillings 1978: 312)

A Subject–Object Asymmetry, Reminiscent of the ECP

Compare (56b) (without the subject) with (57a–c), from Nanni & Stillings (1978: 317–18 fn. 4), who credit Alan Prince with the observation

---

[44] For other such cases see Bianchi (1995: 270), who finds a difference (which I do not find) between noun complement islands like (55a–b), and relative clause islands like (55c). Under an exclusively promotion ('raising') analysis as in Sportiche (2017a: §7.3) (55) should be as bad as (54).

[45] But see the much milder marginality of the presence of a pronominal subject in Italian:

(i)   ?Quelle feste eleganti, [$_{CP}$ (l') esser noi stati ammessi ad una delle quali era stato senz'altro un privilegio], …
Those elegant parties, for us to have been admitted to one of which had certainly been a privilege, …

that the pied-piping of clauses with a *wh*-word in subject position is prohibited:[46]

(57) a. *The men, for whom to be invited to the elegant parties was a privilege, were appropriately appreciative.

      b. *The car, the idea that which might be a lemon was a surprise to them, was painted bright orange.

      c. *The man, whose singing songs loudly disturbed us, finally moved away.

The same subject–object asymmetry is found with the tensed cases in (58), to be compared with (55):

(58) a. *Giorgio, [il solo fatto [che il quale vi abbia scritto]] non depone a vostro favore, ...
          Giorgio, the very fact that who has written to you does not argue in your favour, ...

      b. *Giorgio, [l'idea [che il quale possa rivolgersi a voi]] non vi deve neanche sfiorare, ...
          Giorgio, the idea that who could refer to you should not even come to your mind, ...

      c. *Giorgio, [le voci [che il quale vi ha riferito]] sono pura fantasia ...
          Giorgio, the rumours that who reported to you are pure fantasies ...

      d. *Giorgio, [scusarsi [perché il quale non vi ha salutato]] sarebbe ingiusto ...
          Giorgio, to excuse himself because who has not greeted you would be incorrect ...

Given the unavailability, for the reasons seen above, of a movement derivation of the *wh*-, which could invoke an ECP like violation in the case of the *wh*- in subject position, I leave an account of this subject–object asymmetry to be determined, but see Kayne (1983a: §8.3.3) for an interesting discussion and a possible non-movement account of this subject–object asymmetry.

---

[46] Also see the similar contrasts given in Kayne (1983a: 244–5) and Ishihara (1984: 399) (and Cinque 1982: 273–4; 1995: 90–1 in Italian). Given the illformedness of such cases as (i)a–b with inverted subjects in Italian, the asymmetry, rather than left-branch vs right-branch DPs, seems to be between *wh*-complements of V/P in a right-branching structure vs all other *wh*-phrases in left- or right-branches (as shown in Belletti 1988 only inverted indefinite subjects of unaccusative/passive verbs can remain in the internal argument position). In (i) the inverted *il quale*, which is definite, is thus forced to occupy a VP adjoined position):

(i) a. *Giorgio, [l'essere già arrivato il quale] è sorprendente ...
        Giorgio, the having already arrived who is surprising ...

      b. *Giorgio, [l'averci scritto il quale] non significa niente ...
        Giorgio, the having written to us who means nothing ...

As Andrew Radford observes, pers. comm., (57a) is however fine with the structure [$_{PP}$ for whom] [$_{CP}$ Ø [$_{TP}$ PRO to be..]]. See ... *for whom$_i$* [*for them$_i$ to be invited* ...] also fine for him.

3.1.6 The Syntactic Typology of Non-restrictives

3.1.6.1 Externally Headed Post-nominal Non-restrictives
As seen above, *externally headed post-nominal* non-restrictives of both the integrated and non-integrated type are possible (§3.1.1 and §3.1.2).

3.1.6.2 Externally Headed Pre-nominal Non-restrictives
Despite occasional claims to the contrary (see, for example, Zhang 2001a: §3; Del Gobbo 2001, 2002, 2003, 2004, 2005;[47] Aygen 2003; Meral 2004; Cagri 2005; Krause 2001a, 2001b;[48] Potts 2005; De Vries 2001: 237, 2005: 10–11; 2006: 266; Citko 2008a: §3.2), some genuine cases of externally headed pre-nominal non-restrictives seem to exist. They are for example reported to be possible in Basque (De Rijk 1972: 134), in Korean and Japanese (Tagashira 1972: 217; Kuno 1973: 235; Kamio 1977: 153–9; Kameshima 1989: §4.3.3.2; Krause 2001a: ch. IV: §7, 2001b: §6; Yuasa 2005: §6.3; Ishizuka 2008b: §2), in Turkish (Kornfilt 1997: §1.1.2.3.2; 2011; Göksel & Kerslake 2005: §25.2; Özçelik 2014), in Amharic and Quechua (Wu 2008: §2.2.2.1), in Laz (Kartvelian – Lacroix 2009: §12.2.3; 2012: 84–5),[49] in Sarikoli (Iranian – Kim 2014: 16), in Marathi (Pandharipande 1997: 80–4), in Sidaama (Cushitic – Anbessa Teferra 2012: §5.2.2.2.2), in Silt'i (Ethio-Semitic – Rawda Siraj 2003: 14), in Malayalam and Kannada (Dravidian – Asher & Kumari 1997: §1.1.2.3.2, and Sridhar 1990: 51–2, respectively), in Kharia (Munda – Peterson 2006: 300; Peterson 2011: 410–11), among others.[50]

For principled reasons, as noted above (§3.1.4.2), they are only of the integrated type.[51]

De Vries's (2006: 265) second way to reinterpret 'pre-nominal non-restrictives', namely as '(definite) free relatives followed by an apposition'

---

[47] However, in later works she recognizes the existence of (pre-nominal) integrated non-restrictive RCs in Chinese as well (see Del Gobbo 2010, 2015 and 2017).

[48] Krause (2001a) in fact only denies the existence of an appositive interpretation for pre-nominal RCs with a genitive subject like the Turkish ones, but allows for such an interpretation for those with a nominative subject, possible in Japanese and Korean (but see Kornfilt 2011).

[49] Also see Öztürk & Pöchtrager (2011: 136) on Pazar Laz.

[50] Also see Lehmann (1984: 277 ff). One should actually further distinguish the case of full finite pre-nominal non-restrictives (of languages like, for example, Sarikoli) from pre-nominal non-restrictives of the participial type, possibly comparable to English *his recently deceased father*. One such case is Marathi, according to Pandharipande's (1997: 80–1) description, and possibly Chinese – see the discussion in §3.6).

[51] Relevantly, Lacroix (2012) states that 'Non-restrictive ('appositive') relative clauses use the same strategy as restrictive ones' (p. 84) and Kim (2014) that 'there is no structural difference between restrictive and non-restrictive RCs in Sarikoli' (p. 16).

('*(the one)* *who I love, Jean, lives in Paris*') also appears dubious if Downing (1978: 392) and Keenan (1985: 149) are right in claiming that no language with prenominal relative clauses displays genuine (initial) *wh*-pronouns (see also the discussion in §2.2.3).

3.1.6.3 Internally-Headed Non-restrictives

Although they are occasionally claimed not to be possible (De Vries 2005: 10–11; 2006: 266) internally-Headed non-restrictives are documented in the literature. In particular some of the languages whose IHRCs do not display an indefiniteness restriction (see §2.3) can apparently have non-restrictive IHRCs. See (59):[52]

(59) a. [tuut-ee-raa qung-ee 7ij-aa-n]-raaga'la 7waa-gaa-n
                        (Haida (isolate) – Enrico 2003: 570)
           box-DF-in moon-DF be-EVID-PST-for 3PERS do-EVID-PST
           'He did it for the moon, which was in the box.'
      b. lebu=ki iɲ=te yo=yoʔ=ki peʔ ɲokh=oˀj.
                        (Kharia (Munda) – Peterson 2006: 300; 2011: 407)
           person=P 1S=OBL see=A.PT=P rice eat=A.PT.1S
           'I, who the populace saw, ate rice.'
      c. i dawá dul kal jula ñá̰ká jĕk dáli̱-ñ-ĕ̤
                        (Cabecar – Gonzáles Campos & Lehmann forthcoming: §3.1.4)
           [3 brother.in.law POS.stand tree hand/arm IN] NEG RFL move-D.MID-
           NEG.PFV
           'His brother-in-law, who was standing on the branch, did not move.'

Their properties should also be of the integrated type only, as is apparently the case.

3.1.6.4 Double-Headed Non-restrictives

Double-Headed non-restrictives, of which we saw some examples above, from Italian and English (examples (9a), (10a), and (24)), are only of the non-integrated type, as integrated non-restrictives, like restrictives, are never introduced by a full copy of the (external or internal) Head.[53]

---

[52] On non-restrictive IHRCs, also see the discussion in Culy (1990: ch. 5: §2.4). Kitagawa (2005: §4) claims, following Kuroda's work, that all standard IHRCs in Japanese are non-restrictive. But see §2.3.3 for possible evidence that Japanese IHRCs cannot be non-restrictive. The same claim is made by Jung (1995: §3) for Korean.

[53] Berry and Berry (1999: 162), report that in the Papuan language Abun the double-Headed strategy, which is not common, is limited to non-restrictives.

3.1.6.5   Headless Non-restrictives?

Headless non-restrictives appear instead to be impossible (*He credited, what they had discovered, to someone else* – cf. *He credited that, which they had discovered, to someone else* – Emonds 1979: §2.4); perhaps for principled reasons since the silent antecedent of a Headless RC does not seem to have independent reference and since the Headless RC necessarily involves a 'raising' derivation, which is arguably unavailable in non-restrictives – see §3.1.8 below.

3.1.6.6   Non-restrictive Correlatives

Dayal (1996), on the basis of the ungrammaticality of examples like (60) below, concludes that Hindi correlatives cannot be non-restrictive 'since non-restrictives typically occur with proper names' (p. 182).[54]

(60)   *jo laRkii khaRii hai anu lambii hai   (= ex. (43) of Dayal 1996: 182)
          which girl standing be-PRES Anu tall is
          'Anu, who is standing, is tall.'

The question remains whether this is a property of Hindi/Urdu or of correlatives more generally. Judging from the fact that the closely related Indo-Aryan language Marathi can apparently form non-restrictive correlatives, one has to conclude that the impossibility of (60) is not due to some inherent feature of the correlative construction, but is a property of the grammar of Hindi (which would need to be elucidated). The possibility of non-restrictive correlatives in 'rethorical speech and writing' in Marathi is noted in Gupte (1975: 77), where such examples as (61a–b) are reported (also see Pandharipande 1997: 82–3):[55]

---

[54] Also see Gupta (1986: 34). The same is claimed by Butt, Holloway King & Roth (2007: §4.2) for the Urdu variant of Hindi/Urdu.

[55] The existence of non-restrictive correlatives in Marathi has been independently pointed out to me by Avinash Pandey and Renuka Ozarkar. Renuka Ozarkar gave me the following additional example of a non-restrictive correlative in Marathi:

(i)   ji-ne   maajhyaa-saaThii kaSTa ghet-l-e,   tii   maajhii   aaii   aataa jiwanta naahii.
       REL.fem-   me-for   efforts take-PERF-3P. that my-FEM mother now   alive   not-PRES
       ERG   PLURAL,
       my mother, who took efforts for me, is not alive anymore

In (i) and (61a–b) the correlate in the matrix is more informative than the *wh*-phrase in the RC, as in the restrictive example (i) of fn. 181 in Chapter 2, though in (61) the correlate is not only contextually presupposed (Veneeta Dayal, pers. comm.), but also autonomously referential. Non-restrictive correlatives were apparently also possible in Sanskrit. See Davison (2009: 227).

(61) a. jā-nni   gāt^hā   racali   te   tukārām   mahārāj dehulā   janmale
        REL-INSTR   Gatha   composed that   St.Tukaram Dehu-at was   born
        'St. Tukaram, who composed the Gatha, was born in Dehu.'
     b. gānd^hi-nni   jā-nnā   guru   mānale   te   gok^hale mawāl   hote
        Gandhi-INSTR REL-to teacher   regarded that   Gokhale moderate was
        'Gokhale, whom Gandhi regarded as (his) teacher, was a moderate.'

As a matter of fact, given the possibility of resuming a DP followed by a non-restrictive relative clause with a correlative phrase, as in (62) from Bangla, it should in principle be possible, if the language permits it, to delete the external Head as is possible with the external Head of restrictives:

(62)   bhoddrolok, jini amar āttio, tini bose achen   (Morshed 1986: 38)
          gentleman, who my relative, he sitting is
          'The gentleman, who is my relative, is sitting.'

Thus the possibility of non-restrictive correlatives may simply reduce to whether the language allows deletion of the external Head of non-restrictives (Marathi) or not (Hindi).

Interestingly, non-restrictive correlatives are also attested in other language families. See (63) from Jalonke (of the Central Mande branch of Niger-Congo), and the relative discussion in Lüpke (2005: 131–2):

(63)   N   naaxan a   fala-m'   i   bɛ jɛɛ,   n   saa-xi saar-ɛɛ   ma
          1SG REL   3SG speak-IPFV 2SG for PART, 1SG lie-PF bed-DEF at
          Lit.: which I is speaking to you now, I lie in bed
          I, who am talking to you now, I am lying on the bed

3.1.6.7   Non-restrictive Adjoined Relative Clauses

Walbiri 'adjoined' RCs also appear to be able to enter the non-restrictive construction. See (64) below, from Hale (1976: 90), who adds: '[I]f sentence [(64)] proved to be fully grammatical, with a NP-relative interpretation in which the relative clause is simultaneously construed with the main-clause subject [*maliki-li*] 'dog-erg' and the main-clause object [*minitja*] 'cat', it could not be derived by means of an extraction rule alone – at least not under any straightforward formulation of that rule. But such a sentence would be consistent with the adjunction analysis, since the main and subordinate clauses are linked by NP-coreferentiality [. . .]. In short, the study of NP-relative clauses with split antecedents might provide Walbiri internal evidence against the extraction analysis.' (p. 90).

(64)   maliki-li ka   minitja watjilipi-nji,   kutja-lpa-pala-njanu kulu-ŋku   nja-ŋu.
        dog-erg AUX   cat   chase-nonpast, COMP-**AUXrecip** anger-erg/inst look-past
        the dog is chasing the cat, which were looking at one another angrily

3.1.7   Resumptive Pronouns in Non-restrictives

In a number of Romance dialects non-restrictive RCs (of the integrated type, with an invariant relativizer) require, or allow, resumptive pronouns, unlike restrictive RCs, which do not allow them (Benincà & Vanelli 1982: 35, and, for the wide variation found in the dialects of Italy, Cennamo 1997: §2). This should not be surprising if one considers the fact that integrated non-restrictives, as opposed to restrictives, have a full DP as external Head, so that the internal Head that matches it is also a full DP. If resumptive pronouns stand for DPs (possibly accompanied, when clitic, by a silent DP in a 'big DP' structure) in the case of non-restrictives there is no categorial mismatch between the External Head (DP) and the internal one (the resumptive DP). Resumptive pronouns in ordinary restrictives would instead be more marked, when possible, as they involve a categorial mismatch between the external Head (dP) and the internal one (a resumptive DP) (except for hydras – see §5.1). In this respect they are similar to the *il quale*-restrictives of standard Italian, which are more marked, presumably because the *il quale* internal Head is also categorially a full DP.[56]

3.1.8   No 'Raising' Derivation in Non-restrictive Relative Clauses

For the non-integrated type a 'raising' derivation seems out of the question (given the possibility of the Head and the RC occurring in two separate sentences/fragments of the discourse, also uttered by separate speakers). And in fact, evidence has been adduced to this effect in the literature on English, which only has the non-integrated type. One type of evidence has to do with the absence of reconstruction in (English) non-restrictives (as well as in Italian non-integrated non-restrictives – Bianchi 1995: IV).

It has been noted (Vergnaud, 1974: §2.2; Emonds 1979: §2.6) that an 'idiom chunk' can be associated with a restrictive RC, but not with a non-restrictive one (also see Reed 1975: 183, from where the example in (65a) is taken; Postal 1998: 31, from where example (65b) is taken; Authier & Reed 2005: §3, from where (65c) is taken; Sportiche, Koopman & Stabler 2014: 412, from where (65d) is taken and Arnold & Bargmann 2016, from where (65e) is taken):[57]

---

[56] They seem to be possible to varying degrees in restrictive RCs whose Head has a specific interpretation, but normally impossible if the Head is interpreted generically (see Bianchi 2011; Poletto & Sanfelici 2017: 824–5).

[57] Also see Fabb (1990: 7) and Loock (2010: ch. 1: §2.4.1). The impossibility of an idiom chunk occurring as the Head of a non-restrictive RC also follows from Kayne's analysis. See Kayne (1994: 115). Nonetheless Arnold & Bargmann (2016) note the acceptability of sentences like (i) a–b, and Andrew Radford (pers. comm.) that of (i)c, suggesting a semantically compositional account which may distinguish them from those in (65):

(65)   a.   #He didn't want to take advantage, which he used to take.

b.   *[That much headway], which$_i$ they made t$_i$ on the job, ...

c.   *This is nothing but lip service, which Paul pays to civil liberties whenever he gets a chance.

d.   *Peter is aware of some significant headway, which (by the way) John had made recently.

e.   *The strings, which I hereby promise I will pull for you, will get you that job.

Similarly Reed (1975) gives examples like those in (66) saying that 'appositives never have reflexive heads which are coreferential with a constituent of the embedded sentence' (p. 182) (*pace* Kayne 1994: 112–13) (also see Sportiche, Koopman & Stabler's 2014: 412 from where (66c) is taken):[58]

(66)   a.   #Mary found a picture of himself, which Tom admitted painting.

b.   #Colby returned the recommendations of each other, which Mary and Susan promptly mailed in to Harvard.

c.   *Peter liked some pictures of each other, which (by the way) they acquired yesterday.

Authier & Reed (2005: 638), from where (67a) is taken, and Cardoso & De Vries (2010: §3.2), from where (67b) is taken, also observe that a pronominal within the Head of a non-restrictive cannot be bound by a quantifier within the RC under reconstruction:

(67)   a.   *Two pictures of his$_i$ mother, which every student$_i$ had given Sue, were on the table.

b.   #Let's collect the pictures of his$_i$ children, which [every father]$_i$ likes very much.

(i)   a.   The strings that were pulled for you before, which I hereby promise I will pull for you again, will get you that job.

b.   The strings that I pulled, which I will always pull, were decisive.

c.   I was surprised at them making so much headway, which frankly nobody else could have made.

Alternatively, the contrast between (65) and (i) could perhaps be made sense of if in English non-restrictive RCs *which* is an (E-type) determiner stranded by the deletion under identity of the noun *strings* (Arnold and Bargmann note the similarity with an example involving anaphora: *The strings that I pulled were decisive. I will always pull them.*), or *headway*. If so, *strings/headway* are paired with *pull/make* in both the matrix and the RC in (i), but not in (65d–e), where they are paired only in the RC, not in the matrix (see #*The strings will get you the job*; this may still differ from McCawley's (1981: 137) *Park pulled the strings that got me the job* if, as suggested in §2.1.1, in restrictives there can be partial match between the external and the internal Heads (*strings* KIND – KIND).

[58]   Sportiche (2017a) proposes to account for the lack of reconstruction in English non-restrictives in terms similar to De Vries's (2002) analysis, according to which non-restrictives are actually restrictive RCs modifying a light Head in apposition to the Head of the construction, which is then not in a chain with the RC gap. But see fn. 20 and fn. 31 for potential problems with this analysis.

Finally, a quantified Head in a non-restrictive RC cannot be interpreted under the scope of a quantifier inside the RC. See (68), again from Authier & Reed (2005: 638), which shows that the wide scope reading of *every* is unavailable:

(68)   I talked to two patients, who every doctor in town had examined.

In connection with Inverse Case Attraction in Persian restrictive RCs, which in the Appendix will be argued to be a consequence of 'raising', it is noteworthy that Persian does not permit Inverse Case Attraction in non-restrictives (see §A4.1.5 of the Appendix).

Furthermore, as noted in Borsley (1997: 644–5) and Authier & Reed (2005: §3), the fact that in non-restrictives the Head can be an AP, a VP, a CP or a PP, means that 'raising' would have to posit a structure in which the relative *which* has an AP-trace, a VP-trace, a CP-trace, etc. as its complement, in contrast to interrogative *which*, which never allows categories of this type as complements:[59]

Even integrated non-restrictives appear not to display reconstruction of the Head (Bianchi 1999: ch. 5; 2004: 83 and §3.3.3),[60] which I take at face value as suggesting that no 'raising' derivation is involved.

Another case which appears not to be easily reconcilable with 'raising' is represented by non-restrictives modifying a 1st person pronominal in English, like the one in (69) (see Heck & Cuartero 2008: §7; 2012: 61; Douglas 2015):[61]

(69)   I, who am tall, was forced to squeeze into that VW. (vs *I, who is tall, ...)

As Morgan (1972a: 284) observes, person agreement in English breaks down in contexts of long relativization. See (70):[62]

---

[59] Also see Arnold & Borsley (2010: §2).

[60] Also see Kameshima (1989: 8) for the lack of reconstruction effects in Japanese non-restrictives and Huot (1978) and Resi (2011) for arguments that non-restrictive RCs in French and German, respectively, involve 'matching' rather than 'raising'.

[61] When the 1st person pronoun has non-nominative Case (*me*) the agreement is however in the third person (*He had the nerve to say that to me, who has/*have made him what he is today* – Heck & Cuartero 2012: 62). This suggests that 'only a nominative-marked DP has Person features that can agree with T' (Douglas 2015: 46). As opposed to English, in Italian and Icelandic 1st and 2nd personal pronouns can only be relativized with the integrated non-restrictive *che/cui* and *sem* paradigms and not with the *il quale* and *hver* wh-paradigms. Even when they have non-nominative Case they appear to agree with T in Italian suggesting the presence of a null pro. On Italian see Douglas (2015: §6.1) and on Icelandic Jónsson (2017: 170–1).

[62] Also see Heck & Cuartero (2008, 2012: 77). Douglas (2015: 39) summarizes the basic generalizations as in (i):

    (i) a.   Number agreement between the pronominal head and the RC verb is obligatory.

         b.   Person agreement between the pronominal head and the RC verb is impossible, unless:

         i.   the pronominal head is in the nominative case, and

         ii.   relativisation is short-distance.

For Andrew Radford, though, the sentences in (70) are grammatical.

(70)   a.   *I, who John says the FBI thinks am an anarchist, will always be incoherent.

         b.   *I, who John says Martha believes the FBI thinks am an anarchist, may be losing my grip on banality.

So, *I* in (69)–(70) can hardly be taken to raise, it seems, from inside the RC. The exceptional agreement of the RC verb in (69) with the 1st pers. sing. Head rather than with the 3rd pers. relative pronoun *who* recalls the situation in certain varieties of German where personal pronouns are repeated within the non-restrictive relative clause. See, for example, (71):[63]

(71)   a.   Ich, der *(ich) sechzig bin, . . .

                              (variety of standard German – Itô & Mester 2000)

              Lit.: I, who I sixty am, . . .

              I, who am sixty, . . .

         b.   [du$_i$, ke du$_i$ boast nicht] söllast sbaing!

                              (Cimbrian – Bidese, Padovan & Tomaselli 2012: 16)

              you that you know nothing should shut up

              'You, who know nothing, you should shut up!'

Itô and Mester (2000) claim that default third person agreement with the relative pronoun is not permitted, reporting judgements like the following:

(72)   a.   *Ich, der sechzig ist, . . .

              Lit.: I, who sixty is, . . .;

         b.   *Du, der sechzig ist, . . .

              Lit.: You, who sixty is, . . .

However, Trutkowski and Weiß (2016a, 2016b) report experimental (and other) evidence showing that default third person agreement with the relative pronoun, like that illustrated in (72), is actually possible.[64] This makes a 'raising' analysis dubious. If one were to assume that *ich* and *der* start out together, in a 'big DP', with *der* ultimately stranded by the further raising of *ich*, one would also have to assume that the trace of *ich* does not count for agreement, unlike the overt counterpart of *ich* seen in (71). The way different languages behave in the relativization of 1st and 2nd person pronouns remains

---

[63] Sango is apparently similar. See (i):

     (i)   **mbi** só **mbi** ɛkɛ mará tí zande . . .   (Dreyfuss 1977: 126)

          Lit.: **I**, who **I** am tribe of Zande, . . .

          I, who am of the Zande tribe . . .

[64] Also see von Stechow (1979: 233), where both *Ich, der hier mit dir spricht* and *Ich, der ich hier mit dir spreche* are given as possible, in the second of which, according to him, property abstraction applies vacuously as the sentence contains no 'free variable'. My own small survey with younger speakers has revealed that default third person agreement with the relative pronoun is actually the preferred option for them, the resumptive one being judged 'old style'.

to be investigated in more detail and given a precise characterization. See the cited works for possible accounts.

3.1.9   *Stacking of Non-restrictive Relative Clauses?*

The question of whether non-restrictives can stack or not has been a matter of some controversy. Carlson (1977: 520), Chomsky (1977: 66), Jackendoff (1977: 171), Emonds (1979: 222), Smits (1989: 174), McCawley (1998: 447 and n. 13), and Bianchi (1999: 262), among others, assume that they cannot. McCawley gives the following example and judgement:

(73)   ??Sam Boronowski, who took the qualifying exam, who failed it, wants to retake it.

Others, including Grosu & Landman (1998: 126), Grosu (2000: 112), Kempson (2003), De Vries (2006: 252), Arnold (2007: §4.3.4), Loock (2010: ch. 1: §2.3.3), and Fukui (1986: 232 ff) and Kameshima (1989: §4.4) on Japanese, have instead claimed that they can. See for example (74a–c):

(74)   a.   John, who never finished high-school, who can't in fact even read or write, wants to do a doctorate in astrophysics. (Grosu 2000: 112)
        b.   The sole, which I caught yesterday, which was caught in Scotland, was delicious. (Kempson 2003: 303)
        c.   This man, who came to dinner late, about whom nobody knew anything, ... (De Vries 2006: 252)

Thus, the question remains open for English. In Italian a non-integrated non-restrictive appears to be able to be stacked to an integrated one (see (75a), and §3.5.1 below). But even two integrated non-restrictives can, if pragmatically appropriate (see (75b)), and the same seems true of Japanese (see (75c) from Fukui 1986: 232):

(75)   a.   Gianni, che non è propriamente esperto, il quale poi raramente si dimostra disponibile, ...
              Gianni, who isn't really an expert, who in addition is rarely ready to help ...
        b.   Grezar, che è stato uno dei più grandi calciatori degli anni' 40, di cui purtroppo più nessuno ora si ricorda, è sepolto a Trieste.
              'Grezar, who was one of the greatest football players of the Forties, whom unfortunately now nobody remembers any longer, is buried in Trieste.'
        c.   [$_{NP}$ [$_S$ Osaka-(de)-no kokusai-kaigi-ni sanka-suru koto-ni-natte-iru] [$_S$ America-kara kaette-ki-ta bakari]-no Jonn]-wa ima Tokyo-no hotel-ni tomatte-imasu.
              'John, who is supposed to attend the international conference in Osaka, who just returned from America, is now staying at a hotel in Tokyo.'

3.1.10   Extraposition

Some examples of apparently extraposed non-restrictive RCs are reported for English in Kempson (2003: 302 fn. 4) and Arnold (2007: 288), in Dutch in De Vries (2006: 254) and Cardoso & De Vries (2010: §7.6). See (76), though it is not entirely clear whether such cases are genuine instances of extraposition, or simply a special case of non-adjacency, like that found across discourse (see §3.1.2 above). Also see Ziv (1973) and Ziv & Cole (1974: 777) for arguments against the possibility of extraposition in non-restrictives, and Cinque (2008a: §4.2).[65]

(76)   I saw my mother yesterday, who I hadn't seen for years.

3.1.11   Conclusion

On the basis of some comparative evidence I have argued for the existence of two distinct non-restrictive relative constructions: one essentially identical (except for the position of Merge above DP – see §3.5 – and other minor differences) to the ordinary restrictive construction (and as such part of sentence grammar), the other distinct from the ordinary restrictive construction (with characteristics of the grammar of discourse).[66] Italian and other Romance languages display both constructions; English, (Modern Standard) Romanian, and Polish only the discourse grammar construction; Northern Italian dialects and languages with pre-nominal non-restrictive RCs only the sentence grammar one; while other languages display neither. It thus appears that earlier focus on English, which, as noted, possesses just the discourse grammar non-integrated construction, has had the unfortunate effect of biasing the theoretical analyses proposed in the literature for non-restrictive RCs.

---

[65] In Italian restrictives, for example, extraposition from a preverbal subject is not possible (Cinque 1978: fn. 65; 1982: fn. 28; 1988: §1.1.10) (see (i)a), while non-adjacency of a subject Head and a non-restrictive is possible (see (i)b):

(i)   a.   *?Una pianta era stata usata che non era velenosa
                One plant had been used that was not poisonous.
        b.   Una pianta era stata usata, la quale non era velenosa
                Only one plant was used, which was not poisonous.

Also see Baltin's (1987: fn. 2) claim that non-restrictive RCs in English do not extrapose, based on examples like (i):

(i) *I called John up, whom I couldn't stand.

[66] In other words, both types of non-restrictives differ structurally from restrictives in overt syntax, which is apparently crucial to account for the asymmetries in agreement between restrictives and non-restrictives noted in Arsenijević & Gračanin-Yüksek (2016) for Bosnian/Croatian/Serbian relatives.

3.2   Kind(-Defining) Relative Clauses

One type of RC that is not usually recognized as distinct from ordinary restrictive RCs and which shares properties of both restrictives and non-restrictives, with a specific semantics, is what Benincà (2003, 2012a and 2012c), and Benincà & Cinque (2014), refer to as kind-defining. This type appears to correspond closely to what McCawley (1981: §1 and §2; 1998: ch. 13, section d) called pseudo-relatives (not to be confused with the so-called pseudo-relatives of the Romance linguistic tradition – for which see the brief discussion in §3.4.1.2 below) and in particular to Prince's (1990, 1997) Kind clauses (see also Radford (2019: §1.2). The similarities between the English and the Italian constructions will be noted in the text, which primarily deals with Italian. As will become apparent from the examples to be presented, semantically kind-defining RCs differ from ordinary restrictives in that the proposition expressed by the RC is not presupposed to be true (Benincà & Cinque 2014: §13.4). 'They also differ in that they do not narrow down the reference of the Head [...] but rather serve to mark the semantic class which the Head belongs to' (Benincà & Cinque 2014: 261–2). In typical contexts, where it is a predicate (*He is a guy that (he) gets into a lot of fights* paraphrasable as 'he is such that he gets into a lot of fights'), the Head is in fact non-referential. See Prince's (1997: §5.2) term 'predicational relative clauses', where the RCs 'predicate a property of an entity evoked by the head alone ...' (p. 230). Extended contexts (which may contain an existential/locative predicate) include the object position of verbs like 'have', 'look for', 'meet/run into', 'hear of' (see McCawley 1981: 107), and 'see', 'know' (see Benincà & Cinque 2014: §2.1, and references cited there). In certain languages kind-defining RCs (also) have a distinct relative pronoun introducing them (e.g. Macedonian *kakov* ('qualis') – see (77), from Browne 1970: 269). The same is true of Bulgarian (Iliyana Krapova, pers. comm.) and Hungarian (Anna Szabolcsi, pers. comm.):

(77)   Todor e čovek **kakov** retko k'e vidiš.
       Theodore is man qualis (WH-such) rarely will you-see
       'Theodore is a man such as you'll rarely see.'

In these works, a number of properties are identified which differentiate them from both restrictives and non-restrictives, some being shared with restrictives and some (most) with non-restrictives. See also §3.5 for evidence that their Merge position is different from that of both restrictives and non-restrictives:

1) *Kind-defining RCs naturally admit resumptive pronominals* (different from those 'amnestying island violations') (like non-restrictives and unlike restrictives):

(78)   a.   Gianni è uno che non **gli** si può dire di no.
                'Gianni is someone that you can't say no **to him**.'
        b.   E' un conto che **lo** puoi fare sulla punta delle dita.[67]
                'It's a calculation that you can do **it** on the fingers of your hand.'

Similar cases are found in colloquial English ((79)) (in which *where/whereby* are often found as relativizers – Radford 2019: §2.4), and Yiddish ((80)):

(79)   a.   He was one of those comedians that **he** could make the whole audience laugh without even saying a word. (Prince 1990: n. 3)
        b.   He is the kind of guy that **he** gets into a lot of fights. (Prince 1997: 230)
        c.   I think he is one of those defenders that I don't think Swansea are going to miss **him**. (Andrew Radford's corpus of colloquial English, Andrew Radford pers. comm.)
        d.   He's one of those players [where **he**'s been really unlucky]. (Radford 2019: 84)
        e.   It's one of those things [where you're not sure whether to do **it**]. (Radford 2019: 84)

(80)   a.   Nor ikh bin a yid, vos **ikh** hob lib a sakh tsuker. (Prince 1997: 232)
                but I'm a guy that I like a lot of sugar
        b.   Ikh bin a yid, vos **ikh** es veynik. (Prince 1997: 232)
                I'm a guy that I eat little

2) *Kind-defining RCs can have an independent illocutionary force* (again like non-restrictives and unlike restrictives). See (81a), and (81b) for a parallel case in English:

(81)   a.   E' un uomo a cui avresti mai pensato di doverti un giorno rivolgere?
                He is a man to whom would you ever have expected to have one day to refer?
        b.   It's one of those that do we just push to one side? (Brian Law, BBC Radio 5, from Andrew Radford, pers. comm.)

---

[67] Adapted from Benincà & Cinque (2014: fn. 4), from the original in Collodi's Pinocchio. Ordinary restrictive relatives instead do not admit resumptive pronominals. See (i):

(i)   *Il ragazzo che non (*lo) conosci verrà stasera.
            'The boy that you do not know (him) will arrive tonight.'

3) *Kind-defining RCs can display heavy pied-piping with the* il quale *paradigm*[68] (again like non-restrictives and unlike restrictives).

(82)   a.   E' un fiume [correndo lungo il quale] puoi specchiarti in acque limpidissime.
It is a river running along which you can look at yourself in clear waters.

b.   Ho finalmente trovato una ragazza [per uscire con la quale] non mi dovrò inginocchiare.
I have finally found a girl to go out with whom I will not have to kneel down.

Similar heavy pied-piping seems possible in English sentences that appear to qualify as kind-defining.[69] See (83) and the discussion in Viel (2001: §3.2.5)

(83)   a.   Insomnia is a problem [the effects of which] are felt in the long run. (Viel 2001: 73)

b.   ?Mary Smith is the only woman [whose husband's love for whom] knows no bounds. (see Kayne 2017b: 365).

c.   He is a linguist [articles by whom] the editors always reject. (Horvath 2017: §3.1.1)

d.   This is the kind of woman [proud of whom] I could never be. (Horvath 2017: §3.1.1)

4) *Kind-defining RCs can retain the internal Head* (once again, like non-restrictives and unlike restrictives). See (84), and its English translation, which Andrew Radford tells me is acceptable in a high (archaic) register:[70]

---

[68] These sentences belong to a high register, but possibly not as high a register as that to which the restrictives with heavy pied-piping involving the *il quale* paradigm seen in §2.1.2.1.2 belong.

[69] In contrast to the corresponding restrictives, e.g. ??*We have to avoid the problem the effects of which are not foreseeable.* *?Yesterday I met the woman proud of whom he was.*

[70] Also compare (i)a with (i)b, cited in Cinque (1982: 267–8; 1995: 82–3), the first of which is subjunctive in mood and appears thus to qualify as kind-defining, while the second contains the indicative mood, thus qualifying as a restrictive RC:

(i)   a.   Cercava delle macchine le quali macchine fossero in grado di produrre 10 tennellate di chiodi al secondo.
he was looking for machines which machines would be able to produce 10 tonnes of nails per second

b.   *Non ricordo ora il nome della ragazza della quale ragazza si era invaghito.
'I can't remember the name of the girl with whom (lit. the which girl) he had fallen in love.'

(84) (?) Non era un farmaco col quale farmaco uno potesse facilmente
debellare quella malattia.
it wasn't a medicine with which medicine one could easily wipe out
that disease

5) *Agreement in kind-defining RCs*

An additional property of kind-defining RCs is the fact that they
allow the verb in the relative clause to agree with the subject of the
matrix clause rather than with the relative clause Head, as in (85a),
from fourteenth-century Ligurian, quoted in Parry (2007: 26 fn. 16),
and (85b–c) in Modern Colloquial French, reported in Smits (1989:
329) and Auger (Auger 1994: 77; 1995: 22), respectively :[71]

(85) a. **he'** som quella che lo port**ay** nove meysi e che lo norig**ay** com
lo me' layte.
I am the.one that him I.bore nine months and that him I.fed
him with the my milk
'I am the one that bore him for nine months and that fed him
with my milk.'
b. **Nous** étions ceux qui all**ions** vaincre Hitler.
'We were the ones who would (1pl) vanquish Hitler.'
c. **J**'étais pas une personne que **j**'avais beaucoup d'amis.
'I wasn't a person who had (1sg) a lot of friends.'

To judge from Prince (1997) and Radford (2019), the same appears to
be true of English (see (86)), and of Yiddish (see the examples in (80)
above):

(86) a. I am the kind of person **I** don't like anything gooey on my
hands. (Prince 1997: 225)
b. I'm the type of person **I** like to be positive. (Kroch corpus,
cited in Radford 2019: 13 fn. 5)
c. I'm the kind of guy that **I** like to ask a lot of questions.
(Radford 2019: 13 fn. 5)

6) *Kind-defining RCs are compatible with the presuppositional negative
adverb* mica *in Italian (once again, like non-restrictives and unlike
restrictives).*

The presuppositional negative adverb mica, which is possible in
non-restrictives (see (87a)), renders restrictive relatives ungrammatical, as seen from (87b) see Cinque (1976: 107):

---

[71] For more detailed discussion see Benincà & Cinque (2014: §7).

(87)   a.   Ho salutato Gianni, che non avevo mica visto prima.
              'I greeted Gianni, whom I hadn't at all seen earlier.'
        b.   *Ho invitato anche il ragazzo che non conosci mica.
              'I have also invited the boy that you don't know at all.'

Interestingly, kind-defining relatives behave like non-restrictives (see (88)):

(88)   a.   Sono libri che non voglio mica leggere.
              'They are books that I don't want at all to read.'
        b.   Mario è un uomo che non esita mica a rischiare.
              'Mario is a man that doesn't hesitate at all to take risks.'

7) *Can kind-defining RCs be derived by 'raising'?*

In Benincà & Cinque (2014: §13.6) we tentatively suggested on the basis of the relative acceptability of idiom cases like (89a–b) that kind-defining RCs could be derived by 'raising' (in addition to being derived by 'matching'). But given the compositional nature of the idiom cases (89a–b) (see the discussion in the Appendix: A4.4.1) and the impossibility of scope reconstruction in (89c) it is unclear that they can.

(89)   a.   Questi sono conti che non tornano mica.
              'These are things that don't work out at all.'
        b.   Questa è la parte che deve avere avuto nella vicenda.
              'This is the role that he must have had in the event.'
        c.   E' un/l' esercizio che ogni studente dovrebbe fare. (one >
              every; *every > one)
              'It's an/the exercise that every student should do.'

3.2.1   Subject Contact Relatives in English[*]

Restrictive RCs on a subject which have no relative pronoun nor an overt complementizer are generally ungrammatical in English. See (90):

(90)   a.   *The book will arrive today is interesting. (= example (15c) of Benincà
              & Cinque 2014)
        b.   *?I asked one of my uncles was an engineer and he told me . . .
              (Lambrecht 1988: 321, his (13b))

---

[*] This term is due to Jespersen (1949). Other terms used for the same class of cases are 'zero relatives' (Harris & Vincent 1980), and 'pseudo-relatives' (McCawley's 1981: 7 ff and §2). For the zero relatives found in older stages of the Romance languages, which are possible in many more contexts than English subject contact relatives, see Rohlfs (1968: 193), Scorretti (1991), Benincà (1995), Stark (2016: fn. 1), and Poletto & Sanfelici (2017: §4).

There is however one class of subject contact relatives that seem to be possible in a number of English regional varieties (see Lambrecht 1988; Doherty 1993, 1994; Henry 1995: ch. 6; Berizzi 2001; Herrmann 2003; Benincà 2012d: §2; Haegeman 2015; Haegeman et al. 2015, Williamson 2016). See (91):

(91)   a.   There's a train goes without stopping (Great Manchester County)
        b.   I have a sister lives in Dublin (Belfast English – Henry 1995: 124)
        c.   There was a snake come down the road (Appalachian County)
        d.   There was something [bothered me about the garage]. (Guardian, 23.3.1999, page 5, col 6), from Haegeman (2015: 134)

There is evidence that they make up a constituent with the Head, much like object contact relatives (they turn out to be c-commanded by the Head and by other elements that happen to c-command the Head). See Haegeman et al. (2015) for extensive evidence to this effect, which argues against the root analysis proposed in Henry (1995) and Den Dikken (2005).

Benincà & Cinque (2014: §2.1) note that they appear to occur in the same, characteristic, environments as kind-defining RCs (presentational, existential and copular structures, and as objects of verbs like 'have', 'know', 'see', 'come across' – Hermann 2003: 35–6) with the same semantic properties of kind-defining RCs. For example, Doherty (1994) states that 'a noun phrase modified by a subject contact relative must be interpreted as non-referential' (p. 155). As with Italian kind-defining RCs they appear to allow for resumptive pronouns (see (79d) above, repeated here as (92):[72]

(92)   He is one of those players [where he's been really unlucky].

It is thus tempting to take subject contact relatives of those varieties of English that allow them to be kind-defining.

3.2.2 Verb Second Relative Clauses in German and Dutch

Both Lambrecht (1988: 332) and Den Dikken (2005: §4) assimilate subject contact relatives with German and Dutch Verb Second RCs. While such an assimilation cannot be complete (see, in particular, the differences between the two constructions noted in Haegeman et al. 2015, which seem to suggest that subject contact relatives are fully integrated whereas Verb Second RCs are less so), the contexts in which both are found and the interpretation which

---

[72] But see Loss (2017), where two distinct types of subject contact relatives are distinguished, one (specific to Belfast English and Tok Pisin) allowing resumptive pronouns and the other (specific to Gullah and African American English) not allowing them.

they display seem to point to a close relation between the two and kind-defining RCs. The three main differences between subject contact RCs in English and German/Dutch V2 RCs that Haegeman et al. (2015) point out concern the fact that the former but not the latter appear to form a constituent with the antecedent (§5.2.1), the fact that the former but not the latter appear to be c-commanded by material in the matrix clause containing the antecedent (§5.2.2) and the fact that German/Dutch V2 RCs appear to be restricted to root clauses (§5.3). Given Catasso & Hinterhölzl's (2016) analysis of German V2 RCs as 'regular subordinated relative clauses that due to the specific property of embedded V2 need to be extraposed and are interpreted in a high-adjoined position in the matrix clause' (p. 99), it is possible that these differences are to be attributed to orthogonal factors, thus capturing the essential similarities between the two constructions and kind-defining RCs,[73] though this remains to be looked into in detail. Also see Sanfelici, Schulz & Trabandt's (2017) careful study of German V2 RCs, where they are analysed as embedded root clauses necessarily extraposed like other types of embedded root clauses, and where they are shown not to allow for a 'raising' derivation, since, as opposed to (non-extraposed) verb-final restrictives, they do not admit idiom chunk Heads ((93a) vs b) (see their (31a, c)), reconstruction of anaphors ((94a) vs 94b)) (see their (29a, c)) and *de dicto* readings ((95a) vs (95b) and their (32a, c), which are originally from Gärtner 2002: 35; also see Endriss & Gärtner 2005, Ebert, Endriss & Gärtner 2007, Ravetto 2007, and Catasso 2014).[74]

(93)   a.   *Jeder Student spricht über die großen Reden, die schwingen die Professoren.
        b.   Jeder Student spricht über die großen Reden, die die Professoren schwingen.
              'Every student talks about the grand speeches that the professors give.'

(94)   a.   *Es gab ein Foto von sich₍ᵢ₎, das hat Peter₍ᵢ₎ gestern gefunden.
        b.   Es gab ein Foto von sich₍ᵢ₎, das Peter₍ᵢ₎ gestern gefunden hat.
              'There was a photo of himself that Peter found yesterday.'

---

[73] German V2 RCs share with kind-defining RCs the type of predicate of the matrix clause (which must be existential/presentational or belong to a limited set of verbs comprising 'see', 'know', 'hear', etc.), and the type of antecedent (which is virtually always indefinite).

[74] Viola Schmitt agrees with the judgement in (93) but finds the judgements in (94) and (95) less clear.

In addition to Catasso & Hinterhölzl's (2016) and Sanfelici, Schulz & Trabandt's (2017) evidence for the embedded nature of German V2 RCs, see Kallulli's (2018: fn. 6) argument against a syntactic coordination analysis of V2 relatives à la Gärtner's (2001).

(95)   a.   Maria möchte einen Fisch fangen, der ist kariert. (*de re* only)
        b.   Maria möchte einen Fisch, der kariert ist, fangen. (*de dicto* and *de re*)
              'Maria wants to catch a fish that is chequered.'

In §3.3 and §3.4 I consider infinitival and participial RCs, which have been claimed to have a partially reduced structure (for recent discussion see Douglas 2016: 81 ff and references cited there; but also see Radford 2018: §2.5 and 2019: §1.4).

3.3   Infinitival Relative Clauses

Some languages do not possess infinitival RCs.[75] According to Sabel (2006, 2015) a precondition for having infinitival RCs is that the language possesses the option of filling the CP with an infinitival complementizer.[76] Sabel suggests deriving this generalization from the defective nature of the infinitival left periphery in those languages that do not have a genuine infinitival complementizer. See his works for further discussion.

3.3.1   *Infinitival Relative Clauses in English*
Unlike their finite counterparts, infinitival RCs do not allow an overt object *wh*-phrase in Spec,CP (see (96b), (97b), (98b)), while allowing an overt PP containing a *wh*-phrase (possibly at a higher stylistic level) (see (99)):[77]

---

[75] These comprise German (Sabel 2006, 2015) and Turkish (Kornfilt 1985).

[76] See Sabel's (2015) *Wh-Infinitive-Generalization* (WHIG): 'If wh-movement may terminate in the Spec CP of an infinitive in a language then this language possesses the option of filling the C-system of this (type of) infinitive with an overt complementizer.' (p. 318). German possesses no infinitival interrogatives or infinitival relatives (with *zu*), although it may apparently fill the Spec,CP with a relative pronoun in *'rattenfänger'* constructions (where the infinitival clause is pied-piped to a position adjacent to the Head). See Ross (1967: 205) and Van Riemsdijk (1985, 1994) (*pace* Haider 1985 and Grewendorf 1986). On root *wh*-infinitivals in German see Reis (2003).

[77] As shown by a comparison with Italian (see §3.3.2.4 below) cases such as (i), which are often taken to instantiate infinitival relatives, should not be considered to belong to the same construction:

(i)   a.   The man to fix the sink is here. (Bhatt 2006: 9)
       b.   The first to walk on the moon visited my school yesterday. (Bhatt 2006: 9)
       c.   I'll find a professor to help you. (Breivik 1997: 111)

In fact Williams (1980: §2.3.2), Kayne (1981a: n. 26; 1983b: n. 6), and Sag (1997: 470) take English 'subject infinitival relatives' to involve PRO rather than the trace of *wh*-movement. The fact that object infinitival relatives ((ii)) but not 'subject infinitival relatives' ((iii)) permit long-distance extraction in English (subject to islands – Ross 1967: §6.1.1.3) also seems to suggest

(96)   a.   I finally found a book [[to read __]].
        b.   *I finally found a book [which [to read __]].

(97)   a.   Here is someone [[to work with __]].
        b.   *Here is someone [whom [to work with __]].

(98)   a.   The thing (for you) to be these days is a systems analyst. (Girard &
             Malan 1999: 1)
        b.   *The thing which to be these days is a systems analyst.

(99)   Here is someone [with whom [to work __]].

This closely recalls the situation described above for Italian *che/cui* restrictives, with obligatory deletion of one or the other Head (but see below for the possibility that with infinitival RCs the deletion involves only the internal one, under 'matching').[78] The PP case is possibly more akin to the Italian (more marked) art. + *qual-* (and genitive *cui*)[79] paradigm than to the *che/cui* restrictive paradigm, as it allows (at the same stylistically marked level as (99)), even

---

that the former but not the latter involve A-bar movement (as the trace is case-marked in the former though not in the latter case):

(ii)   a.   Here's a plate for you to make Bob try to begin to force his sister to leave the
              cookies on. (Ross 1967: 389)
         b.   Here's the book$_i$ to try to get John to read t$_i$. (Bhatt 2006: 12)
(iii)   *The man$_i$ for us to try t$_i$ to fix the sink is here. (see Bhatt 2006: 6)
Less clear is how to account for the contrast in (iv) pointed out in Ross (1967: 389):
(iv)   a.   ?Here's a knife for you to say that you cut up the onions with.
         b.   *Here's a knife for you to say was on the table.

Douglas (2016: ch. 3: §4.1) gives as grammatical a sentence similar to (iv)b (see (v)a), contrasting it with the impossible (v)b:

(v)   a.   I found a play for you to prove was written by Shakespeare.
         b.   *I found a play to prove was written by Shakespeare.

[78] Pesetsky (1998: §4) also notes that English infinitival relatives 'mirror with startling fidelity the pattern of French *finite* relative clauses – including the obligatory deletion of *wh* up to recoverability' (p. 350). It thus seems that, as in the restrictive or maximalizing RCs of Italian and French, deletion of the internal Head is obligatory unless it is larger (PP) than the external one. For a review of (some of) the accounts that have been proposed for English infinitival relatives see Hasegawa (1998), who adds another piece to the puzzle from Old and Middle English, where the relative pronoun could be deleted stranding a preposition in COMP: *a foot on to goo* ('a foot on which to go') or *a hous in to drink and ete* ('a house in which to drink and eat'). For further references on English infinitival RCs see Radford (2019: 14 fn. 6).

[79] Recall that genitive *cui* in Italian (*Gianni, la cui figlia è appena arrivata, . . .* 'G., whose daughter has just arrived, . . .') does not belong to the ordinary restrictive *che/cui* paradigm but to the more marked restrictive paradigm of *il quale*. See Cinque (1978: §3.11; 1982: §1.6; 1988: §1.1.6.1.3).

heavier pied-pipings. See (100), and the parallel Italian examples in §3.3.2 below:[80]

(100)   a.   I bought a book the cover of which to decorate with crayons. (Green 1973: 18)

         b.   ?I loaned Maggie a Swiss Army knife with whose corkscrew to open the padlock. (Ross 1967: 390)

         c.   Freudians aren't my idea of people whose word to take. (McCawley 1991: 51)

         d.   ?John is looking for a rich man whose daughter to marry. (Bianchi 1995: 293 fn. 31)

When no *wh*-phrase is present in Spec,CP a 'complementizer', *for*, can occupy the CP, obligatorily followed, in Standard English, by a lexical subject assigned Case by *for*. See (101):[81]

(101)   I finally found a book [for [*(you) to read __]].

If a *wh*-phrase occupies Spec,CP *for* (followed by a lexical subject) is ill formed (see (102), unless the *wh*-phrase and *for* are separated by some other constituent (see (103), from Douglas 2016: 68, and (104), from Radford 2019: ch. 1: §1.4), which recalls the contrast between **I want for you to leave* and *I want very much for you to leave*.

(102)   *Here is a knife with which for you to cut up the onions. (Ross 1967: 389)

(103)   ?I found a thrift-shop in which next year for you to do the Christmas shopping.

(104)   a.   There may be more room [in which perhaps for Manchester United to manoeuvre].

         b.   We need weapons [with which, if necessary, for us to defend ourselves].

         c.   This will provide a better basis [from which eventually for them to get started].

         d.   This is the perfect environment [in which, if they are watered regularly, for petunias to thrive].

---

[80] Pesetsky (1998: 352 fn. 17) gives a sentence comparable to (100a) two question marks, which recalls the degraded status of comparable object cases with heavy pied-piping in French and Italian vs PPs – see §2.1.2.1.2 and fns 44 and 45 of Chapter 2.

[81] See the *\[for-to\]* filter of Chomsky & Lasnik (1977: 442), not operative in other variants of English, like Irish or Appalachian English. Berman (1974: 38 ff), based on such cases as *John*[i] *brought a book for himself/*him*[i] *to read*, argues for a PP rather than CP nature of *for* DP. Yet, as Andrew Radford reminds me, in the case of an expletive subject (*The agenda contained a possible list of topics for **there** to be discussion of in the afternoon session*) the PP analysis is ruled out. For the possibly complex nature of the *for* 'complementizer', see Kayne (2014b; 2017c).

Infinitival RCs in English can also apparently stack, as observed in Sag (1997: 470):

(105)   ?The problems [to solve __] [for you to impress them with __] are the ones in the Times.

Non-restrictive infinitival RCs are apparently severely constrained in English. For Huddleston (1971: 251) the non-restrictive infinitive clause is possible 'only when the subject is relativized'. Compare *The man, to see, is Smith.* with *This scholar, to be found daily in the British Museum, has devoted his life to the history of science* (Quirk et al. 1985: 1270). But see Emonds's (1979: 237) example: *?This room, to teach algebra in, adjoins mine*, and Akiyama (2014) for discussion. Perhaps some of them are reduced non-restrictives (*This scholar, who is to be found* ... etc.). Also see below for apparently non-restrictive infinitival RCs in Italian.

3.3.2   Infinitival Relative Clauses in Italian

Italian infinitival relative clauses have been the object of a number of studies (see Napoli 1976, Cinque 1988: §1.1.5, Bianchi 1991, 2007, and Cinque & Benincà 2018, from where I draw some of the points presented here). On the basis of these analyses Italian infinitival relative clauses appear to be characterized by the following properties:

When the relativization is on the direct object, the relative clause is introduced by the invariant preposition *da*, as in (106):[82]

(106)   a.   Ho trovato [un libro$_i$ da recensire t$_i$.]
             'I have found a book to review.'
        b.   [Il libro$_i$ da recensire t$_i$] è lì sul tavolo.
             'The book to review is there on the table.'

Unmarked infinitival relatives behave like unmarked finite restrictive relatives (compare (107a) with (107b)), and English infinitival relatives, (see (107c)): they cannot involve a relative pronoun, unless the DP is embedded in a PP (see (107c–d):[83]

---

[82] In colloquial Italian *da* may also be used when an oblique argument is relativized, provided that the oblique argument is locally bound by a resumptive clitic:

(i)   a.   Ecco un vaso da metterci dentro dei fiori freschi.
           here's a vase to put in it fresh flowers
      b.   Ha trovato un ragazzo da uscirci assieme tutte le sere.
           she found a boy-friend to go out with him every evening

[83] It thus seems that deletion of the internal Head is obligatory unless the internal Head is larger (PP) than the external one.

(107)   a.   Il vestito che/*il quale hai comprato non ti sta bene.
           'The suit which you have bought does not fit you.'
       b.   Sto cercando un libro da/*il quale leggere.
           I'm looking for a book which to read
       c.   'I'm looking for a book (*which) to read' vs ... 'on which to work'
           (Pesetsky 1998: 350)
       d.   Ho regalato a Gianni un libro con cui passare la serata.[84]
           'I gave G. a book with which to spend the evening.'

The (finite) invariant relativizer *che* is completely impossible in infinitival relatives (see (108)):

(108)   a.   Il vestito che indossi non ti sta bene.
           'The dress that you wear does not suit you.'
       b.   *Le ho comprato un vestito che indossare alla festa.
           'I bought her a dress to wear at the party.'

Like the more marked finite restrictive construction seen in §2.1.2.1.2, there is also a more marked infinitival RC construction employing heavy pied-piping with art. + *qual-* and genitive *cui*. See (109):

(109)   a.   Non ha ancora trovato [un progetto [alla realizzazione del quale]
           dedicare il resto della sua vita]. (Cinque 1988: 454)
           he hasn't found yet a project to the realization of which to dedicate the
           rest of his life
       b.   Ho presentato a Gianni [una persona [ai cui amici] chiedere consiglio]].
           I introduced to G. a person whose friends to ask for advice

Infinitival relatives can be restrictive:

(110)   a.   Lo studente a cui affidare l'incarico è purtroppo appena uscito.
           'The student to whom to entrust the task has unfortunately just left.'
       b.   Abbiamo scelto la stoffa da usare per coprire il divano.
           'We chose the cloth to use to cover the sofa.'

---

[84] There is in fact a stylistically more marked construction discussed in Cinque (1988: §1.1.5.1) which admits the retention of the object art + *qual-* pronoun (see (i)a), much like what appears to be possible in French (see (i)b), as well as constituents heavier than PP (see the examples in (109)).

    (i)   a.   ??Cercava dei preziosi, i quali poter impegnare al Monte prima di dover ipotecare
             la casa. (Cinque 1988: §1.1.5.1)
             Lit.: He was looking for jewels which to be able to pawn at the pawnshop before
             mortgaging his house.
        b.   ??Je cherche un homme, lequel photographier. (Kayne 1976: n. 22)
             Lit.: I'm looking for a man whom to photograph.

Some infinitival RCs seem to belong to the class of kind-defining relative clauses, as they do not identify the referent of the antecedent but express its characteristics. See (111):

(111)   a.   Ho trovato un idraulico a cui affidare il lavoro.
             'I found a plumber to whom to assign the job.'
        b.   Ho trovato una stoffa da usare per coprire il divano.
             'I found a cloth to utilize to cover the sofa.'
        c.   Ho bisogno di un assistente da assumere con fiducia.
             'I need an assistant to (be able to) hire with confidence.'

3.3.2.1   Non-restrictive *da* Infinitival Relatives?
In Cinque (1988: §1.1.5), on the basis of sentences like (112), I had assumed that ordinary infinitival RCs are only restrictive (also see Demirdache 1991: 115):

(112)   a.   *C'era persino Giorgio, a cui parlare di questo.
             'There was even Giorgio, to whom to talk about this.'
        b.   *Lida, di cui essere fieri, è qua.
             Lida, of whom to be proud, is here

It would however seem that some *da* infinitival relatives, like those in (113), can have non-restrictive import:

(113)   a.   Questo libro, da non leggere, parla di Mozart senza alcuna cognizione di causa. (Cinque 1988: 455)
             'This book, not to be read, talks about Mozart, without any real knowledge of the matter.'
        b.   Il suo consiglio, da prendere sicuramente sul serio, è che tu non ti muova.
             'His advice, to be taken seriously, is that you do not move.'

It should however be noted that, while ordinary infinitival relatives are ambiguous between a root possibility ('could') and a root deontic ('should') interpretation (see the next section), the interpretation of these 'non-restrictive' *da* infinitival relatives is necessarily deontic, which makes one think that they are derived through a reduction from a full finite non-restrictive involving the deontic periphrasis *è da* + infinitive:[85]

(114)   a.   Questo libro, che è da non leggere, . . .
             this book, which is not to be read, . . .
        b.   Il suo consiglio, che è da prendere sicuramente sul serio, . . .
             his advice, which is to be taken seriously, . . .

---

[85] See Akiyama (2014) for a comparable derivation of English non-restrictive infinitival relatives from the 'IS TO' construction.

3.3.2.2 Two *da* Infinitival Relatives in Italian

Like English (object and oblique) infinitival relatives (Bhatt 2006 and Hackl & Nissenbaum 2012), Italian infinitival relatives can either have a 'could' (possibility) interpretation (see (115a)) or a 'should' (deontic necessity) interpretation when they are introduced by strong determiners (like definite determiners in subject position or universal quantifiers) (see (115b–c)), or contain a negation (see (115d)). In some cases both interpretations are available (in fact (115a) admits a 'should' interpretation as well).[86]

(115)   a.   Ho finalmente trovato un libro da regalare ai miei figli.
          'I finally found a book (to be able) to give to my children as a present.'
      b.   Questo è il libro da regalare a Gianni.
          'This is the book to give to Gianni as a present.'
      c.   Hanno elencato ogni libro da mettere all'indice.
          'They listed every book to put in the index.'
      d.   Mi hanno segnalato un libro da non regalare ai miei figli.[87]
          'They pointed out to me a book not to give to my children as a present.'

Hackl & Nissenbaum (2012: §1.3.1) argue that under the 'could' interpretations the infinitival relative clause involves 'raising' (promotion) of the internal Head, while under the 'should' interpretation either a 'raising' or an externally Headed derivation is possible. In this paper I do not pursue this aspect of the construction, but point out another difference between the two interpretations. The infinitival relatives with a 'could' interpretation are not (necessarily) islands for extraction ((116a)) while the ones with a 'should' interpretation appear to be islands for extraction ((116b)):[88]

---

[86] See Cinque (1988: §1.1.5.2). Bianchi (1991: 121; 2007: fn. 7) in presenting a sentence like (i) says that infinitival relatives introduced by *da* modifying a subject are always interpreted deontically:

(i)   [Un cane da addestrare] ha morsicato l'istruttore.
       a dog to train bit the instructor

Cinque & Benincà (2018: fn. 3) agree with the judgement for (i), but find cases similar to (i) to be acceptable with the possibility reading if they have a generic tense (even (i) perhaps can be marginally interpreted as 'a dog of the kind that can be trained'):

(ii)   a.   Un libro da (poter) leggere a letto non può essere troppo pesante.
          'A book to (be able to) read in bed cannot be too heavy.'
      b.   Cose da (poter) fare senza spendere troppo si trovano sempre.
          'Things to (be able to) do without spending too much can always be found.'

[87] Giurgea & Soare (2010a: 75) note that negation blocks the possibility reading.

[88] The non-island character of infinitival RCs with the 'could' interpretation recalls the analogous status of modal existential Headless RCs discussed in §2.5.5. The island character of those with a 'should' interpretation might instead be attributed to their reduction from of a RC containing the deontic modal *è da* 'is to'. See above §3.3.2.1.

(116)   a.   I miei figli, ai quali non ho un libro da (poter) leggere alla sera prima che
         si addormentino, . . .
         'My children, to whom I have no book (to be able) to read in the evening
         before they go to sleep, . . .'
         b.   *I miei figli, ai quali ci sono libri da non regalare, . . .
         my children, to whom there are books not to give as a present, . . .

When two infinitival RCs are stacked, one with a 'could' interpretation and the
other with a 'should' interpretation, the order seems to be strict (in my Italian),
the one with the 'should' interpretation following the one with the 'could'
interpretation. See (117a–b):

(117)   a.   Ho trovato un bel libro da leggere in vacanza da far assolutamente
         leggere a nostro figlio.
         I found a nice book to read on holidays to absolutely make our child read
         b.   ?*Ho trovato un bel libro da far assolutamente leggere a nostro figlio da
         leggere in vacanza.
         'I found a nice book to absolutely make our child read on holidays.'

3.3.2.3   Differences between the *da* + Infinitive and the P *cui*/art.+*qual-* Infinitive Construction

Clitic Left Dislocation is possible with the latter but not with the former.
See (118):

(118)   a.   Cercavo un argomento di cui/del quale a voi poter parlare con calma.
         I was looking.for some topic about which to be able to talk to you
         with calm
         b.   *Cercavo qualcosa da a voi regalare per Natale/?*a voi da regalare
         per Natale.
         I.was.looking.for something to to you give for Xmas/to you to give
         for Xmas

A second difference is the fact that the verb in *da* infinitival relatives cannot
be passive ((119a)) (as opposed to English – see the translation of (119a),
grammatical in English), while it can in P *cui*/art.+*qual-* infinitival relatives
((119b)):

(119)   a.   *Cercavano un libro da essere recensito in fretta.
         'They were looking for a book to be reviewed rapidly.'
         b.   Cercavano una medicina con cui/la quale essere curati.
         'They were looking for a medicine with which to be cured.'

A third difference has to do with the bounded nature of infinitival relativization
with *da* vs the unbounded nature of infinitival relativization with P *cui*/art.
+*qual-*. See §3.3.2.5 below.

3.3.2.4 Are There Subject Infinitival Relatives in Italian?

The answer seems to be negative (*pace* Sleeman 2010, 2013). Cases which in English have often been interpreted as subject infinitival relatives (see (120) and (121) below) are perhaps more accurately to be analysed as either purpose control structures ((120)) or, in contexts where the noun is modified by superlatives, by superlative ordinals, or by 'only' ((121)) as structures with a controlled PRO (see fn. 77 above). In fact, they appear to be merged higher than ordinary infinitival relatives (see fn. 140 below). In Italian the former are rendered by a modal finite relative clause (see (122)), while the latter, as well as certain clefts, are rendered with an infinitive introduced by the preposition *a* (see (123)):

(120)   a.   The man to fix the sink is here. (Bhatt 2006: 9)
        b.   I'll find a professor to help you. (Breivik 1997: 111)

(121)   a.   The first to walk on the moon was Armstrong.
        b.   Dolly Parton became the oldest woman to have a no. 1 song.
             (see Sleeman 2013: 319)
        c.   John is the only man to really know her. (see Sleeman 2010: 234)

(122)   a.   L'uomo che deve aggiustare il lavandino è qua.
             'The man to fix the sink is here.'(Lit.: 'The man that has to fix the sink is here.')
             (see *l'uomo da aggiustare il lavandino è qua*)
        c.   Troverò un professore che possa aiutarti.
             I'll find a professor to help you. (Lit.: 'I'll find a professor that may help you.')
             (see *Troverò un professore da aiutarti.* 'I'll find a professor to help you.')

(123)   a.   Il primo **a** camminare sulla luna è stato Armstrong.
             'The first to walk on the moon was Armstrong.'
        b.   Dolly Parton è la donna più vecchia **ad** aver avuto una canzone al primo posto.
             'Dolly Parton became the oldest woman to have a no. 1 song.'
        c.   John è il solo uomo **a** conoscerla veramente.
             'John is the only man to really know her.'
        d.   E' stato Gianni **a** darmi la chiave. (Sleeman 2010: 254; 2013: 325)
             is been Gianni to give-me the key
             'It was Gianni who gave me the key.'

Maiden and Robustelli (2013: 141) observe another apparent case of subject infinitival relative in English (*He's not a man to abandon his friends*, meaning 'He is not a man of the kind that abandons his friends/who would abandon his friends') and note that in Italian the same construction is introduced by *da*

(*Non è un uomo da abbandonare i suoi amici*), but here there is possibly a silent *tale*, which can actually be overt (... *tale da* ...).

A third case of an (apparent) subject infinitival RC in English mentioned in Bhatt (2006: 9) (*The book to be read for tomorrow's class is kept on the table*) has no counterpart in Italian (**Il libro da essere letto per la lezione di domani* ...), as it is possibly based on the modal construction containing the *is to* modal periphrasis in English (see Kayne 2016b), which can contain a passivized verb (*This is to be read by tomorrow*), as opposed to the corresponding modal periphrasis *è da* in Italian, which cannot (**Questo è da essere letto per domani*). Maiden and Robustelli (2013: §7.2.7) note that 'in this construction the infinitive may not be passivized [...]. However, the passive formed with reflexive *si* is possible'(p. 141): *Questo è da leggersi per domani* (also see Burzio 1986: 77 n. 36, after Belletti 1982: *Sono cose da farsi al più presto* '(they) are things SI-to do as soon as possible'.

3.3.2.5 *Da* Infinitival Relatives and Restructuring

As opposed to English, where (non-subject) infinitival relatives are not clause-bounded (can span across two, or more, clauses) (see (124) and the examples (ii) and (iv)a in fn. 77 above), Italian *da* infinitival relatives, as noted in Burzio (1986: 346 ff), are clause-bounded[89] (compare (125) with (124)).

		to regret to have admired	
(124)	He is a person	to convince Maria to invite	(Burzio 1986: 346)
		to suggest that Maria invite	

		da rimpiangere di aver ammirato	
(125)	*E' una persona	da convincere Maria a invitare	(Burzio 1986: 346)
		da suggerire che Maria inviti	

As Burzio (1986: 346–7) also noted, there are however systematic exceptions to the clause-boundedness of *da* infinitival relatives. These are provided by restructuring configurations (see (126), but such exceptions are only apparent since restructuring configurations are arguably mono-clausal – see Cinque 2004a, 2006b):[90]

(126) a. C'è solo una cosa da **dover** fare per domani.
           'There is only one thing to have to do for tomorrow.'
       b. Ho trovato un libro da **poter** leggere in vacanza.
           'I found a book to be able to read on holidays.'

---

[89] This is also true of Romanian (Giurgea & Soare 2010a: 76; 2010b: §2).
[90] Sentences similar to some of those reported in (126) are also noted in Napoli (1976: 307).

c. L'unica cosa da **saper** fare è questa.
    'The only thing to know how to do is this one.'
d. Cercavano un problema da **riuscire a** risolvere subito.
    'They were looking for a problem to manage to solve immediately.'
e. Se c'è una cosa da **provare a** fare subito è questa.
    'If there is something to try and do immediately it's this one.'
f. Ho trovato qualcosa da **far**vi fare.
    'I found something to make you do.'
g. C'è una sola cosa da **cominciare** a fare.
    'There is only one thing to begin to do.'
h. L'unica cosa da **continuare** a fare è questa.
    'The only thing to continue doing is this one.'
i. L'unica cosa da **andare a** fare subito è questa.
    'The only thing to go and do immediately is this one.'
l. C'è un solo libro da **finire** di leggere per domani.
    'There is only one book to finish reading by tomorrow.'
m. L'unica cosa da non **tornare a** fare è questa.
    'The only thing not to return to do (=not to do again) is this one.'

Yet, not all restructuring configurations qualify as exceptions. There appears to be a generalization: only those restructuring predicates which are lower than *potere/dovere* are possible. All higher ones (according to the hierarchy in Cinque 2006b) are impossible. See (127):

(127) a. *Cercava una cosa da non **sembrare** apprezzare.
           he was looking for something not to seem to appreciate
       b. *Questa è una cosa da **soler** fare con calma.
           this is something to be accustomed to do with calm
       c. *Un errore da non **tendere a** fare è proprio questo.
           a mistake not to tend to do is precisely this
       d. *L'unico lavoro da **finire per** accettare è questo.
           'The only job to end up accepting is this one.'
       e. *Se trovate una cosa da **voler/desiderare di** fare ditemelo.
           if you find something to want/desire to do, please, tell me
       f. *L'unica cosa da **smettere di** fare è proprio questa.
           'The only thing to stop doing is precisely this.'

Infinitival relative clauses with P *cui*/art.+*qual-* appear instead to span two (or more) clauses whose verbs are non-restructuring verbs, suggesting the presence of *wh*-movement. See for example (128):[91]

---

[91] This is also true of French. See Huot (1981: 171), cited in Abeillé et al. (1998: fn. 10):

(i) a. Je cherche un projet auquel lui proposer de participer.
         'I am looking for a project to propose to him to take part in.'
     b. Je ne vois personne à qui lui conseiller de s'adresser.
         'I don't see anyone to whom to advise him to refer.'

(128)   a.   Ecco un argomento di cui convincerlo ad occuparsi.
              'Here is a topic with which to convince him to occupy himself.'
         b.   Cercavamo un medico a cui consigliarvi di rivolgervi.
              'We were looking for a doctor to whom to advise you to refer.'

3.3.2.6 'Raising' and 'Matching' in Infinitival Relative Clauses in English[*]

The following grammatical cases with coreference between a Head internal nominal possessor and the subject of the infinitival RC appear to suggest that the Head does not reconstruct into the relative clause, pointing to a non-raising derivation of such RCs in English.

(129)   a.   This is John$_i$'s book for him$_i$ to write his thoughts and feelings in.
         b.   This is the book of John$_i$'s for him$_i$ to write his thoughts and feelings in.

(130)   a.   These are John$_i$'s favourite magazines for him$_i$ to read while in bed
              in hospital.
         b.   These are the favourite magazines of John$_i$'s for him$_i$ to read while
              in bed in hospital.

A raising derivation is apparently also possible, though, as shown by the possibility for a quantifier in the relative clause to bind a pronominal inside the Head ((131a)), by the possibility of an idiom chunk qualifying as the Head ((131b)), and by the possibility for a quantified Head being interpreted under the scope of a quantifier in the subject position of the relative clause ((131c–d)):

(131)   a.   She was looking for a friend of his$_i$ for Mary to tell every boy$_i$ to invite.
         b.   The strings to pull to get him a part in that film are frankly too many.
         c.   The two patients for every surgeon to operate on haven't arrived yet.
         d.   The two books for every one of them to read during the summer are
              all in this box.

As noted in Gračanin-Yüksek (2008: fn. 19), the placement of second position clitics provides evidence that in (at least some) Croatian infinitival RCs the Head is external to the RC. See the example in (132):

(132)   čovjek   [za upoznati   *ga*   s   roditeljima] . . .
         man   for introduce   him.ACC   with   parents
         a man to introduce to one's parents . . .

---

[*] I am indebted to Jamie A. Douglas for the judgements concerning (129) to (131) and for discussion of the issues raised in this section. He notes that in (129a) and (130a) the prenominal possessor may in fact be too high (possibly higher than D) for it to reconstruct into (after having raised out of) the RC. Nonetheless, no Condition C violation is found with postnominal possessors either ((129b) and (130b)).

3.4   Participial Relative Clauses

RCs with present or past participles in English, German, Italian, and other languages are usually considered to be reduced, in the sense that they are taken to lack the higher clausal layers (in particular the IP and CP layers). The main properties adduced in support of this conclusion are: (1) the absence of overt relative pronouns and invariant relativizers, (2) the absence of tense, (3) the absence of overt subjects, and (4) the fact that only externally merged or internally merged subjects, depending on the type of participle involved, can be relativized (see, among others, Williams 1975: 249 ff; Burzio 1981: §3.3, 1986: 150–2 and 193–8; Hazout 2001 ; Siloni 1995: §3; Krause 2001a: §2.1; Cecchetto & Donati 2015: §3.4; Harwood 2018: §5; Douglas 2016: ch. 6).[92]

In particular Harwood (2013, 2015), and Douglas (2016: ch. 6) argue that English present participle RCs have a size that comprises only the Progressive Aspect and Voice projections, while past participle RCs have a size that comes to include the Perfect Aspect projection. See their discussion, which nonetheless leaves certain cases to be accounted for, such as sentences like *Any person having purchased land in Florida in the 1950s should contact this office* (McCawley 1988: 413 fn. 10; 1998: 395–6), which would lead one to the conclusion that Progressive aspect is higher than Perfect aspect, contrary to fact (**John is having purchased land* ... See Chomsky 1957: §5.3, and much later work). Also, see the possibility of high sentential adverbs (*pace* Williams 1975: 251), which would seem to argue against a structure truncated above Perfect aspect, Progressive aspect and Voice.[93]

As Belikova (2008) notes (also see Stanton 2011), the term 'reduced' may in fact be a misnomer as a cross-linguistic characterization of participial RCs since the 'reduced' nature of the participial RCs of certain languages appears to be a consequence of the hybrid (verbal and nominal) nature of participles and of specific independent morphological properties of the language, rather than their intrinsic reduced nature. As she shows, in many languages participial RCs can be structurally complex and the four properties above turn out to be independent from one another, with languages having overt tense but no overt subjects, and languages having no overt tense but having overt subjects (thus being able to relativize non-subjects as well). Also see Doron & Reintges (2006) for

---

[92] For problems with the traditional whiz-deletion analysis see Harwood (2016: §3.1).

[93] Williams (1975: 250–1), Emonds (1976: 166), and McCawley (1998: 396), among others, in fact argue that the *-ing* participles of English participial RCs should not be taken to be identical to progressive *-ing* participles. But see Douglas (2016: ch. 6) for an interesting and thorough discussion of participial RCs.

discussion of languages with temporally marked participles and Krause (2001: ch. 2) for discussion of the two main types of participial RCs: those that allow non-subject and non-local relativization and those allowing only subject and local relativization. The former pattern follows as a consequence of the (genitive) Case assigned to their subject (also see Kornfilt 2005a; Miyagawa 2008, 2011; Csató & Uchturpani 2010; Herd, Macdonald & Massam 2011; Ackerman & Nikolaeva 2013) while the latter pattern (of English, German, Italian and other languages) follows as a consequence of the fact that no nominative Case is assigned to Spec,IP owing to the lack of finite Tense (see Kayne 1994: §8.4), or of genitive Case assignment due to the lack of the appropriate nominal morphology (as well as the non-availability in Italian of the special additional nominative Case assignment from a non-finite V in COMP – Rizzi 1982: ch. 3 – due to the absence of CP). This leaves PRO as the only possible subject, as supported by independent empirical evidence from German, to be reviewed below. Also see Burzio (1986: §3.2) and Cecchetto & Donati (2015: §3.4).

All in all the possibility of high adverbs and of a PRO subject in the 'reduced' RCs of languages like English, German, and Italian, which have participial verbs (see §3.4.1.4 and §3.4.2.2/§3.4.2.3, *pace* Siloni 1995: §3.2) and the possibility of overt (genitive) subjects for the participial RCs of other languages seems to suggest that they are at least IPs.

The exclusively pre-nominal nature of German (Keenan 1985: 144) and Finnish (Matsumura 1982) participial RCs may also be taken as supporting evidence for the pre-nominal Merge of RCs.

Even if structures of different sizes may be involved in the pattern where relativization only targets subjects and is local (see Marvin 2002, 2003),[94] here I will be concerned only with questions relating to the double-Headed nature of participial RCs and (more tentatively) whether they should be taken to involve 'raising' as well as 'matching'.

3.4.1   *Present Participle Relative Clauses*
3.4.1.1   Introduction
Here I address certain aspects of present participle RCs, comparing English and French with Italian, which has a particularly limited set of them (for a

---

[94] For example Bulgarian (as opposed to English, German, and Italian) past participle RCs may, unexpectedly for Cecchetto and Donati's (2020) analysis, relativize the subject of transitive verbs: *ženata pročela knigata* ... Lit.: woman.the read (active participle) book.the 'the woman (who has) read the book ...' (Iatridou, Anagnastopoulou & Izvorski 2001). Marvin (2002, 2003) takes them to involve a larger structure, including a Perfect Aspect projection.

characterization of the classes of verbs that display such participles see Cinque 2017a: §3). After considering how Italian renders those English and French present participles that cannot be rendered in Italian with present participles, I will discuss the nature of the subject of present participle RCs, for which German offers a particularly clear piece of evidence.[95]

3.4.1.2 Present Participles and Pseudo-Relatives in Italian

Italian differs greatly from English and French in the use of present participles in RCs. Its *-ant-/-ent-* present participles are a tiny subset of the *-ing* and *-ant* present participles of English and French. While both English and French can use a present participle in such 'reduced' relative clauses as (133a–b),[96] Italian cannot (133c):

(133)   a.   That noise? It's some boys **playing** outside. (Felser 1999: 88 fn. 56, after Declerck 1981: 138)

        b.   Ce bruit-là? C'est des enfants **jouant** dehors.

        c.   Quel rumore? *Sono dei bambini **giocanti** fuori.

Italian renders the present participles of (133a–b) with a periphrasis that apparently involves a finite restrictive relative clause (see (134)):

(134)   Quel rumore? Sono dei bambini **che giocano fuori**.
       'That noise? It's some boys who (Lit.: that) play outside.'

The difference between (133a–b) and (134) is actually part of a larger difference between Italian and English and French; one suggesting that the apparent finite restrictive relative in (134) may actually not be a genuine relative clause. In all of the contexts of (135) and (136), which also involve present participles in English and French, and which are demonstrably not relatives, Italian uses again what looks like a finite relative clause. See (137):[97]

---

[95] I thank Paola Benincà, Richard Kayne and Clemens Mayr for their helpful comments on a previous draft of this section, which is based in part on Cinque (2017a), itself building on Benincà & Cinque (1991).

[96] German also disposes of present participles of activity and subject-experiencer stative verbs in participial 'reduced' RCs:

(i)   a. Diese drei [in ihren Büros   arbeitenden] Männer   (Cinque 2010a: 54)
        These three in   their offices working   men
        these three men working in their office

     b. Er   ist   ein [sein Studium seit langem hassender] Student.
                                             (Cinque 2010a: 54)
        he   is   a   his   study   since   long   hating   student
        he is a student who has been hating his studies for a long time

[97] On French participial RCs see the references cited below and Douglas (2016: ch. 6: §6).

(135)   a.   I saw him running at full speed. (Kayne 1975: 126)
         b.   She met him coming out of the movies. (Kayne 1975: 126)
         c.   She is there weeping like a willow.

(136)   a.   Je l'ai vu courant à toute vitesse. (Kayne 1975: 128)
               'I saw him running at full speed.'
         b.   Elle l'a rencontré sortant du cinéma. (Kayne 1975: 128)
               'She met him coming out of the movies.'
         c.   Elle est là pleurant comme une Madeleine. (Kayne 1975: 128)
               'She's there weeping copiously.'

(137)   a.   L'ho visto che correva/*corrente a tutta velocità.
               I saw him that he.was.running/running at full speed
         b.   L'ha incontrato che usciva/*uscente dal cinema.
               she met him that she.was.coming/coming out of the movies
         c.   Lei è là che piange/*piangente come una disperata.
               she is there that she.is.weeping/weeping desperately

French, in addition to the present participle cases in (136), also has a variant which looks like the Italian finite relative clause in (137). See (138):

(138)   a.   Je l'ai vu qui courait à toute vitesse. (Kayne 1975: 126)
               I saw him that he.was.running at full speed
         b.   Elle l'a rencontré qui sortait du cinéma. (Kayne 1975: 126)
               she met him that he.was.coming out of the movies
         c.   Elle est là qui pleure comme une Madeleine. (Kayne 1975: 126)
               she is there that she.is.weeping copiously

(138), as well as (137), have however been shown to be constructions differing from genuine relative clauses in a number of ways. See Kayne (1975: 126–9), Radford (1975, 1977: §3.3), Graffi (1980), Guasti (1988). For example, they can only 'relativize' subjects, and allow the apparent 'Head' to be cliticized or passivized, unlike ordinary RCs. Various analyses have been proposed for these constructions, which in the Romance syntax literature are referred to as 'pseudo-relatives'.[98] In addition to the works just cited, see, among others, Declerck (1981, 1982), Guasti (1992, 1993), Rizzi (1992), Cinque (1995), Felser (1999), Scarano (2002), Casalicchio (2013a, 2013b, 2015, 2016a, 2016b), Koopman & Sportiche (2014: §3.1). Also see Grosu (2002: §8) and, for a recent overview of the literature, Graffi (2017).

---

[98] As noted, this construction, termed 'pseudo-relative' in the Romance tradition, should not be confused with McCawley's term pseudo-relative, which appears to correspond to kind-defining RCs (see §3.2 above).

If they are not genuine relative clauses involving A-bar movement to Spec, CP within DP, what kind of empty category then fills the subject position of the *che/qui* clause?

Paduan, a dialect closely related to Italian, offers direct evidence that the subject of the *che* clause in (137) contains a small pro (on the *qui* clause in (138), see §3.4.1.4 below). In finite contexts Paduan, differently from Italian, has obligatory subject clitics for 2nd singular and 3rd singular and plural persons and a small pro for the other persons (see Benincà 1994: 16 n. 1). In contexts corresponding to those in (137), which contain 3rd person subjects (the same would obtain with 2nd person singular subjects), a subject clitic is obligatory. See (139):[99]

(139)   a.   Lo go visto ch'*(el) coreva.
              him I.have seen that he ran
              'I saw him running.'
        b.   La lo ga incontrà ch'*(el) veniva fora dal sinema.
              she him has met that he came out from the cinema
              'She met him coming out of the cinema.'
        c.   La ze là che *(la) pianze a diroto.
              she is there that she cries like a willow
              'She is there weeping like a willow.'

If the constructions in (137) contain a small pro in subject position rather than a variable bound from Spec,CP, then the apparent restriction to the relativization of subjects follows directly as (non-arbitrary) small pro is impossible in object (or any other) position (Rizzi 1986; Cattaneo 2007).

This opens up the possibility that the apparent finite relative clause in (134) could also be a pseudo-relative, although in this case one cannot show it clearly because of the existence of a distinct genuine relative clause modifying

---

[99] In the same contexts, no subject clitic is instead required (in fact possible) with 1st singular and plural and 2nd plural subjects (for the simple reason that no such person subject clitics exist in Paduan). See (i)a–b, which plausibly contain a small pro, as the corresponding Italian sentences:

(i)   a.   I me ga visto che corevo.
              they me have seen that I.ran
              'They saw me running.'
        b.   I ne/ve ga visto che corevimo/corevi.
              they us/you have seen that we/you$_{pl}$ run
              'They saw us/you(pl.) running.'

I thank Paola Benincà for originally pointing out to me the obligatoriness of the subject clitic in Paduan in the contexts of (139), and for providing the relevant examples.

the Head NP (witness the possibility of apparently relativizing also an object, as shown in (140)):

(140)   Quel rumore? Sono dei bambini che abbiamo mandato fuori prima.
        'That noise? It's some boys that we sent outside earlier.'

Indeed, in Paduan, in a sentence corresponding to (134), the subject clitic in contrast to (139) is optional. See (141):

(141)   Sto rumore? Ze dei tozi che (i) zuga fora.
        This noise? It's some boys that (they) play outside
        'This noise? It's some boys playing outside.'

More precisely, I would claim, it is obligatory in the pseudo-relative structure, just as in (139), and impossible in the genuine restrictive relative clause one, as shown by the ungrammaticality of a resumptive clitic in the relativization of a subject ((142a)) (Benincà & Cinque 2014: 260), or object (142b) (Paola Benincà, pers. comm.):

(142)   a.   Un professore che (*el) gaveva dedicà la vita ala scola se gà ritirà.
             'A teacher that (he) had devoted his life to school has retired.'
        b.   Ze dei tosi che (*i) gavemo mandà fora prima.
             'It's some boys that them we have sent outside earlier.'

3.4.1.3   Restrictions on Present Participles

Present participles of the above verbs in reduced RCs in Italian appear to be subject to certain derivational restrictions (which need to be elucidated).[100] The implicit subject can apparently be the subject of an unaccusative verb (see (143)), but not the subject of a passive verb (see (144a)), nor the subject of a raising verb (see (144b)):[101]

---

[100] See Benincà & Cinque (1991) and Cinque (2017a) for a preliminary analysis.

[101] Unlike English and German, where it is apparently possible (see (i) and (ii)):

   (i)   A student appearing to be witty was accepted in the program (Burzio 1981: 230)
          (... seeming to be witty ... is slightly less good – Jamie Douglas, pers. comm.).

   (ii)   a.   der [die Wahlen verloren zu haben scheinende] Kanzler   (Fanselow 1986: 352)
               the [the elections lost to have seeming] chancellor
          b.   der [über seine Ufer zu treten drohende] Fluss   (Fanselow 1986: 352)
               the [over its bank to overflow threatening] river

While unaccusative and passive past participle RCs are possible in Italian, Burzio (1986) notes the impossibility of past participle RCs of unaccusative and raising verbs in English (*A student arrived yesterday, and *A man seemed to know the truth (p. 191) – also see Stanton (2011: 61) (with certain exceptions: *the recently arrived letter* (Kayne 1994: 99),

(143)   a.   Le conseguenze derivantine
             the consequences deriving from it
        b.   il denaro restantemi (Benincà & Cinque 1991: 609)
             the money remaining to me

(144)   a.   *gli oggetti essentivi/venentivi rappresentati
             the objects being represented there
        b.   *un quadro sembrante/apparente raffigurare un paesaggio umbro
             a painting seeming/appearing to represent an Umbrian landscape

3.4.1.4   The Subject of Present Participle 'Reduced' Relative Clauses

I take the subject of present participle reduced RCs in Italian to be PRO, as in German, which displays direct evidence for this conclusion.[102] See the discussion in Cinque (2010a: 55–6) on past participle reduced RCs, based on Fanselow (1986), which I summarize here, adding data on present participle reduced RCs. See also Cecchetto & Donati (2015: §3.4) for the same conclusion concerning present participles in reduced RCs, within a different analysis.

As noted in Fanselow (1986), 'floating' distributive phrases like *einer nach dem anderen* 'one after the other' agree in Case with the DP with which they are construed. See (145a–b):

(145)   a.   Wir$_{Nom}$ haben Maria$_{Acc}$ einer$_{Nom}$/*einen$_{Acc}$ nach dem anderen geküsst.
             we have Maria one after the other kissed
             'We have kissed Maria one after the other.'
        b.   Maria$_{Nom}$ hat die Männer$_{Acc}$ einen$_{Acc}$/*einer$_{Nom}$ nach dem anderen geküsst.
             Maria has the men one after the other kissed
             'Maria kissed the men one after the other.'

As Fanselow further observes, if such floating phrases are construed with the PRO subject of an infinitive, they invariably bear nominative Case. This is particularly evident in such cases as (146), where the controller of PRO bears a different Case:

(146)   Weil ich die Männer$_{Acc}$ überzeugte, PRO Renate einer$_{Nom}$/*einen$_{Acc}$ nach dem anderen zu küssen, . . .
        as I the men convinced Renate one after the other to kiss, . . .
        as I convinced the men to kiss Renate one after the other, . . .

---

although not, for him, *the letter arrived recently* . . ., although *the letter recently arrived* is good for Andrew Radford and *the leaf fallen from the tree* for Douglas 2016: 196), and of raising verbs in Italian (*Un ragazzo sembrato conoscere Maria* 'A boy seemed to know Maria') (Burzio 1986: 194).

[102]   Also see Chomsky (1981: 167) and Kayne (1983b: fn. 6) on English and French.

Now, what we observe in the participial relative clause case is that the floating distributive phrase also appears in nominative Case, irrespective of the Case borne by the Head with which it is construed:[103]

(147)   a.   Wir sahen die [einer$_{Nom}$/*einen$_{Acc}$ nach dem anderen ankommenden] Flüchtlinge$_{Acc}$.
          we saw the one after the other arriving migrants
          'We saw the migrants arriving one after the other.'
   b.   Wir sahen die [einer$_{Nom}$/*einen$_{Acc}$ nach dem anderen angekommenen] Studenten$_{Acc}$.
          we saw the one after the other arrived students
          'We saw the students arrived one after the other.'

This clearly points in participle reduced RCs to the presence of a PRO, with which the floating distributive phrase is construed.[104]

Another possible piece of evidence for the presence of PRO, at least for present participle RCs, comes from a contrast in French pseudo-relatives noted in Guasti (1988). She reports that her informants accept *qui* pseudo-relatives with 3rd person clitics (see (148)) but not with 1st and 2nd person clitics (see (149)):[105]

(148)   a.   Pierre la/le voit qui parle à Jean. (= (44)–(46) of Guasti 1988)
          P. her/him sees that speaks to J.
   b.   Pierre les voit qui parlent à J.
          P. them sees that speak to J.

(149)   a.   ?/*Pierre nous voit qui parlons à Jean. (= (49)–(50) of Guasti 1988)
          P. us sees that we.speak to J.
   b.   ?/*Pierre vous voit qui parlez à Marie.
          P. you$_{pl}$ sees that you$_{pl}$.speak to M.

---

[103] I thank Gisbert Fanselow and Roland Hinterhölzl for providing the relevant judgements. Roland Hinterhölzl marginally accepts also the accusative variant, though preferring the one with the nominative.

[104] Burzio (1981: 231–2) also takes present and past participles to be small clauses with a PRO subject and argues that they can occur in identical structures given that they can be coordinated together, as in examples like (i):

    (i)   Everyone [currently studying SPE] and [invited to the reception] must carry identification.

[105] I have restricted attention here to 1st and 2nd plural persons clitics as the judgements are clearer due to the fact that their inflections on the pseudo-relative verb are clearly distinct from those of 3rd persons (1st and 2nd singular verbal inflections, on the other hand, are not as clearly distinct from 3rd person inflections, pronunciation-wise). I thank Dominique Sportiche for clarifying this point to me.

The fact that non-3rd person agreement on the verb of the pseudo-relative is impossible suggests, as Guasti (1988: §4) herself suggested, that *qui* (in the absence of an operator raised to its left, with which it agrees inheriting its feature specification)[106] has a default 3rd person feature, able to license a 3rd person small pro in the subjacent subject position, but not a 1st or 2nd person small pro.

As Guasti (1988: 45) further observes, this asymmetry disappears when present participles are involved (see (150)), which suggests that a different empty category is licensed which is compatible with all persons.

(150)   a.   Pierre le/la/les voit parlant à Jean (= (51) of Guasti 1988)
             P. him/her/them sees speaking to J.
        b.   Pierre nous voit parlant à Jean (= (54) of Guasti 1988)
             P. us sees speaking to J.
        c.   Pierre vous voit parlant à Marie (= (55) of Guasti 1988)
             P. you$_{pl}$ sees speaking to M.

It cannot be a trace of the clitic in an exceptional case marking configuration as in (151):

(151)   Pierre le$_i$/la$_i$/les$_i$/nous$_i$/vous$_i$ voit [$_{XP}$ t$_i$ parlant à Jean].
        P. him/her/them/us/you$_{pl}$ sees talking to J.
        'P. sees him/her/them/us/you$_{pl}$ talking to J.'

The reason for this is that the XP in such structures (as noted in Kayne 1975: ch. 2 n. 75 and Kayne 1981a: 202) is an island for extraction, just like the corresponding pseudo-relative (see (152a–b)), and unlike the bare infinitive complement of verbs of perception (see (152c) – adapted from Burzio 1986: 301):

(152)   a.   *La fille que$_i$ je l'ai vu embrassant t$_i$
             the girl that I him-have seen embracing
        b.   *La fille que$_i$ je l'ai vu qui embrassait t$_i$
             the girl that I him-have seen that embraced

---

[106] As is plausibly the case in non-restrictive RCs (Guasti 1988: 47). See (i)a–c:

(i)   a.   Moi, qui suis toujours la première à monter dans le bus, cette fois je l'ai raté.
             I, who am always the first to enter the bus, this time I missed it
        b.   Nous, qui jouons du piano, nous avons reçu un prix.
             we, who play the piano, have received a prize
        c.   Venez ici vous, qui êtes toujours les meilleurs.
             come here you, who are always the best

As Dominique Sportiche (pers. comm.) tells me, for him in fact both agreement with 1st/2nd person (more formal) and with 3rd person (more colloquial: *Moi, qui est . . .*) are possible.

c.   Il libro che$_i$ l' ho visto leggere t$_i$ è Moby Dick
the book that him I-have seen read is M.D
'The book which I saw him read is M.D.'

The island character of the present participle phrase and of the pseudo-relative
in (152a–b) (as well as of the Italian equivalent of (152c) – Burzio 1986: 300)
is arguably due to the island character of object secondary predicates
(see Kayne 1975: 128–9). Indeed, even simple AP object secondary predicates
appear to be islands (in Italian).[107] See (153):[108]

(153)   a.   *Il sangue di cui tutti l'hanno visto [coperto t] era il suo
the blood with which everybody saw him covered was his own
b.   *L'uomo con cui$_i$ abbiamo visto Maria [furiosa t$_i$]
the man with whom we saw Maria furious
c.   *Questo è l'unico lavoro di cui vedo anche Mario [stanco t$_i$]
this is the only work of which I have seen even M. tired

---

[107]   Richard Kayne pointed out to me (pers. comm.) that in English extraction of a DP is apparently
possible (*The blood that they saw him covered with was not his own*) as is generally the case
with DP extraction out of adjuncts, although extraction of a PP is worse (*The blood with which
they saw him covered was not his own*) when compared with the acceptable *The coat with
which they covered him.* This is reminiscent of the DP/PP contrast mentioned in Chomsky
(1986: 32) who credits Adriana Belletti with the observation, which I interpreted in Cinque
(1990: ch. 3) as involving genuine extraction in the case of PPs and A-bar binding of pro in the
case of DPs.

[108]   As opposed to the small clauses following verbs of thinking (which appear to be exceptional
case marking configurations containing individual-level APs rather than the stage-level APs of
the small clauses following 'see' or 'meet'):

(i)   a.   Il politico a cui$_i$ la pensavamo [vicina t$_i$].
the politician to whom her.we.thought close
the politician that we considered her close to
b.   Il figlio di cui$_i$ tutti la ritenevano [orgogliosa t$_i$].
the son of whom all her.considered proud
the son that everybody considered her proud of

I assume for (153) a configuration where the object secondary predicate is merged in an
adjunct position higher than the object, (..[$_{YP}$ AP [$_{XP}$ DP V]] and is crossed over by XP after
the verb has crossed over the object. In OV languages this order is displayed directly (though
the object may also scramble above the object secondary predicate). See (i), from Japanese,
and also Shibagaki (2011: 145 and 190):

(i)   Taroo-ga   nama-de   katuo-o   tabeta.   (Koizumi 1994: 35)
Taroo-Nom   raw   bonito-Acc   ate
'Taroo ate the bonito raw.'

It cannot be an A-bar bound trace either, otherwise the following should also be possible:[109]

(154)   *Je l'ai rencontré Jean emmenant au cinéma   (Kayne 1981: 201)
        I her have seen J. taking to the movies

This leaves PRO as the only plausible candidate for the subject of such present participles (see also Kayne 1981a: §4.2.2).[110]

3.4.2   Past Participle Reduced Relative Clauses
3.4.2.1   Introduction

As with present participle reduced RCs past participial RCs are also considered to be reduced, in the sense of lacking CP, and possibly IP. As with present participles the main properties adduced in support of this conclusion are: 1) the absence of overt complementizers, 2) the absence of tense, 3) the absence of external arguments, given that only internal arguments promoted to subject position can be relativized.[111] See, among others, Burzio (1981: §3.3; 1986: 150–2, 193–8); Chomsky (1981: 167); Hazout (2001); Siloni (1995; 1997: ch. 4); Benincà & Tortora (2009), Cecchetto & Donati (2015: §3.4); Harwood (2015); Douglas (2016: ch. 6).[112] The limited goal of this section is to present

---

[109] Hazout (2001) (*pace* Siloni 1995) also analyses Hebrew and Standard Arabic participial relatives as involving no operator movement.

[110] Additional evidence that the overt Head of present participle RCs is merged externally rather than being raised from within the RC, with PRO as the internal Head, may come from the following contrast mentioned to me by Richard Kayne (pers. comm.) ?*the only headway that appears/seems to have been made* ... vs *the only headway appearing/seeming to have been made* ..., where the latter contrasts with (i) of fn. 101, which is well formed as it involves no idiom chunk Head. However, he accepts *The only headway being made these days is in their heads*. It is thus not to be excluded that a 'raising' derivation may also be available to present participle RCs, also considering the possibility of reconstructing the Head in such cases as *I due seggi spettanti a ogni regione dovranno trovare un candidato appropriato*. 'The two seats being due to every region will have to find an appropriate candidate.' (every > two). If so, in such a derivation Case should be able to reach the subject of the (IP) participial RC.

[111] Namely, the derived subjects of passive and pseudo-passive participles (*the students accepted t in the program*; *the rights infringed upon t*; *a man believed t to know the truth* (Burzio 1986: 151–2, 190), *anyone given this opportunity*, and certain active past participles of unaccusative verbs (*the recently arrived letter* – Kayne 1994: 99; ?*the leaf fallen from the tree* – Marvin 2002: 141), but not a subject raised from the complement of raising verbs: *a man seemed to know the truth* (Burzio 1986: 191). For restrictions on relatives with active past participles of unaccusative verbs in English see Burzio (1986: 191), Stanton (2011: 61) and Douglas (2016: §5.1).

[112] See however Krause (2001a) and Alcázar (2007) for past participle RCs with overt subjects allowing relativization of non-subjects; and Sleeman (2017) for a review of the literature on participial RCs.

some evidence for the existence in Romance and Germanic past participle reduced RCs of an IP (though not of a CP) layer, and for the PRO nature of their internal head.[113]

3.4.2.2   Evidence for the IP/TP Nature of Past Participle Relatives

Evidence that in Italian past participle RCs are larger than VP, plausibly as big as IP/TP, (but no larger – see §3.4.2.4), comes, in addition to the evidence for a PRO subject discussed in §3.4.1.4 above and §3.4.2.3 below, from two distinct considerations: (1) the possible occurrence of speaker and subject oriented IP adverbs (see the example in (155)),[114] and (2) the tense interpretation of the participles. Both unaccusative and passive participles have a deictic past tense (not just an anterior tense) interpretation. This can be seen from the fact that they are compatible with deictic past tense adverbs like *la settimana scorsa* 'last week', *ieri* 'yesterday'((156)), but not with deictic future tense adverbs like *la settimana prossima* 'next week', *domani* 'tomorrow' ((157)):

(155)   I film sfortunatamente/presumibilmente persi durante l'ultima guerra sono davvero molti.
the films unfortunately/presumably lost during the.last war are really many
'The films unfortunately/presumably lost during the last war are really many.'

(156)   a.   Gli ospiti arrivati la settimana scorsa sono stati tutti sistemati in albergo.
the guests arrived the week last are been all accommodated in hotel
'The guests who arrived last week have all been accommodated in a hotel.'

---

[113] In Cinque (2010a: §4.2) participial RCs are shown to be merged lower than cardinals ((i)a) (see here §3.5), and are taken to acquire their post-nominal position ((i)b) through the raising of the Head, as typical of head-initial languages:

(i)   a.   [DP the [two [ParticP PROi recently appointed ti] professorsi]]
      b.   [DP the [two [professorsk [ParticP PROi recently appointed ti]] tk]] (i = k)

Sleeman (2011) claims that prenominal participles in Germanic are structurally different from postnominal ones, the latter being bigger (CP) than the former (AspP). This is however not entirely clear given the lack of evidence for a CP structure for either one (see below) and given that the differences between them in terms of presence of complements (for postnominal ones) and agreement with the head (for pre-nominal ones) seem ascribable to independent factors (see Cinque 2010: ch. 4, and Appendix, A6).

[114] The same appears to be true of French ((i)a) and English ((i)b):

(i)   a.   L'étudiant probablement/malheuresement arrêté par la police est un étranger.
                                                            (Douglas 2016: 241)
      the.student probably/unfortunately arrested by the police is a foreigner
      'The student probably/unfortunately arrested by the police is a foreigner.'
      b.   the cakes fortunately eaten by the guests …   (Douglas 2016: 229)

b. Il film visto ieri sarà premiato lunedì.
the film seen yesterday will.be prized Monday
'The film seen yesterday will get a prize on Monday.'

(157) a. *Gli ospiti arrivati la settimana prossima verranno tutti sistemati
in albergo.
the guests arrived the week next will.come all accommodated in hotel
'The guests who will have arrived next week will all be accommodated
in a hotel.'
(cf. *Gli ospiti che saranno arrivati la settimana prossima verranno tutti
sistemati in albergo.* 'The guests who will have arrived next week will
be accommodated in a hotel.')

b. *Il film visto domani sarà premiato lunedì.
the film seen tomorrow will.be prized Monday
'The film seen tomorrow will get a prize on Monday.'
(cf. *Il film che sarà visto domani sarà premiato lunedì.* 'The film which
will be seen tomorrow will get a prize on Monday.')

If the participle involved a relative anterior tense (in Reichenbachian terms
E – R: 'the event time precedes a reference time') rather than a past tense (in
Reichenbachian terms E, R – S 'the event time coinciding with the reference
time precedes the speech time'), (157a–b) should be compatible with a deictic
future tense (as the corresponding finite sentences following them indicate).
But they are only compatible with a deictic past tense.

3.4.2.3 The PRO Nature of the Internal Head of Past Participle Relatives

Following Chomsky (1981: 167–8) and Burzio (1986: §3.2), I take the subject
of past participle RCs in Italian to be PRO. German, as discussed in Cinque
(2010a: 55–6), after Fanselow (1986) gives direct evidence (recalled above in
§3.4.1.4) for this conclusion.[115]

Cecchetto & Donati (2015: §3.4) propose that past participle relatives
involve 'movement of N', which 'from its argument position to its derived
position relabels the structure, conveniently providing the external determiner
with the NP it needs to select' (p. 77). See their (111), reported here as (158):

(158) the [$_{NP}$ [$_N$ philosopher]$_i$ [$_{VP}$ admired [$_N$ ~~philosopher~~]$_i$]

In addition to the evidence just reviewed for taking the internal argument
moved to subject to be PRO, further evidence exists that such an argument has
to be a phrase rather than a bare head N. This phrase can control a PRO

---

[115] Siloni (1995: §4.3.2) argues against PRO in reduced RCs, but see Cinque (2010: 131 n. 34).

(*il nuovo documento*$_i$ [$_{IP}$ PRO$_i$ *archiviato* t$_i$ [*dopo* PRO$_i$ *esser stato letto* t$_i$]] . . . 'the new document filed after being read . . .') and can enter an A-chain in restructuring configurations. See the cases of long passivisation in (159) and those involving raising of a lower subject or object in (160):[116]

(159)   a.   Le case popolari [PRO$_i$ finite di costruire t$_i$ negli anni' 50] . . .
             the social houses finished to build in.the years 50
             the social houses that they finished building in the '50s . . .

        b.   [I bambini e le bambine]$_i$ [PRO$_i$ andati/venuti a prendere t$_i$ a scuola] . . .
             the children gone/come to fetch at school
             the children who were fetched from school . . .

(160)   a.   Un vicino di casa [PRO$_i$ venutomi a t$_i$ chiedere un favore] . . .
             (see Burzio 1986: 334)
             a neighbour come-to-me to ask a favour
             a neighbour who had come to ask me a favour . . .

        b.   i quadri antichi [PRO$_i$ andati t$_i$ persi t$_i$] . . .
             the old paintings gone lost
             the old paintings that have been lost . . .

Whether the Head of 'past participle' RCs may also be derived by 'raising' (see Krause 2001a: 26–7) is not entirely clear. While the Head appears to be reconstructable in sentences like *Sono riuscito a risolvere i due problemi assegnati ad ogni studente*. 'I managed to solve the two problems assigned to every student' (with 'every student' taking scope over 'two problems'), and while certain idiom chunks appear to be possible Heads of such participial RCs (*The recently made headway made it into the newspapers*; *The recently pulled strings finally got him the job*), others idiom chunks appear more difficult (*The recently kept track (of his expenses) got mixed up with other files*; *The recently paid heed (to that question) was later ignored by the Director*. Megan Rae, whom I thank for these judgements, feels that the difference may have to do with the relative referential autonomy of *headway* and *strings* vs *track* and *heed*, which are less referentially autonomous in the idiom. If so, it becomes possible to assume that *headway* and *strings* can actually be external Heads in

---

[116] There is also evidence that such participles are verbal and are to be kept distinct from adjectives morphologically derived from past participles. *Un uomo amatissimo da tutti* 'a man most loved by everybody' (Cecchetto & Donati 2015: 78) contains an adjective – witness the superlative morphology – which however becomes impossible if clausal adverbs are added: **un uomo da poco amatissimo da tutti* 'a man recently most loved by everybody'. See Cinque (2010: ch. 6 n. 1). Also past participles in RCs with clitics attached to them (*le sole persone presentateci* . . . 'the only people introduced to us . . .') cannot be adjectives, as these resist cliticisation (Benincà & Cinque 1991: §2.3).

a 'matching' derivation (also see the discussion on the role of idioms in section A4.4.1 of the Appendix).[117]

3.4.2.4 Evidence for the Lack of a CP Layer (and Other Left Peripheral Layers)*

As noted in §2.5.7, after Jacobson (1995: 460), 'Headless' participial RCs appear not to be possible. See (161):

(161)   a.   *What(ever) displayed in this window will be sold by midnight.
          b.   *Whoever invited to the party is supposed to bring a bottle.

The same seems to be true of Italian:[118]

(162)   a.   *Chi invitato alla festa dovrà portare una bottiglia.
              who invited to.the party will.must bring a bottle
              'He who [is] invited to the party will have to bring a bottle.'
          b.   *Quanti intervistati hanno negato di conoscerlo.
              how many interviewed have denied to know.him
              'Those who$_{pl}$ [were] interviewed denied knowing him.'

The ungrammaticality of (161) and (162) could be blamed on the fact that the *wh*-phrase receives no Case within the 'Headless' RC, due to the absence of finite Tense (see Kayne 1994: §8.4). Nonetheless, the fact that 'Headless' participial RCs appear not to be possible even where no Case licensing is plausibly at issue,

---

[117] The same can perhaps be said of the French cases observed in Vergnaud (1985):

   (i)   a.   La parti en ayant été tiré est à noter.   (Vergnaud 1985: 336)
              'The benefit obtained from it is to be noted.'
          b.   Paul a parlé du parti tiré de cette situation.   (Vergnaud 1985: 347 n. 29)
              'Paul has talked about the benefit obtained from this situation.'

* Also see Hazout (2001). But see the next section for a stylistically marked construction apparently giving evidence for the exceptional presence of a CP.

[118] Apparent exceptions can be accounted for if, as suggested in Donati & Cecchetto (2011: Appendix), *qualunque cosa* and *chiunque* can be external heads (see §2.5.7).

     The same appears to be true of cases involving *quanto* 'what' (see (i)), given the possibility of (ii), especially if compared with *quanti* 'who' (**Quanti arrivati si sono subito sistemati.* 'Those who arrived settled down immediately') given the impossibility of (iii):

   (i)   Quanto pattuito è senz'altro soddisfacente.
        how.much agreed is certainly satisfying
        'What [was] agreed upon is certainly satisfying.'
   (ii)   Ho fatto tutto quanto/Ecco quanto.
        I have done all how.much/here how.much
        'I did everything./Here is what (I did/said).'
   (iii)   *Ho visto quanti/*Ecco quanti.
        I saw how many/here I show many

as is the case in (i)a–b of fn. 163 of Chapter 2, repeated here as (163), appears to suggest that the cause of the ungrammaticality is related to the fact that they contain no CP capable of hosting a *wh*-phrase (see also Chomsky 1981: 167):

(163) a. *L'articolo sarà recensito dove pubblicato
       'The article will be reviewed where published.'
   b. *Quando addormentata, Gianna si mise a russare.
       when fallen asleep, Gianna started snoring
       (cf. *Appena addormentata, Gianna si mise a russare* 'Once fallen asleep, Gianna started snoring', where *appena* is an AdvP plausibly in IP)

The absence of a CP in participial RCs should also account for the impossibility of **the man that sitting on the wall* (Douglas 2016: 192), as well for the ungrammaticality of (164) as opposed to (165), which involves pied-piping of the whole participle phrase to the Spec of the matrix CP:[119]

(164) a. *Questo è il divano sul quale sdraiato comodamente lui di sicuro si sentirà meglio.
       this is the sofa on.the which lain comfortably he himself for sure will. feel better
       'This is the sofa on which comfortably lain he will for sure feel better.'
   b. *That's the screen behind which sat he won't be able to see her.

(165) a. Questo è il divano sdraiato comodamente sul quale lui si sentirà di sicuro meglio.
       this is the sofa lain comfortably on.the which he himself will for sure feel better
       'This is the sofa comfortably lain on which he will for sure feel better.'
   b. That's the screen sat behind which he won't be able to see her.

In addition to the lack of a CP layer that hosts *wh*-relative phrases, there is evidence that past participle RCs also lack Topic and Focus layers (see (166)), which (to judge from finite restrictive, 'Headless', and non-restrictive RCs – see (167)) are lower than the *wh*-relative layer:

(166) a. *Il libro a Carlo regalato(gli) non era adatto alla sua età.[120]
       the book to Carlo given(to.him) was not suitable for his age

---

[119] As apparent from such ordinary adjunct participles as *Sdraiato sul divano, lui si sentirà meglio* 'Lain on the sofa, he will feel better', it is possible for such participles to have a controlled PRO subject.

[120] Cases involving tonic pronouns, like (i), are only apparent cases of ordinary Clitic Left Dislocation/Topicalisation or Focus movement, as the same pronouns (as opposed to full DPs) can also occur in finite relative clauses in between auxiliaries and past participles. See (ii):

      b.   *Il libro A MARIA dato (non a Carlo) era molto costoso.

           the book to Maria(FOCUS) given (not to Carlo) was very expensive

(167)   a.   Il libro che a Carlo/*a Carlo che gli era stato dato solo ieri . . .

           the book that to Carlo/to Carlo that to.him had been given only yesterday . . .

           the book that had been given to Carlo only yesterday . . .

      b.   Hanno intervistato chi questi libri/*questi libri chi li aveva letti (see Benincà 2012b: 33)

           they-have interviewed who these books/these books who them had read

           'They interviewed someone who had read these books.'

      c.   Giorgio, che a Carlo/*a Carlo che non aveva mai parlato, . . .

           Giorgio, who to Carlo/to Carlo who not had ever spoken, . . .

           Giorgio, who had never spoken to Carlo, . . .

In Croatian the placement of 2nd position clitics provides evidence that the Head of past participle RCs is external with respect to the participial RC (Gračanin-Yüksek 2008: fn. 19).[121]

    (i)   Il libro a noi (/*a Carlo) regalato . . .

        the book to us (/to Carlo) given

        the book given to us . . .

    (ii)   il libro che era stato a noi (/*a Carlo) regalato . . .

        the book that had been to us (/to Carlo) given

        the book that had been given to us/to Carlo . . .

[121] Also see the discussion in Salzmann (2017: §2.3.3.2.6 and especially fn. 73). This casts doubts on the necessary 'raising' derivation of such cases as *the headway made so far* . . . (Cinque 2010a: 56), which contain idiom chunks like *headway* that have uses independent of the rest of the idiom (see section A4.4.1 of the Appendix). With idiom chunks that have no such independence, like *granchio* (lit. 'crab', interpreted as 'mistake' when following the verb *prendere* 'catch'), the corresponding participial RC (i)a, is much worse (compare it to the full RC (i)b):

    (i)   a.   *?Il granchio preso ieri non è poi così grave

             the mistake made yesterday (lit. the crab caught yesterday) is not so serious after all

        b.   Il granchio che hanno preso ieri non è poi così grave

             'The mistake that they made yesterday (lit. the crab that they caught yesterday) is not so serious after all.'

Note that the participle of the 'reduced' RC is not derived by reduction from a full passive relative (which also happens to be bad in the idiomatic reading: *Il granchio che è stato presto ieri non è poi così grave*). This is apparently shown by the contrast in (ii), in which the participial idiomatic RC and the corresponding full active, but not the corresponding full passive, idiomatic RC, are grammatical:

    (ii)   a.   La parte avuta da Gianni in questa circostanza non è trascurabile.

             'The role played by Gianni in this circumstance is not negligible.'

3.4.2.5   A Stylistically Marked Partitive Participial Relative Clause with a CP

While, as we have seen, ordinary participial relative clauses in Italian and English appear to lack a CP layer, one stylistically marked participial RC construction exists in Italian that gives evidence for the presence of a CP layer. See the following examples:

(168)   a.   ... spunti creativi, **molti dei quali concretizzatisi** poi nei romanzi.[122]
             ... creative cues, many of which materialized later in novels.

         b.   Da ogni vittima sono stati presi trofei, **molti dei quali ritrovati** in casa di Eugene Tooms.[123]
             'A trophy was taken from each victim, many of which were found in the living quarters of E.T.'

         c.   ..., **alcuni dei quali arrivatici** in seguito a percorsi di natura particolare.[124]
             Some of which arrived to us through a route of a peculiar character.

         d.   ... 74 incunaboli, **due dei quali ritrovati** negli scorsi due anni.[125]
             ... 74 incunabula, two of which found in the last two years.

An alternative possibility involves base generating the partitive genitive outside of the subject[126] (... *spunti creativi, **dei quali/di cui** [molti concretizzatisi poi nei suoi romanzi]*, etc.).

In these constructions there appears thus to be a special nominative Case assignment to the subject (possibly owing to a silent finite Tense), followed in the first of the two alternatives by the movement of the subject to Spec,CP.[127]

---

         b.   La parte che Gianni ha avuto in questa circostanza non è trascurabile.
             'The role that Gianni played in this circumstance is not negligible.'

         c.   *La parte che è stata avuta da Gianni in questa circostanza non è trascurabile.
             'The role that was played by Gianni in this circumstance is not negligible.'

[122] From Marina Buzzoni 'Gli occhi di Laura'. In *Le lingue occidentali nei 150 anni di storia di Ca' Foscari.* 411–25. Venice: Edizioni di Ca' Foscari. 2018 (p. 415).

[123] http://context.reverso.net/traduzione/italiano-inglese/molti+dei+quali

[124] From Carlo Greppi *L'ultimo treno: racconti di viaggio verso il lager.* Rome: Donzelli Editore (p. 206 n. 124).

[125] www.bibliotecauniversitariasassari.beniculturali.it/index.php?it/104/manoscritti

[126] Note that ... [*molti/alcuni/due di cui*]/[*cui molti/alcuni/due*] ... are (sharply) ungrammatical (see §2.1.2.1.1).

[127] The construction is not limited to participial RCs, but seems to encompass other predicative structures. See:

(i)   a.   Vorremmo 5 caffè, due dei quali/di cui (or dei quali) due ristretti.
             we would like 5 coffees, two of which/of which two very short

       b.   C'erano molti studenti, alcuni dei quali/di cui (or dei quali) alcuni con barbe e capelli lunghi.
             there were many students, some of whom/of whom some with beards and long hair

That this Case assignment is limited to a partitive construction is apparent from the ungrammaticality of other non-partitive structures:[128]

(169)   a.   *... spunti creativi, i quali concretizzatisi poi nei romanzi.
             ... creative cues, which materialized later in novels
        b.   *persone, alle quali questo arrivato in seguito a percorsi di natura particolare, ...
             people, to whom this arrived through a route of a peculiar character, ...

3.5   The Different External Merge Positions of the Different Types of Relative Clauses

3.5.1   *The Relative Merge Positions of Non-integrated and Integrated Finite Non-restrictives*

As noted in §3.1, non-integrated non-restrictives are 'outside' the sentence containing the Head, in a structure which is impermeable to sentence grammar relations (Movement, Agree, Binding, etc.) despite the asymmetric c-command relation existing between the Head and the RC under the extension of the LCA to Discourse Grammar. As expected given the higher merger of non-integrated non-restrictives, in head-initial languages, where they are both post-nominal, non-integrated non-restrictive RCs necessarily follow integrated ones. See (170):

(170)   a.   Gianni, che abbiamo contattato ieri, il quale raramente si dimostra disponibile, ...
             Gianni, who (lit. that) we contacted yesterday, who is rarely ready to help, ...
        b.   *?Gianni, il quale raramente si dimostra disponibile, che abbiamo contattato ieri, ...
             Gianni, who is rarely ready to help, who (lit. that) we contacted yesterday, ...

3.5.2   *The Relative Merge Positions of Finite Integrated Non-restrictive and Restrictive Relative Clauses*

In languages in which restrictives remain between the N and the demonstrative, non-restrictives are invariably found outside of the

---

[128] In a number of Central and Eastern Eurasian languages, including some Turkic, Uralic, Tungusic, and Mongolic languages (see Miyagawa 2008 and Ackerman & Nikolaeva 2013, Nikolaeva 2017 for an analysis and a typological overview), as well as in Polynesian languages (see Otsuka 2010 and Herd, Macdonald & Massam 2004, 2011), participial RCs can have an overt subject bearing genitive Case, and can thus relativize other arguments within the RC. I refer to Krause (2001a) and the above articles for discussion of this strategy.

demonstrative.[129] This is true, among other languages, of head-initial Vietnamese (Nguyen 2004: 61–2 – see (171)),[130] Indonesian (Lehmann 1984: 282 – see (172)),[131] Javanese (Ishizuka 2008a: §2),[132] and of head-final Korean (see (173), from Kim 1997: 11),[133] and Japanese (see (174), from Kim 1997: 12):[134]

(171)   a. Tôi thích cái đâm [RC mà cô   ây   chọn] [Dem **này**]. (restrictive)
            I   like   CLF dress that aunt that choose this
            'I like this dress that the aunt has chosen.'

        b. Tôi thích cái đâm [Dem **này**] [RC mà cô   ây   chọn] (non-restrictive)
            I   like   CLF dress this   that aunt that choose
            'I like this dress, which auntie has chosen.'

(172)   a. lelaki [RC yang sedang tidor] [Dem **itu**] . . . (restrictive)
            man   Rel   Prog   sleep   that
            that man that is sleeping . . .

        b. lelaki [Dem **itu**] [RC yang sedang tidor] . . . (non-restrictive)
            man   that   Rel   Prog   sleep
            that man, who is sleeping, . . .

(173)   a. Peter-nun [DP [D **ku**] [RC ton-i manh-un] [NP yeca]]-lul cohahan-ta.
            (restrictive)
            Peter-topic that money-Nom many-AM woman-Acc like-Dec
            'Peter likes the woman who has a lot of money.'

        b. Peter-nun [DP[RC ton-i manh-un] [D **ku**] [NP yeca]]-lul cohahan-ta.
            (non-restrictive)
            Peter-topic money-Nom many-AM that woman-Acc like-Dec
            'Peter likes that woman, who has a lot of money.'

---

[129] An early proposal for a higher attachment of non-restrictive RCs with respect to restrictives is found in Jackendoff (1977: §7.1), based on the relative position of restrictive and non-restrictive RCs when they co-occur (with the former closer to the Head). Additional works pointing to the same structural difference between the two types of RCs include Demirdache (1991: 108–9), Kayne (1994: 112), Grosu (2000: 100), Wiltschko (2012, 2013), Studler (2014: 166). See also Arsenijević & Gračanin-Yüksek (2016) for an argument that restrictive and non-restrictive RCs differ syntactically in terms of attachment.

[130] 'When the RC precedes the demonstrative, the RC restricts the meaning of the noun; when the RC follows the demonstrative, the phrase has a non-restrictive meaning' (Nguyen 2004: 61–2).

[131] '[172](a) ist restriktiv, [172](b) appositiv' (Lehmann 1984: 282).

[132] 'the *sing* RC preceding a demonstrative is a restrictive RC, whereas the *sing* RC following a demonstrative is a non-restrictive RC' (Ishizuka 2008a: §2). Javanese NPs have the order N A Num Dem (Cinque 2005: fn. 19).

[133] Also see J.-R. Kim (1993: §2).

[134] Also see Kameshima (1989: §4.3.3).

(174)   a.   Ano [watashi-ga katta] hon ...   (restrictive)
             that I-Nom bought book
             the book that I bought ...
        b.   [Watashi-ga katta] ano hon ...   (non-restrictive)
             I-Nom bought that book
             that book, which I bought, ...

According to Kameshima (1989: §4.3.3.1) and Ishizuka (2008b), Japanese minimally differs from Korean in that relatives appearing inside a demonstrative have just a restrictive interpretation whereas those appearing outside demonstratives may receive either a restrictive or a non-restrictive interpretation.[135] This suggests that the Merge position of non-restrictives is outside the demonstrative and that of restrictives inside the demonstrative, even though restrictives, in languages like Japanese, can optionally raise across the demonstrative (see Kameshima 1989: 215) to a position lower than the Merge position of non-restrictives (given that 'the natural order, when restrictive and non-restrictive relatives co-occur, is that a non-restrictive precedes a restrictive relative.' Kameshima 1989: 233). The same is apparently true of Turkish. Bayırlı (2017: 85) reports Özçelik's (2014) observation that non-restrictive RCs in Turkish precede the demonstrative ((175a)) while restrictive ones come between the demonstrative and the noun ((175b)):

(175)   a.   Noam'ın   yazdığı   o   şiir   (non-restrictive)
             Noam-GEN   write.REL   that   poem
             that poem, which Noam wrote, ...
        b.   O   Noam'ın   yazdığı   şiir   (restrictive)
             that   Noam-GEN   write.REL poem
             that poem that Noam wrote, ...

This was confirmed to me by Jaklin Kornfilt, pers. comm., who added that when a restrictive RC comes to precede the demonstrative, it follows, if present, a non-restrictive one.[136]

There is indirect evidence that in Italian too, integrated non-restrictives are merged higher than finite restrictive or maximalizing RCs, even if both are found after the noun, as a consequence of the Head raising above them as

---

[135] Ishizuka (2008b: §2) attributes the original observation to Kamio (1977: 153–9).

[136] Özçelik (2014: §4) claims that a PP can apparently be stranded to the right of the Head when the IP raises above it:

(i)   [Noam-ın   ti   yaz-dığ-ı]$_{IP}$ şiir   [sentaks hakkında]$_i$
      Noam-GEN   write-FN.-3.sg.   poem   syntax about
      the poem that Noam wrote about syntax

characteristic of head-initial (and of some non-rigid head-final) languages. This is because integrated non-restrictives (those involving *che* and (P) + *cui*) have to follow finite restrictives/maximalizing RCs, suggesting that the Head raises first around the lower restrictive or maximalizing RC before raising around the higher integrated norestrictive.[137] See (176)–(177):

(176) a. [L'unica persona [che è rimasta]], [che è tra l'altro una persona onesta], è Gianni.
           The only person that is left, who incidentally is an honest person, is Gianni.
       b. *[L'unica persona, [che è tra l'altro una persona onesta], [che è rimasta]] è Gianni.
           The only person, who incidentally is an honest person, that is left, is Gianni.

(177) a. [L'unica persona [su cui possiamo contare]], [che è tra l'altro una persona onesta], è Gianni.
           The only person on whom we can rely, who incidentally is an honest person, is Gianni.
       b. *[L'unica persona, [che è tra l'altro una persona onesta], [su cui possiamo contare]] è Gianni.
           The only person, who incidentally is an honest person, on whom we can rely, is Gianni.

Confirming evidence that integrated non-restrictives are merged above DP (as they modify an autonomously referential phrase), while finite restrictive or maximalizing are below DetP/DemP comes from a contrast in their compatibility with a polarity item licensed by a superlative adjective. Superlative adjectives are internally merged quite high in the nominal extended projection. They can even come to precede cardinal numerals (see (178)), and from that position, presumably c-commanding restrictive or maximalizing RCs, they appear able to license a polarity item inside them (see (179)).[138] As superlative adjectives are below definite determiners (inside DPs) it is to be expected that they will instead be unable to license a polarity item found in an integrated non-restrictive, which is higher than DP. This is precisely what we find (see (180)):

---

[137] This is a fortiori true of non-integrated non-restrictives, which are merged even higher, in the Spec of a discourse grammar Head. As noted above, this was observed for English, which only has non-integrated non-restrictives, by Jackendoff (1977: ch. 7).

[138] Similarly in English (*The blackest two dogs that I've ever seen*) and in Persian, where superlative adjectives are the only adjectives that precede the N, as observed in Kayne (2008a: fn. 15).

(178)   Sono state le più belle due settimane di vacanza di questi ultimi dieci anni.
         'They have been the most beautiful two weeks of vacation in the last ten years.'

(179)   Il suo è il più bel cane che io ho/abbia **mai** visto.
         'His is the most beautiful dog that I have **ever** seen.'

(180)   *Il suo più bel cane, di nome Freddy, che è **mai** stato visto da queste parti, è
         docile.
         his most beautiful dog, named Freddy, which was **ever** seen around here, is
         docile

Concerning finite restrictive RCs, evidence from the more rigid head-final and head-initial languages suggests that they are merged between demonstratives and cardinal numerals. See (181)–(182):

More rigid head-final languages:

(181) a. Dem RC$_{\text{finiteRestr}}$ Num$_{\text{Card}}$ A N
       b. Amharic (Ethio-Semitic, SOV – Beermann & Ephrem 2007: 26),
          [ennäzza   [yayyähuaccäw]   sost   telelleq   weshocc]
          those   that.I.saw   three   big   dogs
          those three big dogs that I saw
       c. Wolaytta (West Cushitic, SOV – Lamberti & Sottile 1997: 215)
          [he   [taa- w   kuttuwa   ehida]   iccashu adussa   laagge-t-I]
          those   me-dat   chicken   that.brought five   tall   friend-PL-NOM
          those five tall friends who brought me a chicken

More rigid head-initial languages:

(182) a. N A Num$_{\text{Card}}$ RC$_{\text{finiteRestr}}$ Dem
       b. Tukang Besi (Malayo-Polynesian, VOS – Donohue 1999: 307, adapted from (20))
          [na   wowine mandawulu **dua-mia [umala   te   pandola]$_{\text{RC}}$ [meatu'e
                                                                                    ai]$_{\text{Dem}}$]$_{\text{KP}}$
          NOM   woman beautiful **two-CLF [fetch.SI art eggplant]   REF-that ANA**
          those two beautiful women who were bringing eggplants
       c. Lango (Eastern Nilotic, VSO – Noonan 1992: 156)
          gwóggî à   dòŋò   **àryó**   [ámê lócə ònèkò]-nì
          dogs   ATT   big   **two**   [Rel-Part man 3sg.kill.Perf]-this
          these two big dogs that the man killed

3.5.3   *The Merge Position of Kind-Defining Relative Clauses with Respect to Restrictive and Non-restrictive Relative Clauses*

Judging from Italian it appears that kind-defining RCs (see §3.2) necessarily occur after ordinary restrictives (see (183)), and before ordinary non-restrictives (see (184)):

(183)   a.   Quello è [[[un ragazzo [che conosco]] [che non esita **mica** a rischiare]].
               'That is a young man that I know that does not hesitate at all to take risks.'

b.   *Quello è un ragazzo [che non esita **mica** a rischiare] [che conosco].
      that is a young man that does not hesitate at all to take risks that I know

(184)   a.   Quelli sono [[[ragazzi [che non esitano **mica** a rischiare]],[che/i quali in ogni caso non hanno mai messo in pericolo nessuno].
              'Those are young men that do not hesitate to take risks, who at any rate never created any danger for anyone.'
         b.   *Quelli sono ragazzi, [che/i quali in ogni caso non ha mai messo in pericolo nessuno], [che non esitano **mica** a rischiare].
              'Those are young men who at any rate never created any danger for anyone, that do not hesitate at all to take risks.'

Under the roll-up derivation of head-initial/medial languages these data show that kind-defining RCs are lower than non-restrictives and higher than ordinary restrictives.

As Radford (2019: 11 fn. 4) observes '[d]ata from the Kroch corpus suggest that the same ordering holds in English, since it contains 27 examples (like those below) in which an antecedent is modified by both a restrictive gap relative and a resumptive kind relative, and in every one of these the restrictive relative precedes the kind relative':

(185)   a.   There's a train [you can take] [that it stops in Chicago] (Ann Houston, Kroch corpus)
         b.   I have a friend [that I talk to] [that we left-dislocate and topicalize all the time] (Wendy C., Kroch corpus)

This ordering is not surprising as we have seen that kind-defining RCs share properties of both restrictive and (especially) non-restrictive RCs.

3.5.4   *The Merge Positions of Unmarked (*che/cui*) and Marked (*il quale*) Restrictive Relative Clauses*

When they co-occur marked (*il quale*) restrictives have to follow unmarked (*che/cui*) restrictives. See Cinque (1982: 267):

(186)   a.   Gli studenti che conoscono bene il tedesco ai quali potrete rivolgervi sono pochi.
              'The students that know German well to whom you will be able to turn are few.'
         b.   *?Gli studenti i quali conoscano bene il tedesco a cui potrete rivolgervi sono pochi.
              'The students who know (subjunctive) German well to whom you will be able to turn are few.'

3.5.5 The Merge Position of Restrictive and of Amount/Maximalizing Relative Clauses

In §1.5 I made the simplifying assumption that restrictive RCs and Amount/ maximalizing RCs are merged in the same position, between demonstratives/ determiners and cardinal numerals. There is however some indication that the two types may be merged in two distinct positions. This comes from their relative order when they co-occur. As with Jackendoff's (1977) conclusion that non-restrictive RCs are merged higher than restrictive RCs, based on the latter having to be closer to the Head when they co-occur, I take restrictive RCs to be merged higher than Amount/Maximalizing RCs since bona fide Amount/ Maximalizing RCs, like those involving a *there*-existential clause, appear to have to occur closer to the Head than an ordinary restrictive RC. See the contrast between (187a) and (187b):

(187)   a.   (?) I suddenly noticed [the three books that there were on your desk [that had earlier been on my desk]]. (Grosu 2012: 7, ex. (8)) vs

   b.   *?I suddenly noticed [the three books that had earlier been on my desk [that there were on your desk]]. (Peter Cole, pers. comm., Megan Rae, pers. comm.)[139]

3.5.6 The Merge Position of Infinitival Relative Clauses and Finite Restrictives

To judge from Sag (1997: 470), who gives the contrasts in (188)–(189), and Larson & Takahashi (2007: §4.3) and Douglas (2016: 169), who give similar contrasts (see (190) and (191), respectively), infinitival RCs are lower (closer to the NP) than finite restrictive RCs:[140]

---

[139] Megan Rae, pers. comm., tells me that the judgement becomes even sharper with *desk* in the *there*-existential clause and *shelves* in the restrictive RC:

   (i)   a.   I suddenly noticed [the three books that there were on your desk [that had earlier been on my shelves]].

   b.   **I suddenly noticed [the three books that had earlier been on my shelves [that there were on your desk]].

[140] The contrast between (i)a and b, seems to indicate that infinitival RCs are also lower than amount/maximalizing RCs:

   (i)   a.   Any book [to review] [that there may be in the list] ...

   b.   ??Any book [that there may be in the list] [to review] ...

Apparent subject infinitival relatives, presumably involving a PRO subject (see fn. 77 and §3.3.2.4 above), can instead follow finite restrictive RCs. See (ii), provided by Andrew Radford, pers. comm.:

(188)   a.   The only person [(for us) to visit][whose kids Dana is willing to put up with] is Pat.

      b.   *The only person [whose kids Dana is willing to put up with] [(for us) to visit] is Pat.

(189)   a.   One book [for us to read] [that Leslie praised] was Sense and Sensibility.

      b.   *One book [that Leslie praised] [for us to read] was Sense and Sensibility.

(190)   a.   Alice spoke to the dealer [to buy tickets from] [that Mary mentioned].

      b.   *?Alice spoke to the dealer [that Mary mentioned] [to buy tickets from].

(191)   a.   That is the book [to read] [that I was about to sell].

      b.   ??That is the book [that I was about to sell] [to read].

3.5.7   The Merge Position of Participial Relative Clauses

Pre-nominal relative clauses in head-final languages are often participial, though this is by no means general (*pace* Keenan 1985: §2.5).[141] Their peculiarity as opposed to the participial RCs of European languages is that their relativization possibilities are not limited to relativizing the external argument in the case of present participles or the internal argument in the case of past participles, and in some languages they may also occur between demonstratives and cardinal numerals, like pre-nominal finite restrictive RCs. Participial relative clauses in Germanic, Slavic, and Romance SVO

(ii)   a.   This is the only book [that deals with Stalin] [to have survived the purge].

     b.   This is the only book [that deals with Chomsky] [to be recommended by Chomsky].

But see McCawley (1998: 440–1) for a sentence in which a genuine infinitival RC follows a finite RC:

(iii)   Here's a topic that the Bargle Foundation is likely to support on which to do research.

[141] Pre-nominal RCs are in fact reported to be finite in many head-final languages. See the case of the Cushitic languages Afar (Bliese 1981: §2.4) and Galla (Oromo) (Mallinson & Blake 1981: 288); of the Omotic language Maale (Amha 2001: 162); of the Munda language Kharia (Peterson 2011: 488); of the Iranian language Sarikoli (Kim 2014: §3.3.1); of the Papuan languages Awtuw (Feldman 1986: 164), Gahuku (Reesink 1987: 217–8), Menggwa Dla (de Sousa 2006: 420), Mian (Fedden 2007: §6.4.5), Oksapmin (Loughnane 2009: 196), Tauya (MacDonald 1990: 289 ff), Usan (Reesink 1987: 217) and Yimas (Foley 1991: 420); of the Caucasian languages Laz (Lacroix 2009: 755), Abkhaz (Lehmann 1984: 72) and Chechen (Komen 2007: 1); of the language isolate Kusunda (Watters 2006: ch. 9); among many others. It would be interesting to know how many head-final languages have finite (exclusively) pre-nominal RCs and how many non-finite (exclusively) pre-nominal RCs, and especially what the two options correlate with.

languages are instead severely limited in the arguments that they can relativize and appear to be merged below cardinal numerals. Rijkhoff (1998: 362) explicitly says that '[i]n Dutch (as well as e.g. in German and Frisian) the preposed participial construction follows the demonstrative and the numeral' (and, we may add, precedes 'direct modification' adjectives, in the sense of Sproat & Shi 1990 and Cinque 2010a). See the examples in (192)–(193) from German, (194)–(195) from English, and (196)–(197) from Bulgarian:[142]

German
(Walter Schweikert, pers. comm.)

(192) a. Diese **drei** [in ihren Büros arbeitenden] Männer
       b. ??Diese [in ihren Büros arbeitenden] **drei** Männer
           'these three men working in their office'

(193) a. Der [kürzlich angekommene] **ehemalige** Botschafter von Chile
       b. ??Der **ehemalige** [kürzlich angekommene] Botschafter von Chile
           [non-parenthetical]
           'the recently arrived former ambassador of Chile'

English
(Tim Stowell and Christina Tortora, pers. comm.)

(194) a. These (other) two [recently completed] plays
       b. *?These (other) [recently completed] two plays

(195) a. The three [recently arrived] former ambassadors of Chile[143]
       b. *?The three former [recently arrived] ambassadors of Chile

---

[142] Romance is less revealing in that participial RCs are (virtually) only post-nominal (Dem Num (A) N (A) RC$_{participial}$ – see Cinque 2010a: 70), so that their position relative to numerals and adjectives is not directly observable. Nonetheless, the fact that in the presence of a finite restrictive RC they have to be closer to the Head than the finite restrictive (see Vergnaud 1974: 173 ff; Kayne 1994: 97) may be taken as an indication that they are lower than finite restrictives, especially if they lack a CP (see §3.4.2.4 above). Also see Meltzer-Asscher (2010: §5.1.2) for an argument that English participial 'reduced' RCs are merged pre-nominally.

[143] Also see Kayne (2005b: 66) (and Kayne 1994: 99 for the reduced relative clause status of *recently arrived*). We would interpret the grammaticality of *That beautiful recently arrived letter* (Kayne 2005b: 66) vs the ungrammaticality of (195b) above as due to the possibility for *beautiful*, though not for *former*, to have a 'reduced' relative clause source (see Cinque 2010a for discussion).

Bulgarian

(Iliyana Krapova, pers. comm.)

(196)   a.   Tezi **trima** [naskoro pristignali] poslanici ot Chili
             these three recently arrived ambassadors of Chile

        b.   *?Tezi [naskoro pristignali] **trima** poslanici ot Chili
             these recently arrived three ambassadors of Chile

(197)   a.   Tezi trima [naskoro pristignali] **bivši** poslanici ot Chili
             these three recently arrived former ambassadors of Chile

        b.   *Tezi trima **bivši** [naskoro pristignali] poslanici ot Chili
             these three former recently arrived ambassadors of Chile

Pronominals can be modified by finite non-restrictives (198a), but apparently not by finite restrictive nor by participial RCs. See (198b–c) (Megan Rae, pers. comm.):

(198)   a.   He, who had recently arrived, added in his two cents and the argument
             continued.

        b.   *The he who had recently arrived added in his two cents and the
             argument continued.[144]

        c.   *A recently arrived he added in his two cents and the argument
             continued.

The case of proper names, which can under the appropriate conditions be modified by all three types of RCs, is different. See (199a–c) (Megan Rae, pers. comm.):

(199)   a.   John, who had recently arrived, added in his two cents and the argument
             continued.

        b.   The John who you know is not the one that I know.

        c.   A recently arrived John added in his two cents and the argument
             continued.

The same state of affairs obtains in Italian, German (Roland Hinterhölzl, pers. comm.) and Bulgarian (Iliyana Krapova, pers. comm.). This can possibly be understood if pronominals are merged in the DP, above the Merge position of

---

[144]   The case of (198b) should be distinguished from such light Headed Free relative clauses as *He/She who says that is wrong* (see Elbourne's 2005, 2013 Voldemort pronouns), as well as from cases like (i), which appear to involve the restrictive relativization of stages of 'you' and 'me', respectively:

(i)   a.   That's not the you that everybody used to love. (Kayne 2017a: fn. 47)

       b.   The me who had recently been admitted to hospital was no longer the me who had
            previously so enjoyed life (Andrew Radford, pers. comm.)

both restrictive and participial RCs, while proper names are merged in NP (though they can raise to DP under certain conditions – Longobardi 1994).[145]

In some languages, pre-nominal RCs appear in the order Dem Num RC A N even if they can relativize more positions than those relativizable in the participial RCs of Germanic, Slavic, and Romance. This is, for example, the case of SOV Karata, an East Caucasian language ((200a)), of SVO Mandarin Chinese (where the RC can also precede demonstratives; see the next section) ((200b)), and of T'in, a Khmuic (Mon-Khmer) language, showing the mirror-image order N A RC Num Dem ((200c)):

(200) a. **Karata** (East Caucasian – Testelec 1998, 277)[146]

hab	k'eda	[dena	raxw-araj]	č'ikororaj	igruška-bdi …
this	two	I	bring-PRT	nice	toy-PL

these two nice toys which I had brought …

b. **Mandarin Chinese** (adapted from Lu 1990, 4 and 20)

na	2-ben	[Lisi mailai de]	youqu	de	yuyanxue	shu
those	two-CL	L. bought DE	interesting	DE	linguistic	book

those two interesting linguistic books that Lisi bought

c. **T'in** (Mon-Khmer – Alves 2001, 5)[147]

siŋ	kluak	?əɲ	[bakɛɛw	thoon]	piaï	naŋ	?ĕen	pəl
pig	white	I	[Mr.Kaew	buy]	two	CLF	that	die

'The two white pigs of mine (that) Mr Kaew bought died.'

How are (Germanic, Slavic, and Romance) participial RCs ordered with respect to finite restrictive or maximalizing RCs? If the former are lower than cardinal numerals and the latter are higher, one should expect the former to be closer to the Head than finite restrictives.[148]

---

[145] I assume as NPs to Spec,DP rather than as N°s to D° (see Giusti 2002: §3.4). They can be complex: *la stessa Lucia di Lammermoor*. Lit.: 'the (very) same L. of L.' vs *Lucia di Lammermoor$_i$ stessa* t_i (both: 'L. di L. herself').

[146] According to Kibrik (1996: 153) this is also the position of (participial) RCs in Godoberi, another East Caucasian language, although he says that heavy participial relative clauses tend to occur leftmost in the NP, which appears to reflect the general long-before-short tendency of head-final languages (see Yamashita & Chang 2001), the mirror image of the short-before-long tendency of head-initial languages. See Kibrik's example (14), given here as (i):

(i)

[im-u-di	kote	se=b=a	b=aXi-bu]	ha=b	łabu=da-la	b=eč'uXa	X.ani
[father-	little	before	N=buy.PST-	this=N	three-CARD-	N=big	horse
OBL-ERG			PART]		COLL		

these three big horses, recently bought by father

[147] The same order is attributed by Simpson (2005: 806) to Khmer.

[148] Even though Sag (1997: 471) reports that for him in English 'reduced relatives may precede or follow *wh*-relatives (including *that* relatives)' (see his examples (i) and (ii)). In (my) Italian

Putting together these data, we arrive at the following structure of Merge for (finite) non-integrated and integrated non-restrictive, (finite) restrictive, amount/maximalizing, infinitival and participial RCs:

(201) $\mathbf{RC_{non\text{-}integr}}$ finite nonrestr $\cdots$ $[\mathbf{RC_{integr}}$ finite nonrestr $F°$ $[DemP\ F°\ [\mathbf{RC_{kind\text{-}def}}$
        $F°\ [\mathbf{RC_{(marked)}}$ finite restr $F°\ [\mathbf{RC_{(unmarked)}}$ finite restr $F°\ [\mathbf{RC_{amount}}\ F°\ [\mathbf{RC_{infin}}$
        $F°\ [[NumP\ F°\ [\mathbf{RC_{partic}}\ F°\ [AP\ F°\ [NP]]]]]$

In addition to the post-numeral position participial RCs can however also be found in certain languages between demonstratives and numerals and even before demonstratives. See the case of Hungarian (202), from Dékány (2016), Turkish (203), from Jaklin Kornfilt, pers. comm., and Chinese (in the next section):

(202)   a.   a három [tegnap talál-t] szép/fehér kavics
             the three yesterday find-ed nice/white pebble
             the three nice/white pebbles that were found yesterday ...
        b.   az én eme [tegnap talál-t] három kavics-om
             the I this yesterday find-ed three pebble
             these three pebbles of mine that were found yesterday ...
        c.   az én [tegnap talál-t] eme kavics-om
             the I yesterday find-ed this pebble
             this pebble of mine that was found yesterday ...

---

participial RCs interpreted restrictively need to be closer to the Head than finite restrictive RCs (see (iii)):

(i)   a.   The bills [passed by the House yesterday] [that we objected to] died in the Senate.
        b.   The bills [that we objected to] [passed by the House last week] died in the Senate.
(ii)   a.   The only people [being added to our group][who were at Harvard] are Jones and Abrams.
        b.   The only people [who were at Harvard] [being added to our group] are Jones and Abrams.
(iii)   a.   I soli ragazzi [invitati alla festa] [che ho riconosciuto] erano i suoi studenti.
             'The only boys invited to the party that I recognized were his students.'
        b.   *I soli ragazzi [che ho riconosciuto] [invitati alla festa] erano i suoi studenti.
             'The only boys that I recognized invited to the party were his students.'

Perhaps (i)b and (ii)b sound possible if understood non-restrictively or as parenthetical restrictive RCs (in Stowell's 2005 sense – see A3.1 of the Appendix).

Participial RCs also appear to be closer to the N than Infinitival RCs. See (iv):

(iv)   a.   I ragazzi [invitati alla festa] [da tenere sotto controllo] ...
             the boys invited to the party to subject to close inspection ...
        b.   *?I ragazzi [da tenere sotto controllo] [invitati alla festa] ...
             the boys to subject to close inspection invited to the party ...

(203) a. o   üç   [Oya-nın oku-duğ-u]   ilginç   kitap
           those three   Oya-GEN read-IND.NOM-3.sg.   interesting book
       b. o   [Oya-nın oku-duğ-u]   üç   ilginç   kitap
           those Oya-GEN read-IND.NOM-3.sg.   three   interesting book
       c. [Oya-nın oku-duğ-u]   o   üç   ilginç   kitap
           Oya-GEN read-IND.NOM-3.sg.   those   three   interesting book
           those interesting three books which Oya read

While the pre-demonstrative position is almost certainly derived by movement (see in particular the evidence from Chinese in the next section), the position between demonstratives and numerals (which is more marginal in Turkish and Chinese) may be another option of external Merge, although that remains to be ascertained (both in Turkish and Chinese the participial RC can also follow those adjectives that can be derived from RCs).

Finally, Larson and Takahashi (2007) observe that prenominal relatives in Chinese (for which also see Del Gobbo 2005), Japanese, Korean, and Turkish exhibit ordering preferences based on whether they express stage-level versus individual-level properties. They found that stage-level relatives are higher than individual-level relatives (if both co-occur individual-level RCs occur closer to N). Participial RCs in Italian, which are obligatorily post-nominal appear to show the same effect in a mirror image (the individual-level participial RC is again closer to the noun than the stage-level one):

(204) a. Le uniche disposizioni **[riguardantici][pervenuteci]** sono queste.
           The only dispositions [**concerning us]** [**arrived]** are these.
       b. *?Le uniche disposizioni **[pervenuteci][riguardantici]** sono queste.[149]

If correct, then, these observations suggest a more fine-grained structure, where participial RCs occupy distinct positions depending on whether they are in the scope of a generic (individual-level) or an existential (stage-level) operator: . . .[NumP F°[**RC$_{redS-L}$** F°[**RC$_{redI-L}$** F° [AP F° [NP]]]]].

This gives the overall hierarchy seen in (205):[150]

---

[149] The order restriction is in fact 'lifted if a substantial pause is inserted between the two relative clauses', as Larson & Takahashi (2007: fn. 2) note for Japanese.

[150] It remains to be seen where Wiltschko's (2012, 2013) German 'descriptive' RCs should be merged. She argues that they attach lower than restrictives (and non-restrictives) and conjectures that they might be similar to Chinese RCs (but see Cabredo Hofherr 2014: §5). She also raises the question of whether RCs could attach at each functional layer of the nominal extended projection, concerning which (205) comes close to giving a positive answer.

On these German 'descriptive' RCs employing reduced determiners also see Brugger & Prinzhorn (1996), and more recently Cabredo Hofherr (2014), where it is argued that only contrastive restrictive RCs are incompatible with reduced determiners in Germanic.

(205)

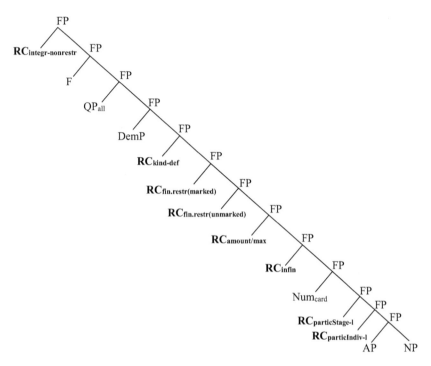

The general question of how this putatively universal structure of Merge (to be thought as purely hierarchical) gets linearized in head-initial and head-final languages cannot be adequately addressed here. I refer to Cinque (2017b) for a movement account of their derivation.

3.6　A Note on Chinese Relative Clauses[*]

In this section, in the light of the different Merge position of the various RC types seen in the previous section, I consider the possibility that Chinese RCs are actually a kind of non-finite/participial RC. The two possible positions of relative clauses in Chinese (the pre-demonstrative one and the post-demonstrative, post-numeral and post-classifier one – see (206)) have since Chao's (1968) characterization of RC1 as 'restrictive' and RC2 as 'descriptive'

[*] Thanks to Jim Huang, Jo-wang Lin, Victor Pan, Waltraud Paul, and Niina Zhang for their judgements and comments on a number of relevant issues. This section covers much of the same material of an article to appear in the journal *Theoretical and Experimental Linguistics*.

(non-restrictive) made Chinese RCs appear quite different from those of other languages (even in conflict with the standard semantics of restrictive and non-restrictive relativization). A comparative perspective may perhaps make Chinese RCs appear less unique.

(206)   **(RC1)** – Demonstrative – Numeral – Classifier – **(RC2)** – (AP)- Noun

As discussed in the previous section, cross-linguistic evidence suggests that finite non-restrictive, finite restrictive, and participial RCs occupy different positions within the nominal extended projection. See (205) above.[151] In particular, the fact we have observed that finite (integrated) non-restrictives are above demonstratives and finite restrictives below demonstratives (and determiners) and above numerals accords with the semantics. Non-restrictives modify something with independent reference, DemP/DP, and are thus outside the scope of DemP/DP; restrictives are instead within the scope of the determiner, which expresses the uniqueness or maximality of the intersection between the set of entities contributed by the Head and those contributed by the relative clause.

As noted, in Chao's (1968: 286) classical work Chinese pre-demonstrative RCs like (207a) are characterized as typically having a restrictive interpretation while post-demonstrative RCs like (207b) are characterized as typically having a 'descriptive' (or non-restrictive) interpretation.[152]

(207)   a.   [[**Dai yanjing de**] na-wei xiansheng] shi shei?   (restrictive)
                wear glasses DE that-CL gentleman is who
                'Who is the gentleman who is wearing glasses (not the one who is not wearing glasses)?'
         b.   [Na-wei [**dai yanjing de**] xiansheng] shi shei?   ('descriptive' (non-restrictive))
                that-CL **wear glasses DE** gentleman is who
                'Who is that gentleman (who incidentally is) wearing glasses?'

In this overall scenario, Chinese is puzzling on at least three counts.[153] First, post-demonstrative RCs (RC2) appear below cardinal numerals (and

---

[151] I abstract away here, as not relevant, from the distinction that has to be made between two types of non-restrictive RCs in head-initial languages with post-nominal RCs (see §3.1 above).

[152] Chao (1968: 286) also adds that '... if a contrasting stress is placed on a modifier, it is used restrictively, so that if *dai yanjing de* in [(207b)] is contrastively stressed, the sentence will have the same restrictive sense as in [(207a)]'. Also see Huang (1982: 68 ff). For Lin (2004: §2.1) no focus is really needed for RC2 to be interpreted restrictively. For a similar, early position see Teng (1981: 14) (as pointed out to me by Waltraud Paul).

[153] It also represents an extremely rare combination of VO order and pre-nominal RCs, typical of Sinitic, except for Hui'an (Southern Min) and Kaiping (Yue), which 'have what seem to be head-initial relatives' (Arcodia 2017: 41).

classifiers) rather than above them (as is the case with finite restrictives);[154] second, pre-demonstrative RCs are typically restrictive rather than, as one should expect, non-restrictive;[155] and third, which is the most puzzling property, the post-demonstrative, post-numeral, post-classifier position of the RC is apparently open to a non-restrictive interpretation (the second and third points appear in conflict with the semantics of restrictives and non-restrictives – see Lin 2004: §4 and §5, Constant 2011: §1.1).

These three puzzles would disappear if we were to analyse Chinese RCs as non-finite (participial-like) RCs. After all the finite/non-finite distinction is not overtly marked in Chinese, so RCs might well be non-finite.[156] This would plausibly mean taking RC2 as the base position, and RC1 as derived from it by movement.

There may in fact be some evidence for this conclusion. The pre-demonstrative position of RCs (and that of other modifiers) appears to be a marked focus position, a fact noted in many works (Chao 1968: 286; Paris 1977: §3.2; L. Zhang 2007: §5.1). The markedness of this position seems confirmed by the counts reported in Ming (2010: §4) and Hsu (2017: 75), where post-demonstrative RCs appear in corpora to be much more frequent than pre-demonstrative ones. See, for example, (208) from Hsu (2017: 75):

---

[154] The position between the demonstrative and the numeral, apparently possible for some speakers (Lu 1998: §5.1; Aoun & Li 2003: 146–7) is felt by many as unnatural (see Lin 2008: fn. 5; Huang, Li & Li 2009: 215; Zhang 2015: fn. 1) and is generally not discussed in any detail, so I set it aside here.

[155] Although, as noted by a number of authors, they can also be interpreted non-restrictively:

(i)   Wo mei zema [laoshishuo biaoxian hen cha de] nage xuesheng. (Lin & Tsai 2015: 113)
       I have.not scold frankly-speaking perform very poor DE that-CL student
       'I did not scold that student, who, frankly speaking, performed very poorly.'

[156] See for example Hsiao (2003: 25): 'Verbs are generally not overtly marked for tense in Chinese'. *Hui*, which can appear within RCs, is occasionally claimed to be a future tense marker. But this is dubious as it can co-occur with a past time adverb like *zuotian* 'yesterday'. See (i), from Hsieh (2002: 15)

(i)   Wo qiantian   zai dianshi li kandao zuotian   taifeng hui lai   de   baodao.
       I   the:day: in TV   see   yesterday   typhoon will come DE   report
           before: inside
           yesterday
       'I saw on TV the day before yesterday the report that the typhoon would come yesterday.'

Thus it is no finite deictic future tense but plausibly only a relative tense or prospective aspect 'be going to/be about to'.

(208)	Corpus	RC1	RC2	
	Academia Sinica Balanced Corpus	21%	79%	(415 sentences)
	Lancaster Corpus of Modern Chinese	28%	72%	(198 sentences)

Both facts thus seem to indicate that RC2 is more basic and that RC1 is more marked (Hsu 2017: 74), also because RC1 displays various restrictions not found with RC2 (Zhang 2015: 375).[157] In fact many have argued that the pre-demonstrative RC is derived from the post-demonstrative (and post-Num Clf) one. See Aoun & Li (2003: 253 n. 21), Lin (2008: §5) and Zhang (2015: §3), among others.

Let me then disregard from now on the derived pre-demonstrative position and consider only RC2, the more basic post-demonstrative, post-numeral, and post-classifier case, attempting to show that it shares properties with the participial RCs of English and Romance rather than with their finite RCs.

In addition to the position below numerals, there are three more properties that Chinese RCs appear to share with English/Germanic and Romance participial RCs occurring after numerals rather than with their finite restrictives.

1) A Chinese RC2 can be interpreted either non-restrictively or restrictively, as noted above. This makes them similar to English post-numeral participial RCs, which can be either non-restrictive (see (209)), or restrictive (see (210)), even if their non-restrictive interpretation (like that of non-restrictive adjectives: *her poor father*) should be kept distinct from that of English (or Romance) finite non-restrictives, which modify a DP/DemP with independent reference (see Cinque 2010a: 52 ff). An English non-restrictive participial RC and a Chinese RC2 interpreted non-restrictively seem to express an inherent property of the NP, modifying something which is still a predicate.[158]

---

[157] There are also certain syntactic differences between pre- and post-demonstrative RCs; for example the fact that only pre-demonstrative RCs can drop the subordinator *de* (see, among others, Wu 2009: §2), that only the post-demonstrative RC *de* can license topicalization and ellipsis (Zhang 2013: 242; 2015: §2.5; Lin & Tsai 2015: 114 ff), and that only post-numeral RCs are possible in existential sentences (Huang 1982: 64). For additional differences see L. Zhang (2007: ch. 3).

[158] See Huang (1982: 103 fn. 30). There is a particular restriction on non-restrictive RCs in Chinese (clearer when they modify a proper name). They are felicitous if they describe a more or less stable property of the Head (an individual-level property). See Lin's (2004) *Condition on Chinese Non-restrictive Relatives* ex. (39).

(209)   a.   Her *recently deceased* father[159]
         b.   The *recently deceased* John Jones was a friend of mine.

(210)   I only met the *newly appointed* colleague, not the others.

   2)   as already noted in the previous section, Chinese RCs are subject to a peculiar ordering restriction not found with finite restrictive RCs. Del Gobbo (2005: §3) and Larson & Takahashi (2007: §2.3) (*pace* Aoun & Li 2003: 150) note that Chinese RCs expressing generic, individual-level properties must occur closer to the noun than those expressing episodic, temporally anchored, stage-level properties. See (211), from Huang (2016: 443), adapted from examples given in Del Gobbo (2005: §3.2).[160]

(211)   a.   [$_{RC}$ wo zuotian kanjian de] [$_{RC}$ xihuan   yinyue de] ren
               I   yesterday   saw   DE   like   music DE person
               the person who likes music who I saw yesterday
         b.   *[$_{RC}$ xihuan   yinyue   de]   [$_{RC}$ wo zuotian kanjian de] ren
               like   music   DE   I   yesterday   saw   DE person

         According to Larson & Takahashi (2007: §1) this restriction is found with the order of English attributive modifiers ((212)) but not with the order between finite restrictives ((213)):

---

[159] Del Gobbo (2017: §6) also notes that English participial reduced RCs can be non-restrictive. In Del Gobbo (2015: §2.4) she points out that pronominal binding by a quantifier in the matrix into a non-restrictive RC is possible in Chinese (but not in English and Italian), providing the example in (i) (= her (51)):

(i)   [Mei yi-ge xuesheng]$_i$ dou wang-bu-liao na yi-ge [$_{RC}$ bangzhu-guo ta$_i$ de] Niu laoshi
       Every one-CL student all forget-not-can that one-CL help-GUO him DE Niu professor
       no student can forget Professor Niu, who helped him

Note however that such binding is possible into a non-restrictive participial RC in Italian (see (iia)), and for me even in the 'integrated' finite non-restrictive (see (ii)b.):

(ii)   a.   Nessuno di loro$_i$ potrà mai dimenticare il prof. Baratto deceduto davanti ai suoi$_i$ occhi.
              no one of them will ever be able to forget Professor Baratto deceased in front of him
        b.   (?)Nessuno dei suoi studenti$_i$ potrà mai dimenticare il prof. Folena, che sicuramente ha costituito per lui$_i$ un modello.
              'No student of his will ever be able to forget Professor Folena, who (lit. that) surely was for him a model.'

[160] Lin (2008) shows that the same relative order holds in pre-demonstrative position (as a consequence, I take, of Rizzi's 1990 Relativized Minimality).

(212)   the   **Thursday** **Thursday** lecture
stage-level individual-level
*individual-level stage-level

(213)   a. the person **[who smokes] [who I met]**
        b. the person **[who I met] [who smokes]**

Larson and Takahashi do not discuss English participial RCs, but to judge from Italian they seem to behave similarly, with individual-level RCs closer to N than stage-level ones, as noted above (see (204)).

3) Chinese RCs2 may also occur closer to the N than adjectives (see (214), from Victor Pan, pers. comm.) (*pace* Lu 1998).[161] They share this property with the participial RCs of English ((215a)), German ((215b)), and Finnish ((215c)) (also see Cinque 2010a: 121 and 131), but not with the English finite restrictives (see (216), from Steven Franks, pers. comm.):

(214)   na-zuo **[pojiu-de]** **[renmen zao** **yi**   **yiqi**   **de]** simiao
          that-CL old-DE   people   early already abandon DE temple
          the old temple that people have already abandoned

(215)   a. that **[beautiful] [recently arrived]** letter
                            (English – Kayne 2005b: 66)
        b. **[kleine] [unter** **dem** **Strassenniveau liegende]** Läden
          (German – Kafka *Der* *Proceß*)
          small   under   the   street-level   lying   stores
          small stores that lie below the level of the street
        c. nämä kolme **[komeaa] [toimstossaan työskentelevää]** miestä
          (Finnish) (Lena Dal Pozzo, pers. comm.)
          these three fascinating   office.INESS working men
          these three fascinating men working in the office

---

[161] Lu (1998: 54) gives the following contrast (see also Lu 1990: 21):

(i)   a. Susumu de   san-ben **[Cyril du-guo** **de]**   **[lan**   **de]** shu
           Susumu DE three-CL Cyril read-Perf DE blue   DE book
           'Sam's three blue books that Cyril read'
        b. *?Susumu de   san-ben **[lan** **de]**   **[Cyril du-guo** **de]** shu
           Susumu DE three-CL blue DE   Cyril read-Perf DE book

Yangyu Sun, pers. comm., reports that for her (i)b becomes possible if there is a pause between [lan de] and [Cyril du-guo de].

(216)   a.   ?Mary tried to interview every candidate **possible that she liked(N AP RC$_{finiteRestr}$)**

        b.   *Mary tried to interview every candidate **(that) she liked possible (N RC$_{finiteRestr}$ AP)**

There are two possible difficulties for the analysis of Chinese RCs as non-finite/participial RCs. The first is that Chinese RCs, unlike English, German, Italian, etc. participial RCs, can have an overt subject (suggesting that some Case is assigned to it).[162] Nonetheless, thinking of Karata (Northeast Caucasian) and T'in (Mon-Khmer)[163] RCs, which as in Chinese are lower than numerals, and are non-finite (participial), and yet license an overt subject, the non-finite nature of Chinese RCs can perhaps still be upheld.[164]

The second difficulty is represented by the unbounded nature of Chinese RCs (217a) and their sensitivity to islands (217b) (Ning 1993: §2.3; Li 2002: §3.1.1; Aoun & Li 2003: §6.3) vs the bounded nature of English and Romance non-finite participial RCs. But once again this might not be too different from the parametric difference existing between English and Italian (Romance) in the non-finite *easy-to-please* construction (unbounded and subject to islands in English (see (218)) but bounded in Italian (219)):

(217)   a.   zhe jiu shi [[ta renwei [ni yinggai t$_i$ zuo zhejian shi de]] fangfa$_i$].
             (Aoun & Li 2003: 177)
             'This is the way that he thinks you should do this work.'

        b.   *zhe jiu shi [[[[ta xihuan [t$_i$ zuo zhejian shi] de] ren] de] fangfa$_i$].
             (Aoun & Li 2003: 177)
             this is the way that he likes the person that does the work

(218)   a.   That book$_i$ was not easy [Op$_i$ to persuade Bill [to read t$_i$]].

        b.   *John$_i$ is easy [Op$_i$ to describe to Bill [a plan [to assassinate t$_i$]]].
             (Chomsky 1977: 104)

[162]   If assigned by (silent) Tense (see Paul 2018a, 2018b) the overt subject would be Nominative; if assigned by a (nominal) participle, as in many head-final and head-initial languages (Krause 2001a), it would be Genitive.

[163]   See (200a) and (200c) above.

[164]   See Krause (2001a: 14–5) on languages that have non-finite 'reduced' RCs with genitive subjects permitting non-subject and non-local relativization. Zhang (2018: 28–9) in fact claims that it is the complementizer DE, which can function like the English complementizer *for* of non-finite clauses, that licenses the Case of the overt subject in Chinese relative clauses.

(219)   a.   Quel libro$_i$ non è stato facile [da leggere t$_i$].
              'That book was not easy to read.'
        b.   *Quel libro$_i$ non è stato facile [da convincere Bill [a leggere t$_i$]].
              'That book was not easy to persuade Bill to read.'

All in all, then, the non-finite (perhaps participial-like) nature of Chinese RCs could still prove to be real.

4 'Strategies' for the Realization of the Internal Head

In this short chapter I recapitulate the different ways in which, within the double-Headed analysis developed above, the internal Head is realized; something akin to what the typological tradition treats under the rubric of 'relativization strategies' (Comrie & Kuteva 2005).

In the present analysis the different ways of realizing the internal Head are primarily dependent on the respective sizes of the internal and the external Heads – whether they fully match in size (giving rise, with the deletion of one or the other Head, to the 'gap strategy', with the possible presence of an invariant relativizer) or not, thus giving rise to the gap strategy with 'relative pronouns/adjectives' or to (one type of) the resumptive pronoun strategy.

4.1 The Gap Strategy with Overt or Silent Invariant Relativizers

As discussed in Chapter 2, one instantiation of the gap strategy is represented by the (obligatory) deletion under non-distinctness of either the external, indefinite (dP), Head (the 'raising' derivational option), or the internal, indefinite (dP), Head: one of the 'matching' derivational options. Depending on the language the presence of an invariant relativizer may be mandatory, as in Italian, or optional (with certain restrictions), as in English. In both cases there will be sensitivity to islands, as movement of the internal Head is involved in both cases. Reconstruction of the overt Head will instead only be present in the 'raising' derivational option.

4.2 The Gap Strategy with Relative Pronouns/Adjectives

Relative 'wh-'pronouns arguably differ from invariant relativizers in at least three ways.

First they generally vary morphologically, encoding some distinctive properties of the internal Head, whether a single one, like the human/non-human

242

distinction of English RCs (*who/which*);[1] or, overtly, more than one, like gender and number, as in the Italian art. + *qual-* paradigm (*il quale/la quale* and *i quali/ le quali*), or gender, number and Case, as in the Bulgarian *kojto* paradigm: *kojto* (masc.,sing.,nom.), *kogoto* (masc.,sing.,acc.), *kojato* (fem.,sing.,nom./acc.), *koeto* (neut.,sing.,nom./acc.), *koito* (masc./fem./neut.,pl.,nom./acc.).

Second, as shown by those languages where they can co-occur with an invariant relativizer, relative 'wh-'pronouns/adjectives appear to occupy a position distinct from that occupied by the invariant relativizer (see the Middle English *which that* case or the *dove che* case of Veneto dialects or the Polish *co ktory* case – §2.1.3).

Third, the fact that their relation to the RC internal position of Merge is characteristically sensitive to islands and incompatible with resumptive pronouns (but see the rare cases in non-island contexts mentioned below) seems to indicate that they come to occupy their position by internal rather than external Merge in the CP area, while invariant relativizers appear to be externally merged in CP, as they are also found in constructions not involving movement, as, for example, in constructions with resumptive pronouns where the relation between the two is not sensitive to islands.[2]

Relative 'wh-'pronouns also differ from invariant relativizers in that, in certain constructions, like the Italian non-restrictive and kind-defining constructions employing the *il quale* paradigm, they show an adjectival use, in which they are followed by a copy of the Head noun (see Chapter 2: fn. 55, and Chapter 3: ex. (9a)).[3] Invariant relativizers on the other hand never show 'adjectival' uses in the non-restrictive and kind-defining relative constructions.

---

[1] As a matter of fact *who* must also encode non overtly number and gender distinctions, as shown by the following examples, from Kroch (1981: 127–8), while *which* presumably only encodes number (non-overtly) – see (ii):
   (i) a.   The men$_i$ who$_i$ we thought t$_i$ would shave themselves$_i$/*himself$_i$ didn't bother.
        b.   The woman$_i$ who$_i$ we thought t$_i$ would shave herself$_i$/*himself$_i$ with the paring knife didn't.
   (ii) a.   The book which we thought was/*were worth a prize . . .
        b.   The books which we thought were/*was worth a prize . . .
[2] The fact that RCs with an invariant relativizer and a gap show in certain languages sensitivity to islands is still compatible with their being directly merged in CP if there is an associated movement of the (silent) internal Head, whether full or reduced, as hypothesized in Chapter 2.
[3] Something that we saw is impossible with the *il quale* paradigm in the restrictive RCs of Italian. Whether in non-restrictive and kind-defining RCs this is a true alternation with an adjectival use or its adjectival use is its only use, with optional (or, in restrictives, obligatory) deletion of the copy of the Head remains to be elucidated.

They can never be followed by a copy of the Head noun (see (i)b of fn. 50 of Chapter 2).

As noted above relative pronouns appear to occur obligatorily in those cases where the internal Head is bigger in size (DP/KP or adposition + DP/KP in finite restrictives and adposition + DP/KP in non-restrictives) than the external one (dP and DP, respectively), with the consequence that no deletion under non-distinctness can obtain (except in languages which allow preposition stranding and/or preposition dangling in COMP – see Chapter 3: fn. 78).

4.3   The Resumptive Pronoun/Epithet Strategy

The literature on resumptive pronouns/epithets in RCs is extensive and I cannot do justice to it in this section, nor to the extensive variation found across languages, across different relative clause constructions and within one and the same construction; even less so can I do justice to the detailed syntax of resumption in particular languages. Here I limit myself to those aspects that bear more directly on the double-Headed analysis with 'raising' and 'matching', with particular attention to the behaviour of resumptive pronouns with respect to movement and reconstruction. For a detailed overview and critical discussion of resumptivity in RCs see Rouveret (2011, 2018), Asudeh (2012), Radford (2019: ch. 2), and references cited there.

One first type of resumptive pronoun or epithet which may be found in RCs is the so called intrusive one found for example in (colloquial) English to rescue sentences that would otherwise violate some condition:[4]

(1)   a.   the guy who I hate almost everything *(**he**) does (Kayne 1981b: 115)
        b.   There was one prisoner that we didn't understand why *(**the guy**) was even in jail (Kroch 1981: 129)
        c.   He's willing to give it a go for Robbie di Matteo, who behind **him** there is Steve Appleton (Radford 2019: 72)
        d.   And then there's the likes of Iaquinta, who I don't think **his** form justified inclusion (Radford 2019: 76 fn. 15)

This type of resumptive pronoun/epithet appears to be non-distinct in character from uses of ordinary pronouns/epithets (McCloskey 2006), and gives no evidence of a movement derivation nor of reconstruction.

---

[4] Some languages, e.g., Chinese, appear not to have resumptives of the intrusive type. See Pan (2016: 35 ff).

Equally non-distinct from uses of ordinary pronouns (but see Adger 2011, and Chidambaram 2013: 90 for certain refinements) is a second type of resumptive pronoun which is systematically available in the RCs of certain languages (sometimes referred to as 'grammatical resumptive').[5] Within this class one must further distinguish resumptives which are optional (in non-island contexts) from those that are obligatory (in non-island contexts). For example, in Hebrew restrictive RCs resumptive pronouns are optional (in non-island contexts) with relativized objects and embedded subjects (in the relativization of the highest subject they are illicit – see Doron 1982; Borer 1984; Shlonsky 1992, 2004). With relativized complements of prepositions (as well as with experiencer objects of psych-verbs or the relativized associates of focus operators like *rak* 'only' or *gam* 'even') they are instead obligatory (in non-island contexts). See Sichel (2014: §2) and Rasin (2016, 2017).

What is more important for our concerns is what derivation ('raising' or 'matching') the different types of resumptives enter. In a 'raising' derivation one should expect them to display movement properties (island sensitivity and especially reconstruction, of quantifier scope, of anaphor and pronominal binding, of idiom chunks), and amount/*de dicto* interpretations, which arguably depend on reconstruction – see Hladnik 2013, 2015; Sichel 2014: 659; Rasin 2017: fn. 8 and relative text, and Bassi & Rasin 2018). In a 'matching' derivation one should instead expect the opposite properties. Hebrew appears to have the two options in one and the same construction, its restrictive RCs. As argued in Rasin (2017), which builds on previous insights of Doron (1982), Shlonsky (1992), Sichel (2014), and Arad (2014) (also see Cole 1976, Borer 1984 and Sharvit 1999a), the resumptive that appears to be optional[6] enters a Head-external/'matching' derivation which blocks reconstruction (just like the resumptive appearing in island contexts). The obligatory resumptive (in non-

---

[5] Sells's (1984) 'intrusive' and 'grammatical' resumptives correspond to Aoun, Choueiri & Hornstein's (2001) 'true' and 'apparent' resumptives and to McCloskey's (2017b) 'intrusive' and 'true' resumptives.

[6] Rasin (2017) argues that optionality is actually an illusion created by the double nature of *še* (which corresponds to the aL and aN complementizers of Irish). In one case it triggers movement leaving an obligatory gap; in the other it licenses binding of an obligatorily base-generated resumptive pronoun. If Rasin is right, the apparent specificity effect of 'optional' resumptive pronouns (Doron 1982; Bianchi 2011) might reduce to the nature of those resumptive pronouns that do not involve any (associated) movement, due perhaps to their full DP status. The fact that some complementizers are incompatible with movement (see the discussion in Rouveret 2011: §2 and in the references cited there) could be interpreted as suggesting that they select a silent operator in the relevant Spec,CP, which turns the resumptive into an operator bound pronoun and prevents at the same time other material from coming to occupy that Spec.

island contexts) can instead enter a 'raising' derivation and show full reconstruction possibilities. Whether the resumptives showing movement and reconstruction properties are to be analysed as the spell-out of the antecedent's trace (see Koopman 1983 on Vata) or the stranded leftovers of a more complex structure containing the trace of the moved antecedent and the resumptive pronoun (see Rouveret 1994 and Willis 2000 on Welsh, and Aoun, Choueiri & Hornstein 2001, Boeckx 2003) is not crucial in the present context. What is relevant is that the gap and the obligatory resumptive cases are compatible with a 'raising' derivation, which permits reconstruction (though apparently not parasitic gap licensing – Shlonsky 1986, *pace* Vaillette 2001: 306 after Sells 1984: 40–1), while the optional resumptive case is only compatible with a Head external/'matching' derivation, which blocks reconstruction. For detailed discussion and relevant examples I refer to Sichel (2014) and Rasin (2017).

A similar situation is found in Lebanese Arabic, where reconstruction is possible in definite (though not in indefinite) restrictive RCs with obligatory resumptive pronouns in non-subject position (in non-island contexts) (Aoun & Li 2003: §4.3).[7]

Also see Persian, where restrictive RCs with resumptive pronouns are still sensitive to island constraints (Taghvaipour 2005: §3.2.3.4) and Kindendeule (Bantu – Ngonyani 2006: §4), where they allow reconstruction. Welsh RCs with 'weak' resumptive pronouns (clitics or agreement) are, according to Tallerman (1983: 197 and 203; and Rouveret 2002, 2008; Willis 2000, 2011), also sensitive to islands, and allow reconstruction, which suggests that movement is involved, although they are not sensitive to principle C, which possibly suggests that a Head-external/'matching' derivation is also available, with obligatory movement of the internal Head stranding a 'weak' resumptive.[8]

---

[7] I follow Aoun & Li (2003: 95 ff) in taking generalized reconstruction to correlate with a 'raising' derivation and with island sensitivity. Guilliot and Malkawi (2007, 2011) have recently argued on the basis of certain French and Jordanian Arabic facts (primarily in dislocation structures) that reconstruction of anaphors and bound pronouns is found even in non-movement derivations containing resumptives within an island (also see Alber 2008 for the claim that Tyrolean RCs with resumptive pronouns 'are not sensitive to islands, but still show reconstruction effects', p. 168). This type of 'reconstruction' is however due in Guilliot and Malkawi's analysis to the presence of a copy of the 'displaced' element inside the island, elided under identity. Also see Rouveret (2008), and Rouveret (2011: 37 ff) for a radical alternative that takes resumption never to involve movement.

[8] I thank Alain Rouveret for relevant discussion. Tallerman observes that island violations are obviated if a strong pronoun (not possible in non-island contexts) is inserted in addition to a

On the other hand, in Irish (McCloskey 1990, 2002, 2017a, 2017b) and Scottish Gaelic (Adger & Ramchand 2005), RCs with resumptive clitics do not involve movement and reconstruction, which suggests the presence of a base-generated silent operator in Spec,CP binding the resumptive.

In certain languages resumptive pronouns, though still marked, are more frequent in non-restrictives (see Chomsky 1982: 58 on Spanish and Bianchi 2004 on Italian) and in kind-defining RCs (see Benincà & Cinque 2014 and §3.2 above) than in restrictives. This is perhaps understandable if we consider the fact that in non-restrictives resumptive pronouns are the same size as the external Head, DP, while in restrictives they are bigger than the external Head, which is a dP. Their markedness in many languages can perhaps be attributed to the availability of an alternative movement derivation that gives rise to a gap with obligatory deletion under non-distinctness.

Base-generated resumptive pronouns, as opposed to those coexisting with movement induce a specific or *de re* interpretation (see Doron 1982, Bianchi 2004, 2011, Bošković 2009 for discussion).

Although more commonly found with RCs introduced by invariant relativizers (like *che* in Italian, or *that* in English), resumptive pronouns are occasionally found (*pace* De Vries 2001: 239) also in RCs introduced by *wh*-pronouns. See for example the case of Middle English (2a), from Viel (2001: 226), that of colloquial Spanish in (2b), that of colloquial English in (2c), from Ross (1967: 433), that of Medieval Latin in (2d), from Bertollo (2014: 15), those of old and colloquial French reported in Touratier (1980: 482–3), and those of Italian reported in Poletto & Sanfelici (2017: 826) after Fiorentino (1999: 32 ff), as well as the examples in the English kind-defining sentences reported in §3.2, and many other colloquial English sentences given in Ross (1967: §6.2.3), Gheoghegan (1975: §6.A), Chomsky (1982: 11), and Radford (2019: §2.1). In Modern Greek non-restrictive RCs, a resumptive pronoun obligatorily co-occurs with a *wh*-phrase even in structural cases (Alexopoulou 2006: §2.2, and references cited there). See (2e) from Alexopoulou (2006: 70).

(2)　　a.　her sleve, **the which** in presence of her fader she had taken **it** from her ryght arme. (Caxton, Blanch., 84)

　　　　b.　yo recuerdo las murallas de la ciudad sobre todo por aquí por la Corredera **las cuales las** tiraron para hacer cases de pisos. (Cortés Rodríguez 1990: 441)

'weak' one. As Rouveret (2011: 15) notes, Welsh thus shows that 'several resumptive strategies may be available in the same language'.

'I remember the walls of the city especially here along the Corredera which they pulled them down to build apartment buildings.'

c.   King Kong is a movie [**which** you'll laugh yourself sick if you see **it**].

d.   **quem** (. . .) sequere **illum** non desinebant. (Chronicon Salaternitanum;) which$_{\text{ACC.SG}}$ to.follow him not stopped$_{\text{3rdPers.PL}}$

e.   O Petros,   **ton**   **opio**   *(**ton**) agapo poli, me ehi stenahorisi.
     the.$_{\text{Nom.Masc}}$ Petros.$_{\text{Nom.Masc}}$ the$_{\text{Acc.Masc}}$ who$_{\text{Acc.Masc}}$ (him) love.$_{\text{1s}}$ a-lot, me has$_{\text{3s}}$ upset
     'Petros, whom I love a lot, has upset me.'

In some such cases, it may not be easy to ascertain whether the resumptive clitics are of the intrusive type, with the relative pronoun merged in Spec,CP, or start out with the relative pronoun in a 'big DP' and end up stranded by the movement of the relative pronoun.

For languages with pre-nominal RCs which make use of resumptive pronouns see Kameshima (1989: ch. 2) for Japanese; Cha (1999: §2.1.1) and Song (2003) for Korean; Meral (2004) for Turkish; Pan (2016) for Chinese; Kapeliuk (2002) for Amharic; Dehghani (2000: 284) for Iranian Azari; and Gandon (2016: §2.2) for several other languages with exclusively pre-nominal RCs.

A variant of the resumptive pronoun strategy is possibly the small pro (i.e., silent pronoun) strategy that is utilized in the relativization of DPs in (certain) islands discussed in Cinque (1990: ch. 3) and in the non-restrictive relativization of 1st and 2nd pronominals in English (see §3.1.8).

4.4   The PRO Strategy

If the evidence discussed in §3.4 for the reduced participial RCs of English, Italian and other languages is correct, the internal Head of the 'matching' derivation is PRO, the evidence for a parallel 'raising' one not being entirely clear.

4.5   The Non-reduction Strategy

I use the term 'non-reduction strategy' here to denote the overtly double-Headed cases found in the languages discussed in §2.4. As seen earlier, in these cases there can either be a full copy of the external Head inside the RC, or the overt external and internal Heads can just partially match, one or the other, or both, being represented by the light/functional nouns associated with the nominal classes of the lexical Heads (see for example (95b) to (95e) of §2.4).

This interpretation differs from that found in the so-called 'non-reduction strategy' discussed in the typological literature as the latter covers two/three cases that are actually different from the double-Headed one, and should be analysed separately. Comrie (1989, 1998) distinguished three subtypes of the non-reduction strategy. The first involves correlative clauses (see here §2.6), 'where the head noun appears as a full-fledged noun phrase in the relative clause and is taken up again by a pronominal or a non-pronominal element in the main clause [...]. The second subtype of the non-reduction strategy, internally headed relative clauses [see here §2.3], covers cases where the head is represented by a full noun phrase inside the relative clause, and has no explicit representation in the main clause [...]. In addition to the above two subtypes [...] the non-reduction strategy covers one more subtype that we have termed elsewhere (see Kuteva & Comrie (forthcoming [2006]) the paratactic relative clause' (Comrie & Kuteva 2005: 6–7). The latter subtype can in fact be taken to be a variant of the correlative subtype since the Head internal to the RC can be resumed by a pronominal or a non-pronominal element in the main clause. The fact that led Comrie & Kuteva to distinguish it from the correlative subtype is the absence of a (wh-)element modifying the Head internal to the RC, but this appears not to be an indispensable ingredient of correlatives (see §2.6).

4.6   The Verb-Coding Strategy[*]

The 'verb-coding' or 'verb-marking' strategy refers in the typological literature to those cases where the syntactic function of the element relativized is expressed by a form of the verb rather than by a relative or personal pronoun. For such a coding to be genuine it must be the case that the form is only available within RCs. So, for example, Comrie (2003: §1) dismisses a number of cases (among which are the present and passive participle RCs of European languages) where the form of the verb apparently distinguishing subject and object relativization is also available in other constructions.

One genuine case of 'verb-coding' strategy is discussed in Andersen (1998). In Madi (Central Sudanic) RCs the verb is a non-finite, nominalized, form and the syntactic function of the relativized element is indicated by a suffix that occurs immediately after the verb stem. ('Depending on its function the relativized NP is either deleted or replaced by a proform' – Andersen 1998: 310.)

---

[*] See Comrie (2003) for a general discussion, as well as Keenan (1985: 161), Andersen (1998), and Pearce (2016) for different distinctions made in the morphology of the RC verb.

When a (singular) subject is relativized it is deleted and the verb has the suffix *-dĩ* (see (3a)). When a direct object is relativized it is deleted and the verb takes the suffix *-lé* (see (3b)). When the complement of a postposition is relativized, the verb takes one of a number of different suffixes depending on the individual postposition, and the postposition is followed by a pronominal suffix (see (3c)).[9]

(3)   a. `ɔtsɛ́    [mã      `-tsī-dĩ]   rì-nī   (Andersen 1998: 310)
            dog   1SG   NF-bite-SUBJ.SG   TERM-DET
            the dog that bit me . . .
        b. àdzú [ɲ´-à   hw`ɛ-lɛ́   má   nʃ]   rì-nī   (Andersen 1998: 312)
            spear 2SG-GEN   give-OBJ   1SG   BEN   TERM-DET
            the spear you gave me . . .
        c. ágɔ´   [ɲ´-à   ʃlí   k`ɛ-rɛ̃   drí-ārú] rì-ī (Andersen 1998: 313)
            man-SG   2SG-GEN   knife   give-LOC   to-3   TERM-DET
            the man to whom you gave a knife . . .

I take deletion to be possible (and indeed obligatory, as with the relativization of subjects and objects in unmarked Italian restrictive relative clauses) when the internal and the external Heads are identical (dPs) and pronoun retention when the size of the two Heads differs.

According to Comrie (2003) other genuine forms of 'verb-coding' are found in Nias (Western Malayo-Polynesian), Lhasa Tibetan and Dolakha Newari (Tibeto-Burman), and in the South American languages Ute, Cuzco Quechua, Macushi, and Apurinã. See for example the case of Nias, whose basic distinction is between subjects and locatives on the one hand and patients and recipients on the other (Comrie 2003: 8) ((4a) and (4b)). In this as well as in the other cases that Comrie discusses the opposition does not correspond in any other respect to a voice system.

(4)   a. asu   [**si**=usu iraono]
            dog   **REL.SBJ**=bite child
            the dog which bit the child . . .
        b. si'ila   [**ni**-be   nama Dali   kefe]
            village advisor   **REL.OBJ**-give   father.MUT Dali   money
            the village advisor to whom Dali's father gave the money . . .

As a matter of fact, the special morphology associated with the RC verb may in some languages have functions different from that of 'argument referencing' of the above type (Pearce 2016: §1). It may mark a special RC Tense or Aspect distinct from that of a main clause, as in Unua (Pearce 2016), Nepali (Genetti

---

[9] See Andersen (1998: §6.3) for the suffixes corresponding to the different postpositions and for adverbial or null alternatives to the postposition + pronominal suffix option.

1992), or Lhasa Tibetan (Comrie 2003); or it may simply indicate a relative subordination, as in Basque; or it may be a form of agreement between the verbal complex and the (external or internal) Head of the RC, as in Blackfoot participle RCs (Johansson 2011: §3.2) and in some Bantu languages (see the next section).

4.7   A Note on Bantu Relative Clauses

Even though in certain Bantu languages the relative marker, an affix in the verbal complex, may appear to vary, and hence distinguish, between subject and object relativization, as in Tshiluba (see below), there is reason to think that this is actually a bound complementizer morpheme agreeing in noun class with the Head, like other nominal modifiers. Compare (5a), with object relativization, and (5b), with subject relativization (the relative affixes are in bold):

(5) a. mu-ntu   **u**-n-aka-bikila   w-avu   (Tshiluba – Cocchi 2004: 67)
        cl.1-man   **1.rel**-1sg.SU-T/A-call   cl.1-come
        the man whom I have called has come
    b. mu-ntu   **ẃ**-aka-kwata   m-buji   (u-dia)   (Tshiluba – Cocchi 2004: 65)
        cl.1-man   **1.rel**-T/A-take   cl.5-goat   (1.SU-eat)
        the man who has taken the goat (eats)

In object relativization the relative affix, a prefix, precedes the subject prefix, while in subject relativization it fuses with the subject prefix (actually changing the low tone of the latter into a high tone – see the corresponding declarative: *mu-ntu ẃ-aka-kwata m-buji* 'the man has taken the goat', and Cocchi 2004: §3 for arguments that Tshiluba relative prefixes are distinct from subject/object affixes).

The complementizer status of Tshiluba relative prefixes appears more clearly if compared with other Bantu languages, where depending on its free or bound (prefixal or suffixal) nature the relative marker gives rise to different affix and word orders.

In Sesotho, for example, where the relative marker is a free morpheme the subject does not invert with the verb in object relative clauses ((6a)), while it does in Chishona, where it is a morpheme bound to the verbal complex, preceding all other affixes ((6b)):[10]

---

[10] The Bantu languages Kindendeule and Kingoni are like Chishona (see Ngonyani 2003).

(6)   a. Setulo   **seo**   basadi   ba-se-rek-ile-ng   kajeno (Demuth & Harford 1999: 43)
         7chair   **7REL**   2women   2AGR-7OBJ-buy-PERF-RL   today
         the chair which the women bought today ...
      b. Mbatya   **dza**-va-kason-era   vakadzi   mwenga
         10clothes   **10REL**-2AGR-sewed-APL   2women   1bride
         clothes which the women sewed for the bride ...

Demuth & Harford (1999) suggest that this word order difference stems from the pro-clitic/prefix nature of the Chishona complementizer, which appears to attract the verbal complex across the subject (arguably to a CP subjacent to the CP hosting the complementizer): 'Thus, a difference in syntactic surface form between Sesotho and Chishona embedded object relatives arises from a difference in the prosodic shape of the relative complementizer' (p. 55).[11] In other Bantu languages however the free complementizer appears nonetheless to attract the verb across the subject (see (7a)). It is only when it is deleted that the verb does not cross over the subject ((7b)):

(7)   a.   kit ki a-swiim-in Kipes zoon ...   (Kihung'an – Takizala 1973: 133)
              chair that bought Kipes yesterday ...
              the chair that Kipese bought yesterday ...
         b.   kit Kipes a-swiim-in zoon ...   (Kihung'an – Takizala 1973: 133)
              chair Kipese bought yesterday
              the chair that Kipese bought yesterday ...

More complex is the case of Swahili, where the different possibilities shown in (8) can reasonably be seen as different ways of providing a host for the relative marker, here a suffix (*vyo* in (8)), either by inserting an invariant relativizer/particle (*amba*) ((8a)),[12] or by raising to its left the entire verbal complex once the subject has raised to Spec IP (when there is no overt tense/aspect affix, as in

---

[11]   Also see Givón's (1972) Universal Pronoun Attraction Principle. Demuth and Harford (1999: n. 6) report the (marked) possibility of a sentence like (i) in Chishona, which appears to involve a topic phrase between the Head and the relative complementizer:
         (i)   ? mbatya   vakadzi   **dza**-va-kasonera   mwenga
               10clothes 2women **10REL**-2AGR-sewed for 1bride
               clothes which the women sewed for the bride
       This possibility is the only one available in Luganda: '[...] when the subject of an object relative clause is a full NP, it is placed between the relative pronoun and the head noun' (Walusimbi 1996: 37):
         (ii)   Omusajja   <Petero>   gwe <*Petero>   a-labye   musomesa
                man   Petero   whom   Ag-have.seen   teacher
                'The man that Peter has seen is a teacher.'
[12]   A combination which, in the KiVumba dialect, can be followed by *kwamba*, 'a complementizer frequently used to introduce indirect discourse [see (i)]' (Andrews 1975: 148–9):
         (i)   watu   amba-o   kwamba   wa   tayari
                    people   amba-Rel   that   SB   ready
                    people who are ready ...

generic sentences (8b)). When the tense/aspect affixes are overt, as in (8c) (see the past tense affix *li*) a more complex derivation is plausibly involved. First the verb (or bare VP) raises above the subject to a Spec,CP subjacent to the complementizer, and then the agreement and tense/aspect morphemes remnant move above the relative marker, providing the needed support for it.

(8)　　a.　vi-tabu amba-**vyo**　　　Juma　　a-li-nunua　　　ni ghali　　　(Cocchi 2004: 67)
　　　　　　cl.8-books part-**8.REL** cl.1-Juma 1.SU-T/A-buy be expensive
　　　　　　'The books which Juma bought are expensive.'
　　　　b.　vi-tabu　　　a-Ø-nunua-**vyo**　　Juma　　　ni ghali　　　(see Cocchi 2004: 66)
　　　　　　cl.8-books　1.SU-buy-**8.REL**　cl.1-Juma　be expensive
　　　　　　'The books which Juma buys are expensive.'
　　　　c.　vi-tabu　　　a-li-**vyo**-nunua　　Juma　　ni ghali　　　(see Cocchi 2004: 66)
　　　　　　cl.8-books 1.SU-T/A-**8.REL**-buy cl.1-Juma be expensive
　　　　　　'The books which Juma bought are expensive.'

The vast parametric variation found in relative clause constructions in the Bantu languages cannot be adequately treated here. For detailed discussion I refer to Demuth & Harford 1999; Ngonyani 2003; Cocchi 2004; Zeller 2004, 2006; Henderson 2006a, 2006b and references cited there. The limited goal of this section was to suggest that Bantu relatives may not be genuine cases of the verb-coding strategy. If anything, Bantu RCs would seem to fall into the gap strategy with (overt or silent) relativizers agreeing with the Head, or in some cases into the resumptive pronoun strategy (see Ngonyani 2006).

4.8　On the Putative Gapless Strategy of East Asian Relative Clauses

It has been claimed that East Asian languages (Japanese, Korean, Chinese, . . .) have no real relative clauses, but use a general adnominal clause in which the external Head is only pragmatically related to the content of the clause (see Matsumoto 1990, 1997; Comrie 1996; Matsumoto, Comrie & Sells 2017). This is based on the fact that the relative clauses of these languages ((9a)–(11a)) have the same form as the gapless adnominal clauses in ((9b)–(11b)), rendered at first sight plausible by the absence of any indication of the role of the putative RC internal position in (9a)–(11a).[13]

---

[13] It should however be noted that even Italian, French, and Spanish, which have ordinary RCs and no obvious adnominal equivalent of (9b)–(11b) (except for the possibility of rendering some of these via the pseudo-relative construction mentioned in §3.4.1.2 – cf. the Italian *l'odore della gomma che brucia* 'the smell of rubber burning' with (10b)), allow in colloquial registers

(9)   a. [gakusei ga hon o   kat-ta] mise   (Japanese – Matsumoto, Comrie & Sells 2017: 6)
              student Nom book Acc buy-Past store
              the store where the student bought the book

         b. [kyaku=ga   niku=o   yaku] nioi   (Japanese – Bugaeva & Whitman 2014: 5)
              guest=NOM   meat=ACC grill smell
              the smell of the guest cooking meat

(10)   a. [John-i   sakwa-lul   kkak-un]   khal   (Korean – Cha 1999: 27)
              John-NOM   apple-ACC   peel-ADN   knife
              the knife with which John peeled an apple

         b. [komwu-ka   tha-nun]   naymsay   (Korean – Cha 1999: 25)
              rubber-NOM   burn-ADN   smell
              the smell of rubber burning

(11)   a. ta xiu-che de fangfa   (Chinese – Li & Thompson 1981: 583)[14]
              he fix-car DE method
              the way he fixed the car

         b. [Lulu tan gangqin]   de   shengyin   (Chinese – Zhang 2008: 1004)
              Lulu play piano   DE   sound
              the sound which is produced by Lulu's playing the piano

There is however evidence that the (a) cases have a relative clause internal gap followed by a silent preposition, and must be distinguished from the (b) cases, which do not have one (see Cheng & Sybesma 2005).[15]

---

for examples very similar to (9a)–(11a), where the thematic role of the RC internal position is not explicit (i.e., where the preposition is unexpressed):

   (i)   a. Il ristorante che abbiamo mangiato ieri non era così buono   (see Cinque 1988: 498)
              Lit.: 'The restaurant that (= in which) we ate yesterday was not so good.'
         b. ... une chose qu'on tient le soulier quand on travaille en cuir   (Fiorentino 1999: 141)
              Lit.: ... one thing that (= with which) one holds the shoe when one works with leather
         c. en el lugar que fue fundada Roma ...   (Fiorentino 1999: 149)
              Lit.: in the place that (= in which) Rome was founded ...

To judge from Maling (1977) and Joseph (1980), Modern colloquial Greek also allows, more liberally than Italian, French and Spanish, deletion of many types of PPs.

[14] In the non-relative counterpart the noun must be the object of the preposition 'with':
   (i)   Ta yong na fangfa xiu che
         he with that method fix car
         'He fixed the car with that method.'

[15] But see Kameshima (1989: §1.3) for arguments that in Japanese even cases like (9b) contain a gap, and Radford (2019: §4.3 ff) for a discussion of this analysis. For English comparable examples like *They were clowning around, which I didn't really care until I found out they had lost my file*, in which there is no apparent gap within the RC, see Collins & Radford (2015). They claim that such supposedly 'gapless' relatives are more properly analysed as containing a gap created by relativization of the object of a 'ghosted' preposition. See however Radford (2019: ch. 4) for at least some cases (those whose non-relative counterparts do not require a preposition) where 'the relation between the relative clause and its antecedent is not explicit (i.e. grammatically encoded by the use of a preposition) but rather implicit (i.e. determined by pragmatic inferencing)' (p. 242).

Cha (1998, 1999) for Korean gives a number of distinct diagnoses which differentiate the two cases, some of which also provide evidence of the presence of a silent gap inside the RC matching the Head in cases of the (10a) type: the possibility in this construction, but not in that in (10b), of replacing the gap with a resumptive pronoun (in which case the preposition is pronounced), of entering a pseudo-cleft sentence, of allowing for the causativization or negation of the verb, and of permitting stacking. On long-distance relativization and island sensitivity and resumption and stacking as diagnoses for differentiating regular RCs from adnominal clauses of the (11b) type in Chinese see Li (2002: §3.1) and Zhang (2008: §2) as well as the discussion in Ning (1993) and Tsai (2008). On the distinction between RCs and the adnominal construction of the (b) cases above in Japanese, Ainu, and other Asian languages see Whitman (2013) and Bugaeva & Whitman (2014). For additional arguments that regular RCs exist in East Asian languages, also see Aoun & Li (2003: §6.6), and Huang (2016) on Chinese, and Kornfilt & Vinokurova (2017), Kornfilt (2018) on Turkish (though perhaps not all of Turkic).[16] Also see Van Riemsdijk (2003).

Similarly elliptical, in Higginbotham's (1984: 229 fn. 1) analysis, are *such that* RCs like (12a–b), in which the understood 'place into which binding is possible' is *of it* (after *sides* in (12a) and *therein* in (12b)) (but they are possibly a subtype of kind-defining RCs – see §3.2):[17]

(12)   a.   Every triangle such that two sides are equal . . .
        b.   The number system such that 2 and 3 make 5 . . .

---

[16] On the possible relative clause source of clausal noun complements, see the discussion in Manzini & Savoia (2003, 2011), Aboh (2005), Kayne (2008b, 2014a), Arsenijević (2009), Haegeman (2010), Manzini (2010, 2012), Krapova & Cinque (2016).

[17] Thanks to Alex Grosu for reminding me of such cases, which according to him, however, may not extend to all comparable cases in Japanese.

5 *Some Residual Questions*

5.1   Coordinated DP Heads: 'Hydras'

Consider examples like those in (1):

(1) a. The boy and the girl who met in Vienna ...   (Jackendoff 1977: 190)[1]
     b. The black dog and the grey horse that hated each other ...   (von Stechow 1979: 57)
     c. The boy and the girl who dated each other are friends of mine.   (Link 1984: 246)

Here, due to the fact that the RC internal predicate requires a plural subject, an analysis involving coordination of two DPs each containing a RC, with subsequent deletion of the RC modifying the first conjunct, is not available: *The boy ~~who met in Vienna~~ and the girl who met in Vienna.*

In such cases it is tempting to assume that the RC merges above the coordinated DPs, but (as required by its restrictive interpretation) still under a DP containing a silent plural determiner that creates the intersection between the external Head and the RC:[2]

---

[1] Jackendoff credits John Robert Ross for pointing out to him cases of this sort.

[2] See Link (1984: 251) and Alexiadou et al. (2000: §1.3). This is also reminiscent of one of the possible analyses suggested in Bobaljik (2017) for Spanish adjectival hydras like (i):

  (i)   a. el teorema y el axioma dependientes uno del otro
          the theorem and the axiom dependent one of.the other
          the theory and axiom dependent on one another
     b. la pianista y la artista austríacas
          the.FSG pianist.SG and the.FSG artist.SG Austrian.FPL
          the Austrian pianist and [the Austrian] artist

'[T]he adjective takes scope over both nouns: its agreement is [...] plural, suggesting that it occurs outside of the conjoined, singular DPs (each of which has its own determiner).' (Bobaljik 2017: 14). Also see Cinque (2004b: 134). The coordination of two singular Headless RCs ((i)) does not (necessarily) give rise to a plural DP. See (i) from Italian and Daskalaki (2005: fn. 9) for a similar property in Greek.

    (i) Chi ha detto questo e anche chi lo ha negato era/?erano in male fede
       (he) who said this and even (he) who denied it was/were dishonest

256

(2)   [DP Dpl° [&P [DPsing the boy] [and [DPsing the girl]]] [CP who met in
        Vienna]]] . . .

This in turn implies that the internal Head, which matches the external one, is also
a potentially plural DP, here represented by the relative pronoun [DP *who*PER-
SONS]. Notice that under a 'raising' analysis of these cases, it is not clear what
intermediate representation would have to be assumed; presumably not [DP D°
[CP *who the boy and the girl met in Vienna*]]. With invariant relativizers, *che* in
Italian, or *that* in English, both a 'raising' derivation with the deletion of the
external Head or a 'matching' derivation with deletion of the internal one seem
possible (see (3)), where both the reading each > 2, with reconstruction, and the
reading 2 > each, without reconstruction, appear available):

(3)   I due ragazzi e le due ragazze che ognuno di voi ha invitato alla festa
        arriveranno in ritardo
        'The two boys and the two girls that each of you invited to the party will
        arrive late.'

The possibility of these readings might suggest that the definite determiners of
the coordinated DPs are actually a function of the spreading of the plural
definite determiner over the indefinite ones (see (4)).

(4)

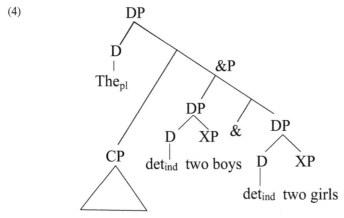

This would account for the fact, noted in Vergnaud (1985: 327 ff), that the
determiners of two or more coordinated Heads have to be similar; whence the
ungrammaticality of (5):[3]

---

[3] This may carry over to quantificational determiners (*pace* Hoeksema 1986: 79, where it is
claimed that '[u]niversally quantified noun phrases, unlike indefinite and definite noun phrases,
do not appear to function as antecedents for hydras.'). See (i) below and (i) of fn. 8.

(5)   *Le général et un aviateur qui se sont concertés   (Vergnaud 1985: 328)
the general and a pilot who talked to each other

This conjecture may be supported by mismatches such as the French cases in (6), noted in Abeillé (2017), where a plural determiner precedes two singular nouns interpreted as a natural pair (6a–b), but also two nouns under a split reading, at least with inanimates (6c):

(6)   a.   Les mari et femme sont d'accord sur le partage des biens.
the.PL husband.SG and wife.SG be.PL agree on the division of.PL property.PL
'The husband and wife agreed on the division of properties.'
       b.   [Mes deux [frère et sœur]]
my.PL two brother.SG and sister.SG
       c.   vos nom et prénom
your.PL name.SG et surname.SG

5.2   Relative Clauses with Split Antecedents

One may distinguish two such cases; one in which the split antecedents occur in two (or more) coordinated sentences characteristically bearing the same grammatical function (subject, object, etc.) (see §5.2.1), and another in which they bear different grammatical functions in one and the same sentence (see §5.2.2).

(i)   a.   Two linguists and one anthropologist who had met at a conference on language planning were among those arrested. (McCawley 1981: 139)
       b.   Every man and every woman who met at the party have left. (Fox & Johnson 2016: 1)

Complications arise with the apparent possibility of coordinating PPs with singular definite DPs triggering plural agreement on the RC predicate. See (ii), and the discussion in Bianchi (1995: 103–6).

(ii) a.   Ho parlato [con [l'avvocato]$_i$] e [con [il giornalista]$_j$] che t$_{i+j}$ si sono interessati al tuo caso.
(Italian – Bianchi 1995: 105) 'I spoke with the lawyer and with the journalist who got interested in your case.'
     b.   Le di un libro al hombre y a la mujer que vinieron.   (Spanish – Camacho 2003: 103)
'I gave a book to the man and to the woman that came.'

A possible alternative would be to assume Den Dikken's (2001) proposal for semantically plural, formally singular NPs, like *committee*, which trigger plural agreement (in British English): [$_{DP}$ pro$_{pl}$ [$_{\&P}$ DP [$_{\&'}$ & DP]]].

For a similar proposal and structure see Citko (2004), and for further discussion of 'hydras' Hoeksema (1986: §9), Smits (1989: §3.1.33), Bianchi (1995: II.10), Suñer (2001), and Fox & Johnson (2016).

5.2.1   Split Antecedents with Identical Grammatical Function
in Coordinate Sentences[*]

RCs with split antecedents in coordinate sentences characteristically bearing the same grammatical function (subject, object, etc.) were originally noted in Perlmutter & Ross (1970), and have since represented an analytical problem for both 'Head-external/matching' and 'raising' analyses of RCs. See (7):[4]

(7)   a.   A man$_i$ entered the room and a woman$_j$ went out who$_{i,j}$ were quite similar.
            (Perlmutter & Ross 1970: 350)
      b.   Every villager envies a relative of his and every townsman admires a friend of his who hate each other. (Hintikka 1974: 172)
      c.   The girl left and the boy arrived who met in Chicago. (Chomsky 1975: fn. 47)[5]
      d.   It is obvious that a man came in and a woman went out who were similar. (Andrews 1975: 119)
      e.   John saw a man and Mary saw a woman [who were wanted by the police]. (Alexiadou et al. 2000: 14)
      f.   Kim likes muffins, but Sandy prefers scones, which they eat with jam. (Arnold 2007: 274)
      g.   John noticed a man and Mary spotted a woman [who it seems were behaving suspiciously]. (Radford 2019: ex. (78))

Other languages possessing RCs with split antecedents include Dutch (8a), from Cardoso & De Vries 2010: §7.7) and Maltese (8b), from Camilleri & Sadler 2016: 121):

---

[*] This construction must be kept distinct (*pace* Cecchetto & Donati 2015: §3.3.5, and Bobaljik 2017: fn. 1) from the construction discussed in §2.5.2. The reason is that languages with pre-nominal relatives appear to have the latter but not the former. See below.

[4] Note that (7b), (7e), (7f) and (7g) have split antecedents in object rather than subject position of the coordinate sentences (*pace* Rochemont & Culicover 1990: 38–9). More difficult seem to be cases where the split antecedents in the coordinated sentences have different grammatical functions. Baltin (2005: 255) gives an example like (i) as ungrammatical:

(i)   *A man entered the room and I saw a woman who were similar.

Also see Moltmann (1992: §2.3). Chaves (2012: §3.4.3) notes that conjunction, but not disjunction, gives acceptable sentences:

(ii)   A man entered and/*or a woman left who were quite similar.

Vergnaud (1974: 184) notes that here too the determiners have to be of the same type:

(iii)   Une/*la femme vient d'entrer et un homme vient de sortir qui se ressemblent beaucoup.
        'A/the woman has just come in and a man has just gone out who look very similar.'

[5] Chomsky (1975: 98) actually says 'To me these examples seem at best quite marginal, and I would question whether anything can be based on them.' (fn. 47). In fact not all languages appear to allow them. See Cardoso (2010: 191–2) on European Portuguese.

(8)   a.   Ik zwaaide naar Anna$_i$ en Jan zwaaide naar Marie$_k$, die$_{i+k}$ overigens
dezelfde jurk aanhadden.
I waved at Anna and Jan waved at Marie, who by.the.way the.same
dress wore:PL
'I waved at Anna, and Jan waved at Marie, who were wearing the same
dress, by the way.'

    b.   Marija t-ħobb it-tuffieħ filwaqt li Rita t-ħobb il-banana, liema frott.
M. 3-love.IMPV.SGF DEF-apple.MASS while COMP R.3-love.
IMPV.SGF DEF-banana.MASS,which fruit.MASS
dejjem j-ieħd-u-h magħ-hom għal-lunch
always 3-take.IMPV-PL-3SGM.ACC with-3PL.ACC for.DEF-lunch
Mary loves apples, while Rita loves bananas, which fruit they always
take with them for lunch

Our tentative interpretation of such cases is that they are possibly to be assimilated to those RCs that (marginally) receive a restrictive interpretation even though they enter a (non-integrated) non-restrictive structure like the restrictives with heavy pied-piping in English (as in examples like *every candidate the father of whom Bill voted for* – Jacobson 1998: 81 – see §2.1.2.2), or the marked restrictives employing the art. + *qual-* paradigm in Italian (see §2.1.2.1.2); constructions not derived by 'raising', in which the *wh*-pronoun is interpreted similarly to an E-type pronoun or a demonstrative.[6]

This interpretation may be supported by the following four facts. First, replacement in English of a *wh*-relative pronoun with *that* (which is otherwise unexceptional with embedded and extraposed restrictives and marginal to impossible with non-restrictives) leads for at least some speakers to much less acceptable sentences. Megan Rae (pers. comm.) finds (7a) with *that* replacing *who* as much worse (see (9a), with her judgement), while Del Gobbo (2015: 88; 2017: 18) gives it as ungrammatical. The example (9b) in the variant with *that* is also given as ungrammatical in Arnold (2004: 30):

(9)   a.   ?*A man$_i$ entered the room and a woman$_j$ went out that$_{i,j}$ were quite similar.

    b.   Kim likes muffins$_i$, but Sandy prefers scones$_j$, which$_{i+j}$/*that$_{i+j}$ they eat with jam.

Second, an example like (10) in Italian is to my ear marginally possible even though it apparently violates the Right Roof Constraint:

---

[6] Recalling the analysis of split antecedents of non-restrictive relatives in Demirdache (1991: 116). Also see Erlewine & Kotek (2015a, 2015b) and Webelhuth, Sailer & Walker (2013: 47), where such cases as (7a) are taken to be similar to *A man$_i$ entered the room and a woman$_k$ went out. They$_{i+k}$ were quite similar.*

(10)   ?[Che [qualcuno$_i$ ci abbia aiutato] e [(che) [qualcun'altro$_j$ si sia aggiunto] è
        stata una vera fortuna], senza i quali$_{i,j}$ tutto questo non sarebbe stato possibile.
        That someone$_i$ helped us and someone else$_j$ joined in was a genuine stroke of
        luck, without whom$_{i+j}$ this would not have been possible.

Third, as noted in Del Gobbo (2010: 406–7; 2015: §2.2; 2017: §2.2) and Lin &
Tsai (2015: 105–6) split-antecedent RCs parallel to (7) above appear not to be
possible in Chinese, even in non-restrictive RCs, which are of the integrated
type (see §3.1.4.2). This may well be a general property of languages with pre-
nominal RCs, which, as seen earlier, do not make use of non-integrated non-
restrictives.[7]

Fourth, as observed in Vergnaud (1985: 335) French RCs with split
antecedents can contain speech act adverbs ((11c)), which are compatible with
non-restrictive ((11a)) RCs but incompatible with ordinary restrictive RCs
((11b)) (but recall the possibility of speech act adverbs in restrictive RCs in
Radford's English, and my Italian, mentioned in §3.1.2):

(11)   a.   Ce colis, qui franchement était très lourd, lui a été remis hier. (non-
              restrictive RC)
              'This parcel, which was frankly very heavy, was handed to him
              yesterday.'
        b.   *Un colis qui franchement était très lourd et une lettre recommandée lui
              ont été remis hier.
              (restrictive RC)
              'A parcel that was frankly very heavy and a registered letter were
              handed to him yesterday.'
        c.   Une femme vient d'entrer et un homme vient de sortir qui franchement
              se ressemblent beaucoup. (RC with split antecedents)
              'A woman has entered and a man has gone out who frankly looked very
              similar.'

For further discussion and different analyses of these split antecedent cases see
Hoeksema (1986), Moltmann (1992: §2.3), Alexiadou et al. (2000: §1.3), De
Vries (2002: 66 ff and ch. 7: §5.2.12), N. Zhang (2007), Cecchetto & Donati
(2015: §3.3.5), Overfelt (2015: §4.5.2)[8] and Fox & Johnson (2016: §2).

---

[7] Jaklin Kornfilt, pers. comm., informs me that examples like (7) above are indeed impossible also
     in Turkish pre-nominal RCs, although examples of 'hydras' are perfectly grammatical.
[8] Overfelt notes that examples like (i) below suggest that a negative polarity item can be licensed
     in the extraposed material even given split antecedence:

     (i)   [$_{DP}$ Every intern]$_1$ left and [$_{DP}$ every employee]$_1$ quit [$_{CP}$ who were in **any** of the
            basement offices]$_1$.

Despite these attempts, it does not seem unreasonable to conclude, with Alexiadou et al. (2000), that '[w]hile it is feasible for an RC to be linked to multiple antecedents by a rule of construal, as in the standard approach, to claim that they are linked by a movement dependency is problematic. It seems rather far-fetched to suppose that the antecedents in [(7e)] could have originated inside the relative clause (say, as a conjoined DP) to then be split and distributed across two clausal conjuncts after raising (a kind of 'reverse' Across-The-Board raising).' (p. 14). Also see Andrews (1975: 119–20), McCawley (1998: 771), Baltin (2005), McKinney-Bock (2013) and McKinney-Bock & Vergnaud (2014) for non-'raising' analyses of these structures.

5.2.2 Split Antecedents with Different Grammatical Functions Belonging to the Same Sentence

The cases of RCs with split antecedents belonging to the same sentence appear to be possible in Italian (and in English) as non-restrictive RCs: (12a) (and its English equivalent (12b), but not as restrictives, as shown by the ungrammaticality of (13a)–(13f):

(12)   a.   Se Carlo$_i$ non amava più Anna$_j$, i quali$_{i,j}$ d'altra parte non si erano mai voluti veramente bene, una ragione c'era.
        b.   if Carlo was no longer in love with Anna, who at any rate never really loved each other, there was a reason

(13)   a.   *The dog is chasing the cat which were fighting (Andrews 1975: 116)
        b.   *A man met a woman yesterday who were similar (Guéron 1980: 648 credited to N. Chomsky)
        c.   *The boy$_j$ looked at the girl$_j$ who$_{i+j}$ both like sports. (De Vries 2002: 67)
        d.   *A man visited a woman (yesterday) who were similar (Baltin 2005: 255)
        e.   *Il ragazzo guardava la ragazza che entrambi amano gli sport (same as (13c))
        f.   *John just wrote a novel and a book has recently been published that are quite similar. (Moltmann 1992: 140)

Yet to judge from Chomsky (1975: fn. 47) referring to what would later be published as ex. (26) in Perkins (1982: 284) similar sentences are apparently possible in Navajo. See (14) (as well as the discussion in Andrews 1975: 116 ff):

(14)   Łééchąą mósi yinoołchééł ahigáné´ę´. (Navajo – Perkins 1982: 284),
        dog$_i$ cat$_j$ it-is-chasing-it-along they$_{i,j}$-are-fighting-REL
        '*The dog$_i$ is chasing the cat$_j$, which$_{i,j}$ were fighting'.

They also appear possible in Walbiri (see ex. (64) of Chapter 3 and Hale's observations reported in the corresponding text), and even in English, provided that the two antecedents are related by a symmetric predicate (see Poschmann et al. 2018, who cite an example like (15), from Hoeksema 1986: 69) (*pace* Moltmann 1992: ch. 2 n. 3):

(15) We always let those boys$_i$ play with those girls$_j$ [who$_{i,j}$ know one another from elementary school].

Once again, such cases of split antecedents are impossible in languages with pre-nominal RCs. See Del Gobbo (2015: §2.2) on Chinese.

A 'raising' analysis for this second type of split antecedent RCs would seem again to require special assumptions.

5.3 Single Head Followed by a Relative Clause with Multiple Relative Pronouns[*]

While the case of RCs with one Head and multiple *wh*-pronouns is ordinarily excluded (see Citko & Gračanin-Yüksek's 2016: §3.1 discussion, references, and their Single Relative Pronoun Restriction), Kayne (2015b) observed the marginal possibility of at least two distinct situations where a RC contains more than one relative pronoun.

In the first, (16), (originally noted in Kayne 1983a: §8.2 and §8.3) the two relative pronouns refer to the same antecedent, the Head of the RC, displaying a parasitic gap flavour (Andrew Radford tells me that he would only accept them if the second pronoun were replaced by *him*) (also see (16d) from Charles Dickens' *A Tale of Two Cities, Book III,* Chapter II. *The Grindstone,* 6th and 7th lines from above):

(16) a. ?John Smith, **whose** wife's feelings about **whom** have changed but little over the years, . . .
      b. ??John Smith, **whose** wife's desire for you to hire **whom**, . . .
      c. ??John, **whose** wife's desire that you befriend **whom** can hardly be called a secret, . . .
      d. . . . the same Monseigneur, the preparation of **whose** chocolate for **whose** lips had once occupied three strong men . . .

As Kayne (1983a: 239 fn. 17) notes, the contrast between (16a) and (17a) below indicates that *whom* is not an anaphor, and the contrast between (16b) and (17b) below that it is not a pronominal, but a nominal, subject to Principle C:[9]

---

[*] For the different case of (apparently) multiple free relative pronouns in Bulgarian, see §2.5.12.

[9] The same Principle C, rather than their Single Relative Pronoun Restriction, may be at the base of the ungrammaticality of the examples in (i), cited in Citko & Gračanin-Yüksek (2016: §3.1), for their restriction would also incorrectly exclude the examples in (16), (18), and (19):

(17)   a.   *John Smith, whose feelings about whom have changed but little over the years, ...

       b.   *John Smith, whose desire for you to hire whom, ...

Comparable cases, with possibly comparable degrees of marginality, are found in Italian. See (18) and (19):

(18)   ?Gianni$_i$, l'avversione dei cui$_i$ dipendenti per il quale$_i$ era ben nota, ...

(19)   ??Gianni$_i$, l'avversione dei dipendenti del quale$_i$ per il quale$_i$ era ben nota, ...
      Gianni, whose employees' dislike for whom was quite well known, ...

I take the contrast between (16c), repeated here as (20a), and (20b), noted in Kayne (1983a: n. 29), and that between (16b), repeated here as (21a), and (21b), to be related to whatever governs the subject–object asymmetry of *wh*-phrases in ordinary heavy pied-piping cases (and possibly in partial *wh*-movement cases – see Cheng 2000: §3). See §3.1.5.1.[10]

(20)   a.   ??John, whose wife's desire that you befriend whom can hardly be called a secret, ...

       b.   *John, whose wife's desire that who befriends you can hardly be called a secret, ...

(21)   a.   ??John Smith, whose wife's desire for you to hire whom, ...
       b.   *John Smith, whose wife's desire for whom to hire you, ...

The case of the Northwest Caucasian languages Adyghe (Hewitt 1979b; Lander 2006, 2010; Caponigro & Polinsky 2008, 2011) and Abkhaz (Hewitt 1979a), where the second relativized constituent can be a clause mate of the first appears to be different. This difference is possibly related to the fact that the relative prefix is identical to the reflexive prefix. I refer to the cited articles for discussion of these multiple relative constructions.

    (i)   a.   *the student **whom** Mary introduced **to whom**
        b.   *student **którego któremu** Maria przedstawiła   (Polish)
           student who.ACC whom.DAT Maria introduced
           Lit.: a student whom to whom Maria introduced
        c.   *mladić **kojega kojemu** je Marija predstavila   (Croatian)
           youth who.ACC whom.DAT AUX Maria introduced
           Lit.: a youth whom to whom Marija introduced

[10] A similar contrast is given in Kayne (2017b: 365):

    (i)   a.   ?Mary Smith, whose husband's desire for me to paint a picture of whom is perfectly understandable, is a very famous linguist.
        b.   *Mary Smith, whose husband's desire for whom to paint a picture of me is perfectly understandable, is a very famous linguist.

(22) a. cəf-ew   **zə**-dež'   txəλ   **zə**-f-je-ǯa-ʁe-xe-r
                                                              (Adyghe – Lander 2006, ex. (1))
          person-ADV **REL**-at   book   **REL**-BEN-3SG(IO)-read-PST-PL-ABS
          a person to whom they were reading a book at his own house
          (Lit.: a person to whom they were reading a book at whose house)

      b. čal-ew   **z**-jat:e   **zə**-λeʁʷə-ʁe-r
                                                              (Adyghe – Lander 2010, ex.(7))
          boy-ADV   **REL**(PR)-POSS+father **REL**(A)-see-PST-ABS
          the boy who saw his own (lit. whose) father

      c. **z**-xarp   **z**-šʷə-z-c'o-z a   a-xac'a
                                                              (Abkhaz – Hewitt 1979a: 166)
          REL-shirt   **REL**-person-**REL**-put_on-IMP:NFIN   ART-man
          the man who was putting on his shirt

In the second type of multiple relativization, (23), the two relative pronouns refer to two distinct antecedents, only one of which refers to the Head of the RC, the other referring to a distinct DP in the matrix clause, much like a pronominal or demonstrative (see (23), from Kayne 2015b).[11]

(23) a. ?That car$_i$ over there belongs to my old friend John Smith$_k$, **whose**$_k$
          long-standing attachment to **which**$_i$ is quite well-known.
      b. ?My old friend Mary Jones$_i$ is still unaware of yesterday's discovery$_k$,
          the capacity of **which**$_k$ to surprise **whom**$_i$ cannot be exaggerated.

Similar cases are possible to some degree in Italian too. See (24):

(24)   ?Il mio vecchio amico Ugo Bonelli$_j$ è ancora all'oscuro della loro scoperta$_i$, la
          cui$_i$ possibilità di piacere al quale$_j$ non può essere esagerata, ...
          My old friend Ugo Bonelli$_j$ is still unaware of their discovery$_i$, the possibility
          of which$_i$ to appeal to whom$_j$ cannot be exaggerated.

Given that in both English and Italian such cases involve pronouns that can appear across discourse,[12] I will interpret them as referring to their antecedents much like E-type pronouns.[13]

---

[11] Also see the (marginal) case reported in Andrews (1975: 121), who credits it to Bill Cantrall, with two *wh*-phrases referring to two Heads belonging to one and the same complex DP:

(i)   ??I scribbled on the cover of a book, which cover of which book was orange.

[12] Recall that the genitive *cui* of (24) does not belong to the *cui* paradigm discussed in §2.1.2.1.1, but rather to the *il quale* paradigm.

[13] For coordinated relative *wh*-phrases modifying a single Head, like *Joan, the oldest sister of whom and the next door neighbor of whom make an amiable couple,* ... (Postal 1972a: 132), see the discussion in Citko & Gračanin-Yüksek (2016).

5.4   'Double Dependence'

The term 'double dependence' ('Konkurrenz' in the German tradition) is used in the literature to refer to cases like those in (25), where the *wh*-pronoun is fronted to the left edge of an island, possibly into the Spec of a TopicP (Cinque 1990: 189 n. 9) (Bianchi 1999: 143–4 and Truswell 2011 reach a similar conclusion).

For this construction in Latin, where it was particularly frequent, see Pizzati (1980) and Maurel (1983, 1989), among others.[14] It is also fairly frequent in old Italian (see, e.g. (25a), with a resumptive clitic typical of topicalization, from Boccaccio, cited in Rohlfs 1968: 196) (also see Bianchi 1999: 143–4 and especially De Roberto 2010: 345–68). On examples of 'double dependence' in (formal) modern Italian, see (25b–d), from Cinque (1978: 59 ff, 1988: §1.1.11); and for similar cases in Early Modern English Truswell (2011), and references cited there.[15]

(25)   a.   In Mugnone si trova una pietra, *la quale chi la porta sopra* non è veduto da niun'altra persona.
   in Mugnone a stone is found, which he who carries it above himself, is not seen by anyone

b.   (?)Una tale ipoteca, *della quale se voi vi liberaste* sareste certamente più felici, . . .
   such a mortgage, of which if you could get rid you would certainly be happier, . . .

c.   (?)Un circolo, *al quale essere ammessi a tali condizioni* è senza dubbio un privilegio, . . .
   a club, to which to be admitted under such conditions is certainly a privilege, . . .

d.   (?) E' un impegno, *dal quale chi mai riuscirà a liberarsi* si sentirà di sicuro più leggero.
   it's a commitment, from which whoever will manage to free himself will certainly feel lighter

---

[14] One example is also given in Ehrenkranz & Hirschland (1972: 26). See (i), which they take (unnecessarily, if we are right) to violate the Complex NP Constraint:

(i)   non politus iis artibus [quas qui tenent] eruditi appellantur   (Cic. Fin. 1, 7, 26)
   not polished in those arts the possessors of which (lit. which those who have) are called erudite

[15] That the *wh*-phrases are still inside the Complex NP island in (25a) and (25d) and the adjunct and subject islands in (25b) and (25c) is suggested by the fact that when the *wh*-phrase is not contiguous to the island the sentences become ungrammatical (see for example: *E' un impegno, *dal quale si sentirà di sicuro più leggero chi mai riuscirà a liberarsi*. vs (25d). I would interpret analogously the Czech contrasts pointed out in Biskup & Šimík (2019). Truswell (2011: 295) claims that in Latin and Hindi (Rajesh Bhatt, pers. comm.) cases of double dependence can also be restrictives, while in both (archaic) Italian and Early Modern English they appear to be possible only as non-restrictives. But see (25a) for a 'Headless' RC case in old Italian.

Also see the quite formal English cases in (26) from Jespersen (1949: 183–4):[16]

(26) a. Until the divinity of Jesus became a dogma, which to dispute was death,
      which to doubt was infamy ... (Jespersen 1949: 183)
  b. The most piteous tale [...] which in recounting this grief grew
      puissant ... (Jespersen 1949: 184)
  c. ... to understand a little more of the thoughts of others, which so soon as
      you try to do honestly, you will discover ... (Jespersen 1949: 202)

That the *wh*-pronouns are still within the island is indicated, as already noted in
fn. 15, by the ungrammaticality of the corresponding cases in which the *wh*-
pronoun is extracted (is no longer contiguous to the island).

5.5   Selective Extraction from Certain Relative Clauses[*]

Apparent violations of the Complex NP Constraint (CNPC, Ross 1967) have
occasionally been reported in the literature, the most prominent case being the
extraction from relative clauses in Scandinavian, documented in work of the
1970s and early 1980s. See Erteschik-Shir (1973: ch. 2; 1982) for Danish,
Andersson (1974, 1982), Engdahl (1980, 1982), Allwood (1976, 1982) for
Swedish, Engdahl (1980), Taraldsen (1978: fn. 6; 1981, 1982) for Norwegian,
and Smits (1989: §4.2.3), Engdahl (1997) and Lindhal (2017) for general
discussion. Some examples are given in (27):[17]

---

[16] The same construction appears possible in Standard German and Bavarian (Grewendorf 2014:
145 dubs it 'Bavarian Extraction'). See (i)a and (i)b–c, respectively. It is possibly based on a
previous topicalization to the edge of the island:

(i) a. Das ist die Frau die wenn du __ heiratest, bist du verrückt.   (Felix 1985: 177)
      this is the woman that if you marry are you crazy
      this is the woman that you are crazy if you marry her
  b. Dies ist da Kerl, mit dem woun i __ tounz, stess i zoum.   (Kallulli 2014: 197)
      this is the guy with whom$_{DAT}$ if I dance, crash I together
      this is the guy, with whom if I dance (with him), I collide
  c. De Mass [wenn i no __ drink], bin i bsuffa.   (Grewendorf 2014: 145)
      this litre$_{ACC}$ if I still drink, am I drunk
      'If I still drink this litre (of beer), I will be drunk.'

[*] This section is an update of Cinque (2010b).

[17] These sentences are known in Swedish as *satsflätor*. Although Maling and Zaenen (1982: 232)
say that 'in Icelandic such extractions seem to be impossible' (also see Platzack 2002: 83), they
also add that one of their informants accepted an example like (i) (see their fn. 6):

(i) Kaffi þekki ég engan á íslandi, sem ekki drekkur
    coffee know I no one in Iceland that not drinks
    coffee, I know no one in Iceland who doesn't drink

(27)   a.   Suppe   kender   jeg   mange   der   kan lide
                                                    (Danish – Erteschik-Shir 1973: 67)
            soup   know   I   many who   like
            soup, I know many people who like

       b.   Johan   känner   jag   ingen   som   tycker om
                                                    (Swedish – Engdahl 1980: 95)
            Johan   know   I   no one   that   likes
            'I do not know anyone who likes Johan.'

       c.   Her er en bok som jeg ikke har møtt noen som har lest
                                                    (Norwegian – Taraldsen 1982: 205)
            here is a book that I not have met anybody that has read

Such violations are apparently possible under rather stringent conditions: the Head of the relative clause must be indefinite (often, but not exclusively, non-specific); the verb of which the Head is an argument must be an existential verb, or a verb like 'know', 'see', 'have', etc. (all 'presentational' cases); and the position relativized in the relative clause from which a constituent is extracted is often, but not exclusively, the subject (see Erteschik-Shir 1973: ch. 2; Taraldsen 1978: fn. 6; Engdahl 1980: 95; 1997, *passim*; Smits 1989: §4.2.3.1–2; Kluender 1992: 243 ff; Rubovitz-Mann 2012; Kush, Omaki & Hornstein 2013: §1.1; Christensen & Nyvad 2014; and Müller 2015, Heinat & Wiklund 2015, Lindahl 2017).[18]

While it is generally assumed in the literature that such violations are present in Scandinavian and absent from Romance languages and English (Engdahl 1997: §7), in Cinque (2010b) some evidence was presented that they are also found, under comparable conditions, in these languages, thus raising the question of whether the CNPC can really be the locus of independent parametric variation. See now Sichel (2018) for a larger overview documenting such selective extraction from relative clauses in Hebrew and other languages.[19]

Engdahl (1997: fn. 28) also reports that her informants found at least some of the corresponding extractions from CNPs in Icelandic and Faroese acceptable.

[18] But see Engdahl (1997: §2) for one example from Norwegian where the subject is extracted from a (free) relative clause on the object, and (i) from Italian in fn. 20 below. Engdahl (1980) argues that cases such as (27) involve movement rather than base generation of a *pro*, and that their acceptability is not due to the fact that they comply with subjacency because extraction occurs from an extraposed clause. The Italian cases discussed below show it even more clearly.

[19] I return to Sichel's analysis below. Some minor differences remain among the languages, having to do with what type of extraction gives the best result (Topicalization, Clitic Left Dislocation, *wh*-relative or interrogative movement), with which embedding predicates give the

Consider the following grammatical Italian sentences, similar to the Scandinavian examples in (27):[20]

(28)   a.   Giorgio, al quale non conosco nessuno che sarebbe disposto ad affidare i propri risparmi, ...
             Giorgio, whom I don't know anybody that would be ready to entrust with their savings, ...
       b.   Ida, di cui non c'è nessuno che sia mai stato innamorato, ...
             Ida, whom there is nobody that was ever in love with, ...
       c.   Gianni, al quale non c'è nessuno che sia in grado di resistere, ...
             Gianni, whom there is nobody that is able to resist, ...

These cases are bona fide cases of extraction as they involve PPs rather than DPs (which could also be base-generated A-bar bound *pro*'s – Cinque 1990: ch. 3).

---

best results (existential or perception predicates, 'know', etc.), and with what counts as the best non-specific indefinite relative clause Head (bare negative quantifiers like *nobody, nothing*, non-negative quantified phrase, like *some, many XP*, etc.), but hopefully these differences may turn out to be related to independent differences among the languages in question. For relevant observations, see Engdahl (1997: §7). Allwood (1982: 32) also mentions the existence of dialect differences in Swedish to the effect that 'eastern dialects are more restrictive than western ones' in their extractions from CNPs. In Kush, Omaki, and Hornstein's (2013) experiments, English appears to show the same pattern of apparent RC-island violations as Scandinavian, but differs from Scandinavian in that extractions are judged to be 'marginal at best'.

[20] Also see the extraction (possible under the same conditions) out of an infinitival relative in Italian with a 'could' interpretation given in Cinque & Benincà (2018: 78). Italian also appears to allow extraction from (at least some) relative clauses that relativize direct objects. See (i):

(i)   Gianni, a cui$_k$ non c'è proprio niente che$_j$ potremmo far avere t$_j$ t$_k$ in giornata, ...
       'Gianni, whom there is really nothing that we could provide him with in one day, ...'

I thank Paola Beninca' and Alessio Muro for checking my judgements on (i) and the sentences in (30).

Given that Clitic Left Dislocation also shows sensitivity to the CNPC (Cinque 1977, 1990: ch. 2), the sentences in (ii) are even closer analogues to some of the Swedish *satsflätor* discussed in the literature on Scandinavian:

(ii)   a.   **A Giorgio**, non c'è niente che **gli** interessi veramente.
             To Giorgio, there is nothing that to-him interests really
             'Giorgio, there is nothing that really interests him.'
       b.   **Di questo argomento**, conosco/ci sono molte persone che **ne** saprebbero parlare molto meglio di me.
             of this topic, I know/there are many people that of-it could talk much better than me
             this topic, I know/there are many people who could speak about much better than me

Their acceptability cannot simply be attributed to the possible extraposition of the relative CP, to the effect that extraction would then only cross a single bounding node (CP). Relative clauses relativizing an oblique argument can also be extraposed ((29)); yet, they resist extraction ((30)):

(29) a. Niénte ha fatto finora di cui potersi vantare con i suoi superiori.
          nothing did he so far about which to boast with his bosses
      b. Non conosco nessuno in questa città con cui potrei parlare di questi argomenti.
          'I know nobody in this town with whom I could talk about these topics.'

(30) a. *I suoi superiori, con i quali$_k$ non ha fatto niente finora [di cui potersi vantare t$_k$], . . .
          his bosses, with whom he did nothing so far about which to boast, . . .
      b. *Sono argomenti di cui$_k$ non conosco nessuno in questa città [con cui potrei parlare t$_k$]
          'These are topics about which I know nobody in this town with whom I could talk.'

Examples similar to (28) are also apparently possible in French ((31)) and in Spanish ((32)):[21]

(31) a. Jean, à qui il n'y a personne qui puisse s'opposer, . . .
          Jean, whom there is nobody that could oppose, . . .
      b. (?)C'est un endroit où il n'y a personne qui voudrait vivre.
          it's a place where there is no one that would like to live
      c. (?)Jean, à qui je ne connais personne qui soit prêt à confier ses secrets, . . .
          Jean, to whom I don't know anybody that would be ready to confide their secrets, . . .

(32) a. Ida, de quien no hay nadie que se haya enamorado alguna vez, . . .
          Ida, whom there is nobody that was ever in love with, . . .
      b. Juan, al que no hay nadie que sea capaz de soportar, . . .
          Juan, whom there is nobody that can stand, . . .
      c. Ese es un sitio en el que no hay nadie que querría vivir.
          this is a place where there is no one that would like to live

---

[21] I thank Vincent Homer, Marie-Claude Paris, and Dominique Sportiche for the French data and María Martínez-Atienza for the Spanish data.

Although it is generally assumed that English disallows extractions from CNPs entirely, in the literature one finds that similar examples are also judged acceptable (to varying degrees, to at least some native speakers). See (33):[22]

(33)　a.　Then you look at what happens in languages that you know and languages that you have a friend who knows. (Charles Ferguson, lecture at the University of Chicago, May 1971; cited in Kuno 1976: 423)

　　　b.　Isn't that the song that Paul and Stevie were the only ones who wanted to record. (Chung & McCloskey 1983: 708)

　　　c.　This is the kind of weather that there are many people who like. (Erteschik-Shir 2007: 163)[23]

　　　d.　This is the child who there is nobody who is willing to accept. (see Kuno 1976: 423)

　　　e.　This is a paper that we really need to find someone to intimidate with. (Kluender 1992: 243)

　　　f.　This is the one that Bob Wall was the only person who hadn't read. (McCawley 1981: 108)

Comparable examples in German ((34), Josef Bayer, pers. comm.; Kvam 1983: 124 fn. 34; Andersson & Kvam 1984: 46), and in Bulgarian ((35), Iliyana Krapova, pers. comm.) are on the other hand apparently ungrammatical.[24]

---

[22] Thanks to David Pesetsky, Andrew Radford, Megan Rae, and Peter Svenonius for sharing their judgements with me. Even though examples such as those in (33) and (i) below were accepted by most of my informants, some informants found them quite marginal, saying that they become better if *that* replaces *who*. Also relevant in this connection are Kayne's (2008a) nn. 30 and 38.

　　(i)　a.　Violence is something that there are many Americans who condone. (McCawley 1981: 108)

　　　　b.　This is a paper that we really need to find someone who understands. (Chung & McCloskey 1983: 708)

　　　　c.　That's one trick that I've known a lot of people who've been taken in by. (Chung & McCloskey 1983: 708)

　　　　d.　This is a paper that we really need to find someone who understands. (Noam Chomsky, cited in Koster 1986: 169)

[23] The example is originally from Erteschik-Shir & Lappin (1979).

[24] Interestingly Brandner and Bräuning (2013) report that Alemannic dialects allow extraction of the Scandinavian type from relative clauses introduced by the invariant particle *wo* (also used in other constructions), provided no *d*-pronoun is also present (see (i), based on their (62) and (64)):

　　(i)　Sottige blueme wüsst i etzt neamed (**der**) **wo** bi üüs verkauft
　　　　such flowers know I now nobody (the) where at our place sells
　　　　such flowers, I now know nobody that sells at our place

(34) a. *Diese Schrift gibt es niemand, der gelesen hat.
          this writing there is nobody who has read

     b. *Johann, dem es keinen Freund gibt, der helfen kann, ...
          Johann, whom (dat.) there is no friend who can help, ...

     c. *Dies habe ich nie jemand getroffen, der getan hat (Kvam 1983: 124
          fn. 34)
          this, I have never met anyone who has done

(35) a. *Ivan, na kojto njama nikoj, kojto/deto može da mu kaže novinata.
          Ivan, to whom there-isn't nobody who/that can-3sg him-Cl.dat tell-3sg
          news-the

     b. *Ivan, na kojto njama nito edin prijatel, kojto/deto iska da mu pomaga.
          Ivan, to whom there-isn't not one friend who/that wants to him help

The languages that appear not to allow for the selective extraction from CNPs discussed here seem to involve relative clauses introduced by 'ordinary' relative pronouns (*welch-*, and *der*, etc., in German, the latter possibly an agreeing relative complementizer – see Chapter 3: fn. 32), or by either 'ordinary' relative pronouns or an exclusively relative complementizer (*kojto*, etc., and *deto*, respectively, in Bulgarian).[25] The languages that instead appear to allow for the selective extraction in question utilize a relative clause introducer which is also used in constructions other than 'ordinary' relative clauses (*som/sem* in Scandinavian; *che/que* in Italian, French, and Spanish).[26] Putting this together with the fact that in English such extractions appear to be possible (or at least more acceptable) if the relative clause is introduced by *that* (or Ø in infinitival and reduced relatives) rather than by 'ordinary' relative pronouns like *who*,[27] it becomes tempting to think that extraction is really not

---

[25] For evidence that the *deto* which introduces emotive factive clauses is the same *deto* which introduces relative clauses (in that the former are in fact hidden relative clauses), see Krapova (2010).

[26] If English *that* and French *que* are a variety of relative pronouns (Kayne 2008a, 2008b, 2010a and Sportiche 2008), then the distinction should be thought of in terms of different types of relative pronouns (see the text below).

[27] Goodluck, Foley and Sedivy (1992: 191 fn. 11) report a similar contrast in Swedish clauses introduced by *som* and by *vilken*, and Platzack (2002: 89) gives the following minimal pair:

(i)   Sådana blommor känner jag en man som/*vilken säljer på torget.
       such   flowers know I a man that/who sells at the market place.
       'I know a man who sells such flowers at the market.'

The same contrast is found in Italian:

(ii)   Il premier, a cui/al quale non sono molti i giornalisti che/*?i quali oserebbero porre una simile domanda ...
       the prime minister to whom the journalists that/who would dare put such a question are not many, ...

out of an 'ordinary' relative clause. See below for the possibility that the RC CP does not even form a constituent with the Head, given the fact that it can 'strand' it under preposing, unlike ordinary RC CPs (see (40) below).

Thinking of languages/dialects that allow 'ordinary' relative pronouns to co-occur with *that* or *che/que*, in the order relative pronoun > *that/che/que* (e.g., Middle English, and various Romance varieties), the fact that extraction is more readily available with *that/che/que* than with 'ordinary' relative pronouns can perhaps be understood in terms of movement through the higher Spec of CP; the one which hosts 'ordinary' relative pronouns, and which is presumably not filled when the complementizers (or 'weak' relative pronouns) *that/che/que* are used.[28] The additional fact that extraction is available only in the presence of indefinite non-specific relative clause Heads may possibly be

---

(cf. *Non sono molti i giornalisti i quali oserebbero porre una simile domanda al premier* 'the journalists who would dare put such a question to the prime minister are not many', possible in the marked restrictive construction discussed in Cinque 1995: §1.5 and here in §2.1.2.1.2).

Those English speakers that do not make a difference between *who* and *that* in (33) and (i) of fn. 22 of this chapter perhaps allow *who* to be in the same class as *that*. See the brief discussion in Chapter 2: fn. 16 and related text.

[28] If 'ordinary' and 'weak' relative pronouns are featurally distinct, and a 'weak' relative pronoun is allowed to pass through the Spec of the higher Comp acquiring its features, then no Relativized Minimality (Rizzi 2004) violation should be triggered. The fact that *deto* in Bulgarian (perhaps also a 'weak' relative pronoun) and *d*-pronouns/agreeing complementizers in German block extraction perhaps indicates the necessary presence of an operator filling the Spec of the higher CP. A potential counterexample to the idea that extraction is blocked out of CNPs introduced by 'ordinary' relative pronouns is represented by Romanian, which apparently allows extractions from CNPs introduced by the relative pronoun *care* ('who, which'). See the examples in (i), kindly provided by Alexandra Cornilescu and Iulia Zegrean:

(i)   a   Ion, pe care nu cunosc pe nimeni care să-l aprecieze pentru ceea ce a făcut, ...
           Ion, who (Acc.) I do not know anybody who appreciates him for what he did, ...
      b   Ion, căruia nu este nimeni care poate să-i reziste, ...
           Ion, who (Dat.) there is nobody who can resist, ...

There is however evidence that *care* in colloquial Romanian has (also) been reanalysed as a 'complementizer' (or 'weak' relative pronoun) (see Grosu 1994: 212). This is clearly shown by examples such as (ii):

(ii)   a.   A venit la noi un elvețian, care proiectul lui l-a interesat pe director (Gheorghe 2004: 279):
           a Swiss came to us, that his project interested the director
      b.   Mândră, mândrulița mea, care m-am iubit cu ea (Gheorghe 2013: 490)
           dear, my dear one, that I was in love with her

understood in terms of the absence of a DP initial (silent) demonstrative/ operator (see Kayne 2008b, end of §10), which would independently block the extraction. As complements, but not adjuncts, can be extracted from these CNPs (see the contrast between (28) and (36a) in Italian, and that between (33b) and (36b) in English), such CNPs seem to qualify as weak islands (Cinque 2010b: 87):

(36)   a.   *E' un modo in cui non conosco nessuno che si sia mai comportato.
             it's a manner in which I don't know anybody who ever behaved
       b.   *Isn't that the color which Paul and Stevie were the only ones who
             painted their yacht? (Postal 1998: 170)

For the conclusion that in Hebrew extraction from CNPs (with the same selective properties found in Scandinavian and Romance) is similar to extraction from a weak island see Sichel (2014: §5.2; 2018). She explicitly claims that extraction is only possible from RCs that involve a 'raising', rather than a 'Head external/matching' derivation, showing that no extraction is possible whenever a 'Head external/matching' derivation is forced 'by a potential Principle C violation or by having an anaphor in the RC Head that must be bound from a position in the matrix clause' (p. 684), or by having an 'optional' resumptive pronoun in the RC. See (37a–c) (Sichel's 2014 (50a), (57a) and (58a), respectively):

(37)   a.   *me-ha-sifria hazot$_2$, od lo macati [sefer$_1$] še-kedai le-haš'il oto$_1$ t$_2$.
             from-the-library this yet NEG found book that-worth to-borrow it
             'From this library, I haven't yet found a book that's worth borrowing.'
       b.   *me-ha-doda hazot$_3$, yeš [kama tmunot bar micva šel dani$_1$]$_2$ 'e-hu$_1$
             lakax t$_2$ t$_3$.
             from-the-aunt this is few pictures bar mitzvah of Dani that-he took
             'From this aunt, there are a few bar mitzvah pictures of Dani that he
             took.'
       c.   *al kir ba-maxlaka$_3$, yeš lo$_1$ rak [tmuna axat šel acmo$_1$]$_2$ še-ani muxana
             litlot t$_2$ t$_3$.
             on wall in.the-department is to.him only picture one of himself that-I
             willing to.hang
             'On a wall in the department, he has only one picture of himself that
             I am willing to hang.'

These contrast with (38a–c) (her (49a), (57b) and (58b), respectively), where nothing forces a 'Head external/matching' derivation (no 'optional' resumptive pronoun inside the RC, no potential Principle C violation, nor a Head internal anaphor bound from a position in the matrix), so that a 'raising' derivation is available:

(38) a. me-ha-sifria hazot$_2$, od lo macati [sefer$_1$] še-kedai PRO le-haš'il t$_1$ t$_2$.
           from-the-library this yet NEG found book that's-worth to-borrow
           'From this library, I haven't yet found a book that's worth borrowing.'
      b. me-ha-doda hazot$_3$, yeš [kama tmunot bar micva šelo$_1$]$_2$ še-hu$_1$ lakax t$_2$ t$_3$.
           from-the-aunt this be few pictures bar mitzvah his that-he took
           'From this aunt, there are a few bar mitzvah pictures of his that he took.'
      c. al kir ba-maxlaka$_3$, yeš rak [tmuna axat šel acmo$_1$]$_2$ še-hu$_1$ muxan litlot t$_2$ t$_3$.
           on wall in.the-department is only picture one of himself that-he willing to.hang
           'On a wall in the department, there is only one picture of himself that he is willing to hang.'

'These examples suggest that it is possible to extract from a RC only if the [H]ead is interpreted within the RC' (Sichel 2014: 685) so that '[t]he restriction of extraction to the raising structure provides evidence of an entirely new sort for the structural ambiguity of RCs' (p. 686) [between a 'raising' and a Head-external/'matching' analysis]. In this particular case, given the non-island character of the construction, it is tempting to assume that it instantiates a bare CP rather than an ordinary complex DP, much like the modal Headless RCs seen in §2.5.5, from which extraction is also possible and which Grosu (1994: Study I, ch. 5) proposed to analyse as bare CPs. The light Headed *ciò/quello che* 'that that' which replaces (*che*) *cosa* 'what' in the Italian 'Headless' construction and that was analysed as a bare CP when appearing after verbs like 'know' also permits extraction:

(39) Gianni, a cui non so quello che direte, . . .
       Lit.: Gianni, to whom I do not know what (lit. that that) you will say, . . .
       Gianni, who I don't know what you will tell . . .

That the (indefinite) Head and the relative clause CP of these 'transparent' RCs may not form a constituent that contains both is possibly indicated by the fact that the relative CP, unlike that of 'ordinary' RCs, can be fronted, stranding the Head. See the contrast in (40):[29]

(40) a. (?)Che fosse in grado di resistergli non c'era proprio nessuno.
           that could resist him, there really was nobody
           'There was nobody that could resist him.'
      b. *Che non fosse in grado di resistergli non inviterei nessuno.
           that could not resist him I wouldn't invite anyone.

---

[29] The respective sources are:

(i)   a. Non c'era proprio nessuno che fosse in grado di resistergli.
           'There was really nobody that could resist him.'
      b. Non inviterei nessuno che non fosse in grado di resistergli.
           'I wouldn't invite anyone that could not resist him.'

This would thus seem to suggest a structure like V [$_{DP}$ nessuno] [$_{CP1}$ [$_{CP2}$ che [$_{IP}$ ....]]], whose precise syntactic and semantic status remains to be understood.[30]

5.6   Residual Points and Puzzles

5.6.1

Hankamer and Postal (1973: 261) noted that while identity of sense pronominalization 'operates with considerable freedom', ignoring islands (e.g. *Jack admits that my gorilla is cute, but he won't listen to the suggestion that we get mine and his together.*) it is still sensitive to the particular *wh*-nature of the genitive NP left behind. Interrogative *whose* is fine but relative *whose* is not:

(41) a. My gorilla is over   **Whose** is that banging at the window?
          there drinking punch.

      b. My gorilla is over   *Melvin, **whose** is banging at the window, is
          there drinking punch.   over there watering the rubber tree.

In Cinque (1982: 270) I noted a similar restriction on the genitive *wh*-pronoun (as opposed to possessive pronouns) in Italian:

(42)   I miei libri sono qua. I suoi (libri) sono spariti/Giorgio, i cui *(libri) sono spariti, ...
        My books are here. His (books) have disappeared/G., whose (books) have disappeared, ...

5.6.2   *Deletions inside Relative Clauses*

Subject to independent differences among languages (Spanish, for example, does not have VP deletion – see Zagona 1988: 6–7; nor does Italian, so Antecedent-Contained VP Deletion is not possible either) many types of deletion are attested within RCs. I simply list here the types of deletion that are mentioned in the literature referring to some of the works that deal with them without attempting an analysis.

---

[30] For a different idea (according to which such extractions are from a complement small clause rather than from a Complex NP, *pace* Christensen & Nyvad 2014), see Kush, Omaki & Hornstein (2009, 2013), which are otherwise quite similar in spirit to the present analysis in doubting that the CNPC could be parameterized differently in different languages.

5.6.2.1 (Antecedent-Contained) VP Deletion (or ACD)

This is available for example in English maximalizing ((43)), but not in restrictive ((44)) RCs:[31]

(43) a. Marv put everything (that) he could in his pockets. (Carlson 1977: 527)
      b. I'll eat whatever you will. (Baltin 1987: 594 fn. 3)

(44) a. *Marv put (some, many, etc.) things he could in his pockets. (Carlson 1977: 528)
      b. *I saw the boy that you did. (as opposed to *I saw the same boy as you did.*)

See the rich literature on it: Bouton (1970), Sag (1976), Williams (1977), May (1985), Baltin (1987), Larson & May (1990), Fiengo & May (1994), Kennedy (1997) (*pace* Hornstein 1994), Fox (2002), Sauerland (2003), among others. I tentatively assume that what is taken to be LF raising of the quantified Head actually takes place in narrow syntax, followed by remnant movement (see Kayne 1998).

In Polish RCs a comparable ellipsis is possible (see (45)), which allows an even more radical deletion with the invariant relativizer *co*, though not with relative pronouns, whereby everything is deleted except the invariant relativizer and the subject. See (46) and the discussion in Szczegielniak (2004: ch. 3).[32]

(45) Ja będę czytać każdą książkę co/którą ty będziesz. (Szczegielniak 2004: 82)
      I will read   every book   that/which you will
      'I will read every book that you will.'

(46) Ja perzeczytałem każdą książkę **co/*którą ty.** (Szczegielniak 2004: 81)
      I read   every book   that/which you
      'I read every book that you did.'

5.6.2.2 Null Complement Anaphora

In Romance, where as noted no VP deletion is available (hence no Antecedent VP Deletion), null complement anaphora appears possible instead, again in maximalizing relatives like 'Headless' RCs, but not in restrictive nor in non-restrictive RCs.[33] See (47), vs (48)–(49):

---

[31] Nor in non-restrictive RCs. For a discussion of apparent cases of ACD in non-restrictives, see Vanden Wyngaerd & Zwart (1991: §2.1.2) and Kennedy (1997: fn. 7).

[32] The same is true of Russian (Szczegielniak 2004: ch. 3). An apparently similar ellipsis of everything in the RC except for the relative pronoun and another constituent is found in Hungarian. But see below §5.6.2.4.

[33] On Null Complement Anaphora see Hankamer & Sag (1976), Depiante (2000) and Cinque (2004a: §7.2 and §7.3), among others.

(47)   a.   Parlava con chi poteva __.
              '(S)he used to speak with whoever (s)he could.'
        b.   Aiutava chiunque poteva __.
              '(S)he would help whoever (s)he could.'
        c.   Ha fatto quanto doveva __.
              '(S)he did what (s)he had to.'
        d.   Ho fatto quello che potevo __.
              'I did what I could.'
        e.   Vedrò (tutti) i libri che potrò __.
              'I'll see (all) the books that I'll be able to.'
        f.   ?Gli ho prestato (tutta) l'attenzione che potevo __.
              'I gave him (all) the heed I could.'

(48)   a.   *Lui è riuscito a vedere il concerto che anch'io volevo/dovevo __.
              'He managed to see the concert that I too wanted/had to __.'

(49)   *Lui è riuscito a vedere Gianni, che anch'io volevo/dovevo __.
        'He managed to see Gianni, whom I too wanted/had to __.'

5.6.2.3 Gapping

As noted in Vergnaud (1985: 330–1) Gapping can apply within the second conjunct of a relative clause:

(50)   La femme a qui Ovide a dédié son ode et Cicéron, son réquisitoire . . .
        the woman to whom Ovid dedicated his ode and Cicero his closing speech . . .

Irrealis/existential/indefinite 'Headless' RCs also allow Gapping ((51a–b)), just like embedded interrogative CPs ((51c)), and unlike ordinary Headless (Free) RCs ((51d)). See the discussion in Chapter 2: fn. 145, from where the examples in (51) are taken:

(51)   a.   Hanno chi invitare oggi e chi __ domani.
              Lit.: they have who to invite today and who tomorrow
        b.   C'è chi preferisce la pasta e chi il riso.
              Lit.: there is who prefers pasta and who rice
        c.   Non ho ancora capito chi ha telefonato a Maria e chi __ a Giuliana.
                                                    (Rizzi 1982: 75 fn. 32)
              I haven't understood who called Maria and who __ Giuliana.
        d.   *Ho punito chi ha telefonato a Maria e chi __ a Giuliana.
                                                    (Rizzi 1982: 75 fn. 32)
              I punished who called Maria and who __ Giuliana.

5.6.2.4   Sluicing
Relative pronouns in English cannot be stranded under sluicing. See (52), from (Kayne 2014a: §14):

(52) a. *We like the students who you invited, but we don't like the professors who.
      b. *We liked the first way in which you presented your results but not the second way in which.
      c. *The stated reason for which they quit is not the same as the real reason for which.

Van Craenenbroeck & Lipták (2006), Lipták & Aboh (2013), Lipták (2015) claim that the ellipsis found in Hungarian RCs, which deletes everything but the relative pronoun and one more constituent is a form of sluicing. See for example (53), which however has the flavour of the correlatives found after the matrix clause in the languages reported in the examples (169) of Chapter 2.

(53) Kornél   azt   a   lányt hívta meg,   akit   Zoltán.
      Kornél that.$_{ACC}$ the girl invited PV REL-who.$_{ACC}$ Zoltán
      'The girl who Kornél invited was the one who Zoltán did.'

5.6.2.5   English Non-restrictives with *which* in VP Deletion and Pseudo-gapping Contexts
Arnold and Borsley (2010) observe a particular use of *which* in English non-restrictives which replaces the gap of ordinary VP deletion and pseudo-gapping. See (54) and (55) respectively:

(54) a. Kim will sing, which Lee won't __.
      b. Kim has sung, which Lee hasn't __.
      c. Kim is singing, which Lee isn't __.
      d. Kim is clever/in Spain, which Lee isn't __.

(55) a. Kim criticized Lee, which he didn't __ Sandy.
      b. Robin will cook the potatoes quickly, which Leslie will __ the beans.

The construction is puzzling, they point out, because auxiliaries do not otherwise take an overt nominal complement, and note that this resembles the case observed in Kayne (1980: §1.3) (see (56)), where a nominal trace but not an overt nominal results in a grammatical output, eventually allowing auxiliaries to take a non-overt nominal complement.

(56) a. John, who I assure you __ to be the best, . . .
      b. *I assure you John to be the best.

There may be a connection to the use of *which* as a 'connector' found in colloquial English sentences like *They didn't want to go to McDonalds, which I wasn't really hungry anyway*, where the antecedent of *which* is the preceding clause. This use is discussed at length in Radford (2019: ch. 4).

Conclusion

In this work a unified analysis of the syntax of relative clauses has been attempted. I have proposed that all of the attested syntactic types of relative clauses (externally Headed post-nominal, externally Headed pre-nominal, internally Headed, double-Headed, 'Headless' (or 'Free'), correlative, and adjoined) are derivable from a single structure. This has been argued to be feasible if a double-Headed structure is assumed, with both a relative clause internal Head and a relative clause external one, to which run-of-the mill operations, like movement, deletion (non-pronunciation), or replacement by a proform, apply. This double-Headed structure underlying all relative clauses also has the consequence that the two main derivational analyses of relative clauses proposed in the literature ('raising' and 'matching') reduce to two minimally different derivational options within one and the same configuration. For restrictive or maximalizing relative clauses, I have argued that when the two Heads are non-distinct, i.e. indefinite dPs, smaller than full DPs as a consequence of the smaller size of the external Head (which is the portion of the extended nominal projection c-commanded by the relative clause, above weak determiners and below all of the strong ones), either Head can become the overt Head deleting the other. When it is the internal Head that by raising to Spec,CP deletes the external one (in the possible presence of an invariant relativizer: *that, che,* etc.), we have the 'raising' derivation (apparently forced in maximalizing relative constructions like amount/degree relative clauses, 'Headless' or 'Free' relative clauses, and (certain) correlative relative clauses). In this case the overt Head is in a chain with the relative clause internal copy and thus 'reconstructs' inside the relative clause. On the other hand, when it is the external Head that from its in situ position, or by raising above it, deletes the internal Head, thus becoming the overt Head (again in the possible presence of an invariant relativizer), we have (one type of) 'matching' derivation. In this case the overt Head will not be in a chain with the relative clause internal copy, and will thus be unable to 'reconstruct' inside the relative clause.

I have also argued that when the two Heads are distinct (e.g. because the internal Head is larger than dP, being inside an oblique DP/KP or inside a PP), no deletion of the internal Head can take place, so that a relative pronoun/ adjective or a resumptive pronoun (preceded by the preposition) will have to be employed. This is a further type of 'matching' derivation, in which the external Head again fails to be in a chain with the relative clause internal copy, thus not 'reconstructing' inside the relative clause. It has also been noted that in some languages resumptive pronouns can enter a 'big DP' structure, part of which moves, so that a 'raising' derivation with full 'reconstruction' becomes possible even in the presence of the resumptive pronoun. Yet another type of 'matching' derivation has been argued to involve a partial deletion of the internal Head stranding a relative modifier, as in finite kind-defining and non-restrictive relative clauses: non-restrictive relative clauses were in fact shown to be realizable cross-linguistically in two different ways – a sentence grammar 'integrated' one (in which the relative clause is merged within the extended nominal projection), and a discourse grammar 'non-integrated' one (in which the relative clause is outside the extended nominal projection). Additional types of 'matching' have been argued to involve a PRO as the internal Head, as in certain participial relative clauses, or an overt (or silent) 1st and 2nd person pronoun in argument position, as in certain non-restrictive relative clauses modifying a 1st or 2nd person pronoun. The existence of these different types of 'matching' derivations should not be taken to weaken the attempted unification, as they are simply different options for realizing the internal Head made available by Universal Grammar (a full, or partial, silent copy of the overt external Head, or a PRO, or an overt, or silent, pronoun or epithet).

In the absence of other A-bar dependencies with multiple copy spell-out in the same language, the existence of relative clauses with both an external and an internal Head overtly spelled out (one of the seven attested types of relative clauses) has been taken to corroborate the postulated double-Headed structure for all relative clause types. This possibility is indeed expected when deletion of one of the two Heads happens not to be forced in some language. The other types of relative clauses, figuring only one, or no, overt Head, have also been shown to be derivable from the same double-Headed structure under both the 'raising' and the (different) 'matching' derivations. Externally Headed pre-nominal relative clauses under the 'raising' derivation involve raising of the internal Head to Spec,CP, followed by raising of the remnant, while under the 'matching' derivation(s) they have been argued to involve backward deletion of the internal Head by the external one. The converse, forwards deletion of the external Head by the internal one, has instead been taken to characterize one family of internally Headed relative clauses with 'matching' only (the one displaying an indefiniteness restriction, insensitivity to islands, and stacking). The other types of internally Headed constructions all involve movement (whence their sensitivity to islands) and different combinations of properties. Externally Headed post-nominal relative clauses have been argued to derive under 'matching' from the leftward movement of the external Head across the relative clause with consequent deletion of the internal Head (a movement typical of head-initial orders) and under the 'raising' derivation from the raising of the internal Head to Spec,CP with consequent deletion of the external Head. 'Free' (apparently Headless) relative clauses have also been argued to involve a silent external Head (actually spelled out in so-called Light-Headed relative clauses) which is licensed by the internal Head necessarily raised to Spec,CP as a consequence of the maximalizing nature of the construction. Correlatives have been argued simply to involve the 'left dislocation' of one or the other of the different types of relative clauses (double-Headed, pre- and post-nominal externally Headed, internally Headed, 'Headless'), resumed by some nominal in the sentence out of which they were dislocated. Adjoined relative clauses have instead been argued to be double-Headed relative clauses where the relative clause CP is either dislocated to the left (in a correlative configuration), or is found at the end of the sentence (in an extraposed configuration).

The independently justifiable proposal that the relative clause is merged, like every other nominal complement or modifier, in the specifier of a functional Head of the nominal extended projection makes even 'matching' derivations compatible with Antisymmetry (which excludes, among other things, the possibility of two XPs being sisters, as was the case in traditional versions of the Head-external analysis of relative clauses).

Evidence has also been presented that ('integrated') non-restrictive, kind-defining, restrictive, maximalizing, infinitival, and participial relative clauses are merged at different heights of the nominal extended projection, thus determining the size of the external Head, which is the constituent immediately c-commanded by the relative clause, the external Head of 'integrated' non-restrictive relative clauses being larger (DP) than the external Head of maximalizing/restrictive relative clauses (dP), which in turn is larger than that of infinitival and participial relative clauses.

Low level parametric differences among languages – the presence of resumptive rather than relative pronouns, how many elements can overtly introduce and/or close off a relative clause, which elements can remain silent, where invariant relativizers are merged with respect to topics and foci, etc. – are numerous. Nevertheless, while numerous, they should not prevent us from seeing the basic underlying unity of all the attested types of relative clauses.

The Appendix which follows contains a summary of the evidence found in the literature (some of which was discussed in the preceding chapters) justifying the existence of a non-'raising' derivation alongside a 'raising' one.

Appendix: Possible Evidence for the Existence of Non-'raising' Derivations

Some evidence mentioned in the text, or in the literature,[1] which apparently motivates a Head-external/'matching' derivation in addition to the 'raising' one, will be schematically recalled in sections A1 to A3. Three phenomena

[1] The following is a (possibly partial) list of works arguing in favour of a Head-external/ 'matching' derivation in addition, for many of these, to the 'raising' one: Andrews (1975: ch. 1), Carlson (1977), Maurel (1983), Heim (1987), Chung (1987: §8.4.4), Smits (1989: §3.1.3), Hirschbühler (1992), Åfarli (1994), Labelle (1996: §8), Borsley (1997, 2001, 2010), Sauerland (1998, 1999, 2003), Bhatt (1999, 2002), Cresti (2000: §4), Kallulli (2000: §2; 2008: §3.2; 2018), Bruening (2001: 229–30 fn. 17), Citko (2001, 2008b), Demeke (2001), Li (2001a, 2001b; 2002: 62), Büring (2002), Fox (2002: §3.2), Hankamer & Mikkelsen (2002: §4), Manninen (2002, 2003), Aoun & Li (2003), Hsiao (2003), Szucsich (2003), Duncan (2004), Szczegielniak (2004, 2005, 2006, 2012) (and Chomsky 2008: fn. 5, after Szczegielniak 2004), Vicente (2004), Adger & Ramchand (2005), Brito (2005), Frascarelli & Puglielli (2005), Heck (2005), Kotzoglou & Varlokosta (2005), Prinzhorn & Schmitt (2005: 498 fn. 2), Hulsey & Sauerland (2006), Kwon, Polinsky & Kluender (2006), Reintges, LeSourde & Chung (2006), Salzmann (2006a, 2006b, 2017: ch. 2; 2019), Schmitt (2006: §1.2.1.2.1.2), Boyle (2007: ch. 6), Caponigro & Polinsky (2008: §1.3), Gračanin-Yüksek (2008, 2010, 2013), Harris (2008), Heck & Cuartero (2008, 2012), Koster-Moeller & Hackl (2008), Leu (2008: §4.3.5), Overfelt (2009), Cheng & Downing (2010), Davis (2010), Hackl & Nissenbaum (2012), Krapova (2010), Miyamoto (2010), Saah (2010), Sevcenco (2010, 2015), Blümel (2011), Citko & Gračanin-Yüksek (2011), Lassiter (2011), Resi (2011), Webelhuth (2011), Bidese, Padovan & Tomaselli (2012), Boef (2012, 2013: §3.3), Gagnon & Mitrović (2012), Koster-Moeller (2012), Struckmeier (2012), Chidambaram (2013: ch. 2), Foley (2013), Huhmarniemi & Brattico (2013), Bağrıaçık (2014), Sichel (2014, 2018), Hladnik (2015: §3.4), Kalivoda & Zyman (2015), Koster (2015: §2), Lin & Tsai (2015: §5.1), Pankau (2015, 2018), Bağrıaçık & Danckaert (2016: §2), Catasso & Hinterhölzl (2016), Deal (2016), Łęska (2016), Douglas (2016), Radford (2016: 394–477; 2019: §1.6), Geraci & Hauser (2017), Giltner (2017), Hill (2017), Jenks, Makasso & Hyman (2017: §4.2 and §4.3), Rasin (2017), Rinke & Aßmann (2017), Sanfelici, Schulz & Trabandt (2017: §5.3.2), Schuurman (2017), Vincent (2017: §7), Webelhuth, Bargmann & Götze (2017, 2019), Wood, Sigurðsson & Nowenstein (2017), Bassi & Rasin (2018),

285

which seem to discriminate between bona fide 'raising' and 'matching' – extraposition, stacking, and weak island sensitivity, despite certain appearances – will then be considered in section A4.

A1   Relative Clauses Failing to Display Reconstruction of the Head

With Aoun & Li (2003: 95 ff) and Hulsey & Sauerland (2006) I take the presence of reconstruction of the RC Head inside the RC to correlate with 'raising' of the internal Head. Conversely I take lack of reconstruction in certain types of RCs as evidence that no 'raising' derivation is involved there. While it is true that movement does not per se force the moved element to be reconstructed in its original position (Sportiche 2017a: fn. 14 and related text), reconstruction should at least be available within a movement chain if something requires it, and unavailable for elements belonging to different chains. Thus, the following cases, where no reconstruction is possible for elements that would seem to require (or permit) it, suggest that a Head-external/'matching' derivation is needed in addition to the 'raising' one, possible in other cases.

Lack of amount readings, and idiom chunk, binding and scope reconstruction in Polish *który*- and Russian *kotoryi*-relatives, as opposed to *co*- and *čto*-relatives (with gaps). See Szczegielniak (2004, 2005, 2006: §3).[2]

Lack of amount readings, and idiom chunk, binding and scope reconstruction in Polish restrictive RCs with resumptive pronouns. See Szczegielniak (2004: §2.13, 2005, 2006).

Lack of reconstruction of Polish *swój* and Croatian *svoj* when in the Head of a restrictive RC. See Borsley (1984: 11–12) and Gračanin-Yüksek (2008). When inside the Head of a Headed RC the anaphors *swój/svoj* must be bound by an antecedent located in the matrix clause, not by one located in the relative clause. This appears to show that the RC Head cannot reconstruct inside the RC pointing to the presence of a 'matching', rather than a 'raising',

---

Chen & Fukuda (2018), Corrêa, Augusto & Marcilese (2018), Hauser & Geraci (2018), Longenbaugh (2019), Sternefeld (2019), Tóth (2019).

Although some of the problems raised in these works for a theory countenancing only a raising derivation may find some solutions (see Kayne 1994, 2010b, 2015b, Bianchi 1999, 2000a, 2004, 2011, De Vries 2002, 2005, 2006, 2009, Henderson 2007, and Sportiche 2017a, 2017b), it remains to be seen if all can. The antisymmetric analysis explored here is compatible with the possibility that both 'raising' and Head-external/'matching' derivations exist.

[2] Szczegielniak (2004: ch. 2; 2006: §3) actually argues that in *co*-relatives the only derivation available is the 'raising' one.

derivation. This contrasts with interrogatives and 'Headless' RCs, where *swój/ svoj* are necessarily bound inside the interrogative and 'Headless' RC under reconstruction. See §2.5.6.

Lack of idiom chunk and quantifier reconstruction in pre-nominal (vs postnominal) RCs in Pharasiot Greek. In Pharasiot Greek only post-nominal RCs involve 'raising' while pre-nominal ones only involve 'matching'. See Bağrıaçık (2014) and Bağrıaçık & Danckaert (2016). See also §2.2, particularly §2.2.2.

Lack of reconstruction in indefinite RCs in Lebanese Arabic (as opposed to definite ones in non-island contexts). See Aoun & Choueiri (1997), Choueiri (2002), Aoun, Choueiri & Hornstein (2001), Aoun & Li (2003: §4.3).

Lack of reconstruction in indefinite RCs in Albanian. See Kallulli (2008: §3.2).

Lack of reconstruction in Adyghe RCs. See Caponigro & Polinsky (2008: §3.1). 'Adyghe relative clauses do not show reconstruction effects and do not preserve idiomatic meaning under relativization' (Caponigro & Polinsky 2008: 83).

Lack of reconstruction in Bosnian/Croatian/Serbian restrictive relative clause. See Gračanin-Yüksek (2010, 2013).

Lack of idiom chunk and anaphor reconstruction in German V2 RCs. See Sanfelici, Schulz & Trabandt (2017); and here §3.2.2.

Lack of quantifier scope reconstruction in Mig'maq restrictive RCs. See Schuurman (2017: ch. 4).

Lack of reconstruction in Chinese RCs with resumptive pronouns. See Aoun & Li (2003: §6.2), Huang, Li & Li (2009: §6.2.3), supported by processing experiments in Hsiao (2003: ch. 6).

Lack of reconstruction in Hebrew restrictive RCs with 'optional' resumptives. See Rasin (2017), Bassi & Rasin (2018) and references cited there.

Lack of reconstruction of anaphors in Georgian preposed *rom*-RCs. See Foley (2013). Anaphors cannot reconstruct inside *rom*-RCs which are preposed. The construction can only involve a 'matching' derivation (Foley 2013: 23).[3]

Lack of reconstruction of anaphors within the Head in Japanese RCs. See Chen & Fukuda (2018).

---

[3] Anaphor reconstruction is also unavailable in extraposed RCs in Georgian.

Lack of reconstruction in non-restrictive relatives (of both types). See Vergnaud (1985: 334), Aoun & Li (2003: 245 n. 18), and §3.1.8 here.

Lack of idiom chunk reconstruction in Bulgarian restrictive RCs when the Head is separated from the invariant relativizer by a topic or focus phrase (as opposed to when there is no such intervening phrase). See the discussion in fn. 67 of Chapter 2, and related text.

Lack of reconstruction in Hungarian Headed RCs. See Tóth (2019).

German RCs with *welch*-pronouns (as opposed to *d*-pronouns) cannot relativize amounts and idiom chunks. See Prinzhorn & Schmitt (2005: 498 fn. 2).

No reconstruction of the Head under the scope of a universal quantifier to yield pair-list readings in the presence of *wh*-pronouns (as opposed to *that*). See (10a–b) of Chapter 2 (after Šimík 2008a).

No reconstruction seems possible with Italian relative pronouns (*cui* or *il quale*). See §2.1.2.1.1 and §2.1.2.1.2.

Possible lack of reconstruction in English infinitival RCs with a Head internal nominal possessor. The Head internal nominal possessor can be coreferent with the subject of the infinitival RC (no Principle C violation: *This is John$_i$'s book for him$_i$ to write his thoughts and feelings in*). See §3.3.2.6. Also see in the same section Gračanin-Yüksek's (2008: fn. 19) argument that in at least some Croatian infinitival RCs the Head is external to the RC.

Heads that never occur in an argument position, including the 'reconstruction' site like Dutch relatives with *datgene* as their Head (Koster 2015: 121)[4] **cannot, it seems, involve 'raising'.**

A2   Relative Clauses Failing to Display Movement – Hence 'Raising'

Non-restrictive RCs on personal pronouns (I, who am …). No 'raising' derivation seems to be available for them. See the evidence from the absence of movement and from repetition of the Head in §3.1.8.

No raising derivation with *wh*-pronouns in certain varieties of English as well as in Russian and Serbian. See Chapter 2: fn. 13, and related text.

---

[4] Also see Koster's (2015: 121 ff) observation concerning Dutch RCs, in which the relative pronoun is an R-pronoun and the Head an ordinary [-R] DP, which cannot be moved from a PP (with preposition stranding).

Lack of movement – hence 'raising' – in Scottish Gaelic as well as Irish and São Tomense creole RCs, as evidenced inter alia by the construction's inability to license parasitic gaps. See Adger & Ramchand (2005: §6).

Insensitivity to islands in Hebrew restrictive RCs with a resumptive pronoun in situ. See Borer 1984: §1.1; Bassi & Rasin 2018: §4; and here §4.3.

Insensitivity to islands in Czech RCs with resumptive pronouns. See Toman 1998: §1.2.

Insensitivity to the Coordinate Structure Constraint in Paduan, e.g. *Queo ze el toso che iu e so pare i ne ga imbroià.* 'That is the boy that he and his father cheated us' (Paola Benincà, pers. comm.).

Insensitivity to islands in IHRCs in Lakhota. See §2.3.1.

Non-restrictive RCs with number or gender mismatch between the relative pronoun and the Head (vs restrictive RCs). They appear to pose a problem for a 'raising' derivation of the Head. See Chapter 3 fn. 9 and related text and example (28).

Insensitivity to islands in Zürich Swiss German RCs. See Van Riemsdijk (1989, 1998, 2008: §9.2.2 and fns 11, 15; Salzmann 2017: ch. 5), except for locative RCs (Van Riemsdijk 2003).

Lack of long distance movement within restrictive RCs (though not within amount/maximalizing RCs) **in Swiss German.** See Bayer & Salzmann (2013: §6.6.1).

Some of Cuzco Quechua externally Headed pre-nominal RCs do not seem to involve movement/'raising' of the internal Head. See Hastings (2004: §3.4.3).

Split antecedents with identical grammatical function in coordinate sentences (see §5.2.1) **and split antecedents with different grammatical functions belonging to the same sentence** (see §5.2.2) pose a problem for a 'raising' derivation of the Head.

One pronoun – two 'binders' (Jacobson 2019: §5.2). In a sentence like *Every third-grade boy invited the (very) relative of his that no fourth-grade boy would (dream of) inviting*, there is a functional reading in which every third-grade boy invites his own mother while no fourth-grade boy would invite his own mother (putting aside the less salient reading in which *his* is bound only by *every third-grade boy*). Jacobson (2019: 331) notes that 'if the head is raised and leaves a complex (functional) trace – so as to have *no 4th grade boy* bind *his*' – then *every third-grade boy* cannot also bind *his*.

A3   Possible Advantages of an Analysis Countenancing Both 'Matching' and 'Raising'

A3.1   *Parenthetical Restrictive Relative Clauses*

Stowell (2005) shows that alongside ordinary restrictives, one should recognize the existence of parenthetical restrictives, as distinct from parenthetical appositives/non-restrictives. The grammaticality of sentences like (1) shows that not all parenthetical relatives are non-restrictive (which would require a *wh*-pronoun with human Heads).

(1)   The guy next door (that I sold my car to) was arrested today.

Three considerations support this conclusion. First, the relative clause in (1) has the flavour of a mid-sentence amendment, as though the speaker, having uttered something, decides that a further restriction is necessary to unambiguously identify the referent, and adds the parenthetical relative to achieve this end. Though the relative clause is parenthetical, its semantic function is to restrict the reference of the head. Second, parenthetical *that*-relatives similar to that in (1) can occur with quantified Heads, something that ought to be impossible if they were non-restrictive, especially in the case of (2b), where the QP does not refer, and (2c), provided by Andrew Radford (pers. comm.), where *ever* needs to be licensed by *no other girl*:

(2)   a.   All the students (that I have managed to speak to, at least) support the president.
       b.   None of the faculty (that I know of, anyway) have said they will attend.
       c.   No other girl (that I have ever met, at least) has swept me off my feet like this.

In these examples, the relative clause clearly functions as a restriction on the quantifier.

A third reason for assuming that the parenthetical *that*-relatives in (1) and (2) are restrictive relatives, rather than non-restrictive *that*-relatives, is that they may never have proper names as their Heads:

(3)   a.   *Jack Martin (that was a grad student here) likes trees.
       b.   *Hilary (that Bill met in college, reportedly) works hard.

Thus, it seems that parenthetical relative clauses can be restrictive.

Stowell (2005) also refers to them as 'repair parenthetical', saying that their status seems to be contingent on their containing a parenthetical adverb.

Now, it seems that they do not allow for 'raising'. So, for example, their Heads do not seem to reconstruct inside the RC: they cannot interact scopally with a quantifier inside the RC (see (4a)), nor can they contain an anaphor bound by the subject of the RC ((4b)), nor can the Head be an idiom chunk to be composed with the predicate of the RC (4c)):[5]

(4) a. The two children (that everyone was assigned, anyway) were difficult.

  b. *?The pictures of each other (that everyone didn't dislike, at least) are these.

  c. *?The amount of headway (that they made, anyway) was slight.

A3.2 Other Possible Advantages

'Hydras' can perhaps receive a simpler analysis in a 'matching' derivation. See §5.1.

Split antecedents in coordinate sentences, which also pose a problem for a 'raising' derivation, may receive a simpler treatment. See §5.2.1, §5.2.2, and Radford (2019: §1.6).

If Head-external (with RC internal *wh*-pronouns) derivations are available, there is no need to assume unattested relative phrases like *who boy* (for a relative like *the boy who you saw yesterday* ... (Aoun & Li 2003: 123), *where place* (for a relative like *the place where I was born* ...). And there is a possible account for the ungrammaticality of *the boy which I like* (Aoun & Li 2003: 121) vis à vis *Which boy do you like?* See §2.1.2.2.

A 'matching' derivation avoids the problem that a [$_{DP}$ D° [$_{CP/ForceP}$ Head ... analysis has with respect to extraposition in German: *Ich habe [den t] getroffen [$_{CP/ForceP}$ Mann den ich mag] (Schmitt 2006: 190).[6]

The availability of a 'matching' derivation may also account for the lack of Principle C violations in sentences such as (5) and (6) in English. See §3.3.2.6[7] for discussion:

(5) a This is John$_i$'s book for him$_i$ to write his thoughts and feelings in.

  b. This is the book of John$_i$'s for him$_i$ to write his thoughts and feelings in.

(6) a. These are John$_i$'s favourite magazines for him$_i$ to read while in bed in hospital.

  b. These are the favourite magazines of John$_i$'s for him$_i$ to read while in bed in hospital.

---

[5] I thank Tim Stowell for discussion and for the relevant judgements.

[6] This is not a problem for the high promotion variant, where the Head is eventually raised outside the CP/ForceP, which, however, faces the difficulties mentioned in fn. 20 of Chapter 1.

[7] The same section reports an argument from Gračanin-Yüksek (2008: fn. 19) to the effect that the Head of (at least some) Croatian infinitival RCs is outside the RC CP.

The availability of a Head-external/'matching' derivation may also avoid the potential problem posed to certain variants of the 'raising' analysis by such sentences as (7a), which would seem to require a movement that violates the Left Branch Condition (see (7b)):[8]

(7)   a.   the student whose brother's band Jonah likes
        b.   the $[_{CP1/ForceP}$ [student$_i$] $[_{CP2}$ [[[who ~~student$_i$~~]'s brother]'s band]$_j$ Jonah likes t$_j$]]

The availability of an external Head may also avoid the problem posed by such sentences as *nobody I know would send me flowers* (see 'I know nobody' – incorrect meaning – as well as **No [I know body]* . . .), *Nowhere I've lived has felt this much like home* (see 'I have lived nowhere' – incorrect meaning – as well as **No [I have lived where]* . . .), and McCawley's (1998: 481 n. 7) *Köchel compiled a catalogue of everything that Mozart wrote* vis à vis **Köchel compiled a catalogue of every work that Mozart wrote,*[9] if *nobody, nowhere, everything,* etc. are something like *nobody$_{person}$* [. . . person], *nowhere$_{place}$* [. . . place] , *everything(=all)$_{thing}$* [. . . thing]. Also see McCawley (1998: 436 ff) for discussion.

The availability of a silent external Head which receives Case from the matrix predicate may also account for certain facts in Inverse Case Attraction in Icelandic, according to Wood, Sigurðsson & Nowenstein (2017). See section A4.1.5 below.

Webelhuth, Bargmann & Götze (2019: §3.2) point out that both 'raising' and (full) 'matching' (but not the external-Head plus a RC internal *wh*-pronoun analysis) miss the following five generalizations:[10]

(i)   In German (see Heck 2005), the dative plural *d*-relativizer *denen* has the same form as the **personal pronoun**, not the same as the determiner (*die Freunde, denen/*den ich vertraue* 'the friends who(m) I trust' vs *Ich vertraue den/*denen Freunden* 'I trust the friends').

(ii)   In German (and English), *wh*-relativizers are homophonous with **interrogative pronouns**, not with interrogative determiners.

---

[8] See Bhatt (2002: 81). As Salzmann (2017: §2.3.3.2.8) notes, a similar point can be made for German.

[9] McCawley notes there that 'the *every-* series can be used even in contexts that allow *all* but not *every*'.

[10] Also see their §3.3.6 on the syntax of adpositions, which are prepositional with an inanimate phrasal complement, but postpositional with an inanimate pronominal (*mit den Anruf* vs *womit*), and are invariably postpositional with a *wh*-relativizer.

(iii) In English, *wh*-relativizers and **personal pronouns**, but not determiners, are characterized by animacy and Case distinctions.

(iv) A DP heading an Ā-chain carries the Case assigned to the foot of the chain.

(v) 'In German determiners govern the declension class of nouns and adjectives they co-occur with.'

Also see Salzmann (2017: §2.3.3.2) for other potential problems for an analysis exclusively countenances 'raising'.

A4   Three Phenomena Discriminating between 'Matching' and 'Raising' – Extraposition, Stacking, and Weak Island Sensitivity – and Some Apparent Exceptions[*]

I consider here three phenomena which have been taken in the literature to be incompatible with the 'raising' derivation, thus justifying the existence of a 'matching' derivation in addition to a 'raising' one: extraposition, stacking, and weak island (in)sensitivity. I will suggest that they are indeed incompatible with bona fide cases of 'raising', and will take them to discriminate clearly between the two derivations. Since certain cases that are usually taken to necessarily involve a 'raising' derivation (those involving anaphor, pronominal, quantifier, and idiom chunk reconstruction) are not incompatible for certain speakers with extraposition, stacking, and extraction from weak islands, I will later consider the possibility that they may also involve (for those speakers) a 'matching' derivation (see §A4.4 below), eventually treating extraposition, stacking, and weak island sensitivity as truly decisive in determining whether 'raising' is involved or not.

A4.1   Extraposition

Consider first Relative Clause Extraposition. It might be thought that Relative Clause Extraposition is incompatible with 'raising' because of certain conflicting requirements holding true of each. Bona fide cases of 'raising', like the different types of amount relatives discussed in Carlson (1977), seem to require that the Head be introduced by strong determiners (definite articles, demonstratives, and universal quantifiers). Compare the grammaticality of (8) with the ungrammaticality of (9), where the Head is introduced by weak determiners (Carlson 1977: 525):

---

[*] This section is an enlarged and updated version of Cinque (2015a).

(8)   a.   The/Those people there were __ at that time only lived a few decades.
       b.   That's all there is __.
       c.   Every lion there is __eats meat.

(9)   a.   *{Some, A} man there was __ disagreed.
       b.   *{Five, Most, Several, Many} men there were __ here disagreed.

On the other hand Relative Clause Extraposition is known to be best with indefinite Heads and bad to various degrees with definite ones. See the contrasts between (10a) and (10b) (from Ziv & Cole 1974: 772) and (11a) and (11b) (from Guéron & May 1984: 6):

(10)   a.   The guy that I met at Treno's yesterday just came in.
       b.   ??The guy just came in that I met at Treno's yesterday.

(11)   a.   I read a book during the vacation which was written by Chomsky.
       b.   *I read that book during the vacation which was written by Chomsky.

Nonetheless Relative Clause Extraposition turns out to be possible even with Heads introduced by strong determiners if some focus is present within the relative clause or if certain focus intensifiers (*very* rather than *only*) precede the Head. See, e.g., the examples in (12):[11]

(12)   a.   The guy just came in that I met at TRENO'S yesterday. (Huck & Na 1990: 54)
       b.   The very man just walked in that I had been telling her about. (Kayne 1994: 124)
       c.   That man came into the room that I was telling you about. (Rochemont & Culicover 1990: 60)
       d.   The student finally arrived who we had been waiting all morning for. (Keenan & Comrie 1977: 80)

With this proviso, let us consider the application of extraposition to bona fide 'raising' relatives in 'Headless' (Free), amount and existential-*there* relatives and relatives on predicates:

A4.1.1   Extraposition in 'Headless' (Free), Amount and Existential-*there* Relatives and Relatives on Predicates

As (13a–i) appear to show, extraposition is barred in these kinds of sentences, which arguably involve 'raising':

---

[11] On the different attachments of extraposed RCs and their consequences for scope, Principle C obviation, etc., see the recent study of Walker (2017) and references cited there.

(13)   a.   *Whatever friends are gone I once had. (from Bresnan 1973, cited in Akmajian & Lehrer 1976: 402 fn. 8) (cf. *Whatever friends I once had are gone.* and ?*The friends are gone I once had.*, also from Bresnan 1973)[12]

        b.   *What is now gone I once had. (cf. *What I once had is now gone.*)

        c.   *What men liked Bob that there were in Austria. (cf. Carlson 1977: 526: *What men that there were in Austria liked Bob.*)

        d.   *?Every doctor rushed to room 222 that there was. (cf. *Every doctor that there was rushed to room 222.*)

        e.   *The one thing is honest [that I want a man to be]. (cf. *The one thing that I want a man to be is honest.* – Heycock 2012: 225)

        f.   *?The gifted mathematician is very rare nowadays that Bill was. (cf. *The gifted mathematician that Bill was is very rare nowadays*)[13]

        g.   *John never became the doctor during his active period that his mother was.[14]

        g.   *?Every pound is worth a fortune that Max weighs. (cf. *Every pound that Max weighs is worth a fortune*)

        h.   *?The (very) way impressed me that he solved the problem. (cf. *The (very) way that he solved the problem impressed me.*)

        i.   *?The longest was two decades that Sheldon had to wait. (cf. *The longest that Sheldon had to wait was two decades.* – Ross 1984: 264)[15]

---

[12] Generally, extraposition of a relative clause not introduced by a *wh*-pronoun or *that* is not possible. However, as noted in the literature, it becomes possible (or at most only slightly marginal) if the subject of the extraposed clause is pronominal (or *there*). See (i)a–d:

(i)   a.   ?A book just came out [I've been meaning to read] (Kayne 1994: 156 n. 20)

      b.   I saw someone yesterday [I hadn't seen for years] (Sag 1997: §6.1, after Dick Hudson, pers. comm.)

      c.   Something happened [I couldn't really talk about] (Sag 1997: §6.1, after Dick Hudson, pers. comm.)

      d.   There was never the problem here [there was there] (Reed 1975: 14)

Under a stranding analysis of extraposition (Kayne 1994: ch. 9) the ungrammaticality of (13)a could be attributed to *whatever friends* not forming a constituent (Kayne 1994: 125; see also Donati & Cecchetto 2011: Appendix). In the analysis of extraposition assumed here, which involves leftward raising of the RC plus remnant movement, along the lines of Kayne (2000), the ungrammaticality of (13a) must be attributed to a reason other than lack of constituency. This appears to be confirmed by the necessity of extraposing with the rest of the RC the German counterpart of English *wh-ever* (*w- auch immer*), which thus behaves as a constituent. See the more detailed discussion in §2.5.6.

[13] On the relativization of such post-copular predicates, see Grosu & Krifka (2005, 2007), who actually distinguish various types and give an analysis which is independent of the reconstruction of the Head into the relative clause, which I still assume here as a consequence of 'raising' (see fn. 26 below). For an alternative to Grosu and Krifka's analysis see Moltmann (2019), who extends to such cases her analysis of intensional relative clauses like *The book that John needs to write.*

[14] Sportiche (2015, example (60)a).

[15] The external and internal Heads of sentences like (13i) plausibly contain a silent AMOUNT OF TIME. Also see the discussion in Ojeda (1982), Bianchi (1999: ch. 2: §6.2),

A4.1.2   Extraposition, Idiom Chunk Relativization, and Anaphor Reconstruction in German

Sanfelici, Schulz and Trabandt (2017: §5.3.2) present evidence that extraposition in German is incompatible with an idiom chunk as Head of the RC (see the contrast in (14)), and with reconstruction of an anaphor within the Head (see the contrast in (15)):

(14)   a.   An der Uni spricht jeder Student über die großen Reden, die die Professoren schwingen.
              'At the university every student talks about the grand speeches that the professors give.'
    b.   *Jeder Student spricht über die großen Reden an der Uni, die die Professoren schwingen.
              'Every student talks about the grand speeches at the university that the professors give.'

(15)   a.   In einer Schachtel gab es ein Foto von sich$_i$, das Peter$_i$ gestern gefunden hat.
              'In a box there was a photo of himself that Peter found yesterday.'
    b.   *Es gab ein Foto von sich$_i$ in einer Schachtel, das Peter$_i$ gestern gefunden hat.
              'There was a photo of himself in a box that Peter found yesterday.'

A4.1.3   Extraposition and Anaphor Reconstruction in Georgian

As noted in Foley (2013: 22–3), in Georgian anaphors cannot be reconstructed inside extraposed RCs. See (16):

(16) a. p̌rezident̩-s$_i$ is   st̩at̩ia tavis   tav$_{i,*j}$=ze moscons, [romeli=c Medea-m$_j$ dacera]
        president-DAT DEM article own self=on like:PRES.3SG [which=REL Medea-ERG write:AOR.3SG]
    b. p̌rezident̩-s$_i$ is   st̩at̩ia   tavis tav$_{i,*j}$=ze moscons, [Medea-m$_j$ rom dacera]
        president-DAT DEM article own self=on like:PRES.3SG [Medea-ERG ROM write:AOR.3SG]
        Both: 'The president$_i$ likes the article about himself$_i$/*herself$_j$ that Medea$_j$ wrote'

A4.1.4   Extraposition and Heim's Ambiguity Sentences

Another case showing that 'raising' is incompatible with extraposition is provided by Harris's (2008) discussion of Heim's (1979) ambiguity sentences.

---

and Huddleston & Pullum (2002: 1060), as well as the impossibility of extraposing the constituent introduced by *che* stranding *quello* in Spec,CP of the *quello che* substitute for the missing (*che*) *cosa* analogue of *what* in 'Headless' RCs in Italian (see §2.5.3).

In Heim (1979) it is noted that a sentence like (17) is ambiguous between the two readings in (18):

(17)   John guessed the price that Mary guessed

(18)   A.   John and Mary happened to guess the same price, but not necessarily anything about one another. John and Mary need not even know of the other's existence.
        B.   John guessed something about Mary; that is, John guessed the answer to the question 'What price did Mary guess?'.

As Harris argues, Heim's (1979) sentences reflect a structural ambiguity: Reading A is derived from a 'matching' relative clause structure and Reading B from a 'raising' one.

Reading B has a meaning comparable to that of a 'Headless' (Free) relative like 'John guessed what(ever) price Mary guessed', which strengthens the idea that Reading B involves 'raising', like 'Headless' (Free) relatives do.

Crucially, what Harris further notes is that Reading B disappears if the relative clause is extraposed (see (19)), thus lending further support to the idea that 'raising' is incompatible with extraposition:[16]

(19)   John guessed [the price t] yesterday [that Mary guessed] (A/#B)

A4.1.5   Incompatibility of Relative Clause Extraposition with one type of Inverse Case Attraction

Another piece of evidence that extraposition is incompatible with bona fide 'raising' appears to be provided by the impossibility of extraposition in some languages when the relative clause displays Inverse Case Attraction.

---

[16] Apparent counterexamples to the idea that extraposition is incompatible with 'raising' are Lisa Selkirk's sentence *There isn't the water in the sink that there is in the bathtub* (pers. comm. to Irene Heim as reported in von Fintel 1999: 5), which was brought to my attention by Cécile Meier, and Richard Kayne's (pers. comm.) *He made the same amount of headway this year that I made last year*. Here, however, the identity of the verbs in the matrix and the relative clause opens up the possibility that *water* and *amount of headway* may be arguments of the matrix clause qualifying as external Heads of the relative clause matched by an identical silent internal Head (WATER and AMOUNT OF HEADWAY), argument of the relative clause verb (see Sportiche 2015: fn. 19, and §A4.4.1 below). Alternatively, they could be interpreted as hidden comparatives (= . . . as there is in the bathtub; . . . as I made last year), which allow extraposition more readily. Notice, in fact, that reading A of Heim's sentence (the one which Harris takes to involve 'matching') is paraphrasable with a comparative: *John guessed the same price as Mary guessed.*

This type of Case attraction, whereby the overt Head of the relative clause bears the Case that would be assigned internally to the relative clause rather than the Case that would be assigned in the matrix, has been taken to depend on a 'raising' derivation of the Head (Andrews 1975: 167; Aghaei 2003, 2006; see also Bianchi 1999: 92–4), but see below for another kind of Inverse Case Attraction which does not seem to depend on 'raising'.

Two Farsi varieties (Dari – as noted in Houston 1974; and Persian – as noted in Aghaei 2003, 2006; also see Payne 1982), one Albanian dialect (that of Xranje – as noted in Bevington 1979), a Finnish variety (Ingrian – as noted in Kholodilova 2013; also see Kholodilova & Privizentseva 2015 on other Finno-Ugric languages), and Icelandic (as noted in Wood, Sigurðsson & Nowenstein 2017: 217) all admit extraposition in the absence of Inverse Case Attraction but ban it in the presence of Inverse Case Attraction, which in these languages arguably involves 'raising'. See the contrasts in (20) through (26) and the comments in Wood, Sigurðsson & Nowenstein (2017: 217) concerning Icelandic.

Dari (Afghanistan Farsi – Houston 1974: 43):

(20)	a.	**doxtar**	**ey**	**(Ø)**	ke	jon	mišnose	inja	æs.
								(No Inverse Case Attraction)	
		girl	ART	(NOM)	COMP	John	know.3	here	be.3
	b.	**doxtar**	**ey**	**ra**	ke	jon	mišnose	inja	æs.
								(Inverse Case Attraction)	
		girl	ART	ACC	COMP	John	know.3	here	be.3

'The girl that John knows is here.'

(21)	a.	**doxtar**	**ey**	**(Ø)**	**inja**	**æs**	**[ke**	**jon**	**mišnose].**
					(extraposition with no Inverse Case Attraction)				
		girl	ART		here	be.3	COMP	John	know.3
	b.	***doxtar**	**ey**	**ra**	inja	æs	**[ke**	**jon**	**mišnose].**
					(extraposition with Inverse Case Attraction)				
		girl	ART	ACC	here	be.3	COMP	John	know.3

'The girl that John knows is here.'

Persian (Iranian Farsi – Aghaei 2006: 81, 85):[17]

(22)   a.   **zan-i** [ke diruz did-i] 'emruz 'injā-st.   (No Inverse Case Attraction)
    woman-RES (NOM) that yesterday saw-2sg. today here-is3sg.

---

[17] As noted in Aghaei (2003), Inverse Case Attraction is not possible in Persian non-restrictive RCs (see (i)), which appears to suggest that in non-restrictives 'raising' is unavailable (see §3.1.8. See also Bianchi 1999, chapters 4 and 5 for a discussion on the lack of reconstruction in (Italian) non-restrictive relatives):

b. **zan-i ro** [ke diruz did-i] 'emruz 'injä-st. (Inverse Case Attraction)
woman-RES (ACC) that yesterday saw-2sg. today here-is3sg.
'The woman who you saw yesterday is here today.'

(23) a. **zan-i** 'emruz 'injä-st [**ke diruz did-i**]. (extraposition with no Inverse Case Attraction)
woman-RES (NOM) today here-is that yesterday saw-2sg.

b. ***zan-i ro** 'emruz 'injä-st [**ke diruz did-i**]. (extraposition with Inverse Case Attraction)
woman-RES ACC today here-is that yesterday saw-2sg.
'The woman is here today who you saw yesterday.'

Albanian dialect of Xranje (Bevington 1979: 273–4):

(24) a. Djali [që e pashë unë] iku.
(No Inverse Case Attraction)
the boy (Nom) [that him saw I] left

b. Djalen [që e pashë unë] iku.
(Inverse Case Attraction)
the boy (Acc) [that him saw I] left
'The boy that I saw left.'

(25) a. Djali iku [që e pashë unë].
(extraposition with no Inverse Case Attraction)
the boy (Nom) left that him saw I

b. *Djalen iku [që e pashë unë].
(extraposition with Inverse Case Attraction)
the boy (Acc) left that him saw I
'The boy that I saw left.'

Ingrian Finnish (Kholodilova 2013: §3.3)
The same is true of Ingrian Finnish. As reported in Kholodilova (2013):
'Inverse Attraction is not compatible with *extraposition* of the relative clause,
which is possible and quite frequent in other cases [. . .]. In [(26)], the relative

---

(i) *'an mard-e mosen ro [ke diruz did-am] 'emruz raft. (Aghaei 2003: 2)
that man-EZ old ACC that yesterday saw-I today went-he
'That old man, who I saw yesterday, went today.'

clause is extraposed, therefore the head cannot undergo Inverse Attraction.'
(p. 100)

(26)   lammas/*lampàn   loikò   koi-n   luon [minkä   miä   eilen   ost-i-n].
        sheep.NOM/sheep-GEN   lie.PRS.3SG   home-GEN   near   what.GEN   I.NOM   yesterday   buy-PST-1SG
        the sheep   lies in front of the house that I yesterday bought
        'The sheep that I bought yesterday is lying in front of the house.'

Icelandic (Wood, Sigurðsson & Nowenstein 2017: 217)
In Icelandic too, Inverse Case Attraction, which is best in RCs modifying a
subject with a RC embedded Dative subject replacing the matrix nominative, is
not possible with extraposition, which is otherwise possible when no inverse
attraction obtains (p. 217).

Wood, Sigurðsson & Nowenstein (2017) also notes that 'the difficulty of
adopting a pure head raising approach to the analysis of our IA data lies in the
fact that the matrix clause shows evidence that the external case is present,
even if it is not pronounced. [...], for example, predicate adjectives will still
bear Nom, even when IA has replaced Nom with Dat. [...] Possibly the
simplest way to describe IA, at our current level of understanding, is to say
that it involves a matching analysis where the matrix copy of the NP is deleted
instead of the embedded copy. We illustrate this schematically in [(27)]:

(27)   a.   the art works.NOM ~~the art works.DAT~~ *sem*__V_{DAT} Ordinary Matching
        b.   ~~the art works.NOM~~ the art works.DAT *sem*__V_{DAT} Inverse Attraction (p. 208)

Not all cases of Inverse Case Attraction apparently involve 'raising'. Gračanin-
Yüksek (2013: §4) provides evidence, based on lack of reconstruction of the
Head, that Inverse Case Attraction in Croatian restrictive RCs does not involve
'raising' of the Head, but rather, following Bader & Bayer (2006: 130), feature
sharing, which extends to Case, between the relative operator (moved to Spec,
CP) and the external Head.[18] Interestingly, in a personal communication, she

---

[18]   Also see now Czypionka, Dörre & Bayer (2018), where it is argued that Inverse Case Attraction
        does not necessarily involve the correlative/left dislocation construction of Old High German
        discussed in Pittner (1995) and Georgi & Salzmann (2014, 2017).

reported that extraposition appears to be allowed in cases like (28), where the Head of the RC arguably realizes the Case assigned RC internally (i.e., in an Inverse Case Attraction case).

(28)   a.   Vidio   sam   brod   jucer   sto   je   isplovio   za   Italiju.
             saw.m.sg   aux.1sg   ship   yesterday   that   aux.3sg   sailed.m.sg   for   Italy.acc
             'Yesterday I saw the ship that sailed to Italy.'
       b.   Vidio   sam   teret   jucer   sto   su   otpremili   u Italiju.
             saw.m.sg   aux.1sg   cargo   yesterday   that   aux.3pl   shipped.m.pl   in Italy
             'Yesterday I saw the cargo that they shipped to Italy.'

That the Head of Croatian restrictive RCs may actually be external to the relative CP is apparently confirmed by the placement of clitics, which are in second position of the clause, after the first constituent (or the first prosodic word), and are clause-bound. As shown in Gračanin-Yüksek (2008: §3.1.2), 'the clitics that originate inside the relative clause follow the relative operator in the specifier of the relative CP, as shown in [(29a)] [and] . . . cannot follow the nominal head of the relative clause, as shown in [(29b)]. (p. 286).[19]

(29)   a.   Vid   kupuje   [NP Sonyjev sat   [CP koji   mu   je   Dan preporučio]].
             Vid   buys   Sony's watch   which   himDAT   AUX   Dan recommended
             'Vid buys the Sony watch that Dan recommended to him.'
       b.   *Vid   kupuje   [NP Sonyjev sat   mu   je   [CP koji   Dan preporučio]].
             Vid   buys   Sony's watch   himDAT   AUX   which   Dan recommended

Clitics originating in a matrix clause whose subject is modified by a RC can instead follow the constituent formed out of the Head and the RC ((30a)), or just the Head, the first prosodic word ((30b)), thus showing that the Head is outside of the RC CP:[20]

(30)   a.   [NP Čovek   [CP koji   laze]]   mu   je   anio   uvredu.
                                                           (Gračanin-Yüksek 2008: 289 fn. 24)
             man   which   lies   himDAT   AUX   brought   offence
             'The man who lies offended him.'
       b.   [NP Čovek mu_i je_j [CP koji laze]]   anio t_i t_j uvredu.
                                                             (Gračanin-Yüksek 2008: 289)
             man   himDAT   AUX   which lies   brought   offence
             'The man who lies offended him.'

---

[19]   Also see the discussion in Salzmann (2017: §2.3.3.2.6). In Croatian 'Headless' (Free) RCs, clitics originating inside the RC follow the Free relative operator, thus showing that the relative operator is in the specifier of the CP rather than in the external Head position (Gračanin-Yüksek 2008: 284).

[20]   Gračanin-Yüksek (2008: 290 fn. 25) notes that both the external-Head account and the 'matching' account can capture the antireconstruction effects in Croatian Headed RCs just mentioned. Yet, she adds, 'neither can capture the reconstruction effects observed in Croatian degree relatives' (fn. 25), suggesting that a 'raising' derivation is also needed.

A4.2   *Stacking*

The second phenomenon incompatible with bona fide 'raising' RCs is Stacking, as already recognized in Carlson (1977) (also see Weisler 1980: 628; Grosu & Landman 1998: 165).[21]

(31)   a.   *Chi hai invitato (chi) non conoscevi è Gianni.   ['Headless' relative]
                He who you invited (who) you did not know is G.

       b.   *Qualunque cosa tu dica (qualunque cosa) tu ritenga importante sarà benvenuta. ['Headless' relative] Whatever you say (subjunctive) you deem (subjunctive) important will be welcome

       c.   *jo laRkii kharRii hai jo ravii kii dost hai, vo (laRkii) bahut lambii hai ['Headless' correlative] (Grosu & Landman 1998: 165)
                which girl standing is which R.gen friend is, that (girl) very tall is
                'The girl that is standing that is a friend of Ravi's is very tall.'

       d.   *The sailor that there was on the boat that there had been on the island died in the explosion. [existential-*there* context]
                (cf. The sailor who was on the boat who had been on the island died in the explosion.)

       e.   *This desk weighs every pound they said it would weigh that I had hoped it would (weigh). [degree relative]

---

[21] I am assuming the following characterization of Stacking (from Stockwell, Schachter & Partee 1973: 442): 'Relative clauses are said to be stacked if a structure exists such that the first clause modifies the head noun, [and] the second modifies the head noun as already modified by the first clause.' Sometimes the existence of Stacking is questioned, by claiming that it is a form of asyndetic coordination. However, cases exist whose intersective import is different (at least for certain speakers, including me) from simple coordination. See, for example, the following two cases:

(i)   a.   Il primo libro che ho letto che mi ha veramente divertito è Alice nel Paese delle Meraviglie.
                The first book that I read that really amused me was Alice in Wonderland.
                (Stockwell, Schachter & Partee 1973: 445) (=/= the first book that I read and that really amused me was Alice in Wonderland.)

       b.   Il solo lavoro che ho letto che mi abbia veramente convinto è il suo.
                The only work that I read that has (subjunctive) truly convinced me is his. (=/= The only work that I read and that has (subjunctive) truly convinced me is his.) (in the second case an overt coordination renders (for me) the sentence ungrammatical: *Il solo libro che ho letto e che mi abbia veramente convinto è il suo.).

Also, the fact that the ungrammatical stacking cases in (31), which involve bona fide 'raising', become grammatical if coordinated (see Carlson 1977: 541, and (ii) here) argues against taking Stacking to be reducible to asyndetic coordination.

(ii)   a.   Chi hai invitato e non conoscevi è Gianni.
                'He who you invited and you did not know is Gianni.'

       b.   Qualunque cosa tu dica e tu ritenga importante sarà benvenuta.
                'Whatever you say (subjunctive) and you deem (subjunctive) important will be welcome.'

f.   *Waylon put what THERE WAS that HE COULD in his pocket. [ACD relativization][22]

g.   *Il bravo idraulico che era che anche suo padre era stato non è facile oggigiorno da trovare.
the good plumber that he was that also his father had been is not easy to find today. [relativization of a predicate]

i.   ?*The way [John drives the car] [that nobody else drives it].[23][manner adverb relativization]

A4.3   Weak-Island Sensitivity

The same bona fide 'raising' RCs that are incompatible with extraposition and stacking turn out to be sensitive to weak islands. See (32) to (37).[24]

Idioms (Rizzi 1990: 78–80; Bianchi 1993):

(32)   a.   L'attenzione che ho deciso di prestare a Gianni è poca.
(Rizzi 1990: 79)
'The attention that I decided to pay to Gianni is negligible.'

b.   *L'attenzione che non ho ancora deciso a chi prestare è poca.
(Rizzi 1990: 80) (*wh*-island)
'The attention that I haven't decided yet to whom to pay is negligible.'

c.   *L'attenzione che non ho prestato a Gianni sarebbe stata cruciale.
(negative island)
'The attention that I did not pay to Gianni would have been crucial.'

d.   *Che credito ti sei pentito di avergli dato?
(Bianchi 1993: 350) (factive island)
'What credit do you regret having put in him?'

Free relatives

(33)   a.   What(ever) he says isn't true.

b.   *Whatever pilots we asked them whether you had contacted . . .
(Postal 1998: 46) (*wh*-island)

c.   *What these players don't weigh is at least 300 pounds.
(Rullmann 1995: 7) (negative island)[25]

d.   *?Whatever friends I am glad I once had are gone.   (factive island)

---

[22] Carlson (1977: 540).

[23] Law (2001).

[24] Sensitivity to weak islands holds at least for those extractions that clearly involve non-referential/non-D-linked operators. Referential/D-linked ones instead possibly involve a 'matching' derivation. On the weak-island sensitivity of RCs involving 'raising' see Sichel's (2014: §5.2; 2018) discussion of the selective extraction from RCs in Hebrew, which she shows behave like weak islands and involve 'raising' (see examples (37)–(38) and related text of §5.5).

[25] Other such cases are however better. See *What a gymnast shouldn't weigh is 300 pounds.* (Andrew Radford, pers. comm.)

Existential-there contexts (Carlson 1977; Bianchi 2002: 203)

(34) a. What meat that there was was soon eaten. (see Carlson 1977: 526)
      b. *What meat I wondered whether there was would not have been sufficient. (*wh*-island)
      c. *What meat there wasn't would have been eaten immediately.
                                                          (negative island)
      d. *What little meat everybody regretted that there was ...
                                                          (factive island)

Lexically selected and unselected adverbials (Rizzi 1990: 78 ff):

(35) a. This is the way that I think he should behave.
      b. *This is the way that I want to know whether he behaved.
                                                          (*wh*-island)
      c. *This is the only way that he didn't behave.
                                                          (negative island)
      d. *This is the way that I regret that he behaved.
                                                          (factive island)

Degree (measure) phrases (see Rizzi 1990: 78–9):

(36) a. John weighed 200 lbs.
      b. *The 200 lbs that I wondered whether he weighed ...   (*wh*-island)
      c. *The 200 lbs that he did not weigh in his youth would be too much.
                                                          (negative island)
      d. *The 200 lbs that I am glad that he weighs would be too much for me.
                                                          (factive island)

Predicate relativization:[26]

(37) a. Non è certo il grande chirurgo che lui ritiene di essere.
          'He is certainly not the great surgeon that he thinks he is.'
      b. *Non è certo il grande chirurgo che si chiedeva come poter diventare.
                                                          (*wh*-island)
          'He is certainly not the great surgeon that he wondered how to be able to become.'
      c. *Riuscirà a diventare il grande chirurgo che suo padre non è?
                                                          (negative island)
          'Will he manage to become the great surgeon that his father is not?'
      d. *Il grande chirurgo che sono contento che sia diventato ...
                                                          (factive island)
          'The great surgeon that I am glad that he became ...'

---

[26] On the necessary 'raising' character of the relativization of DPs in predicate position see Vergnaud (1974: 63–8) and Bianchi (1999: ch. II, §4.2).

A4.4 Extraposition, Stacking and Weak Island Insensitivity of Relative Clauses Putatively Involving 'Raising'

There are a number of RC constructions often taken to involve unequivocally 'raising', which nonetheless appear to allow extraposition, stacking, and extraction from weak islands (to different degrees). I consider them in turn, suggesting in accord with certain claims made in the literature that they may after all not involve 'raising' (or, at least, not exclusively).

As already mentioned, in the end I will let extraposition, stacking, and weak island sensitivity discriminate between bona fide 'raising' and non-'raising' cases, taking them to be reliable diagnostics.

A4.4.1 Do Idiom Chunks Necessarily Involve 'Raising'?

Many cases of RCs on idiom chunks appear to allow extraposition of the relative clause. For example, Hulsey & Sauerland's (2006: 115) sentence, given by them as ungrammatical (*I was shocked by the advantage yesterday that she took of her mother.*) is judged by other speakers as perfectly acceptable, or, at most, only slightly marginal, as are many other such cases. See, for example, (38):[27]

(38)   a.   Every string will be pulled that can be. (Bruening 2015: §2.2).
       b.   Any headway will be highly appreciated that the company is able to make in its negotiations with the unions.
       c.   ?I was bitterly disappointed with the cruel advantage last year that he had taken of his mother and of his sisters and brothers.
       d.   ?The careful track is well known that she was keeping of her expenses.
       e.   I made the same headway last year that he made this year. (Bruening 2015: §5)

Even though it is one of the prototypical cases motivating 'raising', the relativization of idiom chunks is in fact a less than clear diagnostic, for a number of reasons. In the idioms that allow such relativization the relativized nominals appear to retain some referential autonomy (Ruwet 1991: n. 30), which may not exclude the possibility of a matching derivation.[28] Bruening

---

[27] When not indicated, the source of the examples in (38) is Andrew Radford (pers. comm.). Also see the examples in Heycock (2019: §4) based on a survey.

[28] Larson (2017: fn. 24) does not even consider *make headway* an idiom on the grounds that it is compositional. Also see Nunberg, Sag & Wasow (1994) and Webelhuth, Bargmann & Götze (2019: §4) on the compositional/flexible nature of idioms like *pull strings* vs the non-compositional/frozen nature of idioms like *kick the bucket*. To judge from McCawley (1981: 135–6), a further condition seems to be the indefiniteness of the idiom nominal to be relativized (presumably a consequence of the indefiniteness requirement on the internal Head already mentioned).

(2015) (see also Quang 1971: 201) gives examples where idiom chunks can be resumed by pronominals ((39a–c)) (but see Salzmann 2017: § 2.3.1.4.2 for the non-robust status of this observation) and can control a PRO ((40a–c)):[29]

(39)   a.   Every string will be pulled if **it** can be.
       b.   Speaker A: The cat is out of the bag. Speaker B: I know **it** is.
       c.   Speaker A: The beans have been spilled. Speaker B: Yes, **they** have.

(40)   a.   Could the beans have been spilled without PRO being spilled deliberately?
       b.   Headway was made without PRO seeming to be made.
       c.   Strings can be pulled without PRO being pulled in any obvious way.

Ruwet (1991: n. 15), Van Riemsdijk (2000: 226), and Bruening (2015: §5) also mention that in some cases the idiom chunk can be found without the rest of the idiom and still be interpreted idiomatically. See (41):[30]

(41)   a.   I don't regard that as headway. (Ruwet 1991: n. 15, after Higgins 1974)
       b.   Can we characterize this as headway? (Van Riemsdijk 2000: 226; see also Grosu 2003b: 286)
       c.   Headway may be possible with … (Ruwet 1991: n. 15)
       d.   Mary made a lot of headway. (Whitman 2013: 368)
       e.   They had the strings and pulled them. (Bruening 2015: §5 after Riehemann 2001: 75, (73e))

Bresnan and Grimshaw (1978: 388) observe that in some instances the Head can be an idiom chunk related to the matrix verb, rather than to the verb of the relative clause, which (*pace* Sportiche 2015) may pose a problem for a simple

---

On non-relativizable idioms also see the discussion in Bianchi (1993) and De Vries (2002: 78 fn. 13).

[29] Salzmann suggests more generally that 'idioms are not a valid argument for movement, because they can participate in all sorts of non-movement dependencies'; in particular with proforms that cannot involve movement as they can take antecedents across sentences, or even lack a linguistic antecedent. In this idiomatic nominals differ from 'expletive' *there*, which can neither antecede pronouns nor control, thus truly qualifying as 'a valid movement diagnostic'. On the dubious diagnostic value for 'raising' of the relativization of idiom chunks also see Ruwet (1991), Duncan (2004: §2.6.1), Webelhuth, Bargmann & Götze (2017, 2019), and Reşceanu (2014).

[30] On why the idiomatic chunk cannot be used in isolation in all cases (**They were surprised at the headway.*), although it can apparently serve by itself as a matrix clause argument when Head of a relative clause containing the rest of the idiom (*They were surprised at the headway that we made.*), see the interesting suggestions advanced in Bruening (2015: §5).

'raising' derivation (see their example (42a) and similar examples in (42b–d) from the subsequent literature):[31]

(42) a. We didn't *make the amount of headway* that was expected of us.
      b. Parky *pulled the strings* that got me the job. (McCawley 1981: 137)
      c. Bill *made the amount of headway* that Mary demanded. (Hulsey & Sauerland 2006: (47a))
      d. We *made headway* that was sufficient. (Bhatt 2002: fn. 1, credited to one of the reviewers)

In other cases the idiom chunk is shared by both the main and the relative clause (see (43), from Bruening 2015: §6.2.4), which is again problematic for the ordinary 'raising' derivation as the external Merge licensing requirement on the idiom arguably is not fulfilled by the upper occurrence of the verb (also see Webelhuth, Bargmann & Götze 2019: §3.1):

(43) a. John paid the same heed last year that Mary paid.
      b. We can make any headway you can make.
      c. James won't pull any strings that Jill is not willing to pull.

Heycock (2019: 101) also points out that if idiom chunk Heads were necessarily derived by 'raising' they should obligatorily reconstruct, inducing a Principle C violation in sentences like (44), but they do not (see her discussion of cases in the literature where they apparently do):

(44) This represents the only headway on Lucy$_i$'s problem that she$_i$ thinks they have made so far.

All of this seems to me to suggest that a 'matching' derivation must at least be marginally available to idiomatic Heads (see also Bhatt's 2002 discussion in

---

[31] Also see Bresnan's pseudocleft example in (i)a, which is reported in Falk (2010: fn. 6), where the object of *make* is *what*, not *headway* (but see Van Riemsdijk 2000: §2.1), and the *tough*-movement cases (i)b and (i)c, where the idiomatic subject of *hard/easy* is standardly not taken to be directly related via movement to the object position of *make* (see Chomsky 1981: 309 ff), as suggested by the impossibility of an expletive subject in the same position – see (i)d:

(i)   a. What we have to make is more headway!
      b. Tabs are hard to keep on John – he's so elusive! (Joseph 1980: 350 fn. 13)
      c. Headway should be easy to make in cases like this. (Bruening 2015: §5)
      d. *There is hard to believe to have been a crime committed. (Bruening 2015, from Chomsky 1981: 309).

But see Sportiche (2006) for the interesting idea that what moves to the subject position of the 'easy' predicate is not the full DP object of the embedded predicate, but a smaller nominal constituent, subextracted from the embedded Spec,CP. For another 'improper movement' analysis, see Brillman (2015).

his fn. 1), possibly in addition to a 'raising' one, when the idiomatic Head qualifies as an amount (a case to which I return).

The possibility of a 'matching' derivation should also account for the possible cases of Stacking of RCs on idioms (see (45)); a phenomenon which Carlson (1977: §4.3) and Grosu & Landman (1998: §2.7.1) show to be unavailable with bona fide 'raising' RCs (see (46)):[32]

(45)   Jack noticed the headway that WE made __ that the other team miserably
        FAILED to make __. (Aoun & Li 2003: 245 n. 19; example credited to
        Andrew Simpson)

(46)   a.   *The sailor that there was on the boat that there had been on the island
              died in the explosion.
        b.   *This desk weighs every pound they said it would weigh that I had
              hoped it would weigh.

A4.4.2   Anaphor Binding

The apparent binding of an anaphor in the RC Head by an antecedent within the RC (*The picture of himself that John saw hanging in the post office was ugly.* – Jackendoff 1972: 134) is another phenomenon that is often taken to diagnose 'raising' of the RC Head (see Schachter 1973, among many others).

If that were so, the fact that speakers seem to accept the extraposition of the RC even in the presence of such apparent reconstructions of the RC Head would be problematic. For example, Szczegielniak (2005: 75 fn. 39) reports that Pesetsky finds a sentence like (47) perfectly grammatical.

(47)   I saw a picture of himself$_i$ yesterday that John$_i$ also saw.

Once again, however, there are reasons to doubt that an anaphor in the RC Head which is apparently bound by an argument within the RC is an unfailing indication that the Head has raised from inside the RC. Ross (1970), Reinhart & Reuland (1991, 1993), Pollard & Sag (1992), Heycock (2005: 555–6), and

---

[32] Carlson (1977: 540) actually gives as ungrammatical the following sentence with two stacked RCs on the idiom chunk *headway*: **Jake noticed the headway we made that Fred said we couldn't make.* The ungrammaticality may, however, be due to the negation in the second RC, as RCs on *headway* which contain a negation seem to be degraded to begin with (Margaret Speas, pers. comm.), possibly an 'inner island' effect: **?The headway we couldn't make would have been crucial.* (though Andrew Radford finds the following as perfectly acceptable: *The headway that the UN negotiators made (that government representatives hadn't been able to make) was decisive.*, the second RC possibly being a parenthetical restrictive relative in Stowell's 2005 sense).

Jacobson (2019: §6.1) provide evidence that anaphors in picture NPs can be exempt from Condition A of the Binding Theory.[33] If one accepts their arguments, then cases like *the picture of himself$_i$ that John$_i$ saw ...* can no longer be used to motivate reconstruction (and 'raising'). In fact, many have noted that anaphors in picture nouns do not literally need a c-commanding antecedent (under reconstruction). They may find it contextually. See the examples in (48):[34]

(48) a. A picture of himself$_i$ was hanging on John$_i$'s (/*my) wall. (Andrew Radford, pers. comm.)

b. Books about himself$_i$, I think John$_i$ would never buy them. (Peter Cole, pers. comm.)

c. The picture of himself$_i$ in Newsweek dominated John$_i$'s thoughts. (Borsley 2010)

d. The picture of himself$_i$ in Newsweek shattered the peace of mind that John$_i$ had spent the last six months trying to restore. (Borsley 2010)

e. John was really upset. The picture of himself that had hung in the museum had been stolen. (Jacobson 2019: 337)

Jaime Douglas (pers. comm.) reports that he and his British English informants judge sentences like *Mary likes the picture of himself$_i$ that/ which John$_i$ hates* as completely ungrammatical, which casts further doubts on the obligatoriness of reconstruction (and 'raising') of Head-internal anaphors (at least for those speakers). Also see Huhmarniemi & Brattico (2013) on the failure of anaphors within the RC Head to reconstruct in Finnish RCs.

If so, extraposition examples like (47), or stacking cases like (45) or (49), or extractions from weak islands like (50), no longer pose a problem for the conclusion reached above that (bona fide) 'raising' is incompatible with extraposition and stacking and shows weak island sensitivity.

---

[33] Also see Adger & Ramchand (2005: 171 fn. 8), who claim that Scottish Gaelic anaphors can be licensed as logophoric anaphors, without the need for reconstruction. Platzack (2000: §1.1) gives evidence from Swedish against taking reflexives in the relative head as an argument for the 'raising' analysis. Safir (1999: 595) and Cecchetto (2006: 17) also give examples showing that picture-noun reflexivization is not reliable evidence for reconstruction (and 'raising'). If the anaphor is within an idiom chunk Head (as in *The picture of himself that he took ...*) reconstruction is however obligatory and total (Chomsky 1995: ch. 1).

[34] The grammaticality of *Pictures of himself are hard for John to criticize.* (Kayne 1994: 163 n. 68) would be another case in point, at least if the subject of *tough*-movement sentences is not raised from (and reconstructed into) the object position of the associated infinitival clause (but see fn. 31 above).

(49)   The (only) picture of himself that John saw that he finds offensive ...

(50)   The picture of himself that I wonder whether John will like is this one.

Perhaps, if the confound due to logophoric reflexives/reciprocals and implicit PROs in the Head are avoided (see Salzmann 2017: §2.3.1.4.1) by restricting the test cases to unaccusative nominal Heads in languages like Italian that do not have logophoric reflexives (see (50a) – Bianchi 1999: 118–119), then one can indeed see that extraposition is definitely degraded ((51b)):

(51)   a.   Il poeta descrive il [riflesso di se stesso$_i$] che Narciso$_i$ vide __ nella fonte.
              'The poet describes the reflection of himself that Narcissus saw in the fountain.'
        b.   *?Il poeta descrive il [riflesso di se stesso$_i$] in quest'opera [che Narciso$_i$ vide __ nella fonte]
              'The poet describes the reflection of himself in this work that Narcissus saw in the fountain.'

A4.4.3   Pronominal Binding

The same may be true of the binding of a pronominal contained in the RC Head by a quantifier inside the RC (as in *The book on her$_i$ desk that every professor$_i$ liked best* ... – Bianchi 2002: 202)

Alternative semantic analyses have been proposed, by Sharvit (1997, 1999b), Sauerland (1998) and Sternefeld (1998), which permit bound variable interpretations in the absence of c-command by the quantifier (under reconstruction). If so, the wellformedness of (52a–c) again poses no difficulty for the conclusion that (bona fide) 'raising' is incompatible with extraposition, stacking, and extraction from weak islands:

(52)   a.   A book about him$_i$ arrived that every politician$_i$ had hoped would not arrive.
        b.   I saw the book about him$_i$ that every politician$_i$ had hoped would not arrive that finally arrived.
        c.   The book about him$_i$ that I don't know if every politician$_i$ will like ...

For discussion and further references, see Cecchetto (2006) and Cecchetto & Donati (2015: §3.3.4.2).

A4.4.4   Quantifier Scope

Another phenomenon usually taken to be a clear diagnostic for reconstruction (and 'raising' of the Head) is the possibility for a quantifier contained within the RC Head to take narrow scope with respect to another quantifier within the RC (which c-commands it after reconstruction), as in (53):

(53)   I know the two students that each professor invited. (*each* > *two* or *two* > *each*)

If so, the fact that the RC can be extraposed (see (54a)), and that Stacking ((54b)) and extraction from weak islands ((54c)) are possible even under the *each* > *two* interpretation would seem to be a problem for the idea that these phenomena are incompatible with 'raising':[35]

(54)   a. I'll introduce the two students to Mary that each professor invited (*each* > *two* possible, though *two* > *each* is perhaps more immediate)
         b. The two students that each professor recommended that he originally did not want to recommend . . .
         c. The two students that it's high time for each professor to thank for their help . . .

Nonetheless, there is reason to doubt that such scope interactions necessarily always involve reconstruction of the Head containing the quantifier. Generally, strong determiners (like universal quantifiers) are outside restrictive or maximalizing RCs, and do not reconstruct inside the RC (*All the books/no book that I read defended that position.*). Yet there are cases, like the following, where they appear to be able to take narrow scope with respect to a quantifier inside the RC:

(55)   Ford recalled all the '75 models which were put out by a factory of theirs in Detroit.
         (all> a and a > all) (Fodor & Sag 1982: 371, cited in Inada 2008: 3)

All, which precedes *the,* is obviously outside of the restrictive RC and yet it can have narrow scope with respect to the indefinite inside the RC. This seems to show that the apparent scope reconstruction of *all the '75 models* cannot be accounted for by ascribing it to the presence of a copy of the quantifier inside the RC. Rather, Inada (2008) conjectures, such scope construals are via a choice function mechanism (also see Cresti 1995).

A4.4.5   Low Reading of Ordinals and Superlatives

The low reading of ordinals and superlatives discussed in Bhatt (2002) is occasionally also taken as a diagnostic for a 'raising' derivation of the RC Head. However Heycock (2003, 2019) discusses evidence casting doubt on it

---

[35] But see Fox & Nissenbaum (1999), who claim that extraposition blocks reconstruction of the Head into the RC.

as a disgnostic for 'raising'. Also see Sharvit (2007) for evidence that the superlative part does not reconstruct.

A4.5   Conjectures Concerning the Incompatibility of 'Raising' with Stacking, Extraposition, and Extraction from Weak Islands

Stacking

After Grosu & Landman (1998: §2.7.1) I take the incompatibility of stacking with 'raising' (see Carlson 1977: §4.3) to follow from the fact that the Head is interpreted inside the RC and that consequently it 'cannot have this internal interpretation relation to more than one relative clause' (Grosu & Landman 1998: 148).

Extraposition

If in the spirit of Kayne (2000: §15.3), we take RC extraposition to involve attraction of the RC CP 'out of the containing NP/DP' (p. 318), with subsequent movement of the remnant above the raised RC, as shown in (56), then it follows that only the external Head in a 'matching' derivation can be stranded when the RC CP is attracted. In the 'raising' derivation the internal Head is still inside the RC CP and thus cannot be stranded by the raising of the RC; whence the illformedness of the result of the derivation in (57):[36]

(56)   a.   I met [$_{DP}$ a [$_{FP}$ man$_j$ [$_{CP}$ ~~man~~ that asked me about you] t$_j$]] at the party yesterday →

       b.   [[$_{CP}$ ~~man~~ that asked me about you]$_i$ X° [I met [$_{DP}$ a [$_{FP}$ man$_j$ t$_i$ t$_j$] at the party yesterday] →

       c.   [[I met [$_{DP}$ a [$_{FP}$ man t$_i$ t$_j$]] at the party yesterday]$_k$ Y° [[$_{CP}$ ~~man~~ that asked me about you]$_i$ X° t$_k$

(57)   a.   I met [$_{DP}$ a [$_{FP}$ [$_{CP}$ man that asked me about you] ~~man~~]] at the party yesterday →

       b.   [[$_{CP}$ man that asked me about you]$_i$ X° [I met [$_{DP}$ a t$_i$ ~~man~~] at the party yesterday] →

       c.   [[I met [$_{DP}$ a t$_i$ ~~man~~] at the party yesterday]$_k$ Y° [[$_{CP}$ man that asked me about you]$_i$ X° t$_k$

---

[36] Szczegielniak (2005: §3.12) attributes the lack of reconstruction into extraposed RCs in Polish to the island character of the extraposed clause. While such clauses are also islands in Italian (see Cinque 2010b: 83), they appear not to be in other languages, like Norwegian (see Taraldsen 1981). So the question of what ultimately blocks bona fide 'raising' (and reconstruction) when the RC is extraposed remains probably to be sought along the lines explored here.

Extraction from weak islands

As for the incompatibility of 'raising' with extraction from weak islands, it seems that idiom chunks involving amounts, degree (measure) phrases, adverbial phrases, *wh*-phrases in 'Headless' RCs, *wh*-phrases out of existential-*there* sentences, and predicates do not leave copies that count as individual variables which are insensitive to weak islands.

References

Abebe, A. 1990. Relative Clauses in Chaha. A GB Approach. MA thesis. Addis Ababa University. etd.aau.edu.et/handle/123456789/6332

Abeillé, A. 2017. Agreement and interpretation of binominals in French. Paper presented at the CSSP 2017. www.cssp.cnrs.fr/cssp2017/abstracts/An-Abeille.pdf

Abeillé, A., Godard, D., Miller, P. & Sag, I. 1998. French bounded dependencies. In L. Dini & S. Balari, eds., *Romance in HPSG*. Stanford, CA: CSLI Publications. 1–54.

Abels, K. 2003. Successive cyclicity, anti-locality, and adposition stranding. PhD diss. University of Connecticut.

2016. The fundamental left-right asymmetry in the Germanic verb cluster. *The Journal of Comparative Germanic Linguistics* 19: 179–220.

Aboh, E. O. 2005. Deriving relative and factive clauses. In L. Brugè, G. Giusti, N. Munaro, W. Schweikert, G. Turano, eds., *Contributions to the 30th Incontro di Grammatica Generativa*. Venice: Libreria Editrice Cafoscarina. 265–85. hdl.handle.net/11707/757

Ackerman, F. & Nikolaeva, I. 2013. *Descriptive Typology and Linguistic Theory: A study in the morphosyntax of relative clauses*. Stanford, CA: CSLI Publications.

Adger, D. 2011. Bare resumptives. In A. Rouveret, ed., *Resumptive Pronouns at the Interfaces*. Amsterdam: Benjamins. 343–65.

Adger, D., Drummond, A., Hall, D. & van Urk, C. 2017. Is there Condition C Reconstruction? In A. Lamont & K. Tetzloff, eds., *Proceedings of NELS 47. Vol. 1*. Amherst, MA: GLSA. 21–30. ling.auf.net/lingbuzz/003674

Adger, D., Harbour, D. & Watkins, L. 2009. *Mirrors and Microparameters: Phrase structure beyond free word order*. Cambridge: Cambridge University Press.

Adger, D. & Ramchand, G. 2005. Merge vs move: *Wh*-dependencies revisited. *Linguistic Inquiry* 36: 161–93.

Åfarli, T. 1994. A promotion analysis of restrictive relative clauses. *The Linguistic Review* 11: 81–100.

Aghaei, B. 2003. Case attraction: Evidence for raising analysis for relative clauses in Farsi. Paper presented at SALA 23.

2006. The syntax of Ke-clause and clausal extraposition in Modern Persian. PhD diss. University of Texas at Austin. repositories.lib.utexas.edu/handle/2152/2655

Aissen, J. 1972. Where do relative clauses come from? In J. P. Kimball, ed., *Syntax and Semantics. Vol. 1*. New York: Seminar Press. 187–98.

Ajíbóyè, Q. 2001. The internal structure of Yorùbá DP. MS. University of British Columbia. Presented at ACAL 32, UC Berkeley, 25 March.

Akiyama, T. 2014. On restrictions on the use of non-restrictive infinitival relative clauses in English. In L. Gawne & J. Vaughan, eds., *Selected Papers from the 44th Conference of the Australian Linguistic Society, 2013*. University of Melbourne. 335–54. hdl.handle.net/11343/40971

Akmajian, A. & Lehrer, A. 1976. NP-like quantifiers and the problem of determining the head of an NP. *Linguistic Analysis* 2: 395–413.

Alber, B. 2008. Tyrolean A-bar movement: Doubling and resumptive pronoun structures. In S. Barbiers, O. Koeneman, M. Lekakou & M. van der Ham, eds., *Microvariation in Syntactic Doubling*. Syntax and Semantics Vol. 36. Bingley: Emerald. 141–70.

Alcázar, E. A. 2007. A minimalist analysis of participial constructions: Towards a phase account of non-finite structures. PhD diss. University of Southern California.

Aldridge, E. 2004. Internally headed relative clauses in Austronesian languages. *Language and Linguistics* 5(1): 99–129. bit.ly/2QKqY0F

2017. Internally and externally headed relative clauses in Tagalog. *Glossa: A Journal of General Linguistics* 2(1)41: 1–33. DOI: doi.org/10.5334/gjgl.175

Alexiadou, A., Law, P., Meinunger, A. & Wilder, C. 2000. Introduction. In *The Syntax of Relative Clauses*. Amsterdam: Benjamins. 1–51.

Alexiadou, A. & Varlokosta, S. 1996. The syntactic and semantic properties of free relatives in modern Greek. *ZAS Papers in Linguistics* 5: 1–31.

Alexopoulou, T. 2006. Resumption in relative clauses. *Natural Language and Linguistic Theory* 24: 57–111.

Allen, C. L. 1977. Topics in diachronic English syntax. PhD diss. University of Massachusetts, Amherst. bit.ly/2rsBvCR

Allwood, J. S. 1976. The complex np constraint as a non-universal rule and some semantic factors influencing the acceptability of Swedish sentences which violate the cnpc. In J. Stillings, ed., *University of Massachusetts Occasional Papers in Linguistics* 2: 1–20.

1982. The complex noun phrase constraint in Swedish. In E. Engdahl and E. Ejerhed, eds., *Readings on Unbounded Dependencies in Scandinavian Languages*. Umeå: University of Umeå. 15–32.

Almeida, D. A. de A. & Yoshida, M. 2007. A problem for the preposition stranding generalization. *Linguistic Inquiry* 38: 349–62.

Almeida, M. 1989. *A Description of Konkani*. Panaji: Thomas Stephens Konknni kendr.

Alves, M. J. 2001. Noun phrase structure in Mon-Khmer languages. Handout for a presentation made at the Academia Sinica in Taiwan in April. bit.ly/2OiDi6J

Ambadiang, T. 2017. Relative clauses and relativization processes in Nugunu. In G. G. Atindogbé & R. Grollemund, eds., *Relative Clauses in Cameroonian Languages: Structure, function and semantics*. Berlin: Mouton de Gruyter. 67–87.

Amha, A. 2001. *The Maale Language*. Leiden: CNWS Publications. hdl.handle.net/1887/36408

Ananda, L. M. G. 2008. The Cleft Construction in Sinhala. MPhil diss. Jawaharlal Nehru University, New Delhi.

Anbessa Teferra. 2012. *A Grammar of Sidaama: Phonology, morphology, and syntax.* Saarbrücken: LAP Lambert.

Andersen, T. 1998. Verb-coding in Madi relative clauses. *Sprachtypologie und Universalienforschung* 51: 295–326.

Anderson, C. 2005. Two types of Nepali correlatives. In Y. Yadava, G. Bhattarai, R. R. Lohani, B. Prasain & K. Parajuli, eds., *Contemporary Issues in Nepalese Linguistics.* Kathmandu: Linguistic Society of Nepal. 1–12.

Andersson, L.-G. 1974. Topicalization and relative clause formation. *Gothenburg Papers in Theoretical Linguistics* 25.

  1982. What is Swedish an exception to? Extractions and island constraints. In E. Engdahl & E. Ejerhed, eds., *Readings on Unbounded Dependencies in Scandinavian Languages.* Umeå: University of Umeå. 33–45.

Andersson, S.-G. & Kvam, S. 1984. *Satzverschränkung im heutigen Deutsch.* Tübingen: Narr.

Andrews, A. D. III. 1975. Studies in the Syntax of Relative and Comparative Clauses. PhD diss. MIT.

  2007. Relative clauses. In T. Shopen, ed., *Language Typology and Syntactic Description. Volume II: Complex Constructions.* 2nd ed. Cambridge: Cambridge University Press. 206–36.

Annamalai, E. & Steever, S. B. 1998. Modern Tamil. In S. B. Steever, ed., *The Dravidian Languages.* London: Routledge. 100–28.

Anonby, E. J. 2011. *A Grammar of Mambay: An Adamawa language of Chad and Cameroon.* Cologne: Rüdiger Köppe Verlag.

Aoun, J. & Choueiri, L. 1997. Resumption and Last Resort. MS. University of Southern California, Los Angeles.

Aoun, J., Choueiri, L. & Hornstein, N. 2001. Resumption, movement and derivational economy. *Linguistic Inquiry* 32: 371–403.

Aoun, J. & Li, Y.-H. A. 2003. *Essays on the Representational and Derivational Nature of Grammar. The Diversity of Wh-Constructions.* Cambridge, MA: MIT Press.

Arad, T. 2014. The nature of resumptive pronouns. Evidence from parasitic gaps. MA thesis, Tel Aviv University.

Arcodia, G. F. 2017. Towards a typology of relative clauses in Sinitic: Headedness and relativization strategies. *Cahiers de linguistique – Asie orientale/East Asian Languages and Linguistics* 46: 32–72.

Arka, I. W. 2016. Externally and internally headed relative clauses in Marori. In D. Arnold, M. Butt, B. Crysmann, T. Holloway King, S. Müller, eds., *Proceedings of the Joint 2016 Conference on Head-driven Phrase Structure Grammar and Lexical Functional Grammar.* Stanford: CSLI Publications. 23–42. stanford.io/34jTcmL

Arnold D. 2004. Non-restrictive relative clauses in construction-based HPSG. In *Proceedings of the 11th International Conference on Head-Driven Phrase Structure Grammar.* Stanford, CA: CSLI Publications. 27–47.

  2007. Non-restrictive relatives are not orphans. *Journal of Linguistics* 43: 271–309.

Arnold, D. & Bargmann, S. 2016. Idiom licensing in non-restrictive relative clauses (NRCs). Poster presented at PARSEME, 7th General Meeting, Dubrovnik, 26–27 September. bit.ly/34jyvYf

Arnold, D. & Borsley, R. 2008. Non-restrictive relative clauses, ellipsis and anaphora. In S. Müller, ed., *Proceedings of the 15th International Conference on Head-Driven Phrase Structure Grammar*. Stanford, CA: CSLI Publications. 325–45. stanford.io/37BGiCC

2010. Auxiliary-stranding relative clauses. In S. Müller, ed., *Proceedings of the HPSG10 Conference, Université Paris Diderot, Paris 7, France*. Stanford, CA: CSLI Publications. 47–67. bit.ly/37CVe3F

Arsenijević, B. 2009. Clausal complementation as relativization. *Lingua* 119: 39–50.

Arsenijević, B. & Gračanin-Yüksek, M. 2016. Agreement and the structure of relative clauses. *Glossa: A Journal of General Linguistics* 1(1): 17. DOI: doi.org/10.5334/gjgl.12

Arsenijević, B. & Halupka-Rešetar, S. 2013. On the topical nature of non-restrictively used relative pronouns. Paper given at the 35th Annual Conference of the German Linguistic Society, Potsdam, 12–15 March.

Asher, R. E. & Kumari, T. C. 1997. *Malayalam*. London: Routledge.

Assmann, A. 2013. Three stages in the derivation of free relatives. In F. Heck & A. Assmann, eds., *Rule Interaction in Grammar*. Leipzig: Universität Leipzig. 203–45.

Asudeh, A. 2012. *The Logic of Pronominal Resumption*. Oxford: Oxford University Press.

Auger, J. 1994. Pronominal Clitics in Quebec Colloquial French: A Morphological Analysis. PhD diss. University of Pennsylvania. bit.ly/2KSero6

1995. On the history of relative clauses in French and some of its dialects. In H. Andersen, ed., *Historical Linguistics 1993: Selected papers from the 11th international conference on historical linguistics, Los Angeles, 16–20 August 1993*. Amsterdam: Benjamins. 19–32.

Austin, P. 1981. *A Grammar of Diyari*. Cambridge: Cambridge University Press.

Authier, J.-M. & Reed, L. 2005. The diverse nature of non-interrogative *wh*. *Linguistic Inquiry* 36: 635–47.

Aygen, G. 2003. Are there 'non-restrictive' prerelatives in Turkish? *Harvard Working Papers in Linguistics* 8: 199–212.

Bader, M. & Bayer, J. 2006. *Case and Linking in Language Comprehension: Evidence from German*. Dordrecht: Springer.

Bagchi, T. 1994. Bangla correlative pronouns, relative clause order and D-linking. In M. Butt, T. Holloway King & G. Ramchand, eds., *Theoretical Perspectives on Word Order in South Asian Languages*. Stanford, CA: CSLI. 13–30.

Bağrıaçık, M. 2014. Relativization in Pharasiot Greek. MS. University of Ghent.

Bağrıaçık, M. & Danckaert, L. 2016. On the emergence of prenominal and postnominal relative clauses in Pharasiot Greek. MS. University of Ghent.

Baltin, M. 1982. A landing site theory of movement rules. *Linguistic Inquiry* 13: 1–38.

1987. Do antecedent-contained deletions exist? *Linguistic Inquiry* 18: 579–95.

2005. Extraposition. In M. Everaert & H. van Riemsdijk, eds., *The Blackwell Companion to Syntax*. Malden, MA: Blackwell. 237–71.

Barbiers, S. 1995. *The Syntax of Interpretation*. The Hague: Holland Academic Graphics.

2005. Word order variation in three-verb clusters and the division of labour between generative linguistics and sociolinguistics. In L. Cornips & K. P. Corrigan, eds., *Syntax and Variation*. Amsterdam: Benjamins. 233–64.

Barker, C. 2012. Quantificational binding does not require c-command. *Linguistic Inquiry* 43: 614–33.

2019. Evaluation order, crossover, and reconstruction. In M. Krifka & M. Schenner, eds., *Reconstruction Effects in Relative Clauses*. Berlin: de Gruyter. 357–85.

Barss, A., Hale, K., Perkins, E. A. & Speas, M. 1989. Aspects of logical form in Navajo. In E.-D. Cook & K. Rice, eds., *Athapaskan Linguistics: Current perspectives on a language family*. Berlin: Mouton de Gruyter. 317–34.

1992. Logical form and barriers in Navajo. In C.-T. J. Huang & R. May, eds., *Logical Structure and Linguistic Structure: Cross-linguistic perspectives*. Dordrecht: Kluwer. 25–47.

Barwise, J. & Cooper, R. 1981. Generalized quantifiers and natural language. *Linguistics and Philosophy* 4: 159–219.

Basilico, D. 1996. Head position and internally headed relative clauses. *Language* 72: 498–532. www.jstor.org/stable/416277

Bassi, I. & Rasin, E. 2018. Equational-intensional relative clauses with syntactic reconstruction. In U. Sauerland & S. Solt, eds., *Proceedings of Sinn und Bedeutung 22*. Vol. 1. ZASPiL 60. ZAS, Berlin. 143–59.

Battye, A. C. 1989. Free relatives, pseudo-free relatives and the syntax of CP in Italian. *Rivista di Linguistica* 1 (2): 219–46.

Bayer, J. 1984. COMP in Bavarian syntax. *The Linguistic Review* 3: 209–74.

1999. Final complementizers in hybrid languages. *Journal of Linguistics* 35: 233–71.

Bayer, J. & Bader, M. 2007. On the syntax of prepositional phrases. In A. Späth, ed., *Interface and Interface Conditions*. Berlin: Mouton de Gruyter. 157–79.

Bayer, J., Bader, M. & Meng, M. 2001. Morphological underspecification meets oblique case: Syntactic and processing effects in German. *Lingua* 111: 465–514.

Bayer, J. & Salzmann, M. 2013. *That*-trace effects and resumption – How improper movement can be repaired. In P. Brandt & E. Fuß, eds., *Repairs: The added value of being wrong*. Berlin: Mouton de Gruyter. 275–334.

Bayırlı, İ. K. 2017. The universality of concord. PhD diss. MIT. hdl.handle.net/1721.1/113785

Beal, J. C. & Corrigan, K. P. 2002. Relatives in Tyneside and Northumbrian English. In P. Poussa, ed., *Relativisation on the North Sea Littoral*. Munich: Lincom Europa. 125–34.

Beck, D. 2016. Relative clauses in Upper Necaxa Totonac. *Linguistic Discovery* 14: 1–45. DOI:10.1349/PS1.1537-0852.A.469

Beermann, D. & Ephrem, B. 2007. The definite article and possessive marking in Amharic. In F. Hoyt, N. Seifert, A. Teodorescu & J. White, eds., *Proceedings of the Texas Linguistics Society IX Conference*. Stanford, CA: CSLI Publications. 21–32. stanford.io/2qDRiz2

Belikova, A. 2008. Syntactically challenged rather than reduced: Participial relatives revisited. Proceedings of the 2008 annual conference of the Canadian Linguistic Association. bit.ly/2OmzAc3

Belletti, A. 1982. 'Morphological' passive and pro drop: The impersonal construction in Italian. *Journal of Linguistic Reserch.* 2 (4): 1–33.

1988. The case of unaccusatives. *Linguistic Inquiry* 19: 1–34.

2004. Aspects of the low IP area. In L. Rizzi, ed., *The Structure of CP and IP*. New York: Oxford University Press. 16–51.

Benincà, P. 1994. *La variazione sintattica. Studi di dialettologia romanza*. Bologna: Il Mulino.

1995. I dati dell'ASIS e la sintassi diacronica. In E. Banfi, G. Bonfadini, P. Cordin, & M. Iliescu, eds., *Italia settentrionale: Crocevia di idiomi romanzi*. Tübingen: Niemeyer. 131–41.

2003. La frase relativa in fiorentino antico. V° Incontro di dialettologia, University of Bristol, 26–27 September.

2007. Headless relative clauses in Old Italian and some related issues. Handout of a paper presented at the Université de Paris VIII, 13 December.

2010. Headless relatives in some Old Italian varieties. In R. D'Alessandro, A. Ledgeway & I. Roberts, eds., *Syntactic Variation: The Dialects of Italy*. Cambridge: Cambridge University Press. 55–70.

2012a. Frasi relative e strutture copulari. In V. Orioles and P. Borghello, eds., *Per Roberto Gusmani: Studi in ricordo*. Udine: Forum. 251–67.

2012b. Lexical complementizers and headless relatives. In L. Brugè, A. Cardinaletti, G. Giusti, N. Munaro & C. Poletto, eds., *Functional Heads*. The cartography of syntactic structures. Vol. 7. New York: Oxford University Press. 29–41.

2012c. Determiners and relative clauses. *Iberia: An International Journal of Theoretical Linguistics* 4 (1): 92–109.

2012d. Relatives and copular structures. *Padua Working Papers in Linguistics* 5: 29–44. bit.ly/2OkMhUW.

Benincà, P. & Cinque, G. 1991. Participio presente. In L. Renzi & G. Salvi, eds., *Grande Grammatica Italiana di Consultazione. Vol. II*. Bologna: il Mulino. 604–9.

2010 La frase relativa. In G. Salvi & L. Renzi, eds., *Grammatica dell'italiano antico. Vol. I*. Bologna: Il Mulino. 469–507.

2014 Kind-defining relative clauses in the diachrony of Italian. In P. Benincà, A. Ledgeway & N. Vincent, eds., *Diachrony and Dialects: Grammatical change in the dialects of Italy*. Oxford: Oxford University Press. 257–78.

Benincà, P. & Poletto, C. 2004. Topic, focus and V2: Defining the CP sublayers. In L. Rizzi, ed., *The Structure of CP and IP*. The cartography of syntactic structures. Vol. 2. New York: Oxford University Press. 52–75.

Benincà, P. & Tortora, C. 2009. Towards a finer-grained theory of Italian participial clausal architecture. *University of Pennsylvania Working Papers in Linguistics*. 15 (1), Article 4. repository.upenn.edu/pwpl/vol15/iss1/4

Benincà, P. & Vanelli, L. 1982. Appunti di sintassi veneta. In M. Cortelazzo, ed., *Guida ai dialetti veneti IV*. Padova: CLEUP. 7–38.

Berg, R. van den. 1989. *A Grammar of the Muna Language*. Dordrecht: Foris.

Berizzi, M. 2001. The theory of relative clauses and the dialects of English. Thesis. University of Padua.

Berman A. 1974. Infinitival relative constructions. *Papers from the 10th Regional Meeting of the Chicago Linguistic Society*. Chicago: Chicago Linguistic Society. 37–46.

Berman, H. 1972. Subordinate clauses in Yurok – A preliminary report. In P. M. Peranteau, J. N. Levi & G. C. Phares, eds., *The Chicago Which Hunt: Papers from the relative clause festival*. Chicago: Chicago Linguistic Society. 256–61.

Berry, K. & Berry, C. 1999. *A Description of Abun: A West Papuan language of Irian Jaya*. Canberra: Australian National University.

Bertollo, S. 2014. On relatives with a null head: German free relative clauses and clefts. PhD diss. University of Padua. bit.ly/2rsb0xH

Bertollo, S. & Cavallo, G. 2012. The syntax of Italian free relative clauses: An analysis. *Generative Grammar in Geneva* 8: 59–76. bit.ly/33mrBQz

Bertone, C. 2006. La struttura del sintagma determinante nella Lingua dei Segni Italiana (LIS). PhD diss. Ca' Foscari University, Venice. lear.unive.it/jspui/bitstream/11707/313/1/Bertone.pdf

Bevington, G. 1979. Relativization in Albanian dialects. *Folia Slavica* 3: 263–94.

Bhatia, T. K. 1993. *Punjabi*. London: Routledge.

Bhatt, R. 1997. Matching effects and the syntax-morphology interface: Evidence from Hindi correlatives. In B. Bruening, ed., *Proceedings of SCIL 8*. MIT Working Papers in Linguistics 31. Cambridge, MA: MITWPL. 53–68.

1999. Covert modality in non-finite contexts. PhD diss. University of Pennsylvania.

2002. The raising analysis of relative clauses: Evidence from adjectival modification. *Natural Language Semantics* 10: 43–90.

2003. Locality in correlatives. *Natural Language and Linguistic Theory* 21: 485–541.

2005. Correlative clauses. Handout of a course at the 2005 LOT Summer School, Leiden, 16 June. people.umass.edu/bhatt/752-s05/n44.pdf.

2006. *Covert Modality in Non-finite Contexts*. Berlin: de Gruyter.

2015. Relative clauses and correlatives. In A. Alexiadou & T. Kiss, eds., *Syntax – Theory and Analysis. An international handbook*. Vol. 1. Berlin: Mouton de Gruyter. 708–49.

Bhatt, R. & Pancheva, R. 2012. Two superlative puzzles. Paper given at Generative Initiatives in Syntactic Theory (GIST), 22–23 March, University of Ghent.

Bhatt, R. M. 1999. *Verb Movement and the Syntax of Kashmiri*. Dordrecht: Kluwer.

Bianchi, V. 1991. Le relative infinitive e altre strutture modali infinitive in italiano. *Quaderni del Laboratorio di Linguistica* 5: 51–69.

1993. An empirical contribution to the study of idiomatic expressions. *Rivista di Linguistica* 5: 349–85. linguistica.sns.it/RdL/5.2/Bianchi.pdf

1995. Consequences of Antisymmetry for the syntax of headed relative clauses. PhD diss. Scuola Normale Superiore, Pisa.

1999. *Consequences of Antisymmetry: Headed relative clauses*. Berlin: Mouton de Gruyter.

2000a. The raising analysis of relative clauses: A reply to Borsley. *Linguistic Inquiry* 31: 123–40.

2000b. Some issues in the syntax of relative determiners. In A. Alexiadou, P. Law, A. Meinunger & C. Wilder, eds., *The Syntax of Relative Clauses*. Amsterdam: Benjamins. 53–81.

2002. Headed relative clauses in generative syntax. *Glot International*, Part I, 6 (7): 197–204; Part II 6 (8): 235–47.

2004. Resumptive relatives and LF chains. In L. Rizzi, ed., *The Structure of CP and IP. The cartography of syntactic structures*. Vol. 2. New York: Oxford University Press. 76–114.

2007. Wh-infinitives and the licensing of 'Anaphoric Tense'. In M. C. Picchi & A. Pona, eds., *Proceedings of the XXXII Incontro di Grammatica Generativa*. Alessandria: Edizioni dell'Orso. 35–47.

2011. Some notes on the specificity effects of optional resumptive pronouns. In A. Rouveret, ed., *Resumptive Pronouns at the Interfaces*. Amsterdam: Benjamins. 319–42.

Bickel, B. 1995. Relatives à antécédent interne, nominalisation et focalisation: Entre syntaxe et morphologie en bélharien. *Bulletin de la Société de Linguistique de Paris, XC* 1: 391–427.

Bidese, E., Padovan, A. & Tomaselli, A. 2012. A binary system of complementizers in Cimbrian relative clauses. *Working Papers in Scandinavian Syntax* 90: 1–21. bit.ly/37IOscE

Bird, C. B. 1968. Relative clauses in Bambara. *The Journal of West African Languages* 5: 35–47.

Biskup, P. & Šimík, R. 2019. Structure of conditional and (cor)relative clauses: New evidence from locality. MS. ling.auf.net/lingbuzz/004573

Bliese, L. 1981. *A Generative Grammar of Afar*. Arlington: Summer Institute of Linguistics and the University of Texas.

Blümel, A. 2011. *Derjenige* determiner that wants a relative clause. *University of Pennsylvania Working Papers in Linguistics* 17(1): 21–9. https://repository.upenn .edu/pwpl/vol17/iss1/4

Blümel, A. & Liu, M. 2019. Revisiting obligatory relatives in German: Empirical and theoretical perspectives. MS. Georg-August-Universität Göttingen.

Bobaljik, J. D. 2017. Adjectival hydras: Restrictive modifiers above DP. In C. Mayr & E. Williams, eds., *Festschrift für Martin Prinzhorn*. Wiener Linguistische Gazette 82. Vienna: Institute of Linguistics, University of Vienna. 13–22. bit.ly/2KYQxat

Bodomo, A. B. & Hiraiwa, K. 2004. Relativization in Dagaare. *Journal of Dagaare Studies* 4: 53–75.

2010. Relativization in Dàgáárè and its typological implications: Left-headed but internally-headed. *Lingua* 120: 953–83. DOI: doi.org/10.1016/j.lingua.2009.06.008

Boeckx, C. 2003. *Islands and Chains: Resumption as stranding*. Amsterdam: Benjamins.

Boef, E. 2012. Doubling in Dutch restrictive relative clauses: Rethinking the head external analysis. In E. Boone, K. Linke & M. Schulpen, eds., *Proceedings of ConSOLE XIX*. Leiden: Universiteit Leiden. 125–49.

2013. Doubling in relative clauses: Aspects of morphosyntactic microvariation in Dutch. PhD diss. Utrecht University. dspace.library.uu.nl/handle/1874/261909

Bogal-Allbritten, E. & Moulton, K. 2017. Navajo in the typology of internally-headed relatives. *Proceedings of SALT 27*. 700–20. bit.ly/2qELoh3

Bogal-Allbritten, E., Moulton, K. & Shimoyama, J. 2016. Stay inside: The interpretation of internally headed relative clauses in Navajo. Paper presented at the

Canadian Linguistics Association Meeting. elizabethba.files.wordpress.com/2014/03/cla-talk.pdf

Boisson, C. 1981. Hiérarchie universelle des spécifications de temps, de lieu, et de manière. *Confluents* 7: 69–124.

Bokamba, E. & Dramé, M. 1978. Where do relative clauses come from in Mandingo? *Papers from the 14th Regional Meeting of the Chicago Linguistic Society*. Chicago: Chicago Linguistic Society. 28–43.

Bonneau, J. 1990. Logical form and an analysis of the matching effect in free relatives. *McGill Working Papers in Linguistics* 6 (2): 137–66.

1992. The structure of internally headed relative clauses: Implications for configurationality. PhD diss. McGill University.

Borer, H. 1984. Restrictive relatives in Modern Hebrew. *Natural Language and Linguistic Theory* 2: 219–60.

Borsley, R. D. 1984. Free relatives in Polish and English. In J. Fisiak, ed., *Contrastive Linguistics: Prospects and Problems*. Berlin: Mouton. 1–18.

1997. Relative clauses and the theory of phrase structure. *Linguistic Inquiry* 28: 629–47.

2001. More on the raising analysis of relative clauses. MS. University of Essex.

2010. The diversity of relative clauses. Handout of a talk given at the Colchester which hunt – A workshop in relative clauses. 4 June.

Bošković, Ž. 2009. On relativization strategies and resumptive pronouns. In G. Zybatow, U. Junghanns, D. Lenertová & P. Biskup, eds., *Studies in Formal Slavic Phonology, Morphology, Syntax, Semantics and Information Structure: Proceedings of FDSL 7*. Frankfurt am Main: Peter Lang. 79–93.

2012. On NPs and clauses. In G. Grewendorf & T. E. Zimmermann, eds., *Discourse and Grammar*. Berlin: Mouton de Gruyter. 179–242.

2018. On movement out of moved elements, labels, and phases. *Linguistic Inquiry* 49: 247–82.

Bouton, L. 1970. Antecedent contained proforms. In *Papers from the 6th Regional Meeting of the Chicago Linguistic Society*. Chicago: Chicago Linguistic Society. 154–67.

Bowern, C. 2012. *A Grammar of Bardi*. Berlin: Mouton.

Boyle, J. P. 2007. Hidatsa morphosyntax and clause structure. PhD diss. Chicago: University of Chicago.

2016. The syntax and semantics of internally headed relative clauses in Hidatsa. In C. Rudin & B. J. Gordon, eds., *Advances in the Study of Siouan Languages and Linguistics*. Berlin: Language Science Press. 255–87.

Bradley, C. H. & Hollenbach, B. E. 1992, eds., *Studies in the syntax of Mixtecan languages*. Vol. 4. Dallas: Summer Institute of Linguistics and the University of Texas at Arlington.

Bradshaw, J. 2009. Relative-clause bracketing in Oceanic languages around the Huon Gulf of New Guinea. In A. Adelaar & A. Pawley, eds., *Austronesian Historical Linguistics and Culture History: A festschrift for Robert Blust*. Canberra: Pacific Linguistics. 143–61.

Brame, M. 1967. A new analysis of the relative clause: Evidence for an interpretive theory. MS. MIT.

1976. *Conjectures and Refutations in Syntax and Semantics*. New York: North Holland Publishing Co.

Branchini, C. 2014. *On Relativization and Clefting: An analysis of Italian sign language*. Berlin: De Gruyter Mouton and Preston: Ishara Press.

Branchini, C. & Donati, C. 2009. Relatively different: Italian sign language relative clauses in a typological perspective. In A. Lipták, ed., *Correlatives Cross-Linguistically*. Amsterdam: Benjamins. 157–91.

Brandner, E. & Bräuning, I. 2013. Relative *wo* in Alemannic: Only a complementizer? *Linguistische Berichte* 234: 131–69.

Breivik, L. E. 1997. Relative infinitives in English. *Studia Neophilologica* 69: 109–37.

Bresnan, J. 1973. 'Headless' relatives. Mimeograph. University of Massachusetts, Amherst.

Bresnan, J. & J. Grimshaw. 1978. The syntax of free relatives in English. *Linguistic Inquiry* 9: 331–91.

Bretonnel Cohen, K. 2000. *Aspects of the Grammar of Kukù*. Munich: Lincom Europa.

Brillman, R. 2015. Improper movement in tough constructions and gapped degree phrases. *University of Pennsylvania Working Papers in Linguistics* 21: Article 4. repository.upenn.edu/pwpl/vol21/iss1/4

Brito, A. M. 1991. A sintaxe das oraçoes relativas em português. PhD diss. Centro de Linguística da Universidade do Porto.

2005. As relativas não restritivas como um caso particular de aposição. *Actas do XX Encontro Nacional da Associação Portuguesa de Linguística*. Lisbon: Associação Portuguesa de Linguística. 401–19.

Browne, W. 1970. Noun phrase definiteness in relatives and questions: Evidence from Macedonian. *Linguistic Inquiry* 1: 267–70.

1986. *Relative clauses in Serbo-Croatian in comparison with English. The Yugoslav Serbo-Croatian–English Contrastive Project*. Vol. 4. Zagreb, University of Zagreb.

Browning, M. 1987. Null Operator Constructions. PhD diss. MIT.

Brucart, J. M. 1992. Some asymmetries in the functioning of relative pronouns in Spanish. *Catalan Working Papers in Linguistics* 2: 113–43. ddd.uab.cat/record/20988

1999. La estructura del sintagma nominal: Las oraciones de relativo. In I. Bosque & V. Demonte, eds., *Gramatica descriptiva de la lengua española*. Madrid: Espasa Calpe. 395–522.

Bruening, B. 2001. Syntax at the edge: Cross-clausal phenomena and the syntax of Passamaquoddy. PhD diss. MIT. dspace.mit.edu/handle/1721.1/8198

2015. Idioms: Movement and non-movement dependencies. MS. University of Delaware. udel.edu/~bruening/Downloads/IdiomsMovement1.pdf

Brugger, G. & Prinzhorn. M. 1996. Some Properties of German Determiners. MS. University of Vienna.

Brunelli, M. 2006. The grammar of Italian sign language, with a study about its restrictive relative clauses. MA diss. Ca' Foscari University, Venice.

2011. Antisymmetry and sign languages: A comparison between NGT and LIS. PhD diss. University of Amsterdam and Ca' Foscari University, Venice. bit.ly/37J5W8J

Bugaeva, A. & Whitman, J. 2014. Deconstructing clausal noun modifying constructions. *Japanese/Korean Linguistics* 23: 1–12. stanford.io/2ruaQFW

Büring, D. 2002. Orphan attributes. In L. Mikkelsen & C. Potts, eds., *Proceedings of the 21st West Coast Conference on Formal Linguistics*. Somerville, MA: Cascadilla Press. 100–13. bit.ly/37HIJUn

Burton-Roberts, N. 1975. Nominal apposition. *Foundations of Language* 13: 391–419.

Bury, D. 2003. Phrase structure and derived heads. PhD diss. University College London.

Burzio, L. 1981. Intransitive verbs and Italian auxiliaries. PhD diss. MIT.

   1986. *Italian Syntax: A government-binding approach*. Dordrecht: Reidel.

Butler, A. 2002. Relatives and there-insertion. In M. van Koppen, E. Thrift, E. J. van der Torre & M. Zimmermann, eds., *Proceedings of ConSOLE IX*. 28–40. bit.ly/2ruQ4Gk

Butt, M., Holloway King, T. & Roth, S. 2007. Urdu correlatives: Theoretical and implementational issues. In M. Butt & T. Holloway King, eds., *Proceedings of the LFG07 Conference*. Stanford, CA: CSLI Publications. stanford.io/33p2yfY

Cable, S. 2005. Free relatives in Lingít and Haida: Evidence that the mover projects. MS. MIT. bit.ly/2OPoc7J

   2010a. *The Grammar of Q: Q-particles, wh-movement, and pied-piping*. New York: Oxford University Press.

   2010b. Against the existence of pied-piping: evidence from Tlingit. *Linguistic Inquiry* 41: 563–94.

   2012. Pied-Piping: Introducing two recent approaches. *Language and Linguistics Compass* 6 (12): 816–32.

   2013. Pied-Piping: Comparing two recent approaches. *Language and Linguistics Compass* 7 (2): 123–40.

Cabredo Hofherr, P. 2014. Reduced definite articles with restrictive relative clauses. In P. Cabredo Hofherr & A. Zribi-Hertz, eds., *Crosslinguistic Studies on Noun Phrase Structure and Reference*. Syntax and Semantics, Vol. 39. Leiden: Brill. 172–211. bit.ly/2DnFfZb

Cagri, I. M. 2005. Minimality and Turkish relative clauses. PhD diss. University of Maryland, College Park.

Caha, P. 2009. The Nanosyntax of Case. PhD diss. CASTL, University of Tromsø.

Callegari, E. 2014. Why locality-based accounts of the left periphery are unfit to account for its variation. Paper given at the Variation in C Workshop, Venice, 21 October.

Camacho, J. 2003. *The Structure of Coordination: Conjunction and agreement phenomena in Spanish and other languages*. Dordrecht: Kluwer.

Camilleri, M. & Sadler, L. 2016. Relativisation in Maltese. *Transactions of the Philological Society* 114: 117–45. bit.ly/2rvN10B

Canac Marquis, R. & Tremblay, M. 1998. The *wh*-feature and the syntax of restrictive and non-restrictive relatives in French and English. In J. Lema & E. Treviño, eds., *Theoretical Analyses of Romance Languages*. Amsterdam: Benjamins. 127–41.

Cantrall, W. R. 1972. Relative identity. In P. M. Peranteau, J. N. Levi, G. C. Phares, eds., *Papers from the 8th Regional Meeting of the Chicago Linguistic Society*. Chicago: Chicago Linguistic Society. 22–31.

Caponigro, I. 2003. Free not to ask: On the semantics of free relatives and wh-words cross-linguistically. PhD diss. UCLA.

2004. The semantic contribution of *wh*-words and type shifts: Evidence from free relatives cross-linguistically. In R. B. Young, ed., *Proceedings of SALT 14*. Ithaca, NY: Cornell University CLC Publications. 38–55.

2019. In defense of what(ever) free relative clauses they dismiss: A reply to Donati and Cecchetto (2011). *Linguistic Inquiry* 50 (2): 356–71. DOI: doi.org/10.1162/ling_a_00311

Caponigro, I. & Fălăuş, A. 2018a. Free choice free relatives in Italian and Romanian. *Natural Language and Linguistic Theory* 36: 323–63. DOI: doi.org/10.1007/s11049-017-9375-y

2018b. The functional nature of multiple wh- free relative clauses. *Proceedings of SALT 28*. 566–83. bit.ly/37H208q

Caponigro, I. & Pearl, L. 2008. Silent prepositions: Evidence from free relatives. In A. Asbury, J. Dotlačil, B. Gehrke & R. Nouwen, eds., *Syntax and Semantics of Spatial P*. Amsterdam: Benjamins. 365–85. bit.ly/2L0r0xz

2009. The nominal nature of *where, when,* and *how*: Evidence from free relatives. *Linguistic Inquiry* 40: 155–64. DOI: doi.org/10.1162/ling.2009.40.1.155

Caponigro, I. & Polinsky, M. 2008. Relatively speaking (in Circassian). *Proceedings of the 27th West Coast Conference on Formal Linguistics*. Somerville, MA: Cascadilla Proceedings Project. 81–9. www.lingref.com/cpp/wccfl/27/paper1819.pdf

2011. Relative embeddings: A Circassian puzzle for the syntax/semantics interface. *Natural Language and Linguistic Theory* 29: 71–122.

Caponigro, I., Torrence, H. & Cisneros, C. 2013. Free relative clauses in two Mixtec languages. *International Journal of American Linguistics* 79(1): 61–96. bit.ly/2L0FJsx

Cardoso, A. 2010. Variation and change in the syntax of relative clauses. New evidence from Portuguese. PhD diss. University of Lisbon. core.ac.uk/download/pdf/12423109.pdf

Cardoso, A. & De Vries, M. 2010. Internal and external heads in appositive constructions. MS. bit.ly/2XSLFsR

Carlson, G. 1977. Amount relatives. *Language* 53: 520–42.

Carlson, R. 1994. *A Grammar of Supyire*. Berlin: Mouton de Gruyter.

Casalicchio, J. 2013a. *Pseudorelative, gerundi e infiniti nelle varietà romanze: affinità (solo) superficiali e corrispondenze strutturali*. Munich: Lincom Europa. bit.ly/2QWd9fx

2013b. The pseudo-relatives and other correspondent constructions in the Romance languages. In I. Windhaber & P. Anreiter, eds., *Proceedings of the 4th Austrian Students' Conference of Linguistics*. Newcastle upon Tyne: Cambridge Scholars Publishing. 64–84.

2015. La costruzione 'con + DP + pseudorelativa': Proposta per una duplice interpretazione. In *Plurilinguismo/Sintassi: Atti del XLVI Congresso Internazionale di Studi della Società di Linguistica Italiana*. Rome: Bulzoni. 467–82.

2016a. The use of gerunds and infinitives in perceptive constructions: The effects of a threefold parametric variation in some Romance varieties. In E. Bidese, F. Cognola & M. C. Moroni, eds., *Theoretical Approaches to Linguistic Variation*. Amsterdam: Benjamins. 53–87.

2016b. Pseudo-relatives and their left-periphery. A unified account. In E. Carrilho, A. Fiéis, M. Lobo & S. Pereira, eds., *Romance Languages and Linguistic Theory 10: Selected papers from 'Going Romance' 28, Lisbon*. Amsterdam: Benjamins. 23–42.

Catasso, N. 2013. For a headed analysis of free relatives in German and English: The 'free relative economy principle'. *Linguistics Journal* 7: 273–93.

2014. Wie viele Jungs haben Anna geküsst? Zum besonderen Status von V2-Relativsätzen im gesprochenen Deutsch. *Linguistik Online* 67 (5): 45–68. DOI: doi.org/10.13092/lo.67.1599

Catasso, N. & Hinterhölzl, R. 2016. On the question of subordination or coordination in V2-relatives in German. In I. Reich & A. Speyer, eds., *Co- and Subordination in German and Other Languages*. Hamburg: Helmut Buske Verlag. 99–124.

Cattaneo, A. 2007. Italian null objects, resultative/depictive predication, and HAB. *NYU Working Papers in Linguistics* 1.

Cecchetto, C. 2006. Reconstruction in relative clauses and the copy theory of traces. *Linguistic Variation Yearbook* 5: 73–103.

Cecchetto, C. & Donati, C. 2010. On labeling: Principle C and head movement. *Syntax* 13: 241–78.

2011. Relabeling heads: a unified account for relativization structures. *Linguistic Inquiry* 42: 519–60. ling.auf.net/lingBuzz/001014

2015. *(Re)labeling*. Cambridge, MA: MIT Press.

2020. Relabeling participial constructions. In L. Franco & P. Lorusso, eds., *Linguistic Variation: Structure and Interpretation*. Berlin: Mouton de Gruyter. 149–62.

Cecchetto, C., Geraci, C. & Zucchi, S. 2006. Strategies of relativization in Italian Sign Language. *Natural Language and Linguistic Theory* 24: 945–75.

Cennamo, M. 1997. Relative clauses. In M. Maiden & M. Parry, eds., *The Dialects of Italy*. London: Routledge. 190–201.

Čeplová, M. 2007. Infinitives under 'have'/'be' in Czech. In M. Dočekal, P. Karlík & Zmrzlíková, eds., *Czech in Generative Grammar*. Munich: Lincom Europa. 31–45.

Cha, J.-Y. 1998. Relative clause or noun complement clause: Some Diagnoses. MS. University of Illinois at Urbana-Champaign.

1999. Semantics of Korean Gapless Relative Clause Constructions. *Studies in the Linguistic Sciences* 29: 25–41.

Chao, Y. R. 1968. *A Grammar of Spoken Chinese*. Berkeley, CA: University of California Press.

Chaves, R. P. 2012. Conjunction, cumulation and respectively readings. *Journal of Linguistics* 48: 297–344. DOI:10.1017/S0022226712000059

Chen, Y. & Fukuda, S. 2018. An experimental investigation of the reconstruction of anaphors in Japanese relative clauses. In C. Guillemot, T. Yoshida & S. J. Lee, eds., *Proceedings of the 13th Workshop on Altaic Formal Linguistics*. MIT Working Papers in Linguistics 88. Cambridge, MA: MITWPL. 311–18.

Cheng, L. L.-S. 2000. Moving just the feature. In U. Lutz, G. Müller & A. von Stechow, eds., *Wh-Scope Marking*. Amsterdam: Benjamins. 77–99.

Cheng, L. L.-S. & Downing, L. J. 2010. Locative relatives in Durban Zulu. *ZAS Papers in Linguistics* 53: 33–51.

Cheng, L. L.-S., & Sybesma, R. 2005. A Chinese relative. In H. Broekhuis, N. Corver, R. Huybregts, U. Kleinhenz & J. Koster, eds., *Organizing Grammar: Studies in Honor of Henk van Riemsdijk*. Berlin: Mouton de Gruyter. 69–76.

Chidambaram, V. S. 2013. On resumptive pronouns in Slavic. PhD diss. Princeton University.

Chierchia, G. & Caponigro, I. 2013. Questions on questions and free relatives. Handout of a paper presented at Sinn und Bedeutung, Vitoria, Basque Country. bit.ly/2r5EO3f

Chomsky, N. 1957. *Syntactic Structures*. The Hague: Mouton.

1965. *Aspects of the Theory of Syntax*. Cambridge, MA: MIT Press.

1973. Conditions on tranformations. In S. Anderson & P. Kiparsky, eds., *A Festschrift for Morris Halle*. New York: Holt, Rinehart & Winston. 232–86.

1975. Questions of form and interpretation. *Linguistic Analysis* 1: 75–109.

1977. On wh-movement. In P. W. Culicover, T. Wasow, & A. Akmajian, eds., *Formal Syntax*. New York: Academic Press. 71–132.

1980. On binding. *Linguistic Inquiry* 11: 1–46.

1981. *Lectures on Government and Binding*. Dordrecht: Foris.

1982. *Some Concepts and Consequences of the Theory of Government and Binding*. Cambridge, MA: MIT Press.

1986. *Knowledge of Language: Its nature, origin, and use*. New York: Praeger.

1993. A minimalist program for linguistic theory. In K. Hale & S. J. Keyser, eds., *The View from Building 20: Essays in linguistics in honor of Sylvain Bromberger*. Cambridge, MA: MIT Press. 1–52.

1995. *The Minimalist Program*. Cambridge, MA: MIT Press.

2001. Derivation by Phase. In M. Kenstowicz, ed., *Ken Hale: A life in language*. Cambridge, MA: MIT Press. 1–52.

2004. Beyond explanatory adequacy. In A. Belletti, ed., *Structures and Beyond*. The cartography of syntactic structures. Vol. 3. New York: Oxford University Press. 104–31.

2008. On phases. In R. Freidin, C. P. Otero & M. L. Zubizarreta, eds., *Foundational Issues in Linguistic Theory: Essays in honor of Jean-Roger Vergnaud*. Cambridge, MA: MIT Press. 133–66.

2013. Problems of projection. *Lingua* 130: 33–49.

2015. A discussion with Naoki Fukui and Mihoko Zushi. In N. Fukui, ed., *Noam Chomsky: The Sophia lectures*. Sophia Linguistica Working Papers in Linguistics 64. Tokyo: Sophia University. 71–97.

Chomsky, N. Gallego, Á. J. & Ott, D. 2017/2019. Generative grammar and the faculty of language: Insights, questions, and challenges. MS. MIT. ling.auf.net/lingbuzz/003507

Chomsky, N. & Lasnik, H. 1977. Filters and control. *Linguistic Inquiry* 8: 425–504.

Choueiri, L. 2002. Issues in the syntax of resumption: Restrictive relatives in Lebanese Arabic. PhD diss. University of Southern California, Los Angeles.

Christensen, K. R. & Nyvad, A. M. 2014. On the nature of escapable relative islands. *Nordic Journal of Linguistics* 37: 29–45. DOI: 10.1017/S0332586514000055

Chung, S. 1987. The syntax of Chamorro existential sentences. In E. J. Reuland & A. G. B. ter Meulen, eds., *The Representation of (In)definiteness*. Cambridge, MA: MIT Press. 191–225.

Chung, S. & McCloskey, J. 1983. On the interpretation of certain island facts in GPSG. *Linguistic Inquiry* 14: 704–13.

Cinque, G. 1976. 'Mica': note di sintassi e pragmatica. *Annali della Facoltà di Lettere e Filosofia dell'Università di Padova*, 1. 101–12. lear.unive.it/jspui/bitstream/11707/5924/1/Mica.pdf

Cinque, G. 1978. La sintassi dei pronomi relativi 'cui' e 'quale' nell'italiano moderno. *Rivista di grammatica generativa* 3 (1): 31–126. bit.ly/33FwhRN

1979. Left dislocation in Italian: A syntactic and pragmatic analysis. *Cahiers de lexicologie* XXXIV: 96–127.

1981. On Keenan and Comrie's primary relativization constraint. *Linguistic Inquiry* 12: 293–308.

1982. On the theory of relative clauses and markedness. *The Linguistic Review* 1: 247–94. Reprinted with corrections in G. Cinque 1995 *Italian Syntax and Universal Grammar*. Cambridge: Cambridge University Press. 54–103.

1988. La frase relativa. In L. Renzi, ed., *Grande grammatica italiana di consultazione*. Vol 1. Bologna: Il Mulino. 443–503.

1990. *Types of A'- Dependencies*. Cambridge, MA: MIT Press.

1991. *Teoria linguistica e sintassi italiana*. Bologna: Il Mulino.

1994. On the evidence for partial N-movement in the Romance DP. In G. Cinque, J. Koster, J.-Y. Pollock, L. Rizzi & R. Zanuttini, eds., *Paths Towards Universal Grammar: Studies in honor of Richard S. Kayne*. Washington: Georgetown University Press. 85–110.

1995. The pseudo-relative and ACC-ing constructions after verbs of perception. In G. Cinque, *Italian Syntax and Universal Grammar*. Cambridge: Cambridge University Press. 244–75.

1996. The antisymmetric programme: Theoretical and typological implications. *Journal of Linguistics* 32: 447–64.

1999 *Adverbs and Functional Heads: A cross-linguistic perspective*. New York: Oxford University Press.

2002. Complement and adverbial PPs: Implications for clause structure. MS. University of Venice.

2003. The prenominal origin of relative clauses. Paper presented at the Workshop on Antisymmetry and Remnant Movement, New York University, 31 October–1 November.

2004a. 'Restructuring' and functional structure. In A. Belletti, ed., *Structures and Beyond*. The cartography of syntactic structures. Vol. 3. New York: Oxford University Press. 132–91.

2004b. A phrasal movement analysis of the Romanian DP. In A. Minuţ & E. Munteanu, eds., *Studia linguistica et philologica in honorem D. Irimia*. Iaşi: Editura Universităţii 'A. I. Cuza'. 129–42. bit.ly/34JVcVF

2005. Deriving Greenberg's universal 20 and its exceptions. *Linguistic Inquiry* 36: 315–32. bit.ly/2Y8YoHS

2006a. Two types of appositives. *University of Venice Working Papers in Linguistics* 16: 7–56. bit.ly/35ZcMp1

2006b. *Restructuring and Functional Heads*. The cartography of syntactic structures. Vol. 4. New York: Oxford University Press.

2007. A note on linguistic theory and typology. *Linguistic Typology* 11. 93–106. hdl.handle.net/11707/123

2008a. Two types of non-restrictive relatives. *Empirical Issues in Syntax and Semantics* 7: 99–137. www.cssp.cnrs.fr/eiss7

2008b. More on the indefinite character of the Head of restrictive relatives. In P. Benincà, F. Damonte & N. Penello, eds., *Selected Proceedings of the 34th Incontro di Grammatica Generativa*, Padova: Unipress. bit.ly/34HacDS

2009a. The fundamental left–right asymmetry of natural languages. In S. Scalise, E. Magni & A. Bisetto, eds., *Universals of Language Today*. Dordrecht: Springer 165–84. DOI: 10.1007/978-1-4020-8825-4_9

2009b. Five notes on correlatives. In R. Mohanty & M. Menon, eds., *Universals and Variation: Proceedings of Glow in Asia VII 2009*. Hyderabad: EFL University Press. 1–20. bit.ly/2YdzJlu

2010a. *The Syntax of Adjectives: A comparative study*. Cambridge, MA: MIT Press.

2010b. On a selective 'violation' of the complex NP constraint. In J.-W. Zwart & M. De Vries, eds., *Structure Preserved: Studies in syntax for Jan Koster*. Amsterdam: Benjamins. 81–90. bit.ly/2DEGkMm

2011a. Greenberg's universal 23 and SVO languages. In M. Frascarelli, ed., *Structures and Meanings: Cross-theoretical perspectives*. Paris and Rome: L'Harmattan. 75–80. bit.ly/2LjMGoG

2011b. On double-headed relative clauses. *Linguística. Revista de Estudos Linguísticos da Universidade do Porto*. 6: 67–91.

2013a. Word order typology. A change of perspective. In T. M. Biberauer & M. Sheehan, eds., *Theoretical Approaches to Disharmonic Word Orders*. Oxford: Oxford University Press. 47–73. hdl.handle.net/11707/154

2013b *Typological Studies: Word order and relative clauses*. London: Routledge.

2014. Again on tense, aspect, mood morpheme order and the 'mirror principle'. In P. Svenonius, ed., *Functional Structure from Top to Toe*. The cartography of syntactic structures. Vol. 9. New York: Oxford University Press. 232–65.

2015a. Three phenomena discriminating between 'raising' and 'matching' relative clauses. *Semantics-Syntax Interface* 2 (1): 1–27.

2015b. A note on 'other'. In E. Brandner, A. Czypionka, C. Freitag & A. Trotzke, eds., *Charting the Landscape of Linguistics: Webschrift for Josef Bayer*. Konstanz: Universität Konstanz. 22–7.

2017a. On a difference between Italian, and English and French present participle relatives. In C. Mayr & E. Williams, eds., *Festschrift für Martin Prinzhorn*. Wiener Linguistische Gazette 82. 37–50.

2017b. A microparametric approach to the head-initial/head-final parameter. In S. Karimi & M. Piattelli-Palmarini, eds., *Parameters: What are they? Where are they? Linguistic Analysis* 41. 309–66. hdl.handle.net/11707/6084

2018. Some notes on meaningless movement. Paper presented at the University of Geneva, 6 February, and at the 44th Annual Meeting of Generative Grammar, Rome, 1–3 March.

2020. On the double-headed analysis of 'headless' relative clauses'. In L. Franco & P. Lorusso, eds., *Linguistic Variation: Structure and interpretation*. Studies in generative grammar 132. Berlin: De Gruyter Mouton. 169–96. DOI: doi.org/10.1515/9781501505201-011

In preparation. On Greenberg's universal 20: Refinements and replies.

Cinque, G. & Benincà, P. 2018. Notes on infinitival relatives in Italian. In M. Grimaldi, R. Lai, L. Franco & B. Baldi, eds., *Structuring Variation in Romance Linguistics and Beyond: In honour of Leonardo M. Savoia*. Amsterdam: Benjamins. 73–84.

Citko, B. 2000. Parallel merge and the syntax of free relatives. PhD diss. State University of New York, Stony Brook.

2001. Deletion under identity in relative clauses. *Proceedings of NELS 31*. Amherst, MA: GLSA. 131–45.

2002. Anti-reconstruction effects in free relatives: A new argument against the comp account. *Linguistic Inquiry* 33: 507–11.

2004. On headed, headless and light-headed relatives. *Natural Language and Linguistic Theory* 22: 95–126.

2008a. An argument against assimilating appositive relatives to coordinate structures. *Linguistic Inquiry* 39: 633–55.

2008b. Nominal and non-nominal appositives. In A. Antonenko, J. F. Bailyn & C. Bethin, eds., *Formal Approaches to Slavic Linguistics 16: The Stony Brook meeting 2007*. Ann Arbor, MI: Michigan Slavic Publications. 97–114.

2008c. Missing labels. *Lingua* 118: 907–44.

2009. What don't *wh*-questions, free relatives, and correlatives have in common? In A. Lipták, ed., *Correlatives Cross-linguistically*. Amsterdam: Benjamins. 49–79.

2010. On the distribution of *-kolwiek* 'ever' in Polish free relatives. *Journal of Slavic Linguistics* 18: 221–58.

2016. Types of appositive relative clauses in Polish. *Studies in Polish Linguistics* 11 (3): 85–110.

Citko, B. & Gračanin-Yüksek, M. 2011. Wh-coordination in free relatives. MS. University of Washington and Middle East Technical University, Ankara. bit.ly/2P8x5ti

2016. Multiple (coordinated) (free) relatives. *Natural Language and Linguistic Theory* 34: 393–427. DOI: doi.org/10.1007/s11049-015-9306-8

Cocchi, G. 2004. Relative clauses in Bantu: Affixes as relative markers. *Rivista di grammatica generativa* 29: 61–84. bit.ly/2P1a4rW

Colburn, M. A. 1984. The functions and meanings of the Erima deictic articles. *Papers in New Guinea Linguistics* 23: 209–72. sealang.net/archives/pl

Cole, P. 1976. An apparent asymmetry in the formation of relative clauses in modern Hebrew. In P. Cole, ed., *Studies in Modern Hebrew Syntax and Semantics*. Amsterdam: North-Holland. 231–47.

1987. The Structure of Internally Headed Relative Clauses. *Natural Language and Linguistic Theory* 5: 277–302.

Cole, P. & Hermon, G. 1994. Is there LF *WH*-Movement? *Linguistic Inquiry* 25: 239–62.

Collins, C. & Radford, A. 2015. Gaps, ghosts and gapless relatives in spoken English. *Studia Linguistica* 69: 191–235.

Comrie, B. 1981. *Language Universals and Linguistic Typology: Syntax and morphology.* Oxford: Blackwell.

1989. *Language Universals and Linguistic Typology.* 2nd ed. Oxford: Blackwell.

1996. The unity of noun-modifying clauses in Asian languages. In *Pan-Asiatic Linguistics: Proceedings of the Fourth International Symposium on Languages and Linguistics, January 8–10, 1996.* Salaya, Thailand: Institute of Language and Culture for Rural Development, Mahidol University at Salaya. 1077–88.

1998. Rethinking the typology of relative clauses. *Language Design* 1: 59–86.

2003. The verb-marking relative clause strategy, with special reference to Austronesian languages. *Linguistik Indonesia* 21: 1–18.

Comrie, B. & Kuteva, T. 2005. Relativization strategies. *The World Atlas of Language Structures.* Oxford: Oxford University Press. 494–7.

Comrie, B. & Polinsky, M. 1999. Form and function in syntax: Relative clauses in Tsez. In M. Darnell, E. Moravcsik, F. Newmeyer, M. Noonan & K. Wheatley, eds., *Functionalism and Formalism in Linguistics II: Case studies.* Amsterdam: Benjamins. 77–92.

Constant, N. 2011. Re-diagnosing appositivity: Evidence for prenominal appositives from Mandarin. *Proceedings of the 47th Annual Meeting of the Chicago Linguistic Society.* Chicago: Chicago Linguistic Society. 47–61. bit.ly/2LiI16j

Cornilescu, A. 1981. Non-restrictive relative clauses: An essay in semantic description. *Revue Roumaine de Linguistique* XXVI: 41–67.

Corrêa, L. M. S., Augusto, M. R. A. & Marcilese, M. 2018. Competing analyses and differential cost in the production of non-subject relative clauses. *Glossa: A Journal of General Linguistics* 3 (1): 62. DOI: doi.org/10.5334/gjgl.401

Cortés Rodríguez, L. 1990. Usos anómalos del relativo en español hablado. *Revista Española de Lingüística* 20 (2): 431–46.

Coto-Solano, R., Molina-Muñoz, A. & Segura, A. G. 2016. Correlative structures in Bribri. In E. Sadlier-Brown, E. Guntly, & N. Weber, eds., *Proceedings of the Workshop on Structure and Constituency in the Languages of the Americas 20.* University of British Columbia Working Papers in Linguistics 43. 27–41. bit.ly/383hWlq

Craenenbroeck, J. van & Lipták, A. 2006. The crosslinguistic syntax of sluicing: Evidence from Hungarian relatives. *Syntax* 9 (3): 248–74.

Crane, T. M., Hyman, L. M. & Tukumu, S. N. 2011. *A Grammar of Nzadi (B.865): A Bantu language of the Democratic Republic of the Congo.* Berkeley, CA: University of California Press.

Creissels, D. 2006. *Syntaxe générale: Une introduction typologique.* 2 vols. Paris: Hermès.

2009. Les relatives corrélatives: Le cas du malinké de Kita. *Langages* 174: 39–52.

Cresti, D. 1995. Extraction and reconstruction. *Natural Language Semantics* 3: 79–122.

2000. Ellipsis and reconstruction in relative clauses. In *Proceeding of NELS 30.* Amherst, MA: GLSA. 153–62.

Crum, B. & Dayley, J. P. 1993. *Western Shoshoni Grammar.* Boise: Boise State University.

Csató, É. Á. & Uchturpani, M. A. 2010. On Uyghur relative clauses. *Turkic Languages* 14: 69–93.

Culicover, P. W. 2011. A reconsideration of English relative constructions. *Constructions* 2. bit.ly/380l4P9

2013. Topicalization, inversion, and complementizers in English. In P. Culicover, ed., *Explaining Syntax: Representations, structures and computation.* Oxford: Oxford University Press. 212–55.

Culy, C. 1990. The syntax and semantics of internally headed relative clauses. PhD diss. Stanford University.

Czypionka, A., Dörre, L. & Bayer, J. 2018. Inverse case attraction: Experimental evidence for a syntactically guided process. *The Journal of Comparative Germanic Linguistics* 21: 135–88.

Dasgupta, P. 1980. Questions and relative and complement clauses in a Bangla grammar, PhD diss. New York University.

2006. Unifying relativization and control in Bangla. In M. Banerjee et al., eds., *Felicitation Volume of Professor V.N. Jha.* Kolkata: Sanskrit Pustak Bhandar. 138–70.

Daskalaki, E. 2005. The external category of free relatives: Evidence from modern Greek. *Cambridge Occasional Papers in Linguistics* 2: 87–107.

2011. Case mis-matching as Kase stranding. *University of Pennsylvania Working Papers in Linguistics.* 17 (1): Article 10. repository.upenn.edu/pwpl/vol17/iss1/10/

d'Avis, F. J. 2004. In front of the prefield – inside or outside the clause? In H. Lohenstein & S. Trissler, eds., *The Syntax and Semantics of the Left Periphery.* Berlin: Mouton de Gruyter. 139–77.

Davis, H. 2004. Locative relative clauses in St'at'imcets (Lilloet Salish). In *Papers from the 39th ICSNL.* Vancouver: UBC Working Papers.

2010. A unified analysis of relative clauses in St'át'imcets. *Northwest Journal of Linguistics* 4: 1–43. bit.ly/2ONBPFT

Davison, A. 2009. Adjunction, features and locality in Sanskrit and Hindi/Urdu correlatives. In A. Lipták, ed., *Correlatives Cross-Linguistically.* Amsterdam: Benjamins. 223–62.

Dayal, V. 1996. *Locality in wh-Quantification.* Dordrecht: Kluwer.

1997. Free relatives and *ever*: Identity and free choice readings. In *Proceedings of SALT 7.* Ithaca, NY: CLC Publications, Cornell University. 99–116.

Deal, A. R. 2016. Cyclicity and connectivity in Nez Perce relative clauses. *Linguistic Inquiry* 47: 427–70.

Declerck, R. 1981. Pseudo-modifiers. *Lingua* 54: 135–63.

1982. The triple origin of participial perception verb complements. *Linguistic Analysis* 10: 1–26.

Dehghani, Y. 2000. *A Grammar of Iranian Azari Including Comparisons with Persian.* Munich: Lincom Europa.

Del Gobbo, F. 2001. Appositives schmappositives in Chinese. In *UCI Working Papers in Linguistics* 7: 1–25.

2002. Appositives and Chinese relative clauses. In *Proceedings of the 38th Annual Meeting of the Chicago Linguistic Society. Vol. 1. The Main Session.* Chicago: Chicago Linguistic Society. 175–190.

2003. Appositives at the interface. PhD diss. University of California, Irvine.

2004. On prenominal relative clauses and appositive adjectives. In B. Schmeiser, V. Chand, A. Kelleher & A. Rodriguez, eds., *Proceedings of the 23rd West Coast Conference on Formal Linguistics*. Somerville, MA: Cascadilla Press. 182–94.

2005. Chinese relative clauses: Restrictive, descriptive or appositive? In L. Brugè, G. Giusti, N. Munaro, W. Schweikert & G. Turano, eds., *Contributions to the XXX Incontro di Grammatica Generativa*. Venice: Libreria Editrice Cafoscarina. 287–305. hdl.handle.net/11707/757

2007. On the syntax and semantics of appositive relative clauses. In N. Dehè & Y. Kavalova, eds., *Parentheticals*. Amsterdam: Benjamins. 173–201.

2010. On Chinese appositive relative clauses. *Journal of East Asian Linguistics* 19: 385–417.

2015. Appositives in Mandarin Chinese and cross-linguistically. In A. Li, A. Simpson & W.-T. D. Tsai, eds., *Chinese Syntax in a Cross-Linguistic Perspective*. New York: Oxford University Press. 73–99.

2017. More appositives in heaven and earth than are dreamt of in your linguistics. *Glossa: A Journal of General Linguistics* 2(1): 49. DOI: doi.org/10.5334/gjgl.14

Dékány, É. 2016. Relative clauses. Handout of a course at the Eastern Generative Grammar (EGG) School 2016. Tbilisi, Georgia.

Demeke, G. 2001. N-final relative clauses: The Amharic case. *Studia Linguistica* 55: 191–215.

Demirdache, H. 1991. Resumptive Chains in Restrictive Relatives, Appositives and Dislocation Structures. PhD diss. MIT.

Demirok, Ö. 2017a. A compositional semantics for Turkish correlatives. In L. Zidani-Eroğlu, M. Ciscel & E. Koulidobrova, eds., *Proceedings of the 12th Workshop on Altaic Formal Linguistics*. Cambridge, MA: MITWPL. 79–90. bit.ly/3602Njb

2017b. Free relatives and correlatives in wh-in-situ. In A. Lamont & K. Tetzloff, eds., *Proceedings of NELS 47. Vol. 1*. Amherst, MA: GLSA. 271–84.

Demuth, K. & Harford, C. 1999. Verb raising and subject inversion in Bantu relatives. *Journal of African Languages and Linguistics* 20: 41–61.

Depiante, M. 2000. The syntax of deep and surface anaphora: A study of null complement anaphora and stripping/bare argument ellipsis. PhD diss. University of Connecticut.

De Roberto, E. 2010. *Le relative con antecedente in italiano antico*. Rome: Aracne.

de Sousa, H. 2006. The Menggwa Dla language of New Guinea. PhD diss. University of Sydney. ses.library.usyd.edu.au/handle/2123/1341

Diesing, M. 1992. *Indefinites*. Cambridge, MA: MIT Press.

Dik, S. 1997. *The Theory of Functional Grammar*. Berlin: Mouton de Gruyter.

Dikken, M. den 2001. 'Pluringulars', pronouns and quirky agreement. *The Linguistic Review* 18: 19–41.

2005. A comment on the topic of topic-comment. *Lingua* 115: 691–710.

Dimova, E. 2014. A new look at multiple free relatives: Evidence from Bulgarian. Paper given at the 9th Slavic Linguistics Society Annual Conference, University of Washington, Seattle. 19–21 September. bit.ly/35QEhB0

Dimova, E. & Tellier, C. 2015. On multiple free relatives that are not. Paper presented at FDSL 11, Potsdam, 2–4 December. bit.ly/34LPEKo

2018. Bulgarian multiple wh relatives revisited. In S. L. Franks, V. Chidambaram, B. D. Joseph & I. Krapova, eds., *Katerino Mome: Studies in Bulgarian Morphosyntax in Honor of Catherine Rudin*. Bloomington, IN: Slavica Publishers. 79–91.

Dixon, R. M. W. 1977. *A Grammar of Yidiɲ*. Cambridge: Cambridge University Press.

2009. *Basic Linguistic Theory. Vol. 2: Grammatical topics*. Oxford: Oxford University Press.

Dobrovie-Sorin, C. 1994. *The Syntax of Romanian: Comparative studies in Romance*. Berlin: Mouton de Gruyter.

Doherty, C. 1993. Clauses without that: The case for bare sentential complementation in English. PhD diss. University of California, Santa Cruz.

1994. The syntax of subject contact relatives. In *Proceedings of the 29th Annual Meeting of the Chicago Linguistic Society*. 55–65. Chicago: Chicago Linguistic Society.

Dombrowski, A. 2012. Multiple relative marking in 19th century West Rumelian Turkish. *Proceedings of the 38th Annual Meeting of the Berkeley Linguistics Society*. Berkeley, CA: Berkeley Linguistics Society. 79–90. bit.ly/2rN71vH

Donati, C. 2006. On *wh*-head movement. In L. L.-S. Cheng & N. Corver, eds., *Wh-movement: Moving on*. Cambridge, MA: MIT Press. 21–46.

Donati, C. & Cecchetto, C. 2011. Relabeling heads: A unified account for relativization structures. *Linguistic Inquiry* 42: 519–60.

Donohue, M. 1999. *A Grammar of Tukang Besi*. Berlin: Mouton de Gruyter.

2004. A grammar of the Skou language of New Guinea. MS. National University of Singapore. hdl.handle.net/11858/00-001M-0000-0012-7AAC-9

Doron, E. 1982. On the syntax and semantics of resumptive pronouns. *Texas Linguistic Forum* 19: 1–48.

Doron, E. & Reintges, C. H. 2006. On the syntax of participial modifiers. MS. The Hebrew University of Jerusalem.

Douglas, J. 2015. Agreement (and disagreement) among relatives. *Cambridge Occasional Papers in Linguistics* 7: 33–60.

2016. The syntactic structures of relativization. PhD diss. University of Cambridge. ling.auf.net/lingbuzz/003182

Downing, B. T. 1973. Correlative relative clauses and universal grammar. *Minnesota Working Papers in Linguistics and Philosophy of Language* 2: 1–17.

1978. Some universals of relative clause structure. In J. H. Greenberg, ed., *Universals of Human Language. Vol. 4. Syntax*. Stanford, CA: Stanford University Press. 375–418.

Dramé, M. 1981. Aspects of Mandingo grammar. PhD diss. University of Illinois at Urbana-Champaign.

Dreyfuss, G. R. 1977. Relative clause structure in four Creole languages. PhD diss. University of Michigan.

Dryer, M. 2005. Order of relative clause and noun. In M. Haspelmath, M. Dryer, D. Gil & B. Comrie, eds., *The World Atlas of Language Structures*. Oxford: Oxford University Press. 366–7.

Duncan, J. D. 2004. The syntax of headed restrictive relative clauses with special reference to Spanish. PhD diss. Pennsylvania State University. https://etda.libraries.psu.edu/files/final_submissions/2606

du Plessis, H. 1977. Wh movement in Afrikaans. *Linguistic Inquiry* 8: 723–6.

Dwivedi, V. 1994a. Topicalization in Hindi and the correlative construction. In M. Butt, T. Holloway King & G. Ramchand, eds., *Theoretical Perspectives on Word Order in South Asian Languages*. Stanford, CA: CSLI Publications. 91–118.

1994b. Syntactic dependencies and relative phrases in Hindi. PhD diss. University of Massachusetts, Amherst.

Dzameshie, A. K. 1995. Syntactic characteristics of Ewe relative clause constructions. *Research Review (NS)* 11: 27–42. bit.ly/364h7qZ

Ebert, C., Endriss C. & Gärtner, H.-M. 2007. An information structural account of German integrated verb second clauses. *Research on Language and Computation* 5: 415–34.

Ehrenkranz, J. & Hirschland, E. C. 1972. Latin relative clauses. In P. M. Peranteau, J. N. Levi, & G. C. Phares, eds., *The Chicago Which Hunt: Papers from the Relative Clause Festival*. Chicago: Chicago Linguistic Society. 23–9.

Elbourne, P. 2005. *Situations and individuals*. Cambridge: MIT Press.

2013. *Definite Descriptions*. Oxford: Oxford University Press.

Emonds, J. 1976. *A Transformational Approach to English Syntax: Root, structure-preserving and local transformations*. New York: Academic Press.

1979. Appositive relatives have no properties. *Linguistic Inquiry* 10: 211–43.

1985. *A Unified Theory of Syntactic Categories*. Dordrecht: Foris.

Endriss, C. & Gärtner, H.-M. 2005. Relativische Verbzweitsätze und Definitheit. In F. J. D'Avis, ed., *Deutsche Syntax: Empirie und Teorie*. Göteborg: Göteborgs Universitet. 195–220.

Engdahl, E. 1980. Wh-constructions in Swedish and the relevance of subjacency. In J. T. Jensen, ed., *Cahiers Linguisticques D'Ottawa: Proceedings of the Tenth Meeting of the North East Linguistic Society*. Ottawa: University of Ottawa Department of Linguistics. 89–108.

Engdahl, E. 1982. Restrictions on unbounded dependencies in Swedish. In E. Engdahl & E. Ejerhed, eds., *Readings on Unbounded Dependencies in Scandinavian Languages*. 151–74.

1997. Relative clause extractions in context. *Working Papers in Scandinavian Syntax* 60: 51–79. bit.ly/363R6In

Enrico, J. 2003. *Haida Syntax*. Vol. 1. Lincoln: University of Nebraska Press.

Erlewine, M. Y. & Gould, I. 2016. Unifying Japanese relative clauses: Copy-chains and context-sensitivity. *Glossa: A Journal of General Linguistics* 1 (1): 51. DOI: doi.org/10.5334/gjgl.174

Erlewine, M. Y. & Kotek, H. 2014. Intervention in focus pied-piping. In H.-L. Huang, E. Poole & A. Rysling, eds., *Proceedings of NELS 43. Vol. 1*. Amherst, MA: GLSA. 117–30.

2015a. The structure and interpretation of non-restrictive relatives: Evidence from relative pronoun pied-piping. *Proceedings of the 51st Annual Meeting of the*

Chicago Linguistic Society. Chicago: Chicago Linguistic Society. 149–63. hkotek.com/CLS51_Erlewine_Kotek_final.pdf

　2015b. Relative pronoun pied-piping in English non-restrictive relatives. ling.auf.net/lingbuzz/002700/

Erteschik-Shir, N. 1973. On the nature of island constraints. PhD diss. MIT.

　1982. Extractability in Danish and the pragmatic principle of dominance. In E. Engdahl & E. Ejerhed, eds., *Readings on Unbounded Dependencies in Scandinavian Languages.* 175–91.

　2007. *Information Structure: The syntax-discourse interface.* Oxford: Oxford University Press.

Erteschik-Shir, N. & Lappin, S. 1979. Dominance and the functional explanation of island phenomena. *Theoretical Linguistics* 6: 41–85.

Espinal, M. T. 1991. The representation of disjunct constituents. *Language* 67 (4): 726–62.

Evans, G. 1980. Pronouns. *Linguistic Inquiry* 11: 337–62.

Fabb, N. 1990. The difference between English restrictive and non-restrictive relative clauses. *Journal of Linguistics* 26: 57–78.

Fachner, R. 1986. Der Relativsatz im Bambara. Arbeitspapier Nr. 50. Institut für Sprachwissenschaft, Cologne University. bit.ly/2reVbKK

Falk, Y. N. 2010. An unmediated analysis of relative clauses. MS. The Hebrew University of Jerusalem. pluto.huji.ac.il/~msyfalk/Relatives.pdf

Faltz, L. M. 1995. Towards a typology of natural logic. In E. Bach, E. Jelinek, A. Kratzer & B. H. Partee, eds., *Quantification in Natural Languages.* Dordrecht: Kluwer. 271–319.

Fanselow, G. 1986. On the sentential nature of prenominal adjectives in German. *Folia Linguistica* 20: 341–80.

Fedden, O. S. 2007. A grammar of Mian, a Papuan language of New Guinea. PhD diss. University of Melbourne. repository.unimelb.edu.au/10187/2044

Feldman, H. 1986. *A Grammar of Awtuw.* Canberra: Australian National University.

Felix, S. W. 1985. Parasitic gaps in German. In W. Abraham, ed., *Erklärende Syntax des Deutschen.* Tübingen: Narr. 173–200.

Felser, C. 1999. *Verbal Complement Clauses: A minimalist study of direct perception constructions.* Amsterdam: Benjamins.

Fiengo, R. & May, R. 1994. *Indices and Identity.* Cambridge, MA: MIT Press.

Fintel, K. von 1999. Amount relatives and the meaning of chains. MS. MIT. web.mit.edu/fintel/fintel-1999-amount.pdf

　2000. Whatever. *Proceedings of SALT 10.* Ithaca, NY: CLC Publications. 27–39.

Fiorentino, G. 1999. *Relativa debole. Sintassi, uso, storia in italiano.* Pavia: Franco Angeli.

Fleischmann, L. 1981. Bine relativization. MS. Summer Institute of Linguistics, Ukarumpa, Papua New Guinea. www.sil.org/resources/archives/31148

Fodor, J. D. & Sag, I. A. 1982. Referential and quantificational indefinites. *Linguistics and Philosophy* 5: 355–98.

Foley, S. 2013. The syntax of Georgian relative clauses. Honors thesis. New York University. bit.ly/2OLCqHR

Foley, W. A. 1991. *The Yimas Language of New Guinea.* Stanford, CA: Stanford University Press.

Fontana, J. 1990. Is ASL like Diegueño or Diegueño like ASL? A study of internally headed relative clauses in ASL. In C. Lucas, ed., *Sign Language Research. Theoretical Issues*. Washington: Gallaudet University Press. 238–55.

Fox, D. 2000. *Economy and Semantic Interpretation*. Cambridge, MA: MIT Press.

2002. Antecedent contained deletion and the copy theory of movement. *Linguistic Inquiry* 33: 63–96.

Fox, D. & Johnson, K. 2016. QR is restrictor sharing. In K. M. Kim et al., eds., *Proceedings of the 33rd West Coast Conference on Formal Linguistics*. Somerville, MA: Cascadilla Press. 1–16.

Fox, D. & Nissenbaum, J. 1999. Extraposition and scope. A case for overt QR. In *Proceedings of the 18th West Coast Conference in Formal Linguistics*. Somerville, MA: Cascadilla Press. 132–44.

Frajzyngier, Z. 1984. On the origin of *Say* and *Se* as complementizers in Black English and English-based creoles. *American Speech* 59 (3): 207–10.

Frajzyngier, Z., Johnston, E. with Edwards, A. 2005. *A Grammar of Mina*. Berlin: Mouton de Gruyter.

Frascarelli, M. & Puglielli, A. 2005. A comparative analysis of restrictive and appositive relative clauses in Cushitic languages. In L. Brugè, G. Giusti, N. Munaro, W. Schweikert, & G. Turano, eds., *Contributions to the Thirtieth 'Incontro di Grammatica Generativa'*. Venice: Libreria Editrice Cafoscarina. 307–32. hdl.handle.net/11707/757

Fuchs, C. & Milner, J. 1979. *A propos des relatives*. Paris: SELAF.

Fuji, M. 2010. On internally headed relative clauses in Japanese and Navajo. *Journal of the Tokyo University of Marine Science and Technology* 6: 47–58. bit.ly/2LjOiyM

Fukui, N. 1986. A theory of category projections and its applications. PhD diss. MIT.

Fukui, N. & Takano. Y. 2000. Nominal structure: An extension of the symmetry principle. In P. Svenonius, ed., *The Derivation of VO and OV*. Amsterdam: Benjamins. 219–54.

Fulass, H. 1972. On Amharic relative clauses. *Bulletin of the School of Oriental and African Languages* 35: 497–513.

Gagnon, M. & Mitrović, I. 2012. More evidence for the split analysis of relative clauses. Actes du congres annuel de l'Association canadienne de linguistique 2012. Proceedings of the 2012 annual conference of the Canadian Linguistic Association. bit.ly/2DKAusZ

Gandon, O. 2016. La relativisation dans une perspective areale: L'aire Caucase – Anatolie de l'Est – Iran de l'Ouest. PhD diss. Université de Paris Sorbonne, Paris 3.

Gärtner, H.-M. 2001. Are there V2 relative clauses in German? *Journal of Comparative Germanic Linguistics* 3 (2): 97–141.

2002. On the force of V2 declaratives. *Theoretical Linguistics* 28: 33–42.

Geis, M. 1970. Adverbial subordinate clauses in English. PhD diss. MIT.

Genetti, C. 1992. Semantic and grammatical categories of relative clause morphology in the languages of Nepal. *Studies in Language* 16: 405–27.

Georgi, D. & Salzmann, M. 2014. Case attraction and matching in resumption in relatives. Evidence for top-down derivation. In A. Assmann, S. Bank, D. Georgi, T. Klein, P. Weisser & E. Zimmermann, eds., *Topics at InfL*. Linguistische

Arbeitsberichte 92. Leipzig: Institut für Linguistik, Universität Leipzig. 347–95. bit.ly/2DKzzZC

2017. The matching effect in resumption: A local analysis based on case attraction and top-down derivation. *Natural Language and Linguistic Theory* 35: 61–98.

Geraci, C. & Hauser, C. 2017. Amount relatives and head matching: Evidence from French Sign Language. MS. Institut Jean Nicod, Paris.

Gheoghegan, S. G. 1975. Relative clauses in Old, Middle, and New English. *Ohio State University Working Papers in Linguistics* 18. 30–71. bit.ly/2rRRDOC

Gheorghe, M. 2004. *Propoziția relativă*. Pitești: Editura Paralela 45.

2013. Relative clauses. In G. Pană-Dindelegan, ed., *The Grammar of Romanian*. Oxford: Oxford University Press. 483–97.

Giltner, D. 2017. Head-raising and head-matching in Russian relative clauses: Diagnostics study. Honors thesis. University of Washington.

Girard, G. & Malan, N. 1999. Postmodification by infinitive clauses. Something about which to have a bit of a discussion. *Anglophonia: French Journal of English Linguistics*. 3 (6): 31–42. journals.openedition.org/anglophonia/669

Gisborne, N. & Truswell, R. 2017. Where do relative specifiers come from? In E. Mathieu & R. Truswell, eds., *Micro-change and Macro-change in Diachronic Syntax*. Oxford: Oxford University Press.

Giurgea, I. & Soare, E. 2010a. Modal non-finite relatives in Romance. In M. G. Becker & E. M. Remberger, eds., *Modality and Mood in Romance: Modal interpretation, mood selection, and mood alternation*. Berlin: Mouton de Gruyter. 57–80.

2010b. Predication and the nature of non-finite relatives in Romance. In A. M. Di Sciullo & V. Hill, eds., *Edges, Heads, and Projections: Interface properties*. Amsterdam: Benjamins. 191–213.

Giusti, G. 2002. The functional structure of noun phrases. A bare phrase structure approach. In G. Cinque, ed., *Functional Structure in DP and IP*. The cartography of syntactic structures. Vol. 1. New York: Oxford University Press. 54–90.

Givón, T. 1972. Pronoun attraction and subject postposing in Bantu. In P. M. Peranteau, J. N. Levi, & G. C. Phares, eds., *The Chicago Which Hunt: Papers from the relative clause festival*. 190–7. Chicago: Chicago Linguistic Society.

1975. Promotion, accessibility and case marking: Toward understanding grammars. *Working Papers on Language Universals* 19. Stanford University. 55–125.

Göksel, A. & Kerslake, C. 2005. *Turkish: A comprehensive grammar*. London: Routledge.

González Campos, G. & Lehmann, C. Forthcoming. The Cabecar relative clause. MS. University of Erfurt. bit.ly/33H6BUU

Goodluck, H., Foley, M. & Sedivy, J. 1992. Adjunct islands and acquisition. In H. Goodluck & M. Rochemont, eds., *Island Constraints: Theory, acquisition and processing*. Dordrecht: Kluwer. 181–94.

Gorbet, L. 1973. How to tell a head when you see one: Disambiguation in Diegueño relative clauses. *Linguistic Notes from La Jolla* 5: 63–82. grammar.ucsd.edu/sdlp/past.html

1976. *A Grammar of Diegueño Nominals*. New York: Garland.

1977. Headless relative clauses in the Southwest: Are they related? In *Proceedings of the 3rd Annual Meeting of the Berkeley Linguistic Society*. Berkeley, CA: Berkeley Linguistics Society. 270–8.

Gould, Laurie J. 1988. Liberation and Kikuria relative clauses. *Proceedings of the 14th Annual Meeting of the Berkeley Linguistics Society.* Berkeley, CA: Berkeley Linguistics Society. 56–65. bit.ly/2Ri5F72

Gračanin-Yüksek, M. 2008. Free relatives in Croatian: An argument for the comp account. *Linguistic Inquiry* 39: 275–94. bit.ly/383Nw2F

2010. On a matching effect in headed relative clauses. In W. Browne et al. eds., *Proceedings of FASL 18.* Ann Arbor: Michigan Slavic Publications. 193–209. bit.ly/2r2W1ui

2013. The syntax of relative clauses in Croatian. *The Linguistic Review* 30: 25–49.

Graczyk, R. 1991. Relative clauses in Crow. In F. Ingemann, ed., *1990 Mid-America Linguistics Conference Papers.* Lawrence: University of Kansas. 490–504. bit.ly/2rQuvjG

Graffi, G. 1980. Su alcune costruzioni 'pseudo-relative'. *Rivista di grammatica generativa* 5: 117–39. bit.ly/2YcZmD2

2017. What are 'pseudo-relatives'? In R. D'Alessandro, G. Iannàccaro, D. Passino, A. M. Thornton, eds., *Di tutti i colori: Studi linguistici per Maria Grossmann.* Utrecht: Utrecht University Repository. bit.ly/2sIpEBu

Gravelle-Karn, G. J. 2010. A grammar of Moskona: An East Bird's head language of West Papua, Indonesia. PhD diss. Vrije Universiteit, Amsterdam. bit.ly/2OOFwuW

Green, G. M. 1973. The derivation of a relative infinitive construction. *Studies in the Linguistic Sciences* 3: 1–32. www.ideals.illinois.edu/handle/2142/9373

Greenberg, J. H. 1963. Some universals of grammar with particular reference to the order of meaningful elements. In J. Greenberg, ed., *Universals of Language.* Cambridge, MA: MIT Press. 73–113.

Grevisse, M. 1969. *Le bon usage.* Gembloux: Duculot.

1993. *Le bon usage.* 13th ed. Paris: Duculot.

Grewendorf, G. 1986. Relativsätze im Deutschen: Die Rattenfängerkonstruktion. *Linguistische Berichte* 105: 409–34.

2014. Gaps and parasitic gaps in Bavarian. In G. Grewendorf & H. Weiss, eds., *Bavarian Syntax: Contributions to the theory of syntax.* 145–82. Amsterdam: Benjamins.

Grewendorf, G. & Poletto, C. 2015. Relative clauses in Cimbrian. In E. Di Domenico, C. Hamann & S. Matteini, eds., *Structures, Strategies and Beyond: Studies in honour of Adriana Belletti.* Amsterdam: Benjamins. 393–416.

Griffiths J. 2015. On appositives. PhD diss. University of Groningen. bit.ly/34LzWyJ

Griffiths, J. & De Vries, M. 2013. The syntactic integration of appositives: Evidence from fragments and ellipsis. *Linguistic Inquiry* 44: 332–44.

Grimshaw, J. 1975. Evidence for relativization by deletion in Chaucerian English. In *Proceedings of NELS 5.* 216–24.

2005. *Words and Structure.* Stanford, CA: CSLI.

Groat, E. 2012. Headhunting at the edge of the C: A probe-goal analysis for free relative clauses. Paper given at Cologne University, 16 May. bit.ly/37XSduV

Groos, A. & Riemsdijk, H. van 1981. Matching effects in free relatives: A parameter of core grammar. In A. Belletti et al., eds., *Theory of Markedness in Generative Grammar.* Pisa: Scuola Normale Superiore. 171–216.

Gross, M. 1977. *Grammaire transformationnelle du français: Syntaxe du nom.* Paris: Larousse.

Grosu, A. 1986/87. Pied-piping and the matching parameter. *The Linguistic Review* 6: 41–58.

1994. *Three studies in locality and case.* London: Routledge.

1996. The proper analysis of 'missing P' free relative constructions. *Linguistic Inquiry* 27: 257–93.

2000. Type resolution in relative constructions: Featural marking and dependency encoding. In A. Alexiadou, A. Meinunger & C. Wilder, eds., *The Syntax of Relative Clauses.* Amsterdam: Benjamins. 83–120.

2001. The semantic diversity of internally-headed relative clauses. In C. Schaner-Wolles et al., eds., *Naturally! Linguistic studies in honour of Wolfgang Ulrich Dressler presented on the occasion of his 60th birthday.* Torino: Rosenberg & Sellier. 143–52.

2002. Strange relative at the interface of two millennia. *Glot International* 6 (6): 145–67.

2003a. 'Transparent' free relatives as a special instance of 'standard' free relatives. In M. Coene, Y. D'Hulst & L. Tasmowski, eds., *The structure of DPs.* Amsterdam: Elsevier North-Holland.

2003b. A unified theory of 'standard' and 'transparent' free relatives. *Natural Language and Linguistic Theory* 21: 247–331.

2004. The syntax-semantics of modal existential *wh*-constructions. In O. M. Tomić, ed., *Balkan Syntax and Semantics.* Amsterdam: Benjamins. 405–38.

2005. Relative clause constructions and unbounded dependencies. MS. Tel Aviv University.

2009a. The syntax-semantics of Japanese/Korean internally headed relative clause constructions. *Studia Universitatis Babeş-Bolyai, Philologia, LIV* 4: 169–91. bit.ly/35YTfVr

2009b. A refined typology of internally-headed relatives. In *Working Papers in Linguistics, Vol. XI.* Bucharest: University of Bucharest Press. bit.ly/2Pa0Hqf

2012. Towards a more articulated typology of internally headed relative constructions: The semantic connection. *Language and Linguistics Compass* 6 (7): 1–30.

2013. Relative clause constructions and unbounded dependencies. In C. Dobrovie-Sorin & I. Giurgea, eds., *A Reference Grammar of Romanian, Vol. 1: The Noun Phrase.* Amsterdam: Benjamins. 597–662.

Grosu, A. & Hoshi, K. 2016. Japanese internally headed relatives: Their distinctness from potentially homophonous constructions. *Glossa: A Journal of General Linguistics* 1 (1): 32 DOI: doi.org/10.5334/gjgl.104

2018. On the unified analysis of three types of relative clause construction in Japanese, and on the 'salient reading' of the internally headed type. A reply to Erlewine & Gould (2016). *Glossa: A Journal of General Linguistics* 3(1): 34. DOI: doi.org/10.5334/gjgl.577

Grosu, A., Hoshi, K. & Sohn, D. 2013. The Japanese-Korean connection: A contrastive study of the inventory and properties of their IHRCs. MS. bit.ly/2rX6M11

Grosu, A. & Krifka, M. 2005. Relative clause constructions with a post-copular gap. In M. Coene & L. Tasmowski, eds., *On Space and Time in Language.* Cluj-Napoca: Clusium. 379–95.

Grosu, A. & Krifka, M. 2007. The gifted mathematician that you claim to be: Equational intensional 'reconstruction' relatives. *Linguistics and Philosophy* 30: 445–85.

Grosu, A. & Landman, F. 1998. Strange relatives of the third kind. *Natural Language Semantics* 6: 125–70.

2012. A quantificational disclosure approach to Japanese and Korean internally headed relatives. *Journal of East Asian Linguistics* 21: 159–96.

2017. Amount relatives. In M. Everaert & H. C. van Riemsdijk, eds., *The Wiley Blackwell Companion to Syntax*. 2nd ed. Hoboken, NJ: Wiley-Blackwell.

Guasti, M. T. 1988. La pseudorelative et les phénomènes d'accord. *Rivista di Grammatica Generativa* 13: 35–80. bit.ly/2LmIRis

1992. Pseudorelatives and Prepositional Infinitives: A unified account. *Geneva Generative Papers* 1: 53–65.

1993. *Causative and Perception Verbs: A comparative study*. Torino: Rosenberg & Sellier.

Guéron, J. 1980. On the syntax and semantics of PP extraposition. *Linguistic Inquiry* 11: 637–78.

Guéron, J. & May, R. 1984. Extraposition and logical form. *Linguistic Inquiry* 15: 1–31.

Guilliot, N. & Malkawi, N. 2007. Reconstruction without movement. In L. Eguren & O. F. Soriano, eds., *Coreference, Modality and Focus*. Amsterdam: Benjamins. 113–31.

2011. Weak vs strong resumption: Covarying differently. In A. Rouveret, ed., *Resumptive Pronouns at the Interfaces*. Amsterdam: Benjamins. 395–423.

Gupta, S. 1986. *Discourse Grammar of Hindi: A study in relative clauses*. New Delhi: Bahri Publications.

Gupte, S. M. 1975. Relative constructions in Marathi. PhD diss. Michigan State University.

Gutiérrez-Bravo, R. 2013. Free relative clauses in Yucatec Maya. *Sprachtypologie und Universalien Forschung* 66: 22–39.

Haberland, H. & Auwera, J. van der. 1990. Topics and clitics in Greek relatives. *Acta Linguistica Hafniensia* 22: 127–57.

Hackl, M. & Nissenbaum, J. 2012. A modal ambiguity in *for*-infinitival relative clauses. *Natural Language Semantics* 20: 59–81. bit.ly/2PagiGk

Haegeman, L. 1988. Parenthetical adverbials: The radical orphanage approach. In S. Chiba et al., eds., *Aspects of modern English linguistics: Papers presented to Masatomo Ukaji on his 60th Birthday*. Tokyo: Kaitakushi. 232–54.

2010. Locality and the distribution of main clause phenomena. MS. University of Ghent. www.gist.ugent.be/file/79

2012. *Adverbial Clauses, Main Clause Phenomena, and the Composition of the Left Periphery*. The cartography of syntactic structures. Vol. 8. New York: Oxford University Press.

2015. A note on English subject contact relatives. In Á. J. Gallego & D. Ott, eds., *50 Years Later: Reflections on Chomsky's aspects*. Cambridge, MA: MITWPL. 133–45. bit.ly/33JvfUN

Haegeman, L., Weir, A., Danckaert, L., D'Hulster, T. & Buelens, L. 2015. Against the root analysis of subject contact relatives in English. *Lingua* 163: 61–74.

Haider, H. 1985. Der Rattenfängerei muß ein Ende gemacht werden. *Wiener Linguistische Gazette* 35/36: 27–50.

   1988. Matching projections. In A. Cardinaletti, G. Cinque & G. Giusti, eds., *Constituent Structure: Papers from the 1987 Glow Conference*. Dordrecht: Foris. 101–21.

   2000. Adverb placement-convergence of structure and licensing. *Theoretical Linguistics* 26: 95–134.

Haïk, I. 1985. The syntax of operators. PhD diss. MIT. hdl.handle.net/1721.1/14972

Haiman, J. & Benincà, P. 1992. *The Rhaeto-Romance Languages*. London: Routledge.

Hale, K. L. 1976. The adjoined relative clause in Australia. In R. M. W. Dixon, ed., *Grammatical Categories in Australian Languages*. Canberra: AIAS. 78–105.

Hale, K. L. & Platero, P. 1974. Aspects of Navajo anaphora: Relativization and pronominalization. *The Navjo Language Review* 1: 9–28.

Han, C.-H. & Kim, J.-B. 2004. Are there 'double relative clauses' in Korean? *Linguistic Inquiry* 35: 315–37.

Hanink, E. A. 2016. Internally headed relatives and event nominalizations in Washo. *Proceedings of the 42nd Annual Meeting of the Berkeley Linguistics Society*. Berkeley, CA: Berkeley Linguistics Society. 119–34.

   2018. Super light-headed relatives, missing prepositions, and span-conditioned allomorphy in German. *Journal of Comparative Germanic Linguistics* 21: 247–90.

Hankamer, J. & Mikkelsen, L. H. 2002. A morphological analysis of definite nouns in Danish. *Journal of Germanic Linguistics* 14 (2): 137–75. bit.ly/2OMB6V6

Hankamer, J. & Postal, P. 1973. Whose gorilla? *Linguistic Inquiry* 4: 261.

Hankamer, J. & Sag, I. 1976. Deep and surface anaphora. *Linguistic Inquiry* 7: 391–426.

Harbert, W. 1983a. On the nature of the matching parameter. *The Linguistic Review* 2: 237–84.

   1983b. A note on Old English free relatives. *Linguistic Inquiry* 14: 549–53.

   1989. Case attraction and the hierarchization of case. *Proceedings of the Eastern States Conference on Linguistics* 6: 138–49.

   1992. Gothic relative clauses and syntactic theory. In I. Rauch, G. Carr & R. Kyes, eds., *On Germanic Linguistics: Issues and Methods*. 109–46. Berlin: De Gruyter Mouton.

Harris, A. C. 1994. On the history of relative clauses in Georgian. In H. I. Aronson, ed., *Non-Slavic Languages of the USSR: Papers from the fourth conference*. Columbus, OH: Slavica Publishers. 130–42.

Harris, J. A. 2008. On the syntax and semantics of Heim's ambiguity. In N. Abner & J. Bishop, eds., *Proceedings of the 27th West Coast Conference on Formal Linguistics*. Somerville, MA: Cascadilla Press. 194–202. www.lingref.com/cpp/wccfl/27/paper1832.pdf

Harris, M. & Vincent, N. 1980. On zero relatives. *Linguistic Inquiry* 11: 805–07.

Harwood, W. 2013. Being progressive is just a phase: Dividing the functional hierarchy. PhD diss. University of Ghent.

   2015. Being progressive is just a phase: Celebrating the uniqueness of progressive aspect under a phase-based analysis. *Natural Language and Linguistic Theory* 33: 523–73.

2018. Reduced relatives and extended phases: A phase-based analysis of the inflectional restrictions on English reduced relative clauses. *Studia Linguistica* 72: 428–71. ling.auf.net/lingbuzz/002867

Hasegawa, I. 1998. English infinitival relatives as prepositional phrases. *English Linguistics: Journal of the English Linguistics Society of Japan.* 15: 1–27. bit.ly/2DJ2fBY

Hastings, R. E. 2004. The syntax and semantics of relativization and quantification: The case of Quechua. PhD diss. Cornell University. bit.ly/34QR71X

Hauser, C. & Geraci, C. 2018. Relative clauses in French Sign Language (LSF): Some preliminary results. *FEAST* 1: 17–26.

Hazout, I. 2001. Predicate formation: The case of participial relatives. *The Linguistic Review* 18: 97–123.

Heath, J. 2008. *A Grammar of Jamsay.* Berlin: Mouton de Gruyter.

2015. Dogon relative clauses. MS. dogonlanguages.org/sources/dogonrelativeclauses

2017. A grammar of Najamba (Dogon, Mali). Language Description Heritage Library, University of Michigan. bit.ly/2RlZHBN

Heck, F. 2005. Gegen Kopfanhebung in deutschen Relativsätzen. Paper given at the GGS 2005, 7 May. University of Tübingen. bit.ly/2Lj4FLW

2008. *On Pied-Piping: Wh-movement and beyond.* Berlin: de Gruyter.

2009. On certain properties of pied-piping. *Linguistic Inquiry* 40: 75–111.

Heck, F. & Cuartero, J. 2008. Long distance agreement in relative clauses. In F. Heck, G. Müller & J. Trommer, eds., *Varieties of Competition.* Linguistische Arbeitsberichte 87. Leipzig: Institut für Linguistik, Universität Leipzig. 13–48. http://home.uni-leipzig.de/heck/papiere/heckcuartero.pdf

2012. Long distance agreement in relative clauses. In A. Alexiadou, T. Kiss & G. Müller, eds., *Local Modelling of Non-Local Dependencies in Syntax.* 49–83. Berlin: de Gruyter.

Heim, I. 1979. Concealed questions. In R. Bauerle, U. Egli & A. von Stechow, eds., *Semantics from Different Points of View.* Berlin: Springer. 51–60.

1987. Where does the definiteness restriction apply? Evidence from the definiteness of variables. In E. J. Reuland & A. G. B. ter Meulen, eds., *The Representation of (In) definiteness.* Cambridge: Cambridge University Press. 21–42.

Heim, I. & Kratzer, A. 1998. *Semantics in Generative Grammar.* Oxford: Blackwell.

Heinat, F. & Wiklund, A.-L. 2015. Scandinavian relative clause extractions: Apparent restrictions. *Working Papers in Scandinavian Syntax* 94: 36–50. bit.ly/2Loyo6d

Heine, B. & Kuteva, T. 2004. *World Lexicon of Grammaticalization.* Cambridge: Cambridge University Press.

Henderson, B. 2006a. The syntax and typology of Bantu relative clauses. PhD diss. University of Illinois at Urbana-Champaign.

2006b. The syntax of agreement in Bantu relatives. In F. Hoyt, N. Seifert, A. Teodorescu & J. White, eds., *The Morphosyntax of Underrepresented Languages: Proceedings of the Texas Linguistics Society IX Conference.* Stanford, CA: CSLI Publications. stanford.io/2PdyHly

2007. Matching and raising unified. *Lingua* 117: 202–20.

Hendery, R. 2012. *Relative Clauses in Time and Space: A case study in the methods of diachronic typology.* Amsterdam: Benjamins.

Henry, A. 1995. *Belfast English and Standard English: Dialect variation and parameter setting.* New York: Oxford University Press.

Herd, J., Macdonald, C. & Massam, D. 2004. Genitive-relative constructions in Polynesian. In *Proceedings of the 2004 Annual Conference of the Canadian Linguistic Association.* bit.ly/36cOaJB

2011. Genitive subjects in relative constructions in Polynesian languages. *Lingua* 121: 1252–64.

Herdan, S. 2008a. A superlative theory of amount relatives. In C. B. Chang & H. J. Haynie, eds., *Proceedings of the 26th West Coast Conference on Formal Linguistics.* Somerville, MA: Cascadilla Press. 234–42. www.lingref.com/cpp/wccfl/26/paper1677.pdf

2008b. Degrees and amounts in relative clauses. PhD diss. University of Connecticut.

Herrmann, T. 2003. Relative clauses in dialects of English: A typological approach. PhD diss. Albert Ludwig University of Freiburg. bit.ly/2DMKUrU

Hetzron, R. 1978. On the relative order of adjectives. In H. Seiler, ed., *Language Universals.* Tübingen: Narr. 165–84.

Hewitt, B. G. 1979a. The relative clause in Abkhaz (Abžui dialect). *Lingua* 47: 151–88.

1979b. The relative clause in Adyghe (Temirgoi dialect). *Annual of Ibero-Caucasian Linguistics* 6: 134–59.

Heycock, C. 1995. Asymmetries in reconstruction. *Linguistic Inquiry* 26: 547–70.

2005. On the interaction of adjectival modifiers and relative clauses. *Natural Language Semantics* 13: 359–82.

2012. Specification, equation, and agreement in copular sentences. *Canadian Journal of Linguistics* 57(2): 209–40.

2019. Relative reconstructions: Can we arrive at a unified picture? In M. Krifka & M. Schanner, eds., *Reconstruction Effects in Relative Clauses.* Berlin: de Gruyter. 87–112.

Higginbotham, J. 1984. English is not a context-free language. *Linguistic Inquiry* 15: 225–34.

Higgins, F. R. 1974. On the use of idioms as evidence for movement: A cautionary note. MS. University of Massachusetts, Amherst.

Hill, V. 2017. Restrictive relative clauses in Acadian French. *Bucharest Working Papers in Linguistics* XIX (2): 5–27. bit.ly/2ON0gD6

Hinterhölzl, R. 2002. Event-related adjuncts and the OV/VO distinction. In K. Magerdoomian & L. A. Bar-el, eds., *Proceedings of the 20th West Coast Conference on Formal Linguistics.* Somerville, MA: Cascadilla Press. 276–89.

Hintikka, J. 1974. Quantifiers vs quantification theory. *Linguistic Inquiry* 5: 153–77.

Hiraiwa, K. 2003. Relativization in Buli. In G. Akanlig-Pare & M. Kenstowicz, eds., *Studies in Buli Grammar.* Working Papers on Endangered and Less Familiar Languages 4. Cambridge, MA: MITWPL. 45–84.

2005. Dimensions of symmetry in syntax: agreement and clausal architecture. PhD diss. MIT.

2008. The head-internal relativization parameter in Gur: D and its typological implications. In A. Schardl, M. Walkow & M. Abdurrahman, eds., *Proceedings of NELS 38, Vol. 1*. Amherst, MA: GLSA. 371–84.

2009. A note on the typology of head-internal relativization. In P. K. Austin, O. Bond, M. Charette, D. Nathan & P. Sells, eds., *Proceedings of Conference on Language Documentation and Linguistic Theory 2*. London: SOAS.

2017. Internally headed relative clauses. In M. Everaert & H. van Riemsdijk, eds., *The Wiley Blackwell Companion to Syntax*. 2nd ed. Hoboken, NJ: Wiley-Blackwell. doi.org/10.1002/9781118358733.wbsyncom028

Hiraiwa, K., Akanlig-Pare, G., Atintono, S., Bodomo, A., Essizewa, K. & Hudu, F. 2017. A comparative syntax of internally-headed relative clauses in Gur. *Glossa: A Journal of General Linguistics* 2 (1): 27. DOI: doi.org/10.5334/gjgl.40

Hirsch, A. 2016. A compositional semantics for wh-ever free relatives. In N. Bade, P. Berezovskaya & A. Schöller, eds., *Proceedings of Sinn und Bedeutung 20*. 341–58. bit.ly/2P9gCoC

Hirschbühler, P. 1978. The syntax and semantics of wh-constructions. PhD diss. University of Massachusetts, Amherst.

1992. Observations sur les propositions relatives. In L. Tasmowski & A. Zribi-Hertz, eds., *Hommages à Nicolas Ruwet*. Ghent: Communication & Cognition. 284–99.

Hirschbühler, P. & Rivero, M.-L. 1983. Remarks on free relatives and matching phenomena. *Linguistic Inquiry* 14: 505–20.

Hladnik, M. 2013. Recoverability in Slovene relative clauses. In C. S. Rhys, P. Iosad & A. Henry, eds., *Minority Languages, Microvariation, Minimalism and Meaning: Proceedings of the Irish network in formal linguistics*. Newcastle: Cambridge Scholars Publishing. 171–85.

2015. Mind the gap: Resumption in Slavic relative clauses. PhD diss. University of Utrecht.

Hodgson, K. 2018. Word order, information structure and relativization strategies in Eastern Armenian. Paper presented at the International Workshop OV-IS 2018: OV basic word order correlates and information structure. 6–7 December. INALCO, Paris.

Hoeksema, J. 1986. An account of relative clauses with split antecedents. In M. Dalrymple, J. Goldberg, K. Hanson, et al., eds., *Proceedings of the 5th West Coast Conference on Formal Linguistics*. Stanford, CA: CSLI Publications. 68–86.

Hoekstra, J. 2002. Relativisation in Frisian. In P. Poussa, ed., *Relativisation on the North Sea Littoral*. 63–76. Munich: Lincom Europa.

Hofling, C. A. 2000. *Itzaj Maya Grammar*. Salt Lake City: University of Utah Press.

Holler, A. 2003. An HPSG analysis of non-integrated wh-relative clauses in German. *Proceedings of the HPSG03 Conference*. Stanford, CA: CSLI Publications. 163–80. stanford.io/384grUc

2005. *Weiterführende Relativsätze: Empirische und theoretische Aspekte*. Berlin: Akademie Verlag.

Hook, P. E. & Koul, O. N. 1996. Kashmiri as a V-2 language. In V. Swarajya Lakshmi & A. Mukherjee, eds., *Word Order in Indian Languages*. Hyderabad: Booklinks. 95–105.

Hornstein, N. 1994. An argument for Minimalism: The case of antecedent-contained deletion. *Linguistic Inquiry* 25: 455–80.

Horvath, J. 2017. Pied-piping. In M. Everaert & H. van Riemsdijk, eds., *The Wiley Blackwell Companion to Syntax*. 2nd ed. Hoboken, NJ: Wiley-Blackwell. 569–630. DOI: doi.org/10.1002/9781118358733.wbsyncom064

Houston, J. R. 1974. Dari Relative Clauses. *Studies in the Linguistic Sciences*, 4(1): 32–58.

Hsiao, F. P.-F. 2003. The syntax and processing of relative clauses in Mandarin Chinese. PhD diss. MIT. hdl.handle.net/1721.1/7990

Hsieh, M.-L. 2002.Tense as a grammatical category in Chinese. In S.-W. Tang & C.-S. Liu, eds., *On the Formal Way to Chinese Languages*. Stanford, CA: CSLI Publications. 3–20.

Hsu, Y.-Y. 2017. Alternatives and focus: Distribution of Chinese relative clauses revisited. *University of Pennsylvania Working Papers in Linguistics* 23: 73–82. bit.ly/2sKnkd7

Hu, S., Cecchetto, C. & Guasti, M. T. 2018. A new case for structural intervention: Evidence from Wenzhounese relative clauses. *Journal of East Asian Linguistics* 27 (3): 247–73.

Hu, S., Gavarró, A. & Guasti, M. T. 2016. Children's production of head-final relative clauses: The case of Mandarin. *Applied Psycholinguistics* 37 (2): 323–46.

Huang, C. 2008. Relativization in Qiang. *Language and Linguistics* 9 (4): 735–68. bit.ly/2OO977F

Huang, C.-T. J. 1982. Logical relations in Chinese and the theory of grammar. PhD diss. MIT.

  2016. The syntax and semantics of prenominals: Construction or composition? *Language and Linguistics* 17(4): 431–75. bit.ly/2Lp1hzn

Huang, C.-T. J., Li, Y.-H. A. & Li, Y. 2009. *The Syntax of Chinese*. Cambridge: Cambridge University Press.

Huck, G. J. & Na, Y. 1990. Extraposition and focus. *Language* 66: 51–77.

Hucklebridge, S. 2016. Head-internal relative clauses in Tłįchǫ Yatıì. *Toronto Working Papers in Linguistics* 36 . bit.ly/33MhB3v

Huddleston, R. 1971. *The sentence in written English: A syntactic study based on an analysis of scientific texts*. Cambridge: Cambridge University Press.

  1984. *Introduction to the Grammar of English*. Cambridge: Cambridge University Press.

Huddleston, R. & Pullum, G. K. 2002. *The Cambridge Grammar of the English Language*. Cambridge: Cambridge University Press.

Huhmarniemi, S. & Brattico, P. 2013. The structure of Finnish relative clause. *Finno-Ugric Languages and Linguistics* 2 (1): 53–88. bit.ly/2YhaFdv

Hull, G. & Eccles, L. (2001) *Tetum Reference Grammar*. Winston Hills, NSW: Sebastião Aparício da Silva Project.

Hulsey, S. & Sauerland, U. 2006. Sorting out relative clauses. *Natural Language Semantics* 14(2): 111–37.

Huot, H. 1978. Appositions et relatives appositives. *Recherches Linguistiques* 5–6: 103–42.

1981. Constructions infinitives du français: Le subordonnant *de*. *L'information grammaticale* 15: 40–5. DOI: doi.org/10.3406/igram.1982.2342

Huttar, G. L., Aboh, E. O. & Ameka, F. K. 2013. Relative clauses in Suriname creoles and Gbe languages. *Lingua* 129: 96–123.

Iatridou, S. 2013. Looking for free relatives in Turkish (and the unexpected places this leads to). In U. Özge, ed., *Proceedings of the 8th Workshop on Altaic Formal Linguistics (WAFL8)*. Cambridge, MA: MITWPL. 129–52.

Iatridou, S., Anagnostopoulou, E. & Izvorski, R. 2001. Observations about the form and meaning of the perfect. In M. Kenstowicz, ed., *Ken Hale: A life in language*. Cambridge, MA: MIT Press. 189–238.

Inada, S. 2008. Unexpected narrow scope and reconstruction into relative clause. *Linguistic Research* 24: 1–11.

2009. On the 'amount' relativization and its relatives. *Linguistic Research* 25: 85–102.

Isac, D. 2001. Restrictive relative clauses as conjuncts. In M. Andronis, C. Ball, H. Elston & S. Neuvel, eds., *Proceedings of the 37th Annual Meeting of the Chicago Linguistic Society, Vol. 1*. Chicago: Chicago Linguistic Society. 243–57.

2003. Restrictive relative clauses vs restrictive adjectives: An asymmetry within the class of modifiers. In A. M. Di Sciullo, ed., *Asymmetry in Grammar. Vol. 1: Syntax and semantics*. Amsterdam: Benjamins. 27–49.

Ishihara, R. 1984. Clausal pied-piping: A problem for GB. *Natural Language and Linguistic Theory* 2: 397–418.

Ishizuka, T. 2008a. Deriving the order of constituents inside the Javanese DP. MS. UCLA. ling.auf.net/lingBuzz/000769

2008b. Restrictive and non-restrictive relative clauses in Japanese: Antisymmetric approach. MS. Department of Linguistics, UCLA. ling.auf.net/lingbuzz/000808

Itô, J. & Mester, A. 2000. 'Ich, der ich sechzig bin': An agreement puzzle. Jorge Hankamer Webfest. UC Santa Cruz.

Izvorski, R. 1996. The syntax and semantics of correlative proforms. In *Proceedings of NELS 26*. Amherst, MA: GLSA. 133–47.

1998. Non-indicative wh-complements of existential/possessive predicates. In *Proceedings of NELS 28*. Amherst, MA: GLSA. 159–73.

2000. Free adjunct free relatives. In R. Billerey & D. Lillehaugen, eds., *Proceedings of the Nineteenth West Coast Conference of Formal Linguistics*. Somerville, MA: Cascadilla Press. 232–45.

Jackendoff, R. 1972. *Semantic Interpretation in Generative Grammar*. Cambridge, MA: MIT Press.

1977. *X-bar Syntax: A study of phrase structure*. Cambridge, MA: MIT Press.

Jacobson, P. 1995. On the quantificational force of English free relatives. In E. Bach, E. Jelinek, A. Kratzer, B. B. H. Partee, eds., *Quantification in Natural Languages*. Dordrecht: Kluwer. 451–86.

1998. Antecedent contained deletion and pied-piping: Evidence for a variable-free semantics. In *Proceedings of SALT 8*. 74–91. bit.ly/2LmgX6s

2002. Direct compositionality and variable-free semantics: The case of binding into heads. In *Proceedings of SALT 12*: 144–63. bit.ly/2DLU3kv

2019. Deconstructing reconstruction. In M. Krifka & M. Schenner, eds., *Reconstruction Effects in Relative Clauses*. Berlin: de Gruyter. 303–55.

Jacques, G. 2016. Subjects, objects and relativization in Japhug. *Journal of Chinese Linguistics* 44: 1–28.

Janse, M. 1999. Greek, Turkish, and Cappadocian relatives revis(it)ed. In A. Moser, ed., *Greek Linguistics: Proceedings of the 3rd international conference on Greek linguistics*. Athens: Ellinika Grammata. 453–62.

Jayaseelan, K. A. 2001. IP-internal topic and focus phrases. *Studia Linguistica* 55: 39–75.

Jeng, H.-H. 1977. *Topic and focus in Bunun*. Academia Sinica, Taipei. Special publication No. 72.

Jenks, P., Makasso, E.-M. & Hyman, L. 2017. Accessibility and demonstrative operators in Basaá relative clauses. In G. G. Atindogbé & R. Grollemund, eds., *Relative clauses in Cameroonian languages: Structure, function and semantics*. Berlin: Mouton de Gruyter. 17–46.

Jespersen, O. 1949. *A Modern English Grammar on Historical Principles: Part III*. Copenhagen: Einar Munksgaard and London: Allen and Unwin.

Jo, M.-J. 2002. The structure of relative clauses in Korean. *Studies in Generative Grammar* 12: 107–37.

Johannessen, J. B. 1998. *Coordination*. New York: Oxford University Press.

Johansson, S. 2011. Towards a typology of Algonquian relative clauses. In *Workshop on the Structure and Constituency of Languages of the Americas (WSCLA) 16*. 92–104. bit.ly/2Pg0Bx9

Johnson, G. 2015. The morphosyntax of *whatever* in free relatives: Variation and optionality in Appalachian English. Handout of LSA talk. MS. Graduate Center, CUNY. bit.ly/2PgiADz

Jónsson, J. G. 2017. Why *sem* is (still) a complementizer and not a relative pronoun. In N. LaCara, K. Moulton & A.-M. Tessier. *A Schrift to Fest Kyle Johnson*. Department of Linguistics, University of Massachusetts, Amherst. 169–75. scholarworks.umass.edu/linguist_oapubs/1/

Joseph, B. 1980. Recovery of information in relative clauses: Evidence from Greek and Hebrew. *Journal of Linguistics* 16: 237–44.

Julien, M. 2002. *Syntactic Heads and Word Formation*. New York: Oxford University Press.

Jung, Y. 1995. Internally headed relative clauses in Korean. In S. Kuno, ed., *Harvard Studies in Korean Linguistics VI: Proceedings of the 1995 Harvard International Symposium on Korean Linguistics*. Cambridge, MA: Department of Linguistics, Harvard University. 235–48.

Junghare, I. Y. 1973. Restrictive relative clauses in Marathi. *Indian Linguistics* 34(4): 251–62.

Kagan, O. & Pereltsvaig, A. 2012. Motivating the DP projection in languages without articles. In E. Cohen, ed., *Proceedings of Israeli Association for Theoretical Linguistics (IATL)*. Cambridge, MA: MITWPL. 167–78.

Kalivoda, N. & Zyman, E. 2015. On the derivation of relative clauses in Teotitlán del Valle Zapotec. In *Proceedings of the Forty-First Annual Meeting of the Berkeley Linguistics Society*. Berkeley, CA: Berkeley Linguistics Society. 219–43. doi.org/10.20354/B4414110016

Kallulli, D. 2000. Restrictive relative clauses revisited. In *Proceedings of NELS 30*. Amherst, MA: GLSA. 353–62.

2008. Resumption, relativization, null objects and information structure. In J. M. Hartmann, V. Hegedűs, & H. van Riemsdijk, eds., *Sounds of Silence: Empty elements in syntax and phonology*. Amsterdam: Elsevier. 235–64.

2014. Observations on relative clauses in Bavarian. In G. Grewendorf & H. Weiss, eds., *Bavarian Syntax: Contributions to the theory of syntax*. Amsterdam: Benjamins. 183–200.

2018. 'Relative pronouns' as agreeing complementizers: German *welch-*. Forthcoming in I. Frana, P. Menéndez-Benito & R. Bhatt, eds., *Making Worlds Accessible: A Festschrift for Angelika Kratzer*. University of Massachusetts Amherst: Scholarworks.

Kameshima, N. 1989. The syntax of restrictive and non-restrictive relative clauses in Japanese. PhD diss. University of Wisconsin, Madison.

Kamio, A. 1977. Restrictive and non-restrictive relative clauses in Japanese. *Descriptive and Applied Linguistics* 10: 147–68.

Kapeliuk, O. 2002. The relative verb in Amharic in an areal perspective. *Afrikanistische Arbeitspapiere* 71: 33–54.

Karlsson, F. & Sullivan, K. P. H. 2002. The use of relativization in the regional dialect of Swedish spoken in Burträsk. In P. Poussa, ed., *Relativisation on the North Sea Littoral*. Munich: Lincom Europa. 97–107.

Kayne, R. S. 1972. Subject inversion in French interrogatives. In J. Casagrande & B. Saciuk, eds., *Studies in Romance Languages*. Rowley, MA: Newbury House. 70–126.

1975. *French Syntax*. Cambridge, MA: MIT Press.

1976. French relative clauses. In M. Luján & F. Hensey (eds.), *Current Studies in Romance Linguistics*. Washington, DC: Georgetown University Press. 255–99.

1980. Extensions of binding and case-marking. *Linguistic Inquiry* 11: 55–91.

1981a. Binding, quantifiers, clitics and control. In F. Heny, ed., *Binding and Filtering*. London: Croom Helm 191–211.

1981b. ECP extensions. *Linguistic Inquiry*. 12: 93–134.

1983a. Connectedness. *Linguistic Inquiry* 14: 223–49.

1983b. Chains, categories external to S, and French complex inversion. *Natural Language and Linguistic Theory* 1: 107–39.

1984. *Connectedness and Binary Branching*. Dordrect: Foris.

1994. *The Antisymmetry of Syntax*. Cambridge, MA: MIT Press.

1998. Overt versus covert movement. *Syntax* 1: 128–91.

1999. Prepositional complementizers as attractors. *Probus* 11: 39–73.

2000. A note on prepositions, complementizers and word order universals. In *Parameters and Universals*. New York: Oxford University Press. 314–26.

2002. On some prepositions that look DP-internal: English *of* and French *de*. *Catalan Journal of Linguistics* 1: 71–115.

2003. Antisymmetry and Japanese. *English Linguistics* 20: 1–40.

2004a. Here and there. In C. Leclère, E. Laporte, M. Piot & M. Silberztein, eds., *Syntax, Lexis and Lexicon-Grammar: Papers in honour of Maurice Gross*. Amsterdam: Benjamins. 253–73.

2004b. Prepositions as probes. In A. Belletti, ed., *Structures and Beyond*. New York: Oxford University Press. 192–212.

2005a. Some notes on comparative syntax, with special reference to English and French. In G. Cinque & R. Kayne, eds., *The Oxford Handbook of Comparative Syntax*. New York: Oxford University Press. 3–69.

2005b. *Movement and Silence*. New York: Oxford University Press.

2007a. Some thoughts on grammaticalization: The case of *that*. Paper presented at the XVIIIe Conférence internationale de linguistique historique. Université du Québec à Montréal (UQAM).

2007b. On the syntax of quantity in English. In J. Bayer, T. Bhattacharya & M. T. H. Babu, eds., *Linguistic Theory and South Asian Languages: Essays in honour of K. A. Jayaseelan*. Amsterdam: Benjamins. 73–105.

2008a. Some preliminary comparative remarks on French and Italian articles. In R. Freidin, C. Otero, M. L. Zubizarreta, eds., *Foundational Issues in Linguistic Theory: Essays in honor of Jean-Roger Vergnaud*. Cambridge, MA: MIT Press. 291–321.

2008b. Antisymmetry and the lexicon. *Linguistic Variation Yearbook* 8: 1–31.

2010a. *Comparisons and Contrasts*. New York: Oxford University Press.

2010b. More on relative pronouns. Handout of a paper given at the workshop Adjectives and Relative Clauses: Syntax and Semantics, Ca' Foscari University, Venice. 16 June.

2014a. Why isn't *this* a complementizer? In P. Svenonius, ed., *Functional Structure from Top to Toe*. The cartography of syntactic structures. Vol. 9. New York: Oxford University Press. 188–231.

2014b. English *for* as a *wh*-phrase. Handout of a talk given at the workshop Variation in C, Università di Ca'Foscari, Venice. 22 October.

2015a. The silence of heads. MS. NYU. bit.ly/2YkKRxe

2015b. English *one* and *ones* as complex determiners. MS. NYU. bit.ly/2PawjvO

2016a. The unicity of *there* and the definiteness effect. MS. NYU.

2016b. Comparative syntax and English *is to*. *Linguistic Analysis* 39 (1–2): 35–82.

2017a. Clitic doubling, person and agreement in French hyper-complex inversion. MS. New York University.

2017b. A note on some even more unusual relative clauses. In L. R. Bailey & M. Sheehan, eds., *Order and Structure in Syntax I: Word order and syntactic structure*. Berlin: Language Science Press. 363–71.

2017c. English *for* as a *wh*-phrase. Handout of a talk given at the University of Frankfurt, 5 May.

2018. The place of linear order in the language faculty. Handout of a talk at Università di Ca' Foscari, Venice. 16 January. ling.auf.net/lingbuzz/003820

2019. *Questions of Syntax*. New York: Oxford University Press.

Keenan, E. 1985. Relative clauses. In T. Shopen, ed., *Language Typology and Syntactic Description. Vol. II. Complex Constructions*. Cambridge: Cambridge University Press. 141–70.

Keenan, E. & Comrie, B. 1977. Noun phrase accessibility and universal grammar. *Linguistic Inquiry* 8: 63–99.

1979. Data on the noun phrase accessibility hierarchy. *Language* 55: 333–51.

Kemp, W. 1981. Headless relatives and reduced relatives in Quebec French, Rumanian, and Spanish. In W. W. Cressey & D. J. Napoli, eds., *Linguistic Symposium on Romance Languages*. Washington, DC: Georgetown University Press. 248–64.

Kempson, R. 2003. Non-restrictive relatives and growth of logical form. In *Proceedings of the West Coast Conference on Formal Linguistics 22*: 301–14.

Kennedy, C. 1997. Antecedent-contained deletion and the syntax of quantification. *Linguistic Inquiry* 28: 662–88.

Keyser, S. J. 1975. A partial history of the relative clause in English. In J. Grimshaw, ed., *Papers in the History and Structure of English*. University of Massachusetts Occasional Papers in Linguistics 1. Amherst, MA: University of Massachusetts. 1–33.

Kholodilova, M. 2013. Inverse attraction in Ingrian Finnish. *Linguistica Uralica* XLIX (2): 96–116. DOI: 10.3176/lu.2013.2.02

2017. Competition between 'who' and 'which' in Slavic light-headed relative clauses. *Slověne. International Journal of Slavic Studies* 6 (1): 118–47. bit.ly/2s0H7o9

Kholodilova, M. & Privizentseva, M. 2015. Inverse attraction in Finno-Ugric languages. Paper given at the workshop 'Insufficient strength to defend its case': Case attraction and related phenomena. Wrocław, 18–19 September. bit.ly/2YoLSnN

Kibrik, A. E., ed., 1996. *Godoberi*. Munich: Lincom Europa.

Kim, D. 2014. Subordination in Sarikoli. MA. thesis. University of North Dakota.

2017. Topics in the syntax of Sarikoli. PhD diss. Leiden University.

Kim, J.-R. 1993. Restriction and apposition. *Language Research*. 29 (2): 189–99. bit.ly/2s084Zu

Kim, M.-J. 2007. Formal linking in internally headed relatives. *Natural Language Semantics* 15: 279–315.

Kim, Y.-K. 1997. Agreement phrases in DP. *UCL Working Papers in Linguistics* 9: 281–302.

Kitagawa, C. 2005. Typological variations of head-internal relatives in Japanese. *Lingua* 115: 1243–76.

2019. The *pro*-head analysis of the Japanese internally-headed relative clause. *Glossa: A Journal of General Linguistics* 4 (1): 62. DOI: doi.org/10.5334/gjgl.857

Kluender, R. 1992. Deriving island constraints from principles of predication. In H. Goodluck & M. Rochemont, eds., *Island Constraints: Theory, acquisition and processing*. Dordrecht: Kluwer. 223–58.

Knowles, J. 1990. Free relatives. A modified COMP analysis. MS. Simon Fraser University.

Koch, K. 2005. German prenominal modifiers. In M.-O. Junker, M. McGinnis & Y. Roberge, eds., *Proceedings of the 2004 Annual Meeting of the Canadian Linguistic Association*. bit.ly/363BrZu

Koizumi, M. 1994. Secondary predicates. *Journal of East Asian Linguistics* 3: 25–79.

Kojima, Y. 2005. Two types of relative clauses in Modern Georgian. In K. Vamling, ed., *Language, History and Cultural Identities in the Caucasus*. Papers from the conference, 17–19 June, Malmö University. Malmö: Malmö University Press. 156–67. bit.ly/2YqAx6Q

2014. The position of *rom* and the pragmatics of subordinate clauses in Georgian. In N. Amiridze, T. Reseck & M. Topdze Gäumann, eds., *Advances in Kartvelian Morphology and Syntax*. Bochum: Universitätsverlag Dr. N. Brockmeyer. 141–53.

Komen, E. R. 2007. The relative clause in Chechen. Abstract of a paper presented at the Conference of the Languages of the Caucasus, 7–9 December, Department of Linguistics, Max Planck Institute for Evolutionary Anthropology. bit.ly/34TzGh8

Koopman, H. 1983. Control from COMP and comparative syntax. *The Linguistic Review* 2: 365–91.

2000. The Spec head configuration. In *The Syntax of Specifiers and Heads: Collected essays of Hilda J. Koopman*. London: Routledge. 331–65.

Koopman, H. & Sportiche, D. 2014. The *que/qui* Alternation: New analytical directions. In P. Svenonius, ed., *Functional Structure from Top to Toe*. The cartography of syntactic structures. Vol. 9. New York: Oxford University Press. 46–96.

Koopman, H. & Szabolcsi, A. 2000. *Verbal Complexes*. Cambridge, MA: MIT Press.

Kornfilt, J. 1985. Infinitival Relative Clauses and Complementation in Turkish. *Proceedings of the 21st Annual Meeting of the Chicago Linguistic Society*. Chicago: Chicago Linguistic Society. 221–35.

1997. *Turkish*. London: Routledge.

2005a. Agreement and its placement in Turkic nonsubject relative clauses. In G. Cinque & R. S. Kayne, eds., *The Oxford Handbook of Comparative Syntax*. New York: Oxford University Press. 513–41.

2005b. Free relatives as light-headed relatives in Turkish. In H. Broekhuis, N. Corver, R. Huybregts, U. Kleinhenz & J. Koster, eds., *Organizing Grammar: Studies in honor of Henk van Riemsdijk*. Berlin: Mouton de Gruyter. 340–9.

2011. Non-restrictive pre-nominal relative clauses in a head-final language. In E. Erguvanlı Taylan & B. Rona, eds., *Puzzles of Language: Essays in Honour of Karl Zimmer*. Wiesbaden: Harrassowitz. 93–102.

2014. Free adjuncts and non-free relatives in Turkish. In C. Arslan Kechriotis, D. Akar, M. Kelepir, B. Öztürk, eds., *Dilbilim Araştırmaları*. Special issue. Istanbul: Boğaziçi University Publications. 117–29.

2015. Two types of free relatives in Turkish in disguise: One is headed, the other a correlative. In D. Zeyrek, Ç. Sağın Şimşek, U. Ataş & J. Rehbein, eds., *Ankara Papers in Turkish and Turkic Linguistics*. Wiesbaden: Harrassowitz. 132–50.

2018. Turkish complex nominal phrase constructions. In C. Guillemot, T. Yoshida & S. J. Lee, eds., *Proceedings of the 13th Workshop of Altaic Formal Linguistics*. MIT Working Papers in Linguistics 88. Cambridge, MA: MITWPL. 17–33.

Kornfilt, J. & Vinokurova, N. 2017. Turkish and Turkic complex noun phrase constructions. In Y. Matsumoto, B. Comrie & P. Sells, eds. *Noun-modifying clause constructions in languages of Eurasia: Rethinking theoretical and geographical boundaries*. Amsterdam: Benjamins. 251–92.

Koster, J. 1986. *Domains and Dynasties: The radical autonomy of syntax*. Dordrecht: Foris.

2000. Extraposition as parallel construal. MS. University of Groningen.

2015. Relative Clauses: Parallelism and partial reconstruction. In M. van Oostendorp & H. van Riemsdijk, eds., *Representing Structure in Phonology and Syntax*. Berlin: Mouton de Gruyter. 115–40.

Koster-Moeller, J. 2012. Internal DP heads in restrictive relative clauses. In *Proceedings of ConSOLE XVII*: 209–30.

Koster-Moeller, J. & Hackl, M. 2008. Quantifier scope constraints in ACD: Implications for the syntax of relative clauses. In N. Abner & J. Bishop, eds., *Proceedings of the 27th West Coast Conference on Formal Linguistics*. Somerville, MA: Cascadilla Press. 301–09. www.lingref.com/cpp/wccfl/27/paper1844.pdf

Kotek, H. & Erlewine, M. Y. 2015a. Non-interrogative wh-constructions in Chuj. In *Workshop on Structure and Constituency in Languages of the Americas (WSCLA) 21*. 1–3 April 2016, Université du Québec à Montréal.

2015b. Relative pronoun pied-piping in English non-restrictive relatives. MS. McGill University and National University of Singapore.

2015c. Intervention effects in relative pronoun pied-piping: experimental evidence. In N. Bade, P. Berezovskaya & A. Schöller, eds., *Proceedings of Sinn und Bedeutung 20*.

2016. Unifying definite and indefinite free relatives: Evidence from Mayan. *Proceedings of NELS 46, Vol. 2*. Amherst, MA: GSLA. 241–54.

Koul, O. N. 2003. Kashmiri. In G. Cardona & D. Jain, eds., *The Indo-Aryan Languages*. London: Routledge. 895–952.

Kotzoglou, G. & Varlokosta, S. 2005. Clitics in Greek restrictive relatives: An integrated approach. *Reading Working Papers in Linguistics* 8. 27–49.

Krapova, I. 2010. Bulgarian relative and factive clauses with an invariant complementizer. *Lingua* 120: 1240–72.

Krapova, I. & Cinque, G. 2016. On noun clausal 'complements' and their non-unitary nature. *Annali di Ca' Foscari*. Serie occidentale. 50: 77–107. doi.org/10.14277/2499-1562/AnnOc-50-16-4

Krause, C. 2001a. On reduced relatives with genitive subjects. PhD diss. MIT.

2001b. On pre-relatives and appositives. *Proceedings of the 20th West Coast Conference on Formal Linguistics*. Somerville, MA: Cascadilla Press. 332–45.

Krifka, M. 2011. Reconstruction effects in relative clauses. Handout of a paper given at the workshop 'An explanation of condition C effects under apparent reconstruction', Zentrum für Allgemeine Sprachwissenschaft (ZAS), Berlin, 8–9 July. bit.ly/2qjLome

Krifka, M. & Schanner, M. 2019. *Reconstruction Effects in Relative Clauses*. Berlin: de Gruyter.

Kroch, A. 1981. On the role of resumptive pronouns in amnestying island constraint violations. In *Proceedings of the 17th Annual Meeting of the Chicago Linguistic Society*. Chicago: Chicago Linguistic Society. 125–35. bit.ly/3671U8x

Kroeger, Paul. 2005. *Analyzing Grammar: An introduction*. Cambridge: Cambridge University Press.

Kroeker, M. 2001. A descriptive grammar of Nambikuara. *International Journal of American Linguistics* 67: 1–87.

Kuno, S. 1973. *The Structure of the Japanese Language* Cambridge, MA: MIT Press.

1976. Subject, theme, and the speaker's empathy: A re-examination of relativization phenomena. In C. Li, ed., *Subject and Topic*. New York: Academic Press. 417–44.

Kuroda, S.-Y. 1968. English relativization and certain related problems. *Language* 44: 244–66.

1976. Headless relative clauses in modern Japanese and the relevancy condition. In *Proceedings of the Second Annual Meeting of the Berkeley Linguistics Society*. Berkeley, CA: Berkeley Linguistics Society. 269–79.

Kush, D., Omaki, A. & Hornstein, N. 2009. Reanalysing relative clause island effects. Paper presented at 32nd GLOW, Nantes.

2013. Microvariation in islands? In J. Sprouse & N. Hornstein, eds., *Experimental Syntax and Island Effects*. Cambridge: Cambridge University Press. 239–64.

Kuteva, T. & Comrie, B. 2006. The typology of relative clause formation in African Languages. In F. K. E. Voeltz, ed., *Studies in African Linguistic Typology*. Amsterdam: Benjamins. 209–28.

Kvam, S. 1983. *Linksverschachtelung im Deutschen und Norwegischen*. Tübingen: Niemeyer.

Kwon, N., Polinsky, M. & Kluender, R. 2006. Subject preference in Korean. In D. Baumer, D. Montero, & M. Scanlon, eds., *Proceedings of the 25th West Coast Conference on Formal Linguistics*. Somerville, MA: Cascadilla Press. 1–14. www.lingref.com/cpp/wccfl/25/paper1429.pdf

Labelle, M. 1996. The acquisition of relative clauses: Movement or no movement? *Language Acquisition* 5: 65–82. bit.ly/2RpqCNg

Lacroix, R. 2009. Description du dialecte laze d'Arhavi (caucasique du sud, Turquie): Grammaire et textes. PhD diss. Université Lumière Lyon 2. bit.ly/2DQ8UKJ

2012. The multi-purpose subordinator *na* in Laz. In V. Gast & H. Diessel, eds., *Clause Linkage in Cross-Linguistic Perspective: Data driven approaches to cross-clausal syntax*. Berlin: Mouton de Gruyter. 77–103.

Lakshmi Bai, B. 1985. Some notes on correlative constructions in Dravidian. In V. Z. Acson & R. L. Leed, eds., *For Gordon H. Fairbanks*. Honolulu: The University Press of Hawai'i. 181–90.

Lamberti, M. & Sottile, R. 1997. *The Wolaytta Language*. Cologne: Rüdiger Köppe Verlag.

Lambrecht, K. 1988. There was a farmer had a dog: Syntactic amalgams revisited. In S. Axmaker, A. Jaisser & H. Singmaster, eds., *Proceedings of the 14th Annual Meeting of the Berkeley Linguistics Society*. Berkeley, CA: Berkeley Linguistics Society. 319–39. bit.ly/2Pe8x28

Lander, Y. 2006. Multiple relativization in Adyghe. Paper given at the workshop 'Morphosyntaxe des langues du Caucase', INALCO, 13 December. CNRS, Paris. bit.ly/2qk1xYS

2010. Relativization in Shapsug Adyghe. *Rice Working Papers in Linguistics* 2: 75–91. bit.ly/354GxEw

Lander, Y. & Kozhukhar, A. 2015. Successfully looking for syntax in Mehweb Dargwa relative clause constructions. Basic research program working papers of the National Research University Higher School of Economics, Moscow. http://bit.ly/31QnRYI

Larson, R. 1987. 'Missing prepositions' and the analysis of English free relative clauses. *Linguistic Inquiry* 18: 39–266.

1998. Free relative clauses and missing Ps: Reply to Grosu. MS. Stony Brook, State University of New York.

2016. Warlpiri adjoined clauses. Workshop on the internal and external syntax of adverbial clauses. Zentrum für Allgemeine Sprachwissenschaft (ZAS), Berlin, 23 July.

2017. On 'dative idioms' in English. *Linguistic Inquiry* 48: 389–426.

Larson, R. & LaTerza, I. 2017. Revisiting article-S. *Revista Linguística* 13(2): 51–87. bit.ly/366yJ5r

Larson, R. & May, R. 1990. Antecedent containment or vacuous movement: Reply to Baltin. *Linguistic Inquiry* 21: 103–22.

Larson, R. & Takahashi, N. 2007. Order and interpretation in prenominal relative clauses. In M. Kelepir & B. Öztürk, eds., *Proceedings of the 2nd Workshop on Altaic Formal Linguistics (WAFL 2)*. MIT Working Papers in Linguistics 54. Cambridge, MA: MITWPL. 101–120.

Lassiter, D. 2011. Anaphoric properties of *which* and the syntax of appositive relatives. *NYU Working Papers in Linguistics (NYUWPL)* 3: 69–94. bit.ly/33XOFWo

Law, P. 2001. Some issues in English and Chinese relative clauses. Handout for the Study Group on Relative Clauses, Hong Kong Polytechnic University. 29 September.

Lee, F. 2001. Relative clauses without wh-movement. In M.-J. Kim & U. Strauss, eds., *Proceedings of NELS 31*. Amherst, MA: GLSA. 321–31.

Lee-Goldman, R. 2012. Supplemental relative clauses: Internal and external syntax. *Journal of Linguistics* 48: 573–608.

Lees, R. B. 1960. *The Grammar of English Nominalizations*. The Hague: Mouton.

1961. The constituent structure of noun phrases. *American Speech* 36: 159–68.

Lefebvre, C. & Brousseau, A.-M. 2002. *A Grammar of Fongbe*. Berlin: Mouton de Gruyter.

Lefebvre, C. & Fournier, R. 1978. Le relatives en français de Montréal. In *Syntaxe et sémantique du français*. Montreal: Les Presses de l'Université du Québec. 273–94.

Lehmann, C. 1984. *Der Relativsatz: Typologie seiner Strukturen, Theorie seiner Funktionen, Kompendium seiner Grammatik*. Tübingen: Narr.

1986. On the typology of relative clauses. *Linguistics* 24 (4): 663–80.

Łęska, P. 2016. Agreement under case matching in Polish *co* and *który* relative clauses headed by numerically quantified nouns. *Journal of Slavic Linguistics* 24: 113–36.

Leu, T. 2008. The internal syntax of determiners. PhD diss. NYU. ling.auf.net/lingbuzz/000745

2015. Generalized x-to-C in Germanic. *Studia Linguistica* 69: 272–303.

Leung, T. T.-C. 2007a. Syntactic derivation and the theory of matching contextual features. PhD diss. University of Southern California.

2007b. Correlatives and the conditions on chain formation. In *Proceedings of the International Conference on Linguistics in Korea (ICLK 2007)*. Seoul: Seoul National University, KGGC.

2007c. On the typology of correlative constructions. Handout of a paper presented at the conference of the Association of Linguistic Typology (ALT VII) CNRS, Paris, 28 September.

2009. Wh-phrasal movement and adjunction analysis of free relatives. In R. Mohanty & M. Menon, eds., *Universals and Variation.* 161–80. Hyderabad: The English and Foreign Languages University Press.

Li, C. N. & Thompson, S. A. 1978. Relativization strategies in Wappo. *Proceedings of BLS* 4: 106–13.

1981. *Mandarin Chinese: A functional reference grammar.* Berkeley, CA: University of California Press.

Li, Y.-H. A. 2001a. Universal constructions? Relativization in English and Chinese. *Concentric: Studies in English Literature and Linguistics* 27(2): 163–87. bit.ly/2DOWbs0

2001b. Head-final relatives in one family? A comparative study of relativization in Chinese and Japanese. Paper presented at IACL-10/NACCL-13 joint meeting at Irvine, California.

2002. Word order, structure, and relativization. In S.-W. Tang & C.-S. L. Liu, eds., *On the Formal Way to Chinese Languages.* Stanford, CA: CSLI Publications. 45–73.

Lin, J.-W. 2004. On restrictive and non-restrictive relative clauses in Mandarin Chinese. *Tsing Hua Journal of Chinese Studies* 33(1): 199–240.

2008. The order of stage-level and individual-level relatives and superiority effects. *Language and Linguistics,* 9 (4): 839–64. bit.ly/2DUnhO5

Lin, J.-W. & Tsai, W.-T. D. 2015. Restricting non-restrictive relatives in Mandarin Chinese. In A. Li, A. Simpson & W.-T. D. Tsai, eds., *Chinese Syntax in a Cross-Linguistic Perspective.* New York: Oxford University Press. 100–27.

Lindahl, F. 2017. Extraction from relative clauses in Swedish. PhD diss. University of Gothenburg. bit.ly/389ytEF

Link, G. 1984. Hydras: On the logic of relative constructions with multiple heads. In F. Landman & F. Veltman, eds., *Varieties of Formal Semantics.* Dordrecht: Foris. 245–57.

Lipták, A. 2004. Adjunct scope marking: New arguments for Dayal's approach. In K. Moulton & M. Wolf, eds., *Proceedings of NELS 34.* Amherst, MA: GLSA. 405–23.

2009a. The landscape of correlatives: An empirical and analytical survey. In A. Lipták, ed., *Correlatives Cross-Linguistically.* Amsterdam: Benjamins. 1–46.

2009b. ed. *Correlatives Cross-Linguistically.* Amsterdam: Benjamins.

2015. Relative pronouns as sluicing remnants. In K. É. Kiss, B. Surányi & É. Dékány, eds., *Approaches to Hungarian, Vol. 14.* Amsterdam: Benjamins. 187–207.

Lipták, A. & Aboh, E. O. 2013. Sluicing inside relatives: The case of Gungbe. In S. Aalberse & A. Auer, eds., *Linguistics in the Netherlands 2013.* Amsterdam: Benjamins. 102–18.

Loccioni, N. 2017. Comparative superlatives in relative clauses. Handout of a talk at a syntax/semantics seminar at UCLA.

2018. Getting 'the most' out of Romance. PhD diss. UCLA.

Longenbaugh, N. 2019. Agreement mismatch in partitive relatives. *Linguistic Inquiry* 50: 847–61.

Longobardi, G. 1994. Reference and proper names: A theory of N-movement in syntax and logical form. *Linguistic Inquiry* 25: 609–65.

Loock, R. 2010. *Appositive relative clauses in English*. Amsterdam: Benjamins.

Loss, S. S. 2017. Two types of subordinate subject contact relatives. *Snippets* 31: 15–16.

Loughnane, R. 2009. A Grammar of Oksapmin. PhD diss. University of Melbourne. repository.unimelb.edu.au/10187/4788

Lu, B. 1990. The structure of Chinese nominal phrases. In M. Saito, ed., *Comparative Studies on the Structure of Noun Phrases*. Storrs, CT: Department of Linguistics, University of Connecticut. 1–41.

1998. Left-right asymmetries of word order variation: A functional explanation. PhD diss. University of Southern California.

Lüpke, F. 2005. A grammar of Jalonke argument structure. PhD diss. Radboud University, Nijmegen. repository.ubn.ru.nl/handle/2066/19598

MacDonald, L. 1990. *A Grammar of Tauya*. Berlin: Mouton de Gruyter.

Mahajan, A. 1990. The A/A-bar distinction and movement theory. PhD diss. MIT.

2000. Relative Asymmetries and Hindi Correlatives. In A. Alexiadou, P. Law, A. Meinunger, C. Wilder, eds., *The Syntax of Relative Clauses*. Amsterdam: Benjamins. 201–29.

Maiden, M. & Robustelli, C. 2013. *A Reference Grammar of Modern Italian*. London: Routledge.

Maling, J. 1977. A nonrecoverable deletion. In S. E. Fox, W. A. Beach & S. Philosoph, eds., *CLS Book of Squibs*. 66–67. Chicago: Chicago Linguistic Society. people .brandeis.edu/~maling/Maling1977.pdf

1978. The complementizer in Middle English appositives. *Linguistic Inquiry* 9: 719–25.

Maling, J. & Zaenen, A. 1982. A phrase structure account of Scandinavian extraction phenomena. In P. Jacobson & G. K. Pullum, eds., *The Nature of Syntactic Representation*. Dordrecht: Reidel. 229–82.

Mallinson, G. & Blake, B. J. 1981. *Language Typology: Cross-linguistic studies in syntax*. Amsterdam: North-Holland.

Manninen, S. 2002. Extraposition and restrictive relative clauses. *Working Papers of the Department of English in Lund* 2. bit.ly/34XyZ6L

2003. To raise or not to raise: The case of Finnish restrictive relative clauses. *Nordlyd* 31 (4): 668–93.

Manzini, M. R. 2010. The structure and interpretation of (Romance) complementizers. In E. P. Panagiotidis, ed., *The Complementizer Phase: Subjects and operators*. Oxford: Oxford University Press. 167–99.

2012. The status of complementizers in the left periphery. In L. Aelbrecht, L. Haegeman & R. Nye, eds., *Main Clause Phenomena: New horizons*. Amsterdam: Benjamins. 297–318.

Manzini, M. R. & Savoia, L. 2003. The nature of complementizers. *Rivista di Grammatica Generativa* 28: 87–110. bit.ly/33W4cWH

2011. *Grammatical Categories*. Cambridge: Cambridge University Press.

Marvin, T. 2002. Past participles in reduced relatives. In M. van Koppen, E. Thrift, E. J. van der Torre & M. Zimmermann, eds., *Proceedings of ConSOLE IX*. 141–56.

Marvin, T. 2003. Past participles in reduced relatives: A cross-linguistic perspective. *Linguistica* 43: 141–60.

Matsumoto, Y. 1990. Role of pragmatics in Japanese relative clauses. *Lingua* 82: 111–29.

1997. *Noun-Modifying Constructions in Japanese: A frame semantic approach.* Amsterdam: Benjamins.

Matsumoto, Y., Comrie, B. & Sells, P. eds., 2017. *Noun-modifying Clause Constructions in Languages of Eurasia: Rethinking theoretical and geographical boundaries.* Amsterdam: Benjamins.

Matsumura, K. 1982. Two types of relative clauses in Finnish. *Gengo Kenkyu* 81: 60–82. bit.ly/38gGYho

Maurel, J.-P. 1983. Les relatives en latin: 'Raising' ou 'Matching'? In H. Pinkster, ed., *Latin Linguistics and Linguistic Theory.* Amsterdam: Benjamins. 177–96.

1989. Subordination seconde du relatif en latin et théorie du 'COMP'. In G. Calboli, ed., *Subordination and Other Topics in Latin.* Amsterdam: Benjamins. 181–96.

May, R. 1985. *Logical Form: Its structure and derivation.* Cambridge, MA: MIT Press.

Mazaudon, M. 1978. La formation des propositions relatives en tibétain. *Bulletin de la Société Linguistique de Paris* 73: 401–14. bit.ly/3650hbe

McCawley, J. D. 1981. The syntax and semantics of English relative clauses. *Lingua* 53: 99–149.

1988. *The Syntactic Phenomena of English.* Chicago: The University of Chicago Press.

1991. *A Linguistic Flea Circus.* Bloomington, IN: Indiana University Linguistic Club.

1996. An overview of 'appositive' constructions in English. In *ESCOL '95*: 195–211.

1998. *The Syntactic Phenomena of English.* 2nd ed. Chicago: The University of Chicago Press.

2004. Remarks on adsentential, adnominal, and extraposed relative clauses in Hindi. In V. Dayal & A. Mahajan, eds., *Clause Structure in South Asian Languages.* Dordrecht: Kluwer. 291–311.

McCloskey, J. 1990. Resumptive pronouns, A' binding and levels of representation in Irish. In R. Hendrick, ed., *The Syntax of the Modern Celtic Languages.* Syntax and Semantics 23. New York: Academic Press. 199–248.

2002. Resumption, successive cyclicity, and the locality of operations. In S. Epstein & T. D. Seeley, eds., *Derivation and Explanation in the Minimalist Program.* Oxford: Blackwell. 184–226.

2006. Resumption. In M. Everaert & H. van Riemsdijk, eds., *The Blackwell Companion to Syntax.* Malden, MA: Blackwell. 94–117.

2017a. Resumption. In M. Everaert & H. van Riemsdijk, eds., *The Wiley Blackwell Companion to Syntax.* 2nd ed. Hoboken, NJ: Wiley-Blackwell. 3809–38. DOI: doi.org/10.1002/9781118358733.wbsyncom105

2017b. New thoughts on old questions: Resumption in Irish. In J. Ostrove, R. Kramer & J. Sabbagh, eds., *Asking the Right Questions: Essays in honor of Sandra Chung.* University of California Santa Cruz: California Digital Library. 81–102. escholarship.org/uc/item/8255v8sc

McKinney-Bock, K. 2013. Deriving split-antecedent relative clauses. In *University of Pennsylvania Working Papers in Linguistics 19*. 113–122.

McKinney-Bock, K. & Vergnaud, J.-R. 2014. Grafts and beyond: Graph-theoretic syntax. In K. McKinney-Bock & M.-L. Zubizarreta, eds., *Primitive Elements of Grammatical Theory*. London: Routledge. 207–36.

McNally, L. 2008. DP-internal *only*, amount relatives, and relatives out of existentials. *Linguistic Inquiry* 39: 161–9.

McPherson, L. E. 2014. Replacive grammatical tone in the Dogon languages. PhD diss. UCLA. bit.ly/38fecxg

Meakins, F. & Nordlinger, R. 2014. *A grammar of Bilinarra: An Australian Aboriginal language of the Northern Territory*. Berlin: Mouton de Gruyter.

Meier, C. 2015. Amount relatives as generalized quantifiers. MS. Goethe University Frankfurt. bit.ly/2qwOHH2

Meltzer-Asscher, A. 2010. Present participles: Categorial classification and derivation. *Lingua* 120: 2211–39.

Mendia, J. A. 2017. Amount relatives redux. PhD diss. University of Massachusetts, Amherst. scholarworks.umass.edu/dissertations_2/1111

Meral, H. M. 2004. Resumptive pronouns in Turkish. MA thesis. Boğaziçi University.

Milsark, G. 1974. Existential sentences in English. PhD diss. MIT.

Ming, T. 2010. The relative position of demonstratives and relative clauses in Mandarin Chinese. In *Proceedings of the 22nd North American Conference on Chinese Linguistics and the 18th International Conference on Chinese Linguistics. Vol. 2*. Harvard University. 323–40. bit.ly/2PkCD40

Mithun, M. 2012. Questionable relatives. In B. Comrie & Z. Estrada-Fernández, eds., *Relative Clauses in Languages of the Americas: A typological overview*. Amsterdam: Benjamins. 269–300.

Miyagawa, S. 2008. Genitive subjects in Altaic. In *Proceedings of WAFL 4*. MIT Working Papers in Linguistics. Cambridge, MA: MITWPL. 181–98.

2010. *Why Agree? Why Move? Unifying agreement-based and discourse-configurational languages*. Cambridge, MA: MIT Press.

2011. Genitive subjects in Altaic and specification of phase. *Lingua* 121: 1265–82.

Miyamoto, Y. 2010. On Chinese and Japanese relative clauses and NP-ellipsis. *Nanzan Linguistics* 6: 13–46. bit.ly/2OXLw4t

Mohanan, K. P. 1984. Operator binding and the path containment condition. *Natural Language and Linguistic Theory* 2: 357–96.

Moltmann, F. 1992. Coordination and comparatives. PhD diss. MIT.

2019. Intensional relative clauses and the semantics of variable objects. In M. Krifka & M. Schenner, eds., *Reconstruction Effects in Relative Clauses*. Berlin: de Gruyter. 427–54.

Montague, R. 1970. English as a formal language. In B. Visentini et al., eds., *Linguaggi nella società e nella tecnica*. Milan: Edizioni di Comunità. 189–224.

Morgan, J. L. 1972a. Verb agreement as a rule of English. In P. M. Peranteau, J. N. Levi & G. C. Phares, eds, *Papers from the 8th Regional Meeting of the Chicago Linguistic Society*. Chicago. University of Chicago. 278–86.

1972b. Some aspects of relative clauses in English and Albanian. In P. M. Peranteau, J. N. Levi & G. C. Phares, eds., *The Chicago Which Hunt: Papers from the relative clause festival*. Chicago: Chicago Linguistic Society. 63–72.

Moroney, M. 2018. Interpretation of internally-headed relative clauses in Shan. In K. Garvin, N. Hermalin, M. Lapierre, Y. Melguy, T. Scott & E. Wilbanks, eds., *Proceedings of the 44th Annual Meeting of the Berkeley Linguistics Society*. Berkeley, CA: Berkeley Linguistics Society. 197–212. bit.ly/2LqOYCj

Morshed, A. K. M. 1986. *Relativization in Bengali*. Dhaka: University of Dhaka.

Müller, C. 2015. Against the small clause hypothesis: Evidence from Swedish relative clause extractions. *Nordic Journal of Linguistics* 38: 67–92.

Muller, C. 2006. Sur les propriétés des relatives. *Cahiers de Grammaire* 30: 319–37.

Munaro, N. 2000. Free relative clauses as defective *wh*-elements: Evidence from the north-western Italian dialects. *University of Venice Working Papers in Linguistics* 10: 89–120. hdl.handle.net/11707/505

    2001. Free relatives as defective *wh*-elements: Evidence from the north-western Italian dialects. In Y. D'Hulst, J. Rooryck & J. Schroten, eds., *Romance Languages and Linguistic Theory 1999*. Amsterdam: Benjamins. 281–306.

Munro, P. 1974. Topics in Mojave syntax. PhD diss. University of California, San Diego.

Murelli, A. 2011. *Relative constructions in European non-standard varieties*. Berlin: Mouton de Gruyter.

Nakamura, T. 2009. Headed relatives, free relatives, and determiner-headed free relatives. *English Linguistics* 26: 329–55. bit.ly/38d5BLL

Nanni, D. L. & Stillings, J. T. 1978. Three remarks on pied-piping. *Linguistic Inquiry* 9: 310–18.

Napoli, D. J. 1976. Infinitival relatives in Italian. In M. Lujan & F. Hensey, eds., *Current Studies in Romance Linguistics*. Washington, DC: Georgetown University Press. 300–29.

Nedjalkov, V. & Otaina, G. A. 2013. *A Syntax of the Nivkh Language: The Amur dialect*. Amsterdam: Benjamins.

Nefedov, A. 2012. Relativization in Ket. In V. Gast & H. Diessel, eds., *Clause Linkage in Cross-Linguistic Perspective*. Berlin: De Gruyter. 191–224.

Nevalainen, T. & Raumolin-Brunberg, H. 2002. The rise of the relative *who* in early modern English. In P. Poussa, ed., *Relativisation on the North Sea Littoral*. Munich: Lincom Europa. 109–21.

Ngonyani, D. 2003. Aspects of relative clause construction in Kindendeule and Kingoni. In J. Mugane, ed., *Linguistic Typology and Representation of African Languages*. Trenton, NJ and Asmara: Africa World Press. 229–42.

    2006. Resumptive pronominal clitics in Bantu languages. In O. F. Arasanyin & M. A. Pemberton, eds., *Selected Proceedings of the 36th Annual Conference on African Linguistics*. Somerville, MA: Cascadilla Press. 51–9.

Nguyen, T. T. M. 2013. A grammar of Bih. PhD diss. University of Oregon. hdl.handle.net/1794/12996

Nguyen, T. H. 2004. The structure of the Vietnamese noun phrase. PhD diss. Boston University.

Nilsen, Ø. 2000. *The Syntax of Circumstantial Adverbials*. Oslo: Novus Press.

Nikitina, T. 2012. Clause-internal correlatives in Southeastern Mande: A case for the propagation of typological rara. *Lingua* 122 (4): 319–34.

Nikolaeva, I. 2017. The general noun-modifying clause construction in Tundra Nenets and its possible origin. In Y. Matsumoto, B. Comrie & P. Sells, eds., *Noun-Modifying Clause Constructions in Languages of Eurasia: Reshaping theoretical and geographical boundaries*. Amsterdam: Benjamins.

Ning, C. 1993. The overt syntax of relativization and topicalization in Chinese. PhD diss. UC Irvine.

Noonan, M. 1992. *A Grammar of Lango*. Berlin: Mouton de Gruyter.

Nordlinger, R. 2006. Spearing the emu drinking: Subordination and the adjoined relative clause in Wambaya. *Australian Journal of Linguistics* 26: 5–29.

Nunberg, G., Sag, I. & Wasow, T. 1994. Idioms. *Language* 70 (3): 491–538.

Oguri, H. 1976. Form and meaning in the Isirawa noun phrase. *Irian: Bulletin of Irian Jaya Development*. 5 (2): 85–103.

Ojeda, A. E. 1982. Degree relatives and the neuter article in Spanish. *Proceedings of CLS* 18: 407–18.

Ordóñez, F. 2002. Some clitic combinations in the syntax of Romance. *Catalan Journal of Linguistics* 1: 201–24. DOI: doi.org/10.5565/rev/catjl.59

Otsuka, Y. 2010. Genitive relative constructions and agent incorporation in Tongan. In R. Mercado, E. Potsdam & L. Travis, eds., *Austronesian and Theoretical Linguistics*. Amsterdam: Benjamins. 117–40.

Ouhalla, J. 2004. Semitic relatives. *Linguistic Inquiry* 35: 288–300.

    2006. Review of 'Essays on the representational and derivational nature of grammar: The diversity of wh-constructions' by Joseph Aoun & Yen-Hui Audrey Li. Cambridge, MA: MIT Press, 2003. *Language* 82: 649–51.

Overfelt, J. 2009. The syntax of relative clause constructions in Tigrinya. MA thesis. Purdue University.

    2015. Rightward movement: A study in locality. PhD diss. University of Massachusetts, Amherst. bit.ly/2PoKayy

Özçelik, Ö. 2014. An antisymmetric analysis of Turkish relative clauses: Implications from prosody. *Turkic Languages* 18 (1/2): 247–70.

Öztürk, B. & Pöchtrager, M. A. 2011. *Pazar Laz*. Munich: Lincom Europa.

Palmer, F. R. 1961. Relative clauses in Tigre. *Word* 17: 23–33.

Pan, V. J. 2016. *Resumptivity in Mandarin Chinese: A minimalist account*. Berlin: Mouton de Gruyter.

Pancheva Izvorski, R. 2000. Free relatives and related matters. PhD diss. University of Pennsylvania. repository.upenn.edu/dissertations/AAI9965537

Pandharipande, R. 1997. *Marathi*. London: Routledge.

Pankau, A. 2015. The matching analysis of relative clauses: Evidence from Upper Sorbian. In Y. Oseki et al., eds., *Proceedings of the 24th Meeting of Formal Approaches to Slavic Linguistics 24*. Ann Arbor, MI: Michigan Slavic Publications. bit.ly/2Rr75ff

    2018. The matching analysis of relative clauses: An argument from antipronominal contexts. *Journal of Comparative Germanic Linguistics* 21: 189–245.

Paris, M.-C. 1977. Le morpheme 'de' et la relativisation en mandarin. *Cahiers de Linguistique Asie Orientale* 1 (2) 65–76. DOI : doi.org/10.3406/clao.1977.1029

Parry, M. 2007. La frase relativa (con antecedente) negli antichi volgari dell'Italia nord-occidentale, *LabRomAn* 1: 9–32.

Partee, B. H. 1976. Some transformational extensions of Montague grammar. In B. H. Partee, ed., *Montague Grammar*. New York: Academic Press. 51–76.

Patterson, G. & Caponigro, I. 2016. The puzzling degraded status of *who* free relative clauses in English. *English Language and Linguistics* 20: 341–52. DOI: doi.org/10.1017/S1360674315000325

Paul, W. 2018a. Finiteness in Chinese. Handout of a presentation at the Wuppertaler Linguistisches Forum, 24 April.

2018b. Finiteness and tense in Chinese. Abstract, CRLAO, Paris.

Payne, A. M. & Drew, D. E. 1970. *Kamano Grammar Sketch*. Ukarumpa, Papua New Guinea: Summer Institute of Linguistics.

Payne, J. R. 1982. Relativization in the Iranian languages of the USSR. *Folia Slavica* 5: 344–63.

Pearce, E. 2016. Whither realis marking: Loss and specialization in an Oceanic language. *Diachronica* 33(1): 67–94.

Pearson, M. 2000. Two types of VO languages. In P. Svenonius, ed., *The Derivation of VO and OV*. Amsterdam: Benjamins.

Peng, A. E. 2011. Head-final and Head-initial relative clauses in Jambi Teochew. In K. Otaki, H. Takeyasu & S-I. Tanigawa, eds., *Online Proceedings of Glow in Asia: Workshop for young scholars 2011*. Mie University, Japan. 262–76. bit.ly/38c2OCz

Perekhvalskaya, E. 2007. Les propositions relatives en Mwan. *Mandenkan* 43: 47–59. llacan.vjf.cnrs.fr/PDF/Mandenkan43/perexval.pdf

Perkins, E. 1982. Extraposition of relative clauses in Navajo. *International Journal of American Linguistics* 48: 277–85.

Perlmutter, D. M. & Ross, J. R. 1970. Relative clauses with split antecedents. *Linguistic Inquiry* 1: 350.

Perzanowski, D. 1980. Appositive relatives do have properties. In *Proceedings of NELS 10*. Amherst, MA: GLSA. 355–68.

Pesetsky, D. 1998. Some optimality principles of sentence pronunciation. In P. Barbosa, D. Fox, P. Hagstrom, M. McGinnis & D. Pesetsky, eds., *Is the Best Good Enough: Optimality and competition in syntax*. Cambridge, MA: MIT Press. 337–83. ling.auf.net/lingbuzz/repo/ROA/article/000018

Pesetsky, D. & Torrego, E. 2006. Probes, goals and syntactic categories. In Y. Otsu, ed., *The Proceedings of the Seventh Tokyo Conference on Psycholinguistics*. Tokyo: Hituzi Syobo. 25–60. ling.auf.net/lingbuzz/000321

Peterson, J. 2006. Kharia: A South Munda language. Vol. 1: Grammatical analysis. Habilitation thesis. Osnabrück University.

2011. *A Grammar of Kharia: A South Munda language*. Leiden: Brill.

Peterson, P. 2004. Non-restrictive relatives and other non-syntagmatic relations in a lexical-functional framework. In M. Butt & T. Holloway King, eds., *Proceedings of LFG 2004 Conference*. 391–7. Stanford, CA: CSLI Publications.

Peterson, T. H. 1974. On definite restrictive relatives in Mooré. *Journal of West African Languages* IX: 71–8.

Pittner, K. 1991. Freie Relativsätze und die Kasushierarchie. In E. Feldbusch, R. Pogarell & C. Weiss, eds., *Neue Fragen der Linguistik*. Tübingen: Niemeyer. 341–7.

1995. The case of German relatives. *The Linguistic Review* 12: 97–231.

Pizzati, C. 1980. La questione dell'attrazione e della concorrenza del relativo: Il latino come caso tipico. Thesis. University of Padua.

Plank, F. 2003. Noun phrase structure: *An und für sich*, in time, and in space. In F. Plank, ed., *Noun Phrase Structure in the Languages of Europe*. Berlin: Mouton de Gruyter. 3–33.

Platero, P. R. 1974. The Navajo relative clause. *International Journal of American Linguistics* 40: 202–46.

Platzack, C. 2000. A complement-of-N° account of restrictive and non-restrictive relatives: The case of Swedish. In A. Alexiadou, P. Law, A. Meinunger, & C. Wilder, eds., *The Syntax of Relative Clauses*. Amsterdam: Benjamins. 265–308.

2002. Relativization in the Germanic languages with particular emphasis on Scandinavian. In P. Poussa, ed., *Relativisation on the North Sea Littoral*. Munich: Lincom Europa. 77–96.

Poletto, C. & Sanfelici, E. 2014. What's in C? On the nature of relative complementizers and pronouns. Paper given at the 'Workshop on Variation in C', Venice, 21–22 October.

2017. Relative clauses. In A. Dufter & E. Stark, eds., *Manual of Romance Morphosyntax and Syntax*. Berlin: de Gruyter. 804–36.

2018. On demonstratives as relative pronouns. New insights from Italian varieties. In M. Coniglio, A. Murphy, E. Schlachter, & T. Veenstra, eds., *Atypical Demonstratives: Syntax, Semantics and Pragmatics*. Berlin: de Gruyter. 95–126.

Polinsky, M. 2015. Tsez Syntax: A description. MS. Harvard University. ling.auf.net/ lingbuzz/002315

Pollard, C. & Sag, I. A. 1992. Anaphors in English and the scope of binding theory. *Linguistic Inquiry* 23 (2): 261–303.

1994. *Head-Driven Phrase Structure Grammar*. Chicago: The University of Chicago Press.

Pollock, J.-Y. 1992. Opérateurs nuls, *dont*, questions indirectes, et théorie de la quantification. In L. Tasmowski & A. Zribi-Hertz, eds., *De la musique à la linguistique: Hommages à Nicolas Ruwet*. Ghent: Communication & Cognition. 440–63.

Poschmann, C., Bargmann, S., Götze, C., Holler, A., Sailer, M., Webelhuth, G. & Zimmerman, T. E. 2018. Split antecedent relative clauses and the symmetry of predicates. In U. Sauerland & S. Solt, eds., *Proceedings of Sinn und Bedeutung 22, Vol. 2*. ZASPiL 61: 253–70. bit.ly/2YmfuSE

Postal, P. 1971. *Crossover Phenomena*. New York: Holt, Rinehart and Winston.

1972a. Two remarks on dragging. *Linguistic Inquiry* 3: 130–6.

1972b. On some rules that are not successive cyclic. *Linguistic Inquiry* 3: 211–22.

1998. *Three Investigations of Extraction*. Cambridge, MA: MIT Press.

Potts, C. 2002. The lexical semantics of parenthetical-*as* and appositive-*which*. *Syntax* 5: 55–88.

2005. *The Logic of Conventional Implicatures*. Oxford: Oxford University Press.

Poutsma, H. 1916. *A Grammar of Late Modern English*. Groningen: P. Noordhoff.

Prince, E. F. 1990. Syntax and discourse: A look at resumptive pronouns. In *Proceedings of the 16th Annual Meeting of the Berkeley Linguistics Society*. Berkeley, CA: Berkeley Linguistics Society. 482–97.

 1997. On *kind*-sentences, resumptive pronouns, and relative clauses. In G. R. Guy, C. Feagin, D. Schiffrin & J. Baugh, eds., *Towards a Social Science of Language: Papers in honor of William Labov, Vol. 2. Social interaction and discourse structures*. Amsterdam: Benjamins. 223–35.

Prinzhorn, M. & Schmitt, V. 2005. A note on relative pronouns in standard German. In H. Broekhuis, N. Corver, R. Huybregts, U. Kleinhenz & J. Koster, eds., *Organizing Grammar: Linguistic studies in honor of Henk van Riemsdijk*. Berlin: Mouton de Gruyter. 495–504.

Quang, P. D. [McCawley, J.]. 1971. The applicability of transformations to idioms. In *Papers from the 7th Regional Meeting of the Chicago Linguistic Society*. Chicago: Chicago Linguistic Society. 200–05.

Quirk, R., Greenbaum, S., Leech, G. & Svartvik, J. 1985. *A Grammar of Contemporary English*. London: Longman.

Radford, A. 1975. Pseudo-relatives and the unity of subject raising. *Archivum Linguisticum* 6: 32–64.

 1977. *Italian Syntax: Transformational and relational grammar*. Cambridge: Cambridge University Press.

 2009. *Transformational Grammar: A first course*. Cambridge: Cambridge University Press.

 2016. *Analysing English Sentences*. 2nd ed. Cambridge: Cambridge University Press.

 2018. *Colloquial English: Structure and variation*. Cambridge: Cambridge University Press.

 2019. *Relative Clauses: Structure and variation in everyday English*. Cambridge: Cambridge University Press.

Rackowski, A. 1998. Malagasy adverbs. In I. Paul, ed., *The Structure of Malagasy*. UCLA Occasional Papers in Linguistics Vol. 20. Los Angeles: Department of Linguistics, UCLA. 11–33.

Rackowski, A. & Travis, L. 2000. V-initial Languages: X or XP movement and adverbial placement. In A. Carnie & E. Guilfoyle, eds., *The Syntax of Verb Initial Languages*. New York: Oxford University Press. 117–41.

Rasin, E. 2016. Resumptive pronouns across components: Evidence from Hebrew. Abstract for NELS 2016 conference. bit.ly/3656G6g

 2017. Two types of resumptive pronouns: A minimal account of Hebrew interpretive asymmetries. In A. Lamont & K. Tetzloff, eds., *Proceedings of the Forty-Seventh Annual Meeting of the North East Linguistic Society*. Amherst, MA: GLSA. 25–35.

Rasom, S. 2008. Lazy concord in the central Ladin feminine plural DP: A case study on the interaction between morphosyntax and semantics. PhD diss. University of Padua. paduaresearch.cab.unipd.it/268/

Ravetto, M. 2007. Es war einmal ein Königssohn, der bekam Lust in der Welt umher zu ziehen. Die deutschen d-V2-Sätze: synchrone und diachrone überlegungen. *Deutsche Sprache* 35: 239–49. bit.ly/2DOx9sX

Rawda Siraj. 2003. Relativization in Silt'i. MA thesis. Addis Ababa University.

Rawlins, K. 2008. (Un)conditionals: An investigation in the syntax and semantics of conditional structures. PhD diss. UC, Santa Cruz.

Rebuschi, G. 1999. Types de langues et types de constructions: Le cas des correlatives. In A. Sores & C. Marchello-Nizia, eds., *Typologie des langues: Universaux linguistiques*. LINX, special issue. Nanterre: University Paris X-Nanterre. 55–72.

2005. Generalizing the antisymmetric analysis of coordination to nominal modification. *Lingua* 115: 445–59.

2009. Position du basque dans la typologie des relatives corrélatives. *Langages* 174: 25–38.

Reed, A. M. 1975. The structure of English relative clauses. PhD diss. Brandeis University.

Reesink, G. P. 1987. *Structures and their functions in Usan: A Papuan language of Papua New Guinea*. Amsterdam: Benjamins.

Regmi, D. R. 2012. *The Nouns and Noun Phrases in the Bhujel Language: A functional-typological perspective*. Saarbrücken: LAP Lambert Publishing.

Reinhart, T. & Reuland, E. 1991. Anaphors and logophors: An argument structure perspective. In J. Koster & E. Reuland, eds., *Long-distance Anaphora*. Cambridge: Cambridge University Press. 282–321.

1993. Reflexivity. *Linguistic Inquiry* 24: 657–720.

Reintges, C. H., LeSourde, P. & Chung, S. 2006. Movement, *wh*-agreement and apparent *wh*-in-situ. In L.-L.-S. Cheng & N. Corver, eds., *Wh-Movement. Moving On*. Cambridge, MA: MIT Press. 165–94.

Reis, M. 2003. On the form and interpretation of German wh-infinitives. *Journal of Germanic Linguistics* 15 (2): 155–201.

Renck, G. L. 1975. *A Grammar of Yagaria*. Canberra: Australian National University.

Reşceanu, A. 2014. Reconstruction effects in English and Romanian restrictive relative clauses: The case of idioms. *Annals of the University of Craiova* XV: 128–42. bit.ly/2Rs8H8O

Resi, R. 2011. The position of relative clauses in German. *Lingue e Linguaggio* 1: 87–118.

Rett, J. 2006. Pronominal vs determiner *wh*-words: Evidence from the copy construction. *Empirical Issues in Syntax and Semantics* 6: 355–74. www.cssp.cnrs.fr/eiss6/rett-eiss6.pdf

Rezac, M. 2005. The syntax of clitic climbing in Czech. In L. Heggie & F. Ordóñez, eds., *Clitic and Affix Combinations*. Amsterdam: Benjamins. 103–40.

Rice, K. 1989. *A Grammar of Slave*. Berlin: Mouton de Gruyter.

Riehemann, S. Z. 2001. A constructional approach to idioms and word formation. PhD diss. Stanford University.

Riemsdijk, H. C. van. 1978. *A Case Study in Syntactic Markedness: The binding nature of prepositional phrases*. Lisse: The Peter de Ridder Press.

1985. On pied-piped infinitives in German relative clauses. In J. Toman, ed., *Studies in German Grammar*. Dordrecht: Foris. 165–92.

1989. Swiss relatives. In D. Jaspers, P. A. M. Seuren, W. Klooster & Y. Putseys, eds., *Sentential Complementation and the Lexicon: Studies in honour of Wim de Geest*. Dordrecht: Foris. 343–54.

1994. Another note on clausal pied-piping. In G. Cinque, J. Koster, J.-Y. Pollock, L. Rizzi, & R. Zanuttini, eds., *Paths toward Universal Grammar. Studies in honor of Richard S. Kayne*. Washington, DC: Georgetown University Press. 331–42.

1998. Syntax driven (crazy) by morphology: Morphological effects in the choice of relativization strategies in Zürich German. In A. Bruyn & J. Arends, eds., *Mengelwerk Voor Muysken Bij Zijn Afscheid Van De Universiteit Van Amsterdam*. Amsterdam: Department of Linguistics, University of Amsterdam. 67–74.

2000. Free relatives inside out: Transparent free relatives as grafts. In B. Rozwadowska, ed., *PASE Papers in Language Studies: Proceedings of the 8th Annual Conference of the Polish Association for the Study of English*. Wroclaw: University of Wroclaw. 223–33.

2003. East meets west: About relatives in Swiss German. In J. Koster & H. van Riemsdijk, eds., *Germania et Alia: A linguistic webschrift for Hans den Besten*. Groningen: University of Groningen.

2006. Free relatives. In M. Everaert & H. van Riemsdijk, eds., *The Blackwell Companion to Syntax Vol. II*. Malden, MA: Blackwell. 338–82.

2008. Identity avoidance: OCP effects in Swiss relatives. In R. Freidin, C. P. Otero, & M. L. Zubizarreta, eds., *Foundational Issues in Linguistic Theory: Essays in honor of Jean-Roger Vergnaud*. Cambridge (MA): MIT Press. 227–50.

2017. Free relatives. In M. Everaert & H. van Riemsdijk, eds., *The Wiley Blackwell Companion to Syntax*. 2nd ed. Hoboken, NJ: Wiley-Blackwell. DOI: doi.org/10.1002/9781118358733.wbsyncom116

Rijk, R. de. 1972. Relative clauses in Basque: A guided tour. In P. M. Peranteau, J. N. Levi & G. C. Phares, eds., *The Chicago Which Hunt*. Chicago: Chicago Linguistic Society. 115–35.

Rijkhoff, J. 1998. Order in the noun phrase of the languages of Europe. In A. Siewierska, ed., *Constituent Order in the Languages of Europe*. Berlin: Mouton de Gruyter. 321–82.

2002. *The Noun Phrase*. Oxford: Oxford University Press.

Rinke, E. & Aßmann, E. 2017. The syntax of relative clauses in European Portuguese. Extending the determiner hypothesis of relativizers to relative *que*. *Journal of Portuguese Linguistics*, 16 (4): 1–26. DOI: 10.5334/jpl.172

Rivero, M.-L. 1981. Wh-movement in comparatives in Spanish. In W. Cressey & D. J. Napoli, eds., *Linguistic Symposium on Romance Languages*. Washington, DC: Georgetwon University Press. 177–96.

Rizzi, L. 1982. *Issues in Italian Syntax*. Dordrecht: Foris.

1986. Null objects in Italian and the theory of pro. *Linguistic Inquiry* 17: 501–57.

1988. Il sintagma preposizionale. In L. Renzi, ed., *Grande grammatica italiana di consultazione. Vol. I*. Bologna: Il Mulino. 507–31.

1990. *Relativized Minimality*. Cambridge, MA: MIT Press.

1992. Direct perception, government and thematic sharing. *Geneva Generative Papers* 1: 39–52.

1997. The fine structure of the left periphery. In L. Haegeman, ed., *Elements of Grammar*. Dordrecht: Kluwer. 281–337.

2004. Locality and left periphery. In A. Belletti, ed., *Structures and Beyond. The cartography of syntactic structures*. Vol. 3. New York: Oxford University Press. 223–51.

2006. On the form of chains: Criterial positions and ECP effects. In L. Cheng & N. Corver, eds., *On Wh Movement*. Cambridge, Mass: MIT Press.

2010. The cartography of syntactic structures: Criteria, freezing and interface effects. EALing 2010, ENS, Paris, 16 September. bit.ly/38gRcOO

Roberts, T. 1997. Pashto free relatives and triply-filled Comp: Evidence for a headed analysis. *Lingua* 102 (2): 77–85.

Rochemont, M. S. & Culicover, P. W. 1990. *English Focus Constructions and the Theory of Grammar*. Cambridge: Cambridge University Press.

Rohlfs, G. 1968. *Grammatica storica della lingua italiana e dei suoi dialetti, Vol. 2: Morfologia*. Turin: Einaudi.

Rooryck, J. 1994. Generalized transformations and the wh-cycle: Free relatives as bare wh-CPs. In C. J.-W. Zwart, ed., *Minimalism and Kayne's Asymmetry Hypothesis*. Groninger Arbeiten zur Germanistischen Linguistik (GAGL) 37. Groningen: University of Groningen Press. 195–208.

Ross, J. R. 1967. Constraints on variables in syntax. PhD diss. MIT. hdl.handle.net/1721.1/15166

1969a. Adjectives as noun phrases. In D. A. Reibel & S. A. Schane. eds., *Modern Studies in English: Readings in transformational grammar*. Englewood Cliffs, NJ: Prentice-Hall. 352–60.

1969b. Guess who? In R. I. Binnick, A. Davison, G. M. Green, J. L. Morgan, eds., *Papers from the 5th Regional Meeting of the Chicago Linguistic Society*. Chicago: Department of Linguistics, University of Chicago. 252–86.

1970. On declarative sentences. In R. Jacobs & P. Rosenbaum, eds., *Readings in English Transformational Grammar*. Waltham, MA: Ginn. 222–72.

1984. Inner islands. In C. Brugman, et al., eds., *Proceedings of the Tenth Annual Meeting of the Berkeley Linguistics Society*. Berkeley, CA: Berkeley Linguistics Society. 258–65. bit.ly/36dR2FJ

1986. *Infinite Syntax!* Norwood, NJ: Ablex.

Ross, M. 2002. Jabêm. In J. Lynch, M. Ross & T. Crowley, eds., *The Oceanic Languages*. Abingdon: Routledge. 270–96.

Rouveret, A. 1994. *Syntaxe du gallois : Principes généraux et typologie*. Paris: CNRS Editions.

2002. How are resumptive pronouns linked to the periphery? *Linguist Variation Yearbook* 2: 123–84.

2008. Phasal agreement and reconstruction. In R. Freidin, C. P. Otero, & M. L. Zubizarreta, eds., *Foundational Issues in Linguistic Theory: Essays in honor of Jean-Roger Vergnaud*. Cambridge, MA: MIT Press. 167–95.

2011. Some issues in the theory of resumption: A perspective on early and recent research. In A. Rouveret, ed., *Resumptive Pronouns at the Interfaces*. Amsterdam: Benjamins. 1–62.

2018. Computational and semantic aspects of resumption. In A. Rouveret, *Aspects of Grammatical Architecture*. London: Routledge.

Rubovitz-Mann, T. 2012. *Evidential-existentials: An information structure account of extraction from relative clauses*. Saarbrücken: LAP Lambert.

Rudin, C. 1986. *Aspects of Bulgarian Syntax: Complementizers and wh constructions*. Columbus, OH: Slavica Publishers.

2007. Multiple Wh Relatives in Slavic. In R. Compton, M. Goledzinowska, U. Savchenko, eds., *Formal Approaches to Slavic Linguistics 15: The Toronto Meeting 2006*. Ann Arbor: Michigan Slavic Publications. 282–306.

2008. Pair-list vs single pair readings in multiple wh-free relatives and correlatives. In *Kansas Working Papers in Linguistics 30*. 257–67. bit.ly/36jZrrB

Rullmann, H. 1995. *Maximality in the semantics of wh-constructions*. PhD diss. University of Massachusetts, Amherst.

Rumsey, A. 2000. Bunuba. In R. M. W. Dixon & B. J. Blake, eds., *The Handbook of Australian Languages*. Vol. 5. Melbourne: Oxford University Press. 35–152.

Ruwet, N. 1991. On the use and abuse of idioms in syntactic argumentation. In N. Ruwet & J. A. Goldsmith, eds., *Syntax and Human Experience*. Chicago: The University of Chicago Press. 171–251.

Ruys, E. 2011. Semantic reconstruction and the interpretation of chains. In *Proceedings of Sinn und Bedeutung 15*. 515–29. bit.ly/2sRa5Yj

Saah, K. K. 2010. Relative clauses in Akan. In E. O. Aboh & J. Essegbey, eds., *Topics in Kwa Syntax*. Dordrecht: Springer. 91–107.

Sabel, J. 2006. Impossible infinitival interrogatives and relatives. In P. Brandt & E. Fuss, eds., *Form, Function, and Grammar: A festschrift presented to Günther Grewendorf on occasion of his 60th birthday*. Berlin: Akademie Verlag. 243–54.

2015. The emergence of the infinitival left periphery. In U. Steindl et al., eds., *Proceedings of the 32nd West Coast Conference on Formal Linguistics*. Somerville, MA: Cascadilla Press. 313–22. www.lingref.com/cpp/wccfl/32/paper3182.pdf

Sadat-Tehrani, N. 2004. Relative clauses in Yoruba. MS. University of Manitoba.

Saddy, D., Sloan, K. & Krivochen, D. 2019. Whoever that likes relatives … In K. R. Christensen, H. Jørgensen & J. L. Wood, eds., *The Sign of the V: Papers in honour of Sten Vikner*. Department of English, Aarhus University. 523–44. DOI: doi.org/10.7146/aul.348

Safir, K. 1986. Relative clauses in a theory of binding and levels. *Linguistic Inquiry* 17: 663–89.

1999. Vehicle change and reconstruction in Ā-chains. *Linguistic Inquiry* 30: 587–620.

Sag, I. A. 1976. *Deletion and logical form*. PhD diss. MIT.

1997. English relative clause constructions. *Journal of Linguistics* 33: 431–84.

Salzmann, M. 2006a. Reconstruction in German relative clauses: In favor of the matching analysis. In J. Dotlačil & B. Gehrke, eds., *UiL OTS Working Papers 2006*. Proceedings of the second Syntax AiO Meeting in Utrecht, 2005. 65–79. bit.ly/34W6dDs

2006b. Reconstruction in German restrictive relative clauses. In J. van de Weijer & B. Los, eds., *Linguistics in the Netherlands 2006*. Amsterdam: Benjamins. 186–98. DOI: doi.org/10.1075/avt.23.19sal

2006c. Resumptive pronouns and matching effects in Zurich German relative clauses as distributed deletion. *Leiden Papers in Linguistics* 3 (1): 17–50.

2006d. Resumptive prolepsis: A study in indirect A'-dependencies. PhD diss. Leiden University. www.lotpublications.nl/Documents/136_fulltext.pdf

2017. *Reconstruction and Resumption in Indirect A'-dependencies: On the syntax of prolepsis and relativization in (Swiss) German and beyond*. Berlin: Mouton de Gruyter.

2019. A new version of the matching analysis of relative clauses. Combining deletion under recoverability with vehicle change. In M. Krifka & M. Schenner, eds., *Reconstruction Effects in Relative Clauses*. Berlin: de Gruyter. 187–223.

Salzmann, M. & G. Seiler. 2010. Variation as the exception or the rule? Swiss relatives, revisited. *Sprachwissenschaft* 35: 79–117.

Sandfeld, K. 1936. *Syntaxe du français contemporain. Vol. II*. Paris: Droz.

Sanfelici, E., Schulz, P. & Trabandt, C. 2017. On German V2 'relative clauses': Linguistic theory meets acquisition. In E. di Domenico, ed., *Syntactic Complexity from a Language Acquisition Perspective*. Newcastle: Cambridge Scholars Publishing. 63–104.

Sauerland, U. 1998. The meaning of chains. PhD diss. MIT.

1999. Two structures for English restrictive relative clauses. In M. Saito et al. eds., *Proceedings of the Nanzan Glow*. Nagoya: Nanzan University. 351–66.

2003. Unpronounced heads in relative clauses. In K. Schwabe & S. Winkler, eds., *The Interfaces: Deriving and interpreting omitted structures*. Amsterdam: Benjamins. 205–26.

Sauerland, U. & Heck, F. 2003. LF-intervention effects in pied-piping. *Proceedings of NELS 33*. Amherst, MA: GLSA. 347–78.

Saxon, L. 2000. Head-internal relative clauses in Dogrib (Athapaskan). In A. Carnie, E. Jelinek, & M. A. Willie, eds., *Papers in Honor of Ken Hale, Working Papers in Endangered and Less Familiar Languages 1*. 93–108. Cambridge, MA: MITWPL.

Scarano, A. 2002. *Frasi relative e pseudo-relative in italiano*. Rome: Bulzoni.

Schachter, P. 1973. Focus and relativization. *Language* 49: 19–46.

Schlenker, P. 2009. Supplements within a unidimensional semantics I: Scope. MS. Institut Jean-Nicod, CNRS, Paris. ling.auf.net/lingbuzz/002578

2013. Supplements within a unidimensional semantics II: Epistemic status and projection. In S. Kan, C. Moore-Cantwell & R. Staubs, eds., *Proceedings of the Fortieth Annual Meeting of the North Eastern Linguistic Society, Vol. 2*. Amherst, MA: Graduate Linguistics Student Association. 167–82.

2017. The semantics and pragmatics of appositives. MS. Institut Jean-Nicod, CNRS and New York University. ling.auf.net/lingbuzz/002538

Schmitt, V. 2006. Hessian headed relative clauses and the syntactic role of the relative pronoun. MA thesis. University of Vienna.

Schwartz, A. 1971. General aspects of relative clause formation. In *Working Papers on Language Universals 6*. Stanford University, CA: Committee on Linguistics. 139–71. eric.ed.gov/?id=ED094567

Schuurman, M. 2017. Matching relative clauses with numerals and quantifiers in Mi'gmaq. MA thesis. Concordia University, Montreal. bit.ly/2Rqqr4d

Schweikert, W. 2005a. *The Order of Prepositional Phrases in the Structure of the Clause*. Amsterdam: Benjamins.

    2005b. The position of prepositional modifiers in the adverbial space. *Rivista di grammatica generativa* 30: 115–34.

Scorretti, M. 1991. Complementizers in Italian and Romance. PhD diss. University of Amsterdam.

Seki, S. 1983. Semantic properties of non-restrictive relative clauses. *Tsukuba English Studies* 2: 39–62.

Sells, P. 1984. Syntax and semantics of resumptive pronouns. PhD diss. University of Massachusetts, Amherst.

    1985. Restrictive and non-restrictive modification. Report #CSLI-85-28. Stanford University.

Sevcenco, A. 2010. Romanian restrictive relatives: A head raising analysis? *Bucharest Working Papers in Linguistics* XII (2).

    2015. Restrictive and appositive relatives. In V. Hill, ed., *Formal Approaches to DPs in Old Romanian*. Leiden: Brill. 329–64.

Shagal, K. forthcoming. Relative clauses in Uralic. In D. Abondolo & R. Valijärvi, eds., *The Uralic Languages*. London: Routledge.

Sharvit, Y. 1997. The syntax and semantics of functional relative clauses. PhD diss. University of Massachusetts, Amherst.

    1999a. Resumptive pronouns in relative clauses. *Natural Language and Linguistic Theory* 17: 587–612.

    1999b. Functional relative clauses. *Linguistics and Philosophy* 22: 447–78.

    2007. Two reconstruction puzzles. In P. Jacobson & C. Barker, eds., *Direct Compositionality*. Oxford: Oxford University Press. 336–59.

Shibagaki, R. 2011. Secondary predication in Chinese, Japanese, Mongolian and Korean. PhD diss. School of Oriental and African Studies, University of London.

Shimoyama, J. 1999. Internally headed relative clauses in Japanese and e-type anaphora. *Journal of East Asian Linguistics* 8: 147–82.

Shlonsky, U. 1986. Donkey parasites. In J. McDonough & B. Plunkett, eds., *Proceedings of NELS 17*. Amherst, MA: GLSA. 569–79.

    1992. Resumptive pronouns as a last resort. *Linguistic Inquiry* 23: 438–68.

    2004. Resumptive pronouns in Hebrew. Handout of a Seminar held at CISCL, University of Siena, 15 May. bit.ly/2YscrZs

Shougrakpam, D. 2014. Relative clause structure in Manipuri. *IOSR Journal of Humanities and Social Science (IOSR-JHSS)* 19 (10): 11–14. bit.ly/366Pc9M

Shukla, S. 1981. *Bhojpuri Grammar*. Washington, DC: Georgetown University Press.

Sichel, I. 2014. Resumptive pronouns and competition. *Linguistic Inquiry* 45: 655–93.

    2018. Anatomy of a counterexample: Extraction from relative clauses. *Linguistic Inquiry* 49: 335–78.

Sigurðsson, H. A. 2003. The silence principle. In L.-O. Delsing, C. Falk, G. Josefsson, & H. Á. Sigurðsson, eds., *Grammar in focus: Festschrift for Christer Platzack*

18 November 2003. Vol. II. Lund University: Institutionen för nordiska språk. 325–34.

Siloni, T. 1995. On participial relatives and complementizer D°. A case study in Hebrew and French. *Natural Language and Linguistic Theory* 13: 445–87. DOI: doi.org/10.1007/BF00992738

1997. *Noun Phrases and Nominalizations: The syntax of DPs.* Dordrecht: Kluwer.

Šimík, R. 2008a. The source of wh-morphology in questions and relative clauses. *Proceedings of ConSOLE XV.* 273–94.

2008b. Specificity in (Czech) relative clauses. In J. Witkoś & G. Fanselow, eds., *Elements of Slavic and Germanic Grammars: A comparative view.* Frankfurt am Main: Peter Lang. 179–98.

2008c. Czech modal existential wh-constructions as vP-level free relatives. In M. van Koppen & B. Botma, eds., *Linguistics in the Netherlands 2008.* Amsterdam: Benjamins. 121–32.

2011. Modal existential wh-constructions. PhD diss. University of Groningen. www.lotpublications.nl/Documents/269_fulltext.pdf

2017a. Free relatives. MS. ling.auf.net/lingbuzz/003729

2017b. An annotated bibliography on modal existential *wh*-constructions. MS. bit.ly/2DOExEG

2018. Ever free relatives crosslinguistically. In U. Sauerland & S. Solt, eds., *Proceedings of Sinn und Bedeutung 22.* Berlin: ZAS. ling.auf.net/lingbuzz/003919

Simpson, A. 2005. Classifiers and DP structure in southeast Asia. In G. Cinque & R. S. Kayne, eds., *The Oxford Handbook of Comparative Syntax.* New York: Oxford University Press. 806–38.

Singh, U. N. 1980. Relative clause formation in Maithili. *Nepalese Linguistics* 1: 27–39.

Sleeman, P. 2010. Superlative adjectives and the licensing of non-modal infinitival subject relatives. In P. Cabredo Hofherr & O. Matushansky, eds., *Adjectives: Formal analyses in syntax and semantics.* Amsterdam: Benjamins. 233–63.

2011. Verbal and adjectival participles: Internal structure and position. *Lingua* 121: 1569–87. DOI: doi.org/10.1016/j.lingua.2011.05.001

2013. Italian clefts and the licensing of infinitival subject relatives. In K. Hartmann & T. Veenstra, eds., *Cleft Structures.* Amsterdam: Benjamins. 319–42. DOI: doi.org/10.1075/la.208.12sle

2017. Participial relative clauses. In *Oxford Research Encyclopedia, Linguistics.* DOI: dx.doi.org/10.1093/acrefore/9780199384655.013.185

Smith, C. S. 1964. Determiners and relative clauses in generative grammar. *Language* 40: 37–52.

Smits, R. J. C. 1989. *Eurogrammar: The relative and cleft constructions of the Germanic and Romance languages.* Dordrecht: Foris Publications.

Solà, J. 2002. Les subordinades de relatiu. In J. Solà, M. R. Lloret, J. Mascaró, M. Pérez Saldanya, eds., *Gramàtica del Català Contemporani.* Vol. 2. Barcelona: Editorial Empúries. 1641–88.

Sonoda, K. 2006. The non-restrictive relative *that. Health Science Research* 19 (1): 1–5.

Song, J. J. 2001. Relative clauses, ch. 4 of *Linguistic Typology: Morphology and syntax*. Harlow: Longman. 211–56.

2003. Resumptive genitive pronouns in Korean relative clauses: Distribution and explanation. *SKY Journal of Linguistics* 16: 139–60.

Sotiri, M. 2006. Frasi relative in Albanese. In *Padua Working Papers in Linguistics 1*. 1–14. bit.ly/34SK0WO

Sportiche, D. 2006. NP movement: How to merge and move in tough-constructions. MS. UCLA. ling.auf.net/lingbuzz/000258

2008. Inward bound. Splitting the *wh*-paradigm and French relative *qui*. MS. UCLA. ling.auf.net/lingBuzz/000623

2011. French relative *qui*. *Linguistic Inquiry* 42: 83–124.

2015. Neglect (or doing away with late merger and countercyclicity). MS. UCLA. ling.auf.net/lingbuzz/002775

2017a. Relative clauses. Promotion only, in steps. MS. UCLA. ling.auf.net/lingbuzz/003444

2017b. Reconstruction, binding and scope. In M. Everaert & H. van Riemsdijk, eds., *The Wiley Blackwell Companion to Syntax*. 2nd ed. Hoboken, NJ: Wiley-Blackwell. DOI: doi.org/10.1002/9781118358733.wbsyncom002

Sportiche, D., Koopman, H. & Stabler, E. 2014. *An Introduction to Syntactic Analysis and Theory*. Malden, MA: Wiley-Blackwell.

Sposato, A. 2012. Relative clauses in Xong (Miao-Yao). *Journal of the Southeast Asian Linguistics Society (JSEALS)* 5: 49–66. jseals.org/pdf/sposato2012relative.pdf

Sproat, R. & Shih, C. 1990. The cross-linguistics distribution of adjectival ordering restrictions. In C. Georgopoulos & R. Ishihara, eds., *Interdisciplinary Approaches to Language: Essays in honor of S.-Y. Kuroda*. Dordrecht: Kluwer. 565–93.

Sridhar, S. N. 1990. *Kannada*. London: Routledge.

Srivastav, V. 1988. Hindi relative clauses and learnability. In *Cornell Working Papers in Linguistics 8*. 133–60.

1991a. The syntax and semantics of correlatives. *Natural Language and Linguistic Theory* 9: 637–86.

1991b. Wh dependencies in Hindi and the theory of grammar. PhD diss. Cornell University.

Stanton, T. 2011. The reduced relative: A misnomer? *Début: The Undergraduate Journal of Languages, Linguistics and Area Studies* 2(2): 55–65.

Stark, E. 2016. Relative clauses. In A. Ledgeway & M. Maiden, eds., *The Oxford Guide to the Romance Languages*. Oxford: Oxford University Press. 1029–40.

Stechow, A. von. 1979. Visiting German relatives. In R. Bäuerle, U. Egli & A. von Stechow, eds., *Semantics from Different Points of View*. Berlin: Springer. 226–65.

Sternefeld, W. 1998. The semantics of reconstruction and connectivity. Arbeitspapier 97, SFB 340. Tübingen University and Stuttgart University.

2001. Semantic vs syntactic reconstruction. In C. Rohrer, A. Roßdeutscher & H. Kamp, eds., *Linguistic Form and Its Computation*. Stanford, CA: CSLI Publications. 145–82.

2019. Telescoping by continuations. In M. Krifka & M. Schenner, eds., *Reconstruction Effects in Relative Clauses*. Berlin: de Gruyter. 387–403.

Stockwell, R. P., Schachter, P. & Partee, B. H. 1973. *The Major Syntactic Structures of English*. New York: Holt, Rinehart and Winston.

Stowell, T. 2005. Appositive and parenthetical relative clauses. In H. Broekhuis, N. Corver, R. Huybregts, U. Kleinhenz, & J. Koster, eds., *Organizing Grammar: Linguistic studies in honor of Henk van Riemsdijk*. Berlin: Mouton de Gruyter. 608–17.

Struckmeier, V. 2012. A morphologically guided matching approach to German(ic) relative constructions. In P. Ackema et al., eds., *Comparative Germanic Syntax: The state of the art*. Amsterdam: Benjamins. 387–413.

Studler, R. 2014. The morphology, syntax and semantics of definite determiners in Swiss German. In P. Cabredo Hofherr & A. Zribi-Hertz, eds., *Crosslinguistic Studies on Noun Phrase Structure and Reference*. Syntax and Semantics, Vol. 39. Leiden: Brill. 143–71.

Stuurman, F. 1983. Appositives and X-bar theory. *Linguistic Inquiry* 14: 736–44.

Subbārāo, K. V. 2012. *South Asian Languages: A syntactic typology*. Cambridge: Cambridge University Press.

Subbārāo, K. V. & Kevichüsa, M. 2005. Internally Headed Relative Clauses in Sema. In T. Bhattacharya, ed., *The Yearbook of South Asian Languages*. Berlin: Mouton de Gruyter. 255–72.

Suñer, M. 1984. Free relatives and the matching parameter. *The Linguistic Review* 3: 363–87.

2001. The puzzle of restrictive relative clauses with conjoined DP antecedents. In J. Herschensohn, E. Mallén, & K. Zagona, eds., *Features and Interfaces in Romance: Essays in honor of Heles Contreras*. Amsterdam: Benjamins. 267–78.

Szczegielniak, A. 2004. Relativization and ellipsis. PhD diss. Harvard University.

2005. Two types of resumptive pronouns in Polish relative clauses. *Linguistic Variation Yearbook* 5 (1): 165–85. DOI: doi.org/10.1075/livy.5.06szc

2006. Two types of relative clauses in Slavic: Evidence from reconstruction and ellipsis. In M. T. Martínez, A. Alcázar, & R. M. Hernández, eds., *Proceedings of the Thirty-third Western Conference on Linguistics. WECOL 2004. Vol. 16.* 373–85.

2012. Degree phrase raising in relative clauses. In C. Taboada, J. Fernández, M. González, & R. Tejedor, eds., *Information Structure, Agreement and CP*. Amsterdam: Benjamins. 255–74.

2016. Relative constructions with partial labels. MS. Rutgers University.

Szucsich, L. 2003. The structure of relative clauses in Slavic. In P. Kosta et al., eds., *Investigations into Formal Slavic Linguistics, 2*. Frankfurt am Main: Peter Lang. 697–713.

Tagashira, Y. 1972. Relative clauses in Korean. In P. M. Peranteau, J. N. Levi, & G. C. Phares, eds., *The Chicago Which Hunt: Papers from the relative clause festival*. Chicago: Chicago Linguistic Society. 215–29.

Taghvaipour, M. A. 2005. Persian relative clauses, in head-driven phrase structure grammar. PhD diss. University of Essex.

Taglicht, J. 1972. A new look at English relative constructions. *Lingua* 29: 1–22.

Takizala, A. 1973. Focus and relativization: The case of Kihung'an. In J. Kimball, ed., *Syntax and Semantics. Vol. 2*. New York: Seminar Press. 123–48.

Tallerman, M. 1983. Island constraints in Welsh. *York Papers in Linguistics* 10: 197–204.

Tao, H. & McCarthy, M. J. 2001. Understanding non-restrictive *which*-clauses in spoken English, which is not an easy thing. *Language Sciences* 23: 651–77.

Taraldsen, K. T. 1978. The scope of wh movement in Norwegian. *Linguistic Inquiry* 9: 623–40.

1981. The theoretical interpretation of a class of 'marked' extractions. In A. Belletti, L. Brandi & L. Rizzi (eds) *The Theory of Markedness in Generative Grammar*. Pisa: Scuola Normale Superiore. 475–516.

1982. Extraction from relative clauses in Norwegian. In E. Engdahl & E. Ejerhed, eds., *Readings on Unbounded Dependencies in Scandinavian Languages*. Umeå: Almqvist & Wiksell. 205–21.

Taylor, A. J. 1970. Syntax and phonology of Motu (Papua): A transformational approach. PhD diss. Australian National University. bit.ly/2Yvs1n6

Tellier, C. 1989. Head-internal relatives and parasitic gaps in Mooré. In I. Haïk & L. Tuller, eds., *Current Approaches to African Linguistics, Vol. 6*. Dordrecht: Foris. 298–318.

Tellier, C. & Valois, D. 2006. *Constructions méconnues du français*. Montreal: Presses de l'Université de Montréal.

Teng, S.-H. 1981. Deixis, anaphora, and demonstratives in Chinese. *Cahiers de linguistique – Asie orientale* 10: 5–18.

Terzi, A. 1999. Clitic combinations, their hosts and their ordering. *Natural Language and Linguistic Theory* 17: 85–121.

Testelec, Y. G. 1998. Word order in Daghestanian languages. In A. Siewierska, ed., *Constituent Order in the Languages of Europe*. Berlin: Mouton de Gruyter. 257–80.

Thompson, S. 1971. The deep structure of relative clauses. In C. Fillmore & D. T. Langendoen, eds., *Studies in Linguistic Semantics*. New York: Holt, Rinehart and Winston. 79–96.

Thompson, S. A., Park, J. S.-Y., & Li, C. N. 2006. *A Reference Grammar of Wappo*. Berkeley, CA: University of California Press. escholarship.org/uc/item/0dv86220

Thorne, J. P. 1988. Non-restrictive relative clauses. In C. Duncan-Rose & T. C. Vennemann, eds., *On Language: Rhetorica, phonologica, syntactica*. London: Routledge. 424–36.

Thurgood, G., Thurgood, E. & Fenxiang, L. 2014. *A Grammatical Sketch of Hainan Cham: History, contact, and phonology*. Berlin: Mouton de Gruyter.

Tiffou, E. & Patry, R. 1995. La relative en bourouchaski du Yasin. *Bulletin de la Société de Linguistique de Paris* 90 (1): 335–91.

Togeby, K. 1982. *Grammaire française. Vol. 1: Le Nom*. Copenhagen: Akademisk Forlag.

Toman, J. 1998. A discussion of resumptives in colloquial Czech. In Ž. Bošković, S. Franks, & W. Snyder, eds., *Formal Approaches to Slavic Linguistics (FASL) 6: The Connecticut meeting 1997*. Ann Arbor, MI: Michigan Slavic Publications. 303–18.

Tomić, O. M. 2006. *Balkan Sprachbund Morpho-syntactic Features*. Dordrecht: Springer.

Torrence, H. 2005. A promotion analysis of Wolof relative clauses. In *Proceedings of the 31st Annual Meeting of the Berkeley Linguistics Society*. Berkeley, CA: Berkeley Linguistics Society. 107–17.

2013. *The Clause Structure of Wolof*. Amsterdam: Benjamins.

Tosco, M. 2001. *The Dhaasanac Language: Grammar, texts, vocabulary of a Cushitic language of Ethiopia*. Cologne: Rüdiger Köppe Verlag.

Tóth, B. 2019. Arguments for the matching analysis of Hungarian lexically headed relatives. Poster given at ConSOLE 2019, 21–23 February. bit.ly/34XoyjA

Touratier, C. 1980. *La relative, essai de théorie syntaxique*. Paris: Klincksieck.

Tredinnick, V. A. 2005. On the semantics of free relatives with -ever. PhD diss. University of Pennsylvania.

Truswell, R. 2011. Relatives with a leftward island in early modern English. *Natural Language and Linguistic Theory* 29: 291–332.

2012. English and the typology of non-restrictive relative clauses. CLA, 28 May. robtruswell.com/assets/pdfs/CLA_EModE.pdf

Trutkowski, E. & Weiß, H. 2016a. When personal pronouns compete with relative pronouns. In P. Grosz et al., eds., *The Impact of Pronominal Form on Interpretation*. Berlin: de Gruyter. 135–66.

2016b. (Dis-)agreement in relative clauses. Relativsatz-Kolloquium/DFG-Forschergruppe, Goethe University Frankfurt, 12 July. bit.ly/34Wsd19

Tsai, H.-C. J. 2008. On gapless relative clauses in Chinese. *Nanzan Linguistics*. 5: 109–24. bit.ly/2LuH4ba

Uriagereka, J. 1995. Aspects of the syntax of clitic placement in Western Romance. *Linguistic Inquiry* 26: 79–123.

Utzeri, I. 2007. The production and acquisition of subject and object relative clauses in Italian: A comparative experimental study. *Nanzan Linguistics*. 3 (1): 283–313. bit.ly/2RrJlrm

Vai, M. 2018. *Nuove ricerche di sintassi vedica*. Milan: Ledizioni.

Vaillette, N. 2001. Hebrew relative clauses in HPSG. In *Proceedings of the 7th International Conference on Head-Driven Phrase Structure Grammar*. Stanford, CA: CSLI Publications. 305–24. stanford.io/33RsPn7

Vanden Wyngaerd, G. & Zwart, C. J.-W. 1991. Reconstruction and vehicle change. In F. Drijkoningen & A. M. C. van Kemenade, eds., *Linguistics in the Netherlands 1991*. Amsterdam: Benjamins. 151–60.

Vasu, R. 1994. On the nature of wh-trace in Tamil relative clauses. *International Journal of Dravidian Linguistics* 23: 44–64.

Vedovato, D. & Penello, N. 2007. La grammatica del *che* e delle frasi relative: un'esperienza didattica. *Grammatica e Didattica* 1: 85–129. bit.ly/33XihDd

Vergnaud, J.-R. 1974. French relative clauses. PhD diss. MIT.

1985. *Dépendences et niveaux de représentation en syntaxe*. Amsterdam: Benjamins.

Vicente, L. 2004. Inversion, reconstruction, and the structure of relative clauses. In J. Auger, J. C. Clements & B. Vance, eds., *Contemporary Approaches to Romance Linguistics: Selected papers from the 33rd linguistics symposium on Romance languages (LSRL), Bloomington, Indiana, April 2003*. Amsterdam: Benjamins. 361–79.

Viel, V. 2001. The grammar of relative clauses in old and middle English. Thesis. University of Padua.

Vikner, S. 1991. Relative *der* and other C° elements in Danish. *Lingua* 84: 109–36.

Villalobos, M. E. 1994. Bribri, lengua con cláusulas relativas de núcleo interno. *Letras* 29–30: 225–39.

Vincent, J. W. 2017. D-raising in Chamorro relative clauses and other A′ constructions. MA thesis. University of California, Santa Cruz. escholarship.org/uc/item/0jq7096r

Vogel, R. 2001. Case conflict in German free-relative constructions: An optimality-theoretic treatment. In G. Müller & W. Sternefeld, eds., *Competition in Syntax*. Berlin: Mouton de Gruyter. 341–75.

2003. Surface matters: Case conflict in free relative constructions and case theory. In E. Brandner & H. Zinsmeister, eds., *New Perspectives on Case Theory*. Stanford, CA: CSLI Publications. 269–99.

Vries, L. de. 1993. *Forms and Functions in Kombai, an Awyu language of Irian Jaya*. Canberra: Australian National University Press.

Vries, M. de. 2001. Patterns of relative clauses. In T. van der Wouden & H. Broekhuis, eds., *Linguistics in the Netherlands 2001*. Amsterdam: Benjamins. 231–43.

2002. The syntax of relativization. PhD diss. University of Amsterdam. www.let.rug.nl/dvries/pdf/proefschrift-mdevries.pdf

2005. The fall and rise of universals on relativization. *Journal of Universal Language* 6: 125–57.

2006. The syntax of appositive relativization. On specifying coordination, false free relatives and promotion. *Linguistic Inquiry* 37: 229–70.

2009. Specifying coordination: An investigation into the syntax of dislocation, extraposition, and parenthesis. In C. R. Dreyer, ed., *Language and linguistics: Emerging trends*. New York: Nova. 37–98.

2012. Unconventional mergers. In M. Uribe-Etxebarria & V. Valmala, eds., *Ways of Structure Building*. Oxford: Oxford University Press. 143–66.

Vydrina, A. 2017. A corpus-based description of Kakabe, a western Mande language: Prosody in grammar. Vol. I. PhD diss. INALCO, Paris. bit.ly/2sKBNWq

Wali, K. 1982. Marathi correlatives: A conspectus. *South Asian Review* 6: 78–88.

2006. *Marathi*. Delhi: Indian Institute of Language Studies.

Walker, B. R. 2005. Relative clauses in Sinhala. In R. Englebretson & C. Genetti, eds., *Santa Barbara Working Papers in Linguistics 17*. Proceedings from the Workshop on Sinhala Linguistics. University of California, Santa Barbara: Department of Linguistics. 163–71. bit.ly/2YxBWZr

Walker, H. 2017. The syntax and semantics of relative clause attachment. PhD diss. Goethe University Frankfurt. bit.ly/34Zjnjc

Walusimbi, L. 1996. *Relative Clauses in Luganda*. Cologne: Rüdiger Köppe Verlag.

Watanabe, A. 2004. Parametrization of quantificational determiners and head-internal relatives. *Language and Linguistics* 5: 59–97.

2016. Amount relatives in Japanese. In A. Sugawara, S. Hayashi & S. Ito, eds., *Proceedings of the Eighth Formal Approaches to Japanese Linguistics*

Conference (FAJL8). MIT Working Papers in Linguistics. Cambridge, MA: MITWPL. 189–208.

Watters, D. E. 2006. Notes on Kusunda grammar. A language isolate of Nepal. *Himalayan Linguistics Archive* 3: 1–182. escholarship.org/uc/item/83v8d1wv

Watters, J. R. 2000. Syntax. In B. Heine & D. Nurse, eds., *African Languages: An introduction*. Cambridge: Cambridge University Press. 194–230.

2003. Grassfields Bantu. In D. Nurse & G. Philippson, eds., *The Bantu Languages*. London: Routledge. 225–56.

Webelhuth, G. 1992. *Principles and Parameters of Syntactic Saturation*. New York: Oxford University Press.

2011. Capturing collocations and idioms in relative clauses without literal reconstruction. Handout of a talk presented at the workshop on 'Reconstruction Effects in Relative Clauses', Zentrum für Allgemeine Sprachwissenschaft (ZAS), Berlin, 8 July.

Webelhuth, G., Bargmann, S. & Götze, C. 2017. More empirical evidence against the raising analysis of relative clauses. In C. Halpert, H. Kotek & C. van Urk, eds., *A Pesky Set: Papers for David Pesetsky*. MIT Working Papers in Linguistics. Cambridge, MA: MITWPL. 11–14.

2019. Idioms as evidence for the proper analysis of relative clauses. In M. Krifka & M. Schenner, eds., *Reconstruction Effects in Relative Clauses*. Berlin: de Gruyter. 225–62.

Webelhuth, G., Sailer, M. & Walker, H. 2013. Introduction. In G. Webelhuth, M. Sailer & H. Walker, eds., *Rightward Movement in a Comparative Perspective*. Amsterdam: Benjamins. 1–60.

Werth, P. 1974. Some thoughts on non-restrictive relatives. *Linguistics* 142: 33–67.

Weiß, H. 2013. Satztyp und Dialekt. In J. Meibauer, M. Steinbach & H. Altman, eds., *Staztypen des Deutchen*. Berlin: de Gruyter. 763–84.

Weisler, S. 1980. The syntax of *that*-less relatives. *Linguistic Inquiry* 11: 624–31.

Whitman, J. 2013. The prehead relative clause problem. In U. Özge, ed., *Proceedings of the 8th Workshop on Altaic Formal Linguistic*. MIT Working Papers in Linguistics. Cambridge, MA: MITWPL. 361–80.

Wilbur, R. 2017. Internally-headed relative clauses in sign languages. *Glossa: A Journal of General Linguistics* 2(1): 25. DOI: doi.org/10.5334/gjgl.183

Wilder, C. 1999. Transparent free relatives. In K. N. Shahin, S. Blake & E.-S. Kim, eds., *Proceedings of the Seventeenth West Coast Conference on Formal Linguistics*. Stanford, CA: CSLI. 685–99.

Williams, E. 1975. Small clauses in English. In J. P. Kimball, ed., *Syntax and Semantics, Vol. 4*. New York: Academic Press. 249–73.

1977. Discourse and logical form. *Linguistic Inquiry* 8: 101–39.

1980. Predication. *Linguistic Inquiry* 11: 203–38.

Williamson, J. S. 1987. An indefinite restriction for relative clauses in Lakhota. In E. J. Reuland & A. G. B. ter Meulen, eds., *The Representation of (In)definiteness*. Cambridge, MA: MIT Press. 168–90.

Williamson, S. 2016. Subject contact relatives: A cross-dialectal approach. *Calgary (Working) Papers in Linguistics* 29: 41–60. DOI: 10.11575/PRISM/28995

Willis, D. 2000. On the distribution of resumptive pronouns and *wh*-trace in Welsh. *Journal of Linguistics* 36: 531–73.

2006. Against N-raising and NP-raising of Welsh noun phrases. *Lingua* 116: 1807–39.

2011. The limits of resumption in Welsh *wh*-dependencies. In A. Rouveret, ed., *Resumptive Pronouns at the Interfaces*. Amsterdam: Benjamins. 189–221.

Wilson, W. A. 1963. Relative constructions in Dagbani. *Journal of African Languages* 2 (2): 139–44.

Wiltschko, M. 1998. On the syntax and semantics of (relative) pronouns and determiners. *Journal of Comparative Germanic Linguistics* 2: 43–181.

2012. What does it take to host a (restrictive) relative? *Working Papers of the Linguistic Circle of the University of Victoria* 21: 100–45.

2013. Descriptive relative clauses in Austro-Bavarian German. *Canadian Journal of Linguistics* 58 (2): 157–89.

Wood, J., Sigurðsson, E. F. & Nowenstein, I. E. 2017. Inverse attraction in Icelandic relative clauses. In H. Thráinsson, C. Heycock, H. P. Petersen & Z. S. Hansen, eds., *Syntactic Variation in Insular Scandinavian*. Amsterdam: Benjamins. 200–32.

Wu, H.-H. I. 2016. The syntax of correlatives in Isbukun Bunun. *Canadian Journal of Linguistics* 61 (2): 190–210.

Wu, T. 2008. La relativisasion prénominale: Étude comparative sur l'amharique, le basque, le chinois mandarin, le japonais, le quechua et le turc. Mémoire de Master. Département des Sciences du Langage, Lumière University Lyon 2.

2009. Relative clause without complementizer in Mandarin, with reference to Cantonese. 5th international conference on modern Chinese grammar, 28–30 November, Hong Kong Polytechnic University.

2011. The syntax of prenominal relative clauses: A typological study. *Linguistic Typology* 15: 569–623.

Yadroff, M. & Billings, L. 1998. The syntax of approximative inversion in Russian. In Ž. Bošković, S. Franks & W. Snyder, eds., *Formal Approaches to Slavic Linguistics: The Connecticut Meeting (FASL 6)*. Ann Arbor, MI: Michigan Slavic Publications. 319–38.

Yamashita, I. & Chang, F. 2001. 'Long before short' preference in the production of a head-final language. *Cognition* 81: B45–B55. bit.ly/2YnE2uF

Yang, H. S.-F. 2006. On overt and covert *wh*- and relative movement in Hindi and Punjabi. In L. L-S. Cheng & N. Corver, eds., *Wh-Movement: Moving on*. Cambridge, MA: MIT Press. 135–64.

Yanti, J., McKinnon, T., Cole, P. & Hermon, G. 2012. Relative clauses in Jambi Malay and Kerinci Malay. Paper given at the International Workshop on Clause Combining in/around Indonesia, 7–8 October, Tokyo University of Foreign Studies.

Yoshioka, N. 2012. A reference grammar of Eastern Burushaski. PhD diss. Tokyo University of Foreign Studies. repository.tufs.ac.jp/handle/10108/72148

Yuasa, E. 2005. Independence in subordinate clauses: Analysis of non-restrictive relative clauses in English and Japanese. In S. S. Mufwene, E. J. Francis, R. S. Wheeler, eds., *Polymorphous Linguistics: Jim McCawley's legacy*. Cambridge, MA: MIT Press. 135–60.

Zagona, K. 1988. *Verb Phrase Syntax: A parametric study of English and Spanish.* Dordrecht: Kluwer.

Zeller, J. 2004. Relative clause formation in the Bantu languages of South Africa. *Southern African Linguistics and Applied Language Studies* 22 (1/2): 75–93. www.jzeller.de/pdf/SALALSBantuRelativesOffprint.pdf

2006. On the relation between noun prefixes and grammaticalization in Nguni relative clauses. *Studia Linguistica* 60: 220–49. DOI: https://doi.org/10.1111/j.1467-9582.2006.00138.x

Zhang, L. 2007. The two positions of Chinese relative clauses. PhD diss. University of South Carolina.

Zhang, N. N. (2001a). On the absence of non-restrictive relatives (in Chinese). MS. Berlin: ZAS. www.swtang.net/doc/study_appositivies_zhang_2001.pdf

2007. The syntactic derivations of split antecedent relative clause constructions. *Taiwan Journal of Linguistics* 5: 19–48. tjl.nccu.edu.tw/main/uploads/2NiinaNingZhang11.pdf

2008. Gapless relative clauses as clausal licensers of relational nouns. *Language and Linguistics* 9: 1005–28.

2013. *Classifier Structures in Mandarin Chinese.* Berlin: Mouton de Gruyter.

2015. Nominal-internal phrasal movement in Mandarin Chinese. *The Linguistic Review* 32: 375–425.

2018. Deriving existential entailment constructions in Mandarin Chinese. MS. National Chung Cheng University.

Ziv, Y. 1973. Why can't appositives be extraposed? *Papers in Linguistics* 6 (2): 243–54.

Ziv, Y. & Cole, P. 1974. Relative extraposition and the scope of definite descriptions in Hebrew and English. *CLS* 10: 772–86.

Zribi-Hertz, A. & Hanne, J.-F. 1995. Pronoms, déterminants et relatives en Bambara de Bamako. *Linguistique Africaine* 15: 91–135.

Zwart, J.-W. 2000. A head raising analysis of relative clauses in Dutch. In A. Alexiadou, P. Law, A. Meinunger, C. Wilder, eds., *The Syntax of Relative Clauses.* Amsterdam: Benjamins. 349–385.

2005. Ietz over zgn. V2-relatieven in het Nederlands. *Nederlandse Taalkunde* 10: 59–81.

Zwicky, A. M. 2002. I wonder what kind of construction that this example illustrates. In D. I. Beaver et al., eds., *The Construction of Meaning.* Stanford, CA: CSLI Publications. 219–48.

Author Index

Language Index

Subject Index

Lightning Source UK Ltd.
Milton Keynes UK
UKHW021109160920
369980UK00004B/33